C0-AWP-177

Composers of North America

Series Editors: Sam Dennison, William C. Loring, Margery Lowens, Ezra Schabas

Gorgeous Magnolias—
Spotless in splendor
Sad in their beauty
Heavy with perfume

Drawing by Paul Colmorgan.

FOLLOW ME

The Life and Music
of R. Nathaniel Dett

by Anne Key Simpson

Composers of North America, No. 10

The Scarecrow Press, Inc.
Metuchen, N.J., & London
1993

British Library Cataloguing-in-Publication data available

Library of Congress Cataloging-in-Publication Data

Simpson, Anne K. (Anne Key), 1924–
    Follow me : the life and music of R. Nathaniel Dett / by Anne
Key Simpson.
        p.   cm. -- (Composers of North America ; no. 10)
    Discography: p.
    Includes bibliographical references and index.
    ISBN 0-8108-2627-5 (acid-free paper)
    1. Dett, R. Nathaniel, 1882-1943.   2. Composers--United States--
Biography.   3. Afro-American composers--Biography.   I. Title.
II. Series.
ML410.D375S55   1993
780'.92--dc20
[B]   92-36916

Copyright © 1993 by Anne Key Simpson
Manufactured in the United States of America
Printed on acid-free paper

ML 410.D375 music
S 55

Follow Me is dedicated with love
to my kind and patient daddy,
Collis E. Key (1893-1963),
my mother, Ruth P. Key (1891-1978),
who, like Charlotte Dett, was an
expert with the peachtree switch,
and to my cousins,
Margaret and Paul Colmorgan.

CONTENTS

PART II: Musical Works

Illustrations

Musical Examples

xv

FOREWORD

This biographical series is designed to focus attention on significant North American composers of art and folk music from colonial times to the present. Few composers of art music before 1975 had their works performed frequently during their lifetime. Many have suffered from undeserved neglect.

Each volume consists of a substantial essay about the composer and a complete catalog of compositions, published and unpublished. Part I deals with the composer's life and works in the context of the artistic thought and the musical world of his or her time. In Part II the goals of the composer and the critical comments by contemporaries are included, as are illustrations and musical examples. Some works which merit performance today are singled out for analysis and discussion. In Part III the catalog of the composer's output has full publication details and locations of unpublished works. We hope that this series will make readers conscious and appreciative of our North American musical heritage to date.

The books are also intended to help performers and teachers seeking works to use. For them we designed the Part III Catalog of the composer's music to allow a quick search for works the author finds of historic or current interest that may be considered for readings and hearings.

Sam Dennison, William C. Loring, Jr., Margery M. Lowens,
Ezra Schabas, Martha Furman Schleifer.
Series Editors.

PREFACE

During research for *Hard Trials*, a biography of Harry T. Burleigh, issued by Scarecrow Press in this same series, I took a few notes on Nathaniel Dett, who was also gaining recognition in the mid-1910s through leading newspapers and journals. I had not remembered the composer of a clever piano piece called *Juba*, but after hearing a recording of *In the Bottoms* I thought the whole suite should be choreographed, that a Dett renaissance was in order. Nobody was interested. The Dett notes were filed away.

Four years later serious research began. Puzzled over my own motivation, however, I talked with jazz scholar and author Austin Sonnier. His clarification was both direct and amusing. "Hey, man," he said, "it's cause we black folks *have somethin'!*"

Nathaniel Dett, who accomplished his goals with dignity, compassion, and taste, *had somethin'* worth sharing in his career as a pianist, choral director, music educator, composer, and arranger. Self doubts rarely hindered his determination to achieve.

For help in preparing this study, sincere appreciation goes to my constructive editor, Dr. William Loring, who has helped me through a second book; Carl Brasseaux, Assistant Director of the Center for Louisiana Studies, who, without complaint and unselfishly, corrected my myriad mistakes while type-setting and formatting; Glenn Conrad, Director of the Center; the staff of Dupré Library's Reference, Inter Library Loan, Circulation, and Microfilm Departments; Donald E. Loker, Local Historian in Niagara Falls, New York; Fritz J. Malval, Archivist at Hampton University; Joan Landry, the dependable proof-reader; Paul Colmorgan for art work; James Burke for musical notation and James Haygood for input on choral scores; and the Grainger Museum for the Dett/Grainger correspondence.

More special thanks go to the following persons who helped in their capacities as archivists, scholars, music educators, artists, and friends: Vivian Flagg McBrier, Judith Anne Still, Dominique René DeLerma, Arlene Gray, Mildred E. Clark, Millie Wilson, Jean Kreamer, Josephine H. Love, David Cantrell, Elisabeth Slenk, Esme E. Bahn, George Brown, Willis Ducrest, Jean Snyder, Thomas J. Corcoran, Donald Feinstein, Deborah L. Long, Gail M. Pietrzyk,

James McKinney, Sue McBerry, Pamela Bristah, Pamela Scheffel, Roland M. Baumann, David Carmichael, Paul Bierley, Susan Gleason, Dorothy M. Haith, Patricia Middleton, Mary E. Rame, Lucius R. Wyatt, Elizabeth Schaaf, Andy Simons, Rosemary Florrimell, Baron Philippe Roberts-Jones, Lisa Redpath, Agatha P. Kalkanis, Catherine Morgan, Lilias C. Circle, Louise Goldberg, Robin McElheny, Lucia Grosch, Hollee Haswell, D. W. Krummel, Stanley Sadie, Michael F. Manning, Carolyn Rabson, Mary Platt, Mary Yearwood, Judith Halper, Paul Tobin, Nathaniel Phipps, Donald Hayden, Mark LeBlanc, Gene Speyrer, Roland H. Bogardus, Belinda W. Lam, Richard C. Vitzthum, Leo E. Heim, Betty B. Duveneck, and Virginia Wesby, Patricia Willis, Bill Dalton, Tuskegee Institute Archives, Detroit Public Library, Amistad Research Center, and *The Instrumentalist*.

Though the publishers of Dett's music are credited under each musical example, their professional cooperation is greatly appreciated: Boston Music Co., G. Schirmer, Inc., Theodore Presser Company, CPP/Belwin, Inc., Summy-Birchard, Inc., and Warner/Chappell Music, Inc.

Concern and support from Richard and Thetis Cusimano and Christopher Lyons, my family, kept things in perspective.

Anne Key Simpson
Lafayette, Louisiana

xx

INTRODUCTION

Robert Nathaniel Dett (1882-1943) has been considered both a major and a minor Afro-American composer. His compositional techniques, though not complex, marked him as a pioneer in elevating the Negro spiritual and folksong to a high level during his career as a pianist, composer, and choral director.

Dett was ambitious, a perfectionist, but certainly no dreamer nor idealist. Perhaps partially due to the old work ethic which was so much a part of him, he became an indefatigable, driven man, who pushed himself almost inhumanely. The prevailing attitude of both critics and audiences toward music created and performed by black artists caused far less anguish than a constant striving to meet his own personal standards. It is lamentable that Hampton's administration dismissed him after nineteen years of excellence. Somehow he absorbed the blow, and carried on his musical work. A part of his philosophy of life is revealed in "That's So!", one of his poems from *The Album of a Heart*.

> There'd be no Pleasure were there no Pain;
> E'en Sunshine would pall were there no Rain.
> We could not smile, if in all the years
> We'd never shed a few sad tears.
> What need of ambition if all were gain?
> There'd be no Pleasure were there no Pain.

Follow Me is a non-critical study, structured chronologically in both biography and in discussion of musical compositions according to their dates of publication. Hopefully, the majority of previous unintended but compounded errata found in material on Dett will be corrected in this volume.

PART ONE:
Life

PART I

Chapter I

I'll Never Turn Back (1882-1913)

Robert Nathaniel Dett, black Canadian/American pianist, composer, arranger, and choral director, was born in Drummondville, Ontario, on October 11, 1882. His parents were Robert Tue Dett and Charlotte Johnson Dett. Robert Nathaniel, last born of the four Dett children, soon became aware that his ancestors were descendants of escaped slaves who had come to Canada from the United States. At this time the slave-founded town of Drummondville was largely populated by former slaves and their families, many of whom had arrived there via the Underground Railroad, a secret network organized to aid fugitive slaves in escaping to the northern states and Canada.[1]

Ohio, due to the proximity of its long southern and eastern borders to the southern slave states, was the state most heavily engaged in the network's activities. Religious groups of men, women, blacks, and whites from the Quaker, Congregationalist, and Presbyterian faiths were the most concerned in the cause. In Ontario the counties of Essex and Kent were the safest and most prosperous havens, followed by the area between Detroit, Michigan, and Niagara Falls, New York, just across the Niagara River from Niagara Falls, Ontario. The routes of the Railroad converged either at Detroit, Michigan; Erie, Pennsylvania; Sandusky, Ohio; or Niagara Falls, New York.

By 1840 approximately 10,000 slaves had arrived in Ontario, which housed the largest proportion of Canada's almost 60,000 slave population. At this time Negroes were particularly welcome there, where they were permitted citizenship, the buying of land and entrance into common schools, though various churches had established private schools for immigrants. Discrimination was largely social, evident in selection for jury duty, boat riding, and the purchase of spirits in public taverns. In 1904, when Niagara Falls was incorporated as a city, Drummondville was absorbed into its metropolitan area.

Drummondville was named for Major General Gordon Drummond, a British colonial administrator and commander in

the War of 1812-1814. A brief background of this unique town
seems relevant to the Dett family, for Robert Nathaniel Dett
was remembered there posthumously. The following historical
sketch was given by Millie Wilson, Local Historian at the
Niagara Falls (Ontario) Public Library.

With the end of the American Revolution and the
Declaration of Independence by the United States in
1873, the Niagara River became a boundary between that
country and British North America. The latter was laid
out in townships and originally the land now covered by
the City of Niagara Falls was part of a township named
Mount Dorchester.

In 1791 John Graves Simcoe, the first Lieutenant
Governor of Upper Canada (now roughly the Province of
Ontario) gave the name Stamford to the township.
Drummondville was the first community to evolve in
Stamford Township (1831) when it became the south end
of the city. In 1832 Clifton was added, becoming the
central area of the city. Elgen was added as a third
community in 1853, and three years later it amalgamated
with Clifton, which in 1881, by a special act of
parliament, became the Town of Niagara Falls.

At the same time Drummondville's name was
changed to the Village of Niagara Falls (South), which
in 1904 amalgamated to form the City of Niagara Falls.[2]

The Dett Family

Robert Nathaniel Dett's maternal grandmother, Mrs.
Harriet Washington, formerly of the Washington, D. C. area,
arrived by train in Niagara Falls, Ontario, in the late 1850s,
though no records have confirmed her status as either a slave or a
free person. She was previously married to a Mr. Johnson, by
whom she had a son, Nathaniel, and daughter Charlotte
Johnson, the "full maiden name" Dett gave for his mother on
entering Oberlin in 1903. Charlotte Johnson (Dett) (1863-1937)
was born and educated in Niagara Falls, Ontario. Nathaniel

Johnson, Nathaniel Dett's uncle, a graduate of Hastings Law School in San Francisco, became sugar magnate J. D. Spreckels' confidential secretary. Mrs. Washington later lived with the Detts at the corner of Ferry and Temperance Streets until her death, when Nathaniel was about ten. He remembered her as a lady of strong character, locally popular. As a child he was fascinated by her beautifully gentle singing of spirituals, but recalled, after exposure to more formal church hymns, that they sounded slightly strange and unnatural. Mrs. Washington became blind, and Dett later told an interviewer that she always faced the light while singing.[3] Though no obituary has been located, her funeral was said to have been one of the town's best attended.

Charlotte Dett was a strong influence in her family's life. The Dett children were never allowed idleness and were encouraged to aim for perfection in all their pursuits. Copies of library cards for Mrs. Dett and Nathaniel are in the Local History Archives of the Niagara Falls, New York, Public Library. Mrs. Dett has been described as having high ideals, "a gracious, yet commanding lady of forceful personality and strong character," traits she likely inherited from her mother, Mrs. Washington. Always dressed tastefully in the latest fashions, she became well known in the community through her concern for the unfortunate. The 1910 Niagara County (New York) census showed that Mrs. Dett was a businesswoman as well, who, due to financial necessity, was the proprietor of a rooming house which she owned, free of mortgage.

Further visibility was added when she became a member of the County Committee of the Republican Party, through her activities with the National Federation of Women's Clubs, and as an officer in other women's organizations. She was vice-president of the Empire State Federation of Women's Clubs, president of the Phillis Wheatley Club (1915), and a member of the Eastern Star. In 1918 she was a delegate from western New York to the National Association of Colored Women's Convention in Denver.[4] Mrs. Dett's interest in Wheatley and other prominent Negro women continued strongly throughout her life. The *Niagara Falls* (New York) *Gazette*, February 11, 1931, reported that she spoke on radio WEBR (Buffalo, New York) on "The

Achievements of Negro Women," as part of Black History Week. Wheatley was cited as an achiever among black women.

Though in several documents Dett has given Presbyterian as his religious preference, as a boy he and his family attended the British Methodist Episcopal Church in Niagara Falls, Ontario. This church was rededicated as the Nathaniel Dett Memorial Chapel of the BME Church of Canada in 1983.

Nathaniel Dett's father, Robert Tue Dett (1849-1921), came to Drummondville from Reicesterstown, Baltimore County, Maryland. He was thirteen years older than Mrs. Dett. As a railroad porter on the Grand Trunk Lines running into Chicago, and later for the Canadian Pacific Railroad between Montreal, Quebec, and Vancouver, British Columbia, he had little time to spend with his family. Though not a trained musician, he played piano and guitar. After leaving railroad employment he managed a hotel in Niagara Falls, Ontario.[5]

In 1893 the family moved to 362 Second Street in Niagara Falls, New York. This residence was very near the railroad and the house next to the Dett's, built in 1838, was the first schoolhouse in Niagara Falls. Later it became a depot, a structure torn down in 1960.[6] Shortly after the move Mr. Dett became the owner of a saloon on "the other side of the tracks." As Donald E. Loker, Local Historian at the Niagara Falls, New York, Public Library, put it:

> At that time there was a great deal of construction going on and he [Mr. Dett] catered to that crowd and probably the average man in the community did not even know he existed. Not so for Mrs. Dett, however. They did not live together and she reared her boys for a far different life. Both boys were successful.[7]

Though the Detts separated in 1896, there are no documents of a divorce. Loker related that after Mr. Dett was in the saloon business he became involved with a work-related lawsuit. He continued to maintain business, social and civic ties in Chicago, where he sang for a time in a church choir. Mr. Dett lived until 1921, battling an illness for his last two years, one incurred in 1918 while visiting his first grandchild, Nathaniel's daughter

Helen. The obituary in the *Niagara Falls Gazette*, February 21, 1921, spoke of him as "one of the oldest and best known men in the Canadian and American Niagara district."[8]

Samuel, the oldest Dett child (1879-1962), as well as Nathaniel, was a credit to the Dett family throughout his life. As a youngster he enjoyed sports and reading. He and Nathaniel continued their early schooling in Niagara Falls, Ontario, by special permission after the family moved to Niagara Falls, New York, where Samuel held odd jobs as hotel bellboy, bank messenger, helper at the *Niagara Falls Gazette*, and custodian at the First Methodist Church. In 1907 Samuel was asked to be a substitute mail carrier at $400.00 per year for the Niagara Falls Post Office, a job which would require a signed petition, due to the bank's wish to keep him in its own employ. Through the bank's determination, the post office was underhandedly advised against hiring him. Gaining the support of several prominent Niagara citizens, however, the petition was satisfactorily completed and Samuel accepted the job, becoming the city's first Negro postal employee. Before his retirement he had been promoted to postal clerk, then special clerk.

Samuel demonstrated integrity and wisdom through many city endeavors and involvements. He was an honorary thirty-third degree Mason, president of the Niagara Community Center, a charter member of the Retired Men's Service Club, and was active in the equal rights struggle. In 1961, after fifty years of service he was given life membership in the YMCA Hall of Fame. He never married, and continued to live with his mother until her death in 1937, then stayed alone in the home.

Mrs. Mildred Clark, a native of Niagara Falls, New York, was well acquainted with the Dett family. In a letter she related some interesting memoirs of their association.

> When a child starting to my first school (Third Street) instead of walking the streets as I should of done I took a short cut along the railroad tracks to the station loading platform, then up to the school. This took me past the Dett house and often Mrs. Dett would be in the yard and talk to me. She always had cookies for me. Many times I would hear Nathaniel playing the piano.

... Mrs. Dett belonged [to] and held office in many clubs.
... She organized the Black Women's Rally in October
1928 to endorse Herbert Hoover for President. [She] was
president of the Colored Women's Coolidge and Dawes
Club political group in 1920, chaired National
Federation of Women's Clubs Ways and Means
Committee.

Mrs. Clark said that Mrs. Dett was the major influence in her
sons' lives and "they adored her. She was one of the most
remarkable women of the Niagara Frontier. . . . She was also
musical. Played the piano, mandolin, and sang soprano in
various singing groups or at church." Policeman Claude Clark,
Mildred's late husband, was a special friend of Samuel Dett, as
was the postmaster, Mr. Soluri.

A group of men, Mr. Soluri, Claude, Sam, Claude's
brother and some others took in the wrestling matches in
Buffalo and Niagara Falls, Ontario. . . . I invited him
[Sam] to our holiday dinners and always had a birthday
party for him and the group. After Sam retired Claude
did errands for him or took him when he needed to go
somewhere. Mr. Soluri and Claude checked him daily so
they knew he was OK.

For companionship Samuel was given a dog by the Clarks.
Samuel enjoyed many a Sunday dinner and drive with them.
Speaking of the Dett Collection in the Niagara Falls, New York,
Public Library, Mrs. Clark recalled:

One time when at the house Sam said to me, "I have
a trunk full of pictures, music, newspaper clippings, etc.,
of Nathaniel's and I know you would preserve them and
also see they were taken care of so others could enjoy." So
Claude brought them home. On August 19, 1962 when
they checked on Sam they found him dead in the bath
tub. He was 83. They took care of everything and also
the disposing of the things in the house. Also a stone at
the cemetery.[9]

Little has been written on the second Dett brother, Arthur Newton (1880-1889), whose aptitude for mathematics was unusual, and a third child, Harriet, born in 1881, who lived only two years. Arthur's short life was ended by a gunshot during what was initially a harmless Hallowe'en prank. Of this unfortunate accident the *Suspension Bridge Journal*, November 2, 1889, reported: "Arthur Dett, a colored lad of eight years, of Niagara Falls, Ontario, is dead, the result of a Hallowe'en celebration. The cause of death was injuries received at the hands of Patrick Crowley."

A later report in the *Niagara Falls Gazette*, November 6, 1889, explained that some boys were trying to remove a sign on shoemaker Crowley's property. Crowley shot and hit Arthur. Crowley, after realizing his deed, fled to Niagara Falls, New York. By November 13, the *Gazette* revealed that he had been charged with murder and was in jail, awaiting sentencing. Witnesses, including Samuel Dett, also present at the prank, testified, saying that a neighbor carried the wounded Arthur home and stayed until his father, Robert Dett, arrived. Crowley was tried, convicted of manslaughter, and received a six year prison term, according to the *Welland* (Ontario) *Tribune*, May 9, 1890.

Early Musical Training

Of his parents Nathaniel Dett has written:

Both my father and mother were educated and both were musical. Father played the piano a little and the guitar very well, and he also sang baritone. For many years he was first bass at the old Mount Olivet Baptist Church, Chicago. My mother played the piano, sang soprano, and as a regular part of the entertainment interest of the town, was fond of getting up concerts of local talent which were patronized by both colored and white people.[10]

Dett has said that some of his earliest remembrances are of playing the piano, something he just picked up from listening to his mother play. A well-rounded, cultural education for her children seemed to be uppermost in Mrs. Dett's mind. She taught "Nate," as she called him, to recite from memory the poetry of Tennyson and Shakespeare and lengthy passages from the Bible. Besides an appreciation for literature, Mrs. Dett evidently encouraged further creativity in the visual arts. Mention was made of young Nathaniel's watercolor painting in the Niagara Falls, New York *Daily Cataract*, August 30, 1898.[11]

Though family money was not plentiful, the two older brothers, Samuel and Arthur Newton, were given piano lessons with a Mrs. Marshall, an English lady teaching in Niagara Falls, Ontario. As a little tot still wearing dresses, but already the subconscious possessor of a keen musical ear, Nathaniel sometimes went with his brothers to these lessons, apparently delighted at what he heard. He later recalled of the scene at Mrs. Marshall's:

> . . . whenever the teacher left the room for music, which she kept in an adjoining room, I would slip up to her piano and play on it. I enjoyed this hugely . . . because her piano being an upright one, seemed novel compared to our square piano. At the faintest rustle of her skirts, I would dart back to my chair and when she again entered the room, all would be as before.[12]

Mrs. Marshall pretended to leave one day, only to catch Nathaniel by surprise. He said, "She lifted me off the stool and kissed me, so delighted was she by what she had heard."[13] Immediately Mrs. Dett received a note from her, offering to teach Nathaniel free of charge. Thus began his piano study. He admitted to slow progress with actual note-reading, since he could easily play by ear. After hearing Mrs. Marshall play the piece, he imitated her, often adding a fancy ending of his own, or something else that he thought might sound better. Very soon he could no longer trick her. Another note was sent to his mother, who assured Mrs. Marshall that at the next lesson Nathaniel would know the notes.

Threatened with a peach tree switch, which he was asked to fetch from the yard, Nathaniel suddenly stopped improvising and reluctantly learned to read the notes. If he failed to play a note correctly, Mrs. Dett switched his fingers. Though he never inflicted such *rigueur* on his own students, for him at this time it was efficacious. His improvisory skills, however, never far in the background, would later serve him well as an arranger and composer.

Before the move to Niagara Falls, New York, Dett had other teachers, but also continued to learn on his own. Some of his favorite performance war-horses were "Clayton's Grand March," "Tam O'Shanter," and "The Witches' Flight," which he enjoyed playing with his own embellishments for admiring friends.

Once settled in Niagara Falls, New York, Dett and his brother Samuel continued to cross the border each day to attend school in Ontario. John Weiss, an Austrian guest at the Cataract Hotel in Niagara Falls, New York, became Dett's next teacher. Dett remembered how Weiss, the "excitable Teuton," would tear his hair on hearing wrong notes. Needless to say, student and teacher had little rapport. But Dett has credited Weiss with providing the proper interpretation of Beethoven's "Sonata in f minor." Dett had felt that it should be slow and rather sentimental, but Weiss insisted that the printed musical terms be strictly heeded. Other pieces in Dett's repertoire at the time were a popular arrangement of Franz von Suppe's "Poet and Peasant Overture," a transcription from violin of Joachim Raff's "Cavatina," and Josef Haydn's "Gypsy Rondo."

Aware of his natural gifts, Dett's lack of classical repertoire did not bother him too much. He was always assured of an enthusiastic audience, having repeatedly demonstrated a sympathetic, musical touch, creativity of musical ideas, and skill at fashioning and befrilling popular operatic airs of the day into attractive piano solos. He definitely blossomed at salon entertainment of this type, then much in vogue.

At Niagara Falls (Ontario) Collegiate Institute, where Dett was a high schooler, concerts were presented frequently, often by the students themselves. At one such performance, Dett's chum Willie Clipperton, "a fair cherubic Nordic with bright blue eyes and golden hair," was playing a piano piece on the program in

the school's Assembly Hall, infamous for electrical outages. Dett
has recalled:

> Right in the middle of the piece the house was plunged
> in darkness. One could hear the tones of the piano falter,
> presaging the silence all felt to be inevitable.
>
> It happened that I was sitting directly behind
> Principal Dickson who asked me in a whisper whether I
> could play in the dark. (Of course I could! I had loved to
> do so from childhood!) So I slid onto the stage, and
> sliding onto the stool beside Willie who was glad to
> escape to the wings, continued the music, improvising as
> far as possible on his themes, so that it seemed that he
> was really continuing to play.
>
> Quite unexpectedly, with full brilliance, the lights
> returned. The audience shrieked. What on earth
> happened to Willie? Then, as the truth of the situation
> dawned, there was an outburst of uproarious applause,
> probably not all of which was a tribute to the charm of
> the music.[14]

After Dett's parents separated the boys were left in their
mother's care. Now fourteen, Dett took part time employment to
supplement the family income. Selling newspapers proved
unlucrative due to his shyness, but he secured a job as bellboy at
Niagara Falls' Cataract Hotel through his parents' friendship
with the manager. Never actually required to be a regular
bellboy, he was allowed the privilege of playing on a huge, old
Chickering grand piano, whose deep, mellow tone could be heard
throughout the hotel's lower floors. He often played informally
for the Cataract's guests. By now his repertoire was rather large,
but he still relied on his favorites by Beethoven, Suppe, Raff,
and Haydn.

His exposure at the Cataract perhaps enabled him to accept
extra weekly engagements at the Niagara Falls Country Club
during this period. Too, he played the organ in his family's First
Presbyterian Church, presently at 311 Rainbow Boulevard
North, a church built in 1849, still functioning, and boasting a
congregation of approximately 250. The modestly furnished

sanctuary, with stained-glass windows and oak panelling, has been enlarged to twice its original size. A fellowship building has been added behind it. The Detts' first minister there was Albert Bacon, who came in 1893, followed in 1925 by Albertus C. Van Raalte, who held both Charlotte and Nathaniel Dett's funerals.[15] According to soprano Mrs. Elisabeth Slenk, Dett's "Listen to the Lambs" and "Gently Lord, Oh, Gently Lead Us" are still among the choir's favorite anthems.

The Cataract Hotel must have appeared grandiose to the impressionable young Dett. His description of it is awesome:

> The old parlor . . . as it originally stood, was a room of French colonial design, elegant and grand in treatment. It was a very long room, having ten or twelve windows on each side. From the high ceiling hung two elaborate chandeliers, literally small forests of candles from which peeped cupids and shepherdesses of gilt and wrought iron. Flanking the doors at the center of each end of the room and opposite to each other, midway of the long walls, were enormous plate glass mirrors on marble bases, having curved gilt legs. The frames were also of gilt, climaxing in a burst of gilt flowers and vines in high relief. Curved gilt chairs upholstered in damask lined the walls; a cream colored carpet of deep plush with a rose border covered the floor.[16]

During Dett's stint at the Cataract a visitor who introduced himself as Dr. Hoppe, "a friend of Antonin Dvorak," held a rather serious chat with the young pianist, mostly concerning the increasing influence of Indian and Negro melodies on American and other composers, such as Dvorak. At approximately this time Dvorak had just left the directorship of the National Conservatory in New York City, glowing with the richness of Negro and Indian musical heritages. Dett, however, was not impressed with this information which Dr. Hoppe intended as complimentary to the two races. Rather, the naive young Dett revealed embarrassment that musically his race was identified only with the current and frivolous ragtime style. Too, the poignancy of the spirituals, so totally embraced by Dvorak, might have reminded him sorrowfully of his ancestors' slave days. Dr. Hoppe left his business card with Dett, hoping that he might come to Germany to study.[17]

Later, while a student at Oberlin College, Dett fortunately developed a broader, more cheerful perspective of the larger Negro idiom, but even as late as 1918, he commented on the atttitude of a majority of the black race in an interview carried by *Musical America*:

> The Negro people as a whole cannot be looked to as a very great aid in the work of conserving their folk music. At the present time they are inclined to regard it as a vestige of the slavery they are trying to put behind them and to be ashamed of it. Moreover, the prevailing manner of presenting Negro music to the public—the "coon" song of vaudeville or the minstrel show—has not tended to increase appreciation of it, either among the Negro or white races.[18]

One summer (c. 1897) when Dett was still at the Cataract Hotel, he was asked to move enough chairs into the opulent hotel parlor to accommodate an expected large audience who would hear bass singer Fred Butler in a recital. Dett had earlier been friends with Butler's younger brother in Sunday School, where Mr. Butler was the Sunday School superintendent. Despite the fact that Dett was proud that Fred Butler was returning to his native city for the concert, he vowed that he would not carry chairs again unless it was for his own concert. Why, he asked himself, should he not be able to do as much in music as Fred Butler? His vow concerning the chairs was indeed carried out, for later that same summer, at the urgence of a member of the Country Club where Dett played, he set up the parlor for a recital of his own. His brother, Samuel, acted as agent and sold advance tickets, netting about $50.00, to be used for further music study. Assisting Dett on the concert were his mother, who sang, and friend Mrs. Hilda Brown with dramatic readings.

The 1898 City Directory of Niagara Falls listed Mrs. Charlotte Dett and Samuel Dett's residence as a boarding house at 403 Erie Avenue. In the 1899 and 1900 directories Robert Dett and Annie Dett's residences were listed as the Keystone Hotel, 333 Main Street. The unidentified Annie could have been a relative, or possibly a common law wife, according to Donald E. Loker, Local Historian at the Niagara Falls Public Library. An advertisement in the Niagara Falls, New York, *Daily Cataract-Journal*, March 9, 1901, read: "Robert Dett will serve his usual Saturday night lunch this evening at the Keystone Hotel, 333 Main St. Carved turkey is the main attraction."

A few days later, March 13, the same paper mentioned that Robert Dett played the piano on a program at the Public Library featuring the Niagara Frontier. Another item in that paper, May 25, 1901, indicated that Dett's ties with his father were not completely severed: "R. N. Dett will furnish a continuous musical program at the turkey slicing tonight at the Keystone Hotel, 333 Main Street."[19] In the 1900 City Directory Mrs. Charlotte Dett and sons Samuel and Nathaniel, were residing at 181 Riverway, a boarding house. Nathaniel, eighteen at the time, was listed as a clerk at Lynch and Sons, Boots and Shoes, at 115 Falls Street.

The Turn of the Century

In 1900 Dett's piano piece, "After the Cakewalk," was published by the Vander Sloot Music Company in Williamsport, Pennsylvania. It is rarely listed with Dett's Catalog of Works, and possibly soon went out of print. Apparently Dett accepted miscellaneous engagements whenever asked. The *Niagara Falls Gazette*, May 20, 1901, noted that he had played on a "show," "Lost Paradise," at the International Theater. Seats were twenty-five cents. His selection was an original two-step, entitled "Niagara Falls."

In 1901 Dett began piano study with Oliver Willis Halstead at the Halstead Conservatory (now a beauty parlor) in Lockport, New York, twenty miles from Niagara Falls. He probably went to and from lessons by train, as railroads were the principal connections for area travel. Halstead impressed upon Dett the importance of being a serious student, while frankly pointing out and emphasizing both his interpretive and technical deficiencies.

After a year with Halstead, Dett, now nineteen, gave a quite respectable recital, which included the entire Beethoven "Sonata in F major" (Op. 1, No. 2), Chopin's "Nocturne in g minor," Schumann's "Soaring," two of MacDowell's *Sea Pieces*, and a few of his own compositions which were well received.

He continued at the Conservatory until 1903, during which time Halstead encouraged him to make music his career. On March 10, 1903, Dett shared a recital at the Conservatory with two elocutionists and a vocalist. He played his own "Etude in A Flat," "Inspiration Waltzes," "Churning Song," and "Cave of the Winds March."[20] Dett's inspiration for "Cave of the Winds March" undoubtedly came from a visit to the spectacular Falls.

It was once possible to walk behind the Bridal Veil Fall. The experience was very much like entering a cave. The first person to walk behind the fall was Joseph W. Ingraham, who described the winds there as tumultuous and breathtaking. He gave it the name "Cave of the Winds."[21]

Entries in Dett's diaries of 1901-1903 included his fees, ranging from $2.50 to $5.00 for playing at teas and receptions. Once he wrote of playing at a benefit supper without pay, because it was for the church fund. His association with Halstead, which he writes of in the diaries, must have been a godsend, since he had no steady paternal role model at the time. He thought Mr. Halstead was fond of him, writing that "he put his arm around me."

He wrote of his practice hours, whether or not he was inspired, and jotted a poetic fragment here and there. In a few consecutive entries, c. 1902, he mentions a composition done at the Halstead Conservatory, "Churning Song," under guidance of a Dr. Clarke there. Clarke's criticism to Halstead said: "I think the piece shows decided musical ability and it would repay you [Halstead] to take him [Dett] in hand and give him a course in harmony." Knowing that he must recopy the song, Dett wrote in the diary: "Began copying Churning Song today."

In another entry, January 19, 1903, Dett said that he wrote to

Halstead Conservatory, ca. 1975
Photo courtesy of Local History Dept.,
Niagara Falls, New York, Public Library.

London publisher Richard A. Saalfield concerning his "Inspiration Waltzes," piano pieces he wished Saalfield to orchestrate and publish. He wrote that Halstead had told Saalfield "how well he liked me" and that he wanted to send "Churning Song" to Theodore Presser for publication.

After one enjoyable and appreciated chat with Halstead Dett wrote: "Last night I practiced for an hour. Considerable practice today. Somehow I feel a new inspiration for practicing which I imagine is the result of yesterday's conversation with Mr. H." Other of Dett's intermittently readable entries concerned Sunday School attendance and concerts he heard in Buffalo.[22] Apparently such "inspiration" was not prolonged. A letter dated June 10, 1903, from Halstead to Dett indicated that the young student may have missed lessons from time to time. Halstead's concern was indeed admirable. The letter read:

> My Dear Sir and Pupil:
>   I expected you today and I wish to say that you *must* come tomorrow or next day for your lesson because we must work on your recital pieces.
>   We will make a place for you when you come. So come any hour you can. The programs are nearly printed and we must be ready, as the recitals are next week. Yours,
>   Oliver Willis Halstead[23]

* * *

Robert Dett, Nathaniel's father, remained visible, seeming to exemplify the opposite of Halstead's pious behavior. The *Niagara Falls Gazette*, October 24, 1902, carried news that he had been "charged with keeping a disorderly house, the Keystone Hotel on Main Street." His scheduled trial was delayed because Annie Dett, a witness for the defense, was ill, according to her attorney. Speculation on her actual fitness to stand trial was in question, since two physicians had pronouced her recovered, and able to testify. The trial was adjourned for a week. If Annie Dett was then still incapable of appearing in court her evidence would be given by deposition.

On November 10, 1905, approximately three years later, the *Daily Cataract-Journal* again mentioned that Robert Dett, "the colored proprietor of a Main Street resort," is "patiently waiting for a Sixth Street man to become sober enough to be presented with a bill of $2.68, incurred by making repairs to Dett's wine emporium." The offender, who had well-to-do relatives, had brought a party of merrymakers to Dett's establishment and during their revelling the glass front had been broken. Dett planned to take "desperate measures if the Sixth Street man did not pony up, p. d. q."

On the following June 20, 1906, a headline in the *Gazette* read: "Dett and Davy Are at Law." The item concerned Dett's house rent which was past due. There had been a misunderstanding between Dett and his proprietor about trading lunches for rent. The hearing was postponed.

The Oberlin Years (1903-1908)

In 1833 two young Yankee missionaries, the Reverends John J. Shipherd and Philo P. Stewart, resolved to found a College and Colony on the western frontier "to train teachers and other Christian leaders for the boundless, most desolate fields in the West." Their brainchild was supported by Charles Grandison Finney, a famous nineteenth-century revivalist. The first area settler, Peter Pindar Pease, built a log house in the center of Oberlin, Ohio's present site, a dwelling which was Oberlin Collegiate Institute's first classroom. Twenty-nine men and fifteen women were in attendance at the Institute by 1834.

Circulars advertising the school, one of the few white ones then admitting Negroes, stated that "youths are received as members, irrespective of color." In 1850 the Institute was renamed Oberlin College by an act of the Ohio Legislature. Oberlin Conservatory became a part of Oberlin College in 1867, after operating as a private school since 1865. By 1900 approximately one-third of all black graduates of predominately white institutions had graduated from Oberlin.[24]

After finishing his first year at Oberlin in 1904 Dett met a gentlemanly guest of the Cataract Hotel, Mr. Frederic H. Goff. Goff perceived that Dett had special talent, and became interested enough to inquire about his college activities. At Goff's request Dett soon called on him at his office in Cleveland, where he was President of the Cleveland Trust Company. Goff introduced him to various people, then gave him a check for $75.00. Throughout Dett's attendance at Oberlin, Goff assisted him financially. For this generosity and for recognizing his musical possibilities, Dett was forever grateful.[25]

In her biography of Dett, Vivian Flagg McBrier states: "Dett entered college life joyously and completely. His friends during this period remember him as an elegant dresser, popular at parties, respected and appreciated by the faculty and his fellow students."[26] Dett's double-major in piano and composition required a five-year course. The Oberlin Conservatory's reputation was excellent for its thoroughness. Its school motto, "Learning and Labor," was upheld, economy was stressed, and after graduation worthy students launching careers were given even further support.

In Dett's "Memory and Fellowship Book," in the Mesiah Papers and Documents, he kept a Public Recital program from September 15, 1904, though the town of the performance was not on the program. He had played on this occasion "Valse in D Flat" by Moszkowski. On another Public Recital, June 15, 1907, he played the flashy "Finale" from Schumann's *Carnaval*.

Another of Dett's recitals had taken place at the Cataract House on October 11, 1904. On the program headed "Piano Recital of Modern Composers," Dett played compositions by MacDowell, Paderewski, Mendelssohn, and himself, one titled "To Mother." Assisting him were Mrs. Charlotte Dett, soprano, Mrs. Alyda Brown, reader, and Mr. Charles Pierman, barytone.[27]

Dett's first piano teacher at Oberlin was Howard Handel Carter, who had proudly been a fellow student with Theodore Presser in Leipzig. Dett recalls of Carter:

> He held me down with an iron discipline, and I needed it at that time, as I had chiefly played only such music as appealed to me. Now I was initiated into Bach and other masters of complex rhythms, with whom tune

alone was not the most vital element of composition.[28]

During Dett's last year at Oberlin Carter went abroad, leaving his students with George Carl Hastings, who saw Dett through graduation.

Arthur E. Heacox and Freidrich Lehmann were Dett's theory professors at Oberlin. He studied voice with William J. Horner, music history with Edward Dickinson, and organ with both J. R. Frampton and George Whitefield Andrews. Of Dr. Andrews, also his composition professor, Dett has said:

> He was one of the most modest of men but a very great teacher. I believe that, had this man been a publicity agent, he would have been ranked with the foremost teachers of composition of all countries. But he was so retiring that few outside of Oberlin knew him, and it was possible that even there many failed to realize the tremendous genius which was his. He had the uncanny gift of reading the minds as well as the most complex scores of his pupils, and his great unselfishness and devotion to Christian principles gave a rare vitality to all he said or did.[29]

The 1906 *Oberlin Catalog* gave estimates of anywhere from $283.00 to $435.00 to cover expenses for a thirty-six weeks' school year. Maximum itemizations were: Tuition - Harmony and any other two studies, $174.00; Board - including room furnished, $180.00; Lights and Washing - $30.00; Fuel - $15.00; and Piano rent - $36.00. Private lessons at the Conservatory, assessed each term, were offered for half an hour, at an average of $24.00 per term, and class lessons were less expensive. Free "exercises" included a choral class which met four times a week, recitals given by teachers and students, and orchestra practice for all students prepared to enter the Conservatory orchestra. In addition, there was no charge for using the College Library of over 64,000 volumes, nor for use of the 17,000 musical scores in the Conservatory Library. At this time Oberlin Conservatory had a faculty of thirty-three, including its chairman, Dr. Charles W. Morrison.

    Students in the Conservatory degree program were required to
take basic courses in English, Mathematics, History and Civics,
Science, and Foreign Language. Two units of the language
requirement were to be in either Latin or Greek. For the Bachelor
of Music degree the two essential studies were piano-theory and
music history. A third could be selected from organ, singing,
violin, viola, cello, clarinet, oboe, or cornet. Before the senior
year the student must have completed a course in literary work
taken from the basic courses listed above. The Bachelor of Music
degree could possibly be earned in four years, but five were
advised in the catalog.

    Dett had frequent opportunities to perform on student recitals
in Oberlin's Warner Concert Hall where his playing was well
received, especially when he performed his own compositions.
Two particularly popular ones were "Cave of the Winds March,"
published in 1902, and "Inspiration Waltzes" (1903).

    Warner Hall, a gift of Dr. and Mrs. Lucien C. Warner of New
York City, was described as "one of the finest structures ever
erected exclusively for the use of a School of Music." It was four
stories high, built of Amherst stone, with frontages of 120 feet
each on two streets. Its performance hall boasted two Steinway
grand pianos and "a large and exceptionally fine organ of three
manuals and forty stops." Other areas of Warner Hall included
lecture rooms, a library, offices, and 113 classrooms and practice
rooms. It was heated by steam, which was also used to power the
passenger elevator, pump the organs, and provide lighting.[30]

    To help meet expenses Dett directed the choir at Oberlin's
Mt. Zion Baptist Church, where he also had the custodial duty
of stoking the church furnaces.[31] Though Dett was always well
groomed and stylishly dressed, he could not afford to be a big
spender. Arrangements for meals were made with a Mr. and Mrs.
Barnes on Vine Street in Oberlin. A mutual affection grew
between Dett and the Barnes family, who treated him warmly.
"Berceuse," a poem in Dett's collection *The Album of a Heart*
(1911), is dedicated to Louise Kathryn, a Barnes child born in
1908.

    On one occasion at Oberlin Dett was captivated by the
Kneisel Quartet's performance of the slow movement from
Dvorak's "American Quartet." For perhaps the first time he was

able to absorb the concept of using traditional folk tunes in serious music. Of the experience he has written:

Suddenly it seemed I heard again the frail sweet voice of my long departed grandmother, calling across the years; and, in a rush of emotion which stirred my spirit to its very center, the meaning of the songs which had given her soul such peace was revealed to me.[32]

Dett's activities in 1907 were not limited to the Oberlin campus, as indicated by the previously mentioned Public Recitals. A recital shared by Dett and singer T. W. Langston at the Second Baptist Church in Oberlin on December 19, 1907, was announced on a flyer in Folder 5 of the Mesiah Papers and Documents.

Dett believed that education was the key to both self-esteem and freedom from racial intolerance. As a hard worker with an excellent academic record, he was an ideal student for Oberlin. He was elected to Phi Beta Kappa. With his double-major he was Oberlin Conservatory's first black student to finish the five-year course. He received the Bachelor of Music degree on June 25, 1908. Several commencement concerts were given during the week of June 19-25, some featuring ex-graduates, the Oberlin Glee Club, its orchestra, and drama groups. The Mesiah Papers and Documents contain Dett's autograph book of 1908, in which approximately eighty-five classmates autographed a message to him.

Some two weeks before graduation on a June 6 recital, according to a program in the Mesiah Collection, Dett had played two of his own pieces, one dedicated to Professor George Hastings. On the same program he played a composition by Schulz-Evler.[33] A more readable program of this same event from the Dett Collection, NFNYPB, revealed that the whole recital featured Dett's works. Besides the composer's performance of the piano pieces "Il Penseroso" (after Milton, and dedicated to George Hastings) and "Freda," Mr. Upton of the Conservatory faculty played Dett's "Prelude, adagio - ma non troppo," and "Finale" (dedicated to F. H. Goff). Miss Florence Jenny, vocal teacher at the Conservatory, sang "To the Sea" and "Oh

Whisp'ring Tree" (both dedicated to Mrs. F. H. Goff), "Dinah
Kneading Dough," and "Twilight."   Two violin pieces,
"Confessional" (dedicated to fellow student Donald Morrison)
and "My Song" (dedicated to George Andrews), were played by
Morrison.   George Hastings played "Inspiration Waltzes"
(dedicated to Dett's mother).

On June 9 Dett had presented one of his senior recitals, which
included four original compositions: "Nobody Knows the Trouble
I See," arranged for violin and piano, played by Dett and Donald
Morrison; "To the Sea," sung by classmate contralto Helen Mears;
and two other songs, "Twilight" and "Oh, Whisp'ring Tree,"
performed by Miss Florence Jenny. At the graduation ceremony
Dett received first honors in a class of 100 for two of these
compositions.[34]

Dett's senior piano recital on June 15, 1908, was perhaps more
technically taxing.   He played "Adagio" from Beethoven's
"Sonata in d minor," Chopin "Etudes" Op. 25 No. 4 and Op. 10
No. 4, the Chopin "Ballade in g minor," "Barcarolle" by
Moszkowski, Rubinstein's "Etude in c minor," and Strauss'
transcription of Schulz-Evler's "Concert Arabesques."[35]

As a brilliant pianist, Dett had been encouraged by his
instructors to try for the concert stage. An item from the *New
York Age*, July 30, 1908, which showed Dett in a formal portrait,
said of his recent degree from Oberlin: "[One] done in recognition
of his attainments in theory, composition, pianoforte, organ, and
the history of music." Speaking of the possible career of such a
"Negro musical prodigy" the account continued that his

> . . . future has been almost assured by the splendid start
> he has made. . . . Already his original works have
> received attention and commendation from the local
> papers of Ohio.
> . . . Recently he was a guest of honor at a recital of
> his works in Warner Concert Hall. He received warm
> congratulations of the critical-minded people assembled
> there. . . . And now the Oberlin authorities are so
> impressed with the genius of this young man that they
> contemplate sending him to Europe to go on with his
> career.

Dett after graduation from Oberlin Conservatory, 1908.
Photo courtesy of Hampton University Archives.

The writer was obviously impressed that Dett was also a poet, whose previously mentioned settings were performed on his senior recital. The texts of "Twilight," "Oh, Whisp'ring Tree," and "To the Sea" were reprinted within the news item. Mention was made also that Dett's setting of a Paul Laurence Dunbar poem, "Dinah Kneading Dough," was included on the same program.

While at Oberlin Dett sedulously kept class notes for his courses in theory, harmony, counterpoint, music appreciation, and composition, which included scales, chord progressions, and harmony assignments. One heading at the top of the page was "Inverted Suspension." On others were "Auf, auf mein Herz!" and other titles of Bach chorales. One of his own compositions said "Prelude - Respectfully to Mr. Austin [*sic*] Heacox," one of his theory professors. Another said "Small 2 Part Primary Form." Many pages in a manuscript notebook were devoted to his own compositions. One, in the style of a choral, was titled "Gratitudes and Inspirations." Unfortunately, the scores are too dim to read.[36]

In an update for Oberlin's files (undated, but c. 1924) Dett answered the question "What has been the influence of Oberlin on your life?" with "Nothing is good that can be made better, an axiom learned from Dr. Andrews, has been one of the strongest conscious influences in my life." Dett's pick for "Most outstanding former students rendering public service" were President Henry Churchill King (of Oberlin), Dr. Warner (who donated Warner Hall), Dr. Andrews, Mr. Hall, and "the graduate who has been recently honored for his successful experiments in electricity—the name escapes me."[37]

On October 29, 1908, the *New York Age* noted that Dett had played piano solos in Mme Azalia Hackley's annual music festival in Philadelphia, hailing him as a "promising musician." This was quite possibly the beginning of their mutual admiration society. Mme Hackley (1867-1922) became avidly interested in Dett's career, and at the same time he was awed by her good works, not only in his behalf but for other such aspiring Negro musicians as Carl Diton and Clarence Cameron White.

* * *

Besides the *Age, The Crisis*, journal of the National Association for the Advancement of Colored People (NAACP), closely followed the progress of blacks in all fields. Its object, as stated in a first issue of November, 1910, was to give the facts and arguments regarding the current dangers of race prejudice. At ten cents per copy *The Crisis* early on carried advertisements for black schools, studio teachers, hotels, cosmetics, bookstores, and the like. One such ad for the Touissant Conservatory of Art and Music, which offered piano, violin, mandolin, voice culture, and all brass and reed instruments, also boasted art classes for the painting of parasols, fans, bookmarks, pin cushions, lampshades, curtains, screens, piano and mantel covers, and sofa pillows. These were signs of the times. Some of the schools advertising in 1911 were Shaw, Fisk, Wilberforce, Howard, Lincoln College, and Atlanta University.

* * *

An application for a teaching position, filled out by Dett in 1908 and sent to the Board of Education, District of Columbia, revealed that he was five feet, six-and-a-half inches tall and weighed 135 pounds. To the question "When available?" he answered "At any time," and to "Salary desired" he wrote $1,200. "Remarks" about himself read: "I am a young man of Christian character and good habits. Do not use tobacco or alcoholic drinks in any form. Member of First Presbyterian Church." A letter dated September, 1908, to Dett from Louis P. Mehlingen of the D. C. Treasury Department stated that there were no teaching vacancies in the area at that time.[38]

A well put letter of recommendation from Oberlin Professor George Hastings, undoubtedly contributed to Dett's self-esteem, though by this time he had already taken a position at Lane College in Jackson, Tennessee. Dated February 22, 1909, it read:

To whom it may concern:

Nathaniel Dett, O. C. M. 1908, has done the finest kind of work in our Institution, graduating with highest honors in Piano Composition, Organ and all supplementary branches.

As a pianist he is very brilliant, his public performances always creating enthusiasm. His finger technique is finished and his natural musical ability is guided by the spirit of genius. He is a hard worker and a person of the highest character, and in every way a person one takes pleasure in recommending to the confidence of persons of influence.

Piano is not Mr. Dett's only unusual talent. He gave a fine program of his own compositions. His "Inspiration Waltzes" I consider the best piano waltzes written, and I am not alone in this opinion.

In short, I consider Mr. Dett a finely prepared musician of *very unusual* ability, and bespeak for him a brilliant future, and it is a genuine pleasure to recommend him.

Geo. C. Hastings
Ass't. Prof. Piano-forte

The letter, signed by a Notary Public, is in the Dett Collection, NFNYPL.

Dett at Lane College (1908-1911)

Despite the encouragement of Dett's teachers at Oberlin for further study toward a concert career, it was perhaps a wiser choice on his part to stay in America, perform, and teach his people to appreciate good music. Stellar black musicians and writers, such as Samuel Coleridge-Taylor, James Weldon and J. Rosamond Johnson, and Harry T. Burleigh had already broken some ice with the American public, but fierce competition on the concert circuit during the first two decades of the century was increasing rapidly. Numerous fine native pianists, as well as those from Europe, were taking New York and other large cities by storm. In the fall of 1908 Dett accepted a position at Lane College in Jackson, Tennessee.

Under auspices of the Colored Methodist Episcopal Church of America, in January of 1880 four acres of land were purchased for $240.00 for the hill site of Lane College which now overlooks the city of Jackson. When the school opened in November of 1882, with Bishop Isaac Lane as its first principal, its name was C. M. E. High School. Enrollment grew steadily and it soon became Lane Institute. By 1896 a college department was added to the academic department (high school) at which time it was renamed Lane College. Lane attracted both day and boarding students, who came mainly from Texas, Arkansas, Kentucky, Mississippi, and Tennessee.

Dett's duties as Principal of the Music Department included teaching piano, vocal music, and directing the Lane Choral Society. He had had little, if any, choral teaching experience, so actually began to learn on the job. His personality was magnetic and his knack for recruiting exceptional, for in two years he had drawn over 100 students, and was proud of his choir's progress. Too, through the students he was able to expand his knowledge of Negro songs.

On June 1, 1909, the Lane College Choral Society, under Dett's direction presented Sir Frederick Cowen's very popular cantata, *The Rosemaiden,* a work he would present again at Hampton in later years.[39] During this year Lane was able to offer four Bachelor's degrees, in Arts, Science, Divinity, and Music. In the *Vest Pocketbook for Students* the purpose of the founders and promoters of the College was "to provide for the people at the lowest possible cost, an education in all that pertains to moral strength, intellectual power, refinement, and Christian graces in manhood and womanhood." Until 1913 all of the Lane College graduates had been males. Anna L. Cooke gives further insight into the requirements of the College:

> A religious atmosphere was felt throughout the campus. All students were expected to bring a Bible with them, to be present for morning devotions in the college chapel, to attend the college church and Sunday School

regularly, and attend mid-week Prayer Meetings, which were held each Wednesday night. Realizing that freedom was most important in the minds of those who had not been many years removed from slavery, the school recognized as an important date in the school calendar January 1, when Emancipation celebration was held.[40]

One of Dett's first and memorable students in the academic department was Sarah Price (Mrs. Sarah Price Gibbs), a cousin to Bishop Lane, Lane's first principal. McBrier has given Mrs. Gibbs' view of Dett's early public school music course:

> The large class met weekly and the course covered the rudiments of music, scales, notes, syllables and singing. Each student had a textbook and was required to sing alone. Class programs were offered during Assembly and in Chapel for devotions. [Mrs. Gibbs] recalled that he taught the entire Music Department "My Bonnie Lies Over the Ocean."
> The students held him in high respect and considered him genteel and refined.[41]

Mrs. Mattie Lane, Bishop Lane's sister-in-law, worked with Dett at Mother Liberty Church in Jackson, where he was the organist and pianist. Mother Liberty was the first church of the colored Methodist Episcopal denomination established in Jackson. Dett's newly organized community chorus, which welcomed any townsperson who wanted to sing, rehearsed at Mother Liberty and presented pleasing programs in the Jackson area.

Dett's home and off-campus studio, a small squarish cottage, formerly the Lane College Library, was situated near the railroad tracks. According to a photo taken c. 1909, the small house looked to have been moved from another site. Since its foundation was not underpinned, it was likely not too comfortable during the winter. Though he continued to practice and study there after his classroom hours, Dett generously allowed visits from the students who were compelled by his playing.

In 1910 and 1911 Dett went on several short tours as a piano recitalist, though did not neglect his duties at Lane. As a single performer he attracted unprecedented large black audiences at two concerts in Memphis. As a guest of the Inter-se Club of Birmingham, his two fund raising concerts for charity were well received. Other appearances in Mason City and at Alabama State College in Montgomery (then a junior college named Alabama State Normal School for Colored Students) resulted from the second concert in Birmingham. Though no specific date was given, Folder 5 of the Mesiah Papers and Documents contains a program of the operetta *Sylvia*, whose composer was not listed, performed by the Lane College Choral Society in 1910.

By 1911 Dett had written approximately thirty poems, included in a volume published that year in Jackson, titled *The Album of a Heart*. In a highly romantic style, many of them were love poems. Others praised the influence of nature's beauties, philosophy, and music. Several were dedicated to colleagues, students, friends, and family. One titled "The Rubinstein Staccato Etude" was included in James Weldon Johnson's *The Book of Negro Poetry* (1931).[42]

The year 1912 was significant for Dett, marking the composition of his first large piano work, the *Magnolia Suite*, a set of five pieces published that year by Clayton F. Summy. The following year, before Dett left Lane College, he had completed a second piano suite, *In the Bottoms*, which included the still popular "Juba Dance," though Summy did not publish it until later that year, after Dett had taken a position at Lincoln Institute in Jefferson City, Missouri.

Dett's work in Jackson, especially that with the Lane College Choral Society, had left a tremendously favorable impact. He showed not only teaching and recruiting skills, prowess as a performer, poise and discipline, but that he was a builder and an innovator as well. He was invited back to Jackson over the years to present recitals of his own compositions, and to re-organize and conduct the community chorus.

Lincoln Institute (1911-1913)

Dett bore Lane no ill will, but neither could he refuse Lincoln

Institute's salary offer, one three times that he was presently receiving. For a six months' period in the 1913-1914 school year he was to receive $653.00. He accepted the position at Lincoln in preference to another he had been offered at the same time in Kansas City, as Director of Music at the Kansas City High School.

Lincoln Institute, named for Abraham Lincoln, was initially a private school established in 1866 with funds from two United States Infantry companies. The 62nd Infantry donated $4,000.00 and the 65th Infantry gave $1,379.00 in individual contributions, some as large as $100.00, though each soldier received only $13.00 per month for military service. Determined that their black successors would be eligible for higher education denied them as a race, the soldiers gave unselfishly. Since 1879, when the Institute property was transferred to the State of Missouri, Lincoln in essence has functioned as a state university.[43]

Lincoln Institute, which became Lincoln University in 1921, first offered instruction at the post-secondary level in 1877. It was incorporated and became a state institution in 1879, awarding its first degree at the 1891 graduation ceremony.

Dett was one of approximately two dozen full-time faculty members at Lincoln, all required to have the minimum of a Bachelor's degree. A few outstanding students worked as assistants. Dett soon managed to ingratiate himself, all the while maintaining the respect due a professional person. Young Carol C. Damel, son of John W. Damel, a physics and zoology professor at Lincoln, had the honor of delivering fresh milk to Dett in Yates Hall, which later became the school library. Of this routine biographer McBrier wrote: "He [Carol] was directed to knock *gently* on the door, wait and knock *gently* again. If there was no answer, he was to leave the milk outside the door," so as not to disturb Dett's practicing.[44]

When Dett arrived at Lincoln it already had an enthusiastic chamber orchestra of some twenty players, and the voice and piano students were ripe for teaching. Vocal music had always held its own there, partially through highly praised concerts presented for the Missouri Legislature. Any student at Lincoln could take vocal music free of charge, whereas instrumental lessons were twenty-five cents each. Special emphasis was placed on proper methods of breathing, tone production, phrasing, enunciation, part sight-reading, scales, and the learning of songs.

Dett, considered friendly but reserved by many, took little time to socialize, since numerous hours were spent teaching vocal classes and, according to McBrier, approximately 100 piano students. He also directed the chorus (one named for him) and orchestra. As a pianist, he performed at the school and also publicly.

Word of Dett's performances, compositions, and excellent teaching had spread to those interested in the activities of black musicians. His piano suite, *Magnolia*, had drawn the attention of such influential persons as Mme Azalia Hackley, black singer, lecturer, voice teacher, and crusader for the development of Negro folk music. Already aware of his qualifications, Mme Hackley would be instrumental in his moving to Hampton Institute in 1913, where, hopefully, a music school was to be newly established.

On May 4, 1912, while Dett was still at Lincoln, Mme Hackley was invited to Hampton Institute for a song recital and voice demonstration, and returned there in late December to present a Christmas concert.[45] Dett's praise for Mme Hackley has been unbounded. He considered that she did even more as a promoter of Negro music, in her larger scope of activities, than either spiritual arranger Harry T. Burleigh or Henry T. Krehbiel, music critic and author of *Afro-American Folk Songs*.

> . . . Mrs. Hackley, by going all through the country, especially the South, and personally organizing mammoth Negro choruses to sing spirituals in the largest available halls, before large audiences, not only dramatically focused attention on Negro native musical ability, but gave the Negroes themselves a thrill of pride in their own ability and in a racial inheritance of which they were fast becoming ashamed.[46]

Since Mme Hackley was at this time on the faculty of the Washington Conservatory of Music, she had undoubtedly mentioned Dett to its director, Mrs. Harriet Gibbs Marshall. As

the former Harriet Gibbs, Mrs. Marshall (1869-1941) was the
first black American to complete the piano course at Oberlin
Conservatory in 1899.   As a concert performer, teacher and
collector of folk music she worked as an educator in the
Washington, D.C., public schools as well as at the Washington
Conservatory, which opened in 1903.   She was a pioneer in
bringing black concert artists to Washington from all over the
United States.[47]

Evidently, from the content of Dett's letter to Mrs. Marshall,
dated February 24, 1913, while he was still at Lincoln Institute,
she had invited him to participate in one of her coming
productions. Dett's letter read:

> Your letter of the 2nd of Feb. was forwarded to me
> from Kansas City. In reply I would say that I am very
> glad indeed to hear of the movement you have on foot for
> the promulgation of Negro Music and its composers. My
> list of contributions is not a very long one, consisting of the
> "Magnolia" Suite. This Suite comprises five numbers,
> which are described in the enclosed circular.
>
> There is in preparation at present another Suite "In
> the Bottoms" which I hope will appear soon; in some
> ways I think that this last work is even more
> characteristic than the first. I should be very glad to
> send you a complimentary copy of the new work when it
> appears.
>
> Thanking you, and with very best wishes for your
> well deserved success, I am, most truly yours,
>   R. Nathaniel Dett[48]

Dett wrote a later letter to Mrs. Marshall on his personal
letterhead from Lincoln Institute, which said "In recitals of
original compositions" in one corner and "Author *The Album of a
Heart*" in the other. He needed something from her. Dated
April 17, 1913, the letter read:

> I have just heard of your announcement cards of the
> exercises in which you are illustrating the progress of the
> Negro in Music Composition. I am writing to know if I

might have one to show my students by way of encouragement. Stamps are enclosed to cover postage. Congratulating you on your noble work and with best wishes for its unvarying success, I am

Most truly yours

R. Nathaniel Dett[49]

During the summer of 1913 Dett took the opportunity of returning to Oberlin to study with Professor Karl Gehrkens, at the time a prominent and well respected leader in musical pedagogy and public school music. Dett was forever The Student. Study at other institutions of higher learning were to follow in the coming years.

Chapter II

Hampton, My Home by the Sea (1913-1919)

R. Nathaniel Dett is known and will be remembered foremost
for his work at Hampton Institute. He accepted a position on the
Hampton faculty in the fall of 1913, one which he held through
the spring of 1931, having become Director of the Music
Department in 1926. His efforts with the Hampton Institute
Choir, Hampton's various glee clubs, the Hampton Quartet, and
the Hampton Choral Union are praised in practically
everything one reads about him. His excellence as a pianist,
composer, and arranger was outstanding. His ability to work
with and mold large groups resulted in high quality
performances heard by appreciative audiences throughout the
United States, Europe, and Canada. But Dett's years at Hampton
were bittersweet.

Hampton Institute

Founded on a 120-acre estate purchased by the American
Missionary Association of New York, the school was named
Hampton Normal and Agricultural Institute when it opened in
1868. It has been estimated that between 1865 and 1872 more
than $5,000,000.00 was spent organizing American public schools
and such colleges and universities as Hampton, Howard, Fisk,
Atlanta, and Storer.

General Samuel Chapman Armstrong (b. 1839) was the
fortunate choice of the Freedmen's Bureau as Hampton's founder
and first principal. Born of missionary parents, Armstrong grew
up in Hawaii. As a youngster he often accompanied his father,
the Minister of Public Instruction, on school inspection rounds,
absorbing not only a sense of educational responsibility, but true
compassion for less advanced races.

Armstrong completed his education at Williams College in
Williamstown, Massachusetts, where he graduated with honors
in 1862. Entering with the rank of Captain, he made the Union
Army his career for the next six years, by the end of which stint

he had become a Brevet Brigadier General. Two and a half years' training of Negro soldiers in the Eighth and Ninth Regiments, two all-colored groups, fitted him perfectly for the coming administrative duties at Hampton. He was convinced that

> . . . the freedmen had excellent qualities and capacities and deserved as good a chance as any people. Educational methods to meet their needs must include special practical training and take into account the forces of heredity and environment.[1]

Hampton's first fifteen male students were required to do manual labor, and thereafter anyone who could not pay the school fees was allowed to work during the day and attend night classes, which accommodatingly duplicated the daytime ones. This initial student group lived in army barracks until 1871, when the Academy Building was completed with funds from the Freedmen's Bureau and philanthropists from the North. The barracks were then occupied by female students for the following three years, until Virginia Cleveland Hall was finished in 1874. Some of the funding for it was raised by the famous Hampton Singers, with whom General Armstrong went on tour.

Beginning as an elementary school with only two teachers, Hampton soon became a secondary one, whose aim was to train teachers. The modest entrance requirements permitted students up to the age of twenty-five, but did demand certain standards, such as basic skills in reading, writing, and mathematics, plus good physical health and character. After ten years of solid operation, funds from the United States government were donated to enable the attendance of American Indians at Hampton. In its early years heavy emphasis was placed on learning an industrial skill, with less concern for cultural pursuits.

General Armstrong remained Principal of Hampton until his death in 1893, when he was succeeded by Reverend Hollis B. Frissell until 1917. From 1918-1929 James Gregg was Principal, followed by George Phenix. Phenix's appointment was for the fall of 1930, though his assistance actually began in the spring of 1929. In 1927 Phenix had written a review for *The Southern*

Workman, Hampton's journal, of Dett's *Religious Folk-songs of the Negro*. Later, in 1931, by the time Dett left Hampton, Arthur Howe had become Principal. These administrators were all white men, a policy then customary with a majority of Negro schools of similar status. Alonzo Moron, a Hampton graduate originally from the Virgin Islands, became the school's first Negro President in 1948, a position thereafter filled by Negroes.

The Legacy

On January 11, 1913, Mme Azalia Hackley was Hampton's guest for a third time, invited there to conduct a student music festival. Male and female choruses presented folk songs under her direction, and she offered vocal soli in addition to a "demonstration in voice culture."[2] Her timely appearance, coupled with an innate persuasiveness and her longtime association with the Dett family, undoubtedly worked in Dett's behalf, presaging his appointment to the music faculty. Dett himself has admitted: "Through Mrs. Hackley's influence, I went to Hampton Institute in 1913, as director of [vocal] music, and took charge of the choir."[3]

He considered her a woman of extraordinary powers, beauty, and intelligence, for

> . . . she was able to establish and maintain "foreign scholarships" by which she sent abroad two promising Negro students, Carl Diton, pianist, and Clarence Cameron White, violinist, for extended study. So far as I know, this achievement has never been equalled by any member of my race and becomes all the more remarkable when it is remembered that this good woman was herself of limited means.[4]

The new appointment at Hampton Institute would challenge Dett's personal integrity, as well as his academic and musical abilities. He rose to the challenge, indeed, and established a solid reputation through his untiring efforts for the school. One of his most responsible duties was directing the Hampton Choir, assuring its continuing tradition of excellence.

Hampton's first choral group had been organized in 1872 by Thomas P. Fenner, called to Hampton from his teaching position at the conservatory in Providence, Rhode Island. Precedent for such a choir had been set by the enviably successful touring Fisk Jubilee Singers. In emulation Fenner had readied seventeen of Hampton's singers by February of 1873 for a several month's tour, starting in Washington, D. C. The group's division of four sopranos, three altos, six tenors, and four basses was well balanced. This first performance, *a cappella*, included "The Milk-White Horses," "In Search of Liberty," "Ef You Want to See Jesus, Go in de Wilderness," and "The Soldier's Farwell," none of which Dett composed. Afterwards the singers were entertained at Howard University, then interviewed by President Ulysses Grant. Two more concerts were given in Washington before they moved on to Philadelphia and New York.

The *Philadelphia Bulletin*, February 22, 1873, gave high praise:

> The weird, the wild, the grotesque, the pathetic, the religious, and the comic elements in the African nature seem to be all represented in the songs they sing. No language can portray the effect of such songs as "Dust and Ashes," "Swing Low, Sweet Chariot." If Meyerbeer ever heard these songs, he could have introduced them into his operas with a stranger and more striking effect than any chorus in his *Africaine* can produce.[5]

The following year a smaller group was reorganized for another tour through Canada and the Middle West. By the end of a third tour, ending in July, 1875, the group had sung over 500 concerts in Canada and eighteen states, and earned enough money to build Virginia Cleveland Hall within which was a dining room and a chapel.

The hall, designed by architect Richard Morris Hunt, was completed in 1874. Hunt (1827-1895) had earlier designed two academic halls on the Hampton campus. The first, mentioned earlier, "little more than an academic shell," burned in 1879; the second, completed three years later, was fireproof. Virginia

Cleveland Hall, still very much in use, "embodied both Second
Empire and Victorian Gothic elements."[6] Topped with slate
turrets, this huge brick complex of four stories and a basement
tranquilly faces the Chesapeake Bay.

To maintain their academic courses choir members took
school work with them on tour. In concert they used some of
Fenner's arrangements for four-part chorus of folk and plantation
songs, published as a volume in 1874, one complementing
Hampton and Its Students by Mrs. M. F. Armstrong and Helen W.
Ludlow.[7]

According to letters from students of the choir, the group met
with a variety of hospitality and housing on their tours. Even in
St. Catherine's, a city seven miles from Niagara, Ontario, the
two first class hotels refused them accommodations. In some
restaurants waitresses refused to serve them. In contrast,
however, in Cambridge, Massachusetts, they were invited to the
home of Henry Wadsworth Longfellow where they performed.
In Cambridge they also sang at the grave of pro-Civil Rights
Senator Charles Sumner. Adult admissions to their public
concerts were thirty-five and fifty cents, or in some cases three for
one dollar. Children's tickets were twenty-five cents.[8]

Excellence in performance and preservation of the spirituals
remained the Choir's strong points in future years. Fenner's
arrangements of the spirituals were only the beginning of a
wealth soon to follow, including those by Dett, Natalie Curtis-
Burlin, Harry T. Burleigh, and numerous other reputable
arrangers, both black and white.

By the late 1890s Hampton had organized the Hampton
Folklore Society, its own group for the preservation of spirituals,
whose main concern was

> . . . not to obtain any song in a more or less changed or
> mangled condition, as you surely do when you take it out
> of its foreordained and appropriate setting in some part
> of the complicated Negro religious ritual, and adapt it to
> be sung as a regular four-part song by a choir or
> congregation, either white or black. . . . Each one of these
> songs has its place and its history and the work of our
> Society must be to find the place and the history of each

song that it adds to its collection.[9]

For complete accuracy the Society was hoping to record live performances of spirituals, as well as sermons, prayers, and complete religious services, by gramophone, rather than risk inaccuracies in notating them.

Beginnings

Dett inherited a rich structure at Hampton. Besides the enthusiasm of the music students and faculty and Mme Hackley's surveillance, Major Robert Russa Moton, Hampton's Commandant of Male Students, gave his full support to the school's music program. The somewhat military appearance of the male students' uniforms was in no way intended to create a militant atmosphere. John Wesley Work, writing in 1915, said of Hampton's excellence:

At Hampton the spirit and attitude are admirable. It is doubtful if at any place this music [Negro folk songs] is more thoroughly appreciated. Through all these years since its founding, Hampton had steadily collected and published these songs in attractive form. Their editions have been more thorough, more painstaking and more important than those of any other school. . . . The songs have been written and published in their original forms, just as they came from the people, and the harmonies have been written with no particular significance.

In interpretation, Hampton has always done well. She has stood far forward. . . . Virginia has a most interesting and fine class of Negroes. They are full of folk lore, folk song, and folk spirit.[10]

Work continued with praise for Moton and Dett:

It is fortunate for this institution that Major R. R. Moton stands as the chief exponent of this music. His spirit and understanding are commendable. Doubly fortunate is it that Hampton has secured the services of

R. Nathaniel Dett. . . . His arrangement of the folk song,
"Listen to the Lambs," is meritorious and marks the
beginning of the period of development of Negro Folk
Song in Hampton. It would not be surprising if under his
leadership this institution would be the foremost in both
preservation and development.[11]

Moton had written a Preface to Fenner's first edition (1901) of
Religious Folk Songs of the Negro. In it he declared strong
personal feelings regarding spirituals:

Though the words are sometimes rude and the strains
often wild yet they are the outpourings of an ignorant and
poverty-stricken people whose religious language and
ideals struggled for expression and found it through
limited vocabularies and primitive harmonies. They are
not merely poetry. They are life itself in the life of the
human soul mainfesting itself in rude words, wild stories,
and curious tho' beautiful harmonies.[12]

* * *

The Crisis acknowledged Dett's Hampton appointment in its
December, 1913 issue in the section "Music and Art," saying "R. N.
Dett, a colored Canadian, who is teaching music at Hampton
Institute, is a composer of note. Especially notable are two suites
characteristic of Negro life: *In the Bottoms* and *Magnolia*."[13]
Such publicity, though modest, was undoubtedly to Dett's
advantage.

Musical America carried a critique of *In the Bottoms*, which
had recently been published by Clayton F. Summy. In part the
review read:

As the title suggests it deals with things of the
South, things of the cottonfields, of aged negroes,
their sorrows and joys, of those intimate
characteristic touches of humor for which the
Southern negro is famous.

Mr. Dett has more than one interesting moment in

> this suite. The work fairly teems with musical ideas
> that strike the listener as unusual. . . . The composer
> has written a full-page preface of explanation to his
> work—an entirely unnecessary proceeding. Would it
> not have been better to allow the musician who plays
> the music to form his own pictures from the titles?

Comparing this suite to the earlier *Magnolia*, the reviewer
went on:

> Mr. Dett has distinct talent. Some time ago there
> appeared a rather sentimental piano suite from his pen
> which gave little promise of such an excellent gift as is
> shown [here]. . . . The movements of the work vary, some
> of them requiring a well-developed technic for
> performance, others not making any considerable
> demands.[14]

A long list of Mme Hackley's slave-driving suggestions, found
in the Hampton University Archives, had been given to Dett and
the voice teacher, Miss Elizabeth Drew, for the fall semester of
1913, including Christmas programs, library holdings, hymns to
be sung by rote, and the necessary inclusion of sight reading for
the choir. Mme Hackley's plans stated in part:

> Try reading from the History of Music three to five
> minutes, three times a week at prayers. Every month
> give short talks about what has been read. Every quarter
> give a talk or paper on ground covered. Next season,
> Theory of Music. . . . Think out a tentative condensed
> course for a Summer Music School for Teachers in Colored
> Colleges.

No grass grew under Dett's feet as he plunged whole
heartedly into the school's musical activities, though he may
not have been able to implement all of Hackley's well-meant
ideas. On his arrival he had found the pianos in abysmal
condition, a situation gradually remedied. He was smitten with
the overall atmosphere of the place, however, particularly with

the magnolias and other plant life on Hampton's grounds. McBrier described the campus:

> In 1913 Hampton Institute was almost idyllic in its physical beauty. The spacious campus was a picture with its carefully mowed grass, magnificent magnolia and holly trees, abundant shrubbery, formal flower gardens and well-kept buildings. The blue waters of the Hampton River dotted with sail and motor boats passed placidly by the front of the campus, completing the charming picture.[15]

One interesting old brick building, the Hampton Memorial Church, completed in 1886, is still in daily use. Its original pews, floors, and stained glass windows have been maintained. It was designed by architect Joseph Cleveland Cady (1837-1919), a leading exponent of the Romanesque Revival, famous for his austere churches, including the New York Avenue Methodist Episcopal Church in Brooklyn. Both the Hampton and Brooklyn churches have massive square towers. Cady is best known as the architect for the Metropolitan Opera House (1881-1884) and the South Wing of the American Museum of Natural History.[16]

1914

On January 27, 1914, Dett's Hampton Singers presented a program in Carnegie Hall. *The Crisis* reported that

> . . . a chorus of forty from Hampton Institute [was] heard . . . in Negro folksongs illustrating a motion-picture pageant of agricultural life in the South. The Honorable George McAneny, president of the board of aldermen, spoke in behalf of Hampton, the first industrial school for Negroes and Indians.[17]

Mrs. Harriet Gibbs Marshall, mentioned in Chapter I as founder and director of the Washington Conservatory of Music, continued her contact with Dett through correspondence. Similar to Mme Hackley, she was a lady of strong personality and administrative talent. A letter to her from Dett, dated February 9, 1914, indicates that she had suggested some sort of cultural exchange whereby teachers from her Conservatory would give recitals at Hampton, and that Dett would perform at the Conservatory in reciprocation. Dett answered:

Dear Mrs. Marshall:

Your letter of the 15th of January has been on my mind for some little time. I was very glad to hear from you and to receive your congratulations on my being here, and I thank you most heartily for them. In regard to your teachers coming I would say that Major Moton usually handles all of the artist recitals. The Major has been away for a month, and that is why you have not heard from me; however as soon as he returns, I shall be pleased to take the matter up with him.

I should be glad to come to your school for a recital, later in the year, about April, if the arrangements can be made. I have to play in New York about that time and I think that the two dates could be arranged at the same time. I am always glad to hear from you and to learn of the success of your work.

With every wish for your continued prosperity in every way, I am

Yours very truly,
R. Nathaniel Dett[18]

The following March 11 marked the third annual concert of Negro music in Carnegie Hall under auspices and for the benefit of the Music School Settlement. Harry T. Burleigh, Rosamond Johnson, and Abbie Mitchell were soloists. James Reese Europe conducted the Negro Symphony Orchestra, and Will Marion Cook and Burleigh directed the Settlement's eighty-voice chorus. As an entrant in a Settlement sponsored competition, Dett was given second prize at the event for his choral work "Listen to the Lambs." First prize went to Carl Diton, then teaching piano at Paine College in Augusta, Georgia, for his piano arrangement

of four spirituals in five parts: "Pilgrim's Song," "Deep River,"
"Little David, Play on Your Harp," and "Every Time I Feel the
Spirit."[19]

Originally the Settlement had planned to offer $100.00 for
the best composition on a Negro theme by a black resident of the
United States, with guaranteed publication by Schirmer and
Company of New York City. Ultimately, however, the money
was divided into a $75.00 prize for Diton's arrangements and
$25.00 for Dett's "Listen to the Lambs." Diton on occasion
accompanied such outstanding singers as Marian Anderson, Jules
Bledsoe, Catarina Jarboro, and Ezio Pinza, and also concertized
as a piano soloist.

Another letter from Dett to Mrs. Marshall, dated March 14,
1914, somewhat clarified the matter of the exchange concerts,
though evidently Dett did not proofread it for mistakes before
mailing:

> Your letter of the 4th inst. at hand, and in reply
> would say that I have taken up the matter of your
> teaches (sic) coming here with Major Moton, and I regret
> to say that our schedule is so full that ther (sic) is no
> other place for other concerts this year, much as I should
> like to have the students hear some outside talent. If you
> are still minded to have me come you (sic), I think that I
> could arrange to be in your city on the 25th of April.
> Terms for my concerts are Fifty Dollars.[20]

The letter was signed as before. That Dett played at the
Conservatory in April is uncertain.

Integrated with Dett's Hampton duties was the forming of
the Hampton Choral Union, a move urged by President Frissell
for rapport between the community of Hampton and Hampton
Institute. Dett's invitation for an organizational meeting was
well taken, one extended to every musical organization and every
church in the area. The group's first meeting at Clarke Hall
proved rewarding, and rehearsals using campus facilities were
begun almost immediately. The Hampton Choral Union was
described as

. . . another expression of the co-operative spirit of Hampton Institute. . . . The idea is mutual helpfulness, and to promote greater musical interest and appreciation throughout the community. The Union has no president nor vice-president, the affairs being managed by an executive board. The annual membership fee is one dollar; there are fifty-four paid memberships. The average attendance is something over forty; a very large percent of the members are graduates of the school.[21]

On May 5, 1914, Dett gave a recital in Norfolk, Virginia, at the Queen Street Baptist Church, under auspices of the Samuel Coleridge-Taylor Club. An account in the May 9, 1914 *Norfolk Journal and Guide* said: "Mr. Dett's own compositions were enthusiastically received, some eliciting applause before his conclusion. He is a master of the piano, the grace and technique of his execution showing fine training and versatility."

The Choral Union's first public program, planned for May 20, 1914, would feature Harry T. Burleigh as soloist. Burleigh, a graduate of the National Conservatory of Music in New York City, had by this time several published art songs and some instrumental compositions to his credit, as well as arrangements of "Deep River" and other spirituals. He was also known as a distinguished baritone recitalist and oratorio singer, the first Negro to be hired as a musician by St. George's Episcopal Church and the Jewish Temple Emanu-El, both in New York City. Burleigh was in constant demand, frequently invited to sing in such fine homes as J. P. Morgan's. In 1908 Morgan sponsored Burleigh's trip to Europe, where he gave many performances for royalty.

Shortly before the gala scheduled for May 20, a smaller but quite significant concert was held on May 5, featuring Dett as pianist and baritone Burleigh, at the Samuel Coleridge-Taylor Club in Norfolk, Virginia. Dett performed the *Magnolia Suite*, sharing the program with Miss Annie Spiller, soprano, Mrs. Blanche Smith, contralto, Miss Eliza Coppage, reader, and Mr. William Kemp, violinist. Also in early May of 1914 Dett gave a concert in Niagara Falls, New York. Without specifying the exact date, the *Niagara Falls Gazette*, May 12, said of his appearance there:

> R. Nathaniel Dett, one of Niagara's most
> distinguished sons, returned home on Tuesday night, not
> only as a pianist of first rank, but as a scholar of music
> and literature, and thrilled a Howard Hall audience by
> his masterful display during an interesting program.

The awaited concert on May 20, using approximately 800
participants, was actually a joint effort by the Choral Union, the
Institute student body, the Hampton Choir, an orchestra from the
Old Soldiers' Home, and the Hampton Institute Cadet Band,
directed by Professor William O. Tessman. With Burleigh as a
drawing card, and Dett's spectacular work with the singers and
players, the concert in the gymnasium was attended by a crowd
unprecedented on the Hampton campus. *The Crisis*, July, 1914,
reported the attendance at 1,000, plus the Hampton student body.
Due in part to Burleigh's prestige, the *New York Age*, May 7,
1914, had carried an announcement of the concert.

A reviewer for *The Southern Workman* called it "one of the
most successful in years," giving Burleigh high praise for his
varied solo program of operatic selections and plantation
melodies. Among Burleigh's selections were Jules Massenet's
"Legend of the Sage Brush," Coleridge-Taylor's "Corn Song," and
Walter Damrosch's "Danny Deever."[22] For the occasion the
Hampton Choral Union and Hampton Institute Choir combined to
perform Dett's "Listen to the Lambs." An Italian folk song, "The
Gypsy Camp," and Dett's "Hampton, My Home by the Sea" were
offered by all the other participants except the Old Soldiers'
Home Orchestra. The climax of the concert occurred when the
entire ensemble of singers, accompanied by the orchestra,
performed Sir Frederic Cowen's cantata *Rosemaiden*, first
mentioned in Chapter I, which featured four soloists.

As powerful as the Choral Union seemed, it feared sabatoge
by the Hampton Administration whose rulings dictated
unreasonably low fees for their concerts. For the first May
Festival at Hampton Dett had engaged five outside artists to
participate in two of the concerts. They fulfilled their contracts,
despite the poor attendance, but Dett considered the
administration's tactics a severe blow to Hampton's professional

music reputation. Further, the administration stopped all entertainment on campus during World War I, partially due to the withdrawal of numbers of male students who went to the service, and as activities were gradually resumed, music was not included. Another insult was added to the Choral Union when efforts to secure subscribers to the Russian Symphony Concerts were stopped.

> The old time-worn charge that Hampton Institute is opposed to artistic endeavor on the part of Negro people was renewed in many quarters as a direct result of this, and for a while it was the common talk of the barber shops, the great meeting place of the Negro men.[23]

Money earned from the Choral Union's concerts went towards a new piano for the school. Dett was genuinely pleased with the group's dedication. Though the Union continued, its membership decreased. Striving always for an objective, but not always having one, the group dissolved within six years. This was not Dett's only disappointment. He had understood that the establishment of a Department of Music, rather than a continuing music school, would be one of Hampton's priorities and one of his goals. Even with the support and good intentions of Mme Hackley, Dr. Frissell, and Dr. Moton, who was soon to take the presidency of Tuskegee Institute, a Department of Music had not yet developed as such. Dett's opponents, whether persons or factions, have not been clarified, but it is probable that through their prejudice they would not admit to Hampton's musical progress under his aegis.

* * *

On June 3, 1914, Dett performed both the *Magnolia* and *In the Bottoms* suites in Chicago at Symphony Hall on an All Colored Composers' Concert, the first of its kind in the Chicago area. The event, advertising reserved seats for fifty cents and general admission at twenty-five cents, was arranged by tenor William Hackney, who performed works by Burleigh. Unfortunately, Burleigh could not be present. Besides the Dett and Burleigh

works those of Will Marion Cook, Coleridge-Taylor and J.
Rosamond Johnson were programmed.[24]   Other singers
participating were Ernest R. Amos, baritone, and soprano Mme
Anita Patti Brown.   With proper acknowledgement of all
composers represented, Karleton Hackett's review in the *Chicago
Evening Post*, June 4, 1914, was most complimentary of Dett.

> By far the most significant contribution to the evening
> was the playing by Mr. Dett of his two suites for piano.
> . . . Mr. Dett is a pianist of distinct quality and his music
> had an individual note of charm. It was not pretentious,
> did not seek to carry any deep message, nor make a
> propaganda, but was content to express with simplicity
> and intuitive feeling something of the Southland. It was
> not so folksonglike as we had expected, with little
> attempt for racial tone color, but the reflex of an
> individual to whom the things had personal meaning.
> There was melodic feeling, graceful rhythmic form,
> played with an appreciation that made them delightful.

Musical America's reviewer spoke of Hackney as "the
enterprising manager of this concert" who "organized the small
chorus of some thirty mixed voices." Speaking of Coleridge-
Taylor's works he said that the artists "were somewhat ill at
ease, though in the characteristic idiom of the works of J.
Rosamond Johnson and Will Marion Cook the racial traits had
full representation." Continuing about Dett he said that the two
suites were "of genuine originality and decided melodious merit."
Of Dett's piano performance he remarked that he "proved
himself a pianist with an easy, facile technic, an intuitive gift
for tone color and musical talent."[25] Soloists Hackney, Amos, and
Brown were also praised in the review.   The concert was
considered "an excellent beginning and showed ambitious
enterprise on the part of its promoter."
     A reviewer for the *Chicago Record Herald*, musician and
critic Felix Borowski, was also impressed with Dett, believing
that "his abilities . . . qualify him for the leadership of the
musical creators among his people." Borowski felt that Dett's
ideas were "distinguished for originality." He continued with

"Piano playing much less admirable, much less poetic, has often been heard in Orchestra Hall and in concerts much more pretentious than that which had formed the subject of this review." Glenn Dillard Gunn of the *Chicago Daily Tribune* wrote: "It remained for the pianist of the evening [Dett] to show how the characteristic accents of Negro music may be developed into genuine art forms without resorting to imitation of the white man's music."[26]

An undated, unnamed news item from the Hampton University Archives said that during this event Dett was guest of honor at a dinner, before which "the party enjoyed an auto ride through the parks and boulevards . . . and after the sumptuous repast Mr. Dett was guest at a box party to see *Omar the Tentmaker* showing at the Garrick Theater."

On June 13, 1914, *The Freeman*, a Chicago paper, carried an item on Dett, who had apparently played there in public recently. The writer deemed him a better pianist than Coleridge-Taylor, but not a better composer. He praised Dett's *Magnolia Suite* for having a "richness in a variety of themes that were deftly entrancing," and said of his playing that "he gave the best indication of what he will later be if he continues in practice—unaffected."

A letter from Dett to his mother in Folder 8 of the Mesiah Papers and Documents is dated June 18th, without the year. It was most likely 1914, due to its content. Dett comments on both the recent concert with Burleigh at Hampton and another in Chicago when he was piano soloist. After apologizing for typing the letter, rather than writing in longhand, Dett told of an amusing incident connected with the Burleigh concert. A little girl had brought flowers to the stage, and as Burleigh started to take them the child said, "Oh, no, these flowers are for Mr. Dett." And of the concert in Chicago Dett wrote that the *Chicago Defender* "about left me out of it as nearly all of the colored papers seem to do for some reason, but I have never had finer notices from white newspapers." He mentioned also that "the lady in Washington," whose name was omitted, was beginning to "write sweet letters again." He signed the letter with a row of typed x-es (for kisses).

The Crisis for July of 1914 mentioned a "recent" Sunday

Robert Nathaniel Dett, ca. 1918.
Photo courtesy of the Local History Department,
Niagara Falls, New York, Public Library.

service in Weightman Hall at the University of Pennsylvania, using music by Burleigh, Coleridge-Taylor and Dett. No specific compositions or performers were named, but it is likely that Dett did not participate, since the Hampton Choir, traveling aboard the schooner *Hampton*, was at the time on a 100-day tour from Virginia to Maine. The group's last stop on the marathon was at the Collegiate Church of St. Nicholas in New York City on August 30.

A folksong Festival at Symphony Hall in Boston on November 30 received a rather lengthy write-up in *Musical Courier*, December 9, 1914. Two hundred singers participated in the event directed by Mme Hackley. Dett and violinist Clarence Cameron White were soloists. At the time Mme Hackley was director and manager of the Hackley Normal Vocal Institute in Chicago. Most of the choral selections, which had a pleasing effect, were "typical Southern melodies."

> The ensemble was splendid and one was agreeably surprised at the richness of vocal quality in evidence throughout the performance. Nathaniel Dett, a pianist, and also a composer of some note, was heard in his own compositions. The young man is an accomplished player and possesses much talent for composition. His numbers were interesting and displayed much sympathy for the Southland.[27]

Of the same concert the *Boston Herald* said:

> R. Nathaniel Dett, pianist, played his own compositions, two suites, the *Magnolia* and *In the Bottoms*. He also conducted his anthem *Listen to the Lambs*, in which he made effective use of the Negro scale. Mr. White played pieces by Coleridge-Taylor and his own *Berceuse*.[28]

Ending the year 1914, in December Dett directed a choral concert heard by 2,000 people in the Hampton gymnasium. Guest artists were singer Mme Anita Patti Brown and violinist Joseph Douglass. On December 22 guest singer Roland Hayes appeared

Folk Song Festibal

Chorus of 200 Voices

Symphony Hall

Monday Evening, November 30, 1914

Soloists

Mr. R. Nathaniel Dett   Composer-Pianist
Mr. Clarence Cameron White   Violinist

Quartettes, Sextettes, and other arrangements of the
Soulful Folk Songs

The First Folk Song Festival in the New England States
Only Compositions of Colored Composers will be rendered

For the benefit of the

COLUMBUS AVENUE A. M. E. ZION CHURCH,
Boston, Mass.

and the

HACKLEY NORMAL VOCAL INSTITUTE
Chicago, Ill.

Mme. E. Azalia Hackley, Director and Manager

Parquet, First twelve rows,, $1.50   First Balcony, 75cts.
Parquet, $1.00   Second Balcony, 50cts.
Seats now on Sale, Symphony Hall Box Office
Bay State Pharmacy, Cor. Northfield and Tremont Streets
At Churches

Program Courtesy of
Hampton University Archives.

on a concert at Hampton with the Hampton Choral Union in Cleveland Hall Chapel. The program did not list names of Hayes' selections. The choral group performed works by Mozart, MacCunn, Brahms, Burleigh, and Dett. Two soloists from Hampton, Miss Hattie Marshall and Lorenzo Sanders, were also on the program.[29]

Beginning in 1914 Dett was required to make an annual report to Hampton's president, stating his accomplishments and needs and justifying all actions. Copies of these reports have been kept in the Hampton University Archives.

1915

Musical activities at Hampton opened the year 1915 with a flare. A festival with 900 singers and violinist Helen Ware as guest artist was held at Hampton on January 8, 1915. Ware, under the management of Laszlo Schwartz in New York at this time, was advertised in *Musical Courier* with "It has come to pass that when speaking of Hungarian and Slav music, you think of HELEN WARE." At the concert Dett's singers honored Ware with two Hungarian folk songs. A writer for *Musical Courier* said of this offering: "These they sang with that wonderful emotional and rhythmic feeling which characterizes the negroes' musical activities in every field."[30]

Besides some Hungarian melodies and "Chant Negre" by composer/critic A. Walter Kramer, Ware performed the Saint-Saëns Concerto in b minor with Robert Braun as accompanist. Both artists were well received for their spirited playing and musicality. The *Courier* said of Dett's performance:

> Mr. Dett's choral arrangement of "Listen to the Lambs" proved a fine work of musicianship, and in conducting it he brought forth from his chorus those splendid nuances of phrasing that have made his work and the excellent chorus famous in musical circles.[31]

On returning to New York Ware spoke of her experience at Hampton in ecstatic terms, well worth quoting as a tribute:

I have always been interested in the Negroes of our country, and have at all times appreciated their inborn talent for music; therefore it was with great pleasure that I anticipated my visit to Hampton. . . . But I never dreamed of the inspiring sights and sounds that were in store for me.

The students of Hampton are members of a race which has every reason to be sad and yet they are the gladdest people I know of. They are busy from five o'clock in the morning till bedtime, but they sing at their work and are earnest in their studies. They march to luncheon to the time of a splendid band, then as they stand in the great dining hall they chant their thanks for their food. At evening they gather and chant their prayers.

At the concert 900 of them sang plantation songs, also a great chorale developed from one of the songs by Nathaniel Dett, the splendid music director of Hampton school. Such a chorus I have never even imagined. What clear, fresh voices, haunting rhythm, harmony, and most wonderful of all, the crescendoes and decrescendoes, the great fortes and whispering pianissimos!

I was told afterward that they produced the swelling and dying away of a chord by instinct. One by one, without any previous arrangement, they would enter or leave the huge ensemble. One could imagine a great organ played by a hand divine. True, they are inspired by their leader or "major," a large, handsome negro, who sings the song over and then begins to conduct. It was a new experience for me to be entertained in such royal fashion by my audience. I was confident they were all fellow musicians, and I only hope they enjoyed my performance half as well as I enjoyed theirs. The next morning, at six o'clock, I was awakened by a muffled roar of laughing, whistling and singing just outside my window. Like a flash it occurred to me that this place was not Hampton, but "Happy Town." And it is, because of their instinct for music, rhythm and laughter. They work while they learn and sing while they work. There is music and sunshine everywhere.[32]

Dett's "Listen to the Lambs" proved of such impact at the Helen Ware concert that the Hampton administrators insisted it should be performed at the School's forty-seventh Anniversary the following April, when the Honorable William Howard Taft, then president of Hampton's Board of Trustees, would meet with the officials and the student body. The Anniversary concert was a huge success. This was the first time that music had been included in an Anniversary exercise. Dett was particularly pleased that he, as Hampton's first Negro choral director, was able to be a part of such an exciting event.[33]

Each of Hampton's Anniversaries had followed a similar pattern, described in an account in *The Southern Workman*. The purposes were to show vistors (1) something of the student's life before he entered Hampton, (2) as complete as possible an exposition of Hampton's work and spirit, and (3) a follow-up on the graduates as professional people. Several autobiographical essays were read to implement the first purpose. To exemplify school spirit and the nature of education visitors were met at the wharf by the schooner *Hampton* and a band. Exhibits and displays of arts, crafts, and industrial work were scattered strategically over the campus. Healthful food prepared by the students was available for a nominal fee. Practice teaching in a nearby small school was in progress, open to observers.

In a more formal program at the gymnasium several alumni spoke of their professional work since leaving Hampton. President Taft's message was carried in the *Workman*, along with those of other trustees, ministers, and visiting dignitaries from other colleges.

Dett's folklore concert for the occasion was described as "a history of the life and art of the Negro race, an exposition of its present development and a hint of its future possibilities." Selections were Coleridge-Taylor's "By the Waters of Babylon," the folksongs "Let Us Cheer the Weary Traveler" and "Run to Jesus," J. Rosamond Johnson's "Since You Went Away," Burleigh's "Deep River," and Dett's "Soon-a Will Be Done with the Troubles of the Worl'," "Wasn't That a Mighty Day?" (a Christmas song), and "My Jesus Lay in the Grave" (an Easter carol). The reviewer commented that "Wasn't That a Mighty Day?" was very difficult, that "the students had had less

The Hampton Normal and Agricultural Institute

Christmas Concert

Cleveland Hall Chapel, December 22, 1914

Seven forty-five o'clock p. m.

by

HAMPTON INSTITUTE
THE HAMPTON CHORAL UNION
MR. ROLAND W. HAYES, Tenor

Gloria in excelsis, from the "Twelfth Mass" - *Mozart*
THE HAMPTON CHORAL UNION

Old French carol   -   -   -   -   *Gevaert*
DAY SCHOOL

"He was despised," from the "Messiah" - *Handel*
MISS HATTIE MARSHALL

Chorale from "Darkness and Light" - *MacCunn*
DAY AND NIGHT SCHOOL

"Go tell it on the mountain" -   -   *Plantation song*
"Rise up shepherd and follow"   -   *Plantation song*
CAMPAIGN CHORUS

"Sing; O Heavens"   -   -   -   -   -   *Tours*
INSTITUTE CHOIR

Legend of the sage bush   -   -   -   -   *Massenet*
MR. LORENZO SANDERS

Bohemian lullaby   -   -   -   -   -   *Brahms*
TREBLE CHORUS

Songs
MR. ROLAND W. HAYES

"Deep River"   -   -   -   -   -   -   *Burleigh*
THE HAMPTON CHORAL UNION

"Listen to the lambs"   -   -   -   -   -   *Dett*
ENSEMBLE CHORUS

The Hampton Choral Union will present Miss Helen Ware, violinist and famous interpreter of Hungarian music, assisted by a chorus of 900 voices, in the Gymnasium on January 8.

Program courtesy of
Hampton University Archives.

practice with it than the others, and the execution was accordingly less finished." The Easter carol, based on "Listen to the Lambs," was sung "with feeling and appreciation." Actually Dett had made the arrangements for use by the school choir at appropriate seasons. The reviewer concluded:

The concert was Hampton's initial attempt to provide an evening's entertainment consisting largely of difficult and closely-harmonized Negro compositions, and had the faults of execution which might be expected in such a case.[34]

***

On March 20, 1915, Dett, as an alumnus, filled out the annual routine form sent him by Oberlin College. Though he listed his present mailing address as Hampton Institute, Hampton, Virginia, his permanent residence and business address was 362 2nd Street, Niagara Falls, New York, where his mother and brother still resided. His places of employment previous to Hampton were given as Lane College 1908-1911 (Director of Music) and Lincoln Institute 1911-1913 (Director of Music). His positions at Hampton were Director of Music and Director of the Hampton Choral Union. For "honors and distinctions conferred by learned societies" he wrote "honorary member of the Sumner Literary Society of Hampton and Phoebus, 1914." For publications Dett listed *The Album of a Heart* 1911 (A Book of Poems), *Magnolia Suite* 1912 (five numbers for piano), *In the Bottoms* 1913 (five numbers for piano), and *Listen to the Lambs* 1914 (chorus). His church affiliation was still given as Presbyterian.[35]

Students from the Music School Settlement, whose director at the time was J. Rosamond Johnson, participated in a concert at Carnegie Hall, April 13, 1915. Works by Stephen Foster and black composers Johnson, Burleigh, Coleridge-Taylor, W. C. Handy, and Will Marion Cook were presented. In addition, Dett's "Listen to the Lambs," the second prize winner of the year before, was performed on this concert by the Settlement Glee Club, with Miss Mattie Harris, soprano, singing the *obbligato*.

The Honorable Charles W. Anderson was guest speaker. It was a
grand occasion, with Roland Hayes as one of the soloists and
pianist Percy Grainger in the audience.[36]

On April 22 Dett's singers presented a folklore concert at
Hampton. Student soloists Carmen Montion, Frederick C. Kimbo,
and Lorenzo Sanders were featured. *Musical Courier* reported:

> Various choruses and solos were well sung, two negro
> folksongs in the original form being worthy of special
> mention. A composition by Mr. Dett and two of his
> arrangements of negro folksongs aroused the enthusiasm
> of the audience. . . . An outstanding feature was the
> singing of Coleridge-Taylor's unusual "By the Waters of
> Babylon." It was an unusual concert, excellently given
> and much enjoyed.[37]

It had been a tiring but exciting and productive school year.
During the summer of 1915 Dett chose to attend classes at
Columbia University in psychology and public school music
offered by visiting professor Peter Dykema, then Chairman of
the Music Department at the University of Wisconsin. Dykema,
well known for his accomplishments in Community Music, felt
that everybody *could* and *should* sing. Dett made an A in the
music course, and a B in psychology.

That same summer he studied composition briefly with
Arthur Olaf Andersen at the American Conservatory in Chicago.
At nearby Northwestern University in Evanston, Illinois, where
he audited some music classes during this time, he was able to
talk with Northwestern's Music Department Chairman, Peter
Lutkin, also an organist, theorist, choral director and composer,
about the problems encountered by music directors. That summer
Dett met Australian pianist Percy Grainger for the first time. A
letter to Natalie Curtis-Burlin, dated October 15, 1915, indicates
that this was a thrilling experience for him:

> I greatly enjoyed Mr. Grainger. I think he is truly
> wonderful. Five minutes in his presence meant more than
> a month's teaching. I didn't know that I was so
> susceptible to atmosphere. My work in Chicago was quite

successful—thanks to Mr. Grainger and the Chicago teachers. I wrote a Negro violin air, made an arrangement of "Listen to the Lambs" for violin and piano and did also a slow movement for string quartet of an old Negro spiritual.[38]

Dett said in the letter that former editor of the *Chicago Tribune*, Glenn Dillard Gunn,[39] was quite taken with "Listen to the Lambs" and wanted it arranged for the Chicago Orchestra. Dett preferred that Professor Andersen arrange it, and lamented the fact that his duties at Hampton had prevented his sending it to him. "Lambs" by now had sold 1,400 copies, and was being performed by various choral societies. Apparently Summy, publisher of his piano pieces, thought they were too difficult to sell in quantity. The letter continued:

> I was surprised to feel so much prejudice at Schirmer's against the higher development of Negro music. That was the most disappointing thing of the whole summer. Even after Mr. Damrosch recommended two of the choruses they would not have them. As for me, I cannot see why the same principles at work making English folk music a success should not do so for Negro music. Neither do I see why the idea should be so bitterly opposed. Folk music is folk music and development is development.

Before Dett met scholar Natalie Curtis she had already authored the widely acclaimed *Indian's Book* (1907), which contained transcriptions of 200 songs of eighteen North American tribes. By 1915 she had begun what was to become the *Hampton Series Negro Folksongs*, a four-volume set of spirituals and secular pieces, accompanied by a discussion of the harmonic improvisation used in their performance. Curtis frequented the Hampton campus for over a year, listening to the students sing, gathering different versions of the songs which were published in 1918-1919 by G. Schirmer. In their endeavors in this field, she and Dett were of similar mind.

Dett apparently well understood his own needs. Impatient by nature, he must have been inwardly tortured by the injustices

of racial prejudice, especially since he was unable to correct
them. As his letter to Curtis indicated, he fully appreciated the
summer's association with musicians and scholars of high
caliber.

Directed by Carl Diton, a benefit concert was given by the
united choirs of Houston, Texas, on September 29, 1915.
Compositions by Dett, Burleigh, J. Rosamond Johnson, Will
Vodery, and Melville Charlton (organist, composer, and
Burleigh's chief accompanist) were performed. Held at City
Auditorium, the event was billed as "An All-Negro Composers'
Night," with proceeds going to the Drinking Fountain Fund for
Colored Schools.[40]

Seeds sown while studying with Peter Dykema during the
past summer must have sprouted, for Dett was selected as the
first American composer to be represented at the annual
Christmas Festival of the Choral Union in Madison, Wisconsin.
The concert was at the University of Wisconsin Armory on
December 11. *The Crisis* for January, 1916, specified that Dett
was a Negro, but did not make it clear whether he was present to
conduct his "Listen to the Lambs" performed by the Madison
Choral Union. The general tenor of the review, with its
references to ragtime and barber shop harmonies, may well have
been distasteful to Dett:

> Side by side with magnificent musical climaxes is the
> syncopated time, which is so popular with ragtime
> lovers. Almost instantly it changes from grand and
> majestic to some of those good old "barber shop" minor
> chords, which a bunch of fellows like to hold on to.
>
> Often when one voice is carrying a catchy Negro air,
> the rest of the voices are weaving a background of
> harmony around it which carries the production out
> of the realm of ragtime into the realm of the classi-
> cal.[41]

1916—Dett as Professional and Family Man

In its February 11, 1916 issue *The Spectator* (Hamilton,

Ontario) reported that the Elgar Choir sang "a quaint little religious characteristic," Dett's "Listen to the Lambs." It was called "charming" because of its simplicity and deep religious significance.

Dett's third Annual Report to President Frissell, contained in the Mesiah Collection, was made in February of 1916. He commented on the suitable change in his own personal scheduling of five classes per week at 7:00 a. m., and expressed appreciation for gifts of a portrait of Samuel Coleridge-Taylor and a piano board (new teaching tool for introducing the keyboard). Modestly he said how proud he was of his choir, the Choral Union, his piano students, and the progress of the Mandolin Club. In order for the music school to come along even further, however, he listed his "prayers" or requests: academic credits for music work, a course in choir training, a Trade School of Music, recital fees to be paid by the students at the beginning of the year, recital to be considered a part of student education similar to a lecture course, and that Hampton would provide sufficient teachers to implement these requests.

In addition to Dett's larger singing groups, he had by now picked singers for the Hampton Quartet, which was invited to appear at the San Francisco Exposition for one month in the early spring of 1916. After this engagement the Quartet sang several groups of Negro melodies for a large gathering in Symphony Hall in Boston, a concert mentioned in the March, 1916 *Crisis.*

Dett's morale would have soared if he were aware of pianist Percy Grainger's comment in the *Oberlin Alumni Magazine* for May, 1916 (n. p.) quoted from *Musical America*, March 16, 1916. Grainger said:

> As an Australian, I am naturally particularly interested to hear the works of Canadian composers. Of course, Clarence Lucas is famous throughout the whole English-speaking musical world. But perhaps you do not know that R. Nathaniel Dett is also a Canadian. He is head of the music [*sic*] at Hampton Institute, Virginia, and is doing a magnificent work.

Despite engagements with his singers and the demands of

teaching, Dett kept up his piano practice. On April 25, 1916, under auspices of the Dorcas Club of Hampton, Dett gave a recital at the National Soldiers' Home Theatre. Robert R. Moton, now principal-elect for Tuskegee Institute, gave the address. Assisted by the Hampton Institute Male Chorus who sang "Marguerita," "Jonah Man," "Doan' You Cry, My Honey," "I Want to Be Ready," and "Look Away," Dett gave a hefty piano program. It included "Polonaise Brilliante" (Schytte), "Nocturne" (Grieg), "Staccato Etude" (Rubinstein), and portions of his own two suites, *Magnolia* and *In the Bottoms*.[42]

At Hampton's May Festival Cowen's *Rosemaiden* was programmed again, with a chorus of nearly 1,000 under Dett's direction. Vocal soloists for the May 22 occasion were soprano Mrs. F. C. Talbert, contralto Daisy Tapley, tenor George R. Garner, and Paige I. Lancaster, baritone. Miss Helen Elise Smith (who became Mrs. Robert Nathaniel Dett the following December) was the featured pianist.

In August of 1916 Dett was chosen by *Crisis* as one of its "Men of the Month," along with pianist Harry A. Williams and Ford T. Dabney, the first Negro to lead an orchestra on Broadway in New York. *Crisis* cited Dett's "Listen to the Lambs" as one of his best known works, and called him a "young pianist of ability and a promising composer whose work has already commanded the attention of music critics."[43]

Some of the previous "Men of the Month," a few of whom were women, had been Roy W. Tibbs, professor of piano and choral director at Howard; Melville Charlton, organist and accompanist; James Reese Europe, orchestra director; Will Marion Cook, composer and conductor; William H. Tyers, song writer and assistant orchestra conductor to both Europe and Cook; Hazel Harrison, pianist; writer, diplomat, and educator James Weldon Johnson; Jesse E. Moorland, white philanthropist, later a founder of the Moorland-Spingarn Research Center; and singer Anita Patti Brown. In the following two months *Crisis* named Harry T. Burleigh and Marian Anderson as "Men of the Month."

The Hampton Quartet gave a concert before a large audience

Helen Elise Smith
Photo courtesy of Hampton University Archives.

at Duffield, Connecticut, in the early fall of 1916, under auspices of the Banner Fountain Order. No specific date for the event was mentioned by *The Crisis*.[44]

Dett, ever eager to share his professional knowledge, was often called upon by vocal teachers. McBrier points out one such instance, when Mrs. Grace Nicoll of Shinneocock School on Long Island was concerned about literature for her choruses of Negro and Indian students. Not only did Dett send her an ample list of musical selections, but his comments and ideas as well. Stressing patience as a virtue of teaching, along with attractive songs and copies for each singer, and feeling that all students have an urge to make music, he told Mrs. Nicoll that "no extraordinary skill is required to be a good leader or vocal teacher." Dett advised using a blackboard on which to notate troublesome passages, and testing the voices separately with either a simple hymn or ascending and descending scales. If a hymn were used, the student should start it several times on different pitches to determine his range. Moderate vocalization should correct bad tone quality. Anyone over sixteen should know what part he could sing, since his voice has probably matured, according to Dett.

His list for Mrs. Nicoll offered quite a variety of literature from which to choose, including selections from opera and operetta, songs with religious, Indian, and Negro characteristics, anthems, and arrangements of folk tunes. Too, he suggested such compilations as the *Laurel Song Book*, which had its own teaching suggestions; Vols. I and II of *Methodical Sight Reading*, edited by Theodore Presser and containing "plenty of exercise material"; *Standard Song Classics*, for which orchestral accompaniment was available, published by Ginn and Company; and perhaps most excellent of all, Frederick W. Wodell's *Choir and Chorus Conducting* (1909), which he called "splendid." Wodell's instruction book, *How to Sing by Note*, was published in 1915. He also composed an opera and several cantatas, and was for several years conductor of the People's Choral Union of Boston.

Among the recommended religious characteristic pieces were Dett's own "Listen to the Lambs," Burleigh's "Deep River," Coleridge-Taylor's "By the Waters of Babylon," and two melodies of European origin, "Lord Have Mercy" (Russian) and

"Ancient Song in Praise of Heaven and Earth" (Netherlands). Two songs by Will Marion Cook and one by Carl Diton were listed for Negro characteristics, but in a word of caution Dett said to Mrs. Nicoll:

> . . . do not begin with characteristics. Standard numbers of a general nature are far better for many reasons. Characteristics accentuate racial differences and must be used with discretion. Pieces like "Deep River" and "Listen to the Lambs" are perhaps exceptions to this rule because of their treatment.[45]

* * *

Dett was now thirty-four years of age. On October 26, 1916, the *New York Age* carried an announcement of his engagement to New Yorker Helen Elise Smith. An earlier announcement from the American Press Association in an unnamed newspaper, dated April 6, 1916, is in the Hampton University Archives. This item was accompanied by a profile picture of the bride-to-be, who is wearing a lacy or beaded bodice with five strands of pearls, eye spectacles, and a head band with a bow on one side. Her hairdo featured curls in a bun.

Miss Smith was unusually musical as a child and gained early admittance to the Damrosch Institute of Musical Art (now Juilliard), where she studied piano with Sigismond Stojowski and theory with Percy Goetschius. She was this school's first black graduate, and after a seven-year course she received two diplomas and recognition as an honor student. Her prowess as a pianist even caught the favorable attention of critic Henry Krehbiel, who had heard her in concert.

Miss Smith's first teaching experience after graduation had been in her own private studio in New York City. From February through August of 1912 *The Crisis* carried her advertisement which read: "Music, Helen Elise Smith concert pianist. Postgraduate of the Institute of Musical Art. Pupil of Sigismond Stojowski. Teacher of Piano, Theory, Ear Training, etc. 224 East 86th St. New York City." The following fall Miss Smith and violinist David Martin, a North Carolinian, established the

Martin-Smith School of Music in New York City where she served as its Director. Already affiliated with the Music School Settlement, founded in 1911 with Martin as its first Director, she had ample opportunities to perform with such artists as David Mannes, violinist with the New York Symphony.

The Martin-Smith School trained teachers and provided a haven for young artists, such as Marian Anderson and known concert artists as well, some of whom taught there after their retirement. The school presented many worthy concerts featuring the music of black composers, giving little, if any, attention to minstrel or vaudeville entertainers. In 1919, after Rosamond Johnson resigned as Director of the Music School Settlement, the Settlement was absorbed by the Martin-Smith School. After Miss Smith left there to teach at Hampton, Martin's three children, all string players, continued to carry on its solid reputation.

A letter from Miss Smith to Dett a few weeks before their wedding gives some insight into her personal nature. Dated November 17, 1916, it reads:

My dear Nate,

Who under the sun ever heard of such a thing as an overcoat letter? I will admit that it *was* a queer letter, especially the part about the kindergarten. Oh! Oh!

There are quite a few things I have bought to embroider, but as I am so busy now, shall wait and do them later.

I am so glad that you are going to wait until later to buy most of the things, because I do not think that tradespeople are apt to take advantage of a man. They know that men are always impatient and a woman will go through all the shops until she finds something to suit her taste and also her purse.

It will be necessary for you to come to New York as early as possible, the 26th, at any rate, because of our marriage license. Here in N. Y. both parties have to go to City Hall together in order to receive one. Can't get married without it. Our little wedding will take place in St. Philips [sic] Church before the evening service. Then

Mr. and Mrs. Martin are giving us a reception and I think we can take the one o'clock to Baltimore and the boat from there to Virginia. Do you agree? Please say yes.

You must not mind if I forget to send my love each time. It is not because I think any the less of you, my dear, but because in my haste it does not get on paper. My thoughts are of you always, and if I did not love you, why never would I have been willing to "leave my happy home for you." Ma sends love. So do I.

Yours always
Elise

P. S. The postman just brought me the dearest, lovlyist [*sic*] little ring in the world. Thanks. I appreciate it, and accept it with great pleasure. Love and more love, Elise

P. S. II The little flower is the first one to appear on a little water plant of mine, and so I am sending it to you.[46]

On December 27, 1916, at five p. m. Dett and Miss Smith were married in St. Philip's Church, 216 West 134th Street in New York City. Fortunately the Oberlin College Archives kept a wedding invitation, issued by the bride's mother, Mrs. Josephine L. Smith, for Dett, oddly enough, in inquiries for Oberlin's Alumni report for both 1925 and 1935, gave the wedding date as December 27, 1917.

The Dett's first home was Maple Cottage on the Hampton campus, where they would be "at home" on February 1, 1917. The Detts had two daughters, Helen Charlotte Elise, born in 1918, and Josephine Elizabeth, born in 1922, according to McBrier. In the same Oberlin query of 1925, however, Dett gives Helen's birth date as January 26, 1919, and in the 1935 one as January 24, 1919. In the earlier one Josephine's birth date is May 28, 1922, and in the later one it is May 26, 1923. These discrepancies about family matters seem to indicate an absent-minded professor, a preoccupied husband and father. Shortly after the second daughter's arrival Mrs. Dett was appointed to the Hampton music school faculty as a piano teacher and accompanist.

McBrier has stated that though the marriage began happily, it did not remain so, due to basic incompatibility and differing professional attitudes.   The Detts never divorced, however.

> Mrs. Dett did not understand the provincial attitude of the women on the campus nor was she well received by them. Her life had been occupied almost solely by music and she did not adjust well to the social groups and life-style on the Hampton campus. He [Dett], on the other hand, was well liked for his personality, was gracious and full of fun.[47]

McBrier suggests that a slight professional jealousy might have developed between the couple, since Mrs. Dett was so well schooled in theory and counterpoint.   She critiqued Dett's compositions, which constructive advice he "wisely" accepted, however.

Dett's teaching duties demanded at least fifty hours per week, and the remaining time was spent more in composing, writing, and lecturing than with his family.   Mrs. Dett, understandably, was under heavy stress with her own teaching duties and almost the sole care of the girls. She was often left alone when Dett was lecturing or concertizing in other cities. Neither was the home scenario bettered when Mrs. Dett's mother, Mrs. Smith, moved in with them in 1917, and remained until her death.   Dett must have felt in the minority, at times even persecuted, with four women to placate. McBrier gives a dreary picture of the situation:

> [Mrs. Smith] had little regard for her son-in-law and constantly complained that he spent limitlessly on himself and gave his wife barely enough to run the house. The two daughters . . . lacked any depth of understanding for their father. His apparent lack of affection for them was disastrous, for they made little effort to please him and later showed little appreciation for his achievements.[48]

1917-1918

The year 1917 brought no abatement in Dett's activities. According to *The Crisis*, March, 1917, for a tour the past January he had prepared the Hampton Quartet to perform at twenty meetings throughout Massachusetts. Though no date or place was specified, that same issue of *Crisis* mentioned that under Dett's direction the Hampton Choral Union assisted in a recital by David Mannes and his wife Clara, the New York violin-piano duo. The concert was probably at Hampton, however, due to the expense of transporting such a large choir to New York City.

Dett had not forgotten longtime friends in Canada. In an interview with May Stanley, published in June, 1917, he spoke of his four-part choral works which had been dedicated to various Canadian friends and supporters. To Bruce A. Carey, director of the famous Elgar Choir of Hamilton, Ontario, he dedicated "Weeping Mary." The Elgar Choir was the first group to sing his "O, Holy Lord," an *a cappella* folk anthem in eight parts, which he dedicated to them. The occasion was a memorial service to honor Canadian soldiers fallen in battle.[49]

To the Hampton Choral Union he dedicated "I'll Never Turn Back No More," described as "an excellent example of the use of the Negro long-meter as the foundation of a serious music composition." Dett related to interviewer Stanley that he had also dedicated a choral piece, "Music in the Mine," to Percy Grainger. To date, performance-wise, "Listen to the Lambs" was his most successful work, already having been presented by the Church of the Ascension Choir in New York City, the Columbus University Chorus, the Music School Settlement Chorus, and the Syracuse University Chorus in Syracuse. By way of praising Dett's work with a choir of seventy, Stanley mentioned that it sang unaccompanied for campus church services each Sunday morning. The larger group of about 400 voices met for rehearsal twice a week, and a night chorus met once a week.[50]

By early 1917 such personages as Myrtle Moses of the Chicago Opera Association had been guest performer under Hampton Choral Union auspices, as had Harry Burleigh, Roland Hayes, and Clarence Cameron White. No less impressive had been concerts by the Hampton Quartet, one of the three top ones in

America, which had toured extensively with its repertoire of plantation melodies and spirituals.

Though Dett was likely not present, his music and that of Burleigh, Cook, and Coleridge-Taylor were performed for a lecture recital on Indian and Negro music in Ithaca, New York, at the Conservatory of Music.[51] The Hampton Chorus of 700 voices under Dett's direction was mentioned in *The Crisis*, July, 1917, as having given "a fine rendition" of Part I of Mendelssohn's *Elijah*. Baritone soloist for the performance was Dr. Archibald T. Davison of Harvard College, who had been sent to Hampton at this time "to study the music situation there at the request of the General Education Board."[52] The *Musical Courier*, July 19, 1917, carried an item on a lecture recital that the Detts gave at Hampton. Dett spoke on the characteristics of folk music found in individual composers, and Mrs. Dett played examples. Among them were a Scarlatti sonata, a Debussy "Arabesque," Handel's "Harmonious Blacksmith," Liszt's "Hungarian Rhapsodie No. 2," and Coleridge-Taylor's African dance "Bamboula."

On August 14, 1917, a YMCA benefit in Atlanta's Auditorium-Armory drew an audience of 4,000. Twenty-eight area church choirs sang arrangements by Kemper Harreld, violinist and music professor at Morehouse College in Atlanta. Assisting artists were soprano Anna Massey, tenor W. J. Trent, and pianist Fred Hall who played piano works by Dett. Other composers represented were Haydn, Rossini, and Will Marion Cook.

In its October, 1917 issue (n. p.) the *Oberlin Alumni Magazine* called attention to another Dett champion, Frederick H. Martens, writer for *Musical Monitor*. Martens, not only a critic but a poet as well, wrote that "the coming of R. Nathaniel Dett to Hampton as director of music . . . has marked a new epoch in its musical development." He called Dett a "skilled and able theorist who with the primitive music of his race molds this basic material into an art-form." Dett's inspirational and imaginative power gives the form "new facets of beauty," he said. The *Alumni Magazine* continued, citing "Listen to the Lambs" as "the first anthem directly developed out of Negro themes," and "Music in the Mine" "uncommonly effective musically."

* * *

If the death of Hampton President Hollis B. Frissell in the fall of 1917 halted Dett's activities, it was not particularly noticeable. Dett had enough to handle without becoming involved in administrative replacements. For all his good intentions, according to *Crisis* editor W. E. B. DuBois, Frissell may not have done his best to educate the Hampton students. Hampton's graduates were still not considered "educated," because in many cases their background had not fitted them to enter another school of higher learning. Hampton was simply considered a top center in the trade-teaching for Negroes. The argument had been that as Negroes they would never *need* higher education, though many of them wanted it.

DuBois wondered why there had been no closer touch between Negro students and the all-white Board of Trustees, since black members could better voice their needs and give more encouragement for the Negro's self respect. DuBois' editorial concluded:

> I reiterate my respect for the Institution [Hampton] and my firm belief that it has done great good, but I insist that no school which deliberately curtails the training of the talented, refuses to guide her apter students to their greatest development, save in restricted lines, and not only gives her beneficiaries little or no voice in its control, but seems even to harbor and encourage their enemies—no such school is reaching its greatest usefulness.[53]

It was not until May of 1918 that James E. Gregg, trained for the ministry, took the Presidency at Hampton. A few months earlier Dett's choral pieces "Weeping Mary" and "I'll Never Turn Back No More" had been published by J. Fischer. The 1918 April and May issues of *The Crisis* carried Dett's essays "The Emancipation of Negro Music" and "Negro Music of the Present."

Dett directed Hampton's annual spring concert, reported in *Musical Courier*, June 13, 1918. Guest soloist in *Elijah* with a chorus of 500 was composer Geoffrey O'Hara, also an arranger of

spirituals, a leader of soldiers' choruses, and a researcher of
Indian music. Other soloists were contralto Bessie L. Drew, from
the Hampton community, Clara D. H. Smith, a member of the
1918 graduating class, and secretary of the Hampton Choral
Union Dr. T. J. Lattimore. Mrs. Dett was the accompanist.
Cowen's ever popular *Rosemaiden* was again included on the
program. Of the event the *Courier* critic wrote:

> To those who have known Mr. O'Hara as the singer of
> war songs it came as somewhat of a surprise to find that
> this leader of men could throw himself so effectively and
> completely into the spirit of the religious oratorio. . . .
> Mrs. Dett's accompaniments were effective and adequate.
> The Hampton chorus of 500 voices sang with fine spirit,
> tone and attack [winning] hearty applause from the large
> audience.[54]

In July of 1918 Hampton drew 2,000 people for an
Independence Day pageant for which Dett was musical director.
The event was coordinated by Mrs. W. T. B. Williams of the
Hampton music faculty.

During 1918, while World War I still raged, Dett did
extensive traveling as a pianist, lecturer, and observer at Fisk
University, Tennessee State Normal for Colored Youth, Howard
University, Union University, and Storer College. At the War
Department's suggestion he also visited Atlanta University,
Morehouse College, Penn School, Calhoun School, and Tuskegee
Institute. These trips meant absenting himself periodically from
Hampton, a situation with which some of the administration
took issue. In self defense Dett wrote to President Gregg, saying
that his former administrators had considered these excursions
prestigious for Hampton, as well as a personally broadening
experience, useful as an educational tool for the good of the
school.[55]

By now Dett's name as a composer and arranger had reached
a wide teaching and performing circuit. His choral pieces were
being taught in reputable schools and sung by the better church
choirs and leading choral societies. One instance, cited in *The
Crisis*, was at Columbia University during the summer session

Harry T. Burleigh, ca. 1918-1920
Photo courtesy of Dr. David Cantrell.

when Bertha Anderson of Lynchburg, Virginia taught "Listen to the Lambs" to a class of forty as an example of a "Negro Melody."[56] Since his short stay at the American Conservatory of Music in Chicago in the summer of 1915 Dett's piano works had been programmed frequently, not only by Percy Grainger's students, but by Grainger himself.

The December, 1918 issue of *The Southern Workman* reported a Detroit concert on which the Elgar Choir of Hamilton, Ontario performed Dett's "O, Holy Lord" and "Listen to the Lambs." An added account, taken from the *National Notebook*, official bulletin of the National Association of Colored Teachers, commented on "Mr. Dett's skillful management of the music at the summer meeting of the association." His piano solos were said to have "made the distinctive musical hit of the meeting." Dett's "America the Beautiful" was included among the patriotic songs of the National Victory Sing on Thanksgiving Day.[57]

During the fall of 1918, as the war ended, Dett was visited by
William Grant Still a few weeks before he was discharged from
the US Navy. Still was only twenty-three at the time, married,
and a father. He had just been transferred as an entertainer to a
station in Newport News, a short distance from Hampton. Verna
Arvey, Still's second wife, gave an account of the visit:

> [Still] took with him a little piece he had written at
> Oberlin and dedicated to Dett. The older composer [Dett]
> invited him to dinner, then took him to the Institute to
> hear the singing in the evening. He was disappointed by
> two things that evening: the colored girls sat apart from
> the Indian girls, carefully segregated, and Dett's music
> was not performed. Not until many years later was he
> [Still] told that Hampton Institute didn't want Dett to
> program his own works during his tenure there.[58]

If these negative feelings at using Dett's music were correct,
Dett was not daunted by them. That he continued to program his
own works sparingly, however, is indicated by various printed
programs from the school.

Still's insightful daughter, Judith, wrote:

> I think that Dett was an unhappy man, domestically
> and professionally, and he was extremely uptight about
> racial discrimination. He wanted to be the classical
> composer that my father was, but Hampton discouraged
> him—his need to make a living kept him fettered. He
> was, underneath all the sorrow, a very creative and
> intelligent person. (His handwriting says so).[59]

Judith Still explained that Dett's attitude toward her
father mellowed somewhat over the years, that the two "became
great friends."

> In the beginning Dett did not like my father, felt
> threatened by him, and was upset that WGS could make
> a living with his music when Dett had to teach to make

it. My father held nothing against Dett and was always gracious to him. Eventually Dett realized that Still was not trying to "best" him and softened up a bit.[60]

Dett gave two lecture recitals at Tuskegee on December 6 and 8, later reported in the *Tuskegee Student*, December 21, 1918. His lecture topic was "The Difference Between a Musical Arranger and a Musical Composer." While there, he and opera singer Max Weinstein were honored at a reception given by Tuskegee. The same item stated that Dett had recently attended a Song Conference conducted by Peter Dykema, held at Morehouse College in Atlanta, at which he accompanied singer Weinstein.

The Musical Art Society and NANM, 1919

Dett continued to upgrade Hampton's music school. During 1919 he founded the Musical Art Society, one of whose purposes was to promote a recital series attracting concert artists to Hampton, and which would also present the best of Hampton's own students and faculty. The Society still continues as a vital musical force, serving Hampton University and the Hampton metropolitan area. Some of its guest artists during Dett's Hampton years were pianists Harold Bauer and Percy Grainger, singer Marian Anderson, violinist Fritz Kreisler, and such ensembles as the National Symphony directed by Hans Kindler, the John P. Sousa Band, the Denishawn Dancers, the Westminster Choir, the Kedroff Quartet, the Belgian Royal Band, the Ukrainian National Chorus, the Tony Sarg Marionettes, and the Boston Women's Symphony Orchestra, conducted by pianist Ethel Leginska. About the success of the Musical Art Society one writer stated that "through its annual series of concerts and recitals by eminent exponents of music and the dance [it] has made Ogden Hall on the Hampton campus an outstanding cultural center of Tidewater, Virginia."[61]

Dett and the Hampton administrators did not always see eye to eye on matters concerning the Musical Art Society, and there were times when the administrators seemed to be plotting its demise. Dett, however, fought for its continuance. By 1925 a season ticket for the series cost $3.00. A letter dated December 2, 1925 from Dett to the Society's patrons asking for their continued support is in the Niagara Falls, New York, Public Library. Part of the Society's funding in later years came from student fees.

In 1919 Dett became instrumental in other professional but off-campus activities, in particular, helping to found the National Association of Negro Musicians (NANM). As a charter member, Dett was also the first chairman of its advisory board. As early as March of 1916 Clarence Cameron White had sent letters of invitation to prominent black musicians for a meeting that year, one cancelled, however, due to a flu epidemic. Dett sent another letter dated October 22, 1918, for the same purpose as White's, explaining the earlier cancellation, hoping to set a date for the group's first meeting in conjunction with Hampton's annual music festival.

This proposal was re-routed by musician and writer Nora Holt, who held a meeting that spring in her home in Chicago to honor violinist White, at the time scheduled to perform in that city. The denouement was NANM's first conventon, held on July 29-31, 1919, in Chicago when Henry L. Grant of Washington, D.C. was elected its first president, and Holt vice-president. At the time Grant was bandmaster and music education teacher at Chicago's Armstrong High School, and also taught harmony and other musical subjects privately.[62]

Subsequent NANM conventions were held in New York City and in Nashville, Tennessee. Succeeding Grant as president were Clarence Cameron White, and Dett (1924), followed by Carl Diton. NANM's stated purposes were racial unity and advancement, elevation of American Negro teachers' musical standards via a more efficient instructional system, and improvement of the American public's musical taste.[63] Some of the outstanding charter members other than Dett, Holt, Diton, and Grant were Cleota Collins, Lorenzo Dyer, Maude Roberts George, Clara Hutchinson, Edwin Hill, James A. Mundy, Lillian LeMon, J. Wesley Jones, Florence Cole-Talbert, and T. Theodore Taylor.

Annual meetings of the still functioning NANM have been held without fail except in 1942 during World War II. Early on NANM supported and promoted young artists, such as Marian

Anderson, with scholarships and awards. Then in the 1960s its philanthropy was extended to "more mature artists, composers, teachers and music historians for outstanding achievement and contribution to black culture."[64]

* * *

The *National Baptist Review*, May 3, 1919, mentioned that Dett's "Weeping Mary," in quintette version, had closed one of the programs at the twelfth annual session of the National Conference of Music Supervisors, held in St. Louis March 31-April 4. The *Boston Evening Transcript*, December 12, 1919, noted that Dett was present to rise during the applause when Percy Grainger played "Juba" in Jordan Hall in that city.

The Crisis carried a few interesting items during 1919 concerning Dett's music. The March issue mentioned two events, but with no specific date for either: "An Evening with Negro Composers," presented by the Department of English at Western University in Quindaro, Kansas, when compositions of Coleridge-Taylor, Burleigh, Dett, and Rosamond Johnson were performed; and a meeting of the Etude Club in Lima, Ohio, when works by Coleridge-Taylor, Burleigh, and Dett were featured on "The Negro in Music." The November issue noted an organ recital in Kountze Memorial Church, Omaha, Nebraska, when organist Clarence Eddy performed Dett's arrangement of "Mammy," from the *Magnolia* suite, with such success that it had to be repeated.[65]

An earlier item of interest in the October 1919 issue of *Crisis* stated that Dett would take a leave of absence for the coming school term, in order to study at Harvard University and in the Boston area. During Dett's leave Miss Elizabeth Drew, vocal teacher, wrote Dett's annual report for 1919 to President Gregg, and Miss Ruth MacNaughton was in charge of his academic classes.[66]

Chapter III

Go On, Brother (1919-1925)

1919-1920

Dett spent the school year of 1919-1920 in Boston and Cambridge. Letters indicate that in spite of financial difficulties he was enjoying the new scene. One from Dett in Boston to Hampton President James E. Gregg, dated September 27, 1919, was mostly concerned with his courses, and the fact that required attendance to concerts was costly, compared to the free ones at Oberlin. He wrote:

> I appreciate very much indeed the appointment which Hampton has made for me and I am doing my best to make the most of it. I have cashed in my insurance, but it is plainly evident that what funds I shall be able to command will not be adequate for this expensive institution. There is the possibility of outside work that I am hoping for. . . . I saw Dr. Peabody at his beautiful home in Saratoga, and I enjoyed the few minutes he was able to afford me. I was late finding him, having gone out to Yaddo by mistake; and of course I got lost at Yaddo. Who wouldn't get lost in such a place? Yaddo, the seat of Mr. Spencer Trask's estate is beautiful; but therein lies a great deal of the damage, for one lose's one's soul contemplating loveliness.

Unbeknownst to Dett at this time, he was to be a guest at Yaddo for six weeks in the summer of 1941. Spencer Trask was a wealthy business associate of George Foster Peabody.

A letter dated October 8, 1919 acknowleged receipt of some rent money sent to Dett by Gregg. Another letter to Gregg from Dett, October 12, 1919, said that he was enjoying extra courses other than the ones formerly scheduled. He had never seen a professor sitting cross-legged, smoking in class. "I am commencing to understand a different point of view and to look *through* externals," he wrote. He described Pierre Monteaux, then conductor of the Boston Symphony, as a

> marvelous gentleman and musician. He is a small Frenchman with rosy cheeks, very white skin, black hair and dark brown eyes. He is very refined without any suggestion of effeminancy, emotional as one might expect, but above all vastly intelligent. His conducting was characterized by a sane enthusiasm.

Dett also mentioned in the same letter wanting to study organ in case one could be bought for Ogden Hall at Hampton.

Letters from Dr. Archibald Davison, choral director at Harvard, stated that Dett was slighting his choral course in preference to others. Davison doubted that Dett was being idle or disrespectful, but was frankly puzzled by his behavior.[1]

Several references say that Dett studied composition at Harvard, but name no professor, more emphasis being given to his winning of the Bowdoin and Boott Prizes there. The Assistant Curator for University and Public Service at the Harvard University Archives provided this information in August of 1991:

> According to our records R. Nathaniel Dett was a special student at Harvard during the 1919/1920 academic year. In 1920 he received the Bowdoin Prize for his essay, "The Emancipation of Negro Music." Dett also received the Francis Boott Prize in 1920. . . . We have no other records pertaining to Dett.[2]

Arthur W. Foote, with whom Dett was privileged to work that year, had maintained a private studio in Boston for teaching piano, organ, and composition since 1876. Foote, a Harvard graduate in 1874, was also interested in choral music, having been the Harvard Glee Club's "Leader" when he was a student there. In his historical view of music at Harvard, Walter Spalding said of Foote: "The Glee Club's first high level of excellence, both in type of music and in its rendering, was during the leadership of Arthur W. Foote."[3] Foote, along with Horatio Parker and George Chadwick, was considered one of the "Boston Classicists." Though he received two degrees from

Harvard, he never taught there, but was at the New England
Conservatory in Boston from 1921 until his death in 1937.

Dett played a few concerts in the area during this time, but
attended even more, particularly those given by Percy Grainger.
On December 11, 1919, Percy Grainger played Dett's "Juba Dance"
on a recital in Boston's Jordan Hall so successfully that it had to
be repeated. Dett was present to acknowledge the enthusiastic
applause.

In May of 1920 Dett received $100.00 for his essay "The
Emancipation of Negro Music" as one of the Bowdoin Literary
Prize winners, and the same amount as a winner of the Francis
Boott prize for his choral composition "Don't Be Weary
Traveler." Prompt mention of these honors was made in *The
Crisis*, June, 1920.

* * *

The Bowdoin Prizes were first awarded in the early 1780s.
James Bowdoin, the donor, came from a wealthy Massachusetts
family and graduated from Harvard in 1745. In 1783 he became
president of the American Academy of Arts and Sciences, a
supportive and prestigious group of Massachusetts citizens and
Harvard faculty.   Continually involved in Massachusetts
politics, Bowdoin was the state's governor from 1785-1789.
Bowdoin College in Brunswick, Maine, a private co-ed liberal
arts college and the state's oldest institution of higher learning,
is named for him.

In 1824 the stipulated and properly ponderous subjects of the
prize winning essays were either (1) the importance of the study
of the learned languages as a branch of education, or (2) the
antiquity, extent, cultivation, and present state of the empire of
China. A clarification of the prizes read:

> One first premium, being a gold medal of forty dollars;
> and two second premiums, of twenty dollars each, in
> bonds are offered. The candidates will mention their
> standing, as Graduates or Undergraduates, of what class,
> and deliver their performances by the end of June.[4]

The Bowdoin prizes are still being awarded but in a more ample way. Four are open to graduate students in residence, and multiple submissions are permitted, one to each of the specified categories. The prize includes a sum of money, a bronze medal, a sheepskin, and the winner's name printed on the Commencement Program. All winning essays must have been of high merit, and by the early 1980s the highest monetary prizes ranged from $1,000 to $1,500. Similar prizes of $500 to $1,500 were offered to undergraduates. Now, understandably, there is much more leeway in subject and scope than there was in 1824.[5]

The Francis Boott Prize, still being given as late as 1989, was first awarded in 1905, when Boott left $10,000 in his will for this purpose. A news item dated April 27, 1904, shortly after his death that year, stated that prizes of $100.00 would be given for any worthy vocal music composed by a graduate or undergraduate. Submissions would be juried, and in 1904 Arthur Foote was named as an alternate juror in case any of the others declined to serve. In addition the item said:

> . . . it is suggested that the music be neither too ancient nor too modern in its style. It may be religious, original or selected in either Latin or English. If none of the compositions is thought worthy, the amount of the prize is to be added to the fund.[6]

Francis Boott, born in Boston in 1813, graduated from Harvard in 1831, and during the 1860s and early 1870s lived in Florence, Italy, where he studied music with L. Picchianti. Remaining in Florence, in 1881, Boott's daughter married Bostonian Frank Duveneck, a painter and sculptor. After his wife's death in 1888 Duveneck brought their baby to Cincinnati, where he taught until his demise in 1919. Duveneck had gained recognition through an exhibit in Boston in 1875, meanwhile having established an art school in Munich, one later moved to Italy, where his time was divided between Florence and Venice.

Boott's compositions, under the name "Telford," include several string quartets, a mass, a Te Deum, an *a cappella* Miserere, "The Song of Zachariah" (a cantata), and other vocal music. Boott, who lived to be ninety-one, was the oldest alumnus to attend Harvard's graduation in 1903, the year before his death. The *Cambridge Chronicle* reported that at the ceremony he "headed the procession of the alumni through the yard to Memorial Hall." To do him honor on that occasion, the band played his composition, "Viva l'Italia." Boott's best known song was "Here's a Health to King Charles."[7]

Historian Spalding wrote that Boott was "born with a remarkably true and silvery tenor voice," and was heard singing "with perfect intonation in his ninetieth year. Mr. Boott also played well on the flute." Apparently, Boott was quite a colorful character. "Mr. Boott's personality was so striking that he often figured in the literature of the period as the basis for fictitious characters."[8]

According to a rather complete list held by the Harvard University Archives, since the first Boott prize in 1905 there have been approximately a dozen years when no award was made, noticeably so between 1947 and 1951. Several of the winners, however, received prizes more than once. Dett's prize winning choral composition, "Don't Be Weary Traveler," continued to serve him well. By 1982 the Boott Prize was set at $250.00, with stipulations that the entry be of three to eight parts, not exceeding ten minutes duration, accompanied or *a cappella*, and text in either Latin or English, sacred or secular in nature. Efforts were then made to perform the winning composition.[9]

* * *

While in the Harvard area Dett had a chance to hear an earlier choral composition performed. The long established and excellent St. Cecilia Society of Boston presented some of his choral works on April 22, 1920.[10] A reviewer for the *Boston Post*, April 23, 1920, said that "Chariot Jubilee" had "made a deep impression. . . . [Dett's] setting of text realizes the fanaticism, the rhapsodic utterance of the Negro who has religion." Dett used "Swing Low, Sweet Chariot" as a basis for choral composition in extended form. Soloist for "Chariot Jubilee" was Charles C. Bell. Also on the program was well-known singer Eva Gautier.

A belated review of the same concert was carried in the Lockport, New York *Union-Sun and Journal*, May 15, 1920, which read in part: "On this occasion the chorus remained standing after singing and applauded vigorously until Mr. Dett, who was seated in the audience with his mother, was obliged to rise and bow again and again to the great applause." The reviewer noted the presence of Professors Lawrence Erb and Oliver Halstead, and quoted Erb's remark to Halstead after the performance: "If Mr. Dett lives, he will in five years time . . . be as great a composer as Coleridge-Taylor."[11]

The December 1920 issue of *The American Musician* carried Dett's photo and a complimentary article on his accomplishments, including some biographical material and a list of his more popular compositions. The writer did not stint in his praise:

> R. Nathaniel Dett . . . stands in the front rank of American Negro composers, . . . [one] who thinks definitely of his race with respect to music. He is undoubtedly assisted by a pianist of wonderful ability, his wife.

He delineated between the school of belief that Negro music should be presented in its "absolute simplicity, without attempts at elaboration" for American audiences, and the other exponents, including Dett, who believed

> that the better way of preservation lies in development of original themes, development that shall conserve instead of destroy, the original characteristics, and at the same time make them usuable for presentation in concert form.

Mentioning Dett's volume of poetry, *The Album of a Heart*, the writer quoted one of the lines:

> "A melody that haunts and charms" sums up . . . the expressive beauty that is the soul of every song and chorus he writes. And leaving everything else out of

consideration, that is why his compositions are worth knowing and having.

He admitted thinking Dett aloof, impersonal, "not caring for strangers or their comments," before he heard him speak at the NANM convention the past summer, when he radically altered his opinion. Dett, accessible, after all, proved to be

> a plain, ordinary gentleman of easy ways of speech and smooth action. . . . It is a wonderful thing to meet a man or woman who, after attaining a high station in any particular profession, can maintain that plain and ordinary matter-of-fact way which brings to us all friends.[12]

*   *   *

By the end of 1920 Dett had heard his choral piece, "Chariot Jubilee," rehearsed at Syracuse University. This was his first attempt to use thematic material from a Negro spiritual in a larger work. Scored for tenor solo and mixed chorus, accompanied by organ, piano, and orchestra, "Jubilee" had been commissioned in 1919 by Syracuse choral director Howard Lyman, and though not announced until 1921, the work would be programmed on the Syracuse-sponsored Annual Music Festival of Central New York in May of 1921. *The Crisis*, quoting *Musical America's* somewhat florid comment on the work in its December 17, 1920 issue stated:

> [It] impresses one as a truly inspired piece of choral writing. . . . This short score of thirty-one pages may claim to be a masterpiece of its kind. . . . The old spiritual motive "Swing Low, Sweet Chariot," after which the motet is named, has been handled with a master's control. The greatest variety of dynamic and interpretative effects, solo passages with cantillations that stand forth gloriously, splendidly contrasted handling of inner and outer voices in counterpoint that is never dry, vary a sonorous body of choral harmony in

which a mounting stretto of expression, of movement, culminates with passionate intensity in the magnificent allegro finale, rightly marked *con abandon*. The low basses at times have the ritual quality of the Greek Catholic male-choir voices. If . . . Dett had written no other work, his "Chariot Jubilee" would suffice to make his name.[13]

Earlier in 1920 at the Music Supervisor's National Conference in Philadelphia, March 22-26, Peter Lutkin, whom Dett had met at Northwestern University in Chicago, conducted "Listen to the Lambs." The Hampton Choir presented Gilbert and Sullivan's *HMS Pinafore* in Ogden Hall on May 25, according to a program in the Hampton University Archives.

Minus a specific date *The Crisis* (July 1920) mentioned the annual choir concert of New York's St. Mark's M. E. Church, directed by E. Aldama Jackson, organist and choirmaster, given at Carnegie Hall. Works of Dett, Burleigh, Rosamond Johnson and other Negro composers were included on the program. In September of 1920 Dett attended the second annual convention of the NANM in New York, which drew several of the charter members of the preceding year. The program offered concerts and scholarly papers. Among the performers were Dett, Clarence Cameron White, Carl Diton, pianist Helen Hagan, and singers Minnie Brown and Daisy Tapley. Henry L. Grant was re-elected president.

* * *

Neither Dett's exact stay in Boston nor the date of his return to Hampton has been documented. Mrs. Dett had remained at Hampton, performing her teaching and accompanimental duties. In early fall of 1920 soprano Florence Cole-Talbert shared a recital at Hampton with baritone Paige I. Lancaster of Hampton Institute. They were accompanied by Mrs. Dett. Cole-Talbert was one of the leading artists present at the 1920 NANM convention.

Dett had now clarified his aim as a composer: to develop larger and higher art forms, using American Negro folksongs as thematic material. He was back at Hampton in plenty of time to prepare a large scale Christmas concert, which included something for everybody.   Participating in the Christmas selections were vocal and violin soloists, the Hampton Orchestra, the Hampton Institute Girls, Hampton Institute Boys, the Girls' and Boys' Glee Clubs, and the Hampton Choir. The audience joined in singing some of the numbers.

Sometime during this school year Dett received an undated form letter from Mrs. Harriet Gibbs Marshall asking for a contribution to the Washington Conservatory's Endowment Fund. The letter's content indicates the year as 1920, since the Conservatory was founded in 1903. Mrs. Marshall's well-worded plea was to "establish permanently the first school of music founded by colored persons into a National School specializing in Negro Folk Song preservation and development." She wrote:

> Do you not think that seventeen years of continued endeavor on the part of the founders of this school with excellent results, should induce all who believe that Negro Folk Song has its mission, to contribute to this first and necessary campaign?
>
> Believing that you are one with us, we are calling on you to contribute to our Endowment Fund. Our special drive, launched by prominent musicians and patrons, will take place in several cities [during November]. Trusting that our prayerful and earnest appeal will have your moral approval and financial support, we are . . .[14]

Toward the end of 1920 Mme Azalia Hackley had directed a second folksong festival in Detroit. Whether Dett attended or not, he was represented by his compositions, as were Burleigh, Diton, Rosamond Johnson, and Will Marion Cook.[15]

1921

On January 8, 1921, guest soloists Eugene and David Martin, violinist and cellist, and Andrades Lindsay, "pianiste," shared a second Musical Art Society concert with the Hampton Girls' Glee

Club. The Martins were the sons of David Martin, Sr. of the Martin-Smith School of Music, which Mrs. Dett directed before her marriage. One of the Glee Club's selections was Dett's "Done Paid My Vow to the Lord," with Ulysses Elam as soloist.

Guest singer for the Society's next presentation (in January or February)[16] was dramatic soprano Christine Langenhan, with accompanist Edith Reed. Miss Langenhan's selections of art songs and arias, ranging from those by Handel to contemporary composer Charles Wakefield Cadman, were interspersed with the Hampton Choir's singing of Dett's arrangements "I'm So Glad Trouble Don't Last Alway" and "Follow Me."

Dett had gained a fan through his NANM association with lyric soprano Florence Cole-Talbert. She sang some of his spirituals and his "A Thousand Years Ago or More" on a joint recital with violinist Louia V. Jones at Palmer Memorial Institute in Sedalia, North Carolina on February 24, 1921.

Jones was also a saxophonist. As an infantryman in World War I, he was an assistant band leader. During the early 1920s he toured as a concert violinist in duo recitals with various performers, including tenor Roland Hayes and accompanist/singer William Lawrence. From 1930-1960 he headed the strings department at Howard University.

The Hampton Girls' Glee Club assisted pianist Hazel Harrison with two selections, neither of them by Dett, at the fourth Musical Art Society concert on February 26, 1921. Miss Harrison's rather heavy program included difficult transcriptions of operatic arias, Pagannini's violin pieces, and the Bach-Busoni "Chaconne." Nineteen year-old contralto Marian Anderson shared the final concert of the 1920-1921 series on April 2 with the Howard University Glee Club. Accompanists for the occasion were William King (Miss Anderson) and Armand F. Cole (Howard Glee Club). Miss Anderson paid tribute to her race by including Coleridge-Taylor's "Songs of Sun and Shade" and Dett's "Somebody's Knocking at Your Door" and "I'm So Glad Trouble Don't Last Alway" among her selections.

Proudly *The Hampton Student* concluded the concert report by saying:

Musical activities, as shown by the above programs,

have attracted the attention of the following notable music magazines: *Musical Courier, Musical America, Musical Observer, The American Musician, Music and Poetry,* and *The Negro Musician.* Besides these, accounts of the concerts have appeared in many daily or weekly newspapers.[17]

Some of Dett's music was used at the Spring Festival of the Music School Settlement at Town Hall in New York when Laura Elliot directed the chorus. Mention was made in *The Crisis,* April, 1921, that Dett's works (unspecified) were performed at Morehouse College's tenth annual concert. In the same issue the *Graphic* was quoted concerning Mrs. H. King Reavis, a singer on tour in London with Will Marion Cook's Southern Syncopated Orchestra: ". . . [her] number, 'Listen to the Lambs,' a religious Negro melody, was exquisitely rendered."

Correspondence from Mrs. Marshall to Dett indicates that she must have been successful with her campaign of 1920 for the preservation and development of Negro Folk Song. Evidently she had asked to Dett to perform piano solos and assist in a segment on the "interpretation of African life" on a program scheduled for April 24, 1921. He told her by telegram that he would not be able to come. Dated April 5, 1921, it read:

DEAR MRS MARSHALL I WISH YOU EVERY SUCCESS IN YOUR ENDEAVORS BUT AS I AM TOO BUSY HERE TO DO ANY PRACTICING I WOULD RATHER NOT PLAY IF THERE IS ANY OTHER WAY I COULD SERVE YOU I WOULD BE GLAD TO DO SO OUR QUARTETTE DOES NOT KNOW THE CHARIOT JUBILEE I WOULD RECOMMEND THE FOLK SONG SINGERS WITH BEST WISHES
R NATHANIEL DETT[18]

Mrs. Marshall's letter, dated April 13, told Dett that pianist Helen Hagan would take his place, and that a Miss Easmon would replace him in the African life segment. Mrs. Marshall, seemingly determined to obtain Dett's services in some capacity, asked in her letter:

In appreciation of your cordial promise to assist in any way possible, I am asking if you could arrange to have the Hampton Quartette to look over the *second* part of the African melody, on page 114, "Chamalebvu," that they might hum it, possibly behind the scene, with the chorus. It is not difficult and can be learned in three or four rehearsals—and they need not worry about the words. I may not need them, and again they may be of great assistance in adding to the volume of the group that will sing the opening chorus.[19]

It is quite possible that Dett found this "behind the scene" usage of the Hampton Quartet offensive. Though no correspondence indicates his decision on the matter, Dett did comply with Mrs. Marshall's wishes. *The Crisis* for June 1921 stated that the Hampton Quartet had taken part in a concert sponsored by the Washington Conservatory of Music in New York's Town Hall. The *New York Times*, April 25, 1921, noted that the concert was under auspices of both the Washington Conservatory and Tuskegee Institute, that the Hampton Quartet sang work songs and spirituals, and that the Negro actor Charles Gilpin assisted in the program. (Just at that time Gilpin was receiving rave reviews for his performance in Eugene O'Neill's drama *Emperor Jones*.) On the same program the Washington Folk Song Quartet sang Dett's "Chariot Jubilee."

On May 2-4 Syracuse University sponsored the Annual Musical Festival of Central New York, one begun twenty-five years earlier. Among the participants for the five concerts, each of which drew a packed house, were the Cleveland Symphony Orchestra and the 300-voice festival chorus. When Dett's "Chariot Jubilee," dedicated to the Syracuse University Chorus, was performed "the hall was packed to the doors," according to the *Negro Musician*, June, 1921. The account went on:

As considerable mention had been made beforehand in the daily papers and elsewhere, there was a great deal of anticipation of the performance. It was the first time that a Negro composition had been given under such circumstances. Lambert Murphy, the well-known tenor, who has perhaps done more singing on festival occasions than any other singer, sang the solo parts.

At the conclusion of the program the composer was called to the stage to acknowledge the plaudits, and at the second recall brought with him both the artist and conductor to share the honors. The "Chariot Jubilee" proved to be the biggest number of the entire festival.[20]

On May 3 Dett spoke briefly on Negro music at the Syracuse Kiwanis Club luncheon. The city's leading business men were present.

Attention was also paid to the Syracuse concert by the *Oberlin Review*, May 6, 1921. In the pre-concert announcement Dett was called "one of the foremost Negro composers of America," who handled the composition of "Chariot Jubilee" "with a master's skill."

The Hampton Student, May 15, 1921, reviewed "The School Year in Music," giving five full programs of the Musical Art Society 1920-1921 series, plus one of the 1920 Christmas Concert on December 23. Each of the concerts showed both flare and good taste. A December 8 concert, first of the series, was given by four solo singers, each of whom sang an aria or art song. Mrs. Dett accompanied them and played Stephen Heller's piano transcription of Schubert's "Trout" Quintet. Soprano Ravella Hughes' selection was "A Thousand Years Ago or More" by Dett. Guest singers Elizabeth Lennox and Jerome Swinford of New York were white persons. The quartet of soloists each took part in "In a Persian Garden," a then popular song cycle by Liza Lehmann.

"Chariot Jubilee" was performed in early October of 1921 at the Elmwood Music Hall in Buffalo, New York, during a National American Music Festival.[21] In the October 1921 issue of *The Crisis* mention was made of Marian Anderson's recent recital at Young People's Temple in Ocean Grove, New Jersey, on which she included works by Burleigh, Dett, Johnson, and Cook. An item in the November issue mentioned that pianist William S. Lawrence, tenor Granville L. Stewart, and violinist Louia V. Jones were touring in Nova Scotia. Dett's "Rising Sun," "Reflections" by Lawrence, and some of Burleigh's spirituals had particularly pleased their audiences.

* * *

During 1921 and 1922 several black Americans, such as Burleigh, Dett, Roland Hayes, James Weldon Johnson, Rosamond Johnson, Carl Diton, and Clarence Cameron White, to mention a few, had made names for themselves. Beginning to receive growing attention were Marian Anderson, poets Langston Hughes, Countee Cullen, Jessie Fauset, Jean Toomer, and Leslie Pinckney Hill. Artist Laura Wheeler's illustrations were used in *The Crisis*, as well as in other journals. Pianist Eubie Blake and singer Clara Brown were making piano rolls for the Mel-O-Dee Roll Company. Maud Cuney-Hare, who had arranged several spirituals, was touring in concert with singer William Richardson. Paul Robeson's acting career was launched. Unfortunately, Natalie Curtis-Burlin, who had been married to artist Paul Burlin for only three years, died in an auto accident in October of 1921 while she was in France.

* * *

For a glimpse into Dett's sensitivity and thoughtfulness the following recollections from Mrs. Betty Blodgett Duveneck, child of a fellow Hampton teacher, are insightful.

My father, Warren K. Blodgett, was director of the Agriculture Department at Hampton in the early 20s. The Detts lived nearby, were our friends and I took music lessons for a year or two from Mrs. Dett. Coming home from school several of us little girls would sneak into Ogden Hall and listen to Dr. Dett playing.

About 1921, when I was eight, I was in the small room at the Dett home to the right of the door with Mrs. Dett having a lesson. The phone rang, she handed me the baby she was holding (Helen?) and left the room. When she returned, in returning the baby to Mrs. Dett, the baby fell on the floor. She screamed, the baby and I cried and I ran out of the door as Dr. Dett came in to calm us all. I

was terrified that I'd killed the baby and ran the two
blocks home.

Later there was a knock on our door. My mother
answered, me behind her. There was Dr. Dett, with
flowers in his hand, to assure me that the baby was all
right, and asking that I return for music lessons from Mrs.
Dett. I have never forgotten that thoughtful man.[22]

Mrs. Duveneck's mother died in 1922 and was buried in the
school graveyard "as the students sang Swing Low." Her father,
Professor Blodgett, became ill two years later and resigned from
Hampton. Mrs. Duveneck said that her "love of hearing music
started Sunday evenings in Ogden Hall listening to the students
sing."

1922

The John Church Company in New York published Dett's
piano suite *Enchantment* in four separate movements in 1922,
before it was issued as an entity. It was dedicated "In
Appreciation" to Percy Grainger, Dett's staunch champion who
expressed his gratitude for the dedication of the work to himself
as "a great honor and kindness." The program to the suite,
philosophical and poetic, was written by Dett.[23] Dett often
played "Song of the Shrine," the second movement of
Enchantment on his own concerts.

Another important event in 1922, according to several sources,
was the birth of Dett's second daughter, Josephine Elizabeth.
Dett, as previously mentioned, gave the date as 1923 on a query
for the Oberlin Alumni files in 1925. Though both girls had
inherited musical genes from their parents, evident from an early
age, neither pursued music as a profession.

In an interview on September 23, 1991, Miss Cora Reed,
librarian at Hampton University, related that Josephine Dett
was "every bit as good a pianist as her father." Miss Reed's
father, a trade school professor at Hampton, was a contemporary
of Dett's, and the two families were friends. Dett played the
piano "very dramatically" for two Reed family weddings, Miss

Reed said. As children Josephine Dett and Cora Reed were impish, nevertheless, a little afraid of Mr. Dett's seriousness. Miss Reed recalled that for some mischief at the Dett house he once spanked her. Apparently, as Josephine matured, she remained reluctant to abandon her rebellious ways, for she was expelled from Bennett College while a student there. The Dett sisters, Helen and Josephine, were never particularly fond of each other, according to Miss Reed.

When Dett's daughter Helen was three she was cited for her musical ability, according to an undated clipping found in Folder 2 of the Mesiah Collection. The item from *The Brownie Book*, a children's magazine, carried her photo, and said that she liked to imitate her parents' playing.

In 1922 Harry T. Burleigh dedicated his arrangement of "Couldn't Hear Nobody Pray" to Dett. There is no evidence that the two musicians were closer than professional friends, but common interests and mutual respect were certain. Burleigh was even considered aloof by some professional musicians. Both he and Dett were arrangers of spirituals for solo and ensemble, and Burleigh had composed a piano suite, *From the Southland*, published in 1914. Each had received ample publicity. Items on Dett, in fact, had outnumbered those on Burleigh in *Musical Courier* at this time.

The Crisis, April 1922, reported on Dett's choral piece, "Music in the Mine," earlier dedicated to Percy Grainger:

> Among numbers presented at an *a cappella* concert of the Oratorio Society of New York, held at Carnegie Hall, was "Music in the Mine," by R. Nathaniel Dett, the Negro pianist-composer. This number was the only one repeated.[24]

The entire issue of *The Hampton Student*, April 15, 1922, was devoted to the activities of Hampton's music and drama departments. It contained several photos of Dett's choirs and Glee Clubs.

The high caliber of concerts presented by Hampton Institute

continued. On August 11, 1922, violinist Kemper Harreld of
Morehouse College and Dett gave a recital in Ogden Hall. Mrs.
Dett accompanied Harreld in eight selections, and the Alumni
Quartet assisted with one, unnamed on the program. A concert at
the Trinity A. M. E. Church in Baltimore was mentioned in the
September 1922 *Crisis*. Ada Louise Killion played Dett's *In the
Bottoms* suite. In 1925 Killion became the first colored woman to
qualify as Assistant Supervisor of Music in the Baltimore Public
Schools.

During the 1920s Dett often lectured or spoke informally at
Hampton's Ogden Hall Auditorium, and was in steady demand
as a speaker and performer in other areas. He continued to write
on Negro music, while encouraging students to write. His
aspiring group had the name "Epitome," one of whose exercises
was to review concerts presented at Hampton, with the promise
of publication of the best ones. The following rather
romantically expressed excerpts, which remind one of Dett's own
poetry, are from African student Dwight Sumner's review of
pianist Charles Cooper's recital. After listing the compositions
performed Sumner wrote:

> . . . none seemingly possessed so overwhelming a charm as
> that from the pen of the immortal tone-poet, Chopin,
> wherein the *Grave Doppio Movimento* depicts a Polish
> youth of fiery ambition, obsessed with thoughts of home;
> the *Scherzo*, the sound of war ending in a glorious
> triumph; the *Marcia Funebre*, the funeral music for the
> dead warrior; and the *Presto*, the winds whistling over
> his forgotten grave.
>
> To one hailing from the wilds of Africa, war dances
> with their complex rhythms were recalled; forest echoes,
> changing their everlasting *adagios* over the graves of
> chiefs haunted the memory. This was my first experience
> of a piano recital, and after listening to the works of the
> masters, and comparing them with the untutored songs of
> my native land, I realized that music, varied as it is in
> breadth, knows no difference in depth.[25]

The Hampton Normal and Agricultural Institute

KEMPER HARRELD
IN
VIOLIN RECITAL
Assisted by R. NATHANIEL DETT, Pianist, and
HAMPTON ALUMNI QUARTET

HELEN ELISE DETT, Accompanist

OGDEN HALL
Friday Evening, August 11, 1922, 8 o'clock

PROGRAM

1 Sonata in D..*Handel*
(Andante sostenuto, Allegro Larghetto, Allegro)
MR. HARRELD

2. Selection ....Alumni Quartet
3 Suite Op. 34...*Franz Ries*
111. Adagio
V. Allegro vivace.
MR. HARRELD

4. The Deserted Cabin..*Dett*
Barcarolle ....*Dett*
MR. DETT

5. Spanish Serenade ....*Chaminade-Kreisler*
The Old Refrain ....*Kreisler*
Orientale ....*Cesar Cui*
Andantino ....*Lemare*
MR. HARRELD

6 Swanee River (Foster)...*Harreld*
Souvenir de Moscow...*Wieniawski*
MR. HARRELD

Program courtesy of the Hampton University Archives.

Obviously Dett's attitudes and teaching skills are reflected in Sumner's review. McBrier describes Dett as a perfectionist, who

> . . . worked diligently to influence his students to be satisfied with nothing short of the highest attainable. . . . He sought to inspire, rather than dictate, and thereby stimulate and lead students to further growth. Such sincerity, dedication and devotion to his profession earned for him the reputation of being a great teacher.[26]

No doubt Dett was saddened by the passing of his beloved Mme Hackley in December of 1922. She had spent a part of 1920 in Japan at a Sunday School convention, teaching Negro folk songs. A collapse from exhaustion the year before as she toured California preceded her death.

The year 1922 marked the organization of the R. Nathaniel Dett Club of Music and Allied Arts in Chicago. A book titled *Whispers of Love: A History of Music and Allied Arts, 1922-1987*, was published in Chicago by The Club in 1987, indicating that the group was indeed viable for an incredible number of years. Curiously, through an inter-library search in 1992, this book could be located only at the Amistad Research Center (Tulane University) in New Orleans, Louisiana. It contains a wealth of information, though gives no reason for the club's demise in 1987.

The Dett Club began as a result of interest from a group of women students in the Chicago area, pledged at Dett's request to always uphold the standards of good music. At the time Dett said that it was suitable to name it after him "if they mean to do something worthwhile."[27] The Club definitely did something worthwhile, extending its efforts in behalf of not only Negro musicians, but Negroes in other arts fields as well. At first there was actually a waiting list for potential joiners. Initially funds were raised mainly from programs given in private homes, and later in Chicago churches, public halls, or private clubs. Though Dett's compositions were heard frequently, the programmers strove to give all aspiring Negro composers and performers hearings.

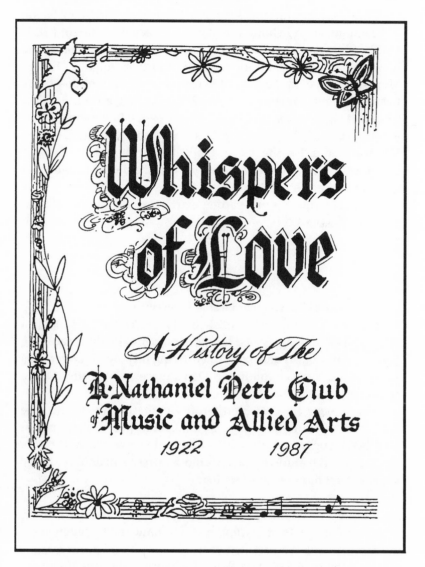

Courtesy of Amistad Research Center,
New Orleans, Louisiana.

At a first meeting on February 20, 1922, Chicagoan Nellie Askew, pianist and choral director, was elected president (1922-1925). She was a graduate of Atlanta University, attended the New England Conservatory of Music, and then entered Chicago Musical College. Askew and the continuing group of go-getters formed a tight, functional camaraderie, and for a time the Dett Club met twice a month. In 1926 it became the first member, as a young club, of the National Association of Negro Musicians (NANM), and by the early 1940s had established its own scholarship fund. As fund raisers the club held dinner dances in some of Chicago's hotels available for Negro socials, such as the Windemere, and annual garden parties at the more affluent members' homes.

1923

The year 1923 was memorable in many ways for Dett. The John Church Company published his *Enchantment* suite as a whole, after having issued its parts separately the preceding year. Dedicated to and performed frequently by Grainger, this set of pieces further confirmed Dett's place as a worthy Negro composer.

On January 16, 1923, Dett wrote George Phenix, at the time Chairman of Hampton's Curriculum Committee. Apparently it had been suggested that fifteen minutes per week for rote teaching to the student body would assuredly maintain a large chorus. Dett did not agree, saying:

> I would recommend the following: That there be Music for all students at Hampton throughout their academic course. For the first two years classes should receive at least three periods a week in class work and one period a week for chorus work; for the last two years two periods of chorus singing a week. I feel very strongly that to try to have the large chorus singing without proper opportunity for the students to prepare it would be futile.[28]

Dett at Hampton, 1923.   Photo courtesy of
Hampton University Archives.

In Early February of 1923 Dett received a supportive letter
from Jesse E. Moorland, co-founder of the Moorland-Spingarn
Research Center at Howard University. One assumes that the
news clipping which he mentions had to do with a coming
performance of Dett's "Chariot Jubilee." It reads:

> I enclose clipping which I am sure will interest you.
> We must not let this valuable material get away from us.
> The other night when in Baltimore I heard a choral
> society rehearsing your motet, "The Chariot Jubilee." It
> was wonderful! When in Detroit a few days ago I told a
> choral leader about this production of yours and he is
> very anxious to get it. I enclose one of his recital
> programs.
> I often think of you and assure you of my interest in
> your creative work. In spite of handicaps we must render
> this great service. I shall be glad to hear from you at any
> time.
>
> With best wishes, I am
> Very truly yours[29]

Born in Ohio in 1863 the remarkable Jesse Edward Moorland
is himself worthy of a biography. Of mixed ancestry, he was
foremost a Congregational clergyman and YMCA executive. Due
to the early deaths of his parents he was raised and partially
educated by his grandfather, later to graduate as class
salutatorian from Howard University in 1891. His various
pastorates were in Massachusetts, Virginia, Tennessee, and
finally in Cleveland, Ohio. As a minister his efforts to develop
a "practical, muscular Christianity," responsive to changing
social conditions, worked favorably with his endeavors in fund-
raising for YMCA buildings and other worthwhile large city
projects of this organization.

After a reluctant retirement from the YMCA in 1923,
Moorland directed his energies to Howard University as a
"professional trustee." His contacts with influential persons
continued throughout his life. The donation of his private
library of Negro materials to Howard in 1914 established the

Moorland Foundation, later to be included in the Moorland-Spingarn Research Center in collaboration with Arthur B. Spingarn. Moorland was awarded honorary degrees from Howard in 1906 and Oberlin in 1924. He died in 1940.[30]

Dett spent a good part of February, 1923 touring the Southern states, playing his own compositions. Appearances were scheduled at Shaw University (Raleigh, North Carolina), Morehouse College (Atlanta, Georgia), the Calhoun School (Calhoun, Alabama), Lane College (Jackson, Tennessee), Fisk University (Nashville, Tennessee), and at Tuskegee Institute (Tuskegee, Alabama). While he was at Tuskegee the workers and students honored him by presenting a program of his music.[31]

A review titled "Nathaniel Dett is Real Artist," with the subtitle "Negro Composer-Pianist Gives a Beautiful Recital at Fisk Chapel," appeared in the *Nashville Banner*, February 27, 1923, after Dett had played at Fisk. Its author was George Pullen Jackson, a somewhat controversial authority on the Negro spiritual. Jackson began the review with "The piano is an obstinate thing," in order to say that Dett was not guilty of the usual lost motion as the player or composer relates through the instrument to his audience. "The lost motion was reduced to a minimum. The piano, under the hand of one who is at once the artist and the tone-poet, obeyed completely." Jackson continued:

> Applause is a variable entity. Sometimes it is sympathetic. Sometimes, very often indeed it is perfunctory, and then it is honestly appreciative. But the determined applause that compelled Mr. Dett to halt the trend of his *Magnolia Suite* to repeat that unspeakably soulful poem-without-words, "Mammy," was proof conclusion that his hearers had had an experience of rare beauty.[32]

An added attraction for the occasion was John Wesley Work, Jr., at the time a member of the Fisk Quartet, as soloist in two groups of Negro songs arranged by Dett. Jackson could not seem to praise Dett enough:

> [Dett] comes to Nashville as one of the very few best

composers of his race, and as one who has been uniquely
successful in translating the rich folk music of his race
into an art form that is already the treasured possession
of the musical world. But the trait in this artist which
sanctifies his work and ennobles it, the trait that
recommends him to both the Negro and the white race, is
his life-purpose. His goal is not money making, it is the
goal of "beautiful living in America." Would that there
were more Nathaniel Detts in both races.

Another review of the same concert was carried in the
Nashville Tennessean, February 27, 1923. In it Dett was called
"one of the most original composers America had yet produced."

Although born in Ontario, Canada, [Dett]
understands the soul and spirit of the Southern Negro,
and has created on the keyboard the most poetic pictures,
full of fancy, and showing a mastery of all the technical
intricacies of modern composition, yet absolutely typical
of the subject. . . . [The spirituals had] an austerity of
accompaniment intended to counteract the jazz tendencies
of the day.

                              * * *

Dett's hope that Hampton would get an organ materialized
in the spring of 1923. On April 25, as a part of Hampton's fifty-
fifth Anniversary "the splendid instrument was first heard by
the public at its formal presentation and dedication," according
to an item in *The Southern Workman*, June, 1923. Written by
Hamptonite Bessie L. Drew and titled "The Frissell Memorial
Organ," the article stated that "an unnamed friend" had
presented $25,000 for the organ to be installed in Ogden Hall in
memory of Hampton's late president, Dr. Hollis B. Frissell.

At this time the unknown donor was revealed by
George Foster Peabody, Hampton's senior trustee, who
made the presentation in the name of his old friend, Gen.
William J. Palmer, who long ago had intrusted a fund to

Mr. Peabody to be used as he might deem wise for the benefit of Hampton Institute. The conception thus came from the kind thought of Mr. Peabody, the devoted friend who has long been keenly interested in the musical life at Hampton.[33]

Mr. Chandler Goldthwaite, organist for the dedication concert, played half a dozen selections, including two of his own composition. Assisting at the concert were the Hampton Girls' Glee Club, directed by Miss Wilhelmina Patterson, and the Boys' Glee Club, directed by Dett. The entire school sang spirituals, under the direction of Paige Lancaster. Dett's group sang Coleridge-Taylor's "Viking Song," Combs' "Her Rose," Schubert's "Sanctus," and his own "Father Abraham." Dett played "Beyond the Dream," "Juba Dance," and "Mammy" from his piano suites.

A "delightful surprise" occurred during the concert when Peabody announced that a life size portrait of Dr. Robert R. Moton had been presented to Hampton by Arthur Curtiss James. The artist, Arthur de Ferraris, had also done portraits of General Armstrong and Mr. Peabody, ones then hanging in the Hampton Library. The Moton portrait was displayed at the concert, later to hang in the lobby of Ogden Hall.[34]

In Texas, some months later, on "An Evening of Music with Negro Composers," the choirs of St. James Baptist and First Christian Churches in Ft. Worth joined in two performances of Dett's "Chariot Jubilee." One was at St. James and the other was on a radio broadcast sponsored by the *Ft. Worth Star Telegram*.[35]

Perhaps a more spectacular performance was held in mid-December in Baltimore, according to the *Evening Sun* of that city, December 15, when 9,000 heard "Chariot Jubilee" and "Listen to the Lambs" as a part of the Baltimore Music Festival. This YMCA sponsored affair at the Fifth Regiment Armory received wide coverage from area newspapers.

* * *

Meanwhile, during the summer of 1923, James Weldon Johnson had received an honorary Doctor of Literature degree from Howard University. The following October David Martin, Sr., died. The Martin-Smith School of Music, to be carried on by his children, had been granted a charter of incorporation in 1921.

1924

A letter from Dett to Hampton President James Gregg, dated January 4, 1924, informed him that he had recently performed with singer Florence Cole-Talbert, and that many favorable reviews followed, though he did not name them. He wrote: "Besides this, I was invited by several of the prominent white musicians of the city [unnamed] into conferences." One wealthy gentleman had offered him a grandly furnished hall whenever he wanted to perform in it, a room "with upholstered chairs and oil paintings covering the walls . . . a room in which no Negro artist has ever appeared and also one to which Negroes are not ordinarily admitted, even as an audience."[36]

Percy Grainger's concert at Hampton on January 18, 1924, was a fitting beginning for the Musical Art Society's activities of the year. His program, including "Juba," was typical in content, and almost identical to one he would perform a few weeks later at the Brooklyn Institute of Arts and Sciences.[37] *The Southern Workman* said of the performance :

> His final number, "Juba," by R. Nathaniel Dett, was played with such a keen sense of rhythm and joyous abandon that at the insistence of the audience it was repeated. Mr. Grainger responded generously to encores and was given as enthusiastic a reception as an artist has ever received at Hampton Institute.[38]

The day before Grainger's concert the Detts had given an informal concert of duo piano and duet selections. Mrs. Dett's "skillful execution of difficult parts won for her much admiration." Dett, on request, played his *Enchantment Suite.* Grainger was present, and spoke on the possibilities of development of Negro folk songs.

PERCY GRAINGER
Composer-Pianist

OGDEN HALL

Friday evening, January 18, 1924, at eight o'clock

PROGRAM

SONATA IN B MINOR, OPUS 58..*Chopin*
    Allegro Maestoso
    Scherzo: Molto vivace
    Largo
    Finale: Presto non tanto

HYMN TO THE TRINITY...*Tschaikowski*
                 HAMPTON INSTITUTE CHOIR

PRELUDE AND FUGUE, C SHARP MINOR..*Bach*
    From "The Well-Tempered Clavichord," Part 1

SONATA IN G MINOR (Brietkopf & Haertel edition, No. 34)
                                                 Scarlatti
SONATA IN G MINOR (Brietkopf & Haertel edition, No. 35)
                                                 Scarlatti

HORNPIPE FROM THE "WATER MUSIC"..*Handel*
    (Arranged for the piano by Percy Grainger)

JACOB'S LADDER...*Negro Folk Song*
                      THE SCHOOL

SYMPHONIC STUDIES, OPUS 13..*Schumann*

LISTEN TO THE LAMBS...*Dett*
                 HAMPTON INSTITUTE CHOIR

IRISH TUNE FROM COUNTY DERRY................................Set by *Grainger*

"COUNTRY GARDENS," ENGLISH MORRIS DANCE..........Set by *Grainger*
    In this piece the composer has wished to express feelings aroused by thoughts
    of the scenery and people of his native land, Australia. It is dedicated to
    the composer's mother.

"JUBA" .... *R. Nathaniel Dett*
            (Born in Drummondsville, Ontario, Canada)
    "Juba" is one of the five numbers from a Suite ("In the Bottoms") pictur-
    ing scenes and moods peculiar to Negro life in the river bottoms of the South.
    "Juba" is the stamping on the ground with the foot, and following it with
    two staccato pats of the hands.

                 STEINWAY PIANO USED

Courtesy of the Grainger Museum,
University of Melbourne.

He paid . . . a fine and generous tribute to the genius of
Mr. Dett as a composer, and told the audience that he
had used his compositions on practically every program
during his extended European concert tour last season,
finding that they were cordially received and   heartily
commended by the best critics.[39]

Mr. Grainger was honored at a reception, assured that he had
made many friends at Hampton.

On January 22 Dett's "Listen to the Lambs" was performed by
the St. Cecilia Club of New York City. The concert was noted in
Musical America, February 2, 1924. On January 27 Dett's Boys'
Glee Club participated in Hampton's Founder's Day activities by
singing selections by Brahms, Burleigh, and and ancient carol,
"Beside the Manger."

Though the date of the broadcast was not specified Dett
received a letter from pianist Doris Rieta Novel, dated
February 11, 1924, apprising him of it. Arranged by William
Henry Hackney for station WDAF in Kansas City, it was titled
an "All Negro Composers' Program," the first of its kind to be
carried over this station. Novel played Dett's "Magnolias,"
"Mammy," "The Place where the Rainbow Ends," and "Juba."

* * *

As his duties at Hampton permitted, Dett toured during most
of February and part of March, 1924, from Canada through
western United States. His first appearance, after leaving
Hampton on February 6, was in Cappahosic, Virginia, where he
played to a crowded house. Next he performed in St. Paul,
where he was feted by the Everywoman's Council and spoke at
several churches in the city. On February 11, 1924, he was piano
soloist for a concert given by the St. Cecilia Choir in Young
Methodist in Winnipeg, Canada. A review from the February 13
Winnipeg Evening Tribune read in part:

. . . the contributions from their choir formed an
appetizing offering; the singing, at its best, was superior
to anything previously accomplished, and because of Mr.

Dett's share in the program, as pianist, it was not
without features of unusual interest and value to all
listeners whose concern with the art of music includes the
study of the important Negro element.

"Juba Dance," a number that could not be accused of being "stale,"
had to be repeated.

More analytically, the same reviewer said that

[Dett's] music splits as to quality into that for the piano
and that for the voice. One feels that if Mr. Dett goes
down to posterity as a composer it will be for his choral
work, unless of course radical changes take place in the
future.

A reviewer for the *Manitoba Free Press*, February 12, 1924,
said: "Dett's compositions, while pleasant and agreeable, are
not profound, and do not deeply appeal to the intellect. The Juba
Dance has an elemental something in it which the other music
lacks."

Under the direction of B. L. Kurth, the St. Cecilia Choir sang
some of Dett's works, one written especially for the occasion but
not named in *The Southern Workman*'s account of the tour in its
April issue. This account stated that "While in the city he
[Dett] had a conference with the leading musicians and spoke
before the Manitoba Teachers' Association. He was delightfully
entertained in Winnipeg, and had the pleasure of witnessing the
Winter Carnival."[40]

While in Winnipeg Dett also gave a lecture/recital of his
own compositions under auspices of the Selkirk Choral Society.
A reviewer for the *Winnipeg Evening Tribune*, February 14, 1924,
commented on the "most enthusiastic" audience who "demanded
the reappearance of the artist again and again." Dett played
the *Magnolia, Enchantment,* and *In the Bottoms* suites, speaking
in detail about their structure, derivation of their themes, and
the use of Negro rhythms and scales. He also accompanied
baritone Stanley Hoban, soloist at the First Congregational
Church, who sang six of Dett's Negro folk song arrangements. Of
their ensemble the *Tribune* reviewer said:

Mr. Hoban produces a smooth luscious tone with a brilliant edge to the upper notes which he used to great advantage in the exacting songs. His interpretation of Negro spirituals was sympathetic, intensely moving, and deeply affected the audience.

Mr. Dett accompanied the songs and added one more detail to make these very beautiful folk tunes receive adequate rendition. Outstanding among them was one entitled "Follow Me," which for dramatic feeling and expressiveness left nothing to be desired. "Somebody's Knocking at Your Door" was Mr. Dett's elaboration into an art song of a brief melodic phrase from a Negro spiritual.

On February 18 Dett played a recital of his own piano suites and his variations on a Negro theme, "Cotton Needs Pickin'," in St. Paul, Minnesota, at People's Church. He also wrote program notes for the event, one sponsored by Everywoman's Progressive Council. Of the concert one reviewer said: "The Magnolia Suite gives evidence of having been written at a very youthful stage in the composer's development, and is a little disappointing in its obviousness." "His Song," from *In the Bottoms* reached "some real heights of imagination," however, and the *Enchantment Suite* showed more sophistication.[41] Again, Dett accompanied baritone Hoban. While in the St. Paul area Dett was given an enthusiastic reception by the Minnesota College and Minnesota University students. His compositions, performed by others, "appeared on the Municipal Organ Sunday Concert program and in a number of the leading churches, both white and colored, while Mr. Dett was in the city."[42]

Dett's next stop was in Detroit, Michigan, for an entire concert of his own compositions. Under auspices of the Detroit Choir's Choral Union a 400-voice chorus gathered to perform four of Dett's choral works, three of which had to be repeated: "Listen to the Lambs," "I'll Never Turn Back No More," and "I'm So Glad Trouble Don't Last Alway." One of the works featured all treble voices. An audience of 4,000 was present. While in Detroit

. . . Mr. Dett was graciously accorded the use of the concert rooms of the Detroit Conservatory, and was made its guest. He also spoke before the Detroit Women's Study Club on "The Message of Negro Music." In this city Mr. Dett had the pleasure of meeting a number of his former pupils and several Hampton workers.[43]

On February 25 Dett was in Cleveland, Ohio, as a guest of the Cleveland Lyricord Singers, who at the time were presenting a series of Negro composers' works in the East Technical High School Auditorium. The *Cleveland Call*, March 1, 1924, called the occasion a "rare musical treat" and Dett "a master of the piano." Dett's picture was on the front of the program. Among other of his compositions Dett played "Juba Dance" and "Mammy's Lullaby." The excellently trained Lyricord Singers were "heartily applauded" in "Don't Be Weary Traveler." A number of local artists performed Dett's works on the concert. In Cleveland Dett met Richard Wagner's son Siegfried who was guest-conducting in the United States at the time, and was privileged to hear some of his compositions, as well as the reading of Wagner and Liszt orchestral scores by the Cleveland Symphony Orchestra.

En route to Oklahoma City, Oklahoma, for a March 1 engagement, Dett played an informal concert at Poro College in St. Louis. In Oklahoma City, he was treated to a concert at Douglass High School, one including his compositions. His own recital in that city, under auspices of the Dett Music Club, was given at the Tabernacle Baptist Church. *The Southern Workman* reported:

A large audience, a third of which were white people, listened to this program made up entirely of works of Negro composers. An interesting feature was the singing of a number of Dett compositions by Mr. Burke Mathis, teacher of agriculture at Langston University, who obtained his B. S. degree at Hampton in 1923 and was a pupil in voice under Mr. Dett.[44]

Stating that "the greater number of the musical folk" did not know that Dett was a Negro, nor a musician of such high caliber, a reviewer for the city's *Daily Oklahoman*, March 2, 1924, said:

> No other musician of his race except S. Coleridge-Taylor . . . has attained the eminence of Dett [who] has served his art better than the English Negro in saving the music lore of the South—of the American Negro race—historically and musically.

This critic ranked Dett in his art as high as James Weldon Johnson, Booker T. Washington, and Paul Laurence Dunbar in their fields. At the concert Dett interspersed his playing with explanatory remarks about the pieces.

Dett's last formal concert of the tour, under auspices of the colored branch of the YWCA, was given in Fort Worth, Texas at the white First Presbyterian Church on February 29. He was assisted by Harry Burleigh and the Harry T. Burleigh Glee Club of that city. The event drew a mixed audience. The following Sunday Dett's "Chariot Jubilee," directed by Bernard U. Taylor, was sung by the Magnolia Avenue Christian Church Choir, a "sympathetic rendering" said to be "most satisfactory." Preceding the program Taylor introduced Dett in a "remarkably fine address and asked him to speak on the meaning of Negro music and the special significance of the Chariot Jubilee."[45] To express his appreciation, Dett played a number of his piano compositions.

Dett returned to Hampton via St. Louis, where he gave a music appreciation demonstration for 1,700 students at Sumner High School. His well received lecture emphasized the use of Negro folk song as a theme for a musical composition.

* * *

During this tour several city choral organizations scheduled performances of Dett's "Listen to the Lambs," according to the *Cincinnati Billboard*, February 16, 1924. *Musical America*, March 15, 1924, mentioned that choral works by Dett, Diton, and Burleigh were performed by the Shaw University Chorus on a

Negro Music Festival in Raleigh, North Carolina, February 26-29. Hampton printed a handsome brochure on Dett shortly after his return. It featured his photo on the cover, a foreword, and several of the above reviews. Diton conducted the Douglass Memorial Chorus in Oberlin, a concert mentioned in the Oberlin *Tribune*, May 16, 1924, which included Dett's arrangement of "Somebody's Knocking at Your Door."

Events of 1924 continued to be particularly rewarding for Dett, not only as a professional musician, but as one interested in drama as well. He had become Director of the Campus Players at Hampton.[46] He was honored during May in his home town of Niagara Falls, New York. As the guest artist for the inauguration of the first Music Week there he worked with 100 white singers performing his choral compositions. At that time he was the first Negro to have this distinctive honor. (He was invited back to participate in Music Week in May of 1925.)

At Hampton's annual spring concert in May of 1924 the choral half, conducted by Dett, was presented as a tribute to Harry Burleigh. On the program were ensemble arrangements of four spirituals, two art songs, *Southland Sketches* for violin and piano, and a processional hymn, all written or arranged by Burleigh. Programs from Hampton spanning over two decades indicated that Dett was eager to use Burleigh's arrangements for his choir, whether on the home campus or on tour.[47] Paul Laurence Dunbar High School in Washington, D.C., honored Dett and Burleigh with a "Burleigh-Dett Program" on June 6, one duplicated the following day, free to the students.[48]

At the fifty-fifth annual commencement of Howard University in June Dett was awarded an honorary Doctor of Music degree by that institution. Also receiving this degree was organist Melville Charlton. President Calvin Coolidge was the principal speaker for the occasion. An inquiry to Clifford L. Muse, Jr., Moorland-Spingarn Research Center Archivist, concerning information on the Howard ceremony revealed very little. Muse replied by letter, August 28, 1991: "After a thorough search of pertinent files, we were unable to find any information about the honorary degree of Doctor of Music that was bestowed on Dr. Dett in 1924 by Howard." There is no documented evidence that Dett ever attended classes at Howard.

Dunbar High School Annual Music Festival

FRIDAY, JUNE 6th, 1924, at 8 o'clock

AN
EVENT
WITH A
PURPOSE
——
PRIDE
IN
ACHIEVE-
MENT

INSPIRING   *ENTERTAINING*

IN HONOR OF

HARRY T. BURLEIGH

AND

R. NATHANIEL DETT

THE PERFORMERS:

Charlotte Wallace Murray, Contralto

and

Afro-American Folk Song Singers

PRICES: Reserved Tickets 75 Cents.   General Admission 50 Cents

Courtesy of the Local History Department,
Niagara Falls, New York, Public Library.

The Shakespeare Club, Hampton, ca. 1924. Dett is located on the bottom step, center. Photo courtesy of Hampton University Archives.

At its 1924 convention in Cleveland Dett was elected president of the National Association of Negro Musicians, whose Advisory Board he had served on since its establishment in 1919. He would take over the presidency the following year and serve through the 1925-1926 term. At the Cleveland meeting "Chariot Jubilee" and "Don't Be Weary Traveler" were performed by the 300-voice Cleveland Associated Chorus, which group Dett guest conducted in "Weeping Mary." Some shorter spirituals of Dett and Diton were performed as well.[49]

For a few weeks during the summer of 1924 Dett studied at Oberlin with his former professor, George Whitefield Andrews. A letter to Hampton's President James Gregg revealed some of his other summer activities. Dett said that he had been advertised as a "drawing card" for the closing concert of the National Association of Teachers in Colored Schools whose convention had recently met. Mention was also made of a later concert in Ft. Worth, Texas, with his vocal student Aubrey Pankey, an occasion including both a white and black choir. The white choir sang "Chariot Jubilee." Dett wrote that Pankey "made a very pleasing impression with his youthful appearance and

expressive voice. He had used his own money to get to Texas . . .
but he earned it all back."

Continuing about himself, he said:

> I have worked very hard here at Oberlin this summer
> under the strict but sympathetic criticism of my great
> friend and teacher Dr. Andrews. . . . He has had me come
> to his home daily, even while he was sick in bed, he
> insisted on my bringing my mss to his bedside where he
> read them over.

Dett had hoped that his wife could join him at Oberlin, but
daughter Josephine was cutting teeth.[50]

* * *

At this time Hampton's music courses belonged to the School
of Education. Each student enrolled in the four-year course for
high school teachers must have two majors, of which music could
be one. Hampton now had a faculty/staff of 250 and 197 college
students. In the fall of 1924 fourteen year-old Dorothy Mainor
(her true name, one later changed to Dorothy Maynor) entered
Hampton as a student. She would be one of the singers in Dett's
choir which gained fame on a European tour in 1930.

That same fall Dett received a letter, dated November 12,
1924, from John Howard Knowles, a piano teacher in Oneida,
New York. Enclosed was a program of Knowles' students' recent
recital with the message, "Talented 15 year old boy played your
piece [Juba] in remarkable manner. We like your music."[51]

1925

On one of the vesper services of Negro spirituals in St.
George's Episcopal Church in New York City, January 25, 1925,
Dett's "Listen to the Lambs" was performed. This series of
vespers was begun in 1924 and continued through 1941, in honor of
St. George's baritone soloist Harry T. Burleigh.[52] On February 17,
1925, two Illinois papers, the *Rockford Gazette* and the *Rockford*

Republic, reported that Dett was assisted in a concert in this city by the Harmony Four Quartet. Dett played his "Sonata in e minor" and parts of his suites, and also spoke on racial elements in his own compositions.

Dett not only had the admiration of Jesse E. Moorland, but that of Arthur B. Spingarn, co-founder with Moorland of the Moorland-Spingarn Research Center at Howard University. Mr. Spingarn, brother of Joel E. Spingarn, donor of the prestigious Spingarn Medal, was a Manhattan lawyer. He succeeded brother Joel in the presidency of the NAACP in 1940, and in 1948 donated his books, newspapers, manuscripts and other relics, collected over a thirty-five year period, to this Center. He died in 1971 at the age of ninety-three.[53]

A letter from Dett to Spingarn, dated February 28, 1925, follows:

My dear Mr. Spingarn:

I feel very flattered indeed that you should express yourself as being interested in my poems. I regret to have to say, however, that there are no more copies left of my book The Album of the (sic) Heart. This collection of poems was published privately some years ago, and strange to say, the edition was quite sold out within a few months. I have hoped several times to make a second publishing of it, but I have never really had the time. The fact is, that my work here at Hampton Institute in teaching and directing, and the management of concerts leaves hardly any time even for the practicing or writing of music, which of course is my profession.

While I have written some verses since being here, they represent the inspiritation and work "of the wee small hours," and there has been no opportunity for collecting and editing them in book form. I recall that there is a copy in the Oberlin College library and also one in the Hampton library here. If I had a spare copy of my book I should be only too happy to send it to you with my compliments, your manifested interest being of itself more than recompense.

In Mr. Robert Kerlin's book of Negro Poets and Their

Poems there is a poem of mine entitled At Niagara
which is regarded by some as being a much better piece of
work than the one in Mr. Johnson's book. I presume that
you have this anthology of Mr. Kerlin's. If not I should
be glad to have one sent you. I am

Very truly yours

R. Nathaniel Dett

Director of Music[54]

Dett received a letter of appreciation concerning a concert by
his Glee Club in New York, probably between March 20 and 24,
though particulars have not been found on the place or occasion.
John Lansill, Executive Secretary of the Hampton-Tuskegee
Endowment Fund, headquartered in New York City, wrote on
March 25, 1925:

Dear Mr. Dett:
We cannot allow this opportunity to pass without
telling you of the excellent impression which you and the
Glee Club made in New York on Monday night. Scores of
people have told us of the great joy which this meeting
gave them.
We realize the personal effort and thought which
you gave to the program to make it the success that it
was, and we are deeply grateful to you.
Your own music, which you rendered so beautifully,
was an inspiration!

Sincerely,

John Lansill[55]

Dett toured again in April of 1925. On April 6 the *Niagara
Falls Gazette* announced that Dett would be honored there on
May 9 during National Music Week. The item viewed Dett as
"rather like the proverbial prophet in his own country—
unhonored in his home town, feted elsewhere. Music Week offers
an opportunity to wipe out this seeming unmindfulness." At the
occasion Dett was one of the guest soloists, and he and his mother
were honored at a reception during the celebration.[56]
A news item from the editor of the *Wichita* (Kansas) *Daily*

Eagle, April 7, 1925, reviewing Dett's concert there on April 6 said:

> Here's a prophecy: within five years this world from Moscow to Shanghai will be whistling Dett's Juba Dance and a lot of Wichita people will be remembering that back in April, 1925, they heard the man who wrote it play it as no one else on earth ever will.

The item continued, quoting Dett, who said that rhythm was the heart of his music.

> Like other artists I must take an outward subject and make it a part of myself before I can give it out in my music. I am a slow worker. I never notice physical fatigue in my work, except such as comes from staring too long at a passage I can't make a go of.

He gave as an example "Mammy" from the *Magnolia Suite*, admitting that he finally had to ask his wife for help.

This particular recital was given for the Coleridge-Taylor Conservatory of Music at Wichita's Roosevelt Auditorium on April 6. Dett played the first movement of his unpublished "Sonata in e minor," and parts of the *Magnolia, Enchantment*, and *In the Bottoms* suites. The Conservatory Chorus sang his "Listen to the Lambs." On April 9 Dett played the same piano works in Kansas City at the Grand Theater, assisted by R. G. Jackson, who directed a 100-voice chorus in "Listen to the Lambs" and a smaller ladies' chorus in Dett's "There's a Meeting Here Tonight" and "Done Paid My Vow to the Lord." On April 14, at Lincoln University, Dett's program was the same as at Wichita on April 6.

On April 23, 1925, Dett was piano soloist on a Douglass Memorial concert in Warner Hall at Oberlin, assisted by the Douglass Memorial Chorus under the direction of Don Morrison. Most of the choral selections were by Dett, one segment of which he conducted. He also played four of his own piano compositions. One of the vocal soloists was Aubrey Pankey, a student of Dett's at Hampton, who "sang several numbers in a pleasing manner," according to the Oberlin *Tribune*, April 24, 1925. The final piece, a "fitting climax to an evening of delightful music," was Dett's "Gently, Lord, Oh Gently Lead Us," which he dedicated to the Douglass Memorial Chorus.

The *Oberlin News*, April 24, 1925, mentioned that Dett had also spoken to the Exchange Club of Oberlin at a noon meeting, "touching on his work and on questions of cooperation between the white and black races." He also discussed the equipment of Hampton Institute and his work there.

An incomplete citation from the *Roanoke World-News*, sometime in 1925, spoke high of Dett's playing in that city: ". . . the experience was a thrilling one from beginning to end. . . . He is a highly interesting personality." His verbal program notes were "admirable." About the suites he played the writer said: "[There is] only one way to get the pure joy of it, and that's to hear him play it. He obtains sonority without a sledge hammer, and he can caress the keys as a bit of plush drapery caresses a plate glass windowpane."

On May 3, 1925, Percy Grainger's second Room Concert was held in the Little Theater in New York City. Some of Dett's works were featured, as well as those of Paul Hindemith, Franz Schreker, Natalie Curtis, and Edvard Grieg. Folder 8 of the Mesiah Collection contains a fan letter to Dett from Wellington Weeks, a teacher in Brooklyn. Dated July 23, 1925, Weeks wrote how glad he was to meet Dett and hear his chorus at the Room Concert. Grainger had played some Dett compositions and Dett conducted his own "Gently Lord, Lead Us On," "Somebody's Knocking at Your Door," "Don't Be Weary Traveler," "I'll Never Turn Back No More," "There Were Shepherds," and "Listen to the Lambs." The words to these compositions were included on the printed program.[57] Mr. Weeks also wrote that one of his students played "Juba Dance" on a studio recital.

An interesting incident, reported in the *Washington Post*, May 6, 1925, occurred at the new Washington, D.C. Auditorium on the preceding day. Dett's choir and Glee Clubs, and other colored singers from the Richmond Treble Clef Club and the Howard University Glee Club, all refused to sing an engagement at the All-American Music Festival, sponsored by the International Council of Women in Washington, because of segregated seating in the balcony of the new hall. Dett contacted Chief Justice William Howard Taft (a Hampton trustee) for advice. Taft asked to be excused from comment, and since Hampton could not be contacted, it became Dett's decision to cancel. The concert was partially saved, however, by some pre-scheduled band offerings. The singers re-scheduled their concert for a few days later in Howard Theater on the Howard University campus. One of Dett's several letters to Hampton's President Gregg that year, reporting on choir trips and courtesies, stated that before this concert messengers came back stage to say that the seating continued to be segregated.[58]

The incident did not go unnoticed. The *New York Times* for both May 6 and May 7, gave quite a detailed account of this unfortunate happening. Mary McLeod Bethune, a delegate to the convention, announced that she and the other Negro women delegates would continue to participate, despite the fact that there was general unrest over the matter with both Negroes and whites. Segregated ticket sales was said to have been the fault of the ticket seller. There was some doubt concerning the wisdom of rescheduling the concert at Howard Theater, since Howard was primarily a Negro university. Apparently, it did not materialize, as it could have been looked upon as another action of segregation.

A community celebration was held in Dett's honor at the Niagara Falls (New York) Auditorium on May 8, 1925. After an address by N. F. Maddever, combined church choirs accompanied by a fifteen-piece orchestra sang Handel's "Hallelujah Chorus" and Dett's "Listen to the Lambs." Dett played from his *Enchantment* and *In the Bottoms* suites, and also accompanied Mrs. Belle Young Smith in his "A Thousand Years Ago or More" and "I'm So Glad Trouble Don't Last Alway."

The Saratogian (Saratoga Springs, New York), May 25, 1925, reported Dett's recent concert at Skidmore College during May Day festivities, at which he gave a short talk, by request, partly in tribute to his mother. His playing was said in the news account to have "won the highest commendation from the noted English performer Percy Grainger who characterized him as among the foremost composers of the present day in America."

During 1925 Dett wisely joined the American Society of

Composers, Authors, and Publishers (ASCAP). Now the new
president of NANM, he posed with a group of eleven gentlemen
for a photo taken at the annual convention held during the week
of August 8 at the Simpson Methodist Episcopal Church in
Indianapolis. All of the men wore suits or long pants except Dett,
who was sporting knickers.[59]

At this seventh annual convention NANM's progress was
duly noted, and its basic tenets were restressed by Dett as
presidential speaker: dedication to the highest and best in
music, and appreciation and support of Negro music and
musicians. Spirituals were presented on several of the programs
by new talent as well as by trained and community groups.[60]
During the meeting a choir-fest was held, allowing Dett to
conduct "Listen to the Lambs" for several different choirs, who
also had prepared his "Weeping Mary" and "Gently Lord, Oh
Gently Lead Us" for performance. The Hampton Quartet, which
had been broadcasting regularly from New York City for the past
three months, also performed at the Indianapolis convention.[61]

From the hand-drawn

"BREAKFAST MUSICAL" program
at Indianapolis, Indiana   (1925)

A sketch from NANM Convention.
Courtesy of the Local History Department,
Niagara Falls, New York, Public Library.

* * *

An item in the Washington *Evening Star*, October 23, 1925, titled "R. N. Dett Approved as Music Director," may have surprised many who knew Dett. Of more significance, however, is Dett's own part in bringing about such a development, a situation not fully explained. Had he become unhappy at Hampton? The *Star* item read:

> Appointment of R. Nathaniel Dett as director of music in the colored public schools was approved by the Board of Education at its meeting Wednesday afternoon in the Franklin School. . . . Recommending Mr. Dett's appointment . . . Garnet C. Wilkinson, first assistant superintendent in charge of colored schools, pointed out that his experience covers a period of more than 14 years as a teacher.

Lane, Lincoln, and Hampton were named as Dett's specific places of experience, as well as his teaching of public school music to "teachers of the southland and to undergraduate students of Hampton Institute."

The Oberlin *Alumni Magazine*, December, 1925, and the December issue of *The Crisis* belatedly mentioned the appointment, which Dett ultimately declined. *The Crisis* reported that

> The Washington colored schools are to be congratulated on the acquisition of Nathaniel R. Dett [sic] as head of their Department of Music. Mr. Dett, who for years has been connected with Hampton, is famous both as director and composer and has recently been made president of the National Association of Negro Musicians.[62]

A letter of congratulation to Dett, before his decision was made known, came from Ferdinand D. Lee, President of the National Memorial Association in Washington, D.C.. It was dated October 26, 1925.

Dear Dr. Dett:

We wish to extend to you our congratulations upon your meritorious appointment as Director of Music in the Public Schools of the District of Columbia.

Believing as we do in your ability and influence among the people of all races, your coming to the Nation's Capital we feel will mean much for the advancement of our people.

As a racial worker, we believe you are interested in the movement inaugurated by the National Memorial Association, we hope for your cooperation with this movement.

We are preparing for a Big Mass Meeting here on the evening of November 17th. We have extended an invitation to the Hampton Quartet, but they have not accepted as yet. If you are in the city on that date, we would be very pleased to be permitted to have you on our program.

Kindly advise at your earliest convenience.

Sincerely yours,

F. D. Lee, President[63]

Dett had probably not discussed leaving Hampton for the new position with his closest friends, even Dean David A. Lane, Jr., at West Virginia Collegiate Institute, indicated by Lane's letter of October 27, 1925.

Dear Dett:

In looking over my Washington paper I came across the announcement of the fact that the Board of Education of that city had approved your appointment as Head of the Department of Music in Public Schools there. I was, of course, surprised, and even now I do not know whether to offer congratulations or not. So I will say, accept my congratulations if you feel that you are to be congratulated.

The thing that is puzzling me, of course, is why you are leaving Hampton, where it has seemed to me you have been doing a job which can be done no where else. I am expecting that you will tell me why before long. With regard to Washington, let me repeat what I believe I have stated to you before, that the tendency of the system there is to make a man a mechanical worker, a cog in a machine—in short, a person whose individuality, energy, and initiative are usually worn down through sheer routine, red tape, etc. Do not let this happen to you.

Best regards to everybody. Let me hear from you soon.[64]

Dett undoubtedly looked upon this appointment as an honor, and obviously underwent much soul-searching before making a decision on the matter. Understandably, the position in Washington would limit his creativity even more than did his duties at Hampton. His well-put letter of declination to Garnet Wilkinson read:

My dear Mr. Wilkinson:

I write to let you know that I have decided to remain at Hampton Institute. I wish to thank you for the efforts you have put forth in my behalf to have me elected Director of Music in your city. I deeply regret the possibility of any embarrassment to you which might be the result of my decision to remain here.

Since I last wrote you I have been waited on by a committee from the Hampton Institute student body, the Executive Committee of the Alumni Association, and still another committee representing a number of the fraternal organizations of the City of Hampton. I had no idea that my work was so far reaching, or so very much appreciated.

The conferences with Dr. Gregg have resulted in such assurances of enlarged opportunities for service that I feel that it would be a mistake to leave a work which has taken so long to establish.

The fear, lest this letter shake somewhat the mutual

esteem which we have so long enjoyed as friends, makes
its composition very difficult for me. I can only rely on
your characteristic broad-mindedness to see things from
my point of view.

    With kindest regards to Mrs. Wilkinson, I am with
renewed assurances of esteem,

                              Faithfully yours,[65]

An undated, unnamed news item in the Dett Collection,
NFNYPL quoted Hampton President James Gregg's telegram to
the Board of Education concerning Dett's decision: "Dr. Dett has
declined the Washington offer and we are glad to say is staying
at Hampton."

                              * * *

Meanwhile, on September 7, 1925, Dett's friend and colleague
John Wesley Work II died, while serving as president of Roger
Williams University in Nashville.   Dett wrote a sincerely
respectful obituary for *The Southern Workman*, saying that
Work was "a man of uncommon gifts," a poet, musician, and
philosopher, who will "be remembered best as a compiler of
Negro melodies and as a devotee to the cause of the advancement
of Negro music."

    Work, one of the few real authorities on Negro folk music,
was at Fisk for twenty-five years and led the student singing and
the Jubilee Singers with "uncommon devotion" and sincere regard
for the spiritual. The tribute continued with an opinion that
might well apply to someone speaking of Dett:

    There is nothing deplorable in the fact that for so many
    years Professor Work was connected with one institution;
    the unfortunate element is that the influence of such a
    man should be bounded largely by college walls.[66]

Continuing the obituary Dett became expansive, mentioning
the accessibility of performances by Negro and non-Negro light
opera companies; the novelty of including spirtuals on concert
programs without a true understanding of them; the minstrelers

as a negative influence; and the "unspeakably grotesque interpretations of Negro idioms by the ever popular jazz orchestras" as overshadowing the "voice of John W. Work, so well qualified to speak . . . on the true meaning of Negro music."

In a pamphlet titled *Armstrong League of Hampton Workers,* October 20, 1925, mention was made of the Musical Art Society's presentations, and of George Foster Peabody's request for a revision of Natalie Curtis-Burlin's *Negro Folk Songs.* Apparently Peabody wished a truer and more accurate representation of the harmonic and rhythmic effects achieved by the Hampton student body's singing of these particular songs. Peabody would continue championing Negro music and Dett's work in the field.

On October 30, at Poro Auditorium in St. Louis, Dett directed a 200-voice chorus under St. Louis Music Association auspices. His *Chariot Jubilee* and *Listen to the Lambs* were sung by the large chorus, and the St. Louis Young Ladies' Glee Club performed *Somebody's Knocking at Your Door.* Dett offered piano solos from his *Enchantment* and *In the Bottoms* suites. He played another concert of his own compositions, including the "Moderato nobile" movement of his "Sonata in e minor," on November 6, 1925, at a First Baptist Church, whose location was not mentioned in an incomplete news item in the Dett Collection, NFNYPL. The Metropolitan Choir of Chicago gave a concert at St. Paul's English Lutheran Church in that city on November 8, 1925, programming Dett's *Weeping Mary* and *Listen to the Lambs.* An organist played his *Mammy,* and a bass soloist sang *Somebody's Knocking at Your Door.*[67]

McBrier lists Dett's compositions published between 1920 and 1925: the piano suite *Enchantment* (1922); five choral works: *Don't Be Weary Traveler* and *There's a Meeting Here Tonight* (1921), *Listen to the Lambs* (1923), *I'm A-Goin' to See My Friends Again* and *Gently, Lord, O Gently Lead Us* (1924); a violin solo, *Ramah* (1923); and seven vocal solos: *Poor Me, O the Land I Am Bound For, The Winding Road,* and *Zion Hallelujah* (1923), *Were Thou the Moon, A Man Goin' Roun' Takin' Names,* and *The Voice of the Sea* (1924).[68]

Chapter IV

Oh Lord, the Hard Won Miles (1926-1930)

1926

At last, in 1926, Dett was officially made Director of Music in the college department at Hampton, the first Negro to hold this position. Sources have not agreed on his title, one stating that he was made Assistant Director, and others giving him the title of Director as early as 1913, or as late as 1927 and 1928. By 1928, however, another Negro department head would be added, biologist Dr. T. W. Turner.

By now Dett's "Juba" was well known and more popular than ever. The Minneapolis Symphony Orchestra played an arrangement of it on a concert in Lafayette, Indiana, February 19, 1926. Program notes hailed Dett as "the foremost among living composers of Negro music, and the first American to utilize Negro folk tunes for classical development."[1] On May 3, 1926, the St. Cecilia Choir of the Western Theological Seminary in Pittsburgh performed Dett's "Don't Be Weary Traveler" at the Bellefield Presbyterian Church.[2]

From Oberlin, Dett's alma mater, he was awarded an honorary Doctor of Music degree at the June commencement of 1926, the first Negro to receive this honor from Oberlin. At least one letter of support for Dett has been retained. L. T. Warner of Bridgeport, Connecticut, wrote to Professor Azariah Root, May 3, 1926:

> My dear Professor Root:
> I am personally acquainted with the three candidates for the Honorary Degree of A. M., and heartily approve them. I think it a happy and fortunate thought to confer the degree of Mus. D. on Nathaniel Dett; he is certainly worthy. The others I know only by reputation and the information that you have given me, but on the basis of that information you can record my vote in the affirmative.
> Very sincerely yours,
> L. T. Warner[3]

126

Dett's citation at this prestigious occasion bears quoting in full because of its particular tailoring to suit his personality. Addressed to "Mr. Chairman" it read:

R. NATHANIEL DETT: Masterful music leader and inspiring composer, active in the work of Hampton Institute.

The most beloved of Roman Poets, looking forward to an old age he was never destined to attain, prayed for two blessings. "May it be granted me, Oh, son of Leto, to spend an old age without disgrace and not without song."

To each race is given its own peculiar gift. Each makes its contribution to our complex life and it is the abiding glory of the Negro race that they have given us song. For our song as the same poet [Horace] has said is a "monument more enduring than bronze, unharmed by any wind, or the measureless lapse of years or the flight of time."

It is thus an especial honor to his Alma Mater that a son of Oberlin has attained high distinction in this the most enduring and most subtle of the arts. I have the honor to present for the degree of Doctor of Music, Nathaniel Dett of the Conservatory class of 1908, a choral director and a beloved teacher at Hampton Institute and a composer of songs.[4]

At the 1926 summer convention of the NANM, hosted by the Philadelphia Academy of Music, Carl Diton was elected president of the organization and Dett became its treasurer. Mrs. Helen Dett was piano soloist on one of the programs.

During the fall of 1926 Dett and his Hampton Choir of eighty voices were invited by the Elizabeth Sprague Coolidge Foundation to perform in the chamber auditorium of the Library of Congress in Washington, D.C.. This was the first such invitation to any group of American students. The *a cappella* concert on December 17 was one in a series sponsored by Mrs. (Frederick S.) Coolidge, who figured prominently in musical activities. As a Harvard supporter, interested especially in organizing chamber groups, she donated funds to bring to Harvard such ensembles as the Ukrainian National Chorus and John P. Sousa's band. She donated Harvard's Sanders Theater, and also gave the Sprague Music Building to Yale in memory of her father, Albert Sprague. Mrs. Coolidge was well aware of and impressed by Dett's productivity at Hampton.

Dett's choir program at the Library of Congress was his usual varied one, using songs from the sixteenth and seventeenth centuries, selections from Russian liturgy, Christmas carols, Thomas Campian's "As By the Streams of Babylon," some of his own arrangements of spirituals and folk songs, and Burleigh's arrangement of "Deep River."

The concert was so well attended that there were not enough programs. It was also well received by the press. A glowing report appeared in the *Christian Advocate*, January 20, 1927, which also carried excerpts from reviews in five Washington newspapers. Speaking of the overall effect of Dett's singers the *Advocate* critic stated:

> When a Negro choir sings a French folk song so that the applause is spontaneous, dispelling the prevalent impression that the spirit of such a piece cannot be given full value by an American choir; when a cultured audience coming primarily to hear Negro singers in a program of Negro folk music is carried beyond the race aspects of its performance into the realm of a universal art knowing no color line, a lasting impression in musical annals has been made. . . . The choir, with whom choral work is but an incident in the training and study at the Institute, singing with clarity and sureness, made the audience marvel. The solo work of Miss Elizabeth Sinkford, soprano, and of Francis J. Minton, baritone, showed surprising gift of voice and finish.[5]

The original lute accompaniment for the Campian work was rearranged by Dett to feature richness in the voices. Dett's arrangements of "Rise Up, Shepherd," "Oh, Hear the Lambs a-Crying," and "Listen to the Lambs" in six and eight voice parts, one of which was repeated, "were enthusiastically applauded."

Other of Dett's arrangements included "Swing Low, Sweet Chariot," "Don't Be Weary, Traveler," and "I'll Never Turn Back No More."

The *Advocate* review added further:

> Dr. Dett carried his choir onto ground formerly considered unsuited to Negro chorus work. That the same feeling and the same quality that have made the spirituals when sung by Negroes popular may be carried over into the entire range of musical composition, was demonstrated at this concert under Dr. Dett's leadership. That this concert begins a new era and reaches a high-water mark in musical achievement is attested to by musical critics in the press comments.[6]

The following newspaper reviews are those carried in the *Advocate*. Speaking of making a "discovery about music in America," the Washington *Times-Herald*, December 19, 1926, wrote poignantly concerning "Oh, Hear the Lambs a-Crying."

> One could have wept with the sadness of it, with the pathos of the voices. But more than the heart of it, there was a choral accent, a sort of syncopation in the rich body of the various choirs that created a new sort of illusion of disturbed emotion. It was one of those fundamental things that is hard to describe. It proved that Dr. Dett has given an arrangement for voices here that requires high choral art to attain, and these were school children! . . . America is rich in a fundamental thing when such art can be produced by the youth among us. The visit of the Hampton Institute Choir writes a page of musical history of which we are justly proud.

Uproarious applause from the audience prompted four encores. The *Times-Herald*'s complimentary statement of Dett was:

> Dr. Dett, whose conducting is reminiscent of Stokowski's work, showed himself still the same fine

musician who won first honors in a class of 1,000 at
Oberlin Conservatory for two of his four programmed
compositions.

The Washington *Evening Star*, December 19, 1926, favorably
compared the expertise of the Hampton singers to that of the
Dayton Westminster Choir, which was also gaining fame for its
excellence. "The work of the Hampton Institute Choir is on an
equal level for the simplicity that art makes natural in choral
work in its finest form."

Wellington Adams, critic for the Washington *Tribune*, wrote
on December 19, 1926: "Strictly speaking, the affair was
distinctive in that for the first time colored singers were accorded
the honor of an appearance in a strictly certified program of
music."

Another editorial in the *Advocate*, from the Brookfield,
Virginia *Union Star*, undated, complimented the decorum of the
singers, as well as the overall performance:

> The attentive attitude and natural modesty of these
> young people added materially to the effectiveness of
> their performance. Not a single act on the part of a single
> singer during the two hours the choir was on stage made
> the slightest jar upon the most sensitive musical
> temperament in the large audience. Evidently the long
> training for such singing had wrought a refining influence,
> and because the refinement of music was deeply felt by
> the singers, its expression produced a like effect upon the
> audience. The expressive sweetness and harmony were
> carried to many homes as a most fitting Christmas
> experience.

The *Niagara Falls Gazette* for January 27, 1927 also gave an
account of the Library of Congress concert, as much a tribute to
Dett as a review. A few years later Dett recalled an amusing
observation in connection with the concert, having overheard a
lady say, "I've been looking at those girls for the past hour, and I
do declare, they've all got straight legs!" Dett, momentarily
puzzled by her remark, told a newsman:

I could not make this out for a long time, but eventually I discovered that this lady thought all Negroes were still brought up in dire poverty, as they were in slavery days, when most of the women suffered from rickets, and that straight limbs among them were unknown.[7]

The particular make-up of the Library of Congress concert may have been different if Carl Engel, then Chief of the Music Division there, had had his way. Engel himself had written some essays on Negro music, and had also been a guest lecturer at Harvard on subjects devoted to the advancement of music. In a letter of February 15, 1926, Engel had asked Dett to compose a quartet for piano, violin, saxophone, and banjo, a somewhat novel and informal combination of instruments. Clarifying the request Engel explained:

The work would be in the form of a suite, or in the regular quartet form of three or four movements. . . a suite of three movements would be the happier form, as it would not be too long, and yet afford enough change for effective contrasts between the various movements. I purposely refrain from using the word "jazz" . . . but I have in mind that the work should have a distinctly racial flavor and yet be in the truest sense first-class chamber music.

Engel also mentioned that $250.00 would be paid on delivery of the manuscript, due by August 1, 1926, and that for nine months afterwards the composition would remain unpublished, with exclusive performance rights belonging to the Library of Congress.

Did Dett consider such a proposal ludicrous? He responded, but not to Engel's satisfaction. Politely put, Dett's reply was nevertheless firm. He refused to feel compromised or be dictated to concerning instrumentation, saying that the result would be "self conscious," "unartistic" and "insincere." He suggested to Engel that "without trying to prescribe for what instruments or combination of instruments any Negro should write, he could be promised a reward for any composition—chamber music if you like—employing an indigenous idiom."

Engel, not yielding either, said that a commission had some right to its own specifications, and he had in mind a "rehabilitation" for the saxophone and banjo, which would "have the merit of being a novelty." He did, however, tell Dett to ignore these stipulations.

Dett's response of March 20, 1926, said that his heavy schedule at Hampton left no time for such composition. He also pointed out, in lecture style, that the Negro church had traditionally never approved of the saxophone and banjo for its musical purposes. Spirituals had always represented the best class of Negro music, and the mind of the higher class Negro would not tolerate these instruments, "which to the bondsman's point of view were instruments of the devil." He continued:

> Also, the long-drawn-out style of the more soulful of Negro songs could not be faithfully portrayed on a banjo, although the saxophone might do this reasonably well; also the associations of the saxophone have not been regarded as respectable, even by people whose racial background is not a religious one. It is evident then, how much more improper such an instrument would be to interpret Negro music truly.

Engel, admitting a fair but incomplete knowledge of Negro music and of the Negro church's influence upon it, did not pursue the issue further, except to suggest that a chain-gang song by Mary Howe be included on Dett's Library of Congress program. Dett did not find Howe's song compatible with the rest of the program, so did not use it. Engel, though bested in the matter, remained professional, leaving his original request for a chamber work open to Dett, who never chose to consider composing it.[8]

A royalty statement sent from O. G. Sonneck, then with G. Schirmer, revealed that from August 1, 1925 to August 1, 1926 Dett received $279.70 for three compositions published by Schirmer to date: "Listen to the Lambs," "Music in the Mine," and "O, Holy Lord."[9]

Though no specific year is given, Verna Arvey, wife of

William Grant Still, wrote that in the mid-1920s Dett came to the Black Swan Phonograph Company in New York for recordings of some of his spiritual arrangements. There at the time was Tourgee de Bose, playing some of Still's first piano compositions. Recalling the incident, Still related to Arvey:

> [Dett's] audible and scornful comment was "Junk!" In later life he [Dett] was friendly, as he had been many years before, but at that time and in that place he seemed to regard the aspirations of younger Negro composers solely as a challenge.[10]

What Dett may not have realized at the time was that Still felt uncomfortable writing for piano, an idiom later improved with concert pianist Arvey's encouragement.

1927

By 1927 news of such American Negro personalities as entertainer Josephine Baker had spread. That spring Baker was in France, popular and doing exceptionally well. According to one report, "her hats, her shoes, her delicate perfumes, her fans, almost everything she owns, are the products of the great artists of Paris. And the money still comes rolling in."[11] Baker was then playing at the Folies Bergere, and in addition had a late night contract with another Parisian club.

Bobbed hair for women was in vogue. Cosmetic ads from Madam C. J. Walker's Manufacturing Company listed everything from shampoo and hair grower to "Tetter Salve to Combat Disease." Mme Walker had become wealthy enough to build a huge home which boasted a $15,000 pipe organ.

More serious happenings, however, were the death of singer Florence Mills, and the fact that writers James Weldon Johnson and Countee Cullen received Harmon Awards for literature. Dett was listed in the 1927 *Who's Who in Colored America*. Announcements were made this year in several issues of *The Crisis* of a European trip for Hampton Institute teachers, one to include France, Holland, Belgium, and England. This year Hampton would offer a new three-year course in music education under Dett's direction. Paramount, producer of "the popular race record," was selling recordings of religious songs and spirituals by the Norfolk Jubilee Quartette for seventy-five cents each.

* * *

Dett's first song collection, *Religious Folk Songs of the Negro as Sung at Hampton Institute*, with an introduction by his former professor Edward Dickinson, was published by the Hampton Institute Press in 1927. Dett explained the nature of these folk songs in his preface to the volume, saying that the tunes and their harmonizations were notated just as they have traditionally been sung at Hampton since 1868. The collection "continues to have a brisk sale yearly throughout the country."[12] As late as 1972 it was still used in Negro music courses in Japan and India.

Within the same year two other books of spirituals were published, *Seventy Negro Spirituals*, compiled by William Arms Fisher, and Eva Jessye's *My Spirituals*. In Fisher's collection ten arrangers were represented, among them Negroes Harry Burleigh and Edward Boatner. Jessye's compilation of sixteen songs, arranged with piano accompaniment, included those she recalled from her childhood. Of Dett's collection a *Crisis* reviewer wrote:

> [It] gives fine evidence of Mr. Dett's work with the student body of Hampton Institute. To the wealth of folk-song material which the students have brought to the Institute, Mr. Dett has applied his own fine musicianship and superior training. The result is an interesting collection of 165 of the religious folk-songs as sung at Hampton. The book is a hymn book in form, in content, and arrangement. As such it will be of great value to all who are interested in the growth of Negro-American folk music and of especial interest and help to those persons who are actively engaged in the preservation of the songs by means of group singing. The editor's introductory chapter is a valuable contribution to literature on the subject.[13]

George Pullen Jackson, who had earlier praised one of Dett's performances, commented critically on *Religious Folk-Songs of the Negro*:

> R. Nathaniel Dett has done excellent editing of the textual material he inherited from the earlier Fenner Hampton compilation (1874) of songs recorded from oral tradition and borrowed from the Fisk collection; and his tunes are musically handled—perhaps too musicianly, for with their inappropriate and over-generous Italian expression, directions, and other artifices, one sees that they are polished up for the technically refined concert stage, a treatment which makes the song less valuable to those who would learn something of Negro folk music as it really was.[14]

An essay in defense of spirituals for concert use appeared in *The Crisis*, February, 1927. The writer, Gamewell Valentine of Sumter, South Carolina, took issue with an item in the *Musical Courier* which labeled the spiritual "futile." Valentine was right on target:

> Are the judgments of [John] McCormack, [Fritz] Kreisler, [Reinald] Werrenrath so fickle as to put futile music on their programs? What did Dvorak see in the spirituals to enjoy them? Was his judgment any good?[15]

The *Christian Science Monitor* reviewed *Religious Folk-Songs of the Negro* more favorably than had Jackson, saying that

> In the best sense of the word these arrangements are authentic, coming directly from the early students who were rooted in the old slave traditions. Dett, in his faithful reproduction of the directness and simplicity of the spirituals, in his avoidance of over-elaborate and sophisticated harmonies, has taken a definite stand against some present tendencies. He has preserved for us the Negro Spiritual, not in an artificial and decorated frame, but in its true native setting.[16]

In the spring of 1927 the Daughters of the American Revolution in Flint, Michigan sponsored a "Nationality in Music" series. On March 20 the featured nationality was American, and Dett was represented by D. J. W. Moore, tenor, who sang his "I'm Goin' to See My Friends Again."[17]

Obviously Dett's compositional output had been recognized by many. In 1927 he was selected to receive the Harmon Award for Creative Achievement in Music, an honor which would be bestowed early in 1928. In September of 1927 Dett was guest of honor at the Niagara Falls, New York, Music League, at which time the League, an all white group, made him an honorary member. As guest speaker he stressed the need for a concert series in a city so "industrially minded," and gave the League constructive suggestions on how to organize such a cultural program.[18]

Dett was formally invited to attend the inauguration of Howard University's new president, Mordecai Wyatt Johnson, on June 10, 1927. Sent by the Board of Trustees and the faculties of Howard, the invitation requested a "reply giving the name, title, and degrees of the delegate by the fifth of May."[19] No further available correspondence confirmed or denied his attendance at the ceremony.

During 1927 several advertisements appeared in *The Crisis* for Bennett College for Women in Greensboro, North Carolina, where Dett would teach in 1937. One of them read: "Climate excellent, campus beautiful; equipment modern; student self-government. Relationship with faculty wholesome and democratic. Faculty composed of college women from the best schools in America."[20] Among the ads also was one for Samuel Huston College in Austin, Texas, another school where Dett would teach briefly in 1935.

Dett was apparently still active with the Epitome group of student writers mentioned in Chapter III. An interesting letter from Dett to poet Countee Cullen, dated July 2, 1927, bears reprinting.

> My dear Mr. Cullen
> Your letter to Mr. Ansley came to me, as all of my Epitome boys are now away for the summer. Practically

all of these are self-supporting young men, and have to make thier [sic] spare time count for the next season's schooling.

We are a young club in writing; we meet once a week, here at my house, which is called Maple Cottage, to read manuscripts and discuss them. All meetings are rather informal, but I think we are learning.

Your trip to the school was greatly appreciated; the Epitome had sepecially [sic] hoped that you would be able to visit one of our meetings as some of our distinguished visitors have done. Mrs. Deland gave the older Epitome a fine talk some years ago, and all that she prophesied about a wave in Negro literature has come true.

Some of our members are now in New York, and I shall be pleased to drop them a line that you have written the club.

Thanking you for your cordial letter, and wishing you long continued success, I am

> Sincerely yours
> R. Nathaniel Dett
> for the Epitome

Added at the bottom of the letter, in Dett's handwriting, was "I am not a typist—as you see by this oblique creation I wished to acknowledge your letter as best I could. Am pleased to learn that you are on Opportunity staff so am enclosing a subscription. R.N.D."[21]

Countee Cullen was born Countee LeRoy Porter in Louisville, Kentucky (a birthplace often given erroneously as Baltimore, Maryland) in 1903. He was adopted and raised by Reverend Frederick Cullen, pastor of New York's Salem Methodist Church. At New York University, where Cullen graduated in 1925, he won Phi Beta Kappa honors and was awarded the Witter Bynner Poetry Prize. His volume of poetry *Color* received a Harmon first gold medal for literature in 1927, by which time he had earned his M. A. at Harvard University.

In April of 1928 the colorful Countee Cullen married W. E. B. DuBois' daughter Nina Yolande. Their elaborate wedding with twelve bridesmaids was featured in the *New York Age*. The honeymoon was combined with Cullen's receipt of a Guggenheim Fellowship, taking him to Paris. The marriage ended in 1930. Cullen taught in public schools, hoping that his continued writing would contribute noticeably to social change. He was a leading figure in the Harlem Renaissance, writing principally of Negritude and its evolution, faith and doubt, mortality, death, love, racial unfairness, and religion.

Cullen's works include six volumes of poetry, one of which he edited, *Caroling Dusk*; some children's books; reviews and other contributions to *The Crisis*, *The Nation*, *Phylon*, and similar contemporary journals. His one novel, *One Way to Heaven* (1932), was not as well received as his poetry, namely *The Black Christ*, *The Medea and Other Poems*, and his last volume *My Lives and How I Lost Them*. His three plays were never published. In the mid-1930s Cullen married Ida Mae Roberson, who lived until 1986. Cullen died in 1946 of uremic poisoning.

* * *

Though it probably had little effect on Dett, who was continually immersed in his work, a student strike which had been brewing at Hampton erupted in the fall of 1927, shortly before the semester's end. The unrest had been partially caused by passage of the Massenburg Bill, which required separation of the races (Negro and Indian) in public halls of Virginia, including those of Hampton Institute. Since the bill's enactment Principal James Gregg had become less and less sociable. Students in general were protesting the lack of justice and freedom in the school regime. Many, some of them prominent school leaders, left the campus. Other students were expelled. The striking students, of course, were considered the bad element.

Letters concerning the situation were later printed in *The Crisis*. One from Principal Gregg stated that he did not wish to comment at this time, that the facts would be found in the December issue of *The Southern Workman*. One mildly shocking incident was reported belatedly in May of 1928: "St. Luke Brown, the colored Hampton student who was arrested for striking a white teacher, was given a jail sentence and a fine of $250." The sentence was suspended, however, "on evidence of the boy's previous good character."[22]

Dett, the sedulous worker, continued in his own realm. He could not have gotten such remarkable results from his choirs without an overall sound structure of operation. He always managed to keep the various vocal parts in balance, and periodically he tested his singers individually. Since the groups performed *a cappella*, he developed a Russian-like basso profundo section for the lowest parts. His patience must have equalled that of Job. As a Dett student McBrier recalled some of his teaching methods:

> The strictest discipline was always maintained; yet an atmosphere of genuinely relaxed pleasure permeated the rehearsal period. Punctuality and regularity of attendance were required; perfection of tone quality, intonation, and interpretation were always sought. The author has seen him spend weeks perfecting one phrase, and never once during that time did the choir evidence boredom. When five o'clock morning rehearsals were added to the regular daily rehearsal schedule, the students still responded.[23]

Dett may or may not have been aware of editor critic H. L. Mencken's retraction of his own statement in September of 1927 that the Afro-American race had done nothing to dignify and develop the music of his race. After much published criticism, Mencken apologized in the *Pittsburgh Courier*, October 1, 1927:

> I forgot Professor R. Nathaniel Dett of the great Afro-American house of learning at Hampton, Virginia. I should have remembered Mr. Dett's anthem "Listen to the Lambs," a genuinely original and moving piece of work. . . . I think [it] is his best. It is dated 1914.

1928

Dett's receipt of a first place Harmon Award was announced on January 12 by interested newspapers. The first award in music

Christmas Concert

BY

The organizations representing the active membership of
the Musical Art Society of Hampton Institute

Dr. R. Nathaniel Dett and Miss Wilhelmina Patterson, conducting
Mr. Ernest H. Hays, organist
Mrs. Nell Hunter, soprano soloist

OGDEN HALL

Thursday evening, December 22, 1927 at seven forty-five

PROGRAM

Grand Chorus .... *Guilmant*
MR. HAYS
Ave Maria .... *Arcadelt*
Ave Maria .... *Tschaikowski*
THE CHOIR
Come, Thou, O Come .... *Bach*
MERCER F. BRATCHER
Wi-um, (Pueblo Lullaby) .... *arranged by Lieurance*
Midnight Carol (Ghosts of the Year) .... *Gaines*
GIRLS' GLEE CLUB
Joy to the World .... *Hymn 112*
CONGREGATION
Come unto Him .... *Handel*
Allelujah .... *Mozart*
Ave Maria .... *Bach-Gounod*
MRS. NELL HUNTER
Prayer from "Iphegenia in Tauris" .... *Gluck*
A Lovely Rose is Blooming .... *Praetorious*
BOYS' GLEE CLUB
Shepherds, Shake Off Your Drowsy Sleep .... *French Folk Song*
There's a Star in de East .... *Negro Folk Song*
THE CHOIR
Birthday of a King .... *Neidlinger*
Cantique de Noel .... *Adams*
Jesu Bambino .... *Yon*
MRS. NELL HUNTER
O Come, O Come, Immanuel .... *Hymn 110*
CONGREGATION
The Outgoing of the Boats .... *Roberton*
Legend .... *Tschaikowski*
It Came upon a Midnight Clear .... *Sullivan*
THE CHOIR
Doxology
CONGREGATION

Program courtesy of Hampton University Archives

was $400.00 and a gold medal, the second, $100.00 and a bronze medal. The music category encompassed song scores, instrumental scores for single instruments or ensemble, scores of oratorio and operas, and performers in drama, instrumental and vocal music. Awards were given in nine cities. Douglas Gordon, music editor of the *Norfolk Ledger Dispatch*, presented Dett's award to him at Hampton on February 12, 1928.

In his verbose and somewhat evangelistically dramatic speech, later printed in *The Southern Workman*, Gordon boasted his own credentials as a music critic. "Because of this [the credentials] no doubt, this honor has been paid me," he said, in reference to presenting Dett's award. He deplored how little most people knew of the stellar Negro representatives in the arts, mentioning achievers "Blind Tom" Bethune, Roland Hayes, Paul Laurence Dunbar, Countee Cullen, Ethel Waters, James Weldon Johnson, and, of course, Dett.

In praise of Dett, Gordon compared his awe on hearing Hayes sing and Dett play, saying that he thought he had now heard everything. He was *convinced* he had heard it all, until he heard Hayes, then Dett's chorus.

> Then I knew again—I knew the truth and [it] was beginning to make me free—that I had known nothing. I heard Dr. Dett play the piano, and I knew again that I had known nothing. I heard his own compositions, and my mind blushed at its ignorance.

Gordon mentioned that a few years ago he, Dett, and a Richmond, Virginia dignitary judged a number of bands in that city at a huge Negro Elks Convention. In choosing the winning band Gordon highly respected Dett's musical experience and opinion. In the award speech he said to Dett, "It is not as Negro musician that you have earned this medal and the less important pecuniary reward that accompanies it, Mr. Dett. It is as a musician." With a quote from Rudyard Kipling, "But there is neither East nor West, Border, nor Breed, nor Birth, when two strong men stand face to face, though they come from the ends of the earth!" he concluded:

Music is the language of all the borders, all the
breeds, all the births. So it is here today, Dr. Robert
Nathaniel Dett, Bachelor of Music, Doctor of Music,
maker of music, maker of music for all the world, I have
the honor to present you the gold medal and pecuniary
reward for that which you have accomplished, the
greatest creative achievement in the field of musical
composition in this year of our Lord, 1927.[24]

Mrs. Charlotte Dett received a special invitation from
Hampton's Principal James Gregg, dated January 27, 1928, to
attend the Harmon ceremony.   She replied eloquently on
February 1.[25] Gregg's and Mrs. Dett's letters follow.

Dear Mrs. Dett:
We at Hampton have rejoiced with you in the fresh
distinction which has come to your son Nathaniel in the
award of the Harmon prize and medal for his outstanding
service in the field of music. The public presentation of
this award has been set for the afternoon of Sunday,
February twelfth. We have felt that it would give us all
especial pleasure and satisfaction if you could be here as
the guest of the Institute on that occasion, the Institute
paying, of course, all travelling expenses connected with
the trip. We hope very much that you can come.
With warm congratulations and all good wishes, I am
Faithfully yours,
James E. Gregg
Principal

Mrs. Dett's letter read:

Dear Sir
I have received your kind invitation to be present at
the presentation of the Harmon Award to my son
Nathaniel, which takes place February 12th.
I shall be both pleased and proud to accept your kind
invitation, and deem it a great privelege (sic) to be able
to visit Hampton Institute again, and to mingle with

those who are making it possible for me to be present under such delightful circumstances.

Again expressing my grateful appreciation I am
Sincerely Yours
Charlotte Dett

Dett's friend, violinist Clarence Cameron White, then Director of Music at West Virginia Collegiate Institute, also received a first place Harmon Award in music. Two first places were given this year, according to the *New York Times*, February 13, 1928, because none was awarded the year before. Artist Laura Wheeler Waring was a first place winner in fine arts. Second places, awarded at the Abyssinian Baptist Church in New York City on February 12, went to William Grant Still, "a composer of New York," and another New Yorker, Edward H. Margetson, organist at the Church of the Crucifixion.[26]

The donor of the Harmon Awards, William Elmer Harmon, who died in July of 1928, had been a New York City realtor and developer of suburbs, whose philanthropic interests were of wide span. He was a generous endower of playgrounds, charities, and a religious motion picture company. The Harmon Award was designed for those who had made worthwhile achievement in the fields of literature, fine arts, industry (business), science (invention), education, religion, and race relations. These seven awards were open to Negroes of American residence, male or female, and an additional eighth could be given to anyone of American residence, regardless of race of sex. Preference, however, was given to persons who were not already well known.

As former Oberlin students, Dett's and White's receipt of a Harmon Award caught the attention of the *Oberlin Tribune* (January 13, 1928), the *Oberlin News* (January 17, 1928), and the *Oberlin Alumni Magazine* (February 1928). The latter also carried a humorous story by John W. Love, printed earlier in the *Cleveland Plain Dealer*, which recalled Dett's early friendship with Mr. Fred H. Goff, mentioned in Chapter II. Love, who met Dett on a train out of Washington, asked him, "Did Mr. Goff ever say what it was that first interested him in you?" Dett replied, "He said he noticed the way I walked."

THE HAMPTON NORMAL AND AGRICULTURAL INSTITUTE

PRESENTATION OF THE HARMON AWARD
FOR CREATIVE ACHIEVEMENT IN MUSIC TO

ROBERT NATHANIEL DETT, DOCTOR OF MUSIC, AND

DIRECTOR OF THE SCHOOL OF MUSIC, HAMPTON INSTITUTE,

IN OGDEN HALL

SUNDAY AFTERNOON, FEBRUARY 12, 1928,

AT 4 O'CLOCK

P R O G R A M

INVOCATION
              REV. LAURENCE FENNINGER, *Chaplain of Hampton Institute*

AMERICA THE BEAUTIFUL ....CONGREGATION

INTRODUCTORY REMARKS
              DR. JAMES E. GREGG, *Principal of Hampton Institute*

LISTEN TO THE LAMBS ....CHOIR

ADDRESS AND PRESENTATION OF THE AWARD
              MR. DOUGLAS GORDON, *Editor of the Norfolk Ledger-Dispatch*

RESPONSE ....DR. DETT

I'LL NEVER TURN BACK NO MORE ....CHOIR

TELL JESUS ....GLEE CLUB

HAMPTON, MY HOME BY THE SEA ....GLEE CLUB

JACOB'S LADDER ....CONGREGATION

BENEDICTION

ALL MUSICAL NUMBERS COMPOSED BY DR. DETT, EXCEPTING THE LAST

Program courtesy of Hampton University Archives.

* * *

On February 1, shortly before the Harmon Award ceremony, the Hampton Institute Glee Club gave a concert at the City Auditorium in Lynchburg, Virginia. Of added interest to the program were Dett's arrangements of "I'm So Glad Trouble Don't Last Alway" for violin and "Somebody's Knocking at Your Door" for saxophone. This program was identical to one given at Hampton on February 4. [27]

The flyer (courtesy of Hampton University Archives) accompanying a photo of the Glee Club, 1928-1929, read:

Twenty-four picked voices, under the capable leadership of Dr. R. Nathaniel Dett, comprise the celebrated Hampton Institute Glee Çlub for its 1928-1929 tour. This noted singing group from Hampton, Virginia, has long since established itself as one of the best male choruses in America.

The Hampton Institute Glee Club has developed, under Mr. Dett's able direction into a peerless singing group, comparable with the very finest Russian, German, or American male choruses.

Not only do they interpret the Negro spirituals and Negro folk songs with peculiar and special effectiveness, but they also render, admirably and flawlessly, modern English songs and classics from the German and Italian music, sung in English.

The Institute has had its celebrated chorus for years and it is safe to say that the splendid ensemble, the fine vocal timbre, the remarkable technique, and the well-chosen repertoire featured by this season's group is unsurpassed in the long years of enviable musical history of the Hampton Institute.

Dr. Dett occupies a most unique place in the realm of contemporary American music history. He has achieved national fame as a composer, as a pianist, and has won considerable distinction as a poet. He appears in a double role with the Glee Club, not only directing their group singing, but also as piano soloist with the club. His

The Hampton Institute Glee Club, 1928-1929 (Dett in tuxedo).
Courtesy Hampton University Archives.

---

repertoire, and also the songs of the Glee Club, will
feature many of his own compositions.

In early February Dett and Hampton students performed at
Hollins College in Virginia. A review of the event in an unnamed
newspaper, found in the Dett Collection, NFNYPL said: "The
twenty-four voices were controlled as an orchestra. . . only better.
. ., not with a baton, but it seemed with a glance." Dett's piano
student Rudolph von Charlton and Dett played solos. Of Dett's
playing the review said: "One can only say that the audience
wished he had played more."

Dett and the choir were busy travelers. At about this time
the *Augusta* (Georgia) *Chronicle*, February 5, 1928, reported a
recital given at the Tabernacle Baptist Church in that city,
saying: "Our white friends came out in the largest numbers that
have been seen in many a day." Remarks of this type by
surprised reviewers were frequently in newspapers during the
mid and late 1920s.

Despite choir activities, Dett managed to fill an engagement
as piano soloist at the Twelfth Annual Concert of the Musical
Club of Harvard, on April 7, 1928, according to an item in Folder 4
of the Mesiah Papers and Documents. He played "Juba Dance"
and "His Song."

During the spring of 1928 the Hampton Choir had gone on

CARNEGIE HALL

MONDAY EVENING, APRIL 16th, 1928
at 8.30

Hampton Institute Choir

from Hampton, Va.

DR. R. NATHANIEL DETT, Conductor

Presented under the Auspices of

THE SOCIETY OF THE FRIENDS OF MUSIC

Programme

SACRED SONGS OF THE EARLY CHURCH

Ave Maria _____Arcadelt (1514-1556)
As by the Streams of Babylon_____Campion (1575-1619)
In Heav'nly Love_____Laurentii (1573-1655)
Now Christ is Risen _____Traditional (Circa 1500)

RUSSIAN LITURGICAL ANTHEMS

Hymn to the Trinity_____Tschaikowski
We Praise Thee_____ Shvedof
Lord, Our God, Have Mercy _____Lvosky

RELIGIOUS COMPOSITIONS BY AMERICAN COMPOSERS

Savior Hear Us When We Pray_____Lily Strickland
Fierce Was The Wild Billow_____Noble

NEGRO SPIRITUALS

Deep River ._____Burleigh
As Children, Walk Ye in God's Love_____Dett

THE NEGRO IDIOM IN MOTETS AND ANTHEMS
BY R. NATHANIEL DETT

Son of Mary
Don't Be Weary, Traveler
Oh, Hear the Lambs A-crying
Listen to the Lambs
Let Us Cheer the Weary Traveler

Management: RICHARD COPLEY, 10 East 43rd Street

Tickets: $2.50, 2.00, $1.50 and $1.00, Tax exempt

Boxes $25.00 and $18.00, Tax exempt, on sale at Carnegie Hall.

Program courtesy of Hampton University Archives.

tour, "singing spirituals to white and colored audiences throughout the South," according to *The Crisis*, April 1928. Their program in Carnegie Hall on April 16, partially sponsored by philanthropist George Foster Peabody, included Russian, early Christian, and Negro music. Their last two selections were Burleigh's arrangement of "Deep River" and Dett's "As Children Walk Ye in God's Love." *The Crisis* said that the concert "has received much striking commendation," and gave excerpts from a few reviews in New York newspapers. One from the *Morning Telegraph* said, "There has been no finer example of choir singing in this season's whole record."[28]

A lengthy review from the New York *Evening Post*, April 17, 1928, favored one of the Russian songs, "Gospodi Pomilui" (in translation "Lord, Our God, Have Mercy") by G. V. Lvovsky, which had to be repeated after the encore, Tschaikovsky's "Legend." The knowledgeable but critical reviewer said:

> Wisely . . . Dett, the conductor, refrained from any individual interpretation, but held to that of the Russians, notably Basile Kibalchich, whose Russian Symphonic Choir recently sang it here.
>
> Some slight flavor was lost because the Hampton choir naturally had to sing the English words. . . and in the endless reiteration . . . they seemed clumsier on the tongue than the Russian. Again it may be that the Negro bass was not as profound and impressive. Otherwise the performance was marvelous. In blend, emphasis on particular notes, rhythm, contrasts of volume and the gradual, breath-taking progression of chords, descending to a pianissimo of infinite beauty, and rising again to the final, desperate entreaty, this choir was magnificent.

The expansive *Evening Post* reviewer compared the looks of pleasant surprise on the audience's faces to those of American tourists who might by chance hear a fine concert at a French Chapelle. He described the applause as "frantic." Continuing, he wrote:

> . . . Negroes should do well with Russian music. They

breathe naturally, stand naturally, sing with ease, know blend and have that same sense of harmony, and their history, too, has been one of oppressions. Their music also shows that utter resignation that is so strangely appealing. No complaint at all, no question, even, as to why the God that made them had to make them so miserable, . . . people of sorrows and acquainted with grief, and possessed of a voice.

Impressed with Dett's program notes, the same reviewer quoted portions from them, in which Dett wrote that Russian music was the second favorite literature of the Hampton Choir. His hope to bring Russian choirs to Hampton had met with much enthusiasm from the students. Dett suggested that a kinship of mutual oppression between the Russian and the Negro could be best expressed through pervading pathos in vocal music, citing in particular certain rhythms, scale formations, and cadences.[29] More comments on the choir ended the *Evening Post* review:

As a whole the choir is splendid. The women's voices have that fresh, girlish quality, without the slightest evidence of strain at any time. The men are virile, healthy, mellow. The solo voices have character and are true. The singers themselves know how to carry a melody, how to let a note fade, and there isn't a white choir on earth that could lift the "Don't Be Weary, Traveler" into rapture as did these dark singers from Virginia.[30]

Reviews of this spectacular Carnegie Hall concert appeared also in the *New York Herald-Tribune* and the *New York Times*. Speaking of the choir's excellence the *Herald-Tribune* writer said:

Their choral technique is unusually sure and skillful, with an absolute precision of attack shown at the start, when Dr. Dett began the concert immediately upon reaching the rostrum. There was notable unity in spirit and execution, a tone marked by strength, smoothness and

praiseworthy depth and color. . . . A few occasional
imperfections, such as top notes when the quality of tone
fell below the general standard, and an exception to the
usual rule of accuracy of pitch, proved unimportant.[31]

Doyen Olin Downes of the *New York Times* also noted the
choir's smoothness, interesting tone qualities, and the "sincere, if
somewhat contained character of the performance. They
demonstrate, perhaps, the best method for a chorus of colored
singers to follow for the sake of technical proficiency." Downes,
however, wished for a more racial interpretation.[32]

Excitement continued to run high within the next few days. A
huge front page headline from the *Washington Tribune*, April 20,
1928, read: "President Coolidge Hears Hampton Choir." The
date of April 20 indicates that the performance which Coolidge
heard was one scheduled in Washington on the same tour. Other
luminaries present were Mrs. Charles G. Dawes and Mrs. Herbert
Hoover. The concert was a benefit for the Trades Building Fund
for the National Training School for Women and Girls. Five
hundred persons were turned away from the First Congregational
Church, which seated a packed 2,000. The reviewer said of the
concert: "Each voice registered its individual touch as diverse as
the members of a profound orchestral group of amazing depth and
vibrancy, and there was an astonishing unity in ensemble that
defied imitation." The *Chicago Defender*, April 27, 1928, noted
that "It was the first time that a chief executive of the nation
had ever attended a concert given here at the national capital by
Race people."

Ending the year 1928 Dett performed with his Hampton
Choir at a meeting of the Virginia Federation of Music Clubs in
Smithfield in December. On the program were Dett's "I'm Going
to Travel," "Gently Lord, O, Gently Lead Us," "Listen to the
Lambs," "O, Hear the Lambs," and "Let Us Cheer the Weary
Traveler." Hampton student Elizabeth Sinkford sang Dett's "A
Thousand Years Ago or More" and "God Understands." Dett
spoke on the development of Negro art composition from the folk
song basis. *The Southern Workman* reported that "Fifty members
of his [Dett's] choir had the pleasure of going to Smithfield with
him over the convenient four-and-a-half mile bridge over the

James."[33]

1929

Seeds planted by the outstanding performance in Carnegie Hall on April 16, 1928, were destined to sprout. As a supportive sponsor of this concert, George Foster Peabody's interest in the Hampton Choir's potential heightened. The fact that he was keen on a European tour for the group is indicated by the following endorsement:

In view of the accomplishment [the Carnegie Hall concert] Mr. Peabody has felt that the singing of the Choir in Europe would have a large international and interracial significance, particularly in those countries with African possessions. He would show them the capacity in music, especially which the Negro is manifesting under the opportunity for development which we are now offering in the United States.[34]

Peabody was a powerful and persuasive figure in America's cultural scene for a number of years, and due to his efforts Dett and the Hampton Choir would, indeed, make a tour of Europe in 1930. Peabody, a patron of the arts, was also a trustee of Hampton Institute from 1884 through 1930. The son of George Henry and Elvira Canfield Peabody, he was born in Columbus, Georgia in 1852. He was educated in private schools, but his love for reading was the true broadening factor which guided his vast knowledge and empathy. Early on he became particularly sympathetic to the Negro's plight.

At age fourteen Peabody went to New York City to work as a clerk in a wholesale dry goods store, bettering his position each year. Being a shrewd young man with an eye for business, he in time affiliated with Spencer Trask, a New York banker whose chief concern was the development of railroads and electric lighting companies. From that point on Peabody's financial future was assured. In 1914 President Woodrow Wilson named Peabody Director and Vice-President of the Federal Reserve

George Foster Peabody, ca. 1927,
courtesy of Hampton University Archives.

Bank of New York, and at one time he was National Secretary to the Democratic Party. He held an honorary doctorate from Harvard University. One of his large philanthropies was the Saratoga Springs (New York) Spa, but smaller scale supportive efforts included modest donations to composer Arthur Farwell's Wa-Wan Press. Peabody died at age eighty-five of a heart attack.[35]

As well as being a Hampton trustee, Peabody was a member of Hampton's Investment Committee. With Roger C. Ogden, former president of Hampton's Board of Trustees for whom Ogden Hall was named, he helped to found both the Southern Conference for Education and the Southern Education Board. He was affiliated with the Jeanes Foundation (for the benefit of rural schools), applying his business acumen to advance the growth of it and other worthy organizations of which he was a part.

In his Introduction to *Dictionary Catalog of the George Foster Peabody Collection of Negro Literature and History*, Fritz J. Malval wrote glowingly but sincerely of Peabody's efforts:

> Peabody, champion of that democracy of the spirit that cannot rest at ease while those less fortunate must suffer for lack of opportunity, felt obligated to donate to the public good the bulk of his accumulations and therefore retired from business so that he might give all his energies to the wide frontier of human welfare. Peabody, the philanthropist, directed his efforts in education in large organized movements and in a discerning and thoughtful interest in individuals, which made his work for others a noble and personal gift.
>
> Appropriately described as a passionate believer in equality of opportunity for all, he demanded full and increasing protection of the rights of all citizens which was the mainspring of his political philosophy. In close association with faculty and students at Hampton Institute, he revealed himself constantly as a man of indomitable spirit "endowed with wide-range sympathies which knew no barrier of race, nationality, or religion, and his death elicited countless tributes to the nobility of his character and the value of his public

services."[36]

* * *

One of Dett's early concerts of 1929 was on January 20, when the choir performed to a huge crowd in the Norfolk, Virginia Armory, under auspices of the Negro Organization Society of Virginia.[37] An equally outstanding off-campus concert by the Hampton Choir was on March 10 in Boston's Symphony Hall, a program identical to the Carnegie Hall concert of April 16, 1928. The *Boston Evening Transcript*, March 11, had these comments:

> As a composer and as a conductor, Dr. Dett discloses the scholarly musician who would create his impressions through careful workmanship. He uses the tools of a composer to knit the characteristic idioms of his race into a compact and designful whole. He has restrained the enthusiasms usually inseparable from these idioms to an ordered and dignified expression. In ensemble they were excellently blended, and since the singers were seldom permitted to apply the full force of their tones, there was never a harsh note or combination of notes emitted.

Selections for this concert were in typical Dett format, including early church music, modern Russian anthems, church music by American composers, and Negro melodies arranged by Dett and others. The *Boston Globe*, March 11, 1929, reported that

> . . . no chorus in recent years has sung with subtler or finer artistry. . . . This chorus, like Roland Hayes, must be judged with no thought of race distinctions; it can take rank right among the leading choruses of the world. . . . The individual voices are remarkably fine. Dr. Dett has trained them in unaccompanied singing with astonishing success.

Young Dorothy Maynor (Mainor), in Dett's choir at the time, caught the *Globe* reviewer's attention. He continued, spelling her name Mainor, as she was known before she took the stage

S Y M P H O N Y   H A L L

SUN. AFT. MAR. 10 AT 3:30 O'CLOCK

HAMPTON INSTITUTE CHORUS

Negro Choir of 60 Mixed Voices from Hampton, Va.

DR. R. NATHANIEL DETT, Conductor

Programme

SACRED SONGS OF THE EARLY CHURCH

Ave Maria	*Arcadelt* (1514-1556)
As by the Streams of Babylon . .	*Campion* (1575-1619)
In Heav'nly Love	*Laurentii* (1573-1655)
Now Christ is Risen . . .	*Traditional* (Circa 1500)

RUSSIAN LITURGICAL ANTHEMS

Hymn to the Trinity	*Tschaikowski*
We Praise Thee	*Shvedof*
Lord, Our God, Have Mercy	*Lvosky*

RELIGIOUS COMPOSITIONS BY AMERICAN COMPOSERS

Savior Hear Us When We Pray . . .	*Lily Strickland*
Fierce Was The Wild Billow	*Noble*

NEGRO SPIRITUALS

Deep River	*Burleigh*
As Children, Walk Ye in God's Love . . .	*Dett*

THE NEGRO IDIOM IN MOTETS AND ANTHEMS
BY R. NATHANIEL DETT

Program courtesy of Hampton University Archives.

name Maynor:

> Good natural voices do not always repay extensive
> and costly cultivation. Yet one felt, hearing Miss Mainor,
> that a philanthropist willing to take a chance on paying
> for the musical education of a young singer might well
> make it possible for her to have the best of musical
> training. There is certainly a chance that she might
> become a great singer, something no experienced reviewer
> would prophesy of most girls with good voices.

Concerning the same concert a critic for the *Christian Science
Monitor*, March 11, 1929, commented:

> In a season replete with choral music, the Hampton
> Institute Chorus, Dr. R. Nathaniel Dett, conductor, set a
> high mark with its concert at Symphony Hall yesterday
> afternoon. . . . The composer's scholarly achievements as
> well as his fine natural ability showed clearly in his
> music.

Many complimentary letters to Dett on his concerts are found
in the Hampton University Archives, including one about the
March 10 performance, from composer Arthur Foote's nephew,
Henry Wilder Foote, who wrote that his uncle, Arthur, was "full
of praise for what he heard."[38] Approximately a week later the
choir performed in Lynchburg, Virginia, assisted by student
soloists Rudolph von Charlton, Charles Flax, and Dett himself,
under auspices of the YWCA. Another concert of mention was on
April 9 in the City Auditorium in Richmond, Virginia. Given by
the Hampton Choir and Glee Club, it was sponsored by the
Hampton Alumni Chapter in that city.[39]
     As if to summarize the preceding events a summer issue of *The
Crisis* carried a photo of the Hampton Choir in which the men,
in dark coats and white pants, are standing behind seated women
in white dresses, all with properly crossed feet, in the style of
genteel ladies. In the photo Dett is sitting midway between the
ladies on the front row. The accompanying article pointed out
that for several years Hampton Institute refused to teach

INSTALLATION OF OFFICERS
OF THE
HAMPTON INSTITUTE GLEE CLUB

for the year 1929–30

MUSEUM

Sunday afternoon, May 5th 1929 at 2:30 o'clock

PROGRAM

Now let ev'ry tongue .... *Bach*
THE GLEE CLUB
Retiring President's Address
MR. SOLOMON PHILIPS
Stilly Night .... *Will Huff*
BRASS QUARTETTE
Awarding of Gold Keys and Certificates
DR. DETT

Raynah Herbert Adams	Spencer Rhone Harrison
William London Briggs	Francis Sylvester James
John Raymond Fisher	Frederick Maddox Lane
Donald Henry Forrest	Charles Henry Wilkinson

Georges William Willis
Hungarian Rhapsody No. 2 .... *Liszt*
MRS. DETT
Installation of officers
REVEREND LAURENCE FENNINGER
God so loved the world .... *Palme*
THE GLEE CLUB

Program courtesy of Hampton University Archives.

Hampton Choir in Hampton Memorial Chapel, 1929.
Courtesy Hampton University Archives.

students instrumental music, and confined all singing to Negro
folk songs. It continued:

> Gradually this custom has yielded to a regular
> instruction, and under Dr. R. Nathaniel Dett there has
> been recently developed . . . a remarkable Institute choir.
> The choir first gained notoriety at the Music Festival in
> the Library of Congress, Washington. Then it came to
> Carnegie, and afterward sang in Norfolk, Richmond and
> Atlanta. Finally at Symphony Hall, Boston, it emerged
> into nation-wide recognition. The critics are unanimous in
> calling this assembly one of the great choruses of the
> world.[40]

On May 25 the Hampton Choir was invited to participate in
a four-choir National Negro Music Festival held in
Philadelphia at the Academy of Music. The other choral groups
were the Howard University Glee Club, the Lincoln University
Glee Club, and the Fisk Jubilee Singers, each of whom gave both
an afternoon and an evening performance that day. The event

was sponsored by the American Inter-racial Peace Committee, whose Executive Secretary was Mrs. Alice Dunbar Nelson. The program was arranged by Alfred Johnson, Supervisor of Music in the Washington Schools. Besides the four choirs, J. Rosamond Johnson, Taylor Gordon, Florence Cole-Talbert, Lucretia Lawson-Love, Carl Diton, Clarence Cameron White, and the colored band from Wanamaker's department store also took part.[41]

A critic for the *Philadelphia Public Ledger* was obviously impressed with the Hampton group, calling its performance "the most superb choral singing of the afternoon and of a kind rarely heard in Philadelphia." He felt that Dett had distinguished himself not only as a composer and pianist, but as a superior choir director, with the "ability to train a chorus virtually to the point of perfection."

Hampton's segment opened with forty male voices singing "On the Sea" by Dudley Buck and "Volga Boat Song." The entire choir then sang "Sky So Bright," "By the Streams of Babylon," and a spiritual, "I'm Going to Travel," all showing "not only the splendid rhythmic feeling which is a heritage of the race, but a development in the art of choral singing that was truly remarkable." The *Ledger* reviewer went on:

> The solo in "By the Streams of Babylon" was beautifully sung by Dorothy Mainor, a member of the Choir, who revealed a superb voice and sympathetic style particularly fitted to works of this character. But the finest work was . . . an encore, the famous Kieff Response of the Russian Church, in which there is a long diminuendo to the faintest pianissimo and an ensuing crescendo to a forte, which was a phenomenal piece of ensemble work and was an effect the like of which has not been heard in Philadelphia in many years. Another encore, . . . a spiritual, "Couldn't Hear Nobody Pray," closed the Hampton Choir's part of the program.[42]

The same reviewer felt that the evening performance was more spectacular, possibly because the singers had grown more familiar with the acoustics, "or perhaps it was the stimulation of a vastly larger audience, for the Academy was almost filled."

Earlier in May Dett had been asked by Mr. W. F. Bohn, assistant to the president of Oberlin College, to do honor to Oberlin at the forthcoming Hampton Anniversary exercises in May of 1929. On May 7 Dett sent the following letter to Mr. Bohn:

It was with extreme pleasure that I received your notice of appointment to represent Oberlin College on the occasion of the sixty-first anniversary exercises of Hampton Normal and Agricultural Institute.

I write now to express my thanks for the honor which my Alma Mater bestowed upon me by such an appointment.

Not having had experience in this sort of thing before, I wonder if you would mind me questioning whether such an appointment ever carries any other responsibility than the receipt of the notification?[43]

* * *

George Foster Peabody arranged through the Palmer Fund for Dett and Ernest Hays, another teacher on the Hampton music faculty, to spend the summer of 1929 studying composition in France with the famed Nadia Boulanger at the American Conservatory at Fontainbleau near Paris. Boulanger was a conductor, organist, and composer who taught harmony, counterpoint, analysis, composition, organ, and other musical subjects to composers, performers, conductors, and musicologists from all over the world. Among her host of renowned American students were Aaron Copland, Virgil Thomson, Roy Harris, Elliott Carter, David Diamond, Douglas Moore, and Marc Blitzstein.

Boulanger (1887-1978) became the director of the American Conservatory at Fontainbleau in 1950, while also teaching at the Paris Conservatoire. She enjoyed many honors and prizes during her long life, including a commandership of the Legion d'honneur, nomination as Maitre de Chapelle to the Prince of Monaco, and membership in the American Academy of Arts and Sciences. Her apartment became known as the "Boulangerie," where she also taught a few students and gave them the opportunity of hearing new compositions by other aspiring composers.[44]

Boulanger's influence on Dett, who was then forty-six, is difficult to estimate, and may not have been as powerful as that of his earlier teachers. His compositional style from 1930 forward did not take any startling or unexpected turns, though his skill with larger forms improved, evidenced in his cantata *The Ordering of Moses*. It is likely that Boulanger, realizing his innate talent and understanding of the Negro idiom, merely guided his imagination and skills, without trying to enforce on him her own ideas.

Dominique-René DeLerma wrote: "This distinguished teacher was impressed with Dett's talents, but, sensitive to the differences in direction of their musical aims, feared imposing her instruction on his native gifts."[45] Boulanger dealt similarly with Negro composer Margaret Bonds ten years later, feeling that Bonds was naturally gifted in the same way as Dett.[46] Composer Ned Rorem has spoken of the works of Boulanger's American students Marc Blitzstein, Samuel Barber, and Aaron Copland as

the first strong non-German-trained utterances we heard. Indeed, Boulanger, herself French to the bone, single-handedly inspired what has come to be the American Sound, on the one hand by stressing . . . the shedding of extraneous Teutonic flab and on the other by admonishing her Yankee flock to exploit home grown products.[47]

Dett's absence from Hampton that summer temporarily spared him any unrest caused by James E. Gregg's resignation as Principal of Hampton. *Crisis* editor W. E. B DuBois wrote that "Mr. Gregg has tried hard but he was set an impossible task and his fault was not to see it sooner." DuBois felt that Hampton, "dealing as she must, mainly with a provincial, narrow-minded small Southern town, . . . was maneuvered into an impossible position in which James E. Gregg became martyr and victim."[48]

DuBois continued his harangue, saying that William Chapman Armstrong, Hampton's first principal, "sought tolerance and silent acquiescence from the Southern whites. Frissell (his sucessor) sought friendship and offered power." When Gregg took over, "white Hampton and white Virginia felt that Hampton belonged to them and that the students were there to sing for them, wait on table, and guide them through the beautiful grounds." He recalled the strike of a few years back, one "by Southern whites to compel Jim Crowing," and a strike by students "against the whole intolerable situation." He was correct in doubting that a Negro could be principal, since it was evident that George P. Phenix, white, would soon fill that position. In conclusion DuBois asked, "Will the white trustees trust a black man to administer eight million dollars' worth of endowment?"[49] Obviously, they would not until years later.

Correspondence between Dett and James Weldon Johnson in the Beinecke Rare Book and Manuscript Library at Yale University indicates that Dett was suggested by Johnson for a Rosenwald Fellowship in 1929. Johnson's advice in helping choose a Rosenwald recipient had been solicited by Edwin R. Embree, president of the Rosenwald Fund at that time. In a letter to Dett, dated June 5, 1929, Johnson asked if he could possibly secure a leave of absence from Hampton in early 1930 to pursue creative work, with aid of this fellowship.

Dett was most appreciative, but declined the offer in a letter of June 18, 1929, asking Johnson if receipt of the fellowship could be postponed until after the projected Hampton Choir's trip to Europe, planned for 1930. Johnson answered at once, urging Dett to arrange his affairs after the trip to accommodate the fellowship. Dett replied on June 27, 1929, saying that the trip would end in June of 1930, but not committing himself to ask for the leave of absence afterwards. A few days later Dett's secretary informed Johnson that he had left Brooklyn for France on July 2, 1929, on the steamer "Columbus." This trip would have been for summer study with Boulanger.

Johnson's wife, Grace Nail Johnson, stated on the back of an envelope, July 1955 (document in Beinecke) that both Dett and Johnson received a Rosenwald Fellowship, though no other available material on Dett mentions his receipt or use of a fellowship by this name. Johnson, in his autobiography *Along This Way*, gives the year of his own receipt as 1929-1930, during which time he reworked some of his poetry.

A native of Florida, Johnson (1871-1938) was the first Negro admitted to the Florida Bar Association. After moving to New York City in 1901, he collaborated with his brother J. Rosamond Johnson on "Lift Every Voice and Sing," a song known as the black national anthem. He translated Enrique Granados' opera *Goyescas* into English for a presentation at the Metropolitan Opera in 1906. He served under U. S. Presidents Roosevelt and Taft as consul in Venezuela and Nicaragua (1906-1912), and as NAACP Field Secretary from 1920-1930. In 1930 he joined the Fisk University faculty as professor of creative literature. The previous year he had been to Japan as a representative to the third biennial meeting of the American Council of the Institute of Pacific Relations.

Other than his autobiography Johnson is best known for a novel, *The Autobiography of an Ex-Colored Man*, and two volumes of poetry, *Fifty Years and Other Poems* (1917) and *God's Trombones* (1927). Johnson and Dett continued to correspond for the next few years. A 1934 letter (in Beinecke) from Johnson to Dett, living in Rochester at the time, again urged him to make time for composition. Johnson's productive life was tragically cut short in 1938 when his car collided with a train.

* * *

The fact that George Foster Peabody had already set wheels in motion for the European choir trip is confirmed by the following document, courtesy of Hampton University Archives. The George Ketcham referred to was Hampton's Field agent at that time.

The Administrative Board, at a meeting held on October 23, 1929

VOTED: That the following statement be presented to the Board of Trustees:

The Administrative Board of Hampton Institute is fully conscious of the steady and untiring interest of members of the Board of Trustees in considering and promoting all projects which are for the advancement of colored races.

Heretofore the interests of Hampton have been chiefly devoted to the Negro and Indian people of this country. Now an opportunity is presented to promote the interest of the Negroes of Africa through influential white people of Europe who are interested in Colonial and Native affairs.

Mr. George Foster Peabody has for a period of some years shown a particular interest in the development of music at Hampton Institute. He has encouraged the Music School. He has furthered the work of the Choir. It has been largely due to his interest that the Choir has been presented before large and important audiences.

The underwriting by Mr. Peabody from the Palmer Fund of the New York concert gave an impetus to the work of the Choir, and Dr. Dett, which has resulted in many effective presentations of the Choir—notably appearances in Boston and Philadelphia.

The interest of Mr. Peabody has prompted him further, to send Dr. Dett abroad this past summer for the purpose of study at the expense of the Palmer Fund, and also to send Mr. George Ketcham abroad for the purpose of investigating opportunities for the Choir in a European tour. Mr. Ketcham returned with the enthusiastic endorsement of some of the most influential people of England and Belgium.

From letters received from Mr. Peabody it is understood that he stands ready to help finance a European tour by the Choir, but that the Palmer Fund has now only a limited balance.

The Administrative Board is unanimously in favor of the proposed trip, provided it can be financed without appropriating from the regular school funds. The Board has discussed the details of the trip, especially those relative to the absence from their classes of members of the Choir, and has agreed that the benefits to the students of a trip abroad will be far greater than the benefits derived from three weeks of school, and proposed to arrange the school work of Choir members who may go on the trip so that they can meet the requirements of their courses.

The Administrative Board hopes that the trustees will consider favorably the proposed trip, and that they may consider it feasible to secure financial assistance without appropriating funds of the Institute. It seems evident from what Mr. Peabody has written that the Palmer Fund may be expected to furnish a considerable portion (possibly as much as 50%) of the cost. It is important that the decision of the Trustees be determined at once if satisfactory European arrangements are to be made.

Tribute was paid to Dett, his choir, and his choral techniques in an item in *The Crisis*, December, 1929, by J. Wesley Jones, then president of NANM and director of the Metropolitan Church Choir in New York City. Of the singers' tone quality Jones said:

The tone he [Dett] secures has been hammered and pounded free from dross, like iron on an anvil. It is so purely pointed that it can flutter but to a breath and yet echo to the farthest reaches. It is so obedient that attack and exit seldom show a laggard. And it is so elastic that it can scale down, without break, that exacting demand in Dett's "Listen to the Lambs," wherein a fortissimo is reduced to a pianissimo unbroken in quality, more like an instrument than a voice color.[50]

1930 - Dett and the Hampton Choir Tour Europe

The year 1930 was probably the most memorable one in Dett's entire career. His efforts in behalf of the music program and its students had been manifold. Among other positive results, by this year he had provided three scholarships for music

Hampton Institute Glee Club

DR. R. NATHANIEL DETT, *Conductor*

OGDEN HALL

Friday Evening, December 6, 1929, at 8:30 o'clock

___

PROGRAM

FOLK SONGS

Swansea Town .... *English Chanty*
Volga Boat Song .... *Russian*
O Shenandoah .... *American Mountain White*
Water Boy .... *Negro Convict*

THE GLEE CLUB

CLASSICS

Bouree for piano .... *Bach*

MR. CHARLES FORD

Ave Maria .... *Tito Schipa*

MR. WALLACE CAMPBELL

A Star .... *Clokey*
Lines with a Rose .... *Clokey*

MR. CAMPBELL AND GLEE CLUB

MODERN

April Rain .... *Oley Speaks*
Rhapsodie No. 4 .... *Liszt*

MR. RUDOLPH CHARLTON

Blow Thou Winter Wind .... *Sarjeant*

MR. CHARLES FLAX

Creation Hymn .... *Rachmaninoff*

THE GLEE CLUB

NEGRO SPIRITUALS

Brother Michael
Daniel Saw the Stone
Father Abraham
Let Us Cheer the Weary Traveler

HAMPTON SONGS

Hampton, My Home by the Sea .... *Dett*
Alma Mater .... *Northern*

___

Musical Art Concert, MARIAN ANDERSON, Contralto
Friday Evening, December 13, 1929
Admission Seventy-five Cents

Program courtesy of Hampton University Archives.

students.[51] It is assumed that now Dett was heavily engrossed in plans for the coming European tour and allowed little to distract him. Of necessity he would test in American concerts new unpublished arrangements to be used for the tour, among them an "Ave Maria" and "As Children Walk Ye in God's Love."

There is no evidence that George Phenix's principalship made any change in Dett's professional activities, except to prompt him to ready his Hampton records for the beginning of the year, indicated by a letter from Dett to his longtime friend Robert R. Moton at Tuskegee Institute. Dated January 8, 1930, the letter reads:

> My dear Dr. Moton:
>
> Enclosed is a memorandum of expenses incurred by me in connection with the trip I made to Washington last spring to confer with you, and which has never been cleared off our books. As the school is after me about this account, if you would okay this and return it, I should be very greatly obliged.
>
> I recently heard at our Directors Meeting that you had been given a Harmon Award, and I wish to congratulate you; but this is small recognition in comparison with the great work you have done, much of which may never be properly appreciated.
>
> With very kindest regards to Mrs. Moton and all the family, as well as the friends at Tuskegee, I am
>
> > Sincerely yours,
> > R. Nathaniel Dett[52]

Such stellar Negro representatives as singers Harry Burleigh, Roland Hayes, and Lillian Evanti, entertainers Josephine Baker and the Williams/Walker duo, artist Laura Wheeler Waring, and sculptress Elizabeth Prophet had already made names for themselves abroad. They had opened the door for others of their race to come.

On January 18, 1930 *Musical Courier* carried a lengthy article on Dett's activities at Hampton, plus a full page announcement of the projected tour of the Hampton Choir to Europe. Included in the item was Hampton's history and its attitudes toward music.

After Dett assumed a position at Hampton he was challenged to present music *a cappella*. "It was his desire, that due to the natural beauty of the Negro voice, there should never be any instrumental accompaniment to religious exercises held [at Hampton]." At this time little *a cappella* music was available, and most Bach choral music was too difficult for untrained singers. Spirituals were not considered for formal concerts, but reserved for more informal evening Chapel service. "Hampton has always manifested a desire to keep the unaccompanied Sunday morning Chapel service distinct from the evening Chapel service."

The article further stated that Tschaikovsky's "Hymn to the Trinity," simple and in folk style, was the ideal number. Students liked its counterpoint, singing first by syllables, not words, "investing their music with a yearning quality and soulfulness discernible only in their spirituals." Dett soon realized the affinity of Russian and Negro music, and "Leading critics of the country recognized in Negro music one of the most beautiful of all folk expressions and in the Hampton Choir the greatest single exponent of the only real American folk music."[53]

By early spring plans were well along for the European tour, due mainly to the urgence of Peabody. Peabody's international interests and connections were prodigious, his list of accomplishments vast. He particularly wanted the Hampton Choir to perform in England, France, and Germany. McBrier explains his reasoning:

> The attitude of the Europeans toward their African colonials was extremely bad, and treatment of these colonial governments was of international concern. It was thought the Choir would be a valid demonstration and convincing argument to these Europeans of the intelligence and ability of the Negro.[54]

Dett himself said that he "was sent" on this tour through Peabody's efforts, in hopes that "such knowledge might have a beneficial effect upon European attitude toward Negroes in foreign possessions."[55] Financial backing for the tour would come from at least two other philanthropists, Arthur Curtiss James,

RICHARD COPLEY
ANNOUNCES

THE FIRST

EUROPEAN TOUR

OF THE CELEBRATED

HAMPTON CHOIR

DR. R. NATHANIEL DETT, CONDUCTOR

Under the Management of
ALBERT MORINI

༺ঌ

SPRING OF 1930

༺ঌ

Management in America	European Management
RICHARD COPLEY	ALBERT MORINI
10 East 43rd St. New York	Vienna IX Hörlgasse 14

From the *Musical Courier*, January 18, 1830 issue.

another trustee of Hampton Institute, and John D. Rockefeller, Jr. Rockefeller's correspondence during this period indicated that he was willing to contribute not only monetarily for the trip, but to help with European introductions as well. Other monies were provided by the Phelps-Stokes Fund in New York.[56]

Meanwhile, Dett was busy filling various engagements, one of which was on February 1 in Chicago at Orchestra Hall. The occasion was one of the concerts in a series sponsored by the Chicago Board of Education in an effort to familiarize Americans with the works of native composers and to give them a clear and comprehensive picture of the musical situation. With Dett was his student, baritone Charles Flax, singing Dett's arrangements of spirituals and other songs.

On February 3 Dett and Flax gave a previously unscheduled concert in Niagara Falls, New York. Mrs. Charlotte Dett, as a member of the Niagara Falls Peace Council, persuaded Dett to play for this group before he returned to Hampton. Flax and Dett received a splendid review in the *Niagara Falls Gazette*, February 4, 1930.

> Those who were present at the impromptu concert last evening were privileged to hear several of Dr. Dett's newest compositions, one among them his setting of "Flower in the Crannied Wall," which has not yet been published.
>
> Mr. Flax has a fine, full baritone, artistically handled. He adds to fine technical training that indefinable quality peculiar to the Negro voice and temperament, a quality which tends to throw into abeyance one's critical powers and to bring forth one's capacity for sheer enjoyment. Dr. Dett's accompaniment left nothing to be desired.

Flax sang "Lead Gently, Lord, and Slow," set to Paul Laurence Dunbar's poem, with "fine feeling" affording "excellent opportunity for an exhibition of legato singing and fine shading." The choral accompaniment, later elaborated, was "strikingly effective." The reviewer was also taken with the "vigorous rhythms and delightful melody" of "The Winding Road," Dett's

Booker Memorial Presbyterian Church

CONCERT

BY
THE HAMPTON INSTITUTE CHOIR
Fifty Voices A Cappella
Dr. R. Nathaniel Dett, *Composer-Conductor*
Auditorium
BOOKER WASHINGTON SCHOOL

Friday Evening, March 28, 1930, at 8:15 o'clock

PROGRAM

Religious Classics
Sky So Bright	*Ancient Spiritual Song*
Sanctus (Men's Voices)	*Schubert*
Now Thank We All Our God	*Cruger-Mendelssohn*

* Negro Motifs
Were You There	*American Negro*
Gently, Lord, O Gently Lead Us	*Bahama Islands*

Russian Anthems
Hymn to the Trinity in C	*Tschaikowski*
We Praise Thee	*Shvedof*
O Praise Ye God	*Tschaikowski*

Negro Anthem
Son of Mary	*Dett*

American Composers
Fierce Was the Wild Billow	*Tertius Noble*
On the Sea (Men's Voices)	*Dudley Buck*
Now the Day Is Over	*Frances McCollin*

Negro Anthems
Ave Maria	*Dett*
O Hear the Lambs a-Crying	*Dett*
Don't Be Weary, Traveler	*Dett*

---

* Settings by Dr. Dett

The School of Music of Hampton Institute cordially invites you to attend a joint recital by Miss Mamie A. Howell of the class of '31 in Piano and Mr. William S. Cooke, of the class of '33 in Voice, Ogden Hall, Sunday afternoon, April 6, 1930, at 4:15. Admission free.

Program courtesy of Hampton University Archives.

setting of Tertius Van Dyke's poem. In presenting it Flax "appeared not only to sing, but to be imbued with the mood dictating the words 'with face to the front and fearless eyes.' It was a veritable challenge to life."

A quiver of excitement went through the crowd as Dr. Dett announced that he would play his "Barcarolle" from the "In the Bottoms" suite. There was present a number of persons who remembered the magic of this selection, as played by Dr. Dett when he appeared in Niagara Falls during its first Music Week. Nor were they disappointed this time; the music rippled along the piano, a living thing that crooned and pleaded and echoed its own lively accents.

The impressed reviewer felt that Flax's voice was perfect for both "Flower in the Crannied Wall" (Alfred Tennyson's poem) and the spiritual "Follow Me," saying that

All the alternating pathos and melancholy of a people down-trodden for centuries is in these spirituals; all their bubbling joyousness and religious ecstacy is revealed in them. The deep flexible voice of Mr. Flax and the sentient fingers of Dr. Dett together evoked significance and beauty.

To conclude the program Dett, as was his custom, played his "Juba Dance," described by the reviewer as "maddening, primitive." Dett was then persuaded to accompany Flax in "My Day," a recently composed love song, explaining that "It is 'My Day' but not my poem," whose author was Daniel S. Twohig.

* * *

The European entourage would consist of Dett, his mother, three chaperones, and forty choir members. An interesting letter dictated April 19, 1930, from Dett to sociologist E. Franklin Frazier, special visiting lecturer at Fisk University, mentions that Mrs. Charlotte Dett would go on the trip.

I should apologize for not having answered your questionnaire, but there has been absolutely no chance to sit down and work out these things. My family has a very interesting history, and I am hoping to piece a good bit of it together while traveling with my mother abroad on this trip, as a large portion of it is hazy in my mind.[57]

In 1932 Frazier became a research professor at Fisk University and in 1934 he moved to Howard University to be chairman of its sociology department. Prominent in sociological societies, Frazier was also a prolific writer, likely wanting information at this time from Dett for his forthcoming book, *The Free Negro Family* (1932). Though Dett may have later given Frazier the needed information, the Dett family was not mentioned by name in his statistical 1932 publication, nor in his *The Negro Family in the US* (1968).

Also on April 19, 1930, Dett received a telegram from his friend Robert Moton which read:

Regret exceedingly I cannot be at White House Tuesday, and must be in Washington Wednesday for the presentation of the Harmon Award. Had hoped to see you off in New York, but impossible now. All Tuskegee joins with Mrs. Moton and myself in wishing you, the choir and the entire party a most pleasant and successful trip and a safe and happy return.[58]

Moton's mention of the White House referred to a concert the choir would give there before departing for Europe.

* * *

Dett has written at least two substantive accounts of the choir's European trip, one included in the essay "From Bell Stand to Throne Room," and a fuller one titled "A Musical Invasion of Europe, the Hampton Choir Abroad."[59] "Invasion" was the leading article in *The Crisis* for December, 1930, with a photo on its cover of the choir aboard ship. The men singers, standing in the rear, wore overcoats but no hats. The ladies were seated with their usual decorum of crossed feet, wearing coats and cloche hats. (A less formal photo of the group aboard ship is used here courtesy of the Local History Department, Niagara Falls, New York, Public Library. Dett, center back, is wearing a beret.)

Dett's account of the send-off from Hampton is touching. After the Easter morning church service (c. April 20 or 21) the "chosen" singers, whom he had selected, met with Hampton's president, chaplain, and friends of the school for a "final consecration and prayer service."

> At six-thirty, the same evening, what seemed to be the whole of Hampton Institute, and a goodly number of citizens of . . . Newport News, Hampton, and Phoebus, gathered at Old Point Comfort docks and amid cheering, the waving of handkerchiefs, crying, and singing, the Hampton Institute Choir set sail.[60]

En route to New York the choir sang for President Hoover on the White House lawn, April 21.[61] On the following evening, April 22, the New York Hampton Club sponsored the choir in a concert at the Metropolitan Baptist Church.[62]

The group of forty-five left New York on April 23, traveling third-class on the French steamer *De Grasse*. Their presence was "the cause of much conjecture," according to Dett's account which gave an interesting observation of curious passengers who regarded the choir as either "Islanders," "A Negro show," or "Entertainers." He wrote:

> But as the dress of the party was quiet, and none drank wine, spoke dialect, or indulged in gambling, these conjectures did not seem to be substantiated, and the mystery deepened. When it was further noted that these young people were reserved in their dancing, orderly at games, unobtrusive at meals and friendly to strangers without making advances, curiosity over-rode convention and inquiries, amounting almost to demands, were made that we tell who and what we were, and wherefrom and whither we were bound.[63]

Hampton Choir, 1930, aboard the *De Grasse*.
Courtesy Local History Department,
Niagara Falls, New York, Public Library.

When the group's identity was clear, a choir from a Negro school, they must surely sing some of the current popular tunes, or in any case, characteristic race tunes, such as "Ole Man River." Without lowering any standards, Dett and the choir did consent to perform for the passengers on April 27. The concert, proclaimed by a beautifully decorated folder, was a benefit to help the Marine Welfare Society. Titled "Concert de Bienfaisance," the occasion in the tourist salon of *De Grasse* drew all of the third class passengers and a smattering of first class ones. It was a huge success, with ovations for chorus, soloists, and conductor. Dett was amazed by the audience's interest in how the choir trip came to be. At the concert, while praising George Foster Peabody's support, he also explained the choir's practice schedule, and spoke of their past success in singing professionally in Carnegie Hall, Symphony Hall, and other prestigious places.

Concerning the personnel of the choir, Dett further explained that only thirteen were regularly enrolled in Hampton's School of Music. The others were from the schools of Business (five);

Education (ten); Home Economics (three); one was an agriculturist; six (two tailors, a tinsmith, a bricklayer, and two auto mechanics) were from the Trade School; and two were Academy students. The well behaved group hoped to rectify the misbehavior in previous years of American touring groups, in particular an American Boy Scout troop and a group of students from Ocean College.

Ten questions which were continually asked of the choir during the European tour were listed by Dett, some quite pertinent, others showing ignorance or naïveté. Summarized, they were: Why are all you Negroes not the same color? As the most backward American element, how did so many of you manage to come on this trip at the same time? Unlike the long period which European culture took to acquire, how did yours come about so quickly? Do black and white people marry in Virginia, and where *is* it? Given the racial prejudice in America, why are black concerts received so enthusiastically? As an American sub-culture, how can a black group appear in European cities under auspices of high ranking American ambassadors and consuls? Europeans are able to speak the language of their traditional countries—why do you not speak African? Because jazz is the Negro element in American music, why does not your choir sing jazz? Why does Hampton need a highly trained religious choir, since it is not church affiliated? Do you like our country?[64]

Though Dett gives no specific dates for concerts in Belgium, in writing about Queen Astrid of Belgium, he called her an "excellent musician" who

> expressed herself as greatly delighted with our work. On being introduced I was lost as to how to address a queen, but I found her simple and unaffected, almost girlish in her enthusiasm over music and our program. To my surprise this simplicity of manner is very characteristic of European titles, quite contrary to the "high falutin'" airs which they are made to assume in our movies.[65]

The following story is the remainder of Dett's account, "Invasion," of the approximately six-week tour in seven countries, England, Holland, Belgium, France, Germany, Switzerland, and Austria.

Receptions in honor of the Hampton Institute Choir overseas began May 1, when the Lord Mayor of Plymouth, accompanied by the Deputy-Mayor and four mace-bearers, all in scarlet robes, met the forty singers as the party landed at the docks of Plymouth.

The Lord Mayor made a thrilling welcoming address, to which Dr. Dett responded. The choir sang the beautiful choral, "Now Thank We All Our God," after which the party led by the Mayor moved in a procession to the railway station, where Mr. Douglas M. Durston, honorary director of the Plymouth Coleridge-Taylor Society decorated Dr. Dett with the Society's pin.

At the second reception at No. 10 Downing Street, London, by Premier Ramsey MacDonald and his daughter Ishbel, attended by many of the nobility not only of England but also of other countries as well, the choir added "Were You There?" as recorded in *Religious Folk-Songs of the Negro*, to the program already given at the request of the Premier. Tea was served by Miss Ishbel MacDonald preceding the choir members' enjoying the rare privilege of being shown through the house and Executive Rooms.

Saturday morning, May 3, at nine-thirty o'clock, the Hampton Choir met the London Press Association and a number of their friends at the YMCA. This was a semi-formal and a very cosmopolitan gathering. The serving of refreshments was continuous, and consequently simultaneous with the conversation which was indulged in by small groups which moved at will from place to place. Accordingly, all present had an opportunity to talk with individual members of the Hampton Choir party, and so a more intimate idea of what we were like was made possible. However, the fact that the choir was made up entirely of students and not professionals did not seem to readily impress itself. Before the close of the morning Mr. Hubert Peet, London journalist, introduced

Dr. Dett who spoke on Negro Music and its development.

An occurrence which received almost world-wide notice was the tribute paid to the choir to the memory of Livingstone at his tomb in Westminster Abbey, concerning which Canon F. Lewis Donaldson of the Abbey wrote in the *Illustrated News* (London) as follows: "As they stood around the grave, and their hymn-song, now pathetic and plaintive, now thrilling and triumphant, rang through the great church, our memories were stirred to recall something of the tragic history of the race, which the white man for centuries had chained in cruel servitude."

The London audiences on both occasions of our formal concerts—Queen's Hall, May 3, and Royal Albert Hall, May 11—greeted us warmly and enthusiastically. The following is from an editorial which appeared in the London newspaper, *The Lady*: "In singing and especially in choral singing we find that amateurs are quite able to hold their own with professionals. Of the three foreign choirs heard in London last week, two, the Hampton Choir of colored singers from Virginia and the Budapest Choir are composed of amateurs, and one, the Denmark Palestrina Choir of professionals drawn from the chorus of Opera at Copenhagen. Their performances could be judged by the same standard."

Between the two London concerts we were in Holland and Belgium. On the way the dikes, the windmills, the miles and miles of tulips, the wooden-shoe clad peasants, chiefly women, working on hands and knees in the fields, made a moving picture which fascinated the students and kept them continuously at the car windows.

Not having opportunity for previous rehearsal in the hall, the Salle du Cercle Artistique, in Antwerp, we were surprised to find that night that it had tricky acoustics, so that in spite of favorable newspaper criticism, we felt that we had not done our best. Next day we rehearsed early at the Beaux Arts in Brussels, and that concert proved to be one of our happiest. Moreover, occupying the royal box was the Queen of Belgium, herself, to whom by royal command I was introduced. By request of the Queen we sang again the Dett setting of "No More Auction Block for Me," which had moved the officials of the Congo Museum in the afternoon at Tervurien, where Governor Louis Frank, former Minister of Colonies, had welcomed us, and Dr. Schoutenden, Director of the Museum, had showed us the world famous collection of African art. One very realistic carved and painted group portraying an African trying to protect his wife from a white trader had moved me to select the spiritual, "No More Auction Block for Me." Preceding the intermission the members of the Belgian Band, whom the choir had entertained at Hampton, made a presentation of an enormous wreath of flowers tied with the Belgian and American colors with words of tribute printed in gold.

We sang at Amsterdam, Rotterdam, and the Hague, before going to France, where we were to appear at the Theatre Champs Elysées, Paris. The Elysées revealed itself a theatre elegant as the audience, which, under the patronage of Ambassador Edge, assembled to greet the Hampton Choir on the night of its Paris debut. A number of Americans were present, but contrary to the effect of a similar group at the Hague they seemed to add to the enthusiasm of the audience. It was here that having been recalled a number of times, we sang the motet, "I'll Never Turn Back No More," on a Negro theme, hoping thereby to terminate the demonstration, but the result was an ovation which even continued after the fire curtain had been lowered. The success of our Paris debut was the more significant when it is recalled that the Hampton Choir was but one of three important concerts occurring the same evening. Enesco, the violinist, a favorite in Europe, was at the Salle Gaveau; De Falla, the Spanish modernist, was giving a recital of his own compositions at the Salle Pleyel, probably the largest concert hall in Paris. Many of my personal friends in Paris who heard the Hampton Choir were also hosts to this great Spanish maestro. Of those who came back stage, I recall M. Pierre Schneider, editor of the *Magasin Musicale*, Paris; Madame Nadia Boulanger of the Fountainbleau School, whose pupil I

had been the summer previous; Louis Schneider of the
Paris-New York Herald; Madame Nordell, soprano and
correspondent for the Martinique *News*; Professor Arthur
Heacox, of the Oberlin Conservatory; John M. Lang,
director of the Music League, Niagara Falls (my home
town); Victor Dunbar, a young Negro who is achieving
European success by giving solo recitals on the clarinet;
and Madame Helen F. Burney. Many members of the
Russian Ballet, who, in the afternoon had been waiting
their turn while we were using the stage, returned that
evening to express appreciation for our use of Russian
numbers.

    While in Paris we made two records for the Pathé
Talking Picture Company which I hear have since been
released in a number of Paris movie houses.

    Our first concert on German soil was at Hamburg, a
city which, on account of its many beautiful waterways,
reminds one of the pictures of Venice. The audience was
small but very enthusiastic. In Berlin we had our pictures
taken in the gardens of the Embassy with the American
Ambassador, Mr. Sackett, a former Tennessean. The
concert that evening was a great success.

    Vienna is an eastern Paris. It is every bit as beautiful
with much the same care-free gayety, open-heartedness,
and love of art. The tendency of many of its citizens it
appears (not unlike that of some of our New Yorkers) is to
estimate all things only in terms of their own city.
Witness this graceful but rather left-hand compliment
which appeared in one of the dailies following our
concert. "We do not know whether or not the members of
the Hampton Choir can blush, but if they can they would
have no occasion to do so, were they compared with the
best of our Viennese choirs."

    I doubt that any group of people were ever more
stared at by Europeans of all classes than was the
Hampton Choir. Of course with the more cultured, there
was an effort to cover the glance somewhat, but the
universal curiosity was undisguisable, and, on taking
thought I would add, excusable; for the glance of the

continental European, when looking at Negroes, is of an entirely different nature generally from that of the average American, under the same circumstances.

In Salzburg, impressed by our impromptu exercises at the tomb of Mozart, a man who himself had been a choral conductor and a director of a symphony orchestra, volunteered his services as guide about the city.   In the Cathedral of Salzburg, he remarked that the acoustics of the building were possibly the best in Europe, whereupon I said it would be pleasant to sing under such ideal circumstances. "It would be very nice if you would sing," our guide said. Noticing that there were a number of people praying, I hesitated. "You may sing," our guide urged, "but," he added lowering his voice, "please don't sing any jazz." (Dear readers, please remember that we were in a cathedral!)

Signalling the choir into formation, we sang an "Ave Maria" in Latin. Our guide was astonished and greatly pleased. As we neared the exit he was full of praise and thanks. "That is a most beautiful Ave," he said, "but I don't believe I ever heard it before. Whose is it?" Not wishing to create a scene within sacred precincts nor to devastate by a single word one who had only shown us kindness, I waited until we were quite outside before saying as softly as I could, "Mine!"

We sang at Geneva, and were given a reception by the Students of the World Christian Federation which was the only direct contact we had with students abroad. Back in Paris, after a month of almost nightly appearances before different audiences, evidence that we had profited by our experiences was indicated by the immediate and unvarying enthusiasm of the audiences.

The last concert abroad was one not scheduled but was given by request on the first-class deck of the *De Grasse*. To this, at the suggestion of the director of the choir, all the third-class passengers were invited.

The returning musicians of the Philharmonic Orchestra and their wives were a large and important part of the audience. Mrs. Richard Copley, wife of our

American manager, was also in attendance. The choir
seemed to sense the presence of fellow musicians and sang
with a will. It was an unforgettable night. The director
of the Hampton Choir was presented to the audience by
Mr. Van Praag. Led chiefly by the members of the
Philharmonic there was a rousing ovation at the
conclusion of the program. Of all successes, none was so
precious to the Hampton Choir as this, for to have
captured the musicians of our own country—that was
achievement.[66]

While the choir was touring several wirelesses were sent to
the *New York Times* from London, Paris, Berlin, and Vienna
about their European performances. One editorial in the *New
York Times* read in part:

> They [the choir] went to sing, not for profit, nor alone
> for pleasure, but to raise up their race in the esteem of the
> world which had enslaved their ancestors, and to prove
> in freedom that it is capable of making a special
> contribution to the happiness of mankind. . . . These
> singers are like the troubadors as they make their way
> from country to country, in that they do not use their
> voices for fee. But theirs is an other world theme and a
> song that has in it the faith and zest of children.[67]

* * *

The exact date of the choir's return is uncertain, but having
been scheduled as a six weeks' tour, they doubtless arrived home
in mid or late June. As a total professional Dett did not mention
in the "Invasion" any unpleasantries which might have occurred
with housing or traveling accommodations. It is a little
surprising, however, knowing his devotion to his mother, that he
did not mention her in the account. One would imagine that she
considered it a great honor to have been on the trip, and was an
excellent and uncomplaining traveler. It is unfortunate that a
four-page, hand written letter to Dett from his mother, dated
July 28, 1930, is too impossibly faded to read, except for the last

line: a row of x-es at the end. Mrs. Dett loved her son Nate very much.[68]

The *Oberlin Alumni Magazine* for May-June of 1930 mentioned the choir's singing engagements in London, and their following itinerary in Belgium, Holland, France, Germany, Switzerland, and Austria. John Lovell, Jr. added to Dett's report of a May performance for Prime Minister MacDonald, who requested the spiritual "Were You There." MacDonald showed the group Mark Symon's painting of the Crucifixion, then hanging at the Royal Academy exhibition, commenting that it bore a similar title to the spiritual and was Symon's modern conception of the Crucifixion. As previously stated, on the same occasion MacDonald's daughter Ishbel requested more spirituals from the group.[69]

One unnamed London paper, dated May 12, 1930, stated that Ishbel

> praised [the choir's] generosity . . . when on the Tower of London's lofty terrace, surrounded by cawing black birds as large as chickens—the famed Tower rooks—the Virginians had given a free concert, rousingly applauded by the tourists.[70]

The *New York Times*, May 4, 1930, noted that the performance at 10 Downing Street was better attended than the one next day at Queen's Hall which got poor publicity. "Ambassador [Charles] Dawes was unable to attend because of a previous engagement in Glasgow but he was represented by members of the embassy staff."

Many of the European papers offered reviews of the Hampton Choir's fabulous performances, copies of which Dett preserved. Some of the headlines read: "Negroes to Sing in Westminster Abbey," "Colored People to Sing in Westminster Abbey," "Negro Singers at Downing Street," "Hampton Negro Choir is Applauded in London," "Hampton Negro Singers Stir British Audience," "Choir of U. S. Negroes Sings for MacDonald," "Premier Moved by Negro Singers Famous Choir at 10 Downing Street," "Staid British Audience Cheers Hampton Choir," "Staid Britons Shout Acclaim as Hampton Negroes

QUEEN'S HALL

Sole Lessees: Messrs. Chappell & Co., Ltd.

Saturday Afternoon, MAY 3, 1930 at .3

Under the Patronage of

His Excellency the American Ambassador General Charles G. Dawes

The First Appearance in London

OF THE

HAMPTON

(VIRGINIA U.S.A.)

CHOIR

Conductor :

Dr. R. NATHANIEL DETT

LIONEL POWELL
161-2 New Bond St.,   *Programme 1/-*
London   ::   W.1

Program courtesy of Hampton University Archives.

Bureau de CONCERTS Marcel de VALMALÈTE, 45-47, rue La Boétie - PARIS (8')
Téléphone : Élysées 79-46   R. C. Seine 311.047

THÉATRE DES CHAMPS-ÉLYSÉES

13-15, Avenue Montaigne

MERCREDI 14 MAI 1930, à 21 heures

POUR LA PREMIÈRE FOIS A PARIS

Sous le Patronage de Son Exc. M. Walter E. EDGE, Ambassadeur des États-Unis

UNIQUE CONCERT

du plus célèbre ensemble mixte nègre (Virginie U. S. A.)

C.Descosty-30

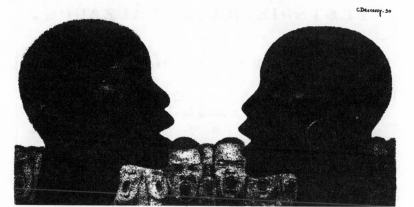

THE HAMPTON CHOIR

(40 chanteurs et chanteuses nègres) sous la direction du

Dr NATHANIEL DETT

Program courtesy of Hampton University Archives.

THE
HAMPTON CHOIR
from Hampton Institute, Virginia

will give a
CONCERT
in
FESTSPIELHAUS, SALZBURG
on
Monday evening, May 26th

❖ ❖

**Full particulars will be found in local announcements.
Tickets may be secured in the usual manner**

❖ ❖

The Negro Choir of 40 members, after singing to
the President of the United States in Washington,
and in the Nave of Westminster Abbey and in
the Queen's Hall and Albert Hall in London, are
visiting seven European countries. The Conductor,
DR. R. NATHANIEL DETT, is one of the most
distinguished Negro musicians. The programme
will include not only the lovely Negro Spirituals,
but Old English and Russian music.

Program courtesy of Hampton University Archives.

Dett with German dignitaries, 1930.
Courtesy Hampton University Archives.

BUREAU de CONCERTS Marcel de VALMALÈTE, 45–47, Rue La Boétie - PARIS-8ᵉ
Tél. : Élysées 79-46   R. C. Seine 311-047

GRANDE SALLE PLEYEL
252, Faubourg St-Honoré

MERCREDI 4 JUIN, à 21 heures
A la demande générale
Sous le Patronage de Son Exc. M. Walter E. EDGE, Ambassadeur des Etats-Unis
SECOND ET DERNIER CONCERT
du plus célèbre ensemble mixte nègre (Virginie U. S. A.)

THE HAMPTON CHOIR
(40 chanteurs et chanteuses nègres)
SOUS LA DIRECTION DU DOCTEUR
Nathaniel DETT

PROGRAMME

Première Partie
I

1. I am seeking for a city . . . . *Spiritual.*
   (Je cherche une cité.)
2. Tis me . . . .   —
   (C'est moi...).
3. I am going to travel . . . .   —
   (Je vais voyager.)

II

BOYS-GLEE-CLUB

1. Shenandoa . . . .
2. Water Boy . . . .

III

1. We praise thee . . . .
   (Nous te louons.)
2. Oh praise ye the Lord . . . . *Tschaïkowsky*
   (Loué soit le Seigneur !)

IV

1. Steal away . . . .
   (Vers Jésus.)
2. Let us cheer the weary traveller . . . . DETT.
   (Réconfortons le voyageur.)

━━━ Entr'acte ━━━

Program courtesy of Hampton University Archives.

Deuxième   Partie

V

1. As by the streams of Babylon . . . . CAMPION.
   (Auprès des flots, à Babylone).

2. Fierce as the wild Billow . . . .
   (Il faisait rage, l'océan sauvage).

VI

1. Dont you weep no more Mary . . . . DETT.
   (Ne pleure plus, Marie).

2. Oh hear the lambs a-crying . . . . DETT.
   (Entendez-vous les agneaux).

VII

BOYS-GLEE-CLUB

1. Brother Michael . . . .
   (Frère Michel).

2. Deep River . . . . BURLEIGH.
   (Rivière profonde).

3. Daniel saw the stone . . . .
   (Daniel a vu la pierre).

VIII

1. Listen to the Lambs. . . . . DETT.
   (Ecoutez les agneaux).

2. Poor mourner got a home at last . . . . DITON.
   (Le pauvre malheureux).

Courtesy Hampton University Archives.

Above and below: Dett and Hampton Choir
in Europe 1930. Courtesy of Hampton University Archives.

Sing," "Le Choeur Nègre de l'Université de Hampton à Paris," and "Het Hampton Gemengd Negerkoor." A photo of the choir walking along the street carrying bags appeared in the *Amsterdam Donderdag* (May 8, 1930). Many other European papers carried excellent photos.[71]

Review excerpts from the following eight European papers were cited by McBrier.[72] The first, undated, is from the *London Spectator*.

> They sing simply. There is no visible effort, no heaving of chests; pure voices rise with miraculous unity from the choir as a whole. If a soloist takes part it is very unobtrusive to the eye. Their attack is faultless, their precision remarkable, and the degree of polish the Choir as a whole attains deserves the highest praise for their conductor, Mr. Dett.

Another longer excerpt, also undated, was from the *London African World*, concerning the concert in Westminster Abbey arranged by the Dean, Dr. Foxley.

> Tears came to the eyes of some in the great congregation at Westminster Abbey on Sunday, as they listened to the impassioned singing of a choir of gifted Negro men and women. Here, in the heart of England's spiritual life, the holiest shrine of her history . . . the Hampton Choir, Virginia, were honored guests. Before their own little service began, they sat in the choir of the Abbey and listened with a tense expression to every word and to every tone of music in the afternoon service.
> After the service [they] proceeded to the tomb of David Livingstone, . . . followed by a multitude of people, among whom were many members of the colored races in London. The singers were welcomed by the Dean, who then invited two of the choir to place wreaths on the tomb of the man who so long ago fought for the rights of slaves in Africa.
> Then came some of the sweetest and most passionate singing the Abbey has known. Not one in the crowd round

these coloured singers is likely to forget their changing moods, the rise from a note as soft and gentle as a whispered prayer to the great burst of triumphant music and the voices cried again and again, "Come along home to Jesus!"

A reviewer for the *Edinburgh-Scotsman* was overcome by the superb performance of the spirituals, "so earnestly and expressively sung." He particularly liked "Were You There?" "Sky So Bright," "Poor Mourner Got a Home at Last," and "As Children Walk Ye in God's Love," saying

> "Deep River" and "Father Abraham" were excellently sung by the male voices, and Mr. Dett's arrangement of Negro idioms in classical form in "O Hear the Lambs a-Crying," "Son of Mary," and "Don't Be Weary Traveler" . . . displayed distinctive possibilities in Negro music. For European ears the most impressive item was the Russian liturgical anthem, "Lord Our God Have Mercy," which, viewed technically, admirably displayed the choir's accomplishments.

From Vienna's *Die Stunde*, May 25, 1930, came the comment: "The Choir has very beautiful voices. . . . The success of the group led by Dr. Dett was great and lasting." Another Vienna paper, *Wiener Allgemeine Zeitung*, May 31, 1930, stated: "Dr. Dett is an eminent musician. Even the last finesses of intonation, phrasing and dynamics are to him no secrets. And his personality is strong enough to transfer his own ability to all who have to follow him."

At least three Swiss papers, cited by McBrier, gave accounts of the concerts. *Zuericher Tagesanzeiger* (Zurich), May 31, 1930, while recalling some flat pitches produced in the Russian numbers, appreciated the "splendid equilibrium of their voices." The *Basler Nachrichten* (Basel), May 28, 1930, called the concerts "artistic experiences" and gave the choir "first place in its kind." *La Semaine à Geneve* (Geneva), June 12, 1930, complimented Dett's direction, and continued: "The perfection of the attack, the suppleness of the interpretation gives a great homogeneity to the choir; if all the voices are not perfect, one must cite a few soloists . . . who have very fine voices." The *Berliner Tageblatt* (Berlin) wrote of the choir's "flawless musical and vocal refinement," saying that "it sings as beautifully as our best a cappella choirs; and it sings more beautifully."[73] Other German papers carried numerous reviews, many of which are in the Hampton University Archives.

A critic for the *London Observer*, May 4, 1930, said of the choir's musicality and technique that

Both tune and attack are excellent; the voices come out at you, without any sort of hesitation, out of silence they do not lose pitch in time, and their tone is rich if without much variety of colour. . . . The fluent chromatics . . . they follow with masterly ease.

The Vienna *Neues Wiener Abenblatt*, May 26, 1930, printed a photo of Dett and the choir. The ladies wore church length white dresses, and the men were in tuxedos.

A flyer for Hampton's Musical Art Series quoted *Le Meuse* (Liege, Belgium) concerning the choir's performance at Palais des Beaux Arts: "The Queen was present at this concert, as well as Mr. Hugh Gibson, the US Ambassador. A palm leaf was presented to Dr. Dett by the Musique des Guides as a remembrance of the cordial reception given them at Hampton two years ago."

After hearing one of the European performances Millard K. Shaler, an American abroad at the time, wrote of his enjoyment to Harvard Professor Harlow, saying that

Mr. Dett is a genius and certainly has the choir wonderfully well in hand; his fault from the point of view of European audiences seems to be too much emphasis on his own productions which, however remarkable, soon get a bit extreme. The choir is wonderful in its execution and the voices are excellent.[74]

* * *

Despite the glowing news reports of the choir's performance

abroad, a spate of letters in the Hampton University Archives
indicate that information sent to Principal Phenix by George
Ketcham, Field Agent for the trip, tended to malign Dett.
Ketcham's letters were gossipy, tattling, and malicious.
Undercurrents swirled ominously. Personalities were in conflict.
Dett had several run-ins with Albert Morini, the musical
manager abroad. Morini and Ketcham seemed to be in a
conspiracy to alter Dett's original programming of so many
spirituals, changes which Dett was determined to resist. Dett
had prepared three different programs for the tour, with a
possible one-fourth to one-third duplication of selections.

Even if all did not go smoothly Morini was soon ready to
capitalize on the choir's success. There is ample correspondence
in the Hampton University Archives between him and incoming
President Arthur Howe at Hampton in an effort to promote
another tour in 1933, though it did not materialize.

In a letter dated July 24, 1930, Dett indicated to Phenix that
he had been asked to make a report on the choir's conduct in
Europe. Whether or not it was required of her, one of the more
unpopular chaperones, Mrs. Annie P. Washington, nevertheless
offered her own evaluation to Phenix, rating Dorothy Mainor
"spoiled," and Charles Flax and Rudolph von Charlton "very
good." [75]

Dett's letter to Phenix, dated August 13, 1930, attempted to
clarify matters.

My dear Dr. Phenix:

You will recall that previous to the choir's going
abroad I came to you and raised quite strong objections to
the chaperones. I did this, because I was certain that the
choice made would fail in securing the proper
cooperation, as neither of the people had had any
experience of that kind before, and they were practically
unknown to the students. I went also to Dr. Moton and
raised the same objections, but he expressed himself as
being powerless because the people had been notified.

Now the thing that I prophesied has come about, and
the aftermath of the trip promises to be an extremely

disagreeable one. I understand that three students have been expelled and another has been put on very severe probation—one year with all restrictions. This information has come to me by roundabout channels. I have not been accorded the ordinary courtesy due a director of being informed when those in charge are disciplined, which I understand is Hampton's regular procedure.

I do not see how you can expect me to work happily with such wholesale disregard of my position. The choir, as well as myself, worked under the greatest handicap at times. I know that the students held endless numbers of meetings trying to devise ways of getting on and of coming to some kind of understanding with the chaperones, especially Mrs. Washington. I am surprised that the Administration Board should have taken such drastic action without having made thorough investigation, and the purpose of this letter is to utter protest.

I should have mentioned this to you before, but the understanding was, as near as I can remember, that as both the chaperones and the students felt they had made mistakes, everything would be called square and no report would be made, but since half the story has been told, I think you should know the whole truth.

Very truly yours,
R. Nathaniel Dett
Director, School of Music[76]

Though emotional unrest over the European trip continued, Dett plunged once again into the fall semester. On September 12, 1930, he performed at a tea in Niagara Falls, New York, honoring Congressman S. Wallace Dempsey. He also spoke to the guests during the afternoon about the Hampton Choir's European trip, mentioning the ovation given them aboard ship by the New York Philharmonic. "Their unstinted praise was, and is, very precious to us," he said.[77] Less than a month later, Dett's compositions would be featured on the Niagara Hudson radio program, to include "Juba" by the Niagara Falls Hudson Orchestra.[78]

An account in the *Norfolk Journal and Guide,* November 1, 1930, titled "Dr. Dett's Artistry Removes Color Line in World of Music," announced that the Hampton Choir would make its first public appearance after the European tour in Norfolk's City Auditorium on November 10. The writer cited Dett and the Hampton Choir, along with Roland Hayes, James Weldon Johnson, George Washington Carver, and poet Countee Cullen as representative cultural ambassadors of the black race. Speaking of Dett as "a great composer and musician" the item said:

> He is a pioneer not only in the developing of primitive folk songs into art forms, but he has freed the Negro ensemble . . . from the confines of the more primitive types of folk song singing by his presentation of certified programs of artistry rather than of race.

Dett's uncanny ability to quickly recognize and mold rough talent as well as his creativity as a poet, was also praised by the reporter, who said: "It is through the work of such individuals as Mr. Dett who by their talent affect the feelings and attitudes of countless hearers through the vehicle of music, that greater sympathy and understanding between races might best flower."

The November 10 concert was given to a sold-out, packed house, as a benefit for scholarships at Hampton. A reviewer for the *Norfolk Ledger-Dispatch,* November 11, 1930, noticed similarities between Russian and Negro folk music and the ease with which the choir sang Russian. He noted that when the tenor line was exposed it was too "white," without sufficient point. "But when the choir sang as a whole, no fault sounded in it."

Featured soloists in Norfolk were Dorothy Mainor and Rudolph von Charlton. Two days later a choir broadcast was scheduled from Washington, D.C. (November 12) as a part of American Education Week.[79]

Dett must have been flattered to receive a letter, dated November 24, 1930, from a former Lincoln University graduate, Mrs. Dorothy Hundley, at this time Director of the R. Nathaniel Dett Glee Club in St. Joseph, Missouri. Aware that Dett was scheduled to appear the following March 17 in Kansas City, she hoped to to book him around that time, either as soloist or with the Hampton Choir, depending on his fee. She wrote: "For two years it has been our one dream and ambition to present you in recital but have hesitated on account of the expense in bringing you from such a distance."[80] No concert in St. Joseph was on the choir's itinerary between March 9 and 21 (see Chapter V), so Dett obviously was previously committed.

An entry on Dett in *Who's Who in Colored America* for 1930-1932 mentioned that the Hampton Glee Club staged a dramatized scene, created by Dett, in December of 1930. Neither the place nor auspice was specified, but the presentation won a gold medal and a cash prize for the Glee Club.[81]

* * *

Dett's professional life would never again be so exciting after the tremendous success of the European tour. This long and steadily built emotional *crescendo* could hardly have climaxed more forcefully, nor could it be duplicated. It was both a rewarding and exhausting experience.

In addition to Dett's glowing account of this adventure, *The Crisis* for December of 1930 also stated that Principal George Phenix died of a heart attack while swimming in the ocean, and would temporarily be succeeded at Hampton by acting principal Frank K. Rogers. Unfortunately, events of 1931 would not be in Dett's favor, after Arthur Howe, a grandson of Samuel Chapman Armstrong, was confirmed as principal.

Chapter V

Trouble Don't Last Alway (1931-1943)

Events of 1931

Following the rave reviews, praises, and admiration of most critics and audiences for Dett's remarkable success on the choir's European tour, one resentful scoffer, Benjamin Stolberg, berated Dett's own account of the trip. Under the by-line of his insulting piece in *The Crisis* of January, 1931, Stolberg was hailed as a "brilliant American writer," often read in *Atlantic Nation*. First, he did not like Dett's "deliberate omission of the racial unpleasantries encountered in Europe by the choir," calling it

> . . . rather poor reporting, of which the unconscious motive was the wrong kind of race pride. But . . . he shows certain race prejudices, so characteristic of the "fine type" American Negro, full of Goodness, Truth and Beauty, that his mental processes form ideal illustrations of just what I mean.

After quoting verbatim four paragraphs of Dett's account concerning the propriety and decorum of the choir, Stolberg ranted on with his attack, poking fun in an unnecessarily ugly manner:

> Lordy, what insufferable prigs this group of young men and women must be! Their dress so quiet! No bad language! Of course, never a drink! No cards! In other words, the sophisticated Dr. Dett accepts Octavius Roy Cohen's caricature of the American Negro and then denies it by turning his young people into sticks. All he forgot to mention is that the youngsters refrained from eating fried chicken and watermelons.

Saying that Dett, "the good musical doctor," maligned his choir, Stolberg saw no reason why they should not play cards, have a drink, or dress less plainly. Dett was trying too hard to

give an image of refinement, and came across as a snob in stating
the choir's repertoire of only "highbrow stuff." Why could they
not sing some spirituals for the "Concert de Bienfaisance," he
asked? Was Dett ashamed of the spirituals?

> Why is it such a racial insult to believe, with common
> horse sense, that the Spirituals *are* "characteristic" of
> the American Negro? Are they characteristic of the
> Roumanians? What perfect nonsense! The Negro is not a
> monstrosity who can feel other people's cultural heritage
> better than his own. And whatever hick from the
> Dakotas may have asked . . . for "Ole Man River," in
> addition to Bach, merely showed his good sense. If the
> Hampton Choir cannot sing spirituals and even play jazz,
> the worse for its musicianship. . . . Dr. Dett's whole
> attitude reeks with a "refined" inferiority feeling and
> all its correlatives of racial shame and racial prejudice.[1]

Stolberg ended his diatribe by saying that the world could
use some "liberal" as opposed to the "old religion." He advised
that the Negro should fight for enlightenment, not merely try to
affect it in a superficial way.

Whether or not Dett was aware of Stolberg's article, it did
not go unnoticed by others. The following month a polite and
somewhat defensive reply from James E. Allen of New York City
appeared in *The Crisis*. Allen pointed out that the students could
not have possibly behaved in any other way than that described
by Dett, given their background and experience of the world. As
representatives of a minority school which needed money they
could not very well dress as flappers and shieks, nor could they
afford to mingle freely with whites. To Stolberg's discontent
Allen remarked: "So after all, Mr. Stolberg, it was a situation
that had to carry a false reaction for the public's sake and a true
reaction from the students' point of view."[2]

* * *

The precise reason for Dett's very gentlemanly letter to Mrs.
Gibbs Marshall, dated January 19, 1931, is unknown, but does

show that the two were still in touch. It read:

> I thank you very much for your kind letter, and any
> time you are at Hampton, I shall be very glad not only to
> extend the right hand of fellowship, but to talk with you
> on any subject that may lie near your heart.[3]

According to a program cover in the Dett Collection,
NFNYPL, on February 21, 1931, Dett played a recital at State
College in Dover, Delaware. Two days later he shared a
program in Brooklyn at a Holiday Morning Musical with
Hampton vocal student Charles Flax, singer Charlotte Murray,
and violinist Alma Creasy. Murray, a friend of Harry T.
Burleigh, had sung for a number of years at New York's Riverside
Church.

The *New York Age*, February 28, 1931, stated that Dett and
Flax performed on February 23 at the Brooklyn YWCA under
auspices of its Education Committee. The reviewer said that
Dett

> . . . as a pianist revealed that he had lost none of the
> virtuosity of those days when he was known as a pianist.
> Ample technique, fluidity of utterance, coupled with
> unusual intelligence in interpretation characterized his
> work. . . . Local pianists who have essayed his Juba
> Dance . . . found something to put into their pianistic cud
> and chew. . . . Mr. Flax . . . brought to his task what was
> evidently a devoted consecration, for whatever his vocal
> limitations might be, there was a singleness of purpose in
> his endeavors. His voice is of considerable force, but is
> lacking resonance and color [with a] tendency to lose its
> singing quality and lapse into the accents of a reader.

On February 24 Dett and Flax presented "A Recital of
Original Compositions" for the Philadelphia Branch of the
NANM. Flax sang ten of Dett's songs and Dett played from his
suites.[4] The *Philadelphia Public Ledger*, February 26, 1931,
reported on this concert, held at the Central YMCA, mentioning
that baritone Flax had been on the European choir tour. Of him

the reviewer said "he has a voice of considerable power and beauty, supplemented by a nice sense of values in the folk music of his race." This was Dett's first appearance in Philadelphia as a soloist. The *Chicago News* (of the same date) carried Dett's views that now Negro performers are selling points for managerial agencies, and that Negro composers are gradually emerging who can measure their stride with white composers, assurances affirmed by the choir's trip abroad.

Dett took no time, nor was it his nature, to rest on his laurels. He was a tightly wired, energetic, restless, driven man, but inordinately pleased that he and the Hampton Choir were in such demand. His previously made plans for a series of concerts in March in the cities of New York, Boston, Buffalo, Cleveland, Detroit, Chicago, St. Louis, Cincinnati, Kansas City, Indianapolis, Washington, and Pittsburgh had already been announced in the New York *Musical American,* January 25, 1931.

The choir's incredible itinerary for a tour of less than two weeks is in Folder 6 of the Mesiah Papers and Documents. Headed "Choir trip itinerary, March 1931," it reads:

9	New York, Carnegie Hall
10	Boston, Symphony Hall
11	Buffalo, Elmwood Music Hall
12	Cleveland, Ohio, Public Music Hall
13	Detroit, Orchestra Hall
14	Toledo, Ohio (?)
15	Free
16	Chicago, Orchestra Hall
17	Kansas City (Kansas or Missouri?) hall not known
18	St. Louis, Odeon Theater
19	Indianapolis, hall not known
20	Cincinnati, hall not known
21	Washington D.C., Washington Auditorium or Constitution Hall

Transportation alone for this marathon cost $6,180.70, according to records in the Hampton University Archives. Besides bookings in these cities George Foster Peabody had

evidently wanted the choir to sing during this tour in Saratoga
Springs, New York. A telegram dated November 17, 1930, from
New York booking agent Richard Copley to Robert Ogden Purves,
Field Secretary at Hampton, indicated that Peabody needed to
guarantee $1,500 for the concert. There is no evidence that the
event materialized. Records indicate that from $1,500 to $2,000
had now become the choir's standard fee for a concert.[5]

The *New York Times* in its weekly schedule of concerts,
March 8, 1931, listed the entire program of varied selections to be
presented in Carnegie Hall by the choir the following evening,
March 9. Among them was Dett's arrangement of "Don't Be
Weary, Traveler." In the same *Times* issue Dett's picture
appeared with an article announcing the concert, which was also
announced in the *New York Review*, March 7, 1931.

On March 10 the choir performed at Symphony Hall in
Boston. Dett wrote to George Foster Peabody immediately after
the Carnegie Hall and Symphony Hall concerts. Addressing
Peabody as "Beloved Friend," the letter, in format more like a
telegram, continued: "Greatly missed seeing you Carnegie Hall.
Back last night and tonight Boston. Splendid success. Am glad
for your sake as well as Hampton's."[6]

Peabody's interest, despite his absence from these concerts,
showed in a letter to Hampton President Arthur Howe, which
enclosed a message from his nephew after hearing the choir in
Boston on March 10. Peabody's nephew wrote:

I think that I can truthfully say that I have never in
my life listened to such a marvelous blending of harmony.
The quality of tone, volume control, unity of attack, and
every factor that goes to make up a perfect result seemed
to be present in abundance. It was a rare evening and one
to be long remembered.

Peabody's own notes to Howe read:

This may interest you—I thought *Times* report very
good—am having it reprinted in *The Saratogian*
tomorrow so that I can send copies to schools in the South
to dent upon them the importance of spirituals as high

grade music. GFP[7]

The *New York Times* review from March 10, 1931, mentioned by Peabody was not run-of-the mill.

Something in the singing of America's old time Negro "spirituals" amid a program of international choral classics by the Hampton Institute Choir last evening at Carnegie Hall caught the imagination of the audience of dwellers in the big city with a sudden power of primitive appeal.

Seated at ease and without their conductor, the twenty-two women and eighteen men crooned or chorused the tender, tragic or dramatic recital of such songs as that of the Crucifixion "Were You There?" One or another solo voice of haunting quality led the refrain, followed by informal seemingly impromptu choral response in harmony that vanished into a breathless pianissimo.

The Hampton Institute Choir has made its bit of history in . . . half a dozen European countries last year. Dr. Nathaniel Dett explained the new and ambitious program here as showing the actual practice of the school [Hampton] today.

A Bach chorale was well-sung, though the voices were not of its more formal type. Russian liturgical airs went even better, with an emotional freedom that earned one great crescendo of the "Litany" as an encore.

They sang their leader's arrangement of a spiritual from the Bahama Islands, his Harvard prize motet of a decade ago, and several more in the manner of the great camp meeting crowds. Secular folksongs of England's seamen and America's mountain whites furnished artistic variety.

The twenty chanted melodies were intoned with feeling and devotion. A result of the foreign tour could be marked in the confidence of the unaccompanied and leaderless numbers as well as in the vivid thrill of these voices that had met with new and fresh response from their less accustomed European audiences.

In an undated review of the March 10 concert at Symphony
Hall in Boston Deems Taylor spoke of the choir's total
effectiveness, saying "The Bach was creditable." He liked the
spirituals best, but thought that they were presented a little
self-consciously. He wrote:

> When Negro singers come to a high note in one of the
> spirituals they—to put it bluntly—holler. And quite
> right, too. Hollering is just what is needed to convey the
> quality of convinced, unquestioning enthusiasm that
> permeates these primitive hymns.[8]

The *Oberlin News-Tribune* proudly announced the Hampton
Choir's concert in Cleveland for March 12, stating that Dett,
class of '08, had received an honorary doctorate from Oberlin,
and that "a number from here are planning to hear his concert in
Cleveland."[9] An even earlier announcement of the event
appeared in the *Cleveland Plain Dealer*, March 8, 1931. The
item reminisced about Dett's early support from F. H. Goff, now
deceased, and his calling Dett "a bellboy in whose intelligence
and energy [Goff] became interested." Now Dett would bring to
Cleveland "the fruits of Goff's generosity and judgment of
character." The item lauded Dett as being responsible for the
continuous success of the Hampton Choir.

Somehow, before the Cleveland concert, Dett and the
Hampton Choir managed a performance in Niagara Falls, New
York, honoring Dett's mother and brother on March 11. According
to the *Niagara Falls Gazette*, March 12, 1931, they gave a
concert in Mrs. Dett's home and were feted at a banquet at the
Buffalo "Y" afterwards. The news account said that "the
students sang their grace, an innovation which made a deep
impression on all present." That evening the choir performed in
Buffalo. The March 1, 1931, First Presbyterian Church *Bulletin*
(Niagara Falls, New York) had announced this concert for March
11, saying that a section of "good seats" had been reserved at
$1.00 each for Niagara Falls people wishing to attend.

The concert on March 12 would be the first time that the
Hampton Choir had sung in Cleveland, according to reviewer
James H. Rogers, who said of the concert in Public Music Hall:

It is long since I have listened to anything so profoundly moving as the spiritual "Were You There." ... Dr. Dett ... is plainly a drillmaster of uncommon quality, and besides a musician with a keen sense of beauty and of the requirements of a well balanced vocal ensemble, a composer of distinction and wide reputation.

He has done wonders with this chorus. Technically it may fairly be called letter perfect. The tone is pliant to a degree, and charmingly shaded. There are impressive fortes to which a capital bass section supplies a full but always mellow foundation; and there are blended, ravishing pianissimos, delightful to hear. . . . We find here all choral virtues. But there is something more . . . that reaches to the depths of human feeling, a grace that goes beyond the confines of race and circumstances.[10]

Rogers noticed the spontaniety of the performance when Dett took a seat, did not conduct, but left the choir on its own to sing a group of spirituals. No scores were used, and no pitch pipe or tuning fork was heard, giving the impression that every one in the group had perfect pitch. Dett's usual format of folk and Russian songs included those of Tschaikovsky and Gretchaninoff, "Swanson Town" (an English sea chantey), "Shenandoah" (the American folk tune), and "Water Boy."

A few days later there were headlines over an inch high in the *Cleveland Gazette*, March 21, 1931: THE HAMPTON CHOIR HIGHLY PRAISED! Reviewer Archie Bell commented: "If other choirs can sing like these brown-skin folk from Hampton, Virginia, why don't they do it?"

On March 13 the choir sang in Detroit at Orchesta Hall. The program's format resembled the one for March 9 in Carnegie Hall, with added spirituals. Three of Dett's arrangements, "Don't Be Weary, Traveler," "Listen to the Lambs," and "Let Us Cheer the Weary Traveler," were performed. The *Detroit Free Press*, March 8, which had noted the coming event, summarized Dett's philosophy:

His aim and ideal with the Hampton Choir has been to project a definite musical thought, developing it to such an extent that technique is a secondary consideration. His method of choosing his candidates for the choir consists in singing the scales and in judging almost impossible intervals to try out the ear. This, of course, is of great importance in unaccompanied singing. Dr. Dett lays great stress on intelligence as being necessary for the best results in his choir, musicianship demanding, he says, intelligence rather than talent.

Preparations for the Chicago performance on March 16 at Orchestra Hall must have caused quite a stir. One Chicago paper reported that the choir was to be met by twenty-five motor cars at the Polk Street Depot and taken to the Vincennes Hotel. They were to be feted with a sight-seeing tour, a dinner, and a dance. Their concert, underwritten by the Chicago Hampton Club, would be broadcast over WMAG.[11] The choir shared a concert in St. Louis, March 18, at the Odeon Theater with Odeon's conductor Spencer Tocus.

Concerning the March 21 concert in Constitution Hall, Mr. Wade Cooper, President of the Commercial National Bank of Washington, D.C., complained in a letter to the Hampton administration that Dett's failure to pack the house was due to programming too many Bach and Russian selections. Cooper himself wanted "America the Beautiful," "When the Saints Go Marching In," and "Onward Christian Soldiers" sung at Chapel "next Sunday evening."[12]

Dett, the enthusiast, faithfully reported on these March 1931 concerts to Hampton President Arthur Howe by telegram. One dated March 10 sent from New York read: "Concert and audience very satisfactory. All send regards to you and to Hampton." The next one from Buffalo dated March 11 said: "Arrived Buffalo. Concert Boston great success. Audience larger and more enthusiastic than New York. Bravos shouted from the floor." At least four more wires followed. Another from Buffalo on March 12 was equally cheerful: "Great crowd last night. Three hundred citizens from my home town Niagara Falls came in a body. Much enthusiasm." From Detroit on March 13 Dett

THE HAMPTON INSTITUTE CHOIR

DR. R. NATHANIEL DETT, *Director*

SATURDAY EVENING	CONSTITUTION HALL
MARCH 21—8:30 ｜9ㄱ\	WASHINGTON, **D. C.**

PROGRAMME

FOLK ANTHEM
　　Gently Lord, O Gently Lead Us ....*Dett*
　　　(Based on a Negro spiritual from the Bahama Islands)
CLASSICS
　　Break Forth O Beauteous Heavenly Light ....*Bach*
　　Sky So Bright ....*Ancient Netherlands (?) Spiritual*
　　As by the Streams of Babylon ....*Campion*
NEGRO SPIRITUALS
　　Fare You Well
　　Were You There
　　Walk Together Children
RUSSIAN LITURGICAL SONGS
　　Cherubim in C ....*Tschaikowsky*
　　As Waves of the Sea ....*Gretchaninoff*
　　O Praise Ye God ....*Tschaikowsky*
NEGRO MOTET
　　Don't Be Weary, Traveler ....*Dett*
　　　(Bowdoin Prize Harvard 1920;
　　　　dedicated to Mr. George Foster Peabody)

INTERMISSION

AMERICAN COMPOSERS
　　Fierce Was the Wild Billow ....*Noble*
　　O Joyful Sound ....*Schlieder*
SECULAR FOLK SONGS
　　Swansea Town (*arr. by Holst*)....*English Sea Chantey*
　　Shenandoah (*Bartholomew*) ....*American Mountain*
　　　　　　　　　　　　　　　　　　　　White
　　Water Boy (*Robinson*) ....*Negro Convict*
　　　　　　　　　Men's Chorus

NEGRO COMPOSERS
　　Stand Still, Jordan (*arr. by Johnson*) ....*Spiritual*
　　Poor Mourner's Got a Home (*arr. by Diton*) *Spiritual*
　　Listen to the Lambs ....*Dett*
　　Let Us Cheer the Weary Traveler ....*Dett*

Program courtesy of Tuskegee Institute Archives.

wired: "Crowd less large. Cleveland appreciation deep, though less spontaneous than heretofore. Many distingues present." Following were messages from Decatur, Illinois, March 17: "Believe many friends made for Hampton by Chicago concert. Cleveland and Detroit also successful"; St. Louis, March 19: "New interest created in Hampton by successful program last night"; and another from St. Louis on the same date: "Concert went good. Crowd good and enthusiastic. St. Louis guarantees. Deserves great credit. Many whites in audience."[13]

Business as usual seemingly continued at Hampton for Dett and the choir after this marathon. He was soon to receive an unexpected blow, however.

Dett's Dismissal from Hampton

The matter of Dett's leaving Hampton was never made satisfactorily clear to either Dett, the students, his colleagues or friends. McBrier pondered the illogic of President Howe's decision: "How could a professor who had contributed so much of himself—beauty, creativity and inspiration—be fired after nineteen years of service?"[14] Apparently there were many subtle, indefinable personality conflicts and undercurrents between Dett and the administration.

Early in July of 1931 President Howe asked for Dett's resignation. That Dett was unmistakably wounded shows in his lengthy letter, dated July 10. After pointing out that he approved of any measure that advanced Hampton Institute, even sacrifices for the cause which must be made in a time of crisis, he managed, however, to inject an amusing note:

> But I cannot resist expressing regret that I have had no opportunity to land a gentle tap on the nose of the person who suggested that I was getting superanuated by giving my age as sixty. According to statistics . . . I was forty-eight my last birthday—"believe it or not!" as Ripley says.[15]

Dett continued the letter, saying that his various duties as choir and Glee Clubs director, advisor to both undergraduate and graduate students, plus time spent in rehearsals and administrative committee meetings, consumed approximately fifty hours per week. If Dett was angry, he tried to control his feelings and state matters as he saw them.

> I am sure you will agree that this was entirely too much for one person to do, for absolutely no time was left for preparation for classes, outside reading, attention to one's friends or social activities; and of course the creative work which I have endeavored to carry on, had to go by the board unless I took the wee small hours for it, as I sometimes was forced to do.

One assumes that the "creative work" was composition. It is interesting, perhaps sad, that Dett did not include his family in the phrase with "friends or social activities."

In the letter Howe was also reminded of Dett's involvement on Sundays with Sunday School and two church services, and of the extra choir rehearsals necessary before tours. He said he did not mean to complain, but was speaking for the consideration of his successor.

> Under the strain of too much work, neither one's patience or spirit is apt to be at its best. I never mentioned to you that the doctor had forbidden my working at all this year, but with the first graduating class in music on my hands, I felt I dare not quit, and I do not know but that I am happier having graduated them than had I taken the recommended rest.

Dett remained rightfully bitter about Howe's action and blatant disrespect for him. A later letter from Dett to Howe, dated September 2, 1931, further vented his feelings of humiliation.

> What concerns me very much is the clause in your letter advising me to keep silent in regard to the future. Eighteen years for one who is busy, as I certainly have

been at Hampton, cannot fail in establishing contacts. Modesty would forbid that I stress either the number or the value of any that I have made while here, but the fact that my compositions have been successful and that they represent an entirely new thought in American music . . . [and] along with the widely advertised work of the Choir, of the School of Music, the Glee Club, and the Musical Art Society—this last representing also, thru the years an outlay of thousands of dollars—have given me such a place in American music, that it is inescapable that the public would concern itself with my movements. Especially have I been led often to believe that members of my own race take a very pardonable pride in what I have accomplished.

Dett mentioned in the letter his compositions "Listen to the Lambs," "Don't Be Weary, Traveler," and "Juba Dance" as exemplary.

Meanwhile, a pre-scheduled meeting of the NANM had taken place at Hampton on August 22-26, 1931, during which the Hampton Choir sang "I'll Never Turn Back No More," Dett's daughter Josephine played Louis Brandt's "Tarantella" for piano, and other students performed selected Dett works. The particular timing of this thirteenth annual meeting of NANM seemed ironical, as it barely preceded Dett's leaving Hampton Institute.

Dett was fortunate to have been granted a leave of absence, with pay, for the school term 1931-1932, which he would spend studying at the Eastman School of Music at the University of Rochester, New York. At Hampton he had been hard pressed to meet expenses on his meager salary of $4,000 per year, even with Mrs. Dett's income. After house rent was subtracted, his check was only $309.50.[16] When he left for Eastman in September Mrs. Dett and their daughters remained at Hampton.

Hampton organist Ernest Hays was appointed acting director in Dett's place. During the months of his direction he received many complimentary letters on his work.[17] Clarence Cameron White (1880-1960) succeeded Hays as the Hampton Choir director, a position he held until 1935, at which time Hampton discontinued its music school as such.[18] White, violinist, composer, and teacher, had earlier helped Mrs. Marshall establish the Washington Conservatory and was one of its first teachers. From 1924 to 1930 White was Director of Music at West Virginia State Institute. After leaving Hampton he taught in Boston and later moved to New York City. To his credit, in addition to musical activities, were several articles in scholarly journals.

* * *

As well as pursuing his studies for a Master of Music degree, which would be granted in 1932 from the Eastman School of Music, Dett toured for some weeks during the fall of 1931 as a piano soloist under state supervision of the Normal Schools of North Carolina.[19] This commitment had possibly been made before Dett knew he was leaving Hampton. Though the area or exact dates of his concertizing have not been defined, mention was made of one concert in Chester, Pennsylvania in November. Edna Coates' review in the *Chester Times*, November 21, 1931, said: "As a pianist Dett ranks high, playing with ease, often with brilliance, and with a melting pianissimo which makes his heavier passages stand out boldly." Assisting Dett on the concert were baritone LeRoy Morlock and a chorus directed by Lawrence Brown.

At Eastman Dett was privileged to study piano with Max Landow, composition and orchestration with Bernard Rogers, counterpoint with Edward Royce, and modern harmony with Howard Hanson. His study was extended through a part of 1933.[20]

Despite President Howe's belligerent determination to oust Dett, Dett was reluctant to yield his position at Hampton. In all frankness and without actually begging Howe to reconsider, Dett did make quite a plea for his case, indicated in a letter to Howe, dated September 28, 1931, which read in part:

> I was taken, as you might say, by your personality and had an enthusiastic feeling that together we could do great things for Hampton. I must honestly add,

however, that you represent the first time in my life that
my instincts have flagrantly misguided me. This is my
19th year as a servant of Hampton Institute. In another
year I could have been retired. No one would have
thought anything had I been given two or even three
years' leave considering the length and quality of my
service to the institution.[21]

The two had clearly reached an impasse. The matter was
closed. Dett would resign officially in 1932. It seemed a cruel
way to handle the situation, after nineteen years of dedication on
Dett's part. The somber news spread rapidly. The press asked
for confirmations and interviews, but apparently failed to get
little from either Dett or Howe, a situation prompting much
speculation and editorializing.

Long repressed stories bordering on gossip surfaced in the
Norfolk Journal and Guide of October 12, 1931, such as the
suggestion that James Gregg, a former Hampton principal, had
let it be known that Dett would have been asked to resign earlier
if he had not been a Negro. Dett had caught disfavor on
Anniversary Day the previous April for inviting a visiting white
organist to perform his own composition, featuring a Negro motif,
a selection not included on the original program. Dett was also
criticized for overlooking the music students as a whole while
giving attention to the more talented ones, and for inflexibility in
changing his programs on the European tour. Also his attempts to
allow the choir more sight-seeing time between engagements in
the foreign countries had been denied. The *Norfolk Journal and
Guide* stated that certain numbers which Dett wished included in
his American concerts were censored by an administrative
committee from Hampton.

A headline in the *Black Dispatch* (Oklahoma City), October
15, 1931, read: "Dr. R. Nathaniel Dett Soon To Take Sabbatical
Year; May Not Return To Hampton." The lengthy, explanatory
item in praise of Dett's good works at Hampton and abroad, bears
quoting in part. Quite different from other reports, it sounds as if
Dett had given an interview to the writer concerning his long
range plans.

The call of pure art has at last reached the heart of the eminent composer-pianist-director, Dr. R. Nathaniel Dett. Dr. Dett, director of the School of Music at Hampton, who takes his sabbatical year during the present term, will probably not return to that institution, but expects to enter upon a plan of creative research work, which his strenuous duties at Hampton would not permit.

When questioned with regard to his decision, Dr. Dett stated that in entering upon his new work, he was actuated by the realization that those who have become truly great in their contributions to the world's music, have dedicated their soul's entirety to the creative phase of artistic endeavor. While he recognizes the dire need for teachers in our colleges, the necessary institutional restrictions do not permit a freedom of artistic expression in the development of untraditional ideas.

. . . reticent about his plans for the future [Dett] was persuaded to give a general outline of the program to which he has dedicated the rest of his life. He stated that his first efforts will be directed toward securing data which, through frequency of occurrence, will establish and confirm a Negro idiom by showing its relation to the oldest existing modes of all folk music. He plans then the collection and harmonization of Negro melodies on a Negro modal basis. In this he agrees with many white critics who have seen that the European harmonic scheme, which is traditional to all schools of music, deflects the Negro composer from the true tendency of his native music.

With this idea as a basis he expects to establish an academy for young Negro creative musicians, and to study Negro native singing for the purpose of preserving and emphasizing folks effects, which will guide the composer true to the principle of using genuine Negro idioms to preserve the pristine spirit of Negro music. There will then be the problem of educating the general public to an appreciation of music based on the true Negro idiom, beginning with the smaller and simpler music

forms. This program will be developed into the creation
of major works such as oratorios, symphonies, operettas
and operas on the Negro folk and folk music basis.

Dr. Dett fully realizes that his plans will require
years of painstaking effort, much sacrifice and many
conflicts, but he considers himself a young man and the
cause most worthy. Dr. Dett is now studying at the
Eastman School of Music at the University of Rochester.

Another similar but shorter item appeared in the *Kansas
City Call,* October 16, 1931.

The retirement of Nathaniel Dett from Hampton
Institute will take from us one of our outstanding
musicians. He leaves active teaching and direction soon
in order to confine himself to creative work. Mr. Dett has
already a considerable reputation because of music he
has written, but he believes he can do still more.

. . . What Mr. Dett has done indicates the possibilities that lie in him. When he retires, in a sense this
generation is the loser, but if he creates music that will
live, he goes from us to become one of the immortals. We
can well afford the temporary loss. Every one of us who
crosses the line into the realm of genius leaves a chain to
which others of us may cling and be lifted.

Men like Dett, Coleridge-Taylor, Clarence White,
and William Dawson by their music are hastening the
day when Negroes will no longer be labeled. Fair play
will not always permit Negro failure to be emphasized
and Negro success to be ignored. Every bit of new territory which the race invades and holds as Mr. Dett now
sets out to do, makes us partners in glory.

The widely circulated *Chicago Defender,* October 17, 1931,
carried news of Dett's dismissal, in part quoted from the *Black
Dispatch.* Items also appeared in such interested papers as the
Savannah (Georgia) *Journal,* October 14, 1931; the *Newport News*
(Virginia) *Star,* October 15, 1931; and the *Afro-American*
(Richmond, Virginia), October 17, 1931, as well as in several
leading black and white papers of the southern and eastern

United States. *The Southern Workman,* however, did not report this news until its March, 1932 issue.[22]

Without support from the Hampton administration, after his strong letters to President Howe, there was little that Dett could do. He must go on with his life, neither allowing his spirit to be broken nor wallow in the non-productivity of self-pity. His inner resources told him that trouble don't last alway, as the spiritual says. No correspondence was located between Dett and his mother about this matter, so one wonders what consolation she had for her beloved son, Nate, or if George Foster Peabody intervened in Dett's behalf.

The Crisis, regarding the dismissal matter, was tactfully brief in its report, simply stating that

> Nathaniel Dett is retiring from his position as Director of Music at Hampton Institute. No reason is given except his desire to "devote himself to creative work." One wonders why this was not made possible at Hampton.[23]

1932-1934

It was true that Dett spent a good portion of time away from Hampton, but largely for the good of the school. Understandably, Howe could possibly have disagreed that the solo appearances were self-gratification for Dett, another factor contributing to his negative attitude. There was even rumor that Dett might have been homosexual, the real reason for his dismissal, of necessity covered up by the administration with other excuses.

Though Dett would now have to plan a new life for himself and his family, he was not soon forgotten by his supporters from Hampton. On January 15, 1932, the Hampton Club of Brooklyn, New York presented him in a piano recital at the Nazarene Congregational Church in that city. He shared the program with a singer, Mrs. Gayla R. Glenn. The *Amsterdam News,* January 23, 1932, reported that he was applauded with enthusiasm, and that the Hampton Club was very much "in accord with Mr. Dett." The *Niagara Falls Gazette,* February 8, 1932, stated that Dett had recently been in Niagara Falls to hear his "Listen to the Lambs" performed by the First Baptist Church

Choir of that city.

Dett lectured in Rochester, New York at the Little Theater Memorial Art Gallery on February 11. In his definition of folk songs he quoted Henry E. Krehbiel:

> Folksongs are the chorus of the heartbeats of the vast folkthoughts and feelings, and in them are preserved feelings of vast antiquity, not only in the words, but also in the music; perhaps there is more feeling in the music than in the words. Music can't lie.[24]

Dett went on to say that the harmony of folksongs evolved naturally.   Helping to demonstrate his lecture was the University of Rochester Glee Club, directed by Theodore Fitch. Dett also demonstrated at the piano, using the first six tones of the scale and playing some of his own compositions. Others assisting at the lecture were Wallace Campbell Rye in some Dett songs, and Karl Blass, violinist.

Though Dett now had no hopes of returning to Hampton, he conducted perhaps his final concert with the Hampton Choir in Norfolk early in March of 1932, an event noted in the *Norfolk Journal and Guide*, March 5. Dorothy Mainor was soloist.

* * *

McBrier felt that Dett's inner spirituality and his love for nature's beauty was reflected in all that he did, that he knew the Kingdom of God was within him and he must search himself inwardly. He had no time for professional or other pettiness. Propelled by his usual extraordinary energy, Dett went to the scholarly work at Eastman with determination and a positive attitude. On June 30, 1932, he received the Master of Music degree in composition. Perhaps the most demanding requirement was that of the thesis, for which he composed "The Ordering of Moses," a "Composition for Chorus and Orchestra" (a work usually called an oratorio), a labor that was to serve him well in coming years.

It is not certain whether Dett asked George Foster Peabody to write in his behalf, or whether Peabody was already aware of Dett's situation and volunteered a letter to Howard Hanson, then

President of the Eastman School of Music. The letter of June 11, 1932, with regard to Dett's creative talents, concerned the possibility of another year of study at Eastman. Hanson, fully aware of Dett's possibilities and ambition, was amenable, and praised his excellent work during the past year at Eastman. Surprisingly, Howe had also written Hanson in Dett's behalf, hoping that Dett could continue another year of study.[25] Was Howe belatedly trying to make amends, assuage his own conscience, or simply avoid Dett for the time being?

Dett, having submitted his formal and final resignation from Hampton after graduation from Eastman in 1932, moved Mrs. Dett and and their daughters to Rochester, where he set up a private teaching studio at 154 East Avenue, Room 309 of the Davis Building. His home address was 577 Plymouth Avenue South until 1937 when he took a position at Bennett College in North Carolina.

In Rochester he continued to lecture and compose. His ongoing compositional works would result in four volumes of Negro spirituals, published in 1936. During 1932 Dett became director of the sixteen-voice American Choir, a group of well paid white singers, which broadcast weekly through the National Broadcasting Company over Station WHAM in Rochester under the auspices of Stromberg-Carlson.

On November 27, 1932, he spoke in New York City to the congregation of Riverside Church, at the invitation of its pastor, Dr. Harry Emerson Fosdick. His subject was "The Religious Significance of the Negro Spiritual." Some of his own compositions were performed for this special vesper service of Negro spirituals, the occasion having been arranged by Riverside's choir director/organist Harold Vincent Milligan. The unnamed, not quite accurate, news item from the Rochester Public Library announcing this event said of Dett:

> Doctor Dett was honored by the invitation, in view of the fact that he is the only living composer who has used the Negro spiritual for classic development after the style of the motets of the early church. In this he has been imminently successful, his works having been performed in practically every country.

* * *

In March of 1933 Dett's works were included on the Institute Musical Series in Niagara Falls, New York. Though performers were not named, Herman Baron Moss spoke about Dett and his compositions.[26] The Institute Musical Series may well have been an outgrowth of Dett's suggestion in 1927 to the Music League in Niagara Falls to organize a concert series. One of Dett's speeches titled "The Negro Composer" was given in Philadelphia at Paul Laurence Dunbar Public School, May 5, 1933.

Results of an interview with Dett were printed in the *Rochester Democrat and Chronicle*, July 19, 1933. Newswoman Augusta S. Anderson, who had paid a visit to Dett's home in Rochester, wrote of his personal treasures which added atmosphere to the general decor. She described the place as a studio "one might find when the occupant is far on in years and has the gleanings of travel through a long career." (Hopefully, the phrase "far on in years" did not strike a sensitive chord with Dett.) Anderson was particularly taken with an African chieftain's robe and matching slippers, brought to Dett by a British West African student at Hampton as a gift from an African who had not met Dett but admired his music. "The robe hangs in the studio like a piece of tapestry. It is like the finest of Irish linen, made, Dr. Dett says, from a plant which is beaten under water until soft. Then the fibre evidently was woven on a hand loom," Anderson wrote in the interview.

She described the Palm and Ribbon wreath as "huge, on which was tied a scarf in the Belgium national colors, black, yellow and red. Across the scarf in gilt letters is Royal Belgian Guards of Brussels." Another fascinating gift was a large hand bag, similar to those made by American Indians, sent to Dett by Sarah Williamson, a former University of Rochester student "whose work he subscribed after she went as a missionary to Africa." Other artifacts were signed woodcuts of personal friend J. J. Lankis, sculptures of the Chinese god of the kitchen and the god of war, and a panel of openwork Japanese carving. Pictures of several celebrities, such as actor Richard B. Harrison (of *Green Pastures* fame) adorned the walls. Anderson was also quite impressed with

. . . a painting on glass of the archbishop's castle at Salzburg where the Rhine begins to flow away from the Alps to the North Sea. This castle, said to be the only one never taken in a siege, because of its high position, can shelter 1,200 persons. The picture shows it lighted in the night.

By the fall of 1933 Dett had begun to organize the Negro Community Chorus in Rochester. In January of 1934 this group shared a concert with the Rochester Orchestra at the Eastman Theater, and on February 15 they gave a concert at the Park Presbyterian Auditorium in Newark.[27] The fact that Dett's mother was still culturally active was indicated by the following news item from the *Niagara Falls Gazette*, February 9, 1934.

Mrs. Charlotte Dett announces that as chairman of the committee on civic celebrations she is preparing a program in observance of Negro History week which will be presented at the Center, February 14, at 8:30 p. m. Both Buffalo and local talent will appear on the program.

In February of 1934 Dett's quite informative article "From Bell Stand to Throne Room," was published by *The Etude*. It contained amusing but pertinent biographical material, as well as thoughts on the Negro spiritual. The *Pittsburgh Courier*, March 31, 1934, carried an item on this article, and Dett's photo with the caption "Genius" above it.

Dett's wife, Helen, still a recitalist, had become active in the Rochester cultural scene. On March 20, 1934, she gave a concert at Berith Kodesh Temple. "Juba Dance" was the only Dett selection on her program, according to an unnamed news item in the Mesiah Papers and Documents.

That Dett was still available for touring as a piano recitalist is confirmed by the following item in the *Niagara Falls Gazette*, March 14, 1934:

Dr. R. Nathaniel Dett, noted pianist-composer,

formerly of Niagara now of the Eastman Conservatory of
the University of Rochester, according to an announcement by the Hutchinson Concert Bureau, has accepted an
invitation to appear in a series of musical concerts in the
southwest beginning the first week in April. The constant
demand for Dr. Dett's services comes from all sections of
the country. The itinerary will include many of the
larger cities of the southwest.

The *Gazette* continued to track Dett's concert route.

Dr. R. Nathaniel Dett, who is giving a most successful
series of concerts in the southwest, was recently presented
in the Boston Avenue Episcopal Church, South Tulsa,
Oklahoma. The church had not presented any colored
artists since the riots of 1921. Dr. Dett was sponsored by
the Race Relations committee, headed by Mrs. C. Faye
Bennett. The concert is reported as a tremendous success.[28]

Though the date was not specified by the *Gazette*, May 3,
1934, another of Dett's concerts on this spring tour was in Parsons,
Kansas. The account stated that on the concert "several evenings
ago" Dett was assisted by Bessie Eads, local lyric soprano, and
the Dett Girls' Glee Club. The *Parsons Sun* (from the May 3
Gazette) gave a complimentary review, saying that Dett had
played his *Enchantment Suite*.

There are many musicians who can reproduce the music of
others in a capable fashion, but only a handful who can
create music such as this. No wonder this talented Negro
is classed among the very best of modern composers. His
music will live long after his nimble fingers cease to
ripple over the keyboard.
    The Negro composer's originality is particularly
outstanding. He strikes out alone and needs no help in
blazing a trail. . . . The program presented a pleasing
variety and ended in whirlwind fashion with the
exceptionally popular "Juba Dance" in which the
wizardry of the pianist's marvelous technique in hand-

ling difficult passages was fully demonstrated.

Dett played selections by other noted composers, revealing "his deep understanding of them and a rare ability in interpreting the music to the greater satisfaction of the hearers."

Before Dett was to perform in Cleveland on May 3 announcement of his concert was made in *The Open Door*, a Wickliffe, Ohio publication. Dett was piano soloist in Cleveland at the Phillis Wheatley Association Auditorium, assisted by the Phillis Wheatley Madrigal Chorus, which sang three of his choral arrangements, "Wasn't That a Mighty Day?," "Weeping Mary," and "Listen to the Lambs." His program "scored a distinct success with an audience that filled the hall," according to the *Cleveland Plain Dealer*, May 4, 1934. The reviewer said of Dett: "His work displays native sensitivity, combined with and disciplined by thorough-going scholastic training. As a piano virtuoso he is not less competent, and he knows how to build a program that appeals to his listeners."

To open the gargantuan program Dett played transcriptions of Bach's "Fantasia and Fugue in g minor" (Liszt), and "Caprice on the Departure of a Loved Brother" (Busoni), which was one of Bach's rare attempts at program music. Following these technically demanding pieces were Brahms' "Rhapsody in b minor," "Danse Negre" by John Boone, and Dett's three suites, *Magnolia, Enchantment,* and the 1928 *Cinnamon Grove.*[29]

The following June Dett chose to visit Oberlin for its centennial celebration. While there he attended an *a cappella* choir concert. Though none of his works was programmed he approved highly of Oberlin's religious spirit, conveyed through the selections which were performed. The report of Dett's appearance in the *Oberlin News*, June 22, 1934, also mentioned that four of his compositions and arrangements had just been published: "Go Not Far From Me, O God," dedicated to the memory of Dr. George W. Andrews, "Drink to Me Only with Thine Eyes," "As By the Streams of Babylon," and "Wasn't That a Mighty Day?". Other previous Dett compositions noted in the article were "Chariot Jubilee," "Listen to the Lambs," his melody for "America the Beautiful," and the recently finished "Ordering of Moses."

An announcement in the *Niagara Falls Gazette,* June 12, 1934, concerning the Chicago World's Fair, "Century of Progress," commemorating the city's 100th anniversary as an incorporated town, read:

> Among the distinguished musicians who will create the huge pageant for the exposition in Chicago this summer will be Dr. R. Nathaniel Dett, of Rochester, who is a native of this city. In Chicago there will be such a gathering of stars that it will be worth a trip to Chicago to meet them. Burleigh, Dett, White, J. Rosamond Johnson, Will Marion Cook, James Weldon Johnson, and a list of stars that would fill this column are creating a pageant that will make history.

Dett's commitment to and attendance at this event may have been pre-empted by another pageant involvement in Rochester. Furthermore, according to the *New York Times,* August 26, 1934, the "huge pageant" depicting the history of the Negro race was narrated by Richard B. Harrison of *Green Pastures* fame, and none of the above composers was mentioned in the item, which stated that the pageant used a cast of 5,000 Negroes, including singers and dancers.

A July 1934 issue of *Musical Courier* mentioned that Dett's tour of the middle West had just ended. Programs included his *Enchantment* suite and works by Bach, Brahms, and Grieg. At his engagement in Wichita, Kansas, the University of Wichita Choir sang several of his works.

That same summer Dett was asked to write incidental music to Edward Hungerford's pageants "Parade of the Years" and "Pathways of Progress" for the centennial anniversary of the city of Rochester. The four-week, one million dollar event began on August 11 with a parade of 7,000 participants and 100,000 onlookers. The pageants depicted the history of Rochester on a stage "capable of containing a counterpart of the old Erie Canal, original boats, oxen, and old railroad train, and modern locomotives."

Hungerford (1875-1948), railroad expert and newsman for the *Rochester Herald, New York Herald,* and *New York Sun,* also wrote "Railroads on Parade," another pageant which was staged at the New York World's Fair. Among his books are *Men of Erie, The Personality of American Cities,* and *Planning a Trip Abroad.* He received an honorary LLD degree from St. Lawrence University in 1936.

Dett was given three weeks to compose the pageant scores which were said to have had a "splendid effect."[30] Dett employed both chorus and orchestra in the scenes depicting the underground railway and the work of Frederick Douglass. The spirituals which he adapted were enthusiastically received. A review of the opening festivities was written by Jean Walrath for the *Rochester Democrat and Chronicle,* August 12, 1934. In praise of Dett's musical contributions she said:

> The music for the spectacle was arranged by Dr. Nathaniel Dett, Rochester composer, and if at any point the pageant failed to stir the audience, it was left to the old tunes to do it. All the songs were there—"Tenting Tonight," "Girl I Left Behind Me," "Annie Laurie," and Dr. Dett's own compositions, without which the drama would have lost some of the highest points of its grandeur.[31]

Another news item concerning the Rochester pageants did not mention Hungerford, but rather Norman S. Wright as Dett's co-writer:

> Music for the dramatic spectacle of the "A Century on Parade" which will be held in Rochester beginning August 11, has been arranged by Dr. Nathaniel Dett, faculty member of Eastman School of Music, who has provided a background of melody for the 15 historical episodes unfolded in Pathways of Progress, name of the spectacle. Dr. Dett's score utilizes original music written for the spectacle by Norman S. Wright.[32]

It should have pleased Dett that in November of 1934 a 200-member black chorus, the Nathaniel Dett Choral Society, was organized in Washington, D.C., largely through the efforts of

Miss Virginia Williams, music educator and critic, who taught in that city at Francis Junior High School. Assisting Miss Williams with rehearsals was Clyde Glass, another Washington musician. In order "to insure his own imprint" Dett served as a consultant, conducting most of the final rehearsals before the concerts which he directed.[33]

1935-1936

Dett obviously found time for a few civic duties in Rochester other than his Community Choir. In his update for the 1935 Oberlin Alumni files he added his presidency of the Rochester branch of the NAACP for 1934-1935, and that he was chairman of the reception committee for newly nationalized citizens, a project of the Rochester Chamber of Commerce. He also mentioned that his oldest daughter, Helen, had graduated from West High School at mid-term and planned to major in physical education at Oberlin. He listed his approximately fifty published compositions and their publishers, but gave no dates of publication.

On January 13, 1935 Dett's Negro Community Choir appeared with the Rochester Civic Orchestra, conducted by Paul White. Admission for the concert was twenty-five cents, stated in an advertisement which read in part: "Another Evening of Delightful Musical Enjoyment, Dr. Dett's Negro Community Choir—Hear one of Rochester's finest singing ensembles in a feast of melody." A brief news item from the *Oberlin Alumni Magazine* mentioned this concert, and also that on January 11 Roland Hayes had sung Dett's arrangement of the spiritual "I'm So Glad Trouble Don't Last Alway" at the Eastman Theatre.[34]

The *Niagara Falls Gazette*, January 23, 1935, noted that Dett played a concert at Howard Hall on January 10, sponsored by the Niagara Falls YWCA. The hall was filled to capacity. The first half of the program included selections by Bach, Beethoven, Brahms, Grieg, and "Concert Caprice" by "Blind" Tom Bethune. The second half was devoted to Dett's own compositions. He played an encore, "Harvest Moon," by a Niagara Falls blind composer, William Wattengel. At the event he was introduced by Alice Babcock Trott as a "son who hitched his wagon to a star and through perseverance succeeded in accomplishing many of his high ideals and ambitions." Mrs. Trott, longtime Niagara Falls piano teacher and organist at the First Presbyterian Church, died in 1959.

Amidst all his serious pursuits, Dett may have been amused had he known of a letter written to Oberlin, dated January 17, 1935, from Aurora, Illinois, which said:

Gentlemen:
    Will you please send me information concerning *Nathaniel Dett*, if he is still teaching & where. Would appreciate it if you would do this at once as I have a paper to write on colored composers. Thanking you in advance I am respectfully,
Mrs. E. A. Rieckman

The secretary of the Oberlin Alumni Records answered Mrs. Rieckman by giving her Dett's business address in Rochester.[35]

One prestigious concert, part of a Music Festival spawned by Williams and Glass, who mustered a 200-voice choir, was given in the Washington Auditorium on April 1, 1935, under auspices of the Nathaniel Dett Choral Society. Among the audience of 1,500 were President and Mrs. Franklin D. Roosevelt, occupying the President's Box with six White House guests, "who by their applause, expressed a keen appreciation for the first night's program of the music festival."[36] Dett was conductor at another Washington concert in early May, celebrating the opening of the Phillis Wheatley YMCA Music Festival, when Mrs. Franklin Roosevelt was again present. Under Dett's direction another 200-voice choir was assisted by baritone LeRoy Morlock, soprano Dorothy Maynor, organist Julius Carroll, and violinist Louia Jones.[37]

Though specific months have not been ascertained, from the fall of 1935 through January of 1936 Dett was a visiting professor at Samuel Huston College in Austin, Texas.[38] At this time one of Dett's earlier protégés, Edward Hammond Boatner, was Director of Music there, a position he took in 1933.

Established in 1875 and chartered in 1877 as Tillotson

Collegiate and Normal Institute, this college first offered
instruction at the post-secondary level in 1881. In 1884 its name
was changed to Tillotson College which became incorporated and
awarded its first degree in 1909. In 1931 it became a four-year
college, and shortly afterward merged with Samuel Huston
College, which had been established in 1876.

Dett's letter to his mother dated December 13, 1935, written
from Samuel Huston relates some of his experiences at the school.
It was hand-printed in letters a half-inch tall with a wide-
tipped pen, for Mrs. Dett's eyesight was failing. The letterhead
said "Visiting Professor in charge of Music at Samuel Huston
College until February 1936" and reads:

Dear Ma

I am glad that you wrote me for I must be getting
absent minded. I was sure that I had written you until I
found this new pen which I bought weeks ago, for just
that purpose.

I have been rather busy. At Thanksgiving the State
Teachers Association met in San Antonio and I was down
for a speech, and I had been widely advertised, but I
took a bad cold so I decided to stay here and take care of
myself, and the two days' rest did me lots of good. I am
now ok again. I also got a new piece copied that I had
been working on and I have sent it off, but have not heard
from the publishers about it. Last Wednesday I
entertained the choir at Paradise Inn. I had promised a
party when "Go Not Far From Me, O God," my new
anthem was all ready. There were about 45. For the first
half hour I had guessing contest on illustrated musical
terms. For instance a man getting a drink in a saloon
represented "a bar," a pint cup and a quart cup
represented "measures." Some sheep bleating and a deaf
man with his hand to his ear represented "Listen to the
Lambs." The funniest one was a donkey between the
Tigris and Euphrates rivers with the City of Sin in the
distance, "Ass by the Streams of Babylon." You ought to
have heard the shriek when this was worked out.

Dett, ca. 1935, courtesy of the
Local History Department,
Niagara Falls, New York, Public Library.

Undated photo of Mrs. Charlotte Dett,
courtesy Local History Department,
Niagara Falls, New York, Public Library.

There was a luncheon of roast turkey and dressing, potato chips and olives, pineapple salad. Before dessert I read an alphabet in rhyme introducing every name of a choir member in a pun. The quartet of boys and a sextet of girls sang, Mrs. Granum, the president's wife, made a beautiful speech.

The place cards carried the blue bonnet flowers of Texas. Table decorations were rosebuds which were afterwards distributed—it has been pronounced the most beautiful and original affair ever given here.

Love and kisses

x x x x   x x x x running to class.

Nate[39]

Dett's teaching duties at Samuel Huston included the direction of a choir, which he mentioned in a letter to Verna Arvey, then living in Los Angeles. Letterhead from his Rochester studio address indicates that he returned to Rochester from Austin during early spring. Arvey, not yet wed to William Grant Still but helping him in a secretarial/editorial capacity, was writing an essay which needed a photograph and accompanying information from Dett. Dated April 4, 1936, Dett's rather coy letter replying to Arvey read:

It was a pleasure, and not a little of a surprise to hear from you. However, I am very glad to be remembered by one so talented.

At the time you wrote me I had no picture of myself; since that time I have been to the photographers, and he has promised to render a caricature bearing my signature if not my features.

I am quite anxious to see and hear what you could possibly say about "little me." I did not know that I was talking with a writer; perhaps I should have been much more guarded in my conversations.

Do you know my latest anthem, "Go Not Far From Me, O God?" I think that this is by far my best chorus; I taught it to my Samuel Huston Choir this past winter, and whenever we did this number, it produced a profound effect,—one which is quite different from the appeal of the well known "Listen to the Lambs."

I do not remember whether or not I told you that I had put words to the "Juba," from the "In the Bottoms Suite." I am so glad to hear of Still and Nathan; please give them both my very kindest regards, and tell them that I should be glad to hear from them direct.[40]

At sometime during 1935 or 1936, when Dett was in California, he contacted Arvey and Still who took him and a white friend (possibly the "Nathan" mentioned in the letter) to Negro Day at the California-Pacific International Exposition then in progress in San Diego. As a white Jewess Arvey's account of the excursion was both observant and interesting:

> As we walked around the Fair grounds, we were awed by the large number of people who followed us to get Dett's autograph. His was a large and loyal following. When lunch time approached, we were told to go to a particular restaurant on the Fair grounds. We did, and there we sat, the four of us (two white and two colored), while waitresses passed us several times, with no sign of recognition. At last Dett asked to see the manager, who informed him that they would not serve Negroes. We left, and like the multitude of other Negroes who had paid their admission fees, ate hot dogs and hamburgers at lunch stands. This is Negro Day at the Fair, in sunny California.[41]

Arvey noticed that when Dett visited groups of Negro musicians in Los Angeles, he asked them to buy and perform works by Negro composers. "At the time we [Arvey and Still] thought he was being a little chauvinistic, but we later realized that the more people buy and perform music, the more it is publicized and the better it is for everyone," she said.[42]

A reminiscence in the *Rochester Democrat and Chronicle*, May 8, 1958, mentioned that Dett and Ernest E. Ahern, director of music at West High School in Rochester, had become friends in the mid-1930s through daughter Helen Dett who was a West

High student then. For the school's spring music festival in 1936 Dett was invited to direct the school choir in "Listen to the Lambs." Mr. Ahern's reaction was highly emotional, for he said:

> I stood in the wings while that beautiful anthem was sung. When it was over I stepped out to thank Dr. Dett and congratulate him. There was no sound of applause. I was surprised. I looked out over the audience and knew why. The audience [was] too busy wiping the tears from their eyes. A moment later the applause began.

Helen Dett graduated from West High this same spring. Among the Mesiah Papers and Documents is part of her yearbook, *The Occident*, inscribed "To Uncle Sam."

In 1936 the Hall & McCreary Company published Dett's four-volume work *The Dett Collection of Negro Spirituals*, which contained seventy songs. Dett's description of the collection was recounted in the *Rochester Democrat and Chronicle*, November 23, 1936.

> It is concerned with giving the uninitiated an under-standing of the religious and folk significance of the spiritual, and vindicating this folk music from the charges of some critics that it is adapted from hymn music. Many of the spirituals are in antique scales, [Dett] points out, and the form of the solo with answering chorus is distinct from the hymn.

McBrier lists no other Dett publications for 1936, but since 1932 the following compositions had been published, according to her "List of Published Works." For chorus were "Somebody's Knocking at Your Door" (Theodore Presser Co., 1932); "Sit Down, Servant" (G. Schirmer, Inc., 1932); "Rise Up Shepherd and Follow" (J. Fischer & Bro., 1932); "Drink to Me Only with Thine Eyes" (J. Fischer & Bro., 1933); and "Juba" (Clayton F. Summy, Co., 1934). Published vocal solos since 1932 included "Melody" (John Church Co., 1932); "Sit Down Servant" (G. Schirmer, Inc., 1932); "O Lord, the Hard Won Miles" (G. Schirmer, Inc., 1934); and "Iorana" (Clayton F. Summy Co., 1935).

1937-1943

Dett began another teaching stint in February of 1937, this time at Bennett College in Greensboro, North Carolina. Still in demand as a performer and lecturer, he was invited to Philadelphia on February 11 to give a lecture/recital, "Problems of a Negro Composer," in Fleisher Auditorium. He played some of his own piano compositions and themes from other of his works.

Announcement was made in the *Rochester Democrat and Chronicle*, February 14, 1937, that the Negro Community Chorus would appear for the second time with the Rochester Civic Orchestra. Selections were to include Edward Elgar's "As Torrents" and five arrangements by Dett ("As By the Streams of Babylon," "Son of Mary," and three unnamed spirituals).

Losing his mother in April of 1937 saddened Dett considerably, for she seems to have been the family member dearest to him. Mrs. Charlotte Johnson Dett's death occurred on April 8, after a long and painful illness. She was seventy-five. "She had been his [Dett's] confidante, advisor, source of inspiration and often his companion."[43] Her funeral was held in the First Presbyterian Church, Niagara Falls, New York. A fitting tribute was paid Mrs. Dett in the *Niagara Falls Gazette* the next day. It spoke of her as "one of nature's noble women," who had "enjoyed the highest esteem and respect of the community." The obituary continued:

> Mrs. Dett was a talented woman, but it was not because of that advantage alone that she grew in the estimation of the people—it was because of an indomitable will that overcame handicaps of life and enabled her to serve the public and to rear a family of which any parent might feel proud.
>
> Mrs. Dett labored all her life in behalf of her people and by them she was regarded as a ministering angel to whom they could carry their troubles and receive advice, counsel and encouragement. She held high place in the councils of many organizations of women because of her powers of leadership and executive ability.

Of the Dett sons the obituary said:

> One of her sons, Dr. R. Nathaniel Dett, has won
> nation-wide distinction as a musician and composer. His
> concerts have been commended by the highest critics.
> Another son, Samuel, holds a responsible government
> position in Niagara Falls.
> These men have succeeded because they had a
> wonderful mother to aid and guide them, and because
> they inherited her fine traits of character and could
> appreciate the value of the legacy that was theirs.
> Women of Mrs. Dett's worth and capacity are too few in
> the world.

Dett was not ashamed to speak of his sadness to his friend
Percy Grainger. He wrote to Grainger, who was also influenced
by his own mother, though in an unhealthily different way:

> I am now an orphan. My mother was always one of my
> main sources of inspiration, always an incentive to more
> and better work, and I know I shall miss her
> unspeakably. Yet, she is done with suffering, and that is
> something. She was in great pain toward the last; her
> fight was heroic.[44]

That same year Grainger had asked Dett to write music
suitable for the high school orchestra which would be featured
that summer at the National Music Camp in Interlochen. Dett,
feeling himself inadequate in this genre, having scored only
Chariot Jubilee and *The Ordering of Moses* for a large
instrumental ensemble, declined Grainger's request.[45]

* * *

Dett's grief over the loss of his beloved mother could not be
completely assuaged, but it must have abated with his ongoing
professional activities. The oratorio, *The Ordering of Moses*, his
thesis composition at Eastman, was premiered on May 7 (a date

given as May 8 in some references) at a gala five-day festival in
Cincinnati. Even as one of the featured composers and the first
Negro to write an oratorio, he was traveling in high company, for
during the festival large works by Beethoven, Vincent d'Indy,
Anton Bruckner, Edward Elgar, and festival conductor Eugene
Goossens were also performed. Alfred Hartzel, the chorus
master, had spent months rehearsing the singers.

Four stars from the Metropolitan Opera, Kirsten Flagstad,
Kathryn Meisle, Frederick Jagel, and Ezio Pinza, took part in the
festival, though only Jagel, singing the role of Moses, was a
soloist in Dett's work. Other soloists for *Moses* were Agatha
Lewis as Miriam, Elizabeth Wysor as the Voice of Israel, and
Alexander Kisselburgh as The Word.

Reviews of *Moses* were numerous and favorable. *Time*, May
17, 1937, called the piece a "novelty and biggest hit of the
Festival, . . . a massive work based on Exodus and involving wild
rhythms and orchestral development of Go Down Moses."

An impressed reviewer for *Musical America* wrote:

It was a stirring spectacle, as the small Negro composer
came onto the stage following the last crashing
syncopation of his work, to see the audience and chorus
rise simultaneously amid a salvo of bravos which lasted
for many minutes.

The oratorio has an intoxicating spiritual flavor, a
number of striking rhythmic devices, and brilliant scoring
which taxes the chorus almost as much as the orchestra.
The frankly sensuous lyric passages, tremendous
climaxes, and above all the pervasive   expressive,
unmistakable melodic and rhythmic stamp of Negro folk
music, combine to give the work its unique character. It
would be a minimizing of the universal almost
cosmopolitan nature of its spiritual quality to give it an
exclusive racial classification.[46]

Though the same reviewer was most taken with the huge
chorus (over 300 voices), "which vied with the orchestra for
leadership," he also complimented the soloists, especially Jagel,

for their musical, artistic, and technical abilities in interpreting *Moses*. He thought that the orchestra "handled the extremely intricate instrumentation with vigor and assurance."

Several critics commented on Dett's lasting ovation, one apparently rarely witnessed at this particular festival. Dwight L. Bicknell wrote that when Dett was called back "the chorus and orchestra rose to their feet as one and cheered him 'to the echo.' A third call was as vociferous as the first." Bicknell called the ovation "rousing" and the audience "wildly enthusiastic."

> Dett's composition is said to be the most important contribution to music yet made by a member of the Negro race, and judging from the reaction of the Festival audience, that statement may be classed as an understatement. . . . Last night's concert was probably the most brilliant, both as to audience and quality of performance, that has been witnessed in many years. One did not have to be versed in the technicalities of music to thoroughly enjoy "The Ordering of Moses," and Berlioz's Requiem Mass, so different in composition, yet similar in giving the audience the utmost satisfaction musically.[47]

The Crisis carried a review from the *Cincinnati Times-Star*, May 8, 1937, excerpts from which read:

> The American Negro may be said to have come into his own, musically speaking. . . . In choosing ["Moses"] as the representative work for the 1937 May Festival Conductor Goossens paid deserved honor to a musical leader of a musically gifted race. Mr. Dett . . . is a man with deep interest and pride in his people [who] has looked into the heart of his people and composed what he saw there. As a result he had added something important to American culture.[48]

May Dearness, society editor for another Cincinnati paper (unnamed) naturally gave more attention in her column to the ladies' satin and chiffon gowns and the box party guests than to the performance. She did allow, however, that Dett's appearance on stage "brought down the house."

Olin Downes, in Cincinnati to cover the premiere for the *New York Times*, was both complimentary and constructively critical in his review on May 9, 1937. Calling *Moses* a "novelty," he felt that the score needed "an even wilder, more emotional treatment than it received," that certain of the solos and recitatives were 'done in the pale white fashion.'" Saying that Dett had done well, he still "has not gone far enough in striking the racial note in this music. There are fine pages; everything is done with knowledge and sincerity. But it is more than half a sophisticated conventionalized style." Downes went on, somewhat philosophically:

> There is a deeper, greater and more powerful thing . . . for the Negro artist to do, . . . which cannot be the way of either imitation or emulation of another race's culture. *The Ordering of Moses*, insofar as it was the expression of a Negro musician, triumphed. The weaknesses are those of a musician educated too well in a conventional mold.

Herman J. Bernfield of the *Cincinnati Inquirer* (May 9, 1937) thought that the greatest work programmed on the festival was Beethoven's *Missa Solemnis*, but that the best received work was Dett's *Moses*. He quoted another *Enquirer* critic, Frederick Yeiser, as saying that *Moses* would have been even more exciting if performed with the same orchestra, but "with the Hall Johnson Choir to supplement the May Festival Chorus . . . and with Marian Anderson, Paul Robeson, Roland Hayes, Adelaide Hall, or Ethel Waters as soloists."[49]

The *Niagara Falls Gazette*, May 12, 1937, reported that *Moses* had been broadcast at the festival, and that Dett was accompanied to the premiere by President and Mrs. David Jones of Bennett College. The newsman, J. M. Pollard, Sr., said that the composition "has been praised by competent critics as a masterpiece. . . . Dr. Dett was ten years in developing the unusual rhythms and musical effects of the oratorio."

The Ordering of Moses, published in 1937 by J. Fischer & Bro., saw several performances in leading American cities in the next year, including one by The Juilliard School of Music (New York) in late March or early April.[50] Other performances were given by the Swedish Choral Society (Chicago), the Worcester Massachusetts Music Festival, October 3-8 of 1938, the Cathedral Choir of the Immanuel Presbyterian Church (Los Angeles), and the Conservatory of Music at the College of the Pacific (Stockton), conducted by J. Russell Bodley. Of the latter performance in early September of 1938, the fifth by well known musical organizations, the *Stockton Evening Record* stated that the impact of Dett's *Moses* was strongly felt, that "it became an emotional experience." There were joyous spontaneous outbursts during the performance of the "unusual oratorio."

In reviewing the Worcester Festival performance *Time*, October 17, 1938, recalling the recent CBS broadcast, said that Dett had "made musical news again." *Moses*, conducted by Albert Stoessel, was on the festival's opening program. "Previously performed in Cincinnati and Manhattan, this tempestuous choral and orchestral work, based on *Exodus*, came near being the hit of the Worcester festival," the review stated. A brief biography of Dett, "long famed as the smart, musically sophisticated leader of the Hampton Institute Choir," whose aim was to "put Negro music on a truly dignified and artistic basis," was included in the item. Other choral pieces scheduled for performance at this festival were Berloiz' *Requiem*, Rachmaninoff's *The Bells*, and Vaughan Williams' *Toward the Unknown Region*. Brazilian singer Bidu Sayao was the featured soloist on Artist's Night.[52]

* * *

Earlier in 1937 the Columbia Broadcasting System had invited composers Dett, Quincy Porter, Robert Russell Bennett, Leo Sowerby, Jerome Moross, and Vittorio Giannini to each write a work for radio broadcast. On the selection committee were composer/critic Deems Taylor, conductor Howard Barlow, Davidson Taylor, assistant to the program director at CBS, and Julius Mattfield, then Music Library Manager for CBS.

Composition guidelines, except for length, were not rigid and the nature of the works was left to the discretion of individual composers with the exception of Giannini, whose work was specified to be an opera. Dett's orchestral work, "American Sampler," was aired on October 2, 1937, conducted by Barlow.

"American Sampler," the first of Dett's works to be based on an idiom or subject other than Negro lore, was never published. The two-part work, divided into "Martyrs" and "Liberators," depicted the Indian invasion of a white American settlement. Based on a true story, it was inspired by a poem of American poet Philip Freneau. Of the work's broadcast *Time*, October 17, 1938, reported:

> Composer Dett has so far been known principally for his choral works and art arrangements of Negro spirituals. But last fortnight he joined the symphonic company of composers [William Grant] Still and [William] Dawson with his sombre, ably orchestrated composition, "American Sampler."

* * *

Dett was now Director of Music at Bennett College. The *Norfolk Journal and Guide*, October 29, 1938, carried a sizable photo of Dett, along with an article saying that he had recently "chalked up" three triumphs in the musical world: *The Ordering of Moses* at the Worcester Festival, Bennett's mid-west choir tour, and the world premiere of his "American Sampler" over radio.

Dett seemed reasonably content with his position at Bennett, a Methodist affiliated women's school with 250 students. His decision to come there was in part influenced by his friendship with Bennett's president, David Jones. Bennett was established in 1873. Advertisements for its advantages had appeared frequently in *The Crisis*. By January of 1927 it had been made a Grade A college for colored women under auspices of the Methodist Episcopal Church. In January of 1940 Bennett was described in *The Crisis* as "A Distinctive College for Daughters of Discriminating Parents—Cultured Atmosphere, Well Trained

Faculty, Ample Facilities."[53]

Dett's previous choir activities had not been structured solely for a women's group, as it would now be. He accepted the situation at Bennett as a challenge, immediately organizing a choir which would soon be a viable touring ensemble. Mrs. Dett, hired to teach piano by Bennett in 1938, seemed socially better adjusted here than at Hampton. Their daughters were both students at Bennett at this time. The music students with whom Dett worked prized him for his integrity, wit, and knowledge, and gave him complete cooperation.

* * *

The day after Easter in 1939 Dett and the Bennett College Choir left on a northern tour. That spring he also found time to visit the Hampton campus. His advice on the place of music in Hampton's newly organized curriculum had been frequently asked by Hampton's president, Malcom S. McClean.[54] Continued contact with McClean prompted an interesting offer for Dett a few years later.

On April 25, 1939, Dett's *Ordering of Moses* was one of the works featured on the Mendelssohn Choir's 1938-1939 season in Pittsburgh. Notes concerning *Moses* in *The Concert Magazine*, the choir's printed program for the season which also included highlights from the *Moses* text, read:

> The new work, "The Ordering of Moses" by R. Nathaniel Dett, prominent colored composer, is ultra-modern in character and decidedly out of the ordinary. It was received with great acclaim at premier performances last season by the New York Oratorio Society and at the Westchester N. Y. Music Festival.

Singing roles were taken by soprano Nell Welsh (Miriam), tenor Philip Sportolari (Moses), baritone W. H. DeVore (Voice of God and The Word), and contralto Eda Kreiling (Voice of Israel). Homer Wickline was the organist.[55] Cesar Franck's *The Beatitudes* comprised the other half of the program, with Ernest Lunt as conductor.

On July 2, 1939, when the NAACP held its annual meeting in Richmond, Virginia, works by numerous Negro composers, including those of Dett, were exhibited at the Public Library through courtesy of the Arthur B. Spingarn Collection. At this meeting Marian Anderson received the Spingarn Medal, presented to her by Mrs. Franklin Roosevelt.[56]

A news item in the *Greensboro Daily News*, October 19, 1939, stated that Dett

> is one of many nationally known persons to be invited by Secretary of State Cordell Hull to participate in a [two-day] conference in Washington on the cultural relationship of America to the other nations of the world. . . . Sunday he [Dett] will speak in Cleveland on "America's Forgotten Song." Dr. Dett states: "Although the song (the spiritual) is always present, we have forgotten its deep religious significance."

The following month Dett led activities for one of Bennett's Chapel Hours to cleverly take a poll concerning his orchestral arrangement of a spiritual. He had been commissioned for it by the American School of the Air, which conducted regular musical broadcasts structured toward educating young America in its country's traditions. "No Auction Block for Me," the spiritual to be arranged, would be aired over CBS on February 13, 1940, played by a full symphonic orchestra if so scored by the arranger.

Dett was spoken of in a news item as "the man who embellished the folk melody for its classic debut, one of American's foremost composers." "No Auction Block for Me" was selected for its musical simplicity and subject interest. As Dett put it, "This song represents what many thought never existed in the mind of the Negro—a protest against his condition."[57]

The poll, in part, was to determine popular sentiment of "swinging the spirituals," a style beginning to gain popularity. The students "overwhelmingly favored classic treatment" of them, though they liked swing music as such.[58] Dett guided the poll on "swing spirituals" with four questions: Do you like this music? Do you think it is close to the spirit of the spirituals? Do you think it has musical value? Does this type music tend to lower or elevate the spiritual? Results of the poll revealed that

> . . . ninety-eight liked the swing style, seventy-three
> disliked it. Seventy-four thought it was not close to the
> pristine spirit of religious song. One hundred were
> assured that the songs in swing type have musical worth;
> fifty-two differed from this opinion. One hundred
> seventeen felt that the spirituals were degraded by the
> swing element; only thirty-six felt that there was an
> elevation because of the swing element.[59]

Ballots of a few students who pleaded no musical background were discarded. The singing in swing style which the students heard in order to vote was taken from "records made by a popular quartet which is regularly heard on the air" (no name given). One of the more insightful answers to the poll, doubtless a reflection of Dett's effective teaching, was: "I like the music, but I don't like the way it was sung; it does not have musical value. I think it lowers the spiritual." Another student wrote: "I do not care particularly for these spirituals; a rather low element seems to have entered in. . . . these are not close to the spirit of the old spirituals."[60]

When interviewed about the balloting Dett seemed pleased that, first

> the girls exhibited keen insight and candor in their
> opinions—that in spite of the fact that they liked the
> rhythm they were not willing to recommend it as
> elevating the spiritual; second, that the students felt
> that the "swing" spirituals had possibilities for
> development into higher forms of musical expression.[61]

Dett was one of several composers asked to make orchestral arrangements of American songs for this CBS broadcast, whose sponsors sought to develop the folk motive. Though not actually bound in format or scoring, Dett's contribution of the orchestrated spiritual was limited to four minutes. He chose to score for a complete string section, one flute, two clarinets, two horns, one trombone, one bassoon, and the standard percussion section.[62]

The all-girl Bennett College Choir toured annually, and in 1940 made a wide swing through the eastern and midwestern states and Canada. Also in 1940 the choir performed on a series of nation-wide broadcasts over CBS. The first one, on March 28, included six of Dett's original compositions.[63]

The same day of the broadcast Dett wrote his publisher, J. Fischer, mainly to thank him for sending some new William Grant Still piano pieces. The letter read:

> Well, our broadcast is over and I am stealing a few minutes. In the interim I have just read, or rather tried to read Still's "Seven Traceries." I want to thank you for sending me this work which I think is highly original with many novel and unique effects. I am anxious to hear in real life that bird that sings in "Wailing Dawn." This passage ought to go down in American music history.
>
> Please extend my congratulations to Still for me.[64]

Perhaps by now Dett had mellowed even more with regard to Still and his compositional reputation. The "bird" passage in "Wailing Dawn" could very well be taken by a trumpet or saxophone.

The *Rochester Democrat and Chronicle*, April 29, 1940, carried an announcement of a concert to be given by the forty-two voice Bennett College Choir in Rochester at the Baptist Temple on May 6. Hailing Dett as a Rochester native (erroneously), and as a "world renowned conductor, pianist, poet and educator," the article named the concert's sponsor as the Rochester branch of the National Association for the Advancement of Colored People, one of Dett's local affiliations, and stated that students in the Bennett Choir were from twenty-two states. The full program for May 6 was also given in the article. It included choral pieces by Gluck, Handel, Bach, Brahms, Dett, and six spirituals, arranger not named.

A later announcement by the same paper, May 5, related that approximately 200 "Rochesterians representing a cross section of the city's music lovers" would sponsor the concert. Names of all sponsors and group captains, about ninety percent of whom were females, were listed.[65]

Besides maintaining his ties with Hampton, the fact that Dett kept his residence in Rochester is indicated on a letterhead. Under his Bennett College address was "Summer address June 1st to September 1st 577 Plymouth Ave. S., Rochester, New York." Perhaps he was already planning to move back there one day.

* * *

In January of 1941 publisher J. Fischer & Bro. issued two spirituals arranged by Dett, "Ride On, Jesus" and "I'm Goin' to Thank God." Under the heading "Song Written for Negro Soprano" the *Detroit Free Press*, January 19, 1941, said that Dett had done "a very fine job of writing." "I'm Goin' to Thank God" was written and set especially for Dorothy Maynor, and "I, for one," said the reviewer, "would be grateful if she'd sing it when she next comes to Detroit."

The *Columbus* (Ohio) *Dispatch*, February 3, 1941, reported that Dett gave a lecture/recital at the YWCA in Detroit the previous evening. His presentation, "The Development of Negro Music," featured readings by the winners of an essay contest whose subject was "The Negro and His Music." No dates in 1941 were specified, but at least two references state that Dett was guest lecturer at Virginia State College in Ettrick, Virginia, and at Northwestern University in Evanston, Illinois, at sometime during that year. While in Evanston he presented a piano recital on June 29 at Wendell Phillips High School in Chicago.[66]

By this time ASCAP had allowed Dett's compositions to be used on Bennett Choir broadcasts, according to spokesman John G. Paine of ASCAP, who stated that "The American Society of Composers, Authors, and Publishers will be very happy to grant special permission to Bennett College for this usage."[67]

Dett's friend, President McClean of Hampton, wrote in March of 1941, offering him a position back on the Hampton faculty. If he accepted, his many duties as stated by McClean would include directing the church choir, playing the organ for chapel, teaching and supervising music in both regular semester and summer school, teaching graduate courses and conducting workshops—a staggering and perhaps bittersweet proposal. Dett's letter of declination, with regard to the organist's duties, showed his integrity and regard for colleagues: ". . . my feeling was that to accept this would be to force Mr. Hays (the organist) from his position, and as his friend I could not do that."[68]

The Richmond, Virginia *Afro-American*, March 29, 1941, announced that the fifty-voice Bennett College Choir, accompanied by Bennett President David Jones and his wife, was to be on tour April 17 through May 2 in Michigan, Ohio, and Virginia, with a scheduled concert at Hampton University on May 1. Another of their concerts, which received ample publicity, was to be at the Asbury Methodist Church in Washington, D.C.[69] Though no date was specified, the tour would include a concert at the Cass Technical High School in Detroit, under auspices of the cultural committee of the Second Baptist Church. Several new works by Dett were to be performed.[70] Cass had an excellent reputation for academic standards and for producing outstanding students. Though it was essentially a technical school, it offered well taught courses in the arts and music.

A review of the Hampton concert on May 1 in the *Norfolk Journal and Guide* said that Dett and the choir were on trial.

> Before such a background the Bennett Choir really proved itself. They sang as if some inner something impelled them to go all out in their singing. There was an inner urge behind the singing of these girls, [and a] confidence and comradeship they have for their director which wouldn't allow them to let down before the "folks." And they didn't! . . . They had the audience at their feet. . . . The quality of tone was pure and unrestrained, . . . well-balanced and soothing to the ear.

Of Schubert's "Sanctus," the highlight of the program, the reviewer said: "Here was well nigh perfect dynamic color." Considered outstanding was Tschaikowsky's "Legend." Dett's "I'll Never Turn Back No More" was also on the program.

The Richmond, Virginia *Afro-American*, May 24, 1941, summarized the response to the choir's tour performances, saying "it was at Hampton Institute that they were accorded the most appreciative reception of the entire tour."

Another complimentary review of the Hampton concert was carried in the Newport News *Daily Press*, May 2, 1941. As usual, the program was a typical Dett one with selections from all periods. The reviewer said:

> ... under sensitive direction a women's choir may present as richly satisfying variety as any male chorus. The fresh young voices . . . showed evidence of splendid discipline and sound musicianship. Particularly notable was the strength of the alto section, which at times achieved an almost monastic austerity.

The only accompanied selection was the "Hallelujah Chorus" from Beethoven's *Mount of Olives*, supported by two Bennett pianists and Hampton organist Ernest R. Hays. The "Legend" by Tschaikowsky "was performed with tenderness an an eye to dramatic contrast." The *Daily Press* reviewer was impressed with the "beauty and feeling" of the alto voice in Burleigh's arrangement of "Sinner, Please Don't Let This Harvest Pass." More popular than the spirituals, however, were two new works by Dett, "Ascapezzo" (dedicated to ASCAP and set to his own words) and a miniature cantata, "Hew Down the Tree," which "really captivated the house," and was predicted to become even more popular than the encore, "Listen to the Lambs," according to the reviewer. The program included Dett's "So We'll Go No More A-Roving" and the Bennett "Alma Mater." As a reminder of Dett's years at Hampton his appearance there, under auspices of the Hampton Roads branch of the National Association of College Women, was said by the reviewer to be "in the nature of a homecoming."

* * *

The *Norfolk Journal and Guide*, May 3, 1941, reported that Dett had signed a contract with Mills Music for all future publications. While pursuing his frantic schedule at Bennett Dett rarely got the desired time for composition. Seeking some seclusion for this purpose, in the summer of 1941 he accepted a six weeks' invitation to Yaddo (Saratoga Springs, New York), the estate of Spencer Trask, deceased banking associate of George Foster Peabody. The Yaddo Corporation had made this estate into an artist colony, not unlike the MacDowell Colony in New Hampshire, but perhaps on a grander scale. Dett was indeed honored to have been invited here, for it meant that his achievements had been recognized. He said of the rewarding experience:

> About twenty-eight or so of these (creative artists) were present during my stay at this unusually beautiful place; most were literary stars, of more or less brilliance. Some were painters, but never more than two musicians were there at a time.[71]

An undated, unnamed news item from the Rochester Public Library revealed that during the Yaddo stay Dett wrote six spirituals (unnamed) "at the request of his distinguished pupil, Miss Dorothy Maynor." Other compositions from Yaddo included two "songs of democracy," three parts of a new piano suite, and several unfinished sketches. The completed selections were under a "two-year classic and educational contract" with Mills Music. "As His Own Soul" and "Desert Interlude," from the new piano suite (*Eight Bible Vignettes*) were expected to be issued by Mills in November of 1941, according to the news item.

A photo of Dett rehearsing a Negro and white choir was in the *Rochester Democrat and Chronicle*, August 21, 1941, above the headline "More White Voices Sought for Dett Interracial Choir." (One of the ladies in the photo looked very much like Dett's wife.) The choir concert, to be a part of Rochester's celebration in transferring the Frederick Douglass Monument from Central Avenue to Highland Park, was scheduled for September 5. In part the item said, " . . . it's brotherhood that shines out in Dr. Dett's new choir, Negroes and whites of Rochester who want to sing their praises in unison to the good life of America."

Direction of the projected 200-voice choir, which Dett had taken on temporarily, was a short term filler before he returned to fall duties at Bennett. Singer enrollment was handled by Reverend James E. Rose, chairman of the celebration committee. "The new interracial choir rehearsed last night in Salem

Evangelical Church, and though it's progressing well . . . it's still not too late for other choristers to join."

Meanwhile, an $8,500 organ had been purchased for Bennett College and on October 31, 1941, it was dedicated in the Annie Merner Pfeiffer Chapel at Bennett. Mrs. Henry Pfeiffer, donor of the chapel building, was present for this occasion and the two services the following day. Dett made an acceptance speech during the preliminaries preceding a dedicatory recital by organist Orrin Clayton Suthern II, who would later succeed Dett as Bennett's music director. Suthern's hefty program included selections from baroque composers through contemporary ones, with program notes for each.[72]

At the next morning's worship service in the Pfeiffer Chapel the Bennett Choir sang "O Friend of Souls" (Bach) and Schubert's "Sanctus." Presiding at the service was Bishop Alexander P. Shaw of Baltimore. The invocation was given by Bishop Lorenzo H. King of Atlanta, and the sermon was delivered by Bishop Robert E. Jones of Columbus. At another service that afternoon to dedicate the Chapel the presidents of Wiley College, Gammon Theological Seminary, and Philander Smith College took part. At this service Dett directed the Bennett Choir in Handel's "Sing Unto God," a spiritual "He Is King of Kings," and in his own "When I Survey the Wondrous Cross," and in addition played a postlude, Godard's "Berceuse," on the new organ.[73]

The *Greensboro Record*, November 11, 1941, announced a recital to be given by the Bennett Choir on November 13 in Greensboro at the Gillespie Park Junior High School. Organizer of the event, Dett's only public presentation in Greensboro for the year, was Miss Eula Tuttle, Gillespie's music director. The choir's program was first class, including selections by Palestrina, Bach, Brahms, Mendelssohn, three spirituals (not Dett's arrangements), and Dett's "I'll Never Turn Back No More," "When I Survey the Wondrous Cross," and "Now Rest Beneath Night's Shadows." The news item said in tribute to Dett:

> As director of the Bennett Choir for the past five years, Dr. Dett has brought honor and recognition to the college through his outstanding achievements in the musical world and through his directorship of the

famous Negro choir. Among his most famous works are
"Listen to the Lambs" and "In the Bottoms," the popular
selection which contains the favorite "Juba Dance."

* * *

Though Dett did not serve in the military during World War
II, by February of 1942 as World War II continued Bennett College
had inaugurated a series of broadcasts "to sustain civilian
morale." These programs included talks by Bennett faculty
members with background music by the Bennett College Choir.[74]
On March 17 Dett played his latest piano composition, "Father
Abraham," at a banquet commemorating the fiftieth anniversary
of the founding of the Chamber of Commerce held at the Niagara
Falls Hotel in Niagara Falls, New York.[75] As the honored
speaker and performer Dett told the audience that "Let Us Cheer
the Weary Traveler" was based on the hardships of the
underground railroad riders, and that "Father Abraham"
derived from both a fourteenth century Hebrew legend and a
Negro spiritual. This appearance was his last one in Niagara
Falls.

From May 3-7, 1942, Annual Music Week was observed in
Pittsburgh at the YMCA on Centre Avenue, under auspices of the
Local Music Teachers and the Citizens' Sponsoring Committee.
Dett again was among high class company. After Harvey Gaul's
opening program on May 3, Dett lectured the following evening on
"Folk and Art Music," assisted by the combined Folkart and
Cardwell-Dawson Choirs under Raymond Walls' direction.
Other eminent speakers were J. Fred Lissfelt, Dean Dixon, and W.
C. Handy. Each was given a page with photo in the printed
program.[76]

The *Chicago Sunday Bee*, June 7, 1942, announced that Dett
was to be piano soloist on June 29 for the first Annual Music
Festival of the Chicago Music Association to be held at Wendell
Phillips High School Auditorium.

Bennett's enrollment had now increased to 400 students, a
statistic which may or may not have directly affected Dett's
work load. In any case he was growing both weary and restless,
still not finding consistent time periods for composition. Too, he

missed the combined large city/university atmosphere and the advantages of both. In September of 1942 Dett gave his resignation to the Bennett administration, an action made public knowledge by mid-October.

A three-fold, updated brochure (ca. 1942) on Dett is in the Dett Collection, NFNYPL, unfortunately not in suitable condition for clear reprinting. His photo is on the front, the other two sections listing his compositions, books, essays, and appearances as a lecturer. Because all eight pieces in his *Bible Vignettes* were listed, this brochure was probably printed after he left Bennett in 1942, although a Greensboro, North Carolina post box address was given on the front. None of his previous college positions was listed. Under the photo and his name were

Distinguished American Composer
Symphony, Oratorio, Chorus,
Suite, Solo
Lecture Recitalist
Contributing Editor
The Cyclopedia of Music and Musicians

Listed places where he had guest lectured were the Columbia Broadcasting System, National Broadcasting Company, the Universities of Nevada, Rochester, Texas, North Carolina (three times), Fisk, and Woman's College of the University of North Carolina; others included were Greensboro College for Women, Rotary Club (Niagara Falls), Obendorfer American Series, Orchestra Hall (Chicago), Wings Over Jordan, Riverside Drive Church (New York), Rosicrucian Temple (San Jose, California), W. P. A. Choir (Oakland, California), Eastern Library Association, and Guilford College. The compositions listed on the brochure will be addressed in Part II of *Follow Me*.

The *New York Age*, October 24, 1942, reported that on the previous day Dett had come to New York for a meeting at the Park Central Hotel of the Song Writers Protective Associaton. As one of the guest speakers he had opportunity to confirm his decision to leave Bennett. Reasons given were that he needed more time to devote to writing and composition. Possibly he planned an autobiography, according to a remark in the *Age*:

"His autobiography will be looked forward to with great interest and will be a great contribution to the musical literature of America." In the item Dett was lauded for his choir tours and work, both at Hampton and Bennett, and for turning out so many successful students: "Dr. Dett is one of the most widely known composers in America, and his compositions are more frequently used than any Negro composer in the country."

Dett's 1942 residence in Rochester was established at 1087 Plymouth Avenue South. A receipt in the Oberlin College Archives indicated that the rent was $265.00 per month. Though Dett yearned to devote himself only to composing, he needed income for the family. Because his financial gain from composition alone was far from adequate he again opened a private studio in Rochester, took lecturing engagements, and directed the choir at St. Simon's Episcopal Church, composing as time allowed.

McBrier included Dett's account of a cultural evening in Rochester on December 1, 1942. Sponsored by the YWCA, Dr. Rachel Davis DuBois (University of the City of New York) held an Inter-Cultural Home Festival and invited as guests the Race Relations Club of the University of Rochester, and "certain other citizens of the city." Several narrations on Christmas customs by guests from various countries provided the entertainment. Dett found Spanish professor Adolpho Ruiz's the most interesting of these, which tale inspired him to write the poem, "A Gypsy's Christmas Gift." Of the poem Dett said:

> I have tried to re-tell Mr. Ruiz's story with only such liberties and indulgencies as are usually allowed an author, with the hope that at least something of the thrill which was mine on hearing this simple folk tale will be yours for the Christmas season.

In rhymed couplets the poem's message is that of an humble repenter, renouncing his gypsy powers, one who must put himself in God's hands to ask forgiveness.[77]

Five compositions for piano were published in 1942 by Mills Music, Inc.: "Desert Interlude," "As His Own Soul," "Bountiful Shepherd," "Martha Complained," and "Father Abraham," all to be parts of *Eight Bible Vignettes* then in progress. Mills also published three of Dett's choral works this year, "Heavenly Union," "Ask for the Old Paths," and "When I Survey the Wondrous Cross." Two vocal solos, "Go On, Brother" and "Hymn to Parnassus," were published by J. Fischer & Bro.

* * *

Dett's work schedule sometimes extended to eighteen hours per day. Though he was beginning to feel the strain of overwork he ignored any similar warning symtoms of ten years earlier. Thinking that a different pace would be provided by a job with the United States Armed Forces, he accepted a directorship of USO (United Service Organization) activities in February of 1943. The following July he was assigned to Fort Custer in Battle Creek, Michigan, where he worked mainly with a Women's Army Corps (WAC) chorus which often toured as an entertainment group. He also organized an All-City Chorus in Battle Creek.[78] Dett's wife remained in Rochester during this time.

In mid-June Dett had appeared in concert both as pianist and conductor at the Shiloh Baptist Church in Washington, D.C.. The Shiloh Choir, ably prepared by Dett's former Hampton colleague, Miss Wilhelmina Patterson, had only one rehearsal with Dett preceding the concert. Part of a review by Glenn Dillard Gunn of the *Washington Times-Herald* was in the *Rochester Democrat and Chronicle,* June 20, 1943. Gunn said with regard to Dett's performance of three of the *Eight Bible Vignettes*:

> The composer spoke, from time to time, on the spiritual as a form of folk art, and on the sacred folk art of the Jews. He has drawn upon both these sources for thematic material developed in a set of piano pieces. . . . The interested public is even more aware of Dett's mastery of the classic motet to the free fantasy, exhibiting many beautiful patterns in voice leading and developing a melodic eloquence which is both racial and individual.

A letter from Dett in Rochester to a Private Robert A. Wilson, dated July 6, 1943, has been preserved in the Dett Collection, NFNYPL. Their personal connection is unclear, but obviously pertained to some interest on Wilson's part in Dett's music. At the time Wilson was based at Alabama Polytechnic Institute. At the top of Dett's letter were the opening bars in over-sized manuscript of his composition then in progress. The letter read:

Dear Private Wilson
I write you from the George Washington Carver Hall 2nd and Elm Streets, N. W. Washington, D. C., where I am at present; you will recall perhaps that I am a   Music Advisor to the USO. This is my third assignment.
Above is the first line of "As His Own Soul" from my new suite, *Bible Vignettes*. At present this is my favorite number. However, very soon it may not be.
With best wishes for lots of good luck, believe me,
Faithfully yours,
Dett

On August 4, 1943, Dett wrote his friend Percy Grainger: "I regret not being able to have stayed over [in Washington] to have heard your concert at Meridian Hill, but as you know, I have to go where the USO sends me."[79] This was perhaps among Dett's last letters.

After the Battle Creek assignment Dett expected to be sent to the West Coast for further USO duty. In September, while on assignment, Dett suffered a heart attack and was hospitalized in Battle Creek. Accumulated exhaustion had left him no reserve with which to fight. He died on October 2, 1943, of another heart attack. Mrs. Dett, of course, was notified at once. Dett would have been sixty-one on October 11. Shortly before his death he had completed *Eight Bible Vignettes*, intended for Grainger, but not yet published as a whole, and was composing the third and fourth movements of a symphony commissioned by Columbia Broadcasting System.

At the time plans were also underway for an All-Dett program in Battle Creek for a First Congregational Church service, which would be under Dett's direction. Rehearsals had already begun with the church choir, whose regular director was Paul H. Eickmeyer, an acquaintance of Dett's at Oberlin. The program, which was to include Dett's two new hymns, "God's Trumpet Wakes the Slumbering World" and "Our God Is Good in Earth and Sky," would now be presented as a memorial service.[80]

Surviving immediate family included Dett's wife, two daughters, Helen (Mrs. Henry Noyes, later Mrs. Helen Hopkins) and Josephine Elizabeth (later Mrs. Josephine Breedlove), a granddaughter, and his brother Samuel. At this time Mrs. Dett lived in Rochester, Mrs. Noyes in Wilmington, North Carolina, and Josephine was a student at Bennett College. It is not certain when or if Mrs. Dett left Rochester, but the Rochester City Directory for 1949 indicated that Josephine had by that time moved to St. Albans, Long Island, New York.

Though Dett's wife and daughters are no longer living, according to persons at Hampton University who knew them, the exact dates of their demises have not been ascertained. Dr. McBrier places Mrs. Dett's death in October of 1950 in Rochester where she had continued to live. When McBrier's biography was published (1977) the daughters were married and had reared families. Mrs. Helen Noyes was a social worker in New York City, mother of six with two grandchildren. Mrs. Josephine Breedlove, mother of three children, lived in Brooklyn. Both Mrs. Hopkins and Mrs. Breedlove were living as late as 1983, for they were guest speakers at ceremonies honoring Dett in 1982 at Hampton and in Niagara Falls, Ontario, in 1983. McBrier mentioned Dett's cousins Mrs. Harriett Johnson Williamson, Dr. Nathaniel Johnson, Nathaniel LeCount Johnson, Mrs. Julia Lavergne Johnson Walker, and Harry Joseph Walker, Jr., all of whom were well educated, professional persons holding responsible positions as musicians, educators, or businessmen.[81]

Hampton administrators wired flowers to the family after Dett's death.[82] The Latimer Funeral Home at 179 Clarissa Street in Rochester was in charge of burial preparations. A funeral service at 2:30 p. m. on October 5 was conducted by Reverend Frank L. Brown in Rochester at St. Simon's Episcopal Church where Dett had served as choir director.

An obituary in the *Rochester Democrat and Chronicle*,

October 5, 1943, quoted Reverend Brown's comment on Dett: "The realm of music has lost an illustrious citizen. Brilliant, versatile, profound, his intense spirituality departed to his works the quality of endurance." Other words of praise for Dett in the same item were by Norman Nairn, music critic of this newspaper: "It was a privilege to have known Dr. Dett; unassuming, this outstanding Negro composer long has occupied a prominent and well-deserved place in contemporary music. He had brought honor to myself and to his race." Reverend Isaiah P. Pogue, Jr., minister of Rochester's Trinity Presbyterian Church, where Dett was formerly organist and choir master, assisted at the service. Miss Isabelle Cash, soprano at St. Simon's, sang Dett's "Super Flumina" (adapted from Hebrew).

An obituary in the *Battle Creek Enquirer and News*, October 4, 1943, stated that Dett had come to that city on the previous August 14 for a six weeks' assignment to direct musical activities at the Hamblin Avenue USO Club. Other of his work involved the organization of a WAC Chorus and a Soldiers' Chorus at Fort Custer, and the establishment of a permanent All-City Chorus. The item mentioned Dett's wife and daughters, his discovery of Dorothy Maynor, his most famous compositions, and the fact that he had composed two hymns while in Battle Creek. "God's Trumpet Wakes the Slumbering World," a processional, was written for the high school and chancel choirs of the First Congregational Church. The other hymn, "Our God is Good in Earth and Sky," Dett dedicated to the Reverend Carleton Brooks Miller of the First Congregational Church, who at the time was observing his silver jubilee as a minister.

Notables attending Dett's funeral, besides Howard Hanson, Director of the Eastman School of Music, were USO music coordinator Dr. Raymond Kendall, who represented national USO headquarters in New York; Joseph J. Ford, director of the Hamblin USO in Battle Creek; Professor Gustav A. Lehmann of the Colgate-Rochester Divinity School, and other Rochester musicians, none of whom was named in the second *Democrat and Chronicle* obituary of October 7, 1943. Dett was buried in his family's plot in Fairview Cemetery, Niagara Falls, Ontario.

Memorial services for Dett included those in Battle Creek and at Bennett College. Oberlin associate Nathaniel Gatlin's eulogy at the Bennett memorial service follows:

> While studying at Oberlin I learned a great deal about Dr. Dett and the esteem in which he was held by college people and people of the village. I was privileged to direct the choir in the church in Oberlin in which Dr. Dett served as choir director. Several of his choir members were in the choir when I accepted the role of director. Through them and others in the village, I got a rather intimate insight into a great man. I never really thought of meeting him and to think of teaching with him never occurred to me.
>
> In June 1938 at his class reunion and my graduation I met Dr. Dett. Somebody had evidently pointed me out to him because after a concert during commencement week as the orchestra was filing by he called to me and introduced himself. After an interview the following day it was indeed an inspiration to look forward to working with him.
>
> To have worked with a man who had achieved international fame as a creator; to have listened in many meetings on the campus to a man who had very definite conviction; to have known a man who worked tirelessly day and night to achieve a purpose thereby destroying any illusion that success is a miracle; to have taught with a very experienced and successful teacher who was forever on the side of the student; and to have conversed with a man who loved God's word and who knew the Bible very well from Genesis to Revelation and had it always at the heart of his creations, are indeed experiences that will live.
>
> I believe that the faculty members who worked with Dr. Dett would agree that he had a superb sense of humor. When in his company there was seldom a dull moment. He nearly always had one laughing about something. In faculty meetings and other meetings he often turned a too serious thought into a laugh. He kept things rather balanced with his sense of humor, whether at choir rehearsals or in meetings. He taught many

important principles of singing to the choir through humor and fun.

The faculty too remembers Dr. Dett as an humble man and surely that trait bespeaks his greatness. One could always sense in his music and in his life that he recognized and was inspired by the integrity of the common, simple living, genuine man of the street and country side. In spite of his fame and achievements he never got beyond the reach nor did he ever indicate a desire to get beyond the reach of those he worked with. He was easy to talk to and always willing to talk to anybody. I have never known him to pass anyone and consciously not speak. He participated in local progressive clubs and civic organizations and he was a watch-care member of the Providence Baptist Church of this city. He lived what he wants his music to express and that is "the kinship of humanity."

Those of us who knew the great man could not help but observe his love of nature. He liked Emerson's idea of nature that nature is the externalization of the soul of God. It was amazing to note his knowledge of plants, trees, birds and animals. One time I remember him saying that nothing spoke as simply, as clearly, as briefly and as profoundly as did nature and that an artist tries to achieve the knack of speaking like nature. He referred to Beethoven as having approached it in the first movement of his Fifth Symphony where he used four notes as the basis of an immortal composition. He referred to Christ as having achieved it in his parables. One never left after having heard his views about nature without a quickened awareness of the great lessons that nature teaches and a deeper respect and admiration for a man who was so profoundly close to nature and the wisdom that is expressed.

As we worked with Dr. Dett we were aware of the fact that he was more than a musician; he was an integrated personality, he was a well-rounded individual with an active interest that touched almost everything. There was hardly a course offered that he didn't have above average knowledge of its contents. He was by no means narrow in his interests and knowledge. I believe that if the faculty was asked to list the fields in which Dr. Dett was successful it would run like this: lecturer, pianist, choral director, critic, educator, writer, composer, philosopher, and friend.

Finally we shall remember Dr. Dett for having helped us realize the meaning of these lines: "I know no brothers, yet all men are my brothers; I am the father of the best that is in them, and they are the fathers of the best that is in me; I am of them, and they are of me; for I am the instrument of God. I AM MUSIC.[83]

A later service, described in one obituary as "simple and impressive . . . in keeping with the dignity of the life he [Dett] led," was held in Niagara Falls, New York. As a well known musician his death was mourned by friends, students, and other professional musicians. Obituaries were carried in many leading newspapers and journals, such as the *New York Times, Chicago Defender, Niagara Falls Gazette, Battle Creek Enquirer and News, Rochester Democrat and Chronicle, Atlanta World, Musical Courier, Musical America, Journal of Negro History,* and *The Etude.* One obituary (paper unnamed), dated October 7, 1943, found in the Dett Collection, NFNYPL spoke of him as "a gentleman in the highest sense of the word. A man of vision and achievement, Nate Dett . . . will ever be counted among Niagara's most distinguished citizens."[84]

Chapter VI

Dett's Professors, Students, and Other Associates

The influence of Dett's mother upon him is inestimable. It is evident that he inherited from her much of his musical talent, a love for nature, art, and literature, and that she gave him moral and spiritual support and a solid sense of values. As a maturing pianist Dett also owed much to Oliver Halstead, his teacher at the Halstead Conservatory, who took a genuine interest in him and made him realize the importance of serious study. George Foster Peabody's concern for and assistance in Dett's pursuits has been discussed in preceding chapters.

The Oberlin Professors (1903-1908)[1]

Dett was fortunate to have had a group of Oberlin's finest professors at the Conservatory from 1903 through 1908. A retrospective overview indicates that teacher quality peaked during these years just after the turn of the century. Howard Handel Carter, George Carl Hastings, Arthur Heacox, Friedrich Lehmann, George Whitefield Andrews, John R. Frampton, and William J. Horner were Oberlin Conservatory graduates, and Edward Dickinson was a graduate of the New England Conservatory. Of these Carter, Hastings, Heacox, Lehmann, and Andrews had studied at the Leipzig Conservatory. Horner, Dickinson, and Frampton had worked in Berlin. Many of their students went from Oberlin to teach at other leading schools of music and some were hired by Oberlin.

Carter (1855-1930), Dett's first piano teacher at Oberlin, was also an organist. While in Leipzig he won a handsome prize for his performance of Schumann's *Concerto in a minor* at a gala concert honoring the King of Saxony. With the exception of two short leaves of absence to again study abroad, Carter taught at Oberlin from 1881 until his retirement as Professor Emeritus in 1923. In 1915 Oberlin awarded him an honorary Master of Arts degree. He was a modest and unassuming person, thinking of himself as merely trying to do his best. His love for music and teaching was said to be "little short of a passionate devotion." He was a nature lover, a bird watcher, and one of Oberlin's more hospitable professors. He was a church organist and also accompanist for the Musical Union.

During Carter's absence from Oberlin Dett was entrusted to George Carl Hastings (1877-1925). After graduating from Oberlin in 1900 Hastings taught there three years before going to Leipzig for further study, returning to Oberlin in 1906 and marrying another piano teacher, Miss Ada Morris. Hastings was a poised gentleman whose playing of Tschaikovsky's piano concerto was called "masterly." His standards of perfection were high for he considered music the most beautiful and perfect of all the arts. He not only imparted musicianship to his students but inspired their aesthetic senses as well.

* * *

Dett studied theory with Arthur Edward Heacox (b. ca. 1871, d. 1952), who also taught counterpoint, and with Friedrich Lehmann (1866-1950). Heacox remained at Oberlin for forty-two years after accepting his position in 1893, with time off only for study abroad. He was a meticulous organizer of presentation material, a sincere friend and counsellor to his students, and his teaching was so effective that he was asked by Oberlin's president to remain on the faculty three years beyond normal tenure. Heacox's special interest was polyphonic structure, though he emphasized keyboard harmony as an adjunct to theory. His publications include *Projects in Orchestration* and *Studies in Keyboard Harmony*. Impatient with mediocrity, he gave every consideration to hard working students.

Before joining the Oberlin faculty in 1902 Lehmann had been Director of Gates Conservatory in Neligh, Nebraska. Besides study in Leipzig and Berlin (in 1912-1913 with William Klatte), he had classes at the Royal Academy and the London Academy of Music in 1924. Lehmann's publications include *Lessons in Harmony, Harmonic Analysis, Simple Counterpoint, Harmonization at the Piano*, and *Analysis of Form in Music*.[2]

* * *

The most colorful of Dett's Oberlin professors was William Jasper Horner (1871-1960) with whom he studied singing. Horner's forty years of service began when he was at Oberlin as an undergraduate in 1896, and ended in 1937 with a full professorship, allowing him to teach harmony, ear training, and public school music in addition to singing. Toward the last of his long life his eyesight and hearing were impaired, though in his prime he was said to have had great vitality and power. General Faculty Minutes from Oberlin, January 17, 1961, recalled that Horner "carried himself like a soldier and his voice had the ring of authority. His teaching was energetic, tireless, and memorable."[3]

Horner was the first of the Oberlin faculty to sing a recital from memory. He and his wife, a pianist and teacher of French, worked closely together as a performing duo, giving private recitals in their home as well as those for the public and the Musical Union. Through Mrs. Horner's influence and guidance Horner realized the importance of the emotional content of song literature, and "with such an attitude he justified the recognition of the performing arts as a legitimate phase of collegiate study." Socially he was a charmer and among his many talents was figure skating. He was thought of as a "courtly gentleman" by his students.

* * *

A 1923 vita of John R. Frampton, available through Oberlin College Archives, does not give his birth date, but indicates that he was a student at Illinois College in Jacksonville from 1897 to 1900. He taught organ on a substitute basis at Oberlin between 1906 and 1908. Shortly before this he was working toward an A. M. degree partly through correspondence with Benjamin Cutter, head of the theory department at the New England Conservatory of Music in Boston. Frampton had obtained a Bachelor of Music degree from Oberlin in 1904, and then taught organ and theory two years at Grinnell College in Iowa. During 1912 to 1913 he studied in Berlin with Josef Lhevinne and Georg Bertram. From Oberlin he went in 1908 to Iowa State Teachers

College in Cedar Falls, where he remained as professor of organ and piano until 1923.

***

Edward Dickinson (1853-1946), who taught Dett music history mingled with the philosophy of music, was also an organist. His first serious study was at the New England Conservatory, and though he was not a Leipzig disciple, he did study further with Eugene Thayer in Boston and with Karl Klindworth and Friedrich Wilhelm Langhans before coming to Oberlin in 1893. Too, he had been an organist in Springfield, Massachusetts, and Director of Music at Elmira College in New York state previous to taking the Oberlin position which he held until 1922. In 1922 Dickinson received the degree of Litt. D. from Oberlin. He authored *Music in the History of the Western Church* (1902), *The Study of the History of Music* (1905), *The Education of the Music Lover* (1911), *Music and the Higher Education* (1915), and *The Spirit of Music of Music* (1925).[4]

* * *

By his own admission Dett's most cherished professor at Oberlin was George Whitefield Andrews, another of his organ teachers who also taught composition. Andrews (1861-1932), mentioned in Chapter I, was a mentor loved and respected by students and colleagues alike. (After Andrews' demise Dett dedicated his choral piece "Go Not Far From Me, O God" to him.) Andrews graduated from Oberlin in 1879, studied in Leipzig, Berlin, and later with Vincent d'Indy and Alexandre Guilmant in Paris. From 1879-1886 he was church organist in Meadville, Pennsylvania; in Toledo, Ohio; and at Oberlin he served as organist for the Musical Union.

Andrews, a charter member of the American Guild of Organists (AGO), was for many years dean of its Northern Ohio chapter. In 1903 Oberlin awarded him an honorary Doctor of Music degree. He toured the United States as a concert organist, particularly in demand for performances at expositions. His published compositions include several pieces for organ and piano, a piano trio, religious songs for baritone, and a Processional and Recessional for choir.[5]

Mme Azalia Hackley

Dett first became professionally associated with Mme Hackley in 1908 when he played at one of her festivals in Philadelphia. Mme Hackley was born Emma Azalia Smith in 1867 in Murfreesboro, Tennessee, and at the age of three moved with her family to Detroit. Her first piano teacher was her mother, who saw that she also had violin and voice lessons. While still a teenager Azalia played piano in Detroit dance orchestras, and as a young member of the Detroit Musical Society she had opportunity to perform vocally. She married in 1894, settled in Denver, attended the university there, and in 1900 received a Bachelor of Music degree. After a year of conducting community and church choral groups she debuted as a singer in Denver (1901), then toured the mid-West as a recitalist.

For the next few years, having moved to Philadelphia, she was music director at the Episcopal Church of the Crucifixion, and in 1904 she organized a 100-voice People's Chorus in that city; then, assisted by some of her students, debuted there as a soloist in 1905. The following year was spent studying with Jean de Reszke in Paris. After another big recital in Philadelphia Hackley determined to promote aspiring black musicians, and for some months neglected her own career in their behalf. She established a scholarship for worthy musicians to study abroad, among them Carl Diton and Clarence Cameron White. She was particularly helpful in advancing the careers of Dett, singers Burleigh, Cleota Collins, and Daisy Tapley, as well as violinists Kemper Harreld and Harrison Emmanuel.

After a last public recital in Chicago in 1910 Hackley toured as a lecturer and workshop presenter, continuing to organize large choirs for special occasions and to raise funds for the Hackley Vocal Normal Institute which she established in Chicago in 1912. Through this extensive touring in behalf of Negro musicians and Negro music she became known as "Our Vocal Teacher." By 1920 signs of physical exhaustion were evident. Mme Hackley suffered a fatal collapse and died in 1922.[6]

Mme Hackley, courtesy Hackley Collection,
Detroit Public Library.

Madame E. Azalia Hackley.
Photo from an original sketch by Carl Owens
in the Hackley Collection, Detroit Public Library.

Musical Courier gave Hackley's work some coverage in 1915 in an item which also explained her basic philosophy of music:

> She believes that the proper study of voice culture will help children spiritually, morally and physically, through control of the will power, the emotions and the muscles; that this study will also cause a general knowledge of other thoughtful refining studies. She believes that because the Negro is vocally gifted that much of the time spent upon technical training could be spent in directing him toward the appreciation of the beautiful in nature, art, poetry, literature and the study of psychology and kindred subjects which would cultivate his observation, thought, taste, and will power.[7]

Oberlin Revisited, Summer of 1913

One reference claimed that Dett was the eternal student because he knew his own inadequacies in the technical intricacies of music. If this is true or not true such self honesty should have been commended, for with periodic renewal Dett's mind and teaching productivity never became stagnant. Before taking a position at Hampton Institute, he returned to Oberlin in the summer of 1913.

Among his professors there was the prestigious and professionally active Karl Gehrkens, with whom he studied public school music. Gehrkens (1882-1975) began teaching at Oberlin just after graduation from the Conservatory in 1905, a position he held until 1942. Besides his teaching duties he edited *School Music* (1925-1934), co-edited with Walter Damrosch and George Gartlan the *Universal Music Series* (1923-1936, teachers' manuals for grade and high schools), and for a time was Supervisor of Music in the Oberlin public schools.

Gehrkens expanded the public school music program at Oberlin Conservatory from its initial six months' duration to a four-year program, culminating in the degree of Bachelor of Public School Music, later Bachelor of Music Education. Some 300 students were enrolled for this course of study when Gehrkens

retired. His greatest contribution was the teaching of teachers
through a well-balanced curriculum of his own formula. After
his retirement he continued to write for journals.

As a studious and well-rounded high schooler Gehrkens was
valedictorian of his senior class. Claiming he was a self-taught
pianist, with a little help from his sister, he recalled the
exciting day that his father went to Cleveland by boat to buy a
piano for the family parlor. He began playing for church at age
twelve.

Gehrkens' first book, *Music Notation and Terminology* (1914),
was the outgrowth of his Master's thesis for Oberlin
Conservatory. Other of his publications were *On Conducting* and
Twenty Lessons in Conducting. He edited the Music Teachers
National Association *Volume of Proceedings* in addition to the
second edition (1934) of *Webster's New International Dictionary*.
His insistence on including music and art in the public school
curriculum gained wide favor. His slogan "Music for every child,
every child for music" was adopted by the Music Educators
National Conference in 1923 when he was its president. In 1939
he received honorary Doctor of Music degrees from Capital
University and Illinois Wesleyan University. Other than music
he was interested in Man's relation to the universe. Despite ill
health which prompted his retirement from Oberlin he lived to
be ninety-two.[8]

Columbia University, Chicago and Evanston
Summer of 1915

Dett was fortunate to study two years later with another fine
music educator, Peter Dykema, who was visiting professor at
Columbia University for the summer of 1915. At the time
Dykema (1873-1951) was chairman of public school music at the
University of Wisconsin where he stayed until 1924, then held a
teaching position at Teachers College, Columbia University for
the next sixteen years.

Like Gehrkens, Dykema was quite active in professional
music organizations, holding numerous offices in them and serving
in an advisory capacity. His early teaching experience was

gained in Illinois and Indiana high schools. He studied at the Institute of Musical Art (now Juilliard) and with Edgar Stillman Kelley in Berlin before taking the Wisconsin position. He was the first editor of the *Music Supervisors Journal* (1914-1921). He is best known for the *Twice 55 Community Song Book* (1919-1927), but also authored numerous articles, a standardized test in music (with Jacob Kwalwasser), and several series of instruction books for band, orchestra, and classroom music. Some of his compositions are "Robin Hood and a Dale" (1936), "The Arrow and the Song" (1940), and "The Three Bears and Goldilocks" (1941).

Dykema was in demand as a guest lecturer on the college and university circuit. In 1948 Lebanon Valley College in Annville, Pennsylvania, awarded him an honorary Doctor of Music degree. As an authority on community music Dykema thought on a grand scale, often combining music and dramatics in his productions. During World War I he served as song leader and Supervisor of Music for the Commission on Training Camp Activities of the War Department.

The writer of a tribute published in *Music Educators Journal* shortly after Dykema's death said:

> Peter would literally rather sing than eat. His success as a leader of community singing was based on his own love for group musical expression. Any person who sat and watched him conduct a large chorus could not fail to note that facial expression which produced an almost hypnotic influence on performers. Put Peter in front of any group, of any age, and it responded.[9]

Dykema, the father of five, loved working with children. The tribute continued:

> It was his love for children, this pleasure in making music with and for them, that kept Peter Dykema young. . . . He was just Peter, lovable, affable, but always that stern sense of honesty and personal integrity that characterized his Dutch ancestors. . . . He never retired in the sense of quitting work. He merely changed his

sphere of action.

[His career] should be a challenge to any young
teacher, for he brought happiness and spiritual uplift to
thousands. People loved him because he gave them
untiring devotion, inspiring leadership, uncompromising
fidelity to truth and beauty.

* * *

Arthur Olaf Andersen (1880-1958), instructor in harmony,
counterpoint and composition, taught at the American
Conservatory in Chicago from 1908 until 1933, and then moved to
Chicago Musical College. His family was "intimately
associated with art," and his musical education was gained both
in America and abroad. His specialty was composition, which
he studied extensively with Vincent d'Indy, George Guirot, and
Alexandre Guilmant in Paris, and with Giovanni Sgambati in
Rome. Andersen had been active professionally in Berlin before
coming to Chicago where he met with immediate and pronounced
success, both as a composer and teacher.

Andersen's students were also successful with their
compositions, several of which, including Dett's "Listen to the
Lambs," were selected for performance at a series of orchestral
concerts in Chicago devoted to American works. Andersen's own
compositions include a ballet, a symphony, *Arizona Sketches* (for
orchestra), and various chamber works.[10]

* * *

Though Dett did not enroll for a class with Peter Christian
Lutkin at Northwestern University in Evanston, Illinois, he did
profit from time spent in professional conversations with him.
Lutkin (1858-1931), a native of Wisconsin, was brought up in
Chicago, where from 1868 he was solo alto in the boy choir of the
Protestant Episcopal Cathedral. By the age of fourteen he was a
fairly decent self-trained organist, but then began lessons with
Mrs. R. Watson and Clarence Eddy.

From 1879 to 1881 Lutkin taught piano at Northwestern
University. For the next three years he worked in Berlin with

pianist Oskar Raif, theorist Woldemar Bargiel, and organist Carl August Haupt, won a scholarship to the Royal Academy, studied piano briefly in Vienna, and lastly composition and piano with Moritz Moszkowski in Paris. After returning to Chicago he was church organist at both St. Clement and St. James. From 1888 to 1892 he taught theory at the American Conservatory.

Meanwhile he was developing ideas for a School of Music at Northwestern, where he became dean in 1895. Lutkin was another of Dett's associates who co-founded the AGO in 1896. In 1900 he received a Doctorate of Music degree from Syracuse University. As a choral conductor his singing groups were instrumental in establishing the Chicago North Shore Festivals in 1908. His lectures from 1908 at the Western Theological Seminary in Chicago were published as *Music in the Church* in 1910. From 1911 to 1920 Lutkin was president of the Music Teachers National Association. Between 1905 and 1918 he was an editor for both the Methodist and Episcopal Hymnals.

Listed among Lutkin's compositions and settings are several Te Deums, Magnificats (some of them *a cappella*), a Jubilate, Psalm 51 (for soli, chorus, and organ), Psalm 137 (*a cappella*), many anthems, solo songs and part-songs, two sacred trios for children, "Romance" for cello and string quartet (or violin and orchestra), nine organ preludes based on hymn tunes, and *Processional March* for organ.[11]

The Incomparable Percy Grainger

During the summer of 1915 in Chicago Dett met pianist Percy Grainger for the first time. Their continued professional friendship and Grainger's high regard for Dett's music has been well documented in personal correspondence and news items. Dett, outwardly conservative in manner and philosophy, seemed a total contrast in personality to Grainger, whose eccentric behavior and professional flair served him well.

Grainger was born in 1882 in Brighton, near Melbourne, Australia, a land he continued to love throughout his life, evidenced by his monetary contributions to the Melbourne and Adelaide Symphony Orchestras, his establishing of the Grainger Museum at the University of Melbourne for his personal papers and documents, and periodic tours to Australia as a concert pianist.

Grainger's psyche, shaped by a bizarre unbringing, was enough to challenge the most astute psychoanalyst. The marriage of his parents, John and Rosa (later Rose), was a stormy one. John Grainger was given to drink, women, tantrums, lying, and boasting, and as a result of his debauchery contracted syphilis, an incurable scourge soon transmitted to Rose. The love that she could not feel for her husband was lavished unhealthily, dotingly upon Percy. She controlled his every thought, his every breath. He was rarely out of her sight, except to pursue his professional activities. After the parents separated, when Percy was about eight, Rose was responsible for his support. She taught piano students, Percy among them. He later worked with Louis Pabst.

Percy was an angelic-looking child with blue eyes and blonde curls. When Rose noticed his precious tresses darkening she applied chemicals to lighten them, a practice Grainger continued even as a man. Her inherited obsession for everything Nordic became ingrained in her son, who was openly anti-Jewish. If he were anti-Negro, even emotionally if not intellectually, the prejudice obviously did not extend to Dett, Diton, and other Negro composers whose works he played. Through his continuing interest in international folk songs, a basis of communication with composers of all races was easily provided. He felt strongly that English and Negro folk songs bore many similarities.

Determined that he would be a performer, not a teacher, Rose moved with him to Germany in 1895, and saw that he worked with the best teachers available, among them James Kwast, and later, Ferruccio Busoni. Edvard Grieg, with whom he coached periodically, became his mentor and friend.

Given some of Grainger's unorthodox ideas on love, lust, flagellation, freedom, and happiness, it is amazing that this brilliant man emerged with even a modicum of sanity. Rose, devasted by moodiness and fits of depression as a result of syphilis, tested Grainger to the extreme, once pretending to be dead just to provoke a confession of his love. He was totally devoted to her, however, and since she dissuaded his association

Percy Grainger, ca. 1925. © 1974 by
The Instrumentalist Co.   Reprinted by permission.

with attractive females, marriage seemed out of the question.[12]

When Grainger and Rose came to America during the 1914-1915 concert season, he was an immediate success. He became an American citizen while serving in the US Army from 1916 to 1918, playing many a concert in khaki uniform. Out of uniform his dress and behavior did not go unnoticed by the critics, some of whom considered them an addition to his charm. Harold Schonberg wrote of him:

> Grainger was . . . a gangling figure with an aquiline face and a formidable mop of hair; a vegetarian; a health faddist, a man who, likely as not, would hike from concert to concert with a knapsack on his back; and a whale of a pianist. . . . He was one of the keyboard originals—a pianist who forged his own style and expressed it with amazing skill, personality and vigor, a healthy, forthright musical mind whose interpretations never sounded forced and who brought a bracing, breezy and quite wonderful out-of-doors quality to the continuity of piano playing.[13]

Grainger frequently arrived early at performance halls to practice for the evening concert, sometimes having to be waked by the attendants who found him napping under the piano. One amusing story from 1930 said that on returning from an out-of-town trip to his home in White Plains, New York, he left his baggage at the train station. Next day he pushed a wheelbarrow the ten blocks to the station, loaded in the baggage, and pushed it back home.[14]

Grainger's article titled "Let Us Sit in Wait No Longer for the Advent of Great American Composers: They Are With Us Already" appeared in a late 1919 issue of *Quarter Notes*, the bulletin of the Brooklyn Music School Settlement. In it he mentioned Dett's "Chariot Jubilee" and "Music in the Mine." On an autographed copy to Dett of the essay, found in the Mesiah Papers and Documents, Grainger wrote: "Most cordial greetings from Percy Grainger, Dec. 1919."

That same month Olin Downes reviewed a Grainger concert for the *Boston Post* (December 12, 1919), calling Dett's "Juba" the "hit of the list played by Grainger." A month earlier (November 1919) *The Southern Workman* had mentioned that some of Dett's compositions were listed in the curriculum of the Chicago Musical College the past summer and were taught and played by Grainger, who intended to play Dett compositions publicly that year. "Juba" proved to be one of his favorite encores. After one New York concert a critic wrote that it was irresistible and the audience insisted on a repetition: "There is a lively, almost frenzied lilt in its rhythm which is most fetching. It revealed Grainger's Griegian art of lifting popular Negro tunes to a high art level without sacrificing their wild abandon."[15]

Though Grainger was admittedly fond of Dett's music, he could not possibly include it on every concert, but often played the "In the Bottoms" suite and used "Juba Dance" as an encore. In the years before 1920 he also had an audience for contemporary American composers Carl Diton and John Alden Carpenter, in addition to Cyril Scott, Claude Debussy, and Frederick Delius, whose works were beginning to be performed in America.

The year 1920 was a popular one for "Juba," with mention of a January 3 concert in the *New York Herald*, January 4; the *New York Times*, January 5; the *New York Citizen*, February 10; and the *San Antonio* (Texas) *Express*, March 10. Other "Juba" performances that year (newspaper unnamed) were on January 8 at the Milliken Conservatory of Music in Decatur, Illinois; January 13 in Lawrence, Kansas; January 18 in Montclair, New Jersey; and in Havana, Cuba, the following December 19. The January 3 concert in Aeolian Hall marked Grainger's first performance of "Juba" in New York City. His program notes read:

> "Juba" is the stamping on the ground with the foot and following it with two staccato pats of the hands. R. Nathaniel Dett is one of the most gifted of contemporary composers, as well as an ardent student and arranger of Negro folk music.[16]

In April of 1922, after a few months of torturous physical and mental illness, Rose Grainger committed suicide by jumping from a window of her apartment. Ironically, some Jewish neighbors provided Grainger with more comfort and sympathy than anyone else. In reply to Dett's own expression of sympathy Grainger sent him a formal printed card edged in black, which read:

Mr. Percy Grainger
thanks you from his heart
for your deeply valued tribute to his beloved mother
and for your kindly sympathy for him
in his tragic loss.

Then by hand Grainger wrote: "Dear Friend heartfelt thanks for your loved sympathy. Your new suite must have been the last or almost the last music she heard from me." He signed it "Lovingly, Percy."[17]

In 1924 Grainger's playing of "Juba" was mentioned in the *Musical Leader* (Chicago) on February 14, at the Biltmore Morning Musicale. On February 25 at the Brooklyn Academy of Music "Juba," depicting "the staccato hop of the Southern Negro . . . [was] one of his best numbers," according to a reviewer for the *Brooklyn Citizen*, February 26, 1924.

On May 3, 1925, the second of Grainger's "Room Music" concerts took place in the Little Theater in New York City. As a conductor and amateur impresario, the programs he arranged for these events were almost as multi-faceted as his own personality. For this particular one Dett conducted Grainger's adaptation for four woodwinds of "Memories of New Mexico" by Natalie Curtis-Burlin, and his own *Negro Folk- Song Derivatives*, sung by the Hampton Choir. Other composers represented that evening were Edvard Grieg, Paul Hindemith, and Franz Schreker.[18]

Fifty musicians participated in the concert, which included encores of Dett's pieces, "simply sung by thirteen young women and fifteen khaki-clad men [Hampton Choir]," in sharp contrast to the chamber works performed by players from the New York Philharmonic Orchestra.[19] Grainger wrote of Dett in the program notes:

R. Nathaniel Dett, in his choral writing, combines cosmopolitan culture and individualistic creative characteristics with a rich heritage of Negro vocal

GRAINGER

— PRESENTS —

TWO SUNDAY EVENINGS
of
ROOM-MUSIC
The LITTLE THEATRE
238 WEST 44th STREET, NEW YORK CITY

April 26th, 1925	May 3rd, 1925 at 8.15 P. M.
at 8.15 P. M.	Works by
All-Grainger	Franz Schreker, R. Nathaniel
Program	Dett, Natalie Curtis,
	Grieg, Paul Hindemith.

PERFORMERS

Conductors: **R. Nathaniel Dett, Frank Kasschau, Percy Grainger**
Baritone: **Erik Bye**
Pianists: **Ernest Hutcheson, Ralph Leopold, Percy Grainger**
Guitarists: **Ralph Leopold, Percy Grainger**

Kasschau's Solo Choir (*Conductor:* **Frank Kasschau**)

SOPRANOS	CONTRALTOS	
C. Andrews	Florence Frommek	
G. Ross	Marion Adam	

TENORS	BARITONES	BASES
Samuel Craig	Elmer Ross	John B. Hamilton
George E. Bennett	Wallace Cannon	Charles Southwick

HAMPTON INSTITUTE CHOIR, About 25 voices
(**Conductor: R. NATHANIEL DETT**)
THIRTY MEMBERS of the NEW YORK PHILHARMONIC ORCHESTRA
(**Orchestra Personnel Manager: Maurice van Praag**)

Piccolo, flute, sopranino sarrusophone, 2 oboes, English horn, heckelphone, 2 bassoons, double-bassoon, clarinet, soprano saxophone, alto saxophone, 2 horns, trumpet, trombone, euphonium, kettle-drums, xylophone, bells, percussion, harmonium, celesta, piano, harp, 4 violins, 2 violas, 3 cellos, 2 basses.

Subscription Tickets $5.50	Single Tickets $3.30

On Sale at Little Theatre Box Office After April 12th
Mail Orders to:—Antonia Sawyer, Inc., Box 446 White Plains, New York.
Owing to the limited capacity of theatre orders will be filled in priority received
NO COURTESY LIST

MGT. ANTONIA SAWYER, Inc.
White Plains, New York.

Flyer courtesy of Grainger Museum, Melbourne, Australia.

traditions. There is in his treatment of blended human voices . . . that innate sonority and vocal naturalness that seems to result only from accumulated long experience of untrained improvised polyphonic singing, such as that of Southern Negroes, South Sea Polynesians and Russian peasants. These things are branches of the very tree of natural communal song.[20]

Despite Rose's feelings toward teaching as a profession for Grainger he had begun seasonal teaching at the Summer Master School of the Chicago Musical College by 1919, continuing until 1928. He missed his mother after her death, of course, but by 1928 felt free to marry artist Ella Strom whom he had met aboard ship en route to Australia. The perfect Nordic type and some years his junior, Ella curiously enough reminded him of his mother. He adored her, and the affection seemed mutual, though Ella was not unaware of his strange tastes and attitudes concerning the intimacies of personal relationships.

Their wedding in the Hollywood Bowl in August of 1928 was one of Grainger's more unique performances. Before an audience of 22,000 Grainger conducted the Los Angeles Philharmonic in "To a Nordic Princess," his tribute to Ella. The wedding ceremony was read by Swedish Lutheran Reverend J. Herman Olsson, while a choir chanted in the background.[21]

Succeeding Albert Stoessel, in 1932 Grainger was appointed department head of the College of Fine Arts, New York University, for one year. He continued to concertize, lecture, record, compose, and write essays concerning the wealth to be found in folk music. Among his compositions are numerous transcriptions of folk songs.

Toward the last of his life this "much-needed musical Puck"[22] was uncomfortably aware of his physical and mental disorientation from terminal stomach cancer. His last words to Ella as she sat by his sick bed were, "You're the only one I really like."[23] The incomparable Percy Grainger died in 1961 in White Plains, New York, and was buried in his beloved Australia.

* * *

The following correspondence between Dett and Grainger is used with permission of the Grainger Museum in Melbourne, Australia.

A one-cent postcard from Dett in Chicago to Grainger in New York City dated September 15, 1915, read:

My dear friend:
I was delighted to hear from you. Will write you in a day or so. Am working at the strings in my instrumentation. I have a splendid teacher who studied many years in Paris. Thanks for what you say of my work. It is only slight as yet. Your playing and your compositions will be an everlasting inspiration to me. Regards to your mother. Dett

Another letter dated September 23, 1915, followed from Dett, still in Chicago:

My dear friend:
I cannot tell you how glad I was and am to receive and have your photo, of how proud I am of it, and with what pleasure I have shown it to my friends and told them of you and your wonderful playing and compositions. I am glad that it is such an excellent likeness for it seems to intensify the already vivid recollection I have of our pleasant meetings.

How is your mother? Please remember me most kindly to her.

My work is going very well. I have made a violin and piano arrangement of "Listen to the Lambs"—last week I wrote a solo for violin with piano.

Yesterday I took in a slow movement for string quartet based on an old Negro folk song. My teacher was much pleased and advised my using it as the middle movement of a work for strings.

In the next three or four days which are left me here I want to finish up two art songs and do something more on my sonata. I was in to see Mr. Summy my publisher yesterday and asked him to send you a copy of the

"Magnolia Suite." He said that all that was needed now was for some great artist to play some of the numbers. Some of our best artists had wanted to, he told me, but were afraid to because the pieces have Negro titles. I shall be leaving very soon for Hampton. I would be very glad to hear from you if you would write me here.

I shall never be able to express my gratitude for the great inspiration you have been to me, and I am most happy to inscribe myself

Your friend

R. Nathaniel Dett

From Hampton, February 25, 1916, Dett wrote:

To Mr. Percy Grainger

The best friend that ever was—Yes, I got yours from Hamilton and one also from Miss Bull who lives in Hamilton now, an English lady who was my Sunday School teacher when I wore dresses—such was the effect of the concert.

How can I thank you; if you were here I should give you a real bear hug. That is the way we used to do in college when words failed expression. I am crazy to study with you, because of the inspiration your personality would be to me. I am going to ask the school for a year off. If I get it what shall I do, where will you be?

I have been thinking of publishing my anthems *myself* as Schirmer rather turned up his nose at the idea of Negro things which were *serious* last summer. Some of their men even disputed whether my themes were Negro—just think of it!

Do you think it would be a good venture to do one's own publishing. It does not seem to be so very expensive. Of course there is considerbale fuss and bother but the returns ought to make it worthwhile. I should be delighted to dedicate something to Mr. [Bruce] Carey in appreciation of his work and also as a fellow countryman. I should like to dedicate something to you too. *You* come *first* remember! Maybe when I get my dances done, I am writing six for the piano, but I never have time to think or work at them long and ideas come and go sometimes before they are completed. You see I am writing you *quick*.

I wish I might hear you play again. How much good that evening did me. I've talked and talked about it, until our people here think that you are the only artist in the world.

How is your mother. My kindest regards to her, and to yourself many, many! With every good wish for you in every way. I am sincerely and gratefully

Yours

R. Nathaniel Dett

On July 26, 1916 Dett wrote from Hampton:

My dear, dear friend

Just the sight of your handwriting to say nothing of the fine letter itself was inspiration for me. How nice of you to want to help one of so little consequence. It is further proof of your true greatness. I went right to work and have worked every day. I hope to have the little tune finished very soon. Also some others. I want to write some character dances for piano and have already sketched out some. I have to go at it with a hurry because I have only the summer to do things of this sort. The work of the school grows daily and as yet I have no additional help. My love to your mother. She is so sweet. No wonder she has such a son. I want to see you, *badly*. I have talked Grainger, Grainger, and now I have to tell my students that of course there are some other pianists for fear they will get the impression that there is only one pianist in the world. They were delighted with your picture which I passed around in my classes. The girls tried to pull your hair. I wish I had gotten your letter a few days earlier. I had just promied Dr. Phenix to stay here this summer when it came. Obviously I should have come straight to New York. I must remain on duty through August. But I can make short trips. So expect to see me.

With kindest of kind regards to both your mother and
yourself I am

Faithfully yours,

R. Nathaniel Dett

A letter written approximately three years later, August 6,
1919, indicated that Dett still hoped to study with Grainger.

My dear dear friend

I hardly know how to thank you for your generosity to
me who am so unworthy. What you have accomplished
in my behalf is wonderful and must bear splendid results.
I glory in the splendid courage (true British) which you
have shown in your convictions. Other great artists have
wanted to play numbers from this and from the
["]Magnolia Suite["] but were *afraid to* because of the
racial character of the music and titles. You see how this
great liberty loving nation is yet slave to the merest show
of conventionalities. America needs most badly such ones
as you who *dare to be*! Thank God for you!

I have good and bad news. Good that Mr. Peabody is
arranging that I have a year off for study. Harvard
University is the place designated and I mean to dig in
and get all I can, though a year is short. There is the
merest possibility that I shall be allowed some time
after returning from Boston for research work among my
own people in the South.

Bad news is that being away from Hampton I won't be
able to have you here for a recital, a thing that I had my
heart set upon.

I enclose you my "The Chariot Jubilee." Do let me
know what you think of it. The orchestra parts are not
yet done. I intend doing them this winter (when I find out
how!) Be candid in your criticisms this is my first
cantata in indigenous ideas and of course it must have its
defects.

Did you see my article in Musical America May 31st
on Mrs. Burlin of course I had to bring you in because of the
great contribution you have made to the world of

developed folk music.

I know your class must have been a great, great success. Had it not have been for having to teach summer school here I had intended to try for it. I used to be a good pianist. I am wondering if I cannot "*come back?*"

Maybe I can be with you next summer. I hope so; at any rate I trust that sometime I can see you in New York and Boston while I am North. Kindest regards to your mother in which my family joins me.

Devotedly yours

R. Nathaniel Dett

Grainger's continued support and interest in Dett and his music was confirmed by his programs. Finally Dett was able to schedule Grainger for a concert on the Musical Art Society series at Hampton on January 18, 1924, which has been discussed in Chapter III.

Grainger's letter to Dett dated March 6, 1925, indicates that Dett had procrastinated in the final details for the coming Room Concert of May 3 in New York. Grainger was polite but seemed more than a little uneasy, perhaps annoyed, that final arrangements had not been completed. His lengthy typed letter reads in part:

Dear Nathaniel,

I am *deeply disappointed* to find in your letter of Feb 21 no *definite* answer to any of my questions. I do not know how many voices you want to bring, so cannot find out from the railroad what the transportation costs would be. You have not sent your items for the 2 groups to be sung by your choir, so I cannot make up my program. You now mention the possibility of your choir assisting at a Carnegie Hall concert for the School. Would that be before the concert . . . May 3 (my date has been definitely fixed for May 3 for some months)? Of course I realize that the school's needs must come first, but if you are to sing for me on May 3 I must stipulate that your choir does not appear in New York this season before that date. . . . [Else] it will be better to put off singing for me until a season when you

The Brooklyn Institute of Arts and Sciences

Monday Evening, Febryary 25, at 8:15 o'clock

1924

Department of Music

PIANO RECITAL

BY

PERCY
GRAINGER

PROGRAM

1. Symphonic Studies, Op. 13.............*Schumann*

2. (a) Prelude and Fugue, C sharp minor.................*Bach*
   (b) Sonata in G minor, Breitkopf & Haertel Edition,
       No. 34 ....*Scarlatti*
   (c) Sonata in G minor, Breitkopf & Haertel Edition,
       No. 35 ....*Scarlatti*
   (d) Hornpipe, from the "Water Music".............*Handel*
       (Arranged for Piano by Percy Grainger)

3. Ballade, Op. 24.......................................*Grieg*

4. (a) "On Hearing the First Cuckoo in Spring".........*Delius*
   (b) "Country Gardens," English Morris Dance..set by *Grainger*
   (c) "One More Day, My John"...............set by *Grainger*
       Based on a sailor's chanty (working song) sung to the
       following words:
              "One more day, my John
              One more day:
              Oh, rock and roll me over,
              One more day."
   (d) "Juba Dance" ....*R. Nathaniel Dett*
       "Juba" Dance is one of the five numbers from a Suite ("In the
       Bottoms") picturing scenes and moods peculiar to the negro life
       in the river bottoms of the South. "Juba" is the stamping on the
       ground with foot, and following it with two staccato pats of the
       hands.

Steinway Piano Used

Program courtesy the Grainger Museum,
Melbourne, Australia.

don't appear before my concert in New York.

I am sorry to have to send you an ultimatum, but, dear friend I cannot help myself. I approached you about this concert several months ago, and you do not give me the definite answers to my business questions that any manager engaging an artist would demand.

Grainger then specified and underlined his needs, giving Dett a deadline of March 16, and saying that he was enclosing a short form for estimating expenses, etc., in order to save Dett time. The letter continued:

My beloved mother & I have always been warmly & affectionately fond of you & your art. I have certainly played JUBA all I could, in Europe as well as U.S. & Canada & intend to make it as well known in Australia in 1926 & in Europe in 1927 as it is in America, if possible.

He wrote in the same letter about Dett's Canadian heritage, and that art should be "one of the meeting-places of all races, without racial, national or local prejudices, jealousies or smallnesses."

Do you know another composer who spends what I do on other composers' works, in time & work & money? I do not. I deserve & expect no CREDIT of this. I do it simply because I am an artist & and art is my life, &, since my mother's death, my one sustaining joy. But I do crave & expect COOPERATION from my fellow- composers where the presentation of their own works is concerned. . . . Dear Nathaniel, if you are harrassed with a few concerts, think of me with 100 concerts this season, trying to get ready big scores involving hundreds of hours of writing in the train, being jerked about all the while. After all, I AM A COMPOSER, & it would not be right for me to let too many other people's practical questions be saddled on me. At any rate, whether I am right or wrong, there is a limit to human powers. And I know that I can only give these concerts of modern music (other composers' & my own) if the composers involved are willing & able to send me their programs in time & answer my business questions in a business way. . . . Here am I wishing to present your more INTIMATE side at a chamber concert with a small choir in a really small hall, in the most serious & esthetic way, as due to your achievements as a leading world composer. All that impression would be destroyed if you appear in a big hall, probably with much the same works, as part of a school propaganda—not of an exclusively musical nature (the propaganda).

Dett definitely got Grainger's "message." In response his telegrams of March 11 and March 13 to Grainger should have put the distressed impresario somewhat at ease, but could not have secured final arrangements.

WHAT WE CAN DO IN WAY OF CHORUS DEPENDS ON WHAT YOU ARE WILLING TO PAY GIRLS VOICES MUCH LIGHTER THAN WOMENS THEREFORE LARGE NUMBER NEEDED FIFTEEN HUNDRED DOLLARS BRING REPRESENTATIVE ORGANIZATION PAYS ALL EXPENSES MAKING NO CHARGE FOR SERVICES PLEASE WIRE IF OK   R NATHANIEL DETT

At the bottom of the telegram, which Grainger evidently mailed back to Dett, Grainger wrote by hand: "Regret 1000 dollars utmost limit theatre very small sure comparatively small choir effective anxious receive letter love yr P.G.

Dett's telegram to Grainger of March 13 indicates that an agreement had been made.

WILL BRING AS MANY AS WE CAN AT PRICE QUOTED PERIOD THERE IS GREAT DIFFERENCE BETWEEN A PROFESSIONAL AND UNTRAINED VOICE ALSO CHORUS VOICES MUST SING TOGETHER MUCH OF THE NEGRO FOLK SONG EFFECTS DEPEND UPON NUMBERS PERIOD THERE IS LITERALLY NO COMPARISON BETWEEN A

PROFESSIONAL VIOLINIST WHO AFTER YEARS OF STUDY ACHIEVES PLAYING IN A SYMPHONY AND A COUNTRY GIRL OR BOY WHO NEVER HAVING HAD A LESSON HAD VOICE ENOUGH TO BE ONE OF THOSE WHO COMPOSE A SCHOOL CHOIR MY CHORUSES ARE DESIGNATED AS NEGRO FOLK SONG DERIVATIVES.

* * *

Grainger and Dett continued to keep in touch. Part of Dett's letter to Grainger, April 27, 1937, concerned Charlotte Dett's death that year, and Dett's declination to compose a band piece for Grainger's National High School Band Camp (mentioned in Chapter V, n 29). The remainder reads:

Dear Percy:
    Your letter occasioned me a real thrill! But I regret to have to state that I never received any of the other letters you refer to. I do not know what could have become of them, as I am well known in Rochester. Of course I should have enjoyed working with you, especially in a place like New York.
    . . . Mrs. Dett, Jr., is quite well and happy; she is still in Rochester. I have been here since February, visiting Director of Music. I came because I could earn more here than at the studio, and because I felt I was needed and appreciated.
    . . . I am to have a new suite published very soon; all of the numbers will reveal an advance in harmony I believe.
    Yes, my "Ordering of Moses" is done and published. It is to have its world premiere Cincinnati Festival Chorus, the Cincinnati Symphony, four soloists, Eugene Goossens conducting, at the Cincinnati Music Festival, May 4-8, 1937. I hope to be going out for the occasion.
    My work is over here about the fourth of June. I go to King's Mountain for a ten day religious conference; after that I am free;—I should love to see you in New York.

My very kindest regards to Mrs. Grainger; if I remember rightly she was at work upon some most unusual etchings, photographs of which I had seen.

With affectionate greetings, always,

Nathaniel

A telegram from Dett in Greensboro to Grainger dated May 25, 1937, indicates that he had received a recording from Grainger of "The Ordering of Moses," made from a broadcast. It read: "THANKS GREATLY PLEASE SEND RECORD HERE AT ONCE FOR COMMENCEMENT."

A letter from Dett to Grainger dated December 29, 1941, was mainly concerned with the "Tropic Winter" suite, a copy of which Dett had sent him.

My dear Percy:

Ever since we bumped into each other at CBS, New York, it has been on my mind to write you. . . . I do not need to tell you how happy I was to see you and regret that, owing to the circumstances, there was no opportunity for a visit.

I think I mentioned to you at that time my new suite, TROPIC WINTER, an autographed copy of which was mailed to you some time ago, but which you evidently did not receive.

I am rather proud of this suite, as I think it represents an advance in musical thought for me, and I never play it over that I do not think of you, especially when I come to the last movement. The object of this letter is to ask you if you can possibly spare the time to play this suite through and then, if you will, let me know how you like it. I am sure it is not necessary for me to reiterate how I esteem your criticism and advice.

With best wishes for happiness and health in the New Year to both you and Mrs. Grainger, I remain as always

Faithfully yours,

Nathaniel

Grainger's reply a few months later from "in the train," April 15, 1942, contains his frank and rather appalling opinion of music for the piano in general. After praising the "richness of texture, the personal and individual quality of the harmonies" in Dett's "Tropic Winter" suite, he said that no piano music was "real or alive" to him; that all of his own music for piano was either a transcription of someone else's piano piece, or a folk tune, or written originally for chorus, orchestra, or band. He continued, saying

> I not only loathe piano music but all the other compromise instruments that foreran the piano (lute, guitar, harpsichord, etc.), in which one player (for convenience as a conductor, or for accompaniment purposes) sums up the whole harmonic texture *that was conceived as polyphonic melody.* I cannot for the life of me see why that should be considered a *full artistic utterance,* when it is merely (as I see it) a most teasing & defrauding compromise. Why geniuses like you, Bach, Grieg can be willing to compose for keyboard instruments I shall never understand.
>
>   . . . I played "Juba Dance" because I sensed it would become a best seller & and because I thought it always rare that a real genius like you are able to write a best seller—when it happens, one should (if one can) help the composer to "cash in" on it. Your choral works (which ARE real to me) I have always talked & written about all I can, because I not only know them to be works of great genius, but also because they are part of my own soul life.

Grainger went on to say that he was not a "natural pianist," had trouble memorizing, disliked the piano as an instrument, and ended the letter by asking

> How can I (being a composer & needing some of my time for composing) keep up my pianistic career & yet learn *as few pieces* as possible? It has been a great problem & a wretched life. But better than starving, of course. I wish I might see you, dear friend & genius! Warm greetings to

you and yours,

Yours ever,

Percy

During Dett's USO stint in 1943 he wrote Grainger at least once, while Grainger was at the National Music Camp in Interlochen, Michigan. Dated August 5, 1943, the letter said in part:

I was flattered that you asked me for the "Bible Vignettes" and I should be glad to send you copies if you will let me know to what address they should be sent. I shall be home until Wednesday of next week which is August 11th. After that, I can be reached care of the Hamblin USO, Battle Creek, Michigan. Do let me hear from you.

It seems a shame that we should drift away from each other after so many happy years of association. You know that I shall always be indebted to you for the interests you have manifested in my work.

With very kindest regards to you and Mrs. Grainger, believe me always as your admirer.

Your friend,

Nathaniel

Natalie Curtis-Burlin

Through his association with Natalie Curtis-Burlin at Hampton, Dett was further convinced that ethnologist and composer were of mutual value in producing publishable collections of folk songs. He has written that ethnologists have sought and found the truth in "the hearts of the common people," but that ethnological research unfortunately has held second place to artistic creation. Records made by these "ambassadors of the unlearned" serve as bridges between nations. Dett has spoken of Burlin as "one of the foremost figures in contemporary music history."[24]

Before Burlin (b. 1875) came to Hampton in 1916 to collect

Negro folk songs for a four-volume *Hampton Series Negro Folksongs* (1918-1919), her *Indian's Book*, published in 1907, had established her reputation as an outstanding ethnologist. By 1918 she had also recorded and published material on the Hopi Indians and Zulu and Vandau tribes in East Africa. The Indian material is recorded on cylinders, owned by the American Museum of Natural History in New York, and housed in the Archives of Traditional Music at Indiana University.

Dett was particularly impressed with the purity of Burlin's harmonizations of Negro songs, which she captured in their primitive, unadorned state and transcribed. Recognizing the timeliness of her project, Dett wrote, poetically, that Burlin could not have begun a century ago "to have caught these wild, weird harmonies of the primitive songs which welled up from a sorrow stricken people like the acutely sweet perfume of broken reeds," songs which serve as "acceptible offerings on the altars of God."[25]

Burlin's *Hampton Series Negro Folksongs* was recorded in 1915 by two self-organized, self-trained male groups: the "First Quartet" and the "Big Quartet." The latter group were Hampton graduates who sang in and around Hampton. Unfortunately, the songs on cylinders have suffered from cracks and incorrect recording speeds, but are still worth hearing. Some of the spirituals in the collection are "Every Time I Feel the Spirit," "Go Down, Moses," and "Listen to the Lambs." Burlin "took great pains" to faithfully represent this Negro music.[26]

As the Hampton students sang their versions of the folk songs Burlin notated them. In April of 1918 some of her songs collected at Hampton were performed on a Schola Cantorum concert in Carnegie Hall. She worked closely at Hampton with African students Kamba Simango and Madikane Qandeyane on her last publication, *Songs and Tales from the Dark Continent* (1920). These same students took part in Mrs. Marshall's previously mentioned folk music presentation at the Washington Conservatory on April 24, 1921.

Fascinated with ethnological pursuits, after attending the St. Louis Exposition in 1904, Burlin forsook her formerly chosen career as a pianist to become a folklorist. She had studied at the National Conservatory in New York, and privately with

Ferruccio Busoni and Arthur Friedheim. In Paris she worked for a
time with Alfred-Auguste Giraudet. With a solid piano
background she was better able to meticulously transcribe the
songs. Other of Burlin's work was in New York with the Music
School Settlement for deprived children.

Many of Burlin's articles were published in *The Southern
Workman, The Craftsman,* and *Musical Quarterly. The Crisis*
quoted Burlin from an undated, untitled *Craftsman* article:

> The American Negroes possess what has been called the
> "harmonic ear." Though utterly without training the
> Negroes improvise alto, tenor, and bass parts to their
> songs with entire ease, and a whole Negro chorus will
> spontaneously break into harmony of real interest to the
> musician as well as of beauty. In the tobacco factories of
> the South and in the fields I have heard ignorant
> Negroes who seemed nearly related to their primitive
> African progenitors sing four-part harmony of a richness
> and charm truly amazing.[27]

Burlin's article "Black Singers and Players" deals in part
with the Hampton student body's incredible ability to
harmonize instinctively, not as a taught routine. When these 900
students attended chapel they were not divided into sections of
soprano, alto, tenor, and bass, but the boys sat together at the
sides with the girls in the middle. Each sang the part that lay
within his range. She said: "The down-trodden black man,
whose patient religious faith has kept his heart still
unembittered, is fast becoming the singing voice of all America."[28]
Burlin was cited in a tribute, "Recognizing Our Debt to Negro
Music," in *Musical America,* December 12, 1919. It would seem
that Burlin's work had just begun at the time of her accidental
death in 1921.

Arthur Foote and Archibald Davison

Dett was granted a year's leave from Hampton during the
1919-1920 academic year, a good part of which was spent
studying with composer Arthur Foote (1853-1937), a Harvard

graduate who taught privately in Boston.[29] Well respected at Harvard, Foote was made chairman of the Harvard Visiting Committee on Music in 1879, which group monitored classes, "suggested important changes of policy and furnished an opportunity for us to hear ourselves as others hear us."[30]

Foote, whose musical training began at the age of twelve, studied with B. J. Lang in Boston and later with John Knowles Paine at Harvard. He received the first M. A. degree in music given by an American university. The Germanic influence detectable in his compositions came about largely through his study abroad with various romantic composers. After a piano debut in Boston in 1876 he became organist at the Church of the Disciples, and later at the First Unitarian Church until 1910. During this time he performed both as a piano soloist and as a chamber player.

Foote's first published compositions were three pieces for cello and piano and three pieces for piano (1882). For the next forty-five years his compositional output included orchestral pieces, chamber works for piano quartets, duos for piano and violin/cello/oboe, string quartet, and songs with orchestra/piano. His chamber music shows decided Brahmsian characteristics. Only forty-two works of his approximately 300 (some unnumbered) had not been published by the mid-1980s,[31] but as recently as 1990 two chamber works were published by Masters Music Publications, Inc.[32]

Besides musical composition and teaching Foote guest lectured, acted as music department chairman at the University of California in Berkeley during the summer of 1911, and authored theory books, piano manuals, and journal articles. He was a founding member of the American Guild of Organists (AGO), active in the Music Teachers National Association, and received honorary doctorates from Trinity and Dartmouth Colleges.[33]

Foote obviously appreciated Dett's dedication to the Hampton choir. In an undated letter to Dett, quite possibly concerning the Boston concert in Symphony Hall, March 10, 1929, he wrote:

The chorus was beautifully trained and responsive.

You must have worked heroically with it to control the
effects of tone and rhythm as you did. You will have
many congratulations, none of them more felt than those
of myself and my wife who was very disappointed at
being prevented attendance at the last moment.[34]

Other of Dett's teachers during his study in Boston were Dr.
Archibald Davison (a visiting professor in theory and choir), a
Mr. Spalding (canon, fugue, composition, and appreciation), and a
Mr. Hill (instrumentation).[35] Choir director Davison was also
organist at Harvard Memorial Chapel, and had made a study of
music work at Hampton for the New York Board of Education.
He was Chairman of the Musical Advisory Board of Boston. In
June of 1917 he sang the bass solos in Dett's presentation of *Elijah*
at Hampton.

Davison's opinion of Hampton stated:

I have been greatly impressed with the singing and music
at Hampton Institute. The devotion to music is very
strong. I wish to congratulate you on your music teaching.
The plantation singing is very good. It corresponds with
the folk singing of France and England. You have the
basis for going forward. All music is derived from the
folk songs. Learn all there is to sing and play.[36]

Letters in the spring of 1920 from Davison to Hampton's
Principal Gregg indicate that Dett was avoiding his Glee Club
rehearsals and organ lessons at Harvard, though Davison would
not have charged him for this instruction. Davison was plainly
distressed that Dett was so evasive, even discussing Dett's
schedule with Gregg in an attempt to clarify the reason for his
absence.   Gregg indicated disappointment that Dett was
unresponsive but could not explain it.

Out of concern Davison invited Dett to dinner, which eased
relations somewhat. Davison's letter to Gregg, April 26, 1920,
said:

I asked him why he didn't give more attention to my
work when he found that he wasn't progressing in the

other lines as he had hoped, and he said he was afraid of giving offense to the instructors with whom he was working. He really is a very talented fellow, but I could wish that he had kept a little more level head during the past year. I will try to crowd into him all the good points I can during the remainder of his stay.[37]

Dett indicated to Davison that Miss Drew, who had taken over his academic courses at Hampton that year, had "stirred things up rather badly."

Dorothy Maynor

In the fall of 1924 Dorothy Leigh Mainor (b. 1910), age fourteen, entered Hampton Institute's college preparatory school, and in 1929 enrolled in its college program, planning to be a home economics teacher. As the daughter of a Norfolk, Virginia Methodist minister, John J. Mainor, she acquired a substantial background of church music. At Hampton she was a flutist in the orchestra and toured abroad with Dett's choir in 1930.

After graduation from Hampton in 1933 with a Bachelor's degree in music, she received a scholarship to study choral conducting with John Finley Williamson at the Westminster Choir School, where she received a Bachelor's degree in 1935. Following a brief teaching stint in Phoenix, a part of the Hampton Roads area, Dorothy Maynor (her professional name) was able to study in the next four years under Wilfred Klomroth and Alan Haughton, with monetary support of patroness Harriet S. Curtis, former Dean of Women at Hampton. During this time she also was a choir director.[38]

Things went steadily uphill after conductor Serge Koussevitsky auditioned her for an August 9, 1939 performance at the Berkshire Festival. Mrs. Gorham Brooks of Brookline, Massachusetts, donor of the Tanglewood estate to the Boston Symphony Orchestra, had been extremely impressed with Maynor's voice and urged Koussevitsky to hear her.

Dorothy Maynor, ca 1940.
Courtesy Hampton University Archives.

SCHOOL OF MUSIC HAMPTON INSTITUTE

STUDENT RECITAL

MUSEUM ANNEX

Thursday Afternoon, December 3, 1931, at 4:30 o'clock

PROGRAM

Prelude and Fugue in C minor (Well-Tempered Clavichord) .... *Bach*
MISS MARTHA ROBINSON
Sonate Pathetique Op. 13 (first movement) .... *Beethoven*
MISS MATILDA PALMER
My Mother Bids Me Bind My Hair .... *Haydn*
Slumber Song .... *Gretchaninoff*
Once in a Blue Moon .... *Fisher*
MISS MARY SHUFORD
MISS ISABELLE FLETCHER, *Accompanist*
Idilio .... *Lack*
MISS MARGARET PHILLIPS
Polish Dance .... *Scharwenka*
MISS MARJORIE DANDY
Whims .... *Schumann*
MISS JOSEPHINE HAMPTON
Rejoice Greatly (Messiah) .... *Handel*
In Autumn .... *Curran*
MISS DOROTHY MAINOR
MISS ISABELLE FLETCHER, *Accompanist*
Polonaise in B flat minor .... *DeLeone*
MISS EDMONIA JOHNSON

Program courtesy of Hampton University Archives.

SCHOOL OF MUSIC   HAMPTON INSTITUTE

RECITAL
BY

Miss Dorothy Mainor

of the Class of '33 in Voice

assisted by

The Hampton Institute Symphonic Orchestra
Mr. Ernest Hays, at the Piano

OGDEN HALL

Sunday Afternoon, May 21, 1933, 4:30 O'clock

PROGRAM

I

Sleep Why Dost Thou Leave Me	*Handel*
A Thought Like Music	*Brahms*
Erlkonig	*Schubert*

II

Aria; Pace, Pace, Mio Dio	*Verdi*
(From the Opera "La Forza del destino")	

III

Hymne au Soleil	*Alexander*
Depuis le jour (Louise)	*Carpentier*

IV

Into the Light	*La Forge*
Iris	*Wolf*
Mountains	*Rasbach*

V

Swing Low, Sweet Chariot	*Burleigh*
Bear the Burden	*C. C. White*
Sit Down, Servant, Sit Down	*Dett*
Wade in de Water	*Burleigh*

Program courtesy of Hampton University Archives.

Her selections for the August 9 performance at the annual picnic, included Handel's "O, Sleep Why Dost Thou Leave Me?" two Mozart arias, and "Depuis le Jour" from Gustav Charpentier's opera *Louise*, repertoire which would serve her well throughout her career. In addition she sang a "final sheaf of spirituals."[39] Noel Straus, *New York Times* reviewer, said of her:

> Miss Maynor . . . roused an audience of 200 to extreme enthusiasm, not alone by her exceptional vocal powers she disclosed, but by her innate expressiveness and her splendid musicianship. . . . Before a highly critical audience composed almost entirely of skilled musicians, Miss Maynor sang with a poise worthy of a veteran of the concert stage—the modest and self-effacing, self-confidence that comes with the knowledge that one is sure of one's mastery of the task in hand. [She] made known a grasp of style, a control of tone, and unusual gifts as an interpreter.[40]

It is true that Dett saw Maynor first, "discovered" her, but promotion of her career as a professional singer was due in great part to the interest of seasoned conductor Koussevitsky. Maynor debuted publicly to a sold out house in Town Hall on November 19, 1939. Olin Downes, reviewing the concert in the *New York Times*, was quite captivated with the tiny coloratura.

> It was without doubt a difficult situation for a young artist of Miss Maynor's intelligence, seriousness and sensibility. She was evidently aware of the impression she was expected to make and under exceptional tension. Before many minutes had passed, she had proved her exceptional equipment.[41]

Downes went on to praise her voice as

> . . . phenomenal for its range, character, and varied resources. . . . Equally adapted to lyric or dramatic and coloratura measures [it] has power as well as rich color.

... a good musician ... a fine ear. With her astonishing
gifts she should be wary of too much singing and too little
deliberate study at this time. She should be able to
reach almost any height as one of the leading concert
singers of her generation.

In 1940 Maynor was under Evans and Salter management,
whose roster included Lawrence Tibbett, Yehudi Menuhin, Helen
Jepson, Rose Bampton, and James Melton. (By 1957 she was listed
with Columbia Artists.) During this year numerous prestigious
engagements followed in New York, at the 1940 Berkshire
Festival, and at the Library of Congress, some with Hungarian-
American accompanist Arpad Sandor, and others with the
leading conductors before capacity audiences. One reviewer
described her voice as "pure and liquid, almost disembodied,"
and her high fortes as "effortless and full-blooded," but was not
too pleased with her German diction.[42] Downes did not like her
interpretation of the "inevitable group of Negro spirituals" on a
Town Hall recital in October of 1940, saying that they were

> ... sung with an artiness that is discouraging. They lose
> their folk quality; they become self-conscious, theatrical,
> whereas no more sincere and inspired music has ever been
> written. ... Nor did we enjoy Nathaniel Dett's finicking
> and artificial arrangements made for Miss Maynor of two
> of the spirituals, one with an echo effect at the end
> which is anything but congruous with the true nature of
> the music.[43]

Maynor was the first Negro to give a solo concert at Coolidge
Hall in the Library of Congress, on December 19, 1940, the
occasion being the first in a series of four to commemorate the
seventy-fifth anniversary of the proclamation of the thirteenth
amendment of the constitution. Among her selections were "My
Day" by Dett, and a group of his spirituals.

In 1942 Maynor married Reverend Shelby Rooks, head of the
divinity school of Lincoln University (Oxford, Pennsylvania) in a
private ceremony in Westminster Choir College Chapel. During
the war years she gave several benefit performances and later

toured abroad.

Reviews of Maynor's singing during the mid-1940s were largely favorable, with only a few remarks about inconsistencies in quality. In a review in late 1947 fan Noel Straus was distressed by her faulty vocalism, inaccurate pitch, and tone production, noticing in the voice a "pronounced waver," which became "hard and explosive."[44]

Maynor was the first Negro to sing at a United States President's inauguration, that of President Harry Truman.[45] She retired from public concertizing in 1963, and by 1964 had opened the Harlem School of the Arts in New York City which initially had twenty students. Four years later it boasted 400. Reverend Rooks was quite instrumental in helping establish the school, supported mainly by contributing church members and such prominent women as Mrs. Serge Koussevitsky, Mrs. Artur Rodzinski, and Mrs. Vladimir Horowitz.[46] Children of all ethnic backgrounds were given music lessons here for a modest fee.

Maynor's aim for the school was not to produce geniuses but to add new dimensions and beauty to children's lives. She tirelessly taught voice and conducted a chorus, retiring as the school's director in 1980 to be succeeded by Betty Allen. In 1985 the school had almost 1200 students. As late as 1991 Maynor lived near the school, a $3,000,000 plant at 645 St. Nicholas Avenue.

Maynor has been given numerous awards and honors, both as a performer and as a humanitarian. In 1940 she received an outstanding performance award from the Town Hall Endowment Series, one for distinguished service in 1941 from the Hampton Alumni Association, and was the first Negro appointed to the Metropolitan Opera Board of Directors. Honorary degrees were given her from Bennett College (1945), Howard University (1960), Duquesne University (1970), Oberlin College (1971), and Carnegie-Mellon University (1972).[47]

Maynor honored Dett posthumously in a production at the Harlem School of the Arts in March of 1976, and in a speech at Hampton on Founder's Day in February, 1977. These tributes will be discussed in Chapter VII.

Eastman Professors Landow, Royce, Rogers
and Hanson, 1931-1933

It is not certain how much study Dett did with the elderly pianist Max Landow, who had become Professor Emeritus at the Eastman School of Music by the mid-1920s. Landow was a romanticist to the hilt, a specialist in Lisztian repertoire which he taught with a flair, in the grand manner of which Liszt himself would have approved. He was exceptionally inspiring to the younger students, and by some magic made the ones of small stature sound like musical giants. At piano juries he gave well-balanced, constructive comments.[48] Too, Dett did very little, if any, work with composer Howard Hanson until 1932-1933, by which time Hanson had recommended his return to Eastman.

Dett studied counterpoint, and perhaps some composition, with Edward Royce during 1931-1932. Royce (1886-1963), son of professor Josiah Royce, the eminent philosopher and music lover, graduated from Harvard in 1907. Before coming to Eastman in 1923, where he taught until 1947, he had studied at the Stern Conservatory in Berlin, and in 1913 he established a music department at Middlebury College in Vermont. From 1916 to 1921 he was head of theory at Ithaca Conservatory.

Royce's best known compositions are two orchestral tone poems, "The Fire Bringers" (1926) and "Far Ocean" (1929), though he left several earlier songs, piano pieces, and miscellaneous works. Some of their titles, "Four Piano Pieces" (1918), "Song" (1921), "Study for Piano (1921), "Three Songs" (1920), and "Variations for Piano" (1921), are rather non-descriptive.[49]

According to Harvard historian Walter Spalding, Royce had perfect pitch and was born "with a remarkable union of emotional and mental qualities."[50] Of his symphonic poem "Far Ocean," which was played at the Eastman School of Music's tenth anniversary, Olin Downes, both in praise and criticism, said that it had

. . . imaginative pages. There is the thought of heaving, vasty deep. The general effect is oceanic, panoramic. Unfortunately this work lacks cohesion. It abounds in sections which are not well connected. Yet it is a finely sincere conception. An effective peroration, which sums up what has gone before, does not recompense for the scrappy and episodic effect of what has preceded.[51]

* * *

Bernard Rogers (1893-1968) was Dett's composition and orchestration professor during his first year at Eastman. As a youngster Rogers was more interested in art, poetry, and architecture than in music, though he did have piano lessons. After hearing a young people's concert conducted by Frank Damrosch he wanted music to be his profession, a situation similar to that of Arthur Farwell on hearing the Boston Symphony for the first time. While Farwell was Supervisor of Municipal Music in New York City (1910-1913), Rogers introduced himself and became his student for an indefinite period. In 1921 Rogers enrolled at the Institute of Musical Art (now Juilliard) and subsequently studied with Hans van den Berg, Ernest Bloch, Nadia Boulanger, Frank Bridge, and Percy Goetschius. Recommended by Farwell, Rogers became a contributing critic to *Musical America* in the early 1920s.

Rogers received financial aid from composition prizes and a Guggenheim Fellowship. From 1929 until 1967 he taught composition and orchestration at Eastman. His most prestigious students have been Peter Mennin, David Diamond, Dominick Argento, and Nathaniel Dett. His passion for art, particularly Japanese art, continued as a powerful influence upon his compositions, which include opera, choral and orchestral works, chamber music, and a few songs with orchestral accompaniment.

Diamond, in *Muscal Quarterly*, April 1947, wrote that Rogers' music combined simplicity and force in all the right proportions. He compared Rogers' use of certain melodic fragments and short rhythmic figures to the pointillistic technique of painters; his harmony to that of Monteverdi and similar madrigalists; and deemed his oratorio *The Passion* his finest work to date. Rogers confined his use of sonata form to the larger symphonic works. Diamond called him "a master of orchestration," whose core of vision is always drama—drama austere and uncompromising.[52]

Rogers composed three operas, one of which, *The Warrior*, was performed at the Metropolitan Opera House in 1947. More durable have been his smaller orchestral works, *Elegy to the Memory of Franklin D. Roosevelt* and *Soliloquy* (for flute and strings), and his cantatas *The Passion, The Exodus*, and *The Raising of Lazarus*.[53]

* * *

By the spring of 1932 Dett was certain that he would not be back on the Hampton faculty, so he made preparations to return to Eastman, this time planning to study modern harmony and composition with Howard Hanson. In the annals of Eastman Hanson looms almost as a god figure, due to his many accomplishments for the School of Music.

A native of Rochester, Hanson was born in 1896 and lived an awesomely productive life until his death in 1981. Before coming to Eastman as Director of the School of Music in 1924, a position he kept unil 1964, he had studied theory with Percy Goetschius, and also had received a B. A. degree from Northwestern University (1916) where he taught during 1915 and 1916. For the following three years he taught in California at the College of the Pacific where he was dean in 1919. For his ballet, California Forest Play of 1920, he won he *Prix de Rome*, and went to live in Rome as the first American prize winner to do so. Invited by Walter Damrosch to direct the New York Symphony Orchestra, Hanson made his conducting debut in 1924, and from that point was in great demand both in the US and Europe for concerts, festivals, and young people's programs.

Hanson was a personal panacea to Eastman, broadening its curriculum, attracting outstanding teachers, and strengthening its orchestras. In 1961 he took the Eastman Philharmonic on an extended European tour. Dett, Jack Beeson, William Bergsma, and Peter Mennin were among his best composition students. Hanson founded the Institute of American Music of the Eastman School "for the publication and dissemination of American music as well as research in the history of twentieth century musical styles."[54]

Hanson was of necessity heavily involved for many years with the leading professional musical organizations. Among his myriad awards and honors were thirty-six honorary degrees, a Pulitzer Prize for his Symphony No. 4, the Ditson Award, the George Foster Peabody Award, election to the National Institute of Arts and Letters (1935), and to the American Academy of the Institute of Arts and Letters (1979).

As a neoromantic composer his most powerful compositional models were Jean Sibelius and Edvard Grieg, and as an orchestrator, Ottorino Respighi. In structure his work resembles Handel and Palestrina. Literary publications by Hanson include *Harmonic Materials of Modern Music: Resources of the Tempered Scale* (1960) and journal articles. Other of his musical articles and reviews were carried in the *Rochester Times-Union*.[55] Musical compositions are two other ballets, six symphonies, shorter orchestral and solo instrumental pieces, works for band, chorus, and half a dozen song cycles.

At Eastman Hanson instigated the American Composers' Concerts as early as May of 1925. Four concerts were given annually until 1935, when the series was replaced by two Symposia of American Music. Annual Festivals of American Music were started in 1931, which continued as late as 1971, involving five or six formal concerts per year.[56] Dett's *Listen to the Lambs* was performed in 1941-1942 and again on the 1943-1944 series. His choral pieces *The Lamb* and *As By the Streams of Babylon* were also on the 1943-1944 series, and during 1959-1960 *The Ordering of Moses* was presented.[57]

Boatner, Von Charlton, Pankey, Flax, and Ryder

Between 1921 and Dett's departure from Hampton, a few of his students who continued in the music field proved worthy of mention. Dett took piano protégé Edward Hammond Boatner (1891-1981) on tour with him through the New England states in the early 1920s, after the versatile Boatner had appeared at Hampton as baritone soloist. They met again later in Boston. Dett never actually taught Boatner, since Boatner did not attend Hampton, but provided him "advice and assistance in his early years."[58]

Boatner was born in New Orleans and received early musical training as the son of a minister. He studied at Western University in Quindaro, Kansas, and at the New England Conservatory. In 1921 he went to the Boston Conservatory on a scholarship. In 1932 he graduated from Chicago Musical College with a Bachelor of Music degree.

As a composer, baritone soloist, and choir director Boatner held various teaching positions, among them one at Samuel Huston College in Austin, Texas, where Dett was hired briefly in 1935 under his Directorship. Boatner's later life was spent in New York City where he maintained a private studio, coaching such stellar singers and actors as George Shirley, and directing choirs in Chicago and the New York area.

In 1964 Boatner was honored by the NANM and in 1979 by the Chicago Music Association for his many years of service to music. His interest in Negro spirituals never waned and to his credit are arrangements of more than 200 spirituals, staples in the concert repertoires of Marian Anderson, Roland Hayes, George Shirley, Paul Robeson, Josephine Baker, Leontyne Price, Nelson Eddy, and other prominent singers. Boatner authored plays, novels, twenty text books, and wrote music for the stage. Artists Anderson, Carol Brice, Ellabelle Davis, and Robeson, among others, have recorded his spirituals.[59]

* * *

During Dett's last years at Hampton he taught Rudolph E. von Charlton (b. 1912, Norfolk, Virginia), a promising piano student. Von Charlton finished a B. A. degree at Hampton in 1931 and in 1939 received the M. Mus. from the University of Michigan in Ann Arbor. By 1948 he had earned a Ph. D. from Columbia University Teachers College. Other study was done at Juilliard and the New England Conservatory. Besides Dett, von Charlton's piano teachers were Percy Grainger and Tobias Matthay.

A singer as well as a pianist, von Charlton toured with Dett's choir while at Hampton. After graduation from 1931 to 1942 he taught at Florida A and M College in Tallahassee, Florida, since 1953 renamed Florida A and M University. From 1942 until 1977 he was Chairman of the Music Department at Prairie View State College in Hempstead, Texas, since 1973 renamed Prairie View A and M University and re-located in Prairie View, Texas.[60] Von Charlton was listed as late as 1989 in the Hampton Alumni Directory. Inquiries sent him in 1991 and 1992 to different Houston addresses, however, brought no response.

* * *

Another person encouraged by Dett was vocal student Aubrey Pankey (1905-1971), who sang in the Hampton Glee Club in the middle and late 1920s. He was also a member of the Hampton Choir when it toured Europe in 1930. At Dett's urgence Pankey pursued a vocal career, going on for further study at Oberlin Conservatory and Boston University. In Boston Pankey studied privately with Arthur Hubbard, and in New York with Alan Haugton, Maynor's teacher. He was able to live in Europe from 1931 until 1940, concertizing and studying with Theodore Lierhammer in Vienna, and Oscar Daniel and Charles Panzera in Paris, a stint likely the result of both Dett's personal endorsement and the support of Hampton's Principal George Phenix. A letter to Dett from Phenix dated June 24, 1930, indicated that Pankey was trying to interest Boston friends in sending him abroad for study. Phenix asked for Dett's input on the matter: "Is he [Pankey] a person of sufficient promise to justify asking any of our friends to help him?"[61]

Baritone Pankey's Town Hall debut on April 28, 1940, received a rather non-committal review in the April 29 *New York Times*, which mentioned that Pankey had made more than 200 appearances in some twenty-four countries of Europe, Asia, and Africa. The "responsive audience" was treated to a rather lengthy and inclusive program, featuring on the first half two Handel arias, some Schubert lieder, art songs by Fauré, Ravel, and Debussy, and "Berceuse" by Theodor Szanto. The second half consisted of songs in Engish by Roger Quilter, Gilbert Spross, Pearl Curran, and a group of Negro spirituals. (This well balanced program is likely a format which Pankey learned from Dett at Hampton.) Pankey's accompanist at Town Hall was Rudolph Schaar.

School of Music Hampton Institute

Recital
BY
MR. RUDOLPH V. CHARLTON
of the Class of '31, in Piano

ASSISTED BY

MISS RUBY E. TRUEHART
of the Class of '31, in Voice

OGDEN HALL

Tuesday evening, January 22, 1929, at seven o'clock

PROGRAM

Sonata, Opus 27, No. 2 (Moonlight) .... *Beethoven*
  Adagio sostenuto
  Allegretto
  Presto agitato

MR. CHARLTON

Caro mio ben (in Italian) .... *Giordani*

MISS TRUEHART

Prelude in C major .... *Chopin*
Nocturne in E-flat .... *Chopin*
Waltz in C-sharp minor .... *Chopin*

MR. CHARLTON

Ah Love! But a Day .... *Mrs. H. H. A. Beach*

MISS TRUEHEART

Hark! Hark, the Lark .... *Schubert-Liszt*
Witches' Dance .... *MacDowell*
Bamboula (African Dance) .... *Coleridge-Taylor*

MR. CHARLTON

Program courtesy of Hampton University Archives.

At the invitation of the Chinese People's Association for Cultural Relations Pankey toured China in 1956, the first American to do so since 1949 when the Chinese Republic was established.[62]

* * *

By 1931 Charles Herbert Flax (1904-1980) was a graduate student in music at Hampton, having worked with Dett after earning a diploma from St. Augustine College in Raleigh, North Carolina, his home state, in 1927. As an undergraduate at Hampton he was baritone soloist with the Hampton Choir on its European tour. "He spoke fondly in later years about the choral imagery painted by Dr. Dett in interpreting the choral literature," a practice which he later used in his own directing.[63] His last degree from Hampton was conferred in 1933.

Flax became Instructor of Music and Voice, Choral Conductor, and Consultant in Dramatics at the George P. Phenix Training School, under Hampton auspices. Highly successful as a choral director, his various organizations performed in churches and schools throughout the Peninsula. At the same time he also was director of the Newport News Choral Society, a community ensemble. Though in 1934 he refused to pursue a concert singing career he was said to "possess a gift of song and an interpretative instinct altogether above average."[64]

Flax's formal education continued at Eastman (1935-1936) and at the Carnegie Institute of Technology in Pittsburgh (1939). In 1939 in the city of Hampton he formed the Crusaders Male Chorus, a group of twelve men from various professions who endearingly referred to him as "Uncle Charlie." Later the Crusaders were called the Ambassadors of Good Will, who said of Flax: "His deep love and devotion to the Crusaders surfaced on one occasion when he admitted that 'not a night goes by that I don't pray for each and every man in the Crusaders.'"[65]

Toward the end of World War II Flax was appointed as a Civilian Technical Advisor to the personnel of the US Navy, at which time he also directed the US Navy Glee Club, and formed a lasting friendship with Noah Ryder, another of Hampton's outstanding music students. Extra assignment was with the

Recital

AUBREY PANKEY, *Baritone*
MRS. DETT, *Accompanist*

OGDEN HALL

Saturday Evening, May 12, 1928, at 7:45 o'clock

PROGRAM

I

Sento Nel Core	*Scarlatti*
Vado Ben Spesso	*Rosa*
O Cessate di Piagarmi	*Scarlatti*
Gia II Sole Dal Gange	*Scarlatti*

II

When I Am Laid in Earth	*Purcell*
Dream Valley	*Quilter*
By a Lonely Forest Pathway	*Griffes*
A Feast of Lanterns	*Bantock*

III

Prologue to "Pagliacci"	*Leoncavallo*

IV

The Crying of Water	*Campbell-Tipton*
Trade Winds	*Keel*
Sea Gypsies	*Loud*

V

Zion Hallelujah	*Dett*
I'm a-goin' to see my friends again	*Dett*
A Man goin' roun' takin' names	*Dett*
Dar's a meetin' here tonight	*Burleigh*

Program courtesy of Hampton University Archives.

Navy's Morale Division, in the Pacific battle area. He later revealed that "Music was one of the important media in which I was able to raise morale."[66]

In 1946 Flax returned to the Hampton area to serve in various capacities, most importantly as choral director and minister of music of the College Chapel Choir, feeling that these duties were some of his most significant ones. He highly prized his association with Roland Carter, a future choral director at Hampton. In the summer of 1970 Flax went to Europe as an advisor to the Hampton Choir, when Carter was its director.

Widely respected, among Flax's honors are the *Norfolk Journal and Guide* Honor Roll (1948), Distinguished Award from the City of Hampton (1966), Hampton Institute Centennial Medallion (1968), and the James Weldon Johnson Humanitarian Award (1973). At Flax's funeral, held in the Hampton Memorial Church on May 5, 1980, two of Noah Ryder's vocal compositions were given by the Crusaders Male Chorus.[67]

* * *

Noah Francis Ryder (1914-1964) enrolled at Hampton in 1931, just as Dett was leaving for study at Eastman. Born in Nashville, Tennessee, Ryder was first taught by his father, and as a teenager showed astute organizational ability with both instrumental and choral groups, as well as talent as an actor. As a Negro student at Cincinnati University, he was not allowed to join any musical organizations. At Hampton he elected to be a physical education major, but fortunately was steered toward music by the athletic director. As stated on Ryder's funeral program:

> [He] was greatly influenced by R. Nathaniel Dett, then head of the music department and also a noted composer and excellent choir director. Later he came under the influence of Clarence Cameron White, the violinist and composer-arranger who succeeded Dett as head of the department, and Ernest Hays, organist.[68]

Ryder was a doer, and said by teacher Irene Cooper to be the most versatile student that Hampton had ever known.[69] He could play nearly all musical instruments. He conducted and made choral arrangements for several singing groups, such as the Orpheus Male Choral Group and the Hampton Institute Double Quartet. His Double Quartet later became the internationally famous Deep River Boys.

After graduation from Hampton in 1935 Ryder taught at Dillard High School (Goldsboro, North Carolina) and then at Palmer Memorial Institute (Sedalia, North Carolina). From 1941-1945 at Hampton he taught theory and directed the college choir. After military service he furthered his education at the University of Michigan and then settled in the Norfolk area, directed the Harry T. Burleigh Glee Club there, composed, and taught at Norfolk State College. With his second wife, Georgia Atkins Ryder, he co-authored "Musically Speaking," a weekly column in the *Norfolk Journal and Guide* from 1950 to 1952.

Ryder's substantial list of published compositions and arrangements are largely Negro folk songs and spirituals. Georgia Ryder's dissertation, "Melodic and Rhythmic Elements of American Negro Folksongs as Employed in Cantatas by Selected American Composers Between 1932 and 1967," includes a discussion of Dett's works in this genre.

Chapter VII

Dett in Retrospect

Continued Interest

Vivian Flagg McBrier, Dett's first in-depth biographer, has appraised his worth as a teacher, composer, and pianist, and also as a "serious social thinker," which concern was reflected in his music, writings, and lectures. Dett entered a scene already in progress, one furthering the Negro's right to recognition due to the efforts of other positive Negro thinkers who had preceded him. "His particular method of reinforcing the fight against the Black Man's disadvantaged status consisted in a positive approach—that of preserving and expanding the unique Afro-American musical heritage."[1]

McBrier regarded Dett as "a simple yet complicated man," possessing "perseverance, intellectual integrity, and a sense of the quality of life," a person continually aware of the common man's problems. He was an idealist, with an "independent spirit, quiet dignity, ready wit, quick humor, creative mind," who derived joy from his work.[2]

Though Dett died some fifty years ago, he has been well remembered and is still honored periodically. The writer of his obituary in the *Journal of Negro History* said of him:

> Dett, a man of great genius, was unfortunate in having had to earn his living by working under those who did not appreciate his genius and ignorantly tried to force him into their own mold. To this a man of vision and great talent could never yield. His career therefore showed a number of transitions which he would not have experienced in a more advanced nation. He was never so successful as to find an angel to relieve him of the drudgery of making a living. Considering the age in which he lived and the imperfections of his employers whom he had to endure, one must concede that he achieved well. Without this sympathetic consideration his creations place him in front rank as a man of creative

genius, but the world would have known him still better
had he been properly appreciated.[3]

* * *

Since Dett's death there have been a respectable number of
news items about him, mainly from the 1960s onward. Since 1949
the *Music Index* had approximately two dozen journal entries on
Dett, including some on posthumously published arrangements,
items on performances and recordings of his works, and
dissertation abstracts. Items in American newspapers have been
more plentiful, however.

Besides McBrier's dissertation on Dett's vocal works (1968) at
least ten more dissertations and/or theses have been done on Dett
in the last three decades, ones to be cited in the Bibliography of
this book. Dr. Jon Michael Spencer, responsible for one of these
dissertations, has also edited a collection of Dett's prose
writings, *The R. Nathaniel Dett Reader, Essays on Black Sacred
Music*, published in 1991 by Duke University Press.

Another forthcoming volume, edited by Dr. Fritz J. Malval,
Hampton University Archivist, will be devoted solely to Dett's
poetry, including miscellaneous heretofore unpublished poems
(some untitled), *Song of Seven* (edited from Dett's manuscript),
some previously published titled poems, and a reprinting of *The
Album of a Heart* from the 1911 edition. Before coming to
Hampton "many years ago" from Haiti Dr. Malval was archivist
of that country's National Library and General Inspector of
Public Libraries. Now he is the veritable Father of the Hampton
University Archives, which collection he began with no money,
using his own car to transport precious volumes and other
materials.

In an interview, September 22, 1991, Malval stated proudly
that the Hampton University Archives, partially through the
interest of George Foster Peabody, housed the first black
collection in an American archive. Originally materials in the
Peabody Room at Collis P. Huntington Library, Hampton
University, numbered 1,400 books and pamphlets, loaned by
Peabody in 1905. In 1908 Peabody made a gift of them. Malval
wrote the Introduction to the two-volume *Dictionary Catalog of*

the George Foster Peabody Collection of Negro Literature and History, issued by Greenwood Publishing Company in 1972. In it he said that the collection held approximately 11,500 monographs and more than 1,700 pamphlets and recorded documents on slavery and reconstruction in the United States. Only 6,000 titles were listed in the first catalog of the Peabody Collection, published in 1940.

After 1908 whole libraries were purchased for the collection from individuals, such as Dr. Phil Broome Brooks, a Washington, D.C. physician, and Wendell P. Dabney, black publisher and editor. Details of the Peabody Collection are listed in Malval's Introduction.

Dett's daughter Helen gave a large portion of Dett's papers, sheet music, etc., to the Hampton University Archives, where Malval and his staff have beautifully organized them both for preservation and to aid researchers. In addition there is a staggering amount of news clippings, correspondence, and financial statements pertaining to the Hampton Choir's European trip in 1930. Other Dett holdings will be discussed later in this chapter, according to the decade in which they materialized.

The 1940s

Before Dett's death in early October of 1943 his oratorio, *The Ordering of Moses*, had been scheduled for performance the following November 26 by the Oratorio Chorus and the St. Louis Symphony Orchestra, conducted by C. Spencer Tocus. The event, held at the St. Louis Opera House (Kiel Auditorium), was a benefit for the People's Art Center. The performers were 200 Negro singers, accompanied by fifty-two white players in the orchestra. It is odd that on the cover of the program Dett's name as composer of *Moses* was omitted.[4]

Word of the performance quickly reached Oberlin College's President Ernest Hatch Wilkins, who was sent a program and review of the concert. He wrote back to W. J. Hutchins of the Danforth Foundation in St. Louis that "the world do move" when such a thing can happen in St. Louis. Wilkins may have been referring to the fact that the 200-voice Negro choir had been accompanied by the all-white orchestra, and that a mixed racial audience of 2,200 attended the concert. Wilkins' letter spoke further of the newly opened Phillis Wheatley Center in Oberlin, a result of the progress of race relations there. "I attended the opening and was pleased to see that almost fifty percent of the audience was white," he said.[5]

The program listed names of all 200 chorus members. *Moses* comprised the concert's second half. Earlier, baritone Aubrey Pankey, former student of Dett, sang eight solos, in addition to "The Word" in *Moses*.

A review, November 27, 1943, in the *St. Louis Globe Democrat*, was very complimentary, calling it "the most ambitious and most important interlaced cultural essay this city has undertaken." Pointing out that the motives in *Moses* were based on "Go Down Moses" and "Let Thy People Go," the reviewer, Harry R. Burke, called Dett's score "intricately developed" from his native Negro tradition "by skillful musicianship as it exploits both that tradition and the complexities of modern harmonization." He praised its brilliance, dramatic power, emotional intensity, and "tremendous climax of jubilation."

Burke, continuing about Conductor Tocus, wrote:

> [*Moses'*] difficulties were surmounted last night by both chorus and orchestra under Mr. Tocus' admirable direction as they responded with avidity and skill to his inspiring leadership. The chorus is . . . the really important soloist, . . . the voice of the whole Negro race in commentary, actually dwarfing the soloists.

But Burke found the soloists impressive: Helen Phillips, Eva Bolar, Sergeant Henry L. Grant (mentioned as NANM president in Chapter II), James E. Tanner (a blind tenor), and Aubrey Pankey. He was pleased with Pankey's singing of the spirituals, but of one of the art songs he said that "dramatic effect impaired its beauty." He called "Listen to the Lambs" "one of the most colorful *a cappella* works ever written."

The *Musical Courier* also carried a review of the concert,

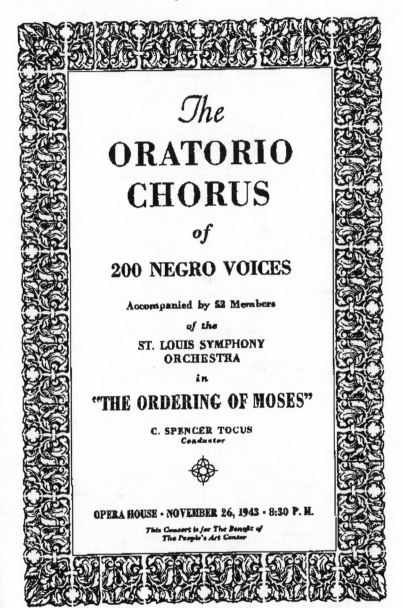

The

ORATORIO
CHORUS

of

200 NEGRO VOICES

Accompanied by 52 Members

of the

ST. LOUIS SYMPHONY
ORCHESTRA

in

"THE ORDERING OF MOSES"

C. SPENCER TOCUS
Conductor

OPERA HOUSE · NOVEMBER 26, 1943 · 8:30 P. M.

*This Concert is for The Benefit of
The People's Art Center*

Program courtesy Oberlin College Archives.

❖ ❖ ❖ ❖ PROGRAM ❖ ❖ ❖ ❖

THE STAR-SPANGLED BANNER...........................*John Stafford Smith*
RUTH E. GREENE—*Accompanist*

I

TRADITIONAL SPIRITUALS

MY LORD'S WRITING ALL THE TIME
DEN MY LITTLE SOUL'S GWINE TO SHINE
SWING LOW, SWEET CHARIOT
IN THAT GREAT GETTIN' UP MORNING

THE ORATORIO CHORUS
LEADERS—JAMES MCFERRIN, JEWEL HUMPHREY, MRS. M. BEASLEY ROBINSON,
LEROY PITCHER

These Spirituals are sung as they appear in "*The Story of the Jubilee Singers*"
(1880), and "*Hampton and Its Students*"—(1874).

II

O THOU BILLOWY HARVEST FIELD...........................*Rachmaninoff*
LIEBESBOTSHAFT..*Schubert*
AVE MARIA...*Schubert*
THE VOICE OF AMERICA...................................*David Guion*
AUBREY PANKEY, *Baritone*

III

A MAN GOIN' 'ROUND TAKIN' NAMES.......................*Arr. by Dett*
STAND STILL, JORDAN.....................................*Arr. by Burleigh*
LORD, I WANT TO BE A CHRISTIAN.........................*Arr. by Payne*
MY GOD IS SO HIGH......................................*Arr. by Pankey*
MR. PANKEY
RUDOLPH SCHAAR, *Accompanist*

IV

LISTEN TO THE LAMBS.......................................*Arr. by Dett*
Sung in Memory of Dr. Dett...................MRS. M. BEASLEY ROBINSON, SOLOIST
SO'S I CAN WRITE MY NAME..........................*Arr. by Noble Cain*

INTERMISSION

V

ORATORIO

THE ORDERING OF MOSES...........................*Dr. R. Nathaniel Dett*
BIBLICAL FOLK SCENE FOR SOLI AND ORCHESTRA
THE TEXT BASED ON SCRIPTURE AND FOLK-LORE

MIRIAM, SOPRANO...*Helen Phillips*
MOSES, TENOR...*James E. Tanner*
THE VOICE OF GOD, BARITONE.......................*Sgt. Henry L. Grant*
THE VOICE OF ISRAEL, ALTO................................*Eva Bolar*
THE WORD, BARITONE.....................................*Aubrey Pankey*
THE CHILDREN OF ISRAEL................................*Oratorio Chorus*
At the time of this "Ordering", Moses was a shepherd, on a hillside—undoubtedly
a young man,—which explains the part assigned to a tenor voice.

PRELUDE..*Orchestra*
ALL ISRAEL'S CHILDREN SORELY SIGHED................*Baritone and Chorus*
O LORD, BEHOLD MY AFFLICTION..........................*Alto and Chorus*
GOD LOOKED ON ISRAEL...................................*Trio and Chorus*
AND FROM A BURNING BUSH.....................................*Chorus*
GOD SPAKE UNTO MOSES..*Chorus*
GO DOWN, MOSES...*Chorus*
LORD, WHO AM I..*Tenor Solo*
AND GOD SPAKE UNTO MOSES....................................*Chorus*
WHO HATH MADE A MAN DUMB?..............................*Baritone Solo*

(PROGRAM CONTINUED)

Is It Not I, Jehovah?................................*Baritone and Chorus*
Go Down, Moses..*Chorus*
Meditation of Moses..*Orchestra*
And When Moses Smote the Water..................*Baritone and Chorus*
March of the Israelites Through the Red Sea..................*Chorus*
The Egyptians Pursue.......................................*Orchestra*
And When They Reached the Other Shore...........*Baritone and Chorus*
I Will Praise Jehovah................................*Tenor and Chorus*
Then Did the Women of Israel...........................*Baritone Solo*
Come Let Us Praise Jehovah....................*Soprano and Treble Chorus*
Sing Ye to Jehovah.................................*Tenor and Chorus*
He is King of Kings........................*Chorus, Tenor and Soprano*

some weeks later, saying that "The chorus sang with superb effect, both as to musical quality and general mechanics, and was a credit to Mr. Tocus' abilities as a choral director."[6]

* * *

On March 3, 1944, Bennett College's Senior Week activities closed with the dedication of a magnolia tree to Dett's memory. At a chapel service Dett's friend, David D. Jones, President of Bennett, spoke of Dett's achievements as a teacher and his helping "others see the finer things of life." Dett's "When I Survey the Wondrous Cross," "So We'll Go No More A-Roving," and "Now Rest Beneath Night's Shadows" were sung by the senior choir. After the service the tree was planted on the campus. "The dedication departed from a tradition in which only women have been previously honored by tree-plantings."[7]

Musical America, May, 1944, gave an account of the recent American Music Festival, founded by Howard Hanson at Eastman, mentioned in Chapter VI. Tribute to Dett was paid in Hanson's speech at Eastman's Founder's Day commemoration. Vocal music for the occasion, dedicated to Dett's memory, included "As By the Streams of Babylon" for mixed choir, with Mari Taniguchi as soprano soloist; "The Lamb," a three-part women's chorus; and "Listen to the Lambs," with soprano soloist Elaine Majchrzak. In addition, Hanson conducted his own *Symphony No. 4* and Roy Harris conducted his stirring "March in Time of War."

The Boston Public Library's entry on Dett states that *The Ordering of Moses* was performed by the Washington Community Chorus at the Metropolitan A.M.E. Church in Washington, D.C., on May 19, 1947.

The 1950s

The Ordering of Moses was performed in Carnegie Hall, June 15, 1951, under auspices of the National Negro Opera Company, founded in 1941 by Mary Cardwell Dawson (1894-1962). Originally the NNOC's purpose was to "provide an outlet for aspiring opera singers and to inspire young artists to study opera."[8] NNOC guilds were established in New York, Chicago, and Washington, D.C. as support agencies when Dawson directed productions in those cities. Dawson had earlier founded the Cardwell School of Music in Pittsburgh, the Cardwell-Dawson Chorus, and from 1939-1941 was president of NANM.

The non-critical review of NNOC's performance in the *New York Times*, June 16, 1951, simply stated that the event was part of a building fund campaign to house the opera company. *Moses* was presented in costume with piano and organ accompaniment. Beatrice Murphy was narrator, and soloists were Thomas Major, Alice Anderson, Joseph Lipscomb, Leo Hagey, and Ethel Hardy Smith. The June 10 *Times* had announced the work as having a "large cast of singers, dancers, and actors." It was recorded at this time for the Voice of America.

Though details of place were not specified, Dett was one of twelve "great teachers" honored during Black History Week in February of 1952 in Baltimore, Maryland.[9]

On March 15, 1954, *Moses*, under Gibson Morrissey's direction, was presented for the first time in Virginia in Roanoke at the American Legion Auditorium. In an announcement, March 9, the *Roanoke World-News* commented that *Moses* was "said to be the most important contribution to the arts yet made by a member of the Negro race." The "vital and ambitious" work would be performed by a large local chorus and the Roanoke Symphony Orchestra. The principal roles were cast as follows: Miriam, Florence Vickland, a dramatic soprano from Lynchburg; Voice of Israel, Mrs. Thilde Beuning-Edele, Hollins College; The Word,

Jack Wimmer, Roanoke; and Moses, Hartwell Philips, Roanoke. The 400-voice choir was drawn from the Andrew Lewis High School and Roanoke College of Salem and the William Byrd High School of Vinton. Roanoke schools participating were the William Fleming and Jefferson High Schools and the National Business College.[10]

Approximately a year later, on February 28, 1955, *Moses* was again presented in Roanoke under Morrissey's direction with a 500-voice choir and the same four soloists.[11]

The *Rochester Democrat and Chronicle*, May 8, 1958, announced an Annual Music Festival on May 9 to be held in West High Auditorium in Rochester, with participation by the high school band, orchestra, and choir of ninety-five singers. The concert, dedicated to Dett, friend of West High's music director Ernest E. Ahern (mentioned in Chapter V), would include "Listen to the Lambs," sung by the choir. "Guest of honor was Dett's daughter, Mrs. Helen Hopkins, flown here at the expense of the Music Department of the school from her home in Jamaica, L. I. [New York]."

The 1960s and 1970s

A revival of interest in Dett is so entwined during the 1960s and 1970s that chronology may be slightly interrupted in the following paragraphs.

An item dated March 2, 1963, sent to Oberlin College Archives from the *Chicago Defender*, stated that five of fourteen new schools were to be named by the Chicago Board of Education in that city in honor of outstanding Negroes.

> Two of the five were Oberlin graduates . . . the late Nathaniel Dett, '08, and Mrs. Mary Church Terrell, '48. . . . Dett was a pianist and composer. He died in 1943. Mrs. Terrell was the first Negro woman ever to serve on a board of education (Washington, DC) and was active in many causes. She died in 1954.

A telephone conversation (December 16, 1991) with Dr. Donald J. Feinstein, principal of the Robert Nathaniel Dett

Elementary School, confirmed its location at 2306 W. Maypole Avenue, District 9. Opened in March of 1963, Dett Elementary presently has 520 students and offers daily classes in piano. Its band program is growing with aid from federal and state funds. A photo of Dett, borrowed at one time for an exhibit at the Afro-American Museum in Chicago, is prominently displayed at the school.[12]

* * *

In 1968 Armstrong Hall, the Fine Arts Building at Hampton University, named for Hampton's founder Samuel Chapman Armstrong, was completed. The right end, named the Dett Wing, includes offices and Dett Auditorium, a multi-purpose hall which seats 180. In it are an organ, a small grand piano, and a portrait of Dett by Daniel Norman Tillman, signed "Tillman" but undated.[13]

Besides a huge bronze bust of Armstrong on a tall pedestal the Dett Wing displays three commemorative plaques in Dett's honor. A pentagon-shaped plaque was erected in 1977 by the Association for the Study of Afro-American Life and History, in cooperation with the Amoco Foundation, Inc. Under a star at the top the nine-line plaque reads: "In recognition of/ R. Nathaniel Dett/ Creative composer, brilliant pianist/ Respected music educator/ Leader of musical groups/ at Hampton Institute/ and Bennett College/ That gained world fame/ 1977."

Another plaque, rectangular in shape and approximately one by one and a half feet, says: "A Landmark of American Music/ R. Nathaniel Dett/ 1882-1943/ Composer, Pianist, Choral Conductor/ Director of Music/ Hampton Institute 1913-1931/ Presented by the/ National Music Council/ Virginia Federation of Music Clubs/ and Exxon." It was unveiled during Hampton's Founder's Day ceremonies, February 28-30, 1977, after Dorothy Maynor had been a guest speaker. Dett's daughter Helen was scheduled to attend the occasion, but her plane was delayed.

The reverent message in capital letters of a third plaque, two feet square, is: "ROBERT NATHANIEL DETT/ 1882-1943/ WHO AS A DYNAMIC SCHOLAR/ COMPOSER, CONDUCTOR, HUMANIST,/ AND MUSIC EDUCATOR HAS/ LEFT A

MUSICAL LEGACY TO/ CONTEMPORARY CREATIVE LIFE. No date or donor is specified on or near the plaque.

* * *

On August 4, 1969, the Hampton Chorus and Orchestra performed *Moses* at Hampton.[14] When the NANM celebrated its Golden Jubilee Anniversary in St. Louis in late summer of 1969, William Levi Dawson was musical director for a presentation of *Moses*. Marian Anderson was Honorary Chairman of the convention and Chicagoan Thomas Charles, a past NANM president, was presiding officer. Soloists in *Moses* were Jeanette Walters, Carol Brice, John Miles, and John Work IV.[15]

Conductor Dawson (1899-1970) entered Tuskegee at age thirteen and studied there seven years, subsequently touring as a trombonist. He received a Master's degree at the American Conservatory of Music in Chicago in 1927, and later studied at Eastman. He was first trombonist with the Chicago Civic Symphony in the late 1920s. While he was choir director at Tuskegee (1931-1956) his choir toured the United States. Dawson was sent to Spain in 1956 as a choral conductor. His compositions include a symphony, chamber works, and numerous arrangements of spirituals. He was awarded an honorary doctorate by Tuskegee in 1955.[16]

* * *

Dett has been well remembered by scholarly biographers, indicated by the fact that Dominique-René De Lerma, author and editor of numerous books, articles, bibliographies, and discographies, was asked in 1970 to contribute an entry on Dett to a supplement of *Die Musik in Geschichte und Gegenwart*. First published in 1949, *MGG* is one of the definitive encyclopedias on music. De Lerma's first reaction was that Vivian Flagg McBrier should write it, from her recently completed dissertation on Dett. At the time, however, McBrier was on sabbatical. Since bibliographer De Lerma already had approximately 100 entries of titles and/or publishers in his personal files pertaining to Dett, he reconsidered, saying, "as soon as that year's seminar was over, I flew to the Library of Congress to see if they had more information than we had gathered."[17]

Extensive research for the *MGG* project put De Lerma in contact with William Lichtenwanger, Carroll Wade, and Elmer Booze at the Library of Congress, Maurice McGill at Hampton, the library personnel at Eastman and Oberlin, and William Grant Still. Too, De Lerma learned that Dett's major publisher, Summy-Birchard, planned to issue an anthology of Dett's piano music.[18] In the late 1960s, while at Indiana University in Bloomington, De Lerma, as Director of the Black Music Center, scheduled a series of performances of Dett's music in that city, Washington, D.C., New Orleans, and Boulder. The programs included *In the Bottoms*, played by Natalie Hinderas, and "Ride on, Jesus," sung by tenor John Patton with Susan Peters, pianist.[19] De Lerma and McBrier contributed substantive introductory sketches on Dett's life and music for Summy-Birchard's *The Collected Piano Works of R. Nathaniel Dett* (1973). De Lerma is presently director of the Center for Black Music Research at Columbia College in Chicago.

* * *

A letter dated April 17, 1972 from Miss Vona Etheridge of the R. Nathaniel Dett Club in Chicago proved that Dett was still popular in that city. Addressed to Oberlin College the letter read:

Dear Oberlin College:

We have a club named R. Nathaniel Dett. We are doing a play on him and we would appreciate background information on him, as far back as possible.

If you are unable to produce any type of information, we would appreciate it very much if you could refer us to such a place. A speeded reply would also be appreciated.

Yours truly,
The R. Nathaniel Dett Club[20]

The "speeded" answer to Miss Etheridge from Gertrude Jacob, Archives Assistant, read:

> Your letter of April 17 just reached this office yesterday afternoon. A search of Dr. Dett's alumni file provides little information which may prove helpful to you in doing a play, but it is hoped that from the assortment of material Xeroxed—a 1927 recital review and commentary, newspaper clippings at the time of Dr. Dett's death in 1943 and the obituary prepared in Oberlin, you can find some of the things you are hoping for.[21]

In part due to the publication of Dett's *Collected Piano Works* in 1973, an appreciation and a revival of interest in him surfaced. Robert Finn, writing for the *Cleveland* (Ohio) *Plain Dealer*, reminisced while announcing a free-to-the-public performance of *The Ordering of Moses* by the Cuyahoga Community College in Cleveland on April 29, 1973:

> Many a young piano student (myself included) has worked away at . . . "Juba Dance" . . . without the slightest notion as to who Dett was, when he lived or what else he may have written.
> With the rise in recent years of interest in black music and musicians, Dett's name has turned up in books and articles as an example of the classically trained American black musician whose contribution has been, until now, unjustly neglected.[22]

The performance at the college was by non-professional musicians and "only a small orchestra," but promised to "give some idea of the flavor and texture of Dett's choral-orchestral efforts," according to Finn, who quoted De Lerma in saying that Dett "was not really at home writing for such large forces." Finn gave full credit in his article to De Lerma's biographical essay in Dett's *Collected Piano Works*, while pointing out the importance of Dett's friendship with Percy Grainger and his post-graduate study with eminent professors. Finn agreed that

Dett indeed understood the piano and how to write for it. His music is not terribly adventurous and only intermittently of virtuoso difficulty, but it is very pianistic, lying well for the hands and sounding well. The six suites reveal two sides of Dett's musical character, his interest in black folklore and in Biblical themes.

Oberlin continued to receive queries in the 1970s concerning Dett. One dated August 10, 1974 from Brooklynite E. Harrison Gordon, then completing a book titled *Black Classical Musicians of the 20th Century*, wanted information on Dett's next of kin. In part his letter to the Oberlin Music Department read:

> Dett is one of the musicians I have included in my book. I must contact the next of kin to check my sketch about him for errors and gain their approval for printing of the sketch. I would appreciate any help you can give me.

In prompt answer to Gordon, W. E. Bigglestone, Oberlin Archivist, wrote on August 19, saying:

> I am afraid we can be of little help to you. When Mr. Dett died he was survived by his wife, Helen Elise Smith Dett, and two daughters, Helen Charlotte and Josephine Elizabeth. I know nothing more about them.

Bigglestone referred Gordon to the previously mentioned Miss Vona Etheridge of Chicago, and to schools where Dett had taught.[23]

* * *

Mrs. Mildred Clark of Niagara Falls, N.Y., was quite insightful concerning the material which Samuel Dett had given her on his brother Nathaniel and the Dett family. She wrote:

Getting along in years myself I wanted what he gave me to be preserved and available to anyone interested to read. I called Mr. Loker at the library [Donald E. Loker, Local Historian at NFNYPL] and asked him if he would like it for the Niagara Falls department. He felt the same way about it as I did, so in 1975, October, I gave it to him.[24]

Mrs. Clark mentioned a shorter biography by McBrier, "published by the local college in 1945, distributed to local art patrons." She might, however, have been speaking of Pope's or Marteena's short unpublished sketch. (See Bibliography of *Follow Me.*) Mrs. Clark's own essay, "Remembering Niagara's Dett," was published February 19, 1989, in the *Niagara Falls Gazette*, in a series titled "Reflections on Black History." She was a guest speaker at some of the memorial services for Dett in the 1980s, as following programs in this chapter will indicate.

* * *

Donald E. Loker and his staff at NFNYPL have meticulously catalogued and preserved the Dett Collection there, largely due to the interest and efforts of Miss Arlene E. Gray, a retired teacher and librarian, now living in Crystal Beach, Ontario. Seven years before her catalog of the NFNYPL Dett holdings (published as *Listen to the Lambs* in 1984) Gray began this special project. As a definitive source book for Dett materials in this particular library, *Listen to the Lambs* has been cross-referenced methodically and carefully. Since its publication Gray has compiled several updated supplements as additional material accumulated.

Listen to the Lambs was made possible in part with funding from an anonymous grant "presented by Msgr. Joseph E. Schieder, patron of the project and friend of the author," and from another grant "in memory of Winston C. Fischer of Niagara Falls, Ontario, . . . made by the Niagara Falls Heritage Foundation of Niagara Falls, Canada, and presented by Mr. George Seibel, City Historian."[25] It has been distributed to libraries and schools from Boston to Los Angeles, as well as to those in Canada and Europe.

By 1987, realizing that *Listen to the Lambs* would not appeal to young students required in their school studies to become acquainted with famous local people, Gray structured a short narrative of Dett's life, titled *Nate, My Son*. Fifty copies were printed that year by In and Out Printing in Niagara Falls, New York.

Gray's long career as a school music teacher and performing musician kept her in touch with Dett's career. She explained that her step-mother was Dett's classmate at the Niagara Falls Collegiate Institute. Her piano teacher, Alice Babcock Trott of Niagara Falls, New York, was one of Dett's devoted patrons. When Miss Trott assigned Dett's piece "Mammy" to Arlene Gray, the young girl did not know who Dett was, nor that Mrs. Charlotte Dett had at one time been Miss Trott's housekeeper.

In 1987 Gray took an active part in the Niagara Falls (New York) High School's program when Dett was the honored guest for National Music Week. She stated: "At the Eastman School of Music, Rochester, New York, Dr. Dett was on the composition faculty when I was doing graduate work in 1932-33."[26] Her uncle had worked with Samuel Dett at the Niagara Falls Post Office. As her main reason for writing *Nate, My Son* she said, "I have always believed in the ability of all people to develop their God-given talents, especially the 'black minority,' at a time when many people did not or would not recognize this fact."[27]

Gray was born in 1909 in Niagara Falls, New York, where she attended elementary and secondary schools. In addition to music degrees (B. M. and M. M.) from the Eastman School of Music, she also received a degree in Library Science from Syracuse University, followed by further study in both fields. Her many professional honors and affiliations testify to her versatility and efficiency. She served for many years as a professional accompanist, both on organ and piano, and established libraries in elementary and high schools where previously there had been none. Her longest teaching position was at LaSalle High in Niagara Falls, New York.

This lovely, dedicated lady never plans to be idle. Her latest publication is *The Hymn: An Analytical Study* (Ridgeway, Ontario, Canada: Smith-Davidson Litho. Ltd., 1991). It is partially dedicated posthumously to "Miss Alice

Arlene E. Gray, ca. 1985,
courtesy the Local History Department,
Niagara Falls, New York, Public Library.

Babcock Trott, author's friend and former piano teacher."

* * *

Donald E. Loker, a specialist in American history, was named Local Historian of the NFNYPL in March of 1979, succeeding Marjorie Williams who died the previous year. He came to Niagara Falls as history master at the former DeVeaux School. He graciously continues to take a keen interest in the treasured volumes, manuscripts, and documents at the NFNYPL. He has been City of Niagara Falls historian, president of the Niagara Falls Historical Society, and secretary of the Niagara County Historical Society.

Modestly vague about his personal past and his years of residence in Niagara Falls, Loker has admitted to arriving there "after receiving a degree in history from Otterbein College in Westerville, Ohio, and being 'involved in Niagara's past ever since.'"[28] Loker has authored a history of the DeVeaux School, a Niagara Falls guidebook, a biography of Sgt. Lewis Leffman (the first regular US army soldier to earn a pension), and *News of the Day*, "a humorous collection of old news stories and items from local newspapers."[29] Loker contributed news items in remembrance of Dett to *Out of the Mist*, newsletter of the Niagara Falls Historical Society, in April/May of 1975 February and March of 1976.

Loker's Local History Department played a prime role in the 1985 Niagara Reservation Centennial, a large scale project allowing him to work closely with the Smithsonian Institute and the Corcoran Gallery of Art in Washington, D.C., and with western New York galleries and state officials. Loker personally designed Dett's cemetery stone, placed in Fairview Cemetery, Niagara Falls, Ontario, where Arthur, Charlotte, and Samuel Dett are also buried. On February 23, 1976, the NFNYPL and the Niagara Falls Historical Society co-sponsored a musical program honoring Dett. At this event the Niagara Falls High School chorus, directed by Mrs. Marva Kincannon, and piano soloist Diane Schackleford were featured. Loker gave a biographical sketch of Dett.

* * *

Besides the collections in the Hampton University Archives and the NFNYPL, substantial holdings on Dett are at the Schomburg Center (New York City Public Library), Bennett College, Oberlin College, Moorland-Spingarn Research Center at Howard University, Sibley Library at the Eastman School of Music, and the Grainger Museum in Melbourne, Australia. Dett scholars would do well to inquire about loan and copying policies, as the regulations vary at these places. For instance, Sibley Library does not permit photo copying of its materials, which include approximately one dozen of Dett's musical manuscripts, his poetry *Song of Seven* (ms), two bound sketchbooks, correspondence, assorted performance programs, published sheet music for organ, voice, solo instruments, choir, and piano, and some of Dett's personal library of books. Also Sibley has musical scores presented to Dett by such friends/composers as Harry Burleigh, Will Marion Cook, William Dawson, Arthur Foote, Percy Grainger, J. Rosamond Johnson, and Geoffrey O'Hara.

* * *

In a personal memoir from Kathleen Reynolds Bruyn, dated March 1, 1976, to Mrs. Edith Cammack in Lewiston, New York, Mrs. Bruyn recalled that Dett had visited in Denver at the home of her friend George Morrison. Dett and Morrison were totally absorbed in playing piano and violin, and when another violinist dropped by "he and Nate romped through Beethoven Sonatas, etc., for hours and I had a heck of a time getting them back to my house for a nine o'clock dinner."[30]

On March 16, 1976, Dorothy Maynor's class at the Harlem School of the Arts in New York City premiered a one-act opera, "The Walls Came Tumbling Down." Composed by Willard Roosevelt and Loften Mitchell, it concerned seventeenth century Negroes living in New Amsterdam. On the same evening Dett was paid a "choreographic tribute" with a dance segment of *In the Bottoms*, created by Charles Neal. Other presentations that evening were choreography of some of Ulysses Kay's spiritual arrangements. Maynor received the annual award given by the New York Committee for Young Audiences from pianist Arthur

THE BOARD OF DIRECTORS OF THE NIAG. FALLS PUBLIC LIBRARY
AND
THE NIAGARA FALLS HISTORICAL SOCIETY, INC.
PRESENT

A PROGRAMME OF THE
MUSIC
OF
NATHANIEL DETT, Ph.D.
(1883 - 1943)
NIAGARA'S BLACK MUSICIAN

THE MIXED CHORUS OF THE NIAGARA FALLS HIGH SCHOOL

MRS. MARVA KINCANNON, VOCAL DIRECTOR

MISS DAWNE SCHACKLEFORD, ACCOMPANIST

7:30 P.M.
THE AUDITORIUM
THE EARL W. BRYDGES LIBRARY
FEBRUARY 23, 1976

Flyer and program courtesy of the
Local History Department,
Niagara Falls, New York, Public Library.

PROGRAMME

Lift Every Voice and Sing........Negro National
                                 Anthem

The Pledge to the Flag...........Miss Teresa L.
                                 Lasher, Program
                                 Chairman, N.F.
                                 Historical Society

Welcome..........................Oswald J. Joerg,
                                 Library Director
                                 N.F. Public Library
                                 Donald E. Loker,
                                 President, N.F.
                                 Historical Society

Let Us Cheer The Weary Traveler..Chorus

Steal Away.......................Chorus

Roll, Jordon, Roll...............Chorus

We Are Climbing Jacob's Ladder...Chorus

Juba Dance.......................Piano Solo,
                                 Miss Schackleford

A Brief Biographical Sketch......Mr. Loker
  of Mr. Dett

My Lord What A Morning...........Chorus

I Belong To The Union Band.......Chorus

Nobody Knows The Trouble I   Vocal Solo, Miss
  See, Lord...................... Valencia Bedgood

Murm'ring Word...................Chorus

Listen To The Lambs..............Chorus

Courtesy of the Local History Department,
Niagara Falls, New York, Public Library.

Rubinstein. A non-enthusiastic critic for the *New York Times*, March 17, 1976, referred to Dett's *In the Bottoms* as "quaintly faded."

A bicentennial celebration of the Triad Chorale at Alice Tully Hall was reported in the *New York Times*, June 7, 1976. The concert, presented the previous evening, featured foremost William Grant Still, but included works by eleven other composers, among whom were Dett, Ulysses Kay, James Bland, W. C. Handy, and Talib Rasul Hakim. The *Times* item stated that "One especially impressive discovery was the final section of The Ordering of Moses by R. Nathaniel Dett (1882-1943), a choral epic on a Handelian scale, bristling with striking dramatic musical ideas." The music was directed by Noel de Costa, who was also to be director of another gala performance for a Dett Centennial in 1982.

As previously mentioned in connection with Armstrong Hall and the Dett Wing within it, Dorothy Maynor was guest speaker for Founder's Day on the Hampton campus on January 28, 1977. Maynor's opening remarks were general, but praise for her experience as a Hampton student was personal and heartfelt. As she proceeded to the subject of Dett she marveled at his ability to overcome an ancestral background of slavery and make a name for himself. As she put it, "Somehow though, as by a hidden cunning, this youngster brought it off; he accomplished the impossible," through his love of music. Speaking of his marriage to Helen Smith, Maynor said that

> . . . it brought into collaboration two richly endowed people whose joint labors over many later years set standards and laid foundations that make us to this day, even as we gather here now, debtors to their diligence and determination.

Hailing Dett as someone wanting to further his race, she described him as a person of "uncommon qualities. He was perceptive, sensitive, proud, bearing a conceit that went well beyond himself, encompassing humankind as bearers of the image of God." Maynor pointed out that though Dett was not born or raised in the South, he nevertheless was

. . . feeling the strange magic of the South's contradictions. . . . This black Canadian had a strange yearning to find out what went on in cotton fields and sugar bottoms. . . . It does not distort the truth for me to say Dett's influence on me was the great Continental Divide that bisected my life.

Though when Maynor entered Hampton she had no intention of making a career of singing, she said that Dett "was the catalyst. . . . Dett had shown me the way. He, so to say, drew me a map and handed it to me." Her address listed Dett's accomplishments at Hampton and cited his dedication to fine performance, "quietly holding before us his own life as a shining instance of striving to do justice to the best that God has bestowed upon us."

She recalled the five o'clock a. m. choir rehearsals, and Dett's deploration of wasted time. "He seemed almost to suffer physical pain," she remembered, "when one of us was late or ill-tempered, or carelessly dressed, or disrespectful of the English language." In conclusion she said candidly:

I am not certain that Hampton appreciated in full measure what Nathaniel Dett gave to Hampton. . . . If I may say so, Mr. President [Hill], the recognition accorded him on this occasion is long overdue. It is for me a gloriously bright moment that I am privileged to salute the memory of Robert Nathaniel Dett— creative spirit, dedicated artist, friend of youth, harbinger of a brighter day for us all.[31]

As already stated, on this occasion a bronze plaque in Dett's honor, now hanging in Armstrong Hall, was presented as an official part of the Bicentennial Parade of American Music.

* * *

Dr. Doris McGinty's review of McBrier's biography of Dett, published in 1977, was on the whole complimentary. McGinty,

professor of music at Howard University, considered the work
definitive, well researched and organized, though pointing out
some deficiencies in correspondence, allowing that these
documents may not have been available at the time of McBrier's
publication. Noting McBrier's inclusion of musical examples in
both the text and the Appendix, she still wished that more
consistency had been observed

> . . . for there are times when the discussion of technical
> aspects of Dett's music within the body of the works
> seems obtrusive. One could also wish for an index because
> of the quantity of useful information contained in the
> volume.

McGinty deemed any minor reservations insignificant beside
Dr. McBrier's major accomplishment, saying that the biography
did exactly what the author intended. It presented Dett as a
serious social thinker as well as an educator and a composer who
"deserves a significant place in American music."[32]

Though the performance was undated, the *Central Opera
Service Bulletin* (Winter 1977/78) reported that Dett's
"children's opera," *The Ordering of Moses*, was produced by the
New York City Intermediate School and the Manhattan School
of Music Prep Division, supervised by Cynthia Auerbach. It was
videotaped. Head Librarian Pamela Bristah at the Manhattan
School of Music confirmed the performance at Martin Luther King
High School, but was not able to supply a specific date nor a
printed program.

The 1980s

The decade of the 1980s marked the 100th anniversary of
Dett's birth. On February 17, 1980, tribute was paid at the First
Presbyterian Church in Niagara Falls, New York, as a part of
Black History Week. The event, with choirs of the host church
and those from New Hope Baptist Church and the Niagara Falls
High School Choir, were directed by Deryk Aird, organist, choir
master, and violinist at the host church. Aird, a former student
of Arlene Gray, performed Dett's "Ramah" for violin. Highlight

of the choral presentation was Dett's "Listen to the Lambs" with soloists Gary Burgess, tenor, and Reverend Leotis Belk, baritone. Burgess at the time was head of the Opera Department at the University of Buffalo. During the week's celebration Dett's music, manuscripts, and letters were on display at the NFNYPL.[33] The program, organized by Arlene Gray, was sponsored by local merchants and citizens, and included a biographical sketch on Dett by Donald E. Loker.

Dett remained popular in Chicago as well as in Niagara Falls. On April 25, 1982, the Monumental Baptist Senior Choir of Chicago, directed by Minister of Music Hortense Love, celebrated his 100th anniversary. A writer from the *Chicago Crusader* for that date remarked that Dett had been friends with such music leaders as Isaac T. Yarborough, J. Wesley Jones, James A. Mundy, and Estella Bonds. The item also included biographical material on Dett and mentioned his best known compositions. Chairman of the event was Clifford A. Eaton, a former Dett student, who as a spokesman of the R. Nathaniel Dett Bi-Centennial Committee wrote the Oberlin Alumni Office that "a letter of commendation from the College commemorating Dr. Dett's birthday would be highly appreciated."[34]

Though the specific date was missing from a 1982 news item in the *Daily Press* (Norfolk, Virginia), the writer was aware of only one performance in honor of Dett's 100th anniversary previous to the one in Norfolk which she was reviewing. She deplored the fact that the music of Dett's contemporaries Igor Stravinsky, Charles Ives, and Charles T. Griffes was more frequently heard than Dett's, attributing the situation to "the American public's love affair with European music and with those whose works are European in nature and feeling."

On the concert, likely in early spring of 1982, held at Christ and St. Luke's Episcopal Church in Norfolk, Dett's *The Ordering of Moses* was given by the I. Sherman Greene Chorale (founded in 1972) and members of the Virginia Philharmonic Orchestra. The reviewer considered *Moses* an "important example of twentieth century writing, . . . important as a thrilling piece of music." She continued:

The work is large and quite beautiful. . . . Its

THE PROGRAM

Master of Ceremonies   *Donald E. Loker*

1.   *The Detts and the Niagara Falls, Ontario years (1880-93)*
                                                  Arthur Jolley

2.   *The Niagara Falls, N.Y. years (1893-1943)*
          a. At this Church and in local musical events
                                            Rev. Russell Stevenson
          b. The Dett family's contribution to this city
                                                Mrs. Mildred Clark

3.   *Chorus:"Let us cheer the weary traveller" Dett*
                                          New Hope Baptist Choir
                                          Mrs. Marva Frails, conducting

4.   *Vocal solo:"Were thou the moon"(c1924) from Dett's book of*
      poetry "Album of a heart"(c1911) Dett
                                            Gary Burgess, tenor
                                            Mrs. Mary Carolyn Neff,accompanist

5.   *Chorus:"Roll, Jordan, Roll"(adaptation of a Negro spiritual)Dett*
                                              N.F. High School Chorus
                                              Mrs. Frails, conducting

6.   *The Professional years (1908-43)*
          a. Greetings from Msgr. Joseph E. Schieder
          b. Presented by Sr. M. Jonelle

7.   *Violin solo: "Ramah"(c1928)   Dett*
                                      Deryck Aird, violinst
                                      Charlene Aird, accompanist

8.   *Vocal solo: "Lead gently, Lord, and slow"(c1924) Dett*
                                      Rev. Dr. Leotis Belk, baritone
                                      Mrs. Johnnie R.A. Belk,accompanist

9.   *Chorus: "Gently, Lord, oh gently lead us"(c1924) Dett*
                                      First Presbyterian Choir
                                      Mr. Aird, conducting

10.   *Introduction of the Guest of Honor*
                                      Rev. Belk

11.   *A Tribute: "R. Nathaniel Dett; his life and work"*
                                      Dr. Vivian Flagg McBrier,author

12.   *Piano solos: "Mammy"(c1912) Dett*
                  "Juba dance" (c1913) Dett
                                      Mrs. Belk, pianist

Program courtesy of the
Local History Department,
Niagara Falls, New York, Public Library.

13. *Combined choruses:"Listen to the lambs" (c1914) Dett*
    First Presbyterian Choir
    New Hope Baptist Choir
    Niagara Falls High School Chorus
                    Mr. Aird, directing
                    Mrs. Neff, organist
                    Mr. Burgess, tenor soloist

THIS PROGRAM IS DEDICATED TO THE MEMORY OF

MISS ALICE BABCOCK TROTT
Former organist of this church
Piano teacher of Mrs. Neff and Miss Gray
Friend of the Dett family

foundation is a rich, dark tapestry with exciting fugal writing above the dark layer for both the chorus and the orchestra. Dett created spectacular musical effects for the orchestra. It is no accompanying vehicle to the choir and soloists, but a full partner in the score. Howard Hanson, once Dett's teacher, does not stand above him. And neither Griffes nor Edward MacDowell could have written such a splendid score.

Praise was also extended to director Carl Haywood of the Greene Chorale, "the best trained choral organization in Tidewater." Saying that the orchestra "gave a distinguished performance" the review concluded: "This was a rewarding musical evening, reminding us of our neglect of American music and the pleasure we deny ourselves in not tapping its rich resources."

The *Buffalo Evening News*, May 6, 1982, announced concerts celebrating Buffalo's Sesquicentennial on one of which Dett's songs were performed. Dett represented the honored area composer for the event.

THE SENIOR CHOIR

of

MONUMENTAL BAPTIST CHURCH

PROUDLY PRESENTS

"A Centennial Celebration Concert "

Featuring The Music of

R. Nathaniel Dett

SUNDAY AFTERNOON, APRIL 25, 1982 — 4:00

**In the Church Sanctuary
729 East Oakwood Boulevard
Chicago**

Mr. Clifford Eaton, Chairman

Mrs. Edna Jordan, President
Miss Hortense Love, Minister of Music

Dr. D. E. King, Pastor

Program courtesy Hampton University Archives.

A quite significant dedication was made in Dett's honor on October 17, 1982, in conjunction with the 126th anniversary of the Dett family's first church in Niagara Falls, Ontario, the British Methodist Episcopal Church on Peer Street. The service was organized in large part by Arlene Gray, Msgr. Joseph E. Schieder, and Donald E. Loker. One of the guest speakers for the occasion was Dr. Vivian Flagg McBrier. After the ceremony a marker, designed by Loker and donated by the Niagara Falls, New York, Historical Society, was unveiled at Dett's gravesite. Rectangular in shape, the stone displays bass and treble clefs and is inscribed with three lines: R. Nathaniel Dett/ 1882-1943/ "Listen to the Lambs."[35]

* * *

The Dett Centennial Committee was not only active in Chicago, but at Hampton as well. Hampton Choral Director, Roland Carter, was chairperson for a four-day celebration in October of 1982 to be held at Hampton. Carter's form letter, dated August 6, 1981, was sent well in advance for participants to make plans for the event. With the purpose of recognizing Dett and of re-introducing his music and poetry through performance, readings, and lectures, the lengthy but well-designed program included such luminary presenters and performers as Dorothy Maynor (keynote speaker), Dr. McBrier, Dr. Eileen Southern, William Dawson, and Dett's daughter Mrs. Helen Dett Hopkins.[36]

Two months earlier, August 8-13, at the sixty-third annual convention of NANM Carter had conducted performances of Dett's "Listen to the Lambs" and "I'll Never Turn Back No More," when 200 musicians sang from memory. "It was not surprising that most of those present did know them and sang them . . . without a score, even observing the dynamics," *The Crisis* reported, quoting Carter.[37] At the meeting, held in Chicago's Bismarck Hotel and the Metropolitan Community Church, Carter conducted a highly successful choral workshop, and was afterwards hailed as a furtherer of Dett's traditions at Hampton.

Another performance of Dett's works was announced in the

October 17, 1982

3:00   *Service at the British Methodist Episcopal Church*

4:00   *Unveiling of monument to Dr. Dett at the*
        Fairview Cemetery, Niagara Falls, Ontario,
        site of his grave in the family plot. The
        stone was purchased through a grant from the
        Niagara Falls, N.Y. Historical Society, Inc. It
        is hoped that a stone will also mark his mother's
        grave sometime in the future.

4:30   *Reception at the Lundy's Lane Historical Museum*
        5810 Ferry Street, Niagara Falls, Ontario

SPONSORING ORGANIZATIONS

The Lundy's Lane Historical Society, the Society in the
city where Dr. Dett was born

The Niagara Falls Historical Society, Inc. (NY) in
the city where Dr. Dett grew to maturity

MASTERS OF CEREMONY

John Burtniak; President of the Lundy's Lane Historical Society

Donald E. Loker; President of the Niagara Falls (NY) Historical
Society

The committee wishes to thank the many people who aided
in the program and in helping to recall the life of
Niagara's outstanding musician. In particular it thanks
Rev. Dr. Harold Jackman, pastor of this B.M.E. Church.

Program courtesy of the
Local History Department,
Niagara Falls, New York, Public Library.

PROGRAMME

Opening remarks and introduction of honored guests

Welcome to British Methodist Episcopal Church
        Rev. Dr. Harold Jackman, pastor

Greetings from Dr. Daniel G. Hill, President of the Ontario
        Black History Society, Toronto, Ontario

"R. Nathaniel Dett, his life and works"
        Dr. Vivian McBrier, biographer, Washington, D.C.

"Mammy", piano solo   Dett
        Dr. Grace Setzer, Faculty member of the Norfolk (VA)
        State College

"Saving the record"   Mildred Clark
        Donor of Dett materials

"Ramah", violin solo   Dett
        Deryck Aird, violinist
        Carolyn Goetzen, accompanist
        Faculty members: Bradley School of Music
            Research Ltd., Niagara Falls, Ontario

"Dett, the man"   Msgr. Joseph E. Schieder
        Procurator: Catholic Diocese of Buffalo

"Juba dance", piano solo   Dett

"A former piano pupil remembers"   Mary Carolyn Neff
        Organist & Choir director, St. Peter's Episcopal
        Church, Niagara Falls, N.Y.

"A bibliography of Dett's works"   Arlene E. Gray
        Author & Co-ordinator of this program

"Listen to the lambs", choral work   Dett
        Recording by Evelyn White Chorale, Washington, D.C.

Closing remarks

                    ****

Ceremony at the Fairview Cemertery, Niagara Falls, Ontario

                    ****

Reception at the Lundy's Lane Historical Museum,
        Peer Street, Niagara Falls, Ontario

New York Times, October 15, 1982, for October 17 at the
Symphony Space at Broadway and 96th Streets in New York
City. Honoring Dett's centennial, works by composers Harry
Burleigh, Carl Diton, Eubie Blake, Samuel Coleridge-Taylor,
Florence Price, Hall Johnson, W. C. Handy, and Eva Jessye were
also presented. The concert was given under auspices of Triad
Presentations founded by Clarissa Cumbo in 1970, as a non-profit
organization for promoting the work of black composers and
artists. Program director and conductor of the chorale was Noel
de Costa, who said:

> Some of the compositional styles of these composers
> were similar, though each had his own special point of
> departure. They accepted the harmonic and contrapuntal
> information from the culture at large, from a European
> source, and they used parts of that. Other parts came
> from their spiritual culture.

The October 15 *Times* item included a brief biography of
Dett. De Costa said further of him:

> He was immersed in the folk experience, which
> influenced, in part, his composition. The other part came
> from his involvement with composition at large. He
> spent every summer at places like Harvard, the Eastman
> School and so forth. He kept abreast of what was
> current, while at the same time he kept his rich
> experience coming out of the Afro-American folk
> spiritual.

Three of Dett's *a cappella* works, "Listen to the Lambs," "As
By the Streams of Babylon" (interpreted from Thomas Campian),
and "Let Us Cheer the Weary Traveler," arranged by Dett as a
short motet, were performed. *Moses* was also presented with
piano accompaniment by Marjorie De Lewis, a thirty-four voice
chorale, and soloists Max Bertrand, Ruth Elmore, Alpha Floyd,
Benjamin Matthews, and John Morrison.[38]
New York Times reviewer Edward Rothenstein said of the
occasion:

It was not just a tribute to a black composer who composed choral music. It was also a tribute to his contemporaries, a generation of black composers that came to maturity well after the end of slavery and finished its work well before the Civil Rights Act.[39]

Pointing out that Dett's music and that of this program's other composers was not in the fashion of blues, jazz, or ragtime Rothenstein continued:

> Their expressions may have derived from folk styles, from the Spiritual, from religious song, but the musical forms often came from the European performance tradition. . . . Dett's "Listen to the Lambs" and his arrangement of "As By the Streams of Babylon" gently combined some aspects of the Germanic chorale with the tradition of the spiritual.

Rothenstein spoke of the Triad Chorale and the soprano soloists as "refined and energetic." Though he approved of Dett's handling of the "Go Down Moses" theme, he was not pleased with the entire *Moses*, "nearly stifled by its oratorio form and its aspirations for the European tradition. Nevertheless, the fine soloists . . . captured a sense of the personal urgency in the music."

* * *

Events honoring Dett continued at Oberlin College in 1983. An October 6 sesquicentennial concert, announced in some detail by the *Oberlin College News Bulletin*, September 23, was to feature works by Oberlin College alumni George Walker, William Grant Still, and Dett. The *Bulletin* release gave short biographies of each composer. At the time Walker was a full professor at Rutgers University. Still had died in 1978. Six of Dett's vocal solos were performed by baritone Ben Holt and accompanist Cliff Jackson: "What Kind of Shoes You Going to Wear?," "Now We Take This Feeble Body," "Hymn to Parnassus," "In That Morning," "Go On, Brother," and "I'm A-Trav'ling to the Grave."

At the same time another remembrance of Dett was underway in Niagara Falls, Ontario, a re-dedication of the British Methodist Episcopal Church. On November 20, 1983, this church was designated as the R. Nathaniel Dett Memorial Chapel of the B. M. E. Church of Canada.[40] Again, Gray and Loker were instrumental in planning the prestigious occasion. At this time the Niagara Falls, New York, Historical Society gave a grave stone for Mrs. Charlotte Dett. Its inscription, composed by Loker, reads:

> The family of Charlotte Washington Dett lived in both Niagara Falls, Ontario and Niagara Falls, New York. Mrs. Dett and her sons Arthur, Nathaniel, and Samuel are all buried here. R. Nathaniel Dett, Mus. D., was an outstanding black composer, pianist, conductor, and poet. Dr. Dett wrote many inspirational religious songs including "Listen to the Lambs."

The four-page program also included Charlotte Dett's obituary from the *Niagara Falls Gazette*, April 9, 1937, a photo of the church, and one of Dett, in addition to Loker's personal biographical sketch of Dett. (Only the actual program is included here, taken from Arlene Gray's 1985 supplement to *Listen to the Lambs*, p. 3.)

Dett was one of six people honored in memory by the Niagara Falls, New York, Historical Society with a tribute in the *Niagara Falls Gazette*, May 26, 1985. Samuel Dett was also honored posthumously by an item in the *Gazette*, February 13, 1987, during Black History Week.

The Ordering of Moses was performed in Houston, Texas, October 11, 1987, in celebration of the 105th anniversary of Dett's birth. The free event, announced in the October 3, 1987 Houston *Informer and Texas Freeman*, was held at Miller Outdoor Theatre, featuring the forty-piece Scott Joplin Chamber Orchestra and chorus, and soloists April Sloan, Cynthia Nelson, Lewis Wilson, and Dorceal Duckins. Conductor Anne Lundy said:

PROGRAMME

WELCOME   Bro. B. Passley[1]
NEGRO SPIRITUALS   Dett
    B.M.E. Angel Childrens' Chorus, Mrs. Phelps, conducting

GREETINGS   Rt. Rev. G.H. Boyce,
                                     General Supt., B.M.E. Church

VOCAL SOLO "O Lord, the hard-won miles"   Dett
    Betty Little Phelps, contralto, Miss Gray, accompanist

GREETINGS   Rev. Harold Jackman[2]

NEGRO SPIRITUALS   Dett
    B.M.E. Church Adult Choir. Mrs. Phelps, conducting

INSTRUMENTAL SOLO   Dett
    Mrs. Nita Chamberlain, B.M.E. Church organist

GREETINGS   Rev. R.H. Blackwood[2]

PIANO SOLO "Mammy"   Dett
    Mrs. Mary Carolyn Neff

INTRODUCTION OF HONORED GUESTS   Miss Gray
    1 Mr. John Burtniak   5 Miss Zetta Mae Miller
    2 Mrs. Mildred Clark   6 Mayor Wayne Thomson
    3 Miss Elizabeth Hopkins   7 Miss Elizabeth Young
    4 Mr. Donald E. Loker

DEDICATION CEREMONY   Rev. Ernest Crawford[1]

FINALE "Listen to the lambs" (piano/organ arr.)   Dett
    Mrs. Dorothy Haynes, organist
    Miss Gray, pianist
                    ****

After the programme

Dedication of a stone for Charlotte Washington Dett (his mother)
    at the Fairview Cemetery, Niagara Falls, Ontario

Participants: Mr. Burtniak, Mrs. Clark, Mr. Loker, Miss Young

The stone was given by the Niagara Falls, N.Y. Historical
    Society as was one for R. Nathaniel Dett in 1982.

    1 Associated with this church
    2 Former pastors of this church

Program of November 20, 1983, in Niagara Falls, Ontario.
Courtesy of the Local History Department,
Niagara Falls, New York, Public Library.

The oratorio highlights Dett's unique classical arrangements of traditional black spirituals. It will be very unusual and interesting for the audience to hear such spirituals as "Go Down Moses" and "He is King of Kings" in a symphonic setting. . . . Black composers' birthdays are so often not recognized in this manner, the way . . . Bach and Vivaldi are celebrated.[41]

On the same program, in addition to *Moses*, some of Dett's arrangements of spirituals were sung by the Wheeler Avenue Baptist Church's Men's Chorus, directed by Clyde Owen Jackson.

The Detroit *Michigan Chronicle*, May 28, 1988, carried a short biographical sketch on Dett in its column "Classical Notes," citing him as one of the "black musicians of the past who have made important contributions to American music." Some of Dett's music (unspecified) was to be performed in Ogden Hall on the Hampton campus December 9, 1989.[42]

The 1990s

A two-day Dett Festival in Chicago, scheduled for the St. Mark United Methodist Church, was announced in the *Chicago Tribune*, October 21, 1990. Soloists were tenor Earl Calloway, sopranos Gloria Brown and Zolla M. Shaver, and saxophonist O'Darie Weathers. Vocal ensembles included the Children's Choir, the Choral Silhouettes, and the Dett Chorale, directed respectively by Evelyn Gaston, Florence M. Smith, and Wallace Cheatham. Cheatham also conducted the Dett Choral Society of Milwaukee in *Moses* in February, 1992, with soloist Paul Adkins.

On March 15, 1992, Gray and Loker co-ordinated an ecumenical service to "kick off" the centennial observance of Niagara Falls (NY) City Charter, featuring works of composers Dett and J. Ernest Rieger, former head of music at Niagara University. Pianists Lucile McElwain and Nancy Haeckl played selections from Dett's suites. Rieger's *The Grand and Mighty Niagara* was performed by Doris Wieloszynski.

In August of 1992 Dr. Raymond Jackson of Howard University was lecturer/recitalist for the New Orleans Institute of

Performing Arts. He spoke on and played compositions from several black American composers, a program similarly presented in Bethesda, Maryland in November of 1991. Parts of *In the Bottoms* were included.

* * *

The fact that Dett made his mark as a pianist, composer, arranger, and choral director is clear. In summary to Part I of this biography, some additional remarks on Dett by persons who knew him professionally seem appropriate. Mrs. Josephine Harreld Love, daughter of violinist and teacher Kemper Harreld, said of Dett in a letter dated August 16, 1991:

> [I] knew him well. He taught with me for several months at Bennett College, my first teaching job. He was brought in to head the Music Department in mid-year. I had been hired in September. He arrived in January. His forte was conducting but he was a fine pianist and all-round musician.
>
> The Dett daughters should be around somewhere, in their 60s or early 70s, if both are living. Not too cooperative, if what I have heard is true. I haven't seen them for over a half-century. [Dett] really was a superb musician. I think his compositions hold up so well.[43]

Professor George Brown, a student at Eastman in the early 1930s, recalls positive memories of Dett. Brown, privileged to have heard Dett guest-lecture in one of his musicology classes, said of him: "He presented himself in a professional and scholarly manner. His clothing, grammar, and delivery were all impeccably correct. Dett carried shining hope of aristocratic culture into all the schools where he taught."[44]

After Dett's death a well-written tribute to him appeared in the *Rochester Democrat and Chronicle*, October 5, 1943. It mentioned that Dett somewhat followed Harry Burleigh's example in elevating the Negro's music, and that Howard Hanson considered Dett the first "to raise Negro melodies to so high an artistic plane." The tribute's excellent summary of Dett as a musician bears quoting in part:

As an influence in the development of a native musical art, Dr. Robert Nathaniel Dett . . . earned his place with the important figures of his generation. He earned that place against the handicaps which the Negro musician faces, . . . by a great gift for musical expression and a character big enough to persist in spite of discouragement. His music today, particularly his choral music, has a recognized place on the concert platform and in the church choirs.

In adaptation of Negro folk tunes to choral and oratorio form, Dr. Dett showed a grasp of the mechanics of the chorus and orchestra and a deep instinct for the classic line.

Rochester is complimented by its close association with the career of Dr. Dett. . . . [He] had many warm friendships here. He had won distinctions in many parts of the world, accepted them with the modesty of a true artist. His death is a loss to musical art, his music a rich legacy to the cultural progress of the future.

PART TWO:
Musical Works

PART II

Chapter VIII

Dett's Piano and Other Instrumental Music

Introduction

Part II of *Follow Me* is devoted to discussion and analysis of Dett's musical works. Whether Dett emerged foremost as a pianist, choral director, composer, or arranger is not as important as the fact that he achieved excellence in each of these pursuits. As a public figure he was a target for criticism, but was never afraid to express himself in composition, conducting, performance, writing, or lecturing.

Aware of the poignancy inherent in Negro folk music, Dett strove to convey his race's longing, griefs, and aspirations, as a creative architect fashions native timber into a substantial structure. He and Harry Burleigh are considered the first Negro Americans to utilize the Negro folk tune for classic development.

DeLerma suggests that had Dett pursued the available musical idioms of his youth, namely the ragtime style of his *After the Cakewalk* (1900), he might have composed successfully for the theater. Further, De Lerma is convinced that the compositional attitudes of Anton Dvorak and Samuel Colerige-Taylor provided impetus for the direction in which Dett chose to go.[1] Interestingly, there are no references to Dett's having met either composer, possibly because Dvorak was at the National Conservatory in New York only from 1892-1895 when Dett was growing up in Niagara Falls. During Coleridge-Taylor's three brief visits to the US (1904, 1906, 1910), Dett was a student at Oberlin and afterwards employed at Lane. Their actual meeting would have been possible, but not likely. During Coleridge-Taylor's first two US visits for concerts of his own music Harry Burleigh was a featured soloist in Washington, D.C. and New York City.

Dett yearned for more time to compose, apart from his heavy and demanding teaching duties, a frustration partially self-inflicted, perhaps subconsciously for self-enhancement, but basically because he was driven by some inner demon to achieve. As a leader he ably commanded a following, hence the title of this book. He did not require cult worship, but rather sought respect for his race through quality and expression in his compositions, which vary in intensity, interest, and perhaps even worth,

351

a judgment true of most composers' works.

Except for the last two piano suites, *Tropic Winter* and *Eight Bible Vignettes* which show influence of contemporary idioms, Dett's style was neoromantic with traditional rhythms and harmonies. McBrier assesses Dett's piano compositions:

> In order fully to appreciate the piano music of R. Nathaniel Dett, it must be understood that he was a true Romanticist. Music to him was an expression of the human soul with all of its subjectivism. It was an expression of hope, love, despair; an instrument for his dreams and poetic longings; a vehicle for his racial messages and love for humanity. Dett was a Romantic in both ideological and technical character. All of his piano compositions are programmatic, expressing a racial trait, nature, or philosophical idea; and most of the compositions are constructed in song-form.[2]

McBrier divided his suites into three periods: (1) *Magnolia* (1912) and *In the Bottoms* (1913); (2) *Enchantment* (1922) and *Cinnamon Grove* (1928); and (3) *Tropic Winter* (1938) and *Eight Bible Vignettes* (1941-1943). She distinguishes those of the first period from the following ones by their "lyrical melodies, simple structures, and unpretentious charm," and points out that the Negro folk-idiom is suggested by syncopation, open fourths, and open fifths.[3]

Dett, by self-admission, was hesitant to compose for orchestra or instrumental ensemble. Consequently, his efforts in these areas compared to those represented by his piano, vocal, and choral works were minimal, and for the most part remain unpublished. The fact that he *did* compose for orchestra toward the end of his life indicates that he still sought the unattainable that drove him to accomplishment. His piano music, the genre which first interested him as a composer, along with his few orchestral works and instrumental pieces will be discussed in this chapter in chronological order. (Chapter IX includes his songs and arrangements of spirituals for solo voice, and Chapter X his choral works.) Mention will be made of several compositions no longer available and/or which were never published.

1900-1909

Dett's earliest piano compositions represent his own playing style, one characterizing the light popular salon music, conventional program music of the time. He later deplored the notion that ragtime was so often associated with the Negro's taste in music. His first published composition was *After the Cakewalk-March-Cakewalk* (1900, Vander Sloot Music Co., Williamsport, PA), a ragtime tune for piano. A copy of *After the Cakewalk* is in the Mesiah Papers and Documents. In the upper left corner is "Arranged by Lee Orean Smith," in the upper right "By Nathaniel Dett." Possibly Dett did not feel competent at notating his own compositions at that time. The melodic pattern of ♪♪♪♪♪♪|♪♪♪♩ with stride bass accompaniment, is in 2/4 meter, typical of rag rhythm. Its form is ABA with a trio, then a return to the B section in a second key. McBrier refers to the piece as a "two-step and polka, as well as a cake walk."[4]

Sketches in the Mesiah Papers and Documents of Dett's early piano and vocal works show frequent use of arpeggiation in the accompaniment. Some of these are "Waltz in the Key of G Major," "The Adieu Waltz" (melody line only with most stems on the wrong side of the notes), "Schwartzbach Gallop," and "Sylvan Stream Polonaise." Neither these nor "Niagara Falls," a two-step for piano from 1901, were published.

Cave of the Winds March for piano was published in 1902 by S. C. Fragard Company in Niagara Falls, New York. McBrier described it as a "vigorous march which uses simple traditional harmony."[5] Reminiscent of old-timey band music, the piece has three themes, all in 6/8 meter. The keys range from G major to C major, back to G major with some chromatic passages for transition. The first and third themes are given in Musical Example No. 1.

Dett's explanation of his inspiration for *Inspiration Waltzes*, published in 1903 reads:

> I awoke one night at midnight and heard, as in a dream, the melodies of this Waltz played over and over, until I again fell asleep. Next morning I found it was still fresh in my memory. I created the Introduction and some other parts to give the whole completeness, but the main themes were truly "Inspirations" or, to put it more poetically were truly "dictated by the Muse."[6]

Inspiration Waltzes for piano was published by Richard Saalfield (London) and dedicated to Mrs. Charlotte Dett, Dett's mother. Saalfield later orchestrated the lilting melodies of the *Waltzes*, for first and second violins, viola, cello, bass, b flat clarinet, flute, drums, and trombone, which parts are preserved in the Mesiah Papers and Documents. "Etude in A flat," mentioned in Chapter I, was composed in 1903, but remains unpublished, as does his piano piece, "To Mother," from 1904.

"Fugue Theme" for piano, dated August 3, 1906, is still in manuscript, according to Arlene E. Gray, author/compiler of *Listen to the Lambs*. Based on a theme by Franz Schrecker, the piece is in b minor, spans 103 measures, and has no time signature, though is in duple meter. Documents in the Dett Collection, NFNYPL state that Dett had copyrights, confirmed by the US School of Music in New York City in 1907, on two pieces for

Cave of the Winds
March and Two Step

Mus. ex. 1, meas. 1-12,   © 1902, S. C. Fragard.

Mus. ex. 1, last 18 meas. © 1902, S. C. Fragard.

violin, "March Up Ye Brothers" and "Chorus from the Unknown," though there is no evidence of their publication.

During 1908, before Dett graduated from Oberlin, he dedicated the piano pieces "Il Penseroso," a miniature suite ("Prelude, Adagio - ma non troppo," and "Finale") and a "Prelude" respectively to Professor George Hastings, Mr. F. H. Goff, and Professor Arthur Heacox, whom he mis-stated as Austin Heacox (see Part I, Chapter I). None of these pieces has been published nor can be located.[7] Other unpublished compositions from 1908 were two pieces for violin, "Confessional," dedicated to Donald Morrison, student violinist at Oberlin, who later became a choral director, "My Song," dedicated to Professor George W. Andrews, and a violin arrangement of "Nobody Knows the Trouble I See." *My Agnes from Niagara* for piano was published by S. C. Fragard in 1909.

About the Piano Suites

Dett was one of the first Negro American composers to compose piano suites. Raoul Abdul wrote in 1977: "In the year of the Bicentennial [1976] it might have been interesting if [Andre] Watts had focused attention on the genuine Black piano works" of Dett, Still, and John Work, rather than "settle for Gershwin's ersatz excursions into Black musical culture."[8]

Dett's first two piano suites, *Magnolia* (1912) and *In the Bottoms* (1913), were published by Clayton F. Summy in Chicago, Illinois. Along with his four later suites they were reissued by Summy-Birchard Company (Evanston, Illinois) in 1973, carefully edited by Drs. McBrier and DeLerma, with the cooperation of Mrs. Helen Dett Hopkins, Dr. Rudolph von Charlton, and Mrs. Harriette E. Williamson. McBrier and DeLerma are responsible for correction of the original printer's errata and for added fingerings.[9]

Eileen Southern reviewed the 1973 edition in 1974, saying

that the collection "is highly recommended, not only for the music historian but also for the performer. Both will enjoy meeting Mr. Dett."[10] She points out the obvious, that his piano music is "laden with cliches," nevertheless calling the dance forms "sparkling and inventive," and some of the slow song forms "quite charming." With a few exceptions separate movements of any of the suites would make effective encores. Parts of the *Bible Vignettes* are suitable as preludes for church services, e. g., "Other Sheep," a variation on an African theme, and "Father Abraham," based on both a Negro spiritual and an ancient Hebrew melody.

Another complimentary review of the 1973 edition appeared in the Detroit *Michigan Chronicle,* July 7, 1973, saying:

> With Summy-Birchard's current publication of this handsome 208-page volume, the piano works of an outstanding Black composer are now again available. The music ranges from short melodic pieces to extended works that require virtuosity. The flavor of the original editions has been preserved through facsimiles of music pages and covers. The only editing is to correct obvious engravers' errors.
>
> Music lovers and their families will both relish and cherish this addition to their home libraries. Music educators will rightly wax with pride in exposing and directing the learning procedures to today's ambitious young. And today's performing keyboard artists (and artist potentials) will thrill anew over the rewarding audience ovations Dr. Dett's masterpiece scores are capable of evoking.

Much has been written about the piano suites and Dett's own performance of them. The Foreword of a brochure on Dett compiled in 1925 stated: "As an interpreter of his own works Dr. Dett brings . . . the double elements of poet and musician, for he is both. . . . To hear Dett play his own compositions is to get a new idea of the Negro race."[11] Frederick H. Martens felt that though the first two piano suites, in addition to *Listen to the Lambs,* had brought attention to Dett, any works which followed would solidify a basis for accurate assessment of him in order to form a more "definite conclusion as to the composer's true status, his importance as a really permanent factor in American composition."[12]

MAGNOLIA

Suite for Piano

by R. Nathaniel Dett

PART I $1.50

No 1 MAGNOLIAS
No 2 THE DESERTED CABIN
No. 3. MY LADY LOVE

PART II $1.50

No 4. MAMMY
No. 5. THE PLACE WHERE
        THE RAINBOW ENDS

CHICAGO
CLAYTON F. SUMMY CO, 64 E. VAN BUREN ST.
WEEKES & CO LONDON

Copyright © 1912 Summy-Birchard, Inc.,
exclusively distributed by Warner Bros. Publications, Inc.,
Secaucus, N.J. Used by permission. License Number F1100592.

1912 (Magnolia)

Each of the five pieces in the *Magnolia* suite shows Dett's love for nature, and pictures a different facet of the southern Negro's life. (1) "Magnolias" is prefaced by Dett's own words: "Gorgeous magnolias/Spotless in splendor/Sad in their beauty/Heavy with perfume." Marked *Moderato molto cantabile* its A section of sixteen measures in D major presents a song-like melody with left hand accompaniment, phrased in bars of two, then four. Pedalling is specific, suggesting that the left hand should be as legato as possible. The B section sounds in b minor, features a conversational echo effect between right and left hands underlaid by syncopation, and after sixteen measures ends in A major with a *fermata*. The next seven measures are in treble clef with an occasional crossover to the bass for dotted rhythms by the right hand. A return to the modified A section is achieved smoothly in the next three measures with intervals of sixths.   A climax is built by a repeated single eighth note passage, soon reinforced with octaves and offbeat chords. Rhapsodic ascending octaves in triplet rhythm in a double *forte*, marked *con molto passione*, invite the A theme's return. After a slight decrescendo the piece builds again with chordal triplets in g minor, f sharp minor, and A major to restate the theme once more before the quiet ending in D major.

(2)   "The Deserted Cabin" is twenty-eight measures in length. In b minor and 12/8 meter, its theme is eminently suitable for a gypsy violin. Unbroken tenths are scored for the left hand. *Fermatas* are well placed for dramatic emphasis; otherwise "The Deserted Cabin," as somber as a funeral march, uses *staccato* bass chords under the more sustained line of the right hand. It ends with the dynamic of *pppp*. (See Musical Example No. 2.)

Dett spoke in his preface of "Cabin's" deep pathos, "expressed in a broad dignified rhythm." Resembling much of the Indian and Hungarian music in minor keys, the Negro origin is evident in similar use of occasional groups of quick notes, leading to a syncopated accent, a device imparting "a touch of tragedy," then breaking suddenly "into the deep yearning expressed in the long notes."

(3) As a contrast "My Lady Love" (A major) begins with a four-measure *pizzicato* vamp, suggesting a sassy dance. Interspersed with two-measure eighth note patterns, the beginning rhythm of the melody is ¢ ♫♫ ♩ |♫♫ ♫♫| varied by ♪♫♩ |♩ ♫♫|

The Deserted Cabin

Mus. ex. 2, meas. 1-8. Copyright © 1912 Summy-Birchard, Inc., exclusively distributed by Warner Bros. Publications, Inc., Secaucus, N.J. Used by permission. License Number F1100592.

and ♪♫♪♫|. As in *Magnolias* there is a minor section in which the right hand melody is in bass clef, while the left hand crosses to the treble. After frollicking through various harmonies as would a coquette deciding on a beau, a return to A major is reached by a *staccato* scale in sixteenth notes.

Dett admits using stop-time, common to the dance idiom, but only hinted at in "Lady Love." He describes it as consisting of two or more strong beats, followed by a sudden silence rhythmically tapped by the feet.

(4) "Mammy," (D flat major), marked *Lento con tenerazza*, is perhaps the freest of *Magnolia's* sections, but staying within its basic rhythmic framework in order to preserve its elementary artistic principle. In the nature of a lullaby it could well be

hummed or crooned by a mammy to her child. (See Musical
Example No. 3.) Beginning at measure 17 Dett scores a new
melody in the left hand, which after eighteen measures
modulates from A major seventh by way of a chromatic bass line
back to the A section. (See Musical Example 4.) Again Dett uses
some unbroken tenths in the left hand.

(5) Twelve pages in rondo-like form comprise "The Place
Where the Rainbow Ends," the longest and most difficult section
of *Magnolia*. Dett based the piece on Paul Laurence Dunbar's
poem of the same name, which in essence says that fulfillment is
not always measured in material wealth, but in terms of personal
joy and aspiration. Dett's piece is reminiscent of both European
salon and ballet music of the time. Beginning with a rather
whimsical thirty-two measure introduction of Polonaise flavor in
G flat major, a theme is finally stated and repeated. After a
Grand Pause the key changes to D flat major and a new short
theme is shared by right and left hands. The A section is
repeated in G flat major.

Following another Grand Pause the C section, in B major, is
like a romantic waltz, enhanced by alternate markings of *molto
meno mosso* and *animato*. Now another section with melody
carried by bold octaves in the left hand is introduced (g sharp
minor), embellished by arpeggiated accompanimental figures in
the right hand with suggested fingerings. Not quite finished
with what he had to say, Dett repeats the C theme in B major,
now with an added obligato. Rather than another G. P., he goes
dramatically into the A and B themes, with slight replacements
of rhythms and motifs.

Then after a bravura buildup with a rhythm pattern of
³⁄₈ ♩♪♪|♪♪♪! etc., leading the listener to think the piece is at an
end, a new short four-measure phrase appears (see Musical
Example No. 5), one gradually flowing with runs and arpeg-

Mammy

Mus. ex. 3, meas. 1-4.

Mus. ex. 4, meas. 17-20.

Meas. 33-38. Copyright © 1912 Summy-Birchard, Inc., exclusively distributed by Warner Bros. Publications, Inc., Secaucus, N.J. Used by permission. License Number F1100592.

giation to a flashy coda of ascending octaves in the left hand. Five chords in G flat major end the piece in grand style.[13]

Dett gained recognition for the Negro folksong without imitating the white man's music. The themes of his suites were original. Maud Cuney-Hare quotes one reviewer who considered "The Deserted Cabin" and "Mammy" "significant examples of this elevation of the folk song to the forms of greater compass, wider contrast and deeper meaning."[14]

McBrier calls "Magnolia" the suite's most "impressive piece" with "immediate appeal," and continues, saying:

> One finds the melody to be poetic, spontaneous, graceful, and sufficient to itself. The harmonic sequences are conventional and the original color is derived from figuration which is contrapuntal. The sum total is a charming early Romantic piano composition.[15]

A critic for the Oklahoma City *Daily Oklahoman*, March 2, 1924, wrote of the suite as a whole that it "was more poetic than deep, but it pictured the South faithfully in 'The Deserted Cabin' and 'My Lady Love.'" Having heard Dett perform the suite, the critic continued, probably with "The Place Where the Rainbow Ends" in mind: "Variations on a theme from a Louisiana dance rioted over the keys in rhythms so ingenious that one was

The Place Where the Rainbow Ends

Mus. ex. 5, meas. 310-324. Copyright © 1912 Summy-Birchard, Inc., exclusively distributed by Warner Bros. Publications, Inc., Secaucus, N.J. Used by permission. License Number F1100592..

constantly alert to catch them, while his [Dett's] habit of pausing for rhythmic effects forced the keenest attention."

1913 (In the Bottoms)

A year after *Magnolia* was published (1912), Dett had finished a second piano suite, *In the Bottoms*, published by Clayton F. Summy Co. in 1913.[16] More often than not *In the Bottoms* is mentioned as a favorite of Percy Grainger, who frequently programmed "Juba Dance," the last section, and used it also as an encore piece. (See Chapter VI.) At least one reference says that Fannie Bloomfield-Zeisler was equally taken with "Juba" and was the first pianist to play it publicly.[17] Queries to the *Chicago Sun-Times*, the *Chicago Tribune* Library, the Chicago Public Library, and to Dr. D. W. Krummel, who authored the Zeisler entry for *The New Grove Dictionary of*

American Music, failed, however, to produce documentation of any programming by Zeisler of Dett's works. Dr. Krummel was unable to supply supportive information, but said: "Remember that FBZ, managing three careers at once, often cancelled; and that the politics of music being what they are *Musical Courier* may have been anti FBZ where others (maybe *Musical Leader*) may have been pro."[18]

Austrian-born Fanny Bloomfield-Zeisler (1863-1927) was a pupil of Theodor Leschetizky. From her incredibly huge repertoire she once gave eight recitals in eighteen days (in San Francisco) without repeating a single selection, according to Harold C. Schonberg. "But at one point," he wrote, "the dynamo short-circuited, and she snapped." After a period of rest for a nervous breakdown in 1906 she made a brilliant comeback, continuing to concertize until shortly before her death.[19]

In the Bottoms, recordings of which continue to be made, is Dett's best known piano work, due in part to the appeal of "Juba Dance." The *Daily Oklahoman* critic in the previously mentioned review, March 2, 1924, called it an "intellectual number," for each part was "true to history and its atmospheric content." While "Night" ("Prelude"), the first section, expressed the Negro's fear of darkness, mystery and dawn, the dashing rhythm of the "Barcarolle" equalled its harmonic depth. "His Song" the critic described as "doleful . . . hummed by an old Negro as he sat by his cabin." He had no comment for "Honey," Part 3, but felt that "Juba" was definitely the suite's climax: "The melodies of the Juba jungle dance were lost, but the eccentric rhythms have been found by Dett and the fury of the dance goes beyond even the quick movements of the Negro in his old jungle assembly."

A recital by Dett in Nashville, Tennessee on February 26, 1923, included his playing of the *Magnolia, Enchantment,* and *In the Bottoms.* Of the latter suite the *Nashville Tennessean* reported the following day:

> "In the Bottoms Suite" was the best of all, the "Prelude" with its open fifths showing the gathering of darkness, lighted only by the flickering candle light in a cabin. After the old Negro has tuned up his banjo, the darkness swallows up everything. "Humoresque" was based on Paul Dunbar's "How Are you Honey?" which the pianist explained might mean much or little, according to the circumstances. "Barcarolle," a boat song of the Mississippi, was beautiful and the celebrated "Juba"

brought a storm of applause.[20]

A review of *In the Bottoms* was given in *Musical America*, November 29, 1913, in the column "New Music - Vocal and Instrumental." The suite "fairly teems with musical ideas, and things of the cotton fields, of aged negroes, their sorrow and joys, of those intimate characteristic touches of humor," peculiar to the Southern negro. Of Dett's own explanatory preface to the work, the reviewer asked: "Would it not have been better to allow the musician who played the music to form his own pictures from the titles?"

He commented on the "atmosphere" lent in the opening "Prelude" by the "banjo effect" of the hollow fifths, but deemed "His Song" the real jewel of the suite, a section "harmonized with taste," saying that Dett "has made it a movement of true musical worth which concert pianists should make their own." Comparing "Honey" to a form of ragtime, he wrote: "It is racy . . . and makes a rousing little solo number, its pentatonic coloring giving it an exotic touch." The reviewer felt that the "rather sentimental" *Magnolia* suite "gave little promise of such an excellent gift as is shown in *In the Bottoms*. He also pointed out that technical difficulty varied in the movements.[21]

Overall observations on *In the Bottoms* have been given from careful analysis by scholar Debra Ann Miles, who calls Dett's "gapped" or alterscale a characteristic of black folk music. For examples she cites these scale rows: C D E G A C (pentatonic), C D E F G A C, C D flat E F G A flat B C, C D E flat F sharp G A flat B C, F A B C D E F G, D E F G A B C D, and A B C D E F G A (Aolian mode). Miles says that his use of a "head motif" creates a cyclic effect, one very popular as a late Romantic period technique. He also used modulations that are in relationships of thirds to each other.

She considers "Barcarolle" Chopinesque. Harmonically "His Song" closely resembles "Night" ("Prelude"), in her opinion, with its emphasis on chords built upon the sixth scale degree, with various spellings and inversions. Dett does not overuse the flatted seventh, as have some Negro composers. He does, however, especially in "Juba," use many fourths and fifths, characteristic of African music. The unifying elements in the suite are the head motif, syncopation of the black folk idiom, use of ninth chords, augmented sixths, appoggiaturas and appoggiatura chords, and the building of chords on the sixth tone of the scale, sometimes on the flatted sixth.[22]

Though no dedication for *In the Bottoms* is given in the 1973 Summy-Birchard edition of Dett's piano music, McBrier states that it was initially for Mr. and Mrs. Fred H. Goff, Dett's longtime friends in Cleveland (see Part I, Chapter I), and that "Juba Dance" was rededicated to Percy Grainger, though gives no date. McBrier finds "considerable craftsmanship in the suite," showing that "a highly creative mind is at work." Though basically of Negro idiom in expression, it is romantic in stylistic treatment.[23]

Dett's own preface to the first edition of *In the Bottoms* says that the work is a continuation of the mood and pictures conjured by the *Magnolia* suite, "but suggests ideas incidental to life in a more particular geographic territory." As programme music, it does not depend on actual folk-song melodies, though it does "musically portray racial peculiarities."

Continuing, he wrote of (1) "Prelude" (or nightfall): "the heavy chords represent the heavy shadows, and the open fifths, the peculiar hollow effect of the stillness; the syncopated melody which occurs, is the 'tumming' [thrumming] of a banjo, which music is, however, only incidental to the gloom." It continues from its *adagio sostenuto* opening for nineteen measures, definitely setting a mood, with duplicate intervals of fifths in right and left hands. From measures 20-36 the tempo picks up slightly, still maintaining the open fifths in the left hand, supporting broken octaves in chromatics and arpeggios in the right hand, settling in the original tonality of D major.

An interlude of ten measures then announces a rhythmic figure for the main theme ♩ ♪♩ ♪♫♩ | ♩. ♩ ‖ with slight variations added, such as a few measures into the key of b minor. Each time this theme is presented chordal texture and higher/lower range are added in both hands. Dett also adds a few crosshand intracacies. In a final section some of the introduction in fifths is restated with slight chordal variations, such as 6/4 chords. By today's recital programming interest this might be considered a ho-hum piece. Dett preferred it to be subdued, mysterious, appearing to come from afar.

(2) Dett wrote of "His Song" in the preface:

The psychological phenomenon is historic, that the moods of suppressed people have oftenest found their most touching expression in song. An aged Negro will sometimes sit for hours in the quiet of the evening, humming an improvised air, whose weird melody seems to strangely satisfy a nameless yearning of the heart.

The same non-excitement of "Prelude" could apply to "His Song," whose theme in d minor is restated with slight variation in both right and left hands. Again Dett scores unbroken tenths. At measure 32 the key changes to D major, remaining until six measures before the end when it returns to d minor. Meanwhile the theme has been reiterated with slight melodic and rhythmic variations. As a piano piece "His Song" is lacking, except for depth in properly produced choral sound. It might better have been a choral work, or used as orchestral background music. As previously mentioned, Dett composed a violin piece titled "His Song" in 1908.   A score is not available to compare with the piano piece.

(3) More lively is the forty-eight measure humoresque "Honey." As music for choreography, phrased with frequent *fermatas*, and liberally sprinkled with such expressive markings as *capriccioso, lusingando, molto meno mosso e parlando, molto teneramente e cantabile*, and *quasi echo*, it should be ripe for interpretation.   With a syncopated left hand pattern of $\frac{2}{4}$ ♪♩ ♪|♪♩ ♪| it also features appoggiaturic grace notes, which sound like anticipated down beats in today's jazz. One wonders if Dett's hand reach easily spanned the lush tenths in "Honey," a flirty, well named piece.

Dett calls the Southern term of endearment "honey" a colloquialism. "It may mean much, little, everything or nothing; the intimation here is one of coquetry." As Dett further states in his introduction "Honey" was inspired by Paul Laurence Dunbar's poem "A Negro Love Song," included in several Dunbar anthologies.   Each of its three rhythmic stanzas, in Negro dialect, has the refrain "Jump back, honey, jump back." The pert last stanza reads:

> Put my ahm aroun' huh wais,'
> Jump back, honey, jump back.
> Raised huh lips an' took a tase,
> Jump back, honey, jump back.
> Love me, honey, love me true?
> Love me well ez I love you?
> An' she answe'd, "'Cose I do" -
> Jump back, honey, jump back.[24]

The poetry of Paul Laurence Dunbar, born in Ohio in 1872, has furnished lyrics for several prominent black song composers, among them Samuel Coleridge-Taylor and Harry Burleigh. Making his name first in dialect verse and short story, Dunbar later tried escaping this writer stereotype in novels dealing primarily with white characters. As a poet Dunbar was also a popular reader, both in the US and abroad, though his physical appearance was not attractive.

Dunbar was editor of the *Indianapolis World* in 1895. As an advocate of aggressive community social action he desired to defend as well as promote his people. He was an assistant in the Library of Congress preceding the contraction of tuberculosis in 1899 which took his life in 1906. His published volumes of poetry include *Lyrics of Lowly Life* (1896), *Lyrics of Love and Laughter* (1903), *Lyrics of Sunshine and Shadow* (1905), and *Complete Poems* (1913). Additionally to his credit are four volumes of short stories and four novels, the last one, *The Sport of the Gods* (1902) arguing that the Southern Negro is unadaptable to urban culture.

(4) "Barcarolle" ("Morning") is in 6/8 meter, typical for a piece of this name. After a brief vamp in ♩ ♪♩ ♪| rhythm, plenty of activity gets underway with a glissando pickup to measure five. A Spanish castanet-like flavor takes over with a melodic rhythmic pattern, still in 6/8 of ♫♩ ♫♩|♫♩♫♩♫♩| etc., the thirty-second notes being ascending scale passages. (See Musical Example No. 6.) In his preface to *In the Bottoms* Dett considered this rhythmic figure one which frequently occurred in ante-bellum folk music, however, one often misused for caricature purposes. He thought of the piece as painting the "pleasure of a sunshiny morning on the Father of Waters."

At measure 21 Dett incorporates four staffs, well marked with pedaling, choosing the right hand to carry the B theme, jumping from one staff to another, while also playing an accompanimental figure. After this *tour de force* the A section's theme is restated briefly with a few harmonic alterations, followed by an eight-measure transition to the B section. The key signature of C major remains throughout the piece. "Barcarolle's" ending is achieved by arpeggiated chords of an altered F eleventh, f minor sixth, and C major. "Barcarolle" is a more interesting piece to program for today's audiences than either "Prelude" or "His Song."

(5) "Juba Dance" (also called "Juba" or "Dance") is just what

Barcarolle

Mus. ex. 6, meas. 1-12. Copyright © 1913 Summy-Birchard, Inc., exclusively distributed by Warner Bros. Publications, Inc., Secaucus, N.J. Used by permission. License Number F1100592.

it implies, a dance using Juba dance rhythms. McBrier states that Dett was not aware until after he composed "Juba Dance" that it was the rhythm of the old New Orleans Juba dance,[25] one originating in Ethiopia along the Juba river. DeLerma has described the juba as a dance "for hands and feet, named after an old African ghost, . . . done to the melody of a single fiddle plus a combination of rhythmic stamps and percussive hand claps."[26] Dett captures this essence well in the stirring "Juba Dance," explaining further in his preface that in the original dance at least one-third of the dancers keep time by stamping and patting while the others dance, though sometimes all will dance frantically at once. Since the fiddler was the total orchestra, he would perch on a box or table, getting ample opportunity to show off his bowing and double stops. Dett cautions against the out-of-character representation that can be given by playing the piece too fast and too boisterously.

The juba dance came from Africa to the US via the West Indies. Its basic elements are a rhythmic stamping, patting, and clapping. Negro slave dancing provided entertainment at the "Big House" on plantations in the South as late as the mid-1940s. Dett's friend Robert Russa Moton even hosted some of these festive evenings when such dances as the juba were performed.[27]

William Henry Lane, an American Negro noted for his Jig dancing, was born a free man (c. 1825), and by 1845 had been acclaimed the greatest dancer of the juba, hence his title "Master Juba." He bested white juba dancer Master John Diamond, somewhat his elder, in two contests in London in the mid-1840s. By 1848 Lane had joined a successful minstrel troupe, but died four years later. Lane's prowess astounded the critics, one of whom wrote: "How could he tie his legs into such knots and fling them about so recklessly, or make his feet twinkle until you lose sight of them altogether in his energy?"[28]

Dett's rollicking "Juba Dance" is exciting and not too difficult for the pianist. A steady rhythm is required for the ragtime-like left hand pattern in 2/4 meter of ♫♪ | ♫♪ |. There are no pedal markings for the A section, in which the initial eight-measure phrase is repeated exactly. At measure 17 a key change from F to C major ushers in a short B section with a walking bass line, punctuated by chords of hand claps as pickups to the downbeats. After the A theme is repeated a new, more song-like and sustained theme is presented in B flat major, and tossed between right and left hands as they cross clefs. Dett's clever use of a descending chromatic bass line (measures 45-48) suggests a respite for the dancer from the more taxing preceding activity.

A variation on the A theme is now presented in g minor (measures 57-72), possibly the most technically demanding part of the piece, due to the intervals of sixths in the right hand. The original key of F major is arrived at in measures 65-72 by another partly chromatic descending bass line. Now the A theme gives way to the ending coda, which begins with a dynamic of *p* in alternating rhythms of ⁴₄ ♫♪ | and | ♫♫ ♫♫ | building

Dance
Juba

54

DANCE
JUBA

Copyright 1913 by Clayton F. Summy Co.
International Copyright

C. F. S. Co. 1465 e   Printed in the U.S.A.

Mus. ex. 7, entire piece. Copyright © 1913 Summy-Birchard, Inc.,
exclusively distributed by Warner Bros. Publications, Inc., Secaucus,
N.J. Used by permission. License Number F1100592.

55

56

58

to chords marked *sf*. A final arpeggio in F major ends the piece. (See Musical Example No. 7.) Performance time for *In the Bottoms* is approximately fifteen minutes.

Arrangements of "Juba Dance" for band and orchestra are mentioned in the *1926-1930* section of this chapter. The orchestration was played over CBS, according to the *New York Age*, September 24, 1938. Dett's own arrangement of the piece for mixed chorus is discussed in Part II, Chapter X of *Follow Me*.

1914-1919

Dett's output of piano or other instrumental music was scant for the first few years after he took a faculty position at Hampton. In her List of Works McBrier mentions Dett's organ composition, "March Negre," first performed at Hampton Institute in 1915 and dedicated to Major Robert Russa Moton.[29]

In 1918 Clayton F. Summy Company published Gordon Blach Nevin's arrangement for organ of Dett's "Deserted Cabin" from the *Magnolia* suite. The key of b minor was retained, as well as the *staccato* punctuation in the organ pedals. One deviation from Dett's original score is obvious in an *ossia*, measures. 12-14, but otherwise Nevin's arrangement follows Dett's piano score closely.[30]

Nevin also arranged for organ "Mammy" and "His Song" from *In the Bottoms*, published by Summy in 1918 and 1921, respectively. Nevin (1892-1943) received an honorary doctorate from Westminster College, where he taught composition and organ from 1932-1943. He was well known as an organist in Cleveland, Ohio, and as a musical arranger in Boston. From 1915-1917 Nevin taught at Hiram College in Ohio. He is the author of *Primer of Organ Registration, First Lessons at the Organ*, and *The Harp and Chimes in Organ Playing*. His compositions, other than those for organ, include the three-volume *Easy Anthems*, a cantata (*Behold the Christ*), and an operetta, *Following Foster's Footsteps*.

By 1919 Dett had completed "Concert Waltz and Ballade" for piano. When he played it for Dr. Glenn Dillard Gunn in Chicago that year, Gunn found it "charming and of significant merit." It remains unpublished.[31]

1920-1925 (Enchantment)

The *Enchantment* suite for piano, first published in 1922 in separate movements by the John Church Company, with branches in Cincinnati, New York, and London, was dedicated to Percy Grainger, "In Appreciation." Grainger deemed the dedication "a great honor and kindness."[32] *Enchantment* unfortunately never gained the popularity that came to *Magnolia* and *In the Bottoms*. A part of Dett's own poetic "program" for the overall mood of the suite reads:

> What seek you? Say! And what do you expect?
> I know not what; the Unknown I would have!
> What's known to me is endless, I would go
> Beyond the end. The last word is still wanting.[33]

This suite, as played by Dett in a concert at Fisk University's Memorial Chapelle, was interpreted by the *Nashville Tennessean* critic, February 27, 1923, as depicting "the experiences of a soul in a temple, addressing an incantation to the Unknown God, bringing in response an answering voice, then a wild, swirling dance ["Dance of Desire"] and "Beyond the Dream."

In the May, 1923 *Oberlin Alumni Magazine, Enchantment* was mentioned by one of Dett's former Oberlin professors, Edward Dickinson in the item "Former Oberlin Students as Composers." *The Southern Workman* had cited *Enchantment* almost a year earlier in its May, 1922 issue, naming Grainger as the grateful and complimentary dedicatee.

McBrier points out Dett's use of chromaticism, altered chords, ornamentation, and improvisatory passages.[34] The writer of a slightly florid but complimentary review of *Enchantment* spoke of the suite as a "working out of an original program," admiring Dett's poetic flair. The reviewer called "Song of the Shrine," the second movement, a "cantilena of real charm" whose broadening development concludes in a chordal song, gradually dying away. He was partial, however, to the third and fourth movements, "Dance of Desire" and "Beyond the Dream," "where so high a general level of attainment is reached." He wrote of "Dance of Desire's" "striking and barbaric orientalism, . . . throbbing tom-toms and primal drum, . . . swaying melody line, and frenetic *presto* ending in octaves," calling it a "splendid passionate evocation of the savage Oriental dance at its musical best."[35] He pointed out that the urgency in "Incantation," the first movement, was mingled with the "mocking" "Song of the Shrine."

Because "Beyond the Dream" attempts a look into the soul's striving for the unattainable, it was a task-setter for the composer. In the manner of a nocturne, it is "instinct with poesy, . . . its melodic themes are harmonized with rare feeling for the evanescent charm and liquid movement of expression for which its program calls." Finally the reviewer again highly commended these last two movements for their "directness of appeal," and "that quality of romance . . . which does so much to vitalize and inspire the best of music, old and new."[36]

Dett himself described *Enchantment* as "A Romantic Suite for the Piano on an Original Program," on the frontispiece of the 1923 edition, which also included a drawing of an ancient temple. This and the Program of the suite precede the first movement, "Incantation," of which he wrote: "A soul obsessed by a desire for the unattainable, journeying on an endless quest, wanders into a pagan temple, and there yields to an overpowering impulse of the moment to utter an Incantation before the shrine of an unknown goddess."

(1) "Incantation," in the key of C sharp minor and marked *un poco agitato, ma moderato*, opens with ascending augmented chords as an accompaniment to the melody carried by the right hand thumb. Within the first four measures Dett has employed *rubato*, suggesting a person running towards something, then continuing to accelerate in a triplet pattern ending at measure 8 in a *ritard*. This is repeated with a slight change in harmony, but with the same sense of urgency. From measures 17 through 46 the A theme is embellished with broken triplet patterns.

In a B section (measures 50-95) of brief tonalities in E major and G major Dett affects a *scherzando* feeling, using more triplets and whole tone progressions, then a chromatic descent in seventh chords leading to B major. *Fermatas* over the next several chord progressions with tenths in the left hand convey that they are to be tasted thoughtfully, passages somewhat reminiscent of Cyril Scott's *Lento* for piano.

The following section (measures 96-140) restates the A theme in various keys. Dett's use of *fermatas* again gives one pause to notice his chord progressions of altered chords, ninth chords, whole tone sonorities, and frequent key changes. Within these measures are two non-connected arpeggios of D major ninth and G sharp major ninth construction. At measure 141 a descending

bravura passage of eighth note octaves duplicated in right and
left hands becomes even more exciting when an accompanimental
figure is added in sixteenth notes, ending suddenly on G sharp
major ninth chords, presaging a resolution in C sharp major. But
instead Dett scores a measure of Grand Pause, then more chords,
each with a *fermata*, one an unexpected E augmented eleventh
chord. *Presto* and *prestissimo* octaves are followed by accelerat-
ing heavy chords carrying a repeated ascending melody of A, C
sharp, D, A. The piece ends with *sf* chords in c sharp minor.

(2) "Song of the Shrine" is definitely the least serious of
Enchantment's four parts. A dreamy bit of fluff, embellishing in
leisurely fashion a theme in cut time, its opening rhythm is
¢ ♩. ♪♩. ♪│♩ ♫♫│♩ ♩ │♩. ♩│ . The melody is sometimes in the
inner voices. Dett's tenths in the left hand now are witten with
an anticipatory grace note, giving the sound of a broken tenth. As
the piece progresses (in measures 39-50) the melody becomes
bolder, chordal, befrilled with fillers of scale passages, a
technique commonly used by improvisory pianists. Of this piece
Dett wrote in his Program preceding it: "From somewhere far
within the shrine a mysterious voice answers - a voice of molten
melody, singing love that may not be."

(3) There is so much color in "Dance of Desire," it could have
been choregraphed and orchestrated to great effect. It is well
marked with accents and for expression, properly sectioned to suit
the interpretation of dance moods. Form-wise it is a rondo, in 2/4
meter throughout. It opens with an accompanimental figure of
♩ ♫│♩ ♫│, one appearing periodically. Syncopation is evident
in the left hand accompanimental figure of │♪♩ ♪│ and another
in the right hand of ♬♬ │♬♬♬♬│.

Other features include a *precipitando* octave passage, some
passges of five sixteenths against two eights, another more
lyrical one of ⅔ ♫♫│ over │♫♫ ♫♫ │, and impressive staggered
octaves culminating in *sf* c sharp minor chords.

Dett describes the scene of this "Dance" as strange shapes,
beckoned by drums and gongs, assembling for a carnival of
passion, into which the soul is irresistibly drawn. A final crash
prompts the revelers to vanish.

(4) Aptly marked *quasi notturno*, "Beyond the Dream" is a
pleasant, somewhat sophisticated salon piece in 3/4 meter. Dett
interestingly achieves syncopation by use of simple hemiola.
Measures 9-16 answer the theme stated in the opening eight measures. (See Musical Example No. 8.) After an interlude of various

broken chords ending in E major a second theme is arranged for the left hand from measures 53 through 60, whose rhythmic

Beyond the Dream

Mus. ex. 8, meas.1-24. © 1922 John Church Company. Used by permission.

Beyond the Dream

Mus. ex. 9, meas. 91-112. © 1922 John Church Company. Used by permission.

pattern is ♩ ♩|♩ ♩|♩. ♩|♩. ♩ 𝄽| , accompanied by the same E seventh chord. It is then repeated in the right hand. A *stretto* section using hemiola ends in a rapid harplike arpeggio. (See Musical Example No. 9.)

A ten-measure improvisory interlude follows with a plaintive five-note motif, repeated in two lower octaves. A clever chromatic augmentation in the right hand arrives at an E seventh chord for a return of the first theme in A major. To carry the melody, Dett now uses broken tenths and broken sixths in the right hand, written with appoggiaturas. The second theme is restated briefly in F major. Toward the end of the piece activity decreases, even to the point of two spaces of a two-measure rest.

Considering the plaintive nature of "Beyond the Dream," it could have been written by the somber Alexander Scriabin. Playing time is estimated at twelve minutes for the four parts of *Enchantment*. Claire R. Reis in *Composers in America* lists an *Enchantment Suite* with harp under Dett's "Orchestral Works," an undated, unpublished arrangement.[37] Explained by Dett in his preface "Beyond the Dream" pictures the soul transfigured, seeing itself as "an ever-shifting shoal of pale, opalescent fire," exuding smoky incense, symbolic of "unsatisfied longing for the unattainable."

* * *

Dedicated "To Dr. Arthur Foote," *Nepenthe and the Muse,* Dett's only other locatable piano piece from 1922, was also published by the John Church Company. In 6/8 meter a pedalpoint bass on D flat serves as an introduction for the uneventful boatsong-like melody beginning in measure 5, one actually more suitable for song words. The bass line rhythmic pattern alternates from ♩ ♩ | to |♩ ♪♩ |. In measure 56 Dett's romantic melody, fit for a concerto theme, is marked *melodia languendo sempre pp gli accompagnamenti zeffiroso.* Over a left hand arpeggiated sweeping accompaniment reminiscent of Liszt or Rachmaninoff the theme (sounding an octave higher and with a pedal tone of D flat) is:

For transition Dett writes an ascending D flat scale (altered), later descending inharmonically (sounding in D major) and ending on an A flat, which serves as a dominant for returning to the original key of D flat and the boat-like rhythm of the piece's beginning. As a pleasant listening piece Dett well captures the mood of nepenthe, the pain-banishing Egyptian drug, once given to Helen of Troy by Queen Polydamna of Egypt.[38]

* * *

Dett's violin piece, *Ramah* (subtitled "Air Characteristic"), was likely suggested by the biblical towns of the same name. In Old Testament geography Ramah was the name of several places in Palestine, such as Ramah of Benjamin and Ramah of Samuel, which were near Jerusalem. With piano accompaniment Dett's *Ramah* was published by the Boston Music Company in 1923. According to a contract drawn up for the piece, dated January 26, 1921 (Dett Collection, NFNYPL), Dett would receive ten percent royalty from sales in all countries of the sheet music, and fifty percent from any recordings. *Ramah's* cost was $.60 per copy.[39]

Oddly enough *Ramah* was not dedicated. In G major and marked *Lento e molto espressivo, Ramah* begins with a two-measure introduction of rolled chords, which continue as an ac-companimental figure lasting for twenty-one measures. The violin melody for the most part has a pattern of triplets, spiced and syncopated by some sixteenth note figures. At measure 22 (see Musical Example No. 10), after a *fermata* and a key change to g minor, the meter changes to 12/8, marked *agitato*, and might present an ensemble problem to less skilled players. At measure 32, marked *declamato*, a variation of the first theme appears, and by measure 38 a return to G major has been reached.

The original theme is transposed, as are the ac-companimental rolled chords, and a variation on measures 22-25 is presented in another tonality, followed by a grandiose restatement of the original theme in the upper octave, a cadenza, then a coda which uses some double stops for the violin. In *Ramah* Dett fully utilized the range of the violin, choosing to score its open low G in a few places.

A letter concerning performances of *Ramah* by touring violinist W. I. Howard, dated January 3, 1925, reads:

> Dear Mr. Dett:
> Your "Ramah" has twice proven to be the hit of my program, so from now on, it shall take the place of the "African Dances" I have used so much. It seems to "take" in spite of my poor interpretation. I hope to improve my interpretation of it as time goes, by repeating it.
> Sincerely,
> W. I. Howard[40]

Though no date is given Reis mentions the unpublished "Listen to the Lambs," a fantasia for violin of eight minutes duration.[41] Since this choral piece, published in 1914, had been

Ramah

Mus. ex. No. 10, meas. 22-27.   Reprinted by permission of the publisher: The Boston Music Co., 172 Tremont St., Boston, MA 02111. © 1923, 1950.

so successful, Dett's arrangement could have been made anytime after that year.

In 1924 Dett was on tour, frequently programming his "Sonata in f minor" for piano. For reasons unknown this work, based on original and folk themes, was not published, nor was his "Sonata in e minor," based on simliar native tunes and played on tour the following year. (See Part I, Chapter IV.) Dett's playing of the "Sonata in e minor" in Rockford, Illinois, was mentioned in the *Rockford Republic*, February 17, 1925: "The concert opened with a skillful rendition of Dett's own Sonata in e minor, moderato mobile, a composition of considerable musical worth."

Another piano piece from 1924, "Cotton Needs Pickin,' Variations on a Negro Theme," was not published. It was based on one of many work songs sung by field hands in the early plantation days. Dett played the "Variations" in St. Paul at People's Church on February 18, 1924. The program, which provided explanatory notes for Dett's selections, is in the Schomburg Collection, New York Public Library. Copyrighted choreograpy of the "Cotton Needs Pickin'" tune by Charles H. Williams is mentioned in an unnamed source in the Dett Collection, NFNYPL, which also has Dett's twenty-measure manuscript of the original tune.

Fair Weather, a sonatine for piano, was published in 1925 by John Church Co., but is no longer in print, according to Thomas Broido of Theodore Presser Company.[42]

1926-1930 (Cinnamon Grove)

At least two arrangements of "Juba Dance" have been made for band, though not by Dett. He did, however, write both words and music for a choral arrangement of it (see Part II, Chapter X). John Philip Sousa's band played "Juba," likely Sousa's own arrangement, in Boston on its thirty-fourth annual tour of America, c. 1926 or 1927. Whether it was performed again when the band played a matinee at Hampton on November 18, 1930, is not documented. Sousa's arrangement was dated May 4, 1926, from his home at Port Washington, Sands Point, New York on Long Island.

Another arrangement, undated, was made by W. Strasser, the manuscript parts for which are in the Sousa Band Library at the University of Illinois.[43] Eileen Southern mentions that a copy of Sousa's manuscript is in the U. S. Marine Corps Museum Band Americana Collection, Washington, D.C.[44]

Arlene Gray's source book, *Listen to the Lambs*, mentions that Henri Verbrugghen's yet unpublished orchestral arrangement of *Juba* was played by the Minneapolis Symphony Orchestra at Purdue University on February 19, 1926. Verbrugghen conducted this orchestra from 1923 until his death in 1934. In 1926 Clayton F. Summy published both a simplified arrangement for piano of "Juba" and a four-hand duet.[45] According to a letter from Percy Grainger's secretary to Dett, dated December 26, 1926, an "Australian Edition" of "Juba" had recently been issued. Dett was asked if he would care to receive a copy.[46]

On a concert in Lynchburg, Virginia, February 1, 1928, two arrangements of Negro songs by Dett were played by violinist

Irving Downer ("I'm So Glad") and saxophonist LeRoy Hardy ("Somebody's Knocking at Your Door"). These were both repeated February 4, 1928, on a concert at Hampton. There is no evidence that these arrangements have been published.

* * *

By 1928 Dett had completed and seen publication by John Church of another piano suite, *Cinnamon Grove*, a rather enigmatic title. Not as popular as Dett's preceding suites, the overall mood of the first three parts is noticeably less active, less difficult for the pianist, and less dazzling as program music, nevertheless presenting some interesting melodies. It requires approximately twelve minutes for performance. Drawing from literary fragments and Negro folk song, the suite reflects Dett's affection for and knowledge of poetry. The melodic lines, featuring chromaticism, ornamentation, and altered chords, seem to have been vocally inspired.

Rather than titling each of the four movements, Dett chose to mark them "Moderato molto grazioso," "Adagio Cantabile," "Ritmo moderato e con sentimento quasi gavotte," and "Allegretto." These titles actually reveal little of the poetic lines which inspired them: "Dear love, for nothing less than Thee," "When thou commandest me to sing," "Was it real?," taken from poems, and "Winter'll Soon Be Over," based on a religious folk song.[47]

(1) "Moderato molto grazioso" was inspired by lines from "The Dreame," a poem of Englishman John Donne (1573-1631). Donne was born a Roman Catholic, educated at Oxford and Cambridge, and after a period of intellectual soul searching he joined the Church of England. In 1621 he was appointed Dean of St. Paul's in London. The four volumes of his published poems, *The Progress of a Soul, An Anatomy of the World, Epithalamium*, and *Divine Poems*, were reprinted in numerous editions after his death.

Donne has been compared to Robert Browning in his directness, intellectuality, and literary grotesqueness. He "delighted in the use of conceits or intricate figures of speech," a strong practice of Elizabethan poets, which he "carried on to highly artificial, often ludicrous conclusions."[48] He is considered the finest of the minor British poets, though in thought he was no saint, choosing in his poetry to express, along with broader views on the contemporary scene, the most intimate details of his love life, which drew added interest from the readers.

Donne's "The Dreame," too lengthy to quote here, is a love poem, rather flowery and impassioned, concerning one's thoughts when waked from a happy dream by his dear one.   In Elizabethan English, its puns are both suggestive and specific. Dett prefaces this first piece with Donne's opening lines: "Dear love, for nothing less than thee would I have broke (sic) this happy dream."

The meter is 4/4 (2/2), with the preferred feeling of two rather than four, as the marking is *con moto* for better flow. It would make a useful and pleasant organ prelude. It is sight-readable and presents no major technical problems except the clarification of the theme in the inner voice, after a key change from F major to C major. Slight embellishments are added when the first theme returns in F major. Strategically placed tenths give a lush sound to this expressive piece, which lends itself well to *rubato*.

(2)   The fact that Dett was inspired by Rabindranath Tagore's religious poetry for "Adagio cantabile" indicates his own tendency toward mysticism and spiritualism, in keeping with his attraction to the Rosicrucians. Tagore's collection *Gitanjali (Song Offerings)* contains 103 religious poems, several of which are in praise of music as a life sustaining force, a gift both from and to God. Dett prefaces this second movement with a part of the second poem in *Gitanjali*: "When thou commandest me to sing, it seems that my heart would break with pride; and I look into thy face, and tears come to my eyes." The remainder of the poem reads:

> All that is harsh and dissonant in my life
> melts into one sweet harmony - and
> my adoration spreads wings like a glad
> bird on its flight across the sea. I
> know thou takest pleasure in my singing.
> I know that only as a singer I come before
> thy presence. I touch by the edge of the
> far-spreading wing of my song thy feet which
> I could never aspire to reach. Drunk with the
> joy of singing I forget myself and call thee friend
> who art my lord.[49]

Calcutta born Tagore (1861-1941) was one of twelve children raised in a wealthy and brilliant Brahmin family, from whose strictures he never seemed to be entirely free. The Tagore household of writers, philosophers, musicians, and artists included the immediate family and close relatives. Tagore gradually became able to express his longing for freedom in poetry, and in founding the "World University" whose ideology embraced freedom from traditional restrictions, held classes in the open air, and welcomed students of all countries. He was knighted in 1913, but relinquished the honor later when Indians in his own country were being massacred under British rule.

Also in 1913 Tagore was awarded a Nobel Prize, fame which intruded upon his longed for solitude. As an international lecturer, "Tall, robed, and bearded, he made a profound physical impression in the West."[50] He was also an artist of unique wash drawings, a singer, and composer, whose *rabindrasangit* style was named after him. His musical ear was ever sensitive to the Bengali language's natural rhythms. It is no wonder that his work appealed to Dett.

The "Adagio cantabile" was printed separately in the October, 1933 *Etude* in a section titled "Fascinating Pieces for the Musical Home." It is almost entirely chordal, easily readable, with a definite songlike melody. A countermelody of small scale patterns is carried in the inner voices and sometimes in the bass line. (See Musical Example No. 11.) Except for a few out of range lower notes "Adagio cantabile" would be suitable as an arrangement for brass choir. Some of Dett's altered ninth chords and their resolutions are almost in popular song idiom.

(3) Dett based "Ritmo moderato e con sentimento quasi gavotte" on Henry Wadsworth Longfellow's poem "Epimetheus or the Poet's Afterthought." Epimetheus was the brother Prometheus, the supposed creator of mankind, whose name means "Forethought," for he was wiser than the gods. Epimetheus, in contrast, "was a scatterbrained person who invariably followed his first impulse and then changed his mind." He bestowed the necessary skills for survival on the animals and sea creatures. In a quandary he called on Prometheus, and subsequently Man was "fashioned in a nobler shape than the animals, upright like the gods."[51] Epimetheus was also the father of Pyrrha by Pandora, the possessor of the wicked magic box from which was unloosed the myriad plagues and sorrows of mankind. Pyrrha became the wife of Deucalion, surviving with him on Mount Parnassus after the deluge sent by Zeus.[52]

The poem describes Epimetheus' torment at having been at-

Adagio Cantabile

"WHEN thou commandest me to sing
it seems that my heart would break
with pride; and I look to thy face,
and tears come to my eyes."

Mus. ex. 11, meas. 1-24. © 1928 John Church Company. Used by permission.

tracted to the *Adagio Cantabile* unpredictable Pandora, calling
her "my Sybil, my deceiver," and wishing for the blissful state of
Elysium. He asks Pandora why Jove created her, if "to win thee
is to hate thee?"[53]

The poetry of Longfellow (1807-1882), renowned American
poet, remains popular. Financial and cultural security was
provided from both parents in an "atmosphere of good breeding"
in the historic family mansion in Portland, Maine. An avid
reader, Longfellow entered Bowdoin College at age fourteen,
having already seen the publication of several poems. His

literary prowess continued to blossom, and after studying languages abroad he accepted a professorship at Bowdoin from 1829 to 1935, then another at Harvard. Though deaths of his two wives saddened him, his productivity was not affected. He was awarded honorary degrees from both Oxford and Cambridge and was the first American honored with a bust in Westminster Abbey (1884).[54]

Dett's preface to this third movement is the first of Longfellow's twelve-stanza poem whose rhyme scheme is ABAAB:

> Have I dreamed? or was it real,
> What I saw as a vision,
> When to marches hymeneal
> In the land of the Ideal,
> Moved my thought o'er Fields Elysian?

Though most gavottes begin on the last half of the measure, Dett chooses to begin his rather march-like but somber piece on beat one. The theme in b flat minor is repeated, developed, and woven together in various keys by ascending and descending single eighth notes and/or well fingered thirds for fifty-three measures. Next a simple but pleasant new theme is introduced in B flat major. The A section is then repeated, exactly, followed by a nine-measure coda, which begins dynamically at *mp* and crescendoes to *ff* as chordal texture is added. One interesting detail in the coda is Dett's use of broken tenths (left hand), descending chromatically for five beats, followed by two measures of chromatic chords with hands in contrary motion.

(4) The fourth movement of *Cinnamon Grove*, "Allegretto," is based on lines from a song in Dett's compilation of *Religious Folk Songs of the Negro* published in 1927. The lines read: "Oh, the winter'll soon be over children, yes, my Lord." Perhaps Dett chose this text to contrast with the more literary works inspiring the preceding movements. He states the opening theme in F major:

The underlying rhythmic figure of ♪♩ ⸀|♪♩ ⸀| in the left hand adds energy. After this opening theme is stated an octave higher

Dett introduces new melodic and rhythmic material in a minor, relying on tritones and fourths for harmonic interest. Syncopation of the first theme is then alternated between the hands with a fragment of the accompaniment also shared. Two short sections of the A theme follow, first in G flat major, then the key signature is cancelled, enabling a return to the key of F major via sequential treatment and whole tone fragments. The theme is now restated in an eighteen-measure G major section. The rest of the piece is loaded with repetition of the original syncopation, and builds dynamically with accented fourths and heavy chords to a frolicksome sixteenth note ascending run, then ends with the cadence V I, marked *sff*. Not overly difficult, this is the showiest piece in the suite, reminding one of the saucy character of "Juba."

1931-1943
American Sampler, Tropic Winter, Bible Vignettes

Ten years elapsed before Dett's fifth piano suite, *Tropic Winter* (1938), was published, though his output of vocal solos and choral works had grown significantly. As mentioned in Part I, Chapter V, Dett composed orchestral incidental music for Edward Hungerford's pageants "Parade of the Years" and "Pathways of Progress" (1934), the scores remaining unpublished, and likely never used again.

In 1937 Dett was one of several American composers invited by the Columbia Broadcasting System to write a work particularly suited to radio (see Part I, Chapter V). According to both Dett and McBrier "American Sampler," Dett's submission, was based on a poem by American poet Philip Freneau titled "Liberators," but an examination of at least half a dozen collections of Freneau's works revealed no title as such. A further inquiry to University of Maryland English Professor Richard C. Vitzthum, author of *Land and Sea* (a study of Freneau's writings), brought this response:

> Sorry; the reference in your follow up of August 25 rings nary a bell. I checked Judy Hiltner's edition of the newspaper verse (done here at MD, incidentally as a dissertation under my direction), found nothing, and have concluded McBrier's allusions erroneous.[55]

Dett's recollection of the Freneau poem was from his boyhood and may well have been another "allusion," though the fact-based story impressed him deeply. In any case, the "Martyrs" and "Liberators" of Dett's composition, named as Gabriel L'Allemaant and Jean de Bréboeuf by McBrier, were real persons, identified more accurately in the *Dictionary of Canadian Biography* as Gabriel Lalemant (1610-1649) and Jean de Brébeuf (dates missing).[56]

The Canadian dictionary makes no mention of their liberation, rather describing their deaths by horrible torture as captives of the Iroquois who raided the small town of Saint-Ignace in Ontario. Both Lalemant and Brébeuf were priests, serving in the late 1640s at Saint-Louis mission. The well-educated Lalemant was born in Paris, and after teaching at several French colleges was sent to Quebec as a foreign missionary in 1646. He and Brébeuf died within hours of each other, perhaps not fully aware of the cruelties inflicted separately upon them.

Unfortunately, "American Sampler," reflecting Dett's sympathy for the priests, has not been published for examination. A heartbreaking account of their last hours revealed that immediately after capture the two were stripped naked and their nails torn out. After separation ungodly torments were suffered by Lalemant, who prayed to God for aid. Among other wounds he received a "hatchet blow on the left ear, which they [the Iroguios] had driven into his brain, which appeared exposed." His body had been literally broiled, "even the eyes, into which those impious ones had thrust burning coals."[57]

Poet Philip Morin Freneau (1752-1832), of French Huguenot ancestry, was born in New York City, and has generally been considered the Poet of the American Revolution. As an ardent, even cantankerous, advocate of Jeffersonian democracy, he expressed his views on many contemporary issues through his writings. Though serious-minded when his principles were at stake, his poetry contained enough humor to maintain communication with his fellow countrymen.

In explaining his idea for "American Sampler" Dett recalled the inspirational lines from Freneau's verses:

> Great guardian of our freedom, we pursue
> Each patriot measure as inspired by you,
> Columbia, nor shall fame deny it owes
> Past safety to the counsel you propose;
> And if you do not keep Columbia free,
> What will, alas, become of Liberty![58]

Untitled Piece from Eastman, 1931.

Courtesy Hampton University Archives.

Untitled Piece from Eastman, 1931.

Oct. 10 '31

Computer printout by Mark LeBlanc.

Of the composition's background Dett said in an interview that "Martyrs" traces the beginnings of the white settlement at St. Ignace to its downfall at the hands of the Indians. "Its significance is symbolic - religion, science, art, medicine, are all rich with the records of martyrs whose lives in the clear blue of history, are even as the galaxy of stars in the glorious flag of the greatest republic."[59]

The unpublished work is in sonata allegro form. Though the principal themes are similar in spirit, their rhythms are contrasting. Dett explained that the four notes constituting the theme of the introduction represent North, South, East and West, which areas are united in a march, stated in e minor. He continued:

> The martyrs are remembered. With a shout the second theme enters in G major; a camp song preludes the recapitulation. Now North, South, East, West are called on to join in a great hymn to Liberty, sung over the moving counterpoint of the bass. Just before the end of the movement there is a modal outburst on the chord of A major. Of ultimate success the Liberators are sure.[60]

* * *

Information is not plentiful on Dett's inspiration and intent for a fifth piano suite, *Tropic Winter*, published in 1938 by Clayton F. Summy. The names of its seven parts are definitely programmatic, indicating that Dett is setting a mood, painting an imaginary scene. Dett wrote to Grainger, "I am proud of this suite, as I think it represents an advance in musical thought."[61] More specifically, some of Dett's compositional devices pointed out by McBrier are use of chords of the fourth, motivic development, shifting tonalities, altered seventh and ninth chords, and escaped notes, identified as non-harmonic tones derived stepwise which leap to a harmonic tone.

(1) McBrier gives an example of shifting tonalities in the first four measures of "The Daybreak Charioteer," the opening section of *Tropic Winter*. Though the key sounds to be G flat major, Dett does not give a key signature. The flashy "Charioteer," marked *pomposo marziale moderato*, is indeed pompous, and might make an even more effective statement if orchestrated. Its underlying triplet rhythm is exploited in chromatic octave passages, crescendoing into heavy G flat major sixth chords. Programmed alone it would not be very interesting.

(2)   The thirty-eight measure "A Bayou Garden" is Dett's most dissonant piano piece to date.   Despite its key signature of two flats there is not one unaltered B flat chord in the piece, which does end, however, on a b flat major seventh chord. The whole piece gives a feeling of indecision, hesitancy, and questioning. As contemporary music it would be more suitable for brass quintet.

(3)   "Pompoms and Fans," marked *grazioso* with a key signature of G major, is much more tuneful. Its opening eight-measure theme is restated, with a few harmonic changes cadencing in D major. Then Dett's directions are for both hands to repeat the above up an octave higher. A second theme using dotted rhythms is treated similarly. A four-measure cadenza followed by a modulatory chromatic treatment leads back to the original theme. Dett makes interesting use of augmentation and chromaticism, as well as some whole tone descending passages in the left hand toward the end.

(4)   A plaintive recitative, *un poco dolente*, opens "Legend of the Atoll," after which the meter changes from 4/4 to 6/4 and a new chordally sustained melody is introduced, one of a lullaby in character, first in b minor, then in D major. Dett skillfully used both major and minor seventh chords and French sixths with disguised spellings.

(5)   Programmed singly "To a Closed Casement" is the choice part of *Tropic Winter*. It also contains many elements of worthy intermediate level teaching pieces, such as balance between accompaniment and melody, bringing out of inner voices, smooth execution of triple against duple rhythms, chordal analysis, and general expressiveness. A tonality of C major is immediately identifiable, departing, however, to keys which rather than resolve go on to a new phrase. Dett dares to use, as he had sparingly before, blues chords of thirteenths and altered ninths.

(6)   "Noon Siesta" is a mood piece which could easily induce a nap by the end of its twenty-eight measures. A two-measure introduction in the right hand in fourths continues as an accompaniment throughout to a simple left hand melody, relieved by the left hand's crossing to the treble staff with a stepwise, sequential chime-like obbligato. The final chord, a rolled G eleventh, is marked *ppp*. The piece has no key signature nor any accidentals.

(7)   The final section of *Tropic Winter*, "Parade of the Jasmine Banners," sounding in the blues idiom, would lend itself

to choreography. Its 6/8 meter has the feeling of an easy two. After changing from E flat major to e flat minor, Dett uses some altered seventh chords, and a descending progression of broken tenth chords as an accompaniment to a second melody in octaves. Both the first and second themes are restated with various embellishments. One passage, marked *pomposo* and *allargando*, features heavy chords, octaves in contrary motion, and is followed by fifths (right hand) and fourths (left hand) played together, giving a brassy or percussive effect. The last chord is an E flat ninth marked *sffz*.

* * *

From 1941-1943 Dett's last suite for piano, *Eight Bible Vignettes*, was composed and first published in separate parts by Mills Music. The previously mentioned Dett brochure issued c. 1942 lists the fourth section of *Vignettes* as "Harps on the Willows" and the fifth as "Bountiful Shepherd." Apparently, as the various segments were completed Dett renamed them or rearranged their order. Neither the title "Madrigal Divine" (the last part) nor the fourth, "Barcarolle of Tears," was listed as such in the brochure. Also possible is that he replaced some of the original drafts with later ones.

Preceding six of the parts is text from the Bible. McBrier stated that Dett was at this time experimenting with "structural changes, harmonic devices, and philosophic ideas. As always his melodic lines are distinctive."[62] At a concert in mid-June of 1943 at the Shiloh Baptist Church, Washington, D.C., Dett spoke about the *Vignettes*, pointing out that the spiritual was a form of folk art, somewhat akin to the sacred folk art of the Jews, both of which were drawn from for the pieces.

Critic Glenn Dillard Gunn, writing of the event in the *Washington Times Herald*, said:

> These are eight original compositions and without parallel in the literature of the instrument. Except as the Bach Choral Preludes have been transcribed for it, or for one or two sacred pieces by . . . Franz Liszt, the piano is entirely the agent of secular expression.
>
> These sacred pieces by Dett are most interesting. They have melodic beauty, rich harmonic variety, and expertly exploit the technical resources of the instrument.
>
> The interested public is even more aware of Dett's mastery of the choral idiom. This runs the gamut from

the classic motet to the free fantasy, exhibiting many beautiful patterns in voice leading, and developing a melodic eloquence which is both racial and individual.[63]

McBrier and DeLerma, in their prefaces to *Collected Piano Works*, have pointed out some general characteristics of the *Vignettes*: Dett's addition of Hebrew flavor, his contrapuntal and chromatic techniques, frequent use of consecutive fifths and sevenths, as well as augmented, diminished and altered sevenths, and ground bass, or ostinato, the unchanging repetition of a short bass phrase, which may be transferred to an upper voice. Seldom used by contemporary musicians, ground bass originated in church music, and lends itself to variations above it.

The separate publication of "Father Abraham" in 1941 prompted a review in *Musical America*. After quoting Dett's own words about the composition the reviewer called his parallel "interesting . . . one that probably would not have occurred to anyone else," a matter of less importance than that

> he has written a richly sonorous piano piece in the form of a majestic idealization of the spiritual form and style with interludes based on fragments of the Hebrew melody. It ranges over the keyboard in massive chords as a piano piece of unique character.[64]

Dett's inspiration for "Father Abraham," the Old Testament patriarch, came from the book of Genesis, specifically XXVI, 3-4. (Though Dett's citation is Genesis, XXIII, 16-18, the text reads the same.) Abraham, according to Dett, was a suitable character to apostrophize in the Negro spiritual, for his goal, the Jew's, and the Negro's was emancipation and "great happiness in some future state." Continuing his explanation of the piece Dett wrote:

> Moreover, from the standpoint of musicology, the interval of the augmented, or "barbaric" second (Byzantium mode) which occurs in the melody of the spiritual, identifies it as belonging more to the great family of oriental folksong than to any offshoot of Moody and Sankeyism, as has been sometimes alleged.[65]

Dett uses parts of both Jewish and Negro tunes, striving for a logical and natural association.

The verses from Genesis say that the Lord will bless and
"multiply thy seed as the stars of the heaven, and as the sand
which is upon the seashore; and thy seed shall possess the gate
of his enemies; and in thy seed shall all the nations of the earth
be blessed." Words from the fourteenth century Hebrew "Father
Abraham" say: "The God of Abraham praise, all praised be his
name, who was, and is, and is to be, and still the same." The less
formal words of the pre-Civil War spiritual, with some variations between versions are: "Father Abraham, sittin' beside the
Holy Lamb, 'way up on the mountain top; my Lord spoke and the
chariot stop."⁶⁶ The ascending melody begins in f minor, and by
the end of the second phrase has an A flat major tonality.

After a rather heraldic opening scored on one treble and three
bass staves, Dett begins to skillfully entwine Hebrew and Negro
versions to resemble antiphonal singing. Snap rhythm gives a
brisk punctuation and dramatic effect, as does a cadenza on an e
minor ninth chord. Some lowered thirds are used to end cadences,
a few of unexpected harmony. The original key of four flats is
cancelled at measure 37 and a thirteen-measure passage filled
with accidentals follows, ending in another cadenza of c minor
ninth harmony; thence by way of C seventh, Dett returns to the
original signature of four flats, this time with a definite f minor
tonality. The spectacular ending of F major chords is preceded by
some stunning repeated chord progressions. This piece is not easy
to read because of enharmonic chord spellings, and calls for a bit
of maneuvering by the pianist from one range of the piano to
another.

"Desert Interlude's" text is from Genesis XXI, 14:

And Abraham rose up early in the morning, and took
bread and a bottle of water, and gave it unto Hagar,
putting it on her shoulder and the child, and sent her
away. And she departed and wandered in the wilderness
of Beer-sheba.

Dett depicts here the banished Hagar's despair at being
responsible for her son Ishmael, as she contemplates the desert's
uncertainties. The bread and water were almost gone, the desert
heat was oppressive, and amidst nostalgic thoughts of her former
home, Hagar was hesitant to make any decision, fearing that
both God and Abraham had forsaken her.

Dett's lovely piece seems a departure from his former
program music, its French flavor reminding one of Ravel or

Poulenc's less pretentious works. Its plaintive melody in a minor is suitable for a flute or oboe air. It is easily sightreadable, and its inner voices are interesting. (See Musical Example No. 12.)

"As His Own Soul," dedicated "To the Memory of Carl," is a hymn-like partsong. Carl, the dedicatee, was not identified further, but since Dett's friend Carl Diton was still living at the time, it was obviously not he. Taken from the first book of Samuel, XVIII, 18, the text of "As His Own Soul" deals with the love between the biblical soulmates David and Jonathan.

Dett's piece is indeed well-knit. It picks up in interest with variations on the two themes, especially in the B section whose theme is embellished in the left hand accompaniment with sixteenth notes in fragmented chromatic passages, not unlike the treatment Rachmaninoff used in some of his Preludes. This piece would well stand alone if progammed without the whole suite. Its key of G flat major adds mellowness.

The 6/4 meter of "Barcarolle of Tears" oddly enough sounds in a blues idiom, whether conceived and/or interpreted in the actual six counts or in a broader two counts per measure. The opening four measures of single notes for the left hand could well be an introduction by a string bass for a torch song, or an interpretive jazz dance. Syncopation and chromatic octave passages in the more heavily textured middle section are almost racuous. A quieter mood, resembling the beginning, ends the piece with an a minor arpeggio though the key signature is three flats.

Dett drew from the book of John, XV, 1 and 5, for "I Am the True Vine." The verses say "I am the true vine and my father is the husbandman," and "I am the vine, ye are the branches." Then Dett adds further Bible text: "He that abideth in me and I in him, the same bringeth forth much fruit, for without me ye can do nothing."

After the initial statement Dett continues to treat it as a fugue, adding a second voice, then a third. Its phrases overlap and there is no point at which the melody is not in progress. About the fugal treatment Dett wrote in the preface: "Because of the triune conception of the Divinity, this fugue is assigned to three voices; and as in the case of the other actual word quotations, the rhythm and flow of the text decided both the inspiration and the treatment of the theme."[67] Though the key signature is four flats, both A flat major and f minor tonalities are featured. Dett's use of the augmented second adds a wistful touch. (See Musical Example No. 13.)

Desert Interlude

Mus. ex. 12, meas. 1-4. Copyright © 1942 by Mills Music, Inc.
Copyright renewed © 1970 by Mills Music, Inc.   International
copyright secured.   All rights reserved.

Mus. ex. 12 (cont'd), meas. 25-32.

I Am the True Vine

Mus. ex. 13, meas. 1-16. Copyright © 1943 by Mills Music, Inc.
Copyright renewed © 1971 by Mills Music, Inc. International copyright secured. All rights reserved.

Martha Complained

Mus. ex. 14, meas. 1-6. Copyright © 1943 by Mills Music, Inc.
Copyright renewed © 1971 by Mills Music, Inc. International copyright secured. All rights reserved.

Martha Complained (cont'd)

Mus. ex. 14, meas. 23-27, 43.

Stories of Martha appear several times in the Bible, but Dett cites no specific biblical verse for "Martha Complained," rather calling her story "legend." Martha, patron saint of good housewives, was mentioned in Luke X, 38-42, for example. She has been a symbol of the active life contrasted with the contemplative life symbolized by her sister Mary. At their home in Bethany Jesus often visited them and their brother Lazarus, the diseased beggar. Martha once complained about the drudgery of house work, saying, "Lord, has thou no care that my sister hath left me alone to serve? Speak to her therefore that she help me." Jesus answered, "Martha, thou art careful and art troubled about many things. But one thing is necessary. Mary hath chosen the best part, which shall not be taken away." Martha later felt that if Jesus had been at their home, Lazarus would not have died. Seeing her grief Jesus wept also, went to the tomb, and, after instructing the sisters to "believe," resurrected Lazarus.

Dett's ground bass, in a triplet figure, does indeed imply that Martha is caught inextricably in her domestic plight. A two-measure introduction of this ostinato in c minor sets the pattern which is to continue for the next twelve measures under a wailing, high-pitched melody, one indicating Martha's discontent. The beats are purposely accented. Then the ground bass is transposed to f minor, culminating in a freer passage of sixteenth notes. Next, two hesitant measures are followed by a descending, ascending passage suggesting despair, then frenzy. (See Musical Example No. 14.) In measure 43 Dett's unusual chord, marked *sfz*, indicates the "last straw," suggesting that Martha had stomped her foot or broken a dish in utter protest. A C major key signature after a *parlando* section suggests that Martha and Jesus have talked out the problem. The last eleven measures, again in C major,` present the opening theme calmly and expressively. The piece ends on a sustained combination of C major ninth and C major sixth chords.

Verse 16 from St. John X inspired "Other Sheep," a term for other people or tribes who needed to receive the Messianic message, persons "outside the pale of the Twelve Tribes." The Bible verse reads: "And other sheep I have, which are not of this fold: them I must bring, and they shall hear my voice; and there shall be one fold and one shepherd."

Dett has stated that the melody (see Musical Example No. 15) was given him by native African Dahklama Simango, a former student. Dett selected it because "it seemed to possess a certain yearning quality suitable for the portrayal of the feelings of those who "longed for light." The opening phrase "is an accompanied setting of the biblical quotation, and as in 'Martha Complained' the divine words are followed by an imaginary Amen by the celestial choir."[68]

"Other Sheep" is in AB form with a coda. The A section is a theme with variations. Dett interestingly introduces some previously unused broken tenths in the right hand to carry the melody, somewhat difficult for small hands to play convincingly. Duplets against triplets comprise one variation in which the melody is alternated between the hands. In another variation repeated octaves are used as an accompanimental figure, which later become ninths, then tenths. Dett uses augmented chords and those with intervals of the French sixth.

The B section, a complete contrast in mood, is in 2/4 meter, suggesting a dance. The left hand accompaniment is for the most part in intervals of fifths, which in addition to fourths are also in the right hand melody. Toward the end of the movement, after a flurry of sixteenth notes, the theme of the A section is reiterated in the left hand with more sixteenths of g minor harmonic scale. Three patterns of ascending loud chords, C major to g minor in snap rhythm, end the piece.

Dett's last published piano piece, "Madrigal Divine," closes the *Vignettes* quietly. It is marked *Moderato molto tranquillo.* The hand span required for its large chords, containing intervals of fourths within them, could make it a difficult piece to execute.

Other Sheep

Mus. ex. 15, meas. 1-24. Copyright © 1943 by Mills Music, Inc. Copyright renewed © 1971 by Mills Music, Inc. International copyright secured. All rights reserved.

It is basically in ABA form, with the repeated A section marked *grandioso*, one requiring accuracy in the left hand skips, including an up to down reversed stride bass figure, rather than the usual down/up skips of this device. The piece ends tranquilly on a C major arppeggio.

In summary the *Eight Bible Vignettes* present quite a different sound from Dett's preceding suites. Despite the fact that six of their inspirations came from Bible texts, each is distinctive in mood, message, and conception. Most of their conversational themes could well be arranged for chorus or vocal solo.

* * *

Mention has been made within the chronology of this chapter of most of Dett's unpublished instrumental works. Claire R. Reis, in *Composers in America*, p. 98, adds to the list "Symphonic Suite in e minor for piano," in manuscript as late as 1947, and "Symphony in e minor," the composition in progress at the time of Dett's death. It had been commissioned by Columbia Broadcasting Company and two movements were completed. At least three other symphonic works, "No Auction Block for Me," "American Sampler," and an orchestral setting of "Tropic Winter" were not published. DeLerma states in his notes on the Denver Oldham piano recording that the string quartet Dett began in Chicago in 1915, mentioned to Natalie Curtis (see Part I, Chapter II), was lost. An unpublished "Andante in F for String Quartet" is listed in the 1944 edition of *Grove's American Supplement*, as is, oddly enough, "The Album of a Heart" (idyllic pieces for piano). Arlene Gray in *Listen to the Lambs*, p. 176, lists as unpublished "a syncopated fantasy" titled "Angel of the Dark." Doubtless there are other lost and unfinished manuscripts which may yet come to light.

Chapter IX

Dett's Compositions and Arrangements
for Solo Voice

Introduction

It is natural that Dett would express himself in song as well as in piano compositions, for his head seemed filled with melodies and poetry, waiting to be joined. His solo vocal works can generally be categorized as (1) art songs or (2) arrangements derived from folk songs and Negro spirituals, some of which he also arranged for chorus.

His substantial output of art songs shows that he was successful outside the Negro idiom, a fact proven in the programming of them by such distinctive singers as Marian Anderson, Caroline Hudson-Alexander, Florence Cole-Talbert, Kathryn Meisle, Roland Hayes, Stanley Hoban, Reinald Werrenrath, and Jerome Swinford. Dett felt strongly, as did Harry Burleigh, however, that use of the Negro idiom was vital in the elevation of the spiritual.

Alvin S. Wiggers, writing for the *Nashville Tennessean*, February 27, 1923, compared Dett's concern in setting the Negro folk song to that of Chopin and Grieg in their native idioms of Poland and Norway. Dett himself has compared the wealth of Negro folk music to the richness of ore in the ground, waiting to be explored and used. Another of his comparisons was to the simple peanut as a wellspring for so many products. For improvements on the natural state Dett has given this example:

> We might try to preserve the tree or the rose because of its beauty and worth. Either one, through the skill of man, may be made presently to disintegrate, later to reappear in other creations of beauty and utility. Even so, the folk song is rich in elements which may be the inspiration of new creations resembling the original as a desk resembles a tree-only in the nature of its material.[1]

Arrangements of spirituals and Negro folk songs are myriad and tomes have been written on their origins. Because many of them are claimed by more than one locale, their melodies, rhythms, and words vary. Therefore, documenting their origins for this biography is unnecessary, considering Dett's absorption of multiple versions through the Hampton students' singing, his own research in the field, and his association with Natalie Curtis-Burlin.

Dett made a serious study of Negro folk song and the Negro spiritual, evidenced in his *Religious Folk-songs of the Negro as Sung at Hampton Institute* (1927) and the four-volume *Dett Collection of Negro Spirituals* (1936). His essays, to be touched upon in the *Appendix* of *Follow Me*, present in detail his concern for these particular genres. He did not claim complete knowledge of the spirituals' origins, but preferred to think of them as a pouring forth of woes of the spirit, first from individual voices, then a blending,

> . . . doubtless repeated until they became consciously or sub-consciously fixed. . . . The children heard these strange instinctive harmonic combinations around the cabin doors, . . . at church meetings, . . . funerals, and at times of jollity. Gradually they became a kind of unwritten literature, a part of the very spiritual essence of a highly emotional people.[2]

Continuing, Dett gives credit to Negro composers Burleigh, White, Dawson, Johnson, Cook, and Diton, who also elevated the spiritual, realizing that notation of them proved difficult, a ritual which

> . . . can only capture a little of what is in the soul of a group of Negroes when in a spirit of devotion they join in singing a spiritual. The spiritual of itself is a form of music. Sometimes I have heard untutored Negro groups chanting the soul songs with no knowledge whatever of what we know as the art of music. I have felt that they become very sincerely the voice of a divine power, as wonderful as that which wakens the magnolias into their gorgeous bloom, hurls a Niagara over a thundering

precipice, wakens the trill of the morning bird or paints
the glories of a sunset sky.[3]

Dett calls the spiritual both an "excrescence and a relic of
slavery," whose simplicity should not be over adorned. He and
Burleigh, however, have both occasionally added to their
arrangements certain chromatic harmonies, which some purists
find unacceptable as a departure from their native element.
Some of the best spirituals have seemed accidentally to take
their harmonies from the melody.

I have attended meetings of old ex-slaves in the
backwoods. Ofttimes when singing their very faces
showed a self-abnegation, wholly different from that one
sees upon the countenance of the average singer,
evidencing that borne on the wings of song they
temporarily had entered another world.[4]

* * *

It is not necessary to analyze each of Dett's works and
arrangements for solo voice, but rather to examine a
representative group from each of the first four decades of the
twentieth century. Mention will be made of some unpublished
songs and of others whose published scores are not available.

Early Vocal Compositions

Among Dett's first songs was "Churning Song," composed in
1903, when he was a student at the Halstead Conservatory.
Despite encouragement from his teachers there, this work was
evidently never published, though a readable manuscript has
been retained in the Dett Collection, NFNYPL. In the general
style of his piano pieces, *Cave of the Winds* and *After the
Cakewalk*, "Churning Song," with words by Sillian M.
Thompson, was dedicated to Mrs. Flora Pierce-Dennis.[5] Lending
themselves perfectly to the song's swinging 6/8 meter,
Thompson's beginning words say:

To and fro, to and fro, slowing swinging the churn;
To and fro, to and fro, crimson roses burn.
Drowsy scarlet poppies sway
Where the morning breezes play
To and fro, to and fro, waves the nodding fern, etc.

"Churning Song's" six-measure introduction is followed by two miniature ABC sections, separated by a four-measure piano interlude. Except for a few octave skips for the voice it could be easily sung by a child. (See Musical Example No. 16.)

Before his first published vocal solo in 1918 Dett, as a student at Oberlin, had composed a few vocal works, ones remaining unpublished. In the Mesiah Papers are sketches for "Oh, Whisp'ring Tree," with an arpeggiated harp-like accompaniment, and "Lost Love," a song in waltz time. Other miscellaneous sketches and fragments of vocal works are also in this collection, though the scores and words are too dim to reproduce.

1918

The rather humorous army camp folk song *Go On, Mule!* published in 1918 by J. Fischer & Bro., was a collaboration of Dett and Reverend J. Fletcher Bryant. An account of it in the *Newport News and Star*, October 11, 1918, called it

a folk-lore patriotic song, something entirely new in the realm of music, . . . a distinct hit—an expression of unusual experience. It is full of Negro pathos, yet apropos, making both the lyrics and rhythm characteristic. J. Fischer & Bros . . . predict that its future will be a brilliant one and it cannot be purchased under fifty cents a copy.

This song was said in the same report to have grown out of Reverend Bryant's experiences as YMCA Secretary. During June

Churning Song

Mus. ex. 16,   meas. 1-47, by permission of Local History Department, Niagara Falls, New York Public Library.

Churning Song (Cont'd)

of 1918 Dett spent a few days assisting with the music at Camp Hill in Newport News, Virginia.⁶ He could possibly have met Bryant here or at any one of several bases while he was concertizing in the southeastern US that summer. Information from the national YMCA Archives at the University of Minnesota confirms that from March through December of 1918 Bryant was at both Camp Hill and in the Tidewater district, and also spent time at bases in Texas and Florida. He was an Oberlin graduate who later became a Congregationalist minister. He did war relief work in religion and physical education, largely with Negro American soldiers, during WW I for the YMCA. In 1923 Bryant was pastor of St. Paul Methodist Church in Pueblo, Colorado. In 1924 Dett and Fletcher would again join talents on *I'm Goin' to See My Friends Again*, an arrangement of a Negro folk song.

Dett's syncopated accompaniment for *Mule*, resembling a rag tune and marked "In slow and well marked time," is simple but catchy. The song might truly have had a "brilliant future" had it been staged in a musical with an army chorus and a live mule. In two verses the words urge the mule to do its duty to help win the war. The solo is answered by a chorus. The refrain begins with the shouted words "Go on, mule!" followed by a percussive high sound imitating a "mule driver's cluck."

Solo:	Go on, mule!
	Git up thar, till I say whoa!
Chorus:	Till I say whoa!
Solo:	Till I say whoa!
	You must help win this war,
	And don't say no.
Chorus:	And don't say no.

1919

During 1919 the John Church Company published Dett's art songs *Magic Moon of Molten Gold* and *A Thousand Years Ago or More*, both with words by Frederick H. Martens. Martens (1874-

1932) studied in his home city of New York with theorist Max Spicker and pianists H. C. Timm and William Barber. From 1907 he made his name as a contributing writer to *Musical America, London Musical Record, The Art of Music, Musical Quarterly, Vogue,* and *Vanity Fair.* He was a charter member (in 1914) and later a director of ASCAP. Martens was librettist for several operettas and cantatas, and his poems have been set by Charles Wakefield Cadman, Gilbert Spross, Harry Burleigh, Walter Kramer, Ole Speaks, Leo Ornstein, Dett, and other American composers. His books include *Leo Ornstein: The Man, His Ideas, His Work* (1918), *Violin Mastery* (1919), *Art of the Prima Donna and Concert Singer* (1923), *Book of the Opera and the Ballet* (1925), and *A Thousand and One Nights* (1926).[7]

The fifteen-page *Magic Moon of Molten Gold* is one of Dett's longer art songs. In 3/4 meter, the accompaniment carries an insistent right hand rhythmic figure of   in thirds, fourths, and sixths, while the left hand doubles the chromatic melody of the voice line an octave lower. After thirty-six measures of this treatment Dett wrote a 2/4 bar, marked *piu accel,* then returned to the beginning rhythmic pattern. Following a sixteen-measure piano interlude, the first theme returns. Next is a B section of twenty-four measures with a new accompanimental figure (arpeggiated) under a gradually ascending voice line, ending on an altered a minor ninth chord. A return to the A section grows in intensity and interest by use of heavier chords which reiterate the beginning rhythmic figure.

Scored for high voice, the song's range is from D to high A flat. Good vocal technique is needed for sustaining several high Gs and the A flat. Martens himself called *Magic Moon* "a serenade at St. Pierre," and said that Dett "gave its full meed of sensuous tonal charm to the imagery of the text. It is no pale, graceful serenade suited to a colder clime, but an ardent melody a-tremble with Creole passion."[8]

One documented performance of *A Thousand Years Ago or More* was at Hampton by Ravella Hughes on December 8, 1920.[9] Another one in 1922, reported in the April *Southern Workman,* was at a public recital in Cleveland, by Mrs. Hudson, who received special favorable comment in local papers.

Martens' words concern the mythological Ethiopian King Memnon, slain by Achilles in the Trojan War. The statue at Thebes of Amenhotep III, called the "vocal Memnon," has been associated with King Memnon. Imagery is affected on the words "This silver bracelet softly rang" with an ascending run in the accompaniment, marked *delicatezza*. The bracelet is later spoken of in the text as "the gaud you wore," so apparently the lovely female wearing it had attracted Memnon's attention. Within the song three of the poem's phrases are reiterated for emphasis: "A thousand years ago or more," "When Memnon in the dawning sang," and "Before the legions came that way." Dett intersperses ninth and eleventh chords with arpeggiated, harp-like figures in the accompaniment. The song is partly *recitativo* with a sustained lyrical section presenting some rather difficult vocal intervals. From the beginning key signature of five flats Dett goes to four sharps, cancels this for a two-measure piano passage, then returns to the original five flats. Performed by an amateur the song might sound fragmented, with its *fermatas* and *recitando rubato* markings.

Martens wrote that Dett's scoring for *A Thousand Years Ago or More* "calls up a Nilotic reminiscence with a poesy of imagination, a delicacy and beauty of melodic utterance that could not better express the soul of the poem." Continuing about both settings of his poems, he said that Dett had definitely set a "hallmark, a standard on his work as a composer . . . which cannot well be questioned. And for all this lovers of the sincere and beautiful in music may be grateful."[10]

* * *

In 1919 Church published Dett's arrangements of three spirituals: *Somebody's Knocking at Your Door, I'm So Glad Trouble Don't Last Alway,* and *Follow Me.* In true spiritual style there is much repetition of words and phrases, a situation Dett relieves with variations in the accompaniment.

Somebody's Knocking at Your Door simply says that somebody who "knocks like Jesus" is knocking at the sinner's door, asking why does the sinner not answer. Dett's clever "knocks" are in *staccato* duplet and triplet patterns, followed by rests. (See Musical Example No. 17.) This comical piece is ripe for interpretation, and could either be programmed in a group of spirituals or make a unique encore. After the theme, underlaid with chords, is restated several times, Dett then changes the mood with twenty measures of arpeggiated accompaniment which also carries the theme while the voice is holding out the phrase. (See Musical Example No. 18.)

The chordal accompaniment of the spiritual *I'm So Glad Trouble Don't Last Alway* (from Dett's own collection) resembles some of Burleigh's accompaniments. The chords, used mainly for rhythmic support, are neither contrived nor sophisticated. As in today's gospel music, the chords do not carry the melody of the voice line. The simple repeated words are: "I'm so glad trouble don't last alway, Lord, O my Lord! what shall I do? make more room, Lord, in my heart for Thee."

Dett's arrangement of *Follow Me*, taken from Mrs. Catherine Fields-Gay's collection of spirituals, is by far the most dramatic of the 1919 output. In the Foreword to his first volume of *The Dett Collection of Negro Spirituals* Dett was particularly proud to "pay tribute to the memory" of Mrs. Fields-Gay, "for many years familiarly known as Miss 'Cash' Fields, late of the town of Hampton Virginia." He continued:

> She was a child with some of the first free slaves, who, after the war, were brought by boat to Hampton. She acquired wealth and an education which included a knowledge of music. But to the day of her death, she loved the spirituals which she sang with a frail, slightly false but very affecting voice. Many of the best songs of my collection were sung to me by Mrs. Gay.[11]

The message of *Follow Me*, put simply, is to turn to the Lord for guidance and trust him to relieve burdens, as did the biblical fisherman Peter, who later would "dwell at God's right hand." This text must have had tremendous appeal to Dett as a choral director, teacher, leader, bible scholar, and deeply religious person.

Somebody's Knocking at Your Door

Mus. ex. 17, meas. 13-16. © 1919 Theodore Presser Company. Used by permission.

Mus. ex 17, meas. 78-87. © 1919 Theodore Presser Company. Used by permission.

Mus. ex. 18, meas. 88-93.   © 1919 Theodore Presser Company.   Used by permission.

The song's key of f minor is maintained throughout. It is laden with expressive markings, and the singer is advised to pronounce the word "fishing" as "fishin'." Somewhat declamatory and in typical spiritual jargon Dett adds "a" to "a-fishing" and to "took-a me." The mostly chordal accompaniment is uncomplicated, expressive, and supportive. About midway through the arrangement Dett reuses as an interlude the opening six measures of the spiritual, then returns to the A section with a different harmonization. After sustaining a high F an optional third space C or a high A flat is offered as the singer's final note.

The 1920s

Four years elapsed before the publication in 1923 of Dett's next art songs and arrangements of folk songs for solo voice. This year Theodore Presser published *The Winding Road*, Dett's setting of a poem by Tertius van Dyke. The song opens with an ascending/descending triplet figure in the accompaniment, suggestive of a curving road. A march-like mood is set by the marking *Marziale*. Van Dyke's words speak of the brave heart "that has no fears," continuing with

> Though what we see at the turn of the road
> Is hidden from you and me,
> Yet with a heart that is free of a vain disguise
> And face to the front, and fearless eyes
> We will dare whatever we see.

Percussive triplets in the accompaniment $\frac{2}{4}$ ♩ 𝅘𝅥𝅮𝅘𝅥𝅮𝅘𝅥𝅮 ♩ 𝅘𝅥𝅮𝅘𝅥𝅮𝅘𝅥𝅮| are scored against duplets in the voice line. Dett uses no complex chords, but offers an interesting whole-tone passage after the phrase "Whenever the wild winds blow" while the word "blow" is sustained. He marked this sweep of triplets *rapido zeffiroso e molto crescendo*, after which the dynamic intensity decreases to *pp*, then is suddenly *forte* again in the measures returning to the first theme. The last four measures feature a *bravura* passage for the piano while the singer is holding the word "see." In mood *The Winding Road* reminds one of the equally stirring *Stout Hearted Men* from Sigmund Romberg's *The New Moon*.

Poet Tertius van Dyke (1886-1958) likely included "The Winding Road" in his *Songs of Seeking and Finding*. He was born in New York, the son of Reverend Henry van Dyke, who won fame as an author, teacher, minister, and diplomat. Before his ordination as a Presbyterian minister in 1913, Tertius received degrees from Princeton, Union Theological Seminary, and Oxford. He was a Phi Beta Kappa at Princeton, which institution awarded him the D. D. degree in 1948. Some of his pastorates were at the Park Avenue and Spring Street Churches in New York City.   As Congregational minister in Washington, Connecticut in 1936, he was also headmaster of Gunnery School. He worked at The Hague as his father's secretary, and was on several prestigious church and missionary boards. Besides *Songs of Seeking and Finding* he authored *Light My Candle* and co-authored, with his father, *Henry Van Dyke*, a biography, and *The Guidepost*, a series of syndicated news articles.[12]

Presser also published *Open Yo' Eyes* in 1923, Dett's setting of his own dialect poem from *The Album of a Heart* (1911). In strophic form and in 2/4 meter, *Open Yo' Eyes* begins with a ten-measure introduction, which is repeated exactly between the verses and again as a postlude. Dett words provide a glimpse into plantation homelife of children reluctant to rise and get on with the day's work. The repeated words "Open yo' eyes" are used as a refrain. Except for the execution of high Fs, Gs, and an A this song presents no difficulty for the singer. (See Musical Examples Nos. 19 and 20.)

Clever and catchy, *Open Yo' Eyes* should fare well, either programmed in a group or used as an encore. Some of Dett's dialectical substitutions are "ter" for "to," "de" for "the," "kivver" for "cover," "dey" for "they," and "wid" for "with." In addition, he omits the ending g on "creakin'" and "risin'."

Zion Hallelujah, published by John Church (1923) in a series of Negro folk song derivatives, followed the previously discussed *Follow Me, I'm So Glad Trouble Don't Last Alway*, and *Somebody's Knocking at Your Door*. Others in the series published this year were *O, The Land I'm Bound For*, dedicated to tenor Lloyd Hickman, frequent soloist with the Douglass Memorial Chorus in Oberlin in the 1920s, and *Poor Me*.

Dett's *Zion*, referring to the biblical land of true believers, has different words and tune from the pre-Civil War folk song titled *Oh, Zion Hallelujah*, which is in a minor key. At the top of Dett's arrangement is "From the Collection of R. N. D. Sung by Miss Baytop." Miss Baytop was possibly a student or associate at Hampton Institute.

Dett's tempo marking is *Lento con molto tranquillo*. The key is D flat major. The vocal line is well sustained by continuous eighth notes, whose changing harmonies heighten in interest each of the numerous times the phrase "O Zion, Hallelujah" is stated. The words say simply, "O Zion, Hallelujah, city, bright and fair, I hope and pray I'll meet you there." The phrases build dynamically with each repetition, ending at *ff* for the voice. The *legato* accompaniment's inner voices are beautifully entwined, lending a prayerful mood. H. H. White, however, reviewing a concert by baritone Wilson Lamb, who programmed *Zion* with two other Dett songs, called the accompaniment "too

Open Yo' Eyes

Mus. ex. 19, meas. 11-18. © 1923 Theodore Presser Company. Used by permission.

Meas. 73-76.

Mus. ex. 20, meas. 82-97.   © 1923 Theodore Presser Company.   Used by permission.

elaborate and instrumental."[13]

Baritone Reinald Werrenrath (1883-1953), to whom *Zion* was dedicated, was a champion of both Dett and Burleigh. News items confirm that during the mid-1920s he frequently programmed Dett's song on his recitals in Carnegie and Symphony Halls in New York and Boston. He was soloist at Dett's Baltimore concert on December 15, 1923, as part of that city's music festival. Though Werrenrath was born in New York state, he was partial to Canada and its composers, one of whose patriotic songs, *Take Me Back to Canada* by O. F. Beck, he recorded. He also recorded Dett's *Follow Me* for Victor.[14]

Werrenrath first studied with his father, a noted oratorio tenor, then with Carl Dufft, Frank King Clark, Arthur Mees, Percy Rector Stephens, and later with Herbert Witherspoon and David Bispham. He debuted in 1907 at a Worcester Festival, directed the University Heights Choral Society in 1914, and in February of 1919 made his first appearance at the Metropolitan as Silvio in *Pagliacci*. Other of his operatic roles were Escamillo (*Carmen*) and Valentin (*Faust*), but more often he was heard as a recitalist and oratorio performer, and as part of the Victor Opera Quartet with Lucy Marsh, Sophie Braslau, and Lambert Murphy.

* * *

In 1924 John Church published two of Dett's art songs, *Were Thou the Moon* and *The Voice of the Sea*, and his arrangement of two Negro folk songs, *A Man Goin' Roun' Takin' Names* and *I'm Goin' to See My Friends Again.* Texts of both art songs were taken from his *The Album of a Heart.*

The twenty-five measure *Were Thou the Moon* is quite romantic in concept. Dett's poem says:

Were thou the moon, and I the flowing sea,
We could not bide as they do, far apart;
My swelling flood must fling its arms to thee,
And draw thee to the love deeps of my heart.

These words are repeated to an entirely different melody and harmonization. The song is not demanding on either singer or pianist. A one-measure introduction in 4/2 meter establishes a syncopated rhythm over the downbeats, basically ♩ ♩ ♩♩ ♩|
♩ ♩♩ ♩| . In true Dett fashion it is generously and specifically marked for expressivness.

Were Thou the Moon was dedicated to "Mr. J. Stanley Hoban, Baritone." John Stanley Hoban was born in Dunoon, Scotland in 1900 and at age twenty moved to Winnipeg, Canada, where he studied voice with Burton Kurth. Later he worked with Herbert Witherspoon in New York and in London with Harry Plunkett Greene. He gained fame as a pioneer in Canadian broadcasting, and as a soloist with the leading Canadian symphonies and the Winnipeg Philharmonic Choir. From 1925 to 1943 he taught voice in Winnipeg, moved to Seattle, Washington in 1946, continuing to teach, and from 1968-1976 he directed workshops for the National Association of Teachers of Singing (NATS).[15]

Contained in thirty-two measures, four of which are an introduction, the text of Dett's *The Voice of the Sea* reads:

All day long from my window
I gaze on the shadowy sea
Whose solemn sound, so deep, profound,
Seems alone, alone for me.

'Tis the song of the mighty spirit
Whose inmost life is peace;
But from the pain of a love in vain,
The heart finds no release.

The underlying rhythm is similar to the syncopation in *Were Thou the Moon*. Dett adds triplet figures and some left hand crossovers to the treble clef in the accompaniment. The song's lowest note is A, and goes only up to a D.

It was dedicated to contralto Kathryn Meisle (1899-1970), who has been described as one of "the formidable" mezzos at the Metropolitan in the mid-1930s.[16] Trained as a pianist in Philadelphia from the age of five, she gave concerts there when she was nine, and as a teenager was pianist for a silent film theater, was a church soloist, and sang in a vocal quartet. In 1920 she debuted as soloist with the Minneapolis Symphony Orchestra, and again in 1923 with the Chicago Opera Company as Erda in *Siegfried*. On April 4, 1924, Meisle sang at Hampton Institute. Before debuting at the Metropolitan in 1935 she was quite successful as a soloist with leading orchestras throughout the US and Europe. She also recorded for Brunswick, Victor, Columbia, and privately for the Metropolitan.[17]

Ample coverage in music journals and the *New York Times* usually showed Meisle in a formal portrait wearing a handsome fur-trimmed gown. In private life she was the wife of concert manager Calvin Franklin. She favored American composers, and believed that church choir participation provided excellent oratorio training. During the 1920s she was featured extensively on radio, both as a soloist and with the Baldwin Quartet. A *New York Times* critic said of her expertise in Verdi's *Requiem*: "Miss Meisle knows the art of projecting tone without recourse to forcing, and her singing was uniformly characterized by deep sincerity and musicianship."[18]

Meisle's Metropolitan debut as Azucena in *Il Trovatore* was scheduled for March 2, 1935, but she stepped in for the indisposed Rose Bampton on February 28 as Amneris in *Aida*, then proceeded to fulfill the March 2 engagement. She was well-received in both roles.[19] She continued at the Metropolitan until 1938, then chose to perform as a recitalist. In September of 1937 she was soloist at the Worcester Festival when Dett's *Listen to the Lambs* was performed, having sung a solo role in *The Ordering of Moses* at its Cincinnati premiere the preceding May.

* * *

The culprit in *A Man Goin' Roun' Takin' Names* (Church, 1924) is actually Death, goin' roun' takin' lives. Dett's arrangement of the Negro folk song was based on the singing of it by Captain Walter R. Brown at Hampton Institute. Brown enrolled at Hampton in 1907 and after completing the Normal Teacher's Course became Head of Industrial Arts at Morehouse College. In 1915 Dr. Robert R. Moton, as Commandant of Cadets, called Brown back to Hampton as his assistant, and by 1930, he was given, as Moton had been, the title "Major," and subsequently was appointed Dean of Men.

In 1944 he was elected secretary of Hampton's Board of Trustees. In 1958 Brown's forty-two years of service were recognized in a dedicatory service by the graduating class of that year, by which time he had become treasurer of the National Alumni Association and coordinator of alumni activities on a local and national level. A written tribute to him for the occasion said in part:

> You have given yourself beyond the requirements of your position as friend, leader, and a true inspiration to the "Hampton Family." To find such an individual as you is a rare occurrence, for by your presence life at Hampton has been made more beautiful.[20]

Somewhat in the style of Burleigh's arrangements, the theme of *Man Goin' Roun'* is shared equally in the vocal line and the accompaniment. After a four-measure introduction, announcing the theme, this simple but beautifully touching song, marked *Largo mestamente* (slowly and plaintively), says that Death has caused pain by taking a mother and father. Dett uses an augmented chord to point up the word "pain." The song's mood is one of resignation as well as reverence.

Major Walter R. Brown
Undated photo, courtesy Hampton University Archives.

It is dedicated "To Mr. Jerome Swinford." Baritone Swinford (1893-1976) graduated from Princeton in 1915. After joining the US Navy in 1917 he was put in charge of music in the Tidewater District, and was also song leader for the US Naval Training Station in Norfolk, Virginia. In an interview during this time he said that it was "absolutely pitiable" to see how worn the phonograph records were in the training camps, not from abuse, but from use. He expressed how important music was to the enlisted men's morale.[21] After the armistice in 1919 he organized the official Navy Glee Club as a traveling entertainment group, for which he was soloist.

In the early 1920s Swinford began serious voice study with the elderly Frederick Bristol in New York, soon gaining fame, under his own management, as an oratorio singer in several of that city's churches. Additional engagements were with the symphony orchestras in New York, Detroit, Minneapolis, St. Louis, Philadelphia, and Los Angeles. Swinford felt a genuine "call" to teach, however, and fortunately was able to combine this profession with a singing career for several years. As a performer on the college and university circuit he sang at

Hampton in 1921 on the Musical Art Series. His sensible suggestions for recital programming were stated in an essay, "College Programs Must Differ from Those of Usual Concerts, Says Singer," which in essence said that an artist should always approach audiences with listenable selections given in the spirit of creating a love for music.[22]

TOWN HALL

113 West 43rd Street

Friday Evening

OCTOBER 11th

at 8:30

Recital by

JEROME

SWINFORD

BARITONE

Program for Swinford's October 11, 1929 Concert
Courtesy Sarah Lawrence College.

Sometimes classified as a *basso cantante*, Swinford was deemed an excellent interpreter of spirituals. His voice was said to be "a splendid one, deep and resonant." He consistently "created a splendid impression" with his "voice of gorgeous quality and a command of style which bespeaks extensive cultivation."[23] Though one concert at Town Hall, October 11, 1929, found him in less than good voice, his reviews on the whole were quite favorable: "The singer's musicianship compensated largely for some vocal shortcomings, however, and his program gave manifest pleasure to an audience of good size."[24]

In 1928 Swinford became a charter faculty member at the then new Sarah Lawrence College in Bronxville, New York, and in 1944 was elected to their Board of Trustees. He remained there until retirement in 1967, then taught privately in New York City.[25]

* * *

As previously mentioned in connection with *Go On, Mule!* Dett collaborated again with Reverend J. Fletcher Bryant on an arrangement of *I'm A-Goin' to See My Friends Again*, dedicated to tenor Roland Hayes.[26] Hayes (1887-1976) sang at Hampton in 1914, just as his career was beginning to bud. He was a consummate artist who gained fame both in the US and abroad, and one of the young American Negroes furthered professionally by Harry Burleigh. In turn, Hayes was a champion of Burleigh's music, and helped aspiring Negro singers.

Hayes grew up in Georgia and Tennessee, sang in a church choir as a teenager in Chattanooga, studied Caruso recordings and music fundamentals with Arthur Calhoun, and later attended Fisk University. Between 1911 and 1929 he studied voice with Arthur Hubbard, George Henschel, and Amanda Ira Aldridge. He toured with the Fisk Singers in 1911 when it was a professional quartet, and rarely turned down other singing engagements, while mainly supporting himself in non-musical occupations. After several years of concertizing at Negro churches and colleges, and in Boston and other American cities, he went abroad to study and perform.

By 1923 Hayes was well established as a leading American singer, and this year was the first Negro to sing with a major orchestra, the Boston Symphony. In 1924 he was awarded the Spingarn Medal. In 1948 his *My Songs: Afro-American Religious Folksongs* was published, and in 1950 he became a faculty member at Boston University. "His repertory was large and richly varied, consisting primarily of lieder but also including works from the Renaissance to contemporary times, particularly Negro spirituals."[27] Hayes remains an awesome and well respected figure in the history of Negro musicians.

The text of *I'm A-Goin' to See My Friends Again*, similar to the hopeful *Zion, Hallelujah*, expresses a desire to join loved

ones in Zion, the Promised Land. The vocal line, which goes up to
G, stays within the G major arpeggio, with the exception a few F
sharps. When the words say "and when I reach that Promis'd
Land, side by side with them I'll stand," the accompaniment
moves to the piano's high register, as if Zion is a high goal to be
attained. Dett uses both "Hallelujah" and "Ahallelu" in the
phrase "I'm a-goin' to see my friends again, Ahallelu," then
"Hallelujah, Lord, Hallelujah Lord." (See Musical Example No.
21.) The accompaniment, supportive and easily readable, opens
with an eight-measure introduction, half of which is used again
as an interlude. Snap rhythm in both piano and vocal parts add
energy.

In 1926 Church published *God Understands*, a certificate of
royalty (1926) for which is in the Dett Collection, NFNYPL. A
news item from the *Niagara Falls Gazette* (November 18, 1930),
mentioned that Nell Hunter performed it in Howard Hall as
part of Niagara's Music Week celebrations.[28]

Words to *God Understands* are by Katrina Trask (1853-1922),
also known as dramatist and poet Kate Nichols, who in private
life was Mrs. George Foster Peabody at the time of her death.
She was formerly the wife of Spencer Trask, Peabody's banking
partner and longtime friend who owned Yaddo Estate in Saratoga
Springs, New York. Katrina was interested in the arts and world
peace, a philanthropist in her own right. The Trasks had four
children, all of whom died in infancy, tragedies memorialized by
Katrina in privately presented dramas of her own writing. As
early as 1900 plans were made to bequeath Yaddo, which boasted
several hundred acres of woodlands, a well-tended rose garden,
and an enviable library, to the creative arts. Dett was a guest
there in the summer of 1941.

Unfortunately, Trask was killed in a train accident in 1909.
Earlier his wife had generously founded St. Christina's School
and St. Christina's Hospital for Crippled Children as further
memorials to her children. During World War I she saw that
food was grown at Yaddo for the Allied cause. Her first play, *In
the Vanguard*, had eight printings and sold 20,000 copies. Other
of her dramas presented publicly were *The Little Town of
Bethlehem*, *Without the Walls*, and *Mors et Victoria*. Katrina
died of pneumonia after less than a year of marriage to Peabody,

I'm A-Goin' to See My Friends Again

Mus. ex. 21, meas. 37-52.   © 1924 John Church Company.   Used by permission.

who had named his own Saratoga Springs home "Katrina Trask Hall," to be used for welfare work.

Completing Dett's solo songs for the decade were *My Day* and *Lead Gently, Lord, and Slow*, both published by Church in 1929. *My Day*, undedicated, is one of Dett's few love songs. Its touching poem, by Daniel S. Twohig,[29] reads:

> The twilight falls, our day of love is past;
> Our day of dreams, would it might ever last,
> Yet this one day will always be my own

Because you shared it, dear, with me, alone!
The twilight wanes and leaves a world of night,
The pale stars beam, and shed a holy light;
Now in a dream, I see you still, my own,
In fancy at love's shrine with me, alone!

Dett's pleasant setting offers nothing unusual, but the accompaniment's syncopated figure, seldom duplicating the vocal line, lends a sense of passion. Conceived for low voice, the range is from low B up to E. There are four skips of a seventh in the vocal line, which could be awkward for an inexperienced singer, though they fit naturally into the harmonic progression.

Lead Gently, Lord, and Slow, set to a text by Paul Laurence Dunbar, discussed in Chapter VIII, was one of two dozen sacred songs which Church published before 1930. Some other composers included in this series were Geoffrey O'Hara, Charles G. Spross, Mana-Zucca, and W. H. Neidlinger. Dett's *Lead Gently* was available for both high and low voice (keys of F and C major), with ranges from D to G and A to D. Dunbar's words ask the Lord's patience in leading a weak, groping, perhaps doubting, being. Dett's accompaniment to the three-verse song is largely chordal, and would be suitable for organ as well as piano. Supportive and interesting for its countermelody, it seldom duplicates the vocal line. His sequential patterns, both for voice and piano, the step-wise descending bass line, and chord progressions are skillfully handled. (See Musical Example No. 22.)

The 1930s

One of Dett's two publications by G. Schirmer, Inc. for solo voice was *Sit Down, Servant* (1932), also published by Schirmer in a choral arrangement this same year. A manuscript of the solo, dated 5/5/32, is in the Hampton University Archives. Called on the manuscript a "Negro folk song scena [*sic*]" and on the published copy a "Negro folk-scene for low or medium voice and piano," its explanation on both copies reads: "A weary Mammy, dozing by the fireside, dreams that the Lord of Heaven bids her 'rest a

Lead Gently, Lord, and Slow

Mus. ex. 22, meas. 45-60.   ©1929, John Church Company.   Used by permission.

little while.'"

The words are repeated over and over, essentially saying sit down, servant, rest a little while. I know you're tired as I was tired. On the score Dett's direction for the word "tired" is: "The division of the word tired recognizes the common pronunciation ti-erd, which the spelling fails to indicate." Each time "sit down" is sung the rhythm is ♪♩, a pattern stated in the introduction and repeated on most downbeats. Measures 58-67, marked *ff*, end in a diminuendoing *melisma* (69), marked *calmato* to the end. (See Musical Example No. 23.) An asterisk at measure 58 suggests the "moan" or "tone" of a Negro preacher, "delivered with unction and a considerable carrying of the voice." The rhythm of the *melisma*, marked *largamente*, is (2/2) ♪♩ ♫♬♩♬♩♬♪♪|, with all but the first note on "sit" to be sung on "down."[30] The total range of the song is only a ninth.

Sit Down, Servant

Mus. ex. 23, meas. 58-61. Copyright © 1932 (Renewed), G. Schirmer, Inc. International copyright secured. All rights reserved. Used by permission.

In 1934 Schirmer published Dett's sacred song *O Lord, the Hard-won Miles*, a setting of Dunbar's words in which the Lord is asked to soothe the weariness and aches of one whose life has been difficult. In ABA form, the keys of the song are E flat major, B flat major, and E flat major. Though in its reverent mood it resembles *Lead Gently, Lord, and Slow*, the continuous eighth-note rhythm of the accompaniment adds urgency, and shows Dett's sensitivity to inner voices. This lovely piano part, which rarely duplicates the voice line, could almost stand alone as a keyboard solo. Some sixteenth-note passages are included for the piano in measures 26 through 28 to provide a transition between the key change from B flat to E flat. *Hard-won Miles* would make an excellent church offertory solo.

Iorana, first published by Summy in 1935, was later included in *Negro Art Songs*, an anthology edited by Edgar Rogie Clark for Edward B. Marks Music Corporation (1946). Obviously Clark deemed Dett's work representative, for he said in his Introduction:

> I have endeavored to select as faithfully as possible the compositions which sincerely represent a particular composer in rhythmic, harmonic and melodic figure. . . . The title of this volume aptly describes the object of this work, namely, to present in a single low-priced album an interesting variety of art songs by Negro composers that will meet the needs of present day singers . . . of all ages.[31]

Iorana (pronounced Ee-o-ra-na) is subtitled "Tahitian Maiden's Love Song," and "Dedicated to Robert Gibbings, Esq." Its words are by J. Henry Quine, whose exact identity as a poet has not been established. The *New York Times*, June 24, 1915, carried an article by a John H. Quine, titled "A Nameless Nationality," which advocated calling US citizens, including natives and naturalized persons, "Unisians." He reasoned that this term had the same number of syllables as "America," and should be substituted for the latter in our patriotic songs.

Other references in the *Times* were to baritone John Quine, recitalist and performer with the Society of American Singers in 1918. In 1919 and the early 1920s some of Quine's more intimate art song recitals were in Aeolian Hall and Town Hall in New York. In programming Quine strove for a wide variety of styles and periods. Critic Richard Aldrich spoke of Quine as an intelligent singer, and, though not highly complimentary of his voice quality, appreciated his expressiveness and flexibility. "A besetting sin in his singing is a tendency to scoop, both up and down," Aldrich said, thereby preventing accuracy and precision.[32] Another reviewer of a Town Hall recital the following fall said that Quine sang with "quiet taste, discrimination of style, and marked advance in commanding an audience's attention."[33]

Which, if either, of these Quines wrote the poem *Iorana* has not been determined. On the other hand, information on the dedicatee, Robert Gibbings, is plentiful. In 1932 Gibbings authored a book titled *Iorana*, a record of his sojourn to Tahiti, which was illustrated with his own woodcuts. Gibbings was born in Cork, Ireland in 1889. He first studied medicine, but soon chose as a profession art and engraving for which he was better suited. In World War I , while serving with the Royal Munster Fusiliers at Gallipoli, he was shot through the throat and subsequently discharged from military service with the rank of Captain.

As director of Golden Cockerell Press in Berkshire (1923-1933) he illustrated many of its publications and authored several books of his own. He was an avid traveler who loved seas and rivers, and as such was the first to make pencil drawings on xylonite under the sea. His passion for submarine life is discussed in his semi-autobiographical *Blue Angels and Whales* (1938). In a self-constructed flat-bottomed boat Gibbings traveled more than 50,000 miles over salt water, visiting five continents.

Other of his publications are *Twelve Wood Engravings* (1921), *The Seventh Man* (1930), *Coconut Island* (1936), *John Graham, Convict* (1937), *Sweet Thames Run Softly* (1940), *Coming Down the Wye* (1942), *Lovely is the Lea* (1945), *Over the Reefs* (1948), *Sweet Cork of Thee* (1951), *Coming Down the Seine* (1953), *Trumpets from Montparnasse* (1955), and *Till I End My Song* (1957). From 1936 to 1942 Gibbings lectured on book production at the University of Reading. In 1938 the National University of Ireland conferred an honorary M. A. degree upon him.

He has been described by one biographer as tall and massively built, "with twinkling eyes, aquiline features, and a beard, . . . great natural charm, a fund of Irish humour, and an exceptional store of miscellaneous knowledge of birds, fishes, plants, geology, and archaeology."[34]

Gibbings' obituary in the *New York Times*, January 21, 1958, stated that he was "a born writer blessed with a distinctive and often beautiful style. His puckish humor, his recondite learning, and his gift for diverting anecdote enrich all his works." Though they were contemporaries, Dett probably did not know the remarkable and colorful Robert Gibbings, unless they met in London during Hampton's 1930 choir tour. There is no indication that Gibbings included the US in his travels.

Dett's score of *Iorana*, which has two verses, is more elemental than exotic. In an art deco vein, a rather stylized drawing of a Tahitian maiden adorns the cover of the 1935 Summy issue. Though no credit for the art work is given, a mere glance at Gibbings' finely wrought engravings almost certainly proves that the illustration is not his.

In ABAB form with a coda *Iorana* begins in 3/8 meter with a key signature of two flats, and an eight-measure introduction. The accompaniment unexcitingly follows the vocal line, sometimes in a lower octave, for the following ninety measures. Slight relief is afforded at measure 66 by a change to 2/4 and a key change at measure 68 to G major. This section is marked *quasi havanera*, with the typical underlying rhythm in the accompaniment of ♪♫♩ | ♪♫♩ |. This rhythm originated in Africa and combined with many Habanera melodies from middle and southern Spain. In its simplest form, as used by Dett in this accompaniment, it became the rhythm characteristic of Spanish and Latin American music.

The passion of Quine's words, which say, "Love me now and love me ever, kiss me now and leave me never, Iorana, Iorana, Iorana!" is somehow not enhanced by Dett's unimaginative accompaniment. He interjects, perhaps as a novelty, an altered C eleventh chord, which is sustained under the singer's *quasi cadenza*, reminding one of an improvised tag on a blues tune.

Arrangements for Dorothy Maynor, 1940-1943

In the early 1940s Dett was asked by Dorothy Maynor, then in the prime of her career, to make at least six arrangements of spirituals for concert use. These were obviously the arrangements he began at Yaddo during the summer of 1941. The first of these, *Ride On, Jesus*, was published by J. Fischer & Bro. in 1940. August Maekelberghe of the *Detroit Free Press* commented on this arrangement in connection with another setting published by Fischer at the same time:

> Dett has done a very fine job of writing. "I'm Goin' to Thank God" is a lament written with such intensity of feeling as to compel a perception of the sighs of a race down-trodden through the ages. . . . "Ride On, Jesus" is entirely in contrast, . . . almost as gay in rhythm as the other is sad in tune.[35]

Ride On, Jesus is dissimilar in words, tune, and rhythm to *Ride on, King Jesus*, set by Burleigh, Hall Johnson, and other arrangers. Dett's inscription above the title reads: "Setting requested and made especially for Miss Dorothy Maynor." The range is from middle C to an optional high B flat. On her recording with Arpad Sandor, made at the Library of Congress in 1940, Maynor takes the high B flat. The joyous mood of the piece in 2/4 meter is aided by the clipped piano rhythm of ♪ᵣ ♪ᵣ | ♪ᵣ ♪ᵣ | and a half-step/step-wise descending bass line combined with a stride bass figure. (See Musical Example No. 24.) The text is mainly in dialect, omitting the "g" on "ing" endings, the "t" on "Baptis'," using "hebben" for "heaven," "mo'n-in'" for "morning," "jes" for "just," "t" for "to," and "de" for "the."

The other spiritual from 1940, *I'm Goin' to Thank God*, is not listed with Dett's other arrangements dedicated to Maynor. On the previously mentioned 1940 recording Maynor sings a spiritual titled *I'm Goin' to Tell God*, Dett's music with her alterations in wording

In 1942 Mills Music, Inc. published *Go On, Brother!* another Maynor request. On its cover is "Featured with success by Miss Dorothy Maynor." *Go On, Brother!*, marked *Andante serioso*, is only thirty measures in length, including a four-measure introduction which states the vocal motif to follow. Interestingly, there are only two short rests (a sixteenth and an eighth) for the singer. Dett cleverly avoids duplicating the

Ride on, Jesus!

Mus. ex. 24, meas. 33-36. Copyright © 1940 by J. Fischer & Bro.
Copyright renewed c/o CPP/Belwin, Inc., Miami, FL 33014.
International copyright secured. All rights reserved.

Mus. ex. 24, meas. 45-49. Copyright © 1940 by J. Fischer & Bro.
Copyright renewed c/o CPP/Belwin, Inc., Miami, FL 33014.
International copyright secured. All rights reserved.

voice line in the accompaniment by alternating supportive chords
with a sixteenth-note figure. (See Musical Example No. 25.) The
words of *Go On, Brother!* urge striving for a place in Heaven, one
recognizable by the bell's toll. The declamatory phrase "Glory
and honor, praise the Lord" ends the song at a dynamic of *ff*, with
a *fermata* over the word "the" on a high A flat.

Go on, Brother!

Mus. ex. 25, meas. 13-23. Copyright © 1942 by Mills Music, Inc.,
1619 Broadway, New York, NY. International copyright secured. All
rights reserved.

   Four more arrangements for Maynor were published by Mills
in 1943: *I'm A-trav'ling to the Grave, Now We Take This Feeble
Body, What Kind of Shoes You Going to Wear?,* and *In That
Morning.* Though *I'm A-trav'ling to the Grave* is marked *Ritmo
quasi march funebre,* it is in a major key (G). The accompaniment
is almost totally chordal, in either half or quarter-note rhythms,
except for a four-measure passage in eighth notes under the words
"My mother died a-shouting, singing Glory Hallelujah!" and
three short descending passages of thirty-second notes

highlighting the words "the grave," "a-trav'ling," and "down."

Based on the Negro funeral hymn, the message says that the time has come to "lay this body down" in death, which need not be a grim thought, but a welcomed one. With Maynor in mind, toward the song's end Dett scored a sustained high G with a *portamento* indicated down to the G below.

Now We Take This Feeble Body was "Especially arranged at the request of Miss Dorothy Maynor."[36] Suitably marked *Adagio doloroso* Dett again uses a sustained, chordal accompaniment. One can well imagine a funeral procession on foot, actually carrying a "dear old brother" to be buried. The ending words say "Now we lift our mournful voices as we gather 'round the grave, and we weep as we sing, Hallelujah." Dett's ending is quite poignant and effective, featuring a countermelody in the accompaniment and another *portamento* for the voice. (See Musical Example No. 26.)

A definite change in mood is presented in the livelier, happier spiritual *What Kind of Shoes You Going to Wear?*, referring to the "golden slippers" which prompted many versions of the same song. Spiritual scholar Newman I. White traces its popularity back to 1827 as a favorite religious song of the whites in the early nineteenth century. It is still used extensively in Southern revivals.[37]

Though the song's range is a ninth (E flat to F), it stays from E flat to C until the last four measures. Dett's frivolous accompanimental figures under the words "golden slippers" and "golden crown" add sass. Every time the second strain of "Yes, yes, yes, my Lord, I'm going to join the heav'nly choir, Yes, yes, yes, my Lord, I'm a soldier of the cross" is sung Dett cleverly varies the right hand figure of the accompaniment over the left hand's descending A flat scale presented earlier. The wearer is indeed elated, dressed in her golden shoes, golden crown, and long white robe, playing her sweet golden harp.

Since Dett's *In That Morning* uses the same words as the spiritual set by Harry Burleigh under the title *You May Bury Me in the Eas'*, a few comparisons and contrasts may be of interest. Dett's twenty-six measures are marked *Lento expressivo*; Burleigh's twenty-two measures are simply *Lento*. Both are in

Now We Take This Feeble Body

Mus. ex. 26, meas. 27-39. Copyright © 1943 by Mills Music, Inc., 1619 Broadway, New York, NY. International copyright secured. All rights reserved.

minor keys, and the initial statement of the melody is the same, but is soon treated dissimilarly with embellishments and rhythmic alterations. Burleigh's arrangement has no meter changes, whereas Dett's jumps frequently from 8/8 to 10/8, back to 8/8, including one measure of 6/4 just before the last two 8/8 measures.

To maintain Dett's slow tempo (M. M. ♪ = 72) in some of the higher *tessitura* would tax even the best of singers, and despite the wished-for doleful effect, the song requires movement. In three instances Dett scores a brief fanfare in the accompaniment when "the trumpet sound" is mentioned, two of which are on an augmented D chord. On the last word, "morning," he uses a slower fragment in C major of military taps.

Other Vocal Compositions from 1942

Two undedicated songs were issued by Mills in 1942, *The Soul of America, Defend!* and *Hymn to Parnassus*. *Soul of America* has many characteristics commonly found in military tunes, including rhythmic patterns, percussive effects, and the potential for an easy band arrangement. In measures 9-12 the vocal melody is repeated with some harmonic variation in the accompaniment and a change in clef. (See Musical Example No. 27.) Later on the words "liberty" and "America" have rhythmic patterns of $\frac{2}{4}$ ♫♩ | and | ♪♫♩ | .

Opposite Dett's name as composer on the first page of the score is ASCAP's logo. Since no lyricist is named, one assumes that the words are by Dett. The two verses are separated by the sprightly, repeated refrain "Liberty, our watch word, carry on to the end, the soul of America, defend!" Dett's purpose in composing this tune is not documented, though his concern for American military efforts during World War II may have prompted it. It was probably one of the "songs of democracy" which he began at Yaddo estate in the summer of 1941, to be used on Bennett Choir broadcasts during 1942.

An unnamed news item from the Bennett College Archives, dated April 4, 1942, stated that Dett's *Hymn to Parnassus* was sung on the twelfth "defense" broadcast, one sent over the North Carolina radio network. The soloist was Lottie McCoy, at the time a senior at Bennett and president of the Student Senate.

The words of Verse I (Anonymous) seem more comfortable for the singer than Dett's words to the second verse. One bit of prosody is evident when, in the line "nor lower than the peak of your desire," Dett sets the word "than" on the downbeat. Any awkwardness, however, could be absorbed in the sweep of the phrase. More distressing to the listener might be Dett's own words to the second verse, e. g., his use of "ev'n" for "even," "'yond" for "beyond," and "t'ward" for "toward," each within moving eighth-note passages. Careful diction and musicianship are required to make this song convincing.

Soul of America, Defend!

Mus. ex. 27, meas. 1-12. Copyright © 1942 by Mills Music, Inc., 1619 Broadway, New York, NY. International copyright secured. All rights reserved.

The accompaniment, fortified with textured chords which change on each eighth-note, is vastly more interesting than the vocal line, which it seldom duplicates. It is decidedly more sophisticated and contemporary than the rather ill-suited, archaic words. The key signature of C major does not change, though there are enough accidentals in the chords to keep the pianist's attention. Meter changes are from 4/4, 2/4, 3/4, 4/4, 3/4, 4/4, 3/4, to 4/4.

Assessment

Dett's contribution to American art song literature, though not prodigious, was sincere, substantial, expressive, and composed in a style similar to that of his contemporaries, combining the elements of Romanticism and Impressionism with a small dash of jazz and ragtime. He offers nothing contrived, technically insurmountable, or recondite. As a keyboardist his accompaniments lie well for the piano, and for the most part are easily readable. Like Burleigh's art songs in their sentimentalism, Dett's are also shades of yesteryear.

Far more programmable are Dett's arrangements of spirituals and Negro folk songs. Their overall conception shows his natural affinity for this genre, in which syncopation, either in slow or fast meter, plays a prominent part, as does snap rhythm, an energizer in Negro music.

Though Dett's solo arrangements of these tunes are highly commendable, his choral arrangements of some of the same, to be discussed in Chapter X, are more challenging and exciting, both to the performer and the listener. Clara Schumann said that Robert Schumann scored symphonically for the piano. One could say that Dett scored chorally for the piano, for he continually wrote into the accompaniment inner voices and other linear progressions which could equally well be sung.

Chapter X

Dett's Choral Music

Introduction

Since the majority of Dett's choral compositions were inspired by or based on folk songs and spirituals, a few remarks concerning his views on these genres are in order. His earliest choral publications were issued in 1914, shortly after he came to Hampton. What better testing ground could he have had than the Hampton Choir and the historic Hampton campus?

After an interview with Dett in 1918, May Stanley described Hampton as a "delightful setting" for Dett's "inspirational labors:"

> The broad grounds, . . . the shaded walks; the satiny sheen of magnolia trees lifting up great white blossoms to the June sunshine; the sparkling waters of Hampton Roads, seen at intervals through the trees, make up an ideal surrounding for one who is gathering and interpreting the melodies of the Southland.[1]

The reverent attitude for spirituals which Dett imparted to the Hampton Choir carried over to their beautiful singing of them, especially the ones which he set, and largely accounted for the group's high rank in choral circles. By 1930, as Dett prepared choral repertoire for the European tour, he felt safe in testing some of his new but unpublished settings.

Regarding Dett and his work at Hampton, a writer for the *Norfolk Journal and Guide*, November 1, 1930, said:

> He is a pioneer not only in the developing of primitive folk songs into art forms, but he has freed the Negro ensemble through his choir from the confines of the more primitive types of folk song singing by his presentation of certified programs handled in distinctly professional manner on a plane of artistry rather than of race.[2]

Dett felt that though a religious element dominated the spirituals, they were too crude in their natural form to be used in a formal church service. He explained that his works based on spirituals and folk tunes were *not* "in any sense arrangements," saying:

> The folk character is gained in some instances from only a line of folk song, serving merely as a theme upon which an entirely new composition is created. All the material used in the development of the folk song is, as far as possible, derived from the folk song sources or very closely imitates folk song style.[3]

In his article, "As the Negro School Sings," Dett deplored the commercialization of the spirituals, stating that Negro schools, rather than Negro churches, were the best place for their preservation:

> Unless the Negro school, where Negro songs are sung, where Negro youth is in the making, and where the Negro idiom is most natural and best understood, add to their responsibilities the making of musicians who can intelligently handle this native art, there   can be but little hope for the future of Negro music.[4]

During the late nineteenth and early twentieth centuries choral groups from Fisk, Hampton, Tuskegee, Wilberforce, and Atlanta University were largely responsible for shaping performance tradition of arranged Negro spirituals.   Their audience appeal brought black and white groups together in public halls. After World War I some of the most famous non-academically affiliated choirs were Wings Over Jordan, the Hall Johnson Choir, the Eva Jessye Choir, the Coleridge-Taylor Society, the Mundy Choristers, and the Legend Singers. Following their success in the 1920s the Negro choirs from Fisk, Hampton, Tuskegee, Morehouse, Spelman, Howard, Wilberforce, Shaw, Talladega, Rust, and Virginia State College became the most important group of musicians "presenting stylistic performances of arranged Negro spirituals."[5]

As Dett continued to compose, his choral music was regarded by many as more appealing and outstanding than his piano compositions.   A writer for the *Rochester Democrat and Chronicle*, June 20, 1943, said:

The interested public is even more aware of Dett's
mastery of the choral idiom. This runs the gamut from
the classic motet to the free fantasy, exhibiting many
beaufiful patterns in voice leading, and developing a
melodic eloquence which is both racial and individual.

McBrier considered Dett's choral compositions in smaller
forms his most durable works, pointing out that their

> . . . vitality and dramatic effects . . . are motivated by the
> use of rhythms, melodies, and idioms borrowed from the
> spirituals, as well as Dett's musicality. Further, his
> knowledge of voice kept him within the confines of good
> vocal writing. His effective use of dynamics, his
> successful experimentation with a variety of forms, his
> knowledgeable selection and creation of textual material,
> and his technical skill, all combine to make him an
> excellent choral composer.[6]

McBrier continues that Dett's choral pieces should be
classified as original works, because of his elaboration and other
compositional techniques employed in their construction. Her list
of these include using either the entire folk song/spiritual or a
mere fragment, absolute or relative repetition of the theme,
expansion, contraction, variation or inverson of the melodic
ideas, rhythmic diminution or augmentation, textual mutations
and repetitions, and antiphonal or contrapuntal treatment. By
relying on his own creativity, Dett learned that composition of
Negro music could be related to the spiritual in style only.[7]

Admitting that rhythm is the most vital element in music,
Dett, in his various essays on Negro music, has pointed out two
basic characteristics of the folk song and spiritual: syncopation
and natural suitability for harmonization, particularly in the
frequency of open fourths (African origin) and fifths. Also
evident in some of the spirituals are the Mixo-Lydian mode,
using the flatted seventh, as in "Roll, Jordan, Roll;" the Aeolian
mode ("Ho Everyone That Thirsts!"); the Dorian mode ("Run to
Jesus" and "Calvary's Mountain"); the pentatonic scale ("Steal
Away" and "Swing Low, Sweet Chariot"); and the native
Hungarian scale ("Go Down Moses").[8]

Choral scholar Carl Gordon Harris, Jr. wrote in 1971 that
Dett described the rhythm of the spirituals as a steady pulse

with no distinction between primary and secondary beats, which should be of equal intensity.[9] On Harris' list of select choral music by Dett are *The Ordering of Moses, City of God, I'll Never Turn Back No More, Listen to the Lambs, Now Rest Beneath Night's Shadows, Rise Up Shepherd and Follow Me, The Lamb,* and *Wasn't That a Mighty Day?*

In 1972 Arthur Lee Evans, whose dissertation was similar in subject to Harris', named Dett among a dozen or so arrangers who have retained the "warmth, spirit, and character of the original spiritual."[10] Evans observed that much of Dett's choral music resembles the nineteenth century Russian style of choral part-writing by free use of *divisi* in all parts, particularly for the lower male voices. Dett frequently used the *fermata* at climaxes, and "achieved melodic, rhythmic, and harmonic effects by the judicious use of dynamic and tempo indications." Along with his "personal expressiveness" he "managed to stay within the classical shadow of Burleigh's concept of form and design," though his arrangements are more advanced than Burleigh's in expansion of his style toward the motet by use of bolder harmonies and dynamics.[11]

Evans noticed that Dett almost entirely avoided dialect except in *Listen to the Lambs,* with the words "all a-crying." Dett's "melody and harmony often shift through quickly moving chromaticism, but never go too far away from the original tonal center. This touch of chromaticism serves to embellish the basic harmonic structure prior to cadences." Other characteristics of his arrangements are word painting and "affective devices." For example in *I'll Never Turn Back No More* (1916), each "no" in all voice parts is repeated with an upward, emphatic melismatic sweep.[12]

Terry Lee Fansler also comments on Dett's infrequent use of dialect and the pentatonic scale. Of Dett's choral pieces Fansler says:

> [They] reflect a dramatic intensity that results from careful indications in the score of the proper tempo and dynamic nuance, and from the use of subtle text painting. Tasteful harmonic sequences and unexpected codas give evidence of Dett's skill as a composer.[13]

Though there are many discrepancies in dates of publication, an examination of several lists of Dett's choral works places the

approximate number at forty, exclusive of the collections
Religious Folk-Songs of the Negro and *The Dett Collection of
Negro Spirituals*, and the more extended works *Chariot Jubilee*
and *The Ordering of Moses*. With the exception of these last two,
Juba, and half a dozen or so shorter works, Dett's choral
compositions are intended to be performed *a cappella*, the piano
scores, containing just the voice parts, designated for rehearsal
only. The following discussion and analysis does not include all
of Dett's choral works, since some scores are out of print, or
unavailable for other reasons.

Compositions in 1914

Dedicated "To all Lovers of Hampton," *Hampton! My Home
by the Sea* was published in 1914 by the Hampton Normal and
Agricultural Institute. In typical barbershop and old timey Glee
Club style, its harmony offers nothing complicated to the singers.
Each of its two verses is followed by an eight-measure refrain.
Dett's words in the first verse read:

> When the glorious day has paled away,
> Great moons in splendor shine, at Hampton;
> Hark! how sweetly on the air,
> Then the bells of evening chime, at Hampton!
> Now the night o'erflown with gladness,
> Pours its joys from shore to shore.
> The dreaming waters sparkle,
> And old caves of ocean roar!
> All the world is filled with music
> Echo answer o'er and o'er, "Hampton!"
>
> Refrain:
> Shout, shout the chorus, o'er mountain, vale and plain,
> The noble deeds, the hearts that would be free!
> Then in a sweeter, yet more tender strain,
> Sing Hampton, my home by the sea!

The second verse is much in the same vein. Extolling the
virtues of the school's magic atmosphere, it ends with the lines
"What tones divinely tragic, ring with high celestial sound! 'Tis
the blood of all the Martyr'd Faithful crying from the ground,

Hampton!" and the same refrain follows. Phrasing is well marked by rests and *fermatas*, perhaps accounting for the split measures at the end of most of the scores. In the key of A flat major, the tenor and alto voices most often carry the moving, modulatory parts. Dett uses snap rhythm effectively on the words "sparkle" and "tragic." This school song was programmed several times while Dett taught at Hampton. It also decorated the Dett family Christmas card in 1929.

* * *

One of Dett's most significant and frequently performed choral works, which undoubtedly first established his compositional skills in this genre, was *Listen to the Lambs* (Schirmer, 1914) about which much has been written. As the first composer to use the theme of a spiritual as the main melody of an anthem, Dett said of *Lambs*:

> I recall that I wrote "Listen to the Lambs" out of a feeling that Negro people, especially the students of Hampton Institute, where I was then teaching, should have something musically which would be peculiarly their own and yet which would bear comparison with the nationalistic utterances of other people's work in art forms.[14]

Dett was a genius at adding flavor to original melodies. *Lambs* is often referred to as a motet or an anthem in the form of a motet. The term motet, also applicable to the anthem, implies a sacred vocal composition, unaccompanied, and in contrapuntal style.

Lambs' well expressed message is taken from Bible text Isaiah 40:11, when Jesus instructs Simon Peter to "feed the lambs" and "tend the sheep" of humanity. The words repeatedly say, "Listen to the lambs, all a-crying. He shall feed his flock like a shepherd, and carry the young lambs in his bosom." Under the title Dett calls *Lambs* "a religious characteristic in the form of an Anthem." Choral scholar Carl Gordon Harris calls it "a study in contrasts, . . . characterized by alternation between full and partial choir, diatonic and chromatic motion, and dynamic extremes."[15]

The unaccompanied *Lambs*, in ABA form, is for an eight-part chorus of mixed voices. It is more expressive than difficult. The melody of the A sections, in d minor, is pentatonic, derived from a traditional spiritual, and for the first seven measures is treated as a dialogue between the women's and men's parts. Measures 8-12 are *tutti*, followed by five measures of dialogue, then the ending thirteen measures are *tutti*, the last four scored in unison in whole notes of D, C, D, D. The highest note for soprano in this section is A on the word "cry," which moves down to a D on the "ing" syllable.

Evans feels that in constructing *Lambs* Dett set the text "in the voice range where the desired effects can be expediently achieved."[16] He classifies the piece as difficult and describes the dialogue of the A sections as "wailing."

The B section, in F major, features a tempo change marked *meno mosso*, and a solo for the soprano section (with rests for the altos), underlaid with a seven-measure hum (F major chord) in the men's parts, *con bocca chiusa*. When the sopranos repeat the phrase Dett drops the hum and goes back to words for all parts. Following this the words are repeated in a different rhythm, then there is another humming passage which adds the altos under the original soprano solo. Next Dett uses to good effect a sustained descending chromatic movement (measures 62-74) in the alto line whose rhythm is duplicated by the tenors while the sopranos and basses chant "in his bosom." (See Musical Example No. 28.)

Fansler looks at this reiteration of "in his bosom" as reassurance to the listener that the Lord will care for his flock, and of the ending measures of the piece he writes: "The doleful cry of the lambs is skillfully depicted in the coda before the voices intone a solemn amen in unison." He considers that the "arrangement of voice parts and harmonic effects in the concluding section vividly portray the 'condition of crying lambs' as representative of human suffering and bondage."[17]

A clever modulatory passage follows (measures 75-78), ending on an A major chord with the word "listen." Dett's directions here are to "Prolong the n of the last syllable of listen into a hum." (See Musical Example No. 29.) The last A section at measure 79, a shorter variation of the opening one, is scored fuller, enabling the building climax on the word "all." It is preceded by two measures of unison eighth notes for the basses and tenors on the words "Listen to the lambs a-crying." Another high A for the sopranos descends step-wise over the next ten measures, ending on the D below. The last four measures are in

Listen to the Lambs

Mus. ex. 28, meas. 62-74. Copyright © 1914 (Renewed), G. Schirmer, Inc. International copyright secured. All rights reserved. Used by permission.

Listen to the Lambs

Mus. ex. 29, meas. 75-83. Copyright © 1914 (Renewed), G. Schirmer, Inc., International copyright secured. All rights reserved. Used by permission.

unison (D) on the word "Amen," marked *pp*.

This is a powerful, timeless, and dramatic piece. Other full analyses of *Lambs* are given by Evans and Harris in their dissertations. Harris called the B section a "miniature arch form," and considers the end repetitions a common feature of the spiritual style, evolving from:

> . . . a need to musically expand a short, simple textual idea. The idea of alternating textures may be related to the traditional performance practice of "lining" a hymn by the leader for the benefit of the congregation which might not know the words or the melody.[18]

McBrier states that Dett later arranged *Lambs* for four-part women's voices, which may be the publication by Schirmer in 1923 included in her List of Published Works, though this was not specified. An undated flyer from Carl Fischer listed as available four choral arrangements of *Lambs*: SSAATTBB, SSAA with soprano solo, SAB, and SATB (*a cappella*). McBrier also mentions that Dett scored *Lambs* for orchestra, an arrangement apparently never published. In her analysis of the choral piece she sums up Dett's several devices for creating excitement:

> One text set against another in a different voice; male vocal quality against quality of women's voices; steady moving rhythm against syncopated rhythm; the step-wise ascending and descending movement of the basses and tenors; the climactic soprano A (fortissimo) descending to a final close with all voices in unison; the varying and extreme dynamic levels. . . . But withal, it is the relentless repetition of "all a-crying" which drives the composition to its high point.[19]

Lambs has been considered "especially worthy of note" by Benjamin Brawley, though he calls it a "carol." Of Dett as a choral director Brawley said that "he has trained one of the best choirs in the country," and of him as a choral composer that he "has the merit, more than most of attempting things in large form."[20] Edith Borroff wrote of *Lambs*: "It uses both African and European elements to produce a fabric that the nearly exhausted European tradition alone could not provide. Such works are prophetic."[21]

Lambs even got the attention of H. L. Mencken, author, editor, and critic, who declared it "the only really good Negro composition." Will Marion Cook, obviously in disagreement, took umbrage at Mencken's statement and wrote an open, sarcastic letter to him:

> "Listen to the Lambs" by Dett, is an old Negro melody elaborated and developed as if by a third rate white composer. The development is distinctly not Negroid. Maybe that is why you "land" the lambs. . . . Maybe "The Lambs" is the only Negro composition you have had time to hear. You are a very busy man. Maybe if you ask some dealer for "Song of the Cotton Field" (Porter Grainger), "Rain Song," "Exhortation," "On Emancipation Day," "Lover's Lane" (by Will Marion Cook) and others, you might find them Negroid. The World has. Please Mr. Mencken stick to familiar subjects such as pawn shops, programs and pennies and stop Van-Vechtening and Mencken-ing my race."

Cook's letter was signed "A Negro Composer, able to sit up and take nourishment, or if you prefer, punishment."[22]

By 1925 the SSAATTBB arrangement of *Lambs* was still popular. From August 1 to 1925-August 1, 1926 its sales were higher by far ($1887.90) than other of Dett's works published by Schirmer, including *O, Holy Lord* ($276.30), *Music in the Mine* ($463.75), and the SSA arrangement of *Lambs* ($279.60). Dett's ten percent royalties for this period on these particular pieces, however, netted a mere $290.75.[23]

Lambs has been performed widely by small church choirs, and larger ones such as the Church of the Ascension on Fifth Avenue and Tenth Streets in New York, the Second Presbyterian Church, 21st and Walnut Streets in Philadelphia, and by university choral groups, including the Columbia and Syracuse University Choruses. It was also sung on tour by the National Ukrainian Chorus and the Westminster Choir.

Compositions from 1916-1919

Schirmer published two more of Dett's choral works in 1916,

O, Holy Lord and *Music in the Mine.* The latter is sometimes erroneously referred to as a piano piece. *O, Holy Lord,* an *a cappella* anthem for eight-part mixed chorus based on a spiritual, was first presented on October 5, 1916 by the Elgar Choir of Hamilton, Ontario, to whom it was dedicated. This premiere in Hamilton, conducted by Bruce Carey, was a part of the Field of Honor Memorial Service for Canadian soldiers fallen in battle. (More will be said of Carey as the dedicatee of Dett's *Weeping Mary,* published in 1918.)

Evidence of *O, Holy Lord*'s continued success was reported in *The Southern Workman,* April, 1922:

> The Emanuel Choir of LaGrange, Illinois, composed of 65 men and boys, gave "O, Holy Lord" at a recent service. Referring to its rendition Mr. William Ripley Dorr, the director of the choir said: "I do not think we have ever done anything which has prompted more people to tell me how much they enjoyed it than this beautiful anthem."[24]

Evans classifies *O, Holy Lord* as difficult, "expressive and highly meditative."[25] Evelyn Davidson White considers it of medium difficulty.[26] The words, taken from "The Story of the Jubilee Singers," according to Dett's inscription, are in two phrases, repeated over and over throughout the piece: "O, Holy Lord, Done with sin and sorrow." Despite a marking *Lento con molt' espressione,* it moves, due to its several descending lines in thirds. The key signature is one sharp, and a G major tonality is usually maintained in the phrases "O, Holy Lord," but in most of the "Done with sin and sorrow" phrases a feeling of e minor dominates, arrrived at by a flatted seventh (D to E) in the bass line on "sorrow."

Basses and tenors have the opening eight measures, altos join at measure 9, and sopranos at measure 17. Dett's *divisi* writing provides a full texture, one spread in places over three octaves. A second, more sustained section in half and whole notes is set in C major, but after eight measures the basses repeat a chant six times on the words "Done with sin and sorrow," at which point the key signature of one sharp is restored. The remaining nine measures, beginning with a D major chord, modulate with a series of ascending step-wise chords in parallel motion to e minor. In the last five measures, marked *p molto rit. e dim.* and ending *pp,* the sopranos sustain an E, the alto and tenor move slightly, and the lower basses go by small skips and steps from E down to low E.

* * *

Music in the Mine, according to Dett's collaborator Frederick Martens, "drew wider attention to Mr. Dett's masterly employ of the valuable thematic material he knows so well." Described as "the occupational chorus," the piece was based on the characteristic "cries" of the miners, "much in the spirit of Jannequin's old seventeenth-century secular motet on the street cries of Paris."[27]

On February 21, 1922, *Music in the Mine* was featured on an *a cappella* concert by the Oratorio Society of New York at Carnegie Hall, conducted by Albert Stoessel with tenor Ernest Davis as soloist. According to *The Southern Workman* (April 1922) *Mine* was the only work on the program which had to be repeated, a fact not mentioned in Richard Aldrich's *New York Times* review the following day. He called this particular concert an "experiment," a departure from the Society's usual programming in that only *a cappella* works were performed, with one exception, conductor Stoessel's setting of Walt Whitman's *Beat, Beat, Drums!* Aldrich said that this was *Mine*'s first performance, perhaps meaning the first by a professional group.

Dett's inscription informs that the piece was "based on traditional airs transcribed by the composer after the singing of Mr. Ralph Stoney and one unknown." Stoney studied at Hampton from 1908-1915, aided by a monetary scholarship, meanwhile working as a janitor and in the Hampton Commissary. A remark on his 1909 Trade Report from the Hampton Archives said: "A peculiar fellow, hard to understand, does not as yet realize the importance of keeping up to his agreement, but I think he means well." Stoney trained as a carpenter, was injured when he fell from a scaffold in 1910, but soon recovered. In 1913, as Center for the basketball team, he was selected for the Middle Atlantic States All-Star College Eleven.

Stoney contributed a poem, "The Blues," and a short essay about fishing, "Muddying," to the *Hampton Student* in 1915, both written with a sense of style and humor. After graduation he taught carpentry at Bordentown, New Jersey and later did construction work in Newport News, Virginia. He died in 1974 and was buried in the Hampton Cemetery.

Under the title of *Mine* are the words "An unaccompanied Folk-song Scena for Tenor Solo and Mixed Chorus," and above it "To my dear friend and fellow composer Mr. Percy Aldridge Grainger."[28] Dett scored only four parts, plus the tenor solo, rather than eight for *Mine,* but plenty of activity gets underway after the first narrative is given in the opening bars. (See Musical Example No. 30.) Dett's instruction for the execution of grace notes, which are subsequently scored on the words "mine" and "time" is: "Sing the grace notes on the beat." In measures 13-29 the words continue: "Set out for the mine. Bid my boss good morning! Sir, I'm here on time! Hammer starts to ringing, music in the mine."

In the following section, marked *Grazioso con moto,* the meter changes from 3/4 to 2/4. Alto, tenor, and bass provide a four-measure introduction with the repeated words "Klang dum dum" (measures 30-33). Dett specifies a continuous tap by "light steel bars" on the first beat of each measure, a pattern strengthened by four eight-note taps per measure toward the end of the piece. At measure 34 the soprano section joins in, sharing the melody with the soloist while the alto and men's parts remain accompanimental, except for a showy two-measure passage in sixteenth notes taken by the bass in measures 88-89. (See Musical Example No. 31.) On the syllable "Dna" Dett's intended pronunciation was "a" as in "arm," and on "Li" "i" as in "line."

The beginning meter of 3/4 is reinstated for the last three measures of this delightful piece, with the words "Music in the Mine" in the chorus parts under a sustained high A flat for the soloist on the syllable "Dna."

* * *

I'll Never Turn Back No More (SATB with tenor or soprano solo, and SSAA), published in 1918 by J. Fischer & Bro., was performed widely in US churches, and included in the 1922 repertoire of New York City's Church of the Ascension. "Affectionately dedicated to my two choirs, the Hampton Choral Union of the Hampton-Phoebus Community, and the Institute Choir of the Hampton Normal and Agricultural Institute" was Dett's inscription, along with "Theme traditional after the singing of Mr. Dola Miller. Additional texts from Church Hymns and Tunes."

Music in the Mine

Mus. ex. 30, meas. 1-12. Copyright © 1916 (Renewed), G. Schirmer, Inc. International copyright secured. All rights reserved. Used by permission.

Music in the Mine

Mus. ex. 31, meas. 34-39. Copyright © 1916 (Renewed), G. Schirmer, Inc. International copyright secured. All rights reserved. Used by permission.

Dola Francis Schofield Miller, born and raised in Biltmore, North Carolina, entered Hampton in 1910 and graduated in 1915 as a brickmason. His student work report was consistently good. In 1913 he was assistant secretary of his Trade Class, and in 1915 played the role of Baptista in Hampton's production of *The Taming of the Shrew.* As a professional brickmason in Asheville, Miller also sang in a church choir there. *The Southern Workman,* February, 1918, mentioned him in connection with the publication of Dett's *I'll Never Turn Back No More.* In the fall of 1930 Miller became head of the brickmasonry division at Tuskegee.

I'll Never Turn Back has been considered a good example of the use of Negro long-meter as the foundation of a serious composition. Long-meter may be described as a four-line stanza in iambic measure (long, short, long short), each line containing eight syllables. With variations, such as a few notes scored on the second beat for the inner voices, Dett has observed the long-meter limits. Evans cites Romans 6:23, Isaiah 25:10, and John 11:26 for the piece's biblical text, calling the music "festive and dramatic."[29] The verse from Isaiah does not seem as pertinent to the text as do those of Romans and John, which say that sinners will likely die for their misdeeds, but they must continue to "believe" in the Lord and hope for salvation. The words are very repetitious, as are the six melismas and triplet figures on the word "no" nearly every time it is used. Perhaps Dett meant to insert a hint of fear by using this device, as if the voice were shaking.

The high tessitura of the tenor (or soprano) solo in measures 45-52, hovering on F, G, and A, should add a wailing or pleading effect, depending on the voice quality of the soloist. A similarly high passage follows for the soprano section. Dett injects drama in his strategic use of *fermatas* and with one *cesura* after the phrase "God, your maker asks you why?" A return to the original choral section shows some harmonic changes, though the piece is not difficult harmonically. A polyphonic "Amen," using fragments of the original refrain theme, makes up the last four measures, dynamically marked *pp.*

* * *

This same year, 1918, Fischer issued *Weeping Mary.* Martens wrote of it and *I'll Never Turn Back* that they "cannot well be bettered as examples of how to enrich, by means of a sympathetic harmonization, the original simple contour of the spiritual without doing injury to its essentially folksong character."[30]

The dedication on *Weeping Mary*, an Afro-American folksong, reads "To my esteemed friend Mr. Bruce Carey." Conductor of the previously mentioned Elgar Choir, Carey (1876-1960) was born in Hamilton, Ontario, and after studying in London and Leipzig returned there to settle until his death. Frequently a guest conductor of choral groups throughout Canada and the US, he conducted the "sesquicentennial choir" of Philadelphia in 1927,[31] and the following year the Mendelssohn Club Chorus of the same city when two Dett compositions were performed (January 27, 1928), at a concert also featuring Lawrence Tibbett.

In 1933, due to the death of its longtime leader Dr. J. Ford Wolle, Carey was invited to direct the annual Festival of the Bethlehem (Pennsylvania) Bach Choir, a prestigious and internationally known chorus founded in 1880. Some days after his first concert with the 240-voice choir a supportive letter appeared in the *New York Times*, March 26, 1933, which in part said: "Dr. Carey has won the admiration of all the members of the Bach Choir."

For the next two years, and also in 1938, Carey directed this festival, which featured the Philadelphia Symphony with the larger 260-voice choir and drew listeners from twenty-four states, England, Ontario, and Chile, according to the *New York Times*, May 28, 1938. In 1935 Carey was director of vocal music at Girard College in Philadelphia, and in 1936 was awarded an honorary Doctor of Music degree from the Moravian Seminary and College for Women in Bethelem.

The repetitive words of *Weeping Mary* say:

> Is there anybody here like weeping Mary?
> Call upon your Jesus and He'll draw nigh.
> O, glory, glory, hallelujah!
> Glory be to my God, who rules on high.
> Weeping Mary, why so long aweeping?
> Call upon your Jesus and He'll draw nigh.

This mournful, expressive tune is for SATB, with a short, moaning soprano solo of high tessitura in measures 21 and 22, then descending in range in measure 23 and 24. Basically in c minor, the key feeling hints at E flat major and g minor in several

passages. Dett's first full measure presents an unconventional
departure from the interval one is accustomed to hearing in this
melody: the soprano sings on the words "Is there anybody here" E
flat, F, G, G, G, E natural, F, the E natural rather than an E flat of
the key signature on the "dy" of "body." One is reminded of
Burleigh's more conventional solo arrangement of the song in d
minor, in which on the same syllable uses an F rather than an F
sharp.

Detts makes good use of *fermatas,* and each time on the last
syllable of "upon" he marks a *ritard.* In measures 30, 32, 58, and
59 the four parts are scored in octaves, adding hollowness but
urgency as well. Dynamic markings range from *f* and *sf* in the
higher ranges to *pp* at the end. For variation and emphasis Dett
wrote some dotted rhythms in the piece. *Weeping Mary,* open to
individual interpretation and expressiveness, would seem a
pleasure for the choral conductor.

* * *

Other than *The Soul of America, Defend!,* a vocal solo
mentioned in Chapter IX, *America the Beautiful,* with words by
Katherine Lee Bates, was Dett's only documented published
patriotic setting. It was issued by J. Fischer & Bro. in 1918, and
also printed by permission in *The Crisis* (December 1918) under
the heading "A National Hymn."[32] Of Dett's setting Frederick
Martens said, "America the Beautiful, a fine patriotic chorus . . .
is a personal reaction to the spirit of the times."[33] One wonders if
Dett thought, or hoped, that his version of the song would
replace or rival the earlier setting of Bates' poem, attributed to
Samuel Ward.

A note concerning Bates' inspiration for the poem was put
simply in the *Reader's Digest Family Song Book:* "A trip to
Pike's peak, in 1893, inspired poetess Bates to write these
patriotic words."[34] Both Ward and Dett's arrangements are in C
major, and a few of their rhythmic patterns are similar. (See
Musical Example No. 32.). Ward's music had previously been
used for two hymns, *O Mother Dear, Jerusalem* and *Materna,* for
which he is best known.

Ward (1848-1903) spent his entire life in Newark, New York,
as a dealer in musical instruments. According to *The New Grove
Dictionary of American Music,* it is not known who actually set
Bates' poem of 1895 to Ward's music, published in 1910, after his

America the Beautiful

Mus. ex. 32.   Copyright © 1918 by J. Fischer & Bro.   Copyright renewed c/o. CPP/Belwin, Inc., Miami, FL   33014.   International copyright secured.   All rights reserved.

death.   By the mid-1890s Bates (1859-1929) had edited and authored several published volumes of poetry and *American Literature*, a "sprightly and anecdotal" textbook.   She was educated at Wellesley College in Massachusetts, her birthplace, and at Oxford, returning to Wellesley to teach literature until retirement in 1925.   As time permitted she also wrote verse drama for children, travel books, and juvenile fiction.   "America the

Beautiful" was later included in her collection *America the Beautiful and Other Poems* (1911).[35]

* * *

The year 1919 was quite productive for Dett. Church published *I'm So Glad Trouble Don't Last Alway* (SSA), *Somebody's Knocking at Your Door* (SATB), *Done Paid My Vow to the Lord* (SSA with baritone or alto solo), and *Chariot Jubilee* (mixed chorus and tenor solo). C. C. Birchard published *O Mary, Don't You Weep* for community singing (mixed voices, unaccompanied) this same year, according to McBrier, and confirmed by Alain Locke in *The New Negro*, who gives Birchard's listing as Laurel Octavo No. 134. It is not available for analysis.

I'm So Glad is one of Dett's few choral pieces with performance accompaniment, in this case constructed mostly of full chords in half notes and a few passages in quarters for the left hand in place of a bass line. There is a little more activity, however, in the six-measure introduction, in the interludes of measures 22-26, 43-47, and in a six-measure postlude similar to the introduction. A simple, syncopated pattern of four eighth notes, the last tied to a quarter note, is used every time the words "trouble don't last" and "Lord in my heart" occur. The piece should not present problems either to singers or accompanist.

Done Paid My Vow, a Negro spiritual, also has an accompaniment. Half-note chords comprise most of the accompaniment, with a more lively figure of sixteenth notes in measures 18 and 38. Dett's dynamics begin at p and end at ff. The key is g minor. Dett's inscription says that this spiritual, "a song much beloved by Booker T. Washington," was adapted from a song in the collection of G. Lake Imes, on whom the Hampton Archives could furnish no information.

Dett has marked the piece *Molto moderato ed serioso, un poco rubato*. After an eight-measure introduction the soloist states the theme and initial message: "Done paid my vow to the Lord, and I never will turn back. I will go, shall go to see what the end will be." In measure 16 the three choral parts enter as the first theme is repeated by the sopranos. The soloist enters again at measure 20, singing through to measure 36, sometimes with the added other parts. The words "will go" and "shall go" are echoed from soloist to chorus and back. Dett's harmonies, aided by the accompaniment, are interesting and full. The last nine measures are marked *Molto allargamente* and *Grandioso* at a dynamic of *ff*. The last three measures have more *ritards*, adding to the seriousness of the message.

Of *Done Paid My Vow* and *I'm So Glad Trouble Don't Last Alway* Martens wrote:

> We need only compare these lovely, haunting religious *chorals* of the slave states as Nathaniel Dett presents them, with some of the *soi-disant* anthems and "sacred songs" of the day in order to realize the gulf that yawns between the truly inspired and the commercially motivated in devotional music.[36]

The Chariot Jubilee (1919)

Based on a Negro spiritual *The Chariot Jubilee*, published by Church in 1919, was composed "at the request" of Professor Howard Lyman, Syracuse University Chorus conductor at the time. Martens called it "an inspired piece of choral writing," and along with the other publications felt that it would "establish beyond all chance of doubt that he [Dett] is moving up and on, and is showing a deeper quality of inspiration, a richer and more matured finish of musicianship." Explaining that the "request" or "occasion" number usually means dry, academic, and lacking in interest, Martens said that *Chariot* "should go far to destroy the general belief in the uninspired nature" of such works.[37]

Chariot, an eight-part motet or small oratorio, scored for mixed chorus, tenor, and orchestra (also piano or organ), was Dett's first use of the spiritual in extended form, and marked "an intensified concern on [his] part for the preservation and elevation of the spiritual for use in the church and by his choruses at Hampton."[38] A critic for *Musical America* called it "a masterpiece of its kind, a truly inspired piece of choral writing."[39] Benjamin Brawley termed it "a superb production."[40] Martens was also full of praise for *Chariot*, admiring its logical but informal musical development, built on a few themes handled with masterly control.[41]

Chariot was published with orchestral parts "for hire." It was not formally premiered, however, until May of 1921 by Lyman and the Syracuse University Chorus, the dedicatees, at the Syracuse University Music Festival. (See Chapter III for more details of its success.) Perhaps this was the awaited occasion which would draw an educated audience, thereby enhancing Dett's prestige. Tenor soloist was Lambert Murphy, and the Cleveland Symphony accompanied.

Massachusetts native Lyman (1879-1980), a 1909 graduate of the New England Conservatory, had been conducting and teaching voice at Syracuse since 1912, a position he held until 1945. Concurrently he was director of music at the Methodist Church on the campus. "In his extreme old age he took shelter at the Folts Home in Hermiker, New York," where he died at the age of 101.[42]

An examination of the score, with organ accompaniment, fully playable by a pianist, reveals the many intracacies of Dett's creative imagination. *Chariot's* message is basically one of salvation for the believer, with the chariot as a symbol of the promised land. A lengthy, sustained introduction of forty measures marked *Adagio* in 2/2 meter announces the "Swing Low, Sweet Chariot" motif in five fragments. The first vocal entrance by the tenor solo on the words "Down from the heavens a golden chariot swinging" is followed by gradual entrances in the choral voices over a sustained G major chord in the accompaniment. The chorus continues to punctuate in quarter notes on the words "swing low" and "low" to the close of the first section.

The meter changes to 4/2 at measure 68, and after four measures of chorus, *a cappella*, the organ enters again with only the basic voice parts. After another four measures, during which the female and male voices sing different words, the tenor soloist joins again for the following ten measures. Under the soloist is an interesting *divisi* scale progression in the men's parts, culminating in a forceful high A to B for the soloist in measure 85.

For the next nine measures the words "God made a covenant for the glory of His grace, thru our Lord and Savior Jesus Christ" are repeated, temporarily sounding in b minor. At measure 95 the key signature changes to two sharps, and Dett writes a section, still in 4/2 meter, of duplets against triplets for the chorus only, alternating between the key harmonies of b minor and D major.

The dynamics gradually increase as this powerful section builds to a huge climax at measures 111-112, when the "Swing Low" motif returns. The accompaniment now becomes sparse or uses only one sustained chord per measure for measures 113-122. Here, after a *molto ritard* marking, Dett injects excitement with a percussive effect for the male voices, which continues through measures 123-130. (See Musical Example No. 33.) Meanwhile the women's voices repeat the words "Salvation, sweet cov'nant of our Lord, I shall ride up in the Chariot in that morning!"

At measure 131 the tenor soloist enters again, effecting a *declamato* mood, alternating for the next few measures with the chorus through his *cadenza* in measure 137. (See Musical Example No. 34.) From measures 140-144 Dett again uses the percussive "tell it" pattern of Example 33, after which a richly scored three measures end boldly with the "Swing Low" theme on an A seventh chord with a *fermata*. This would indicate next a D major tonality in resolution, but instead Dett resolves the A seventh chord to a G 6/4, leading to the original key of G major.

The concluding section of *Chariot* marked *agitato et accel. quasi stretto* sweeps the listener right along with repeated triplets on D, then G in the bass line, underlying the other three parts. The organ adds excitement with its dotted rhythms and syncopation for these ten measures, ending in a broadened passage and *fermata* over a D ninth chord. The next six measures (158-163), *a cappella*, end at *ff* on an A seventh with another *fermata*, resolving again to a G 6/4 chord. At this point, measures 164 and 165, the tenor sings his last entrance alone. Three measures of chorus follow on the words "Coming for to carry me" and on the word "home" Dett changes the meter to 2/2, and marks the concluding twenty-three measures *Allegro, con abandon*, as the words "O Hallelujah" are repeated throughout by the chorus. *Chariot* ends joyfully.

Compositions from 1920-1926

During the year 1920 none of Dett's compositions was published. In 1921 Church published *There's a Meeting Here Tonight* (SSA) and the more famous *Don't Be Weary, Traveler*, a six-part, unaccompanied chorus for mixed voices. *Meeting*, dedicated to the St. Cecilia Society of Boston,[43] is based on a Negro spiritual. Its rollicking accompaniment is similar to *Juba* in rhythmic patterns and tempo. (See Musical Example No. 35.) Each time the alternating A and B sections are presented Dett makes slight changes in the harmony, rhythm, or voicing, both in the vocal line and accompaniment.

Effective execution of this piece calls for the utmost energy.

The Chariot Jubilee

Mus. ex. 33, meas. 122-123. © 1919 John Church Company. Used by permission.

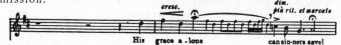

Mus. ex. 34, meas. 136-137. © 1919 John Church Company. Used by permission.

The words say "Get you ready, there's a meeting here tonight. I know by your daily walk there's a meeting here tonight," and as they are repeated the altos sing "Hallelujah!" Continuing, the sopranos sing "You heavenly breth'ren, how do you do? and does your love continue true? There's a meeting here tonight," etc. The song's climax is reached on the word "walk." This arrangement would make a delightful encore piece, quite a different version from the one in Dett's *Religious Folk-Songs of the Negro* (1927).

Don't Be Weary, Traveler, "Motet on Negro Folk Song Motives," was dedicated "To the Honorable George Foster Peabody with grateful acknowledgments." It is scored for mixed voices in six parts, unaccompanied. It won the Francis Boott Prize at Harvard in 1920. (See Chapter II concerning the Boott Prize and Chapter IV for biographical material on Peabody.)

There's A Meeting Here Tonight

Mus. ex. 35, meas. 1-8. © 1919 John Church Company. Used by permission.

The key of b minor is maintained for approximately two-thirds of the piece, during which section the words "Don't be weary, traveler, come along home to Jesus! Ye shall find rest unto your souls" are repeated, with the marking *Andante molt' espressivo*. A substantial solo for tenor or baritone and a shorter one for soprano are included in this section, closed by a four-measure "Amen" in the choral parts. Next, at measure 93, the key changes to B major, repeating the opening theme, now marked *Con anima non troppo allegro*. At measure 110 Dett interestingly treats the voices in canon fashion, beginning with the bass and going upward in order. (See Musical Example No. 36.)

Don't Be Weary Traveler

Mus. ex. 36, meas. 110-117. © 1921, John Church Company. Used by permission.

Don't Be Weary, Traveler is one of Dett's longer works, and though written rather early in his career as a choral composer, is one of his finest. McBrier cites measures 49-56, when the tenor (or baritone) soloist enters, as an example of solo with choral responses and textual repetition:

> Soloist: All ye that labor,
> Chorus: Come along home, come along to Jesus.
> Soloist: And are heavy laden,
> Chorus: Come along home to Jesus!

* * *

McBrier lists an SSA arrangement of *Listen to the Lambs*, published by Schirmer in 1923. In 1924 John Church published *I'm A-Goin' to See My Friends Again* for mixed chorus. The vocal solo arrangement of this work has been discussed in Chapter IX.

Gently, Lord, O Gently Lead Us, "A Bahama Folk Song in the form of an anthem," was also published in 1924 by Church. Dett took the melody from *Bahama Songs and Stories*, originally compiled by Charles Lincoln Edwards in 1895. The words were also the text of a hymn by Thomas Hastings, whose hymns "Come Ye Disconsolate" and "Hail to the Brightness" are still included in Methodist and Baptist hymnals.

Hastings (1784-1872) was born in Connecticut, but spent most of his life in New York state. Interested in practical music, he led a village chorus in Clinton, New York. His first collection of hymns, was published as *Musica Sacra* in 1815, and others followed, some in collaboration with Lowell Mason. Hastings' hymns, numbering around 1,000, are ranked with Mason's as the finest American hymns of their time. Hastings was editor of the weekly *Western Recorder*, and his several published literary works include poems, choir history, and essays on musical aesthetics. His best known hymns are "Rock of Ages," and in topical index "Retreat," "Zion," and "Ortonville."

Gently, Lord was dedicated to the Douglass Memorial Chorus at Oberlin, established in 1922 by Don Morrison out of friendship for Dett, and named for the famous Negro freedman Frederick Douglass. Viable until the mid-1930s under this name, the chorus was then adopted by the Wings Over Jordan choir which frequently broadcast over national radio. Oberlin professor

FIRST CONGREGATIONAL CHURCH
Monday, April 30, 1923

PROGRAM

PART I

Chorus, "The Lee Shore,"	- -	*S. Coleridge Taylor*
Piano Numbers,	- - - -	*R. Nathaniel Dett*

From, "In The Bottoms"
"His Song"
"Barcarole"
"Juba"

Mr. Dett

Men's Chorus, "Drake's Drum,"	-	*S. Coleridge Taylor*
Girl's Chorus, "A Page from Homer,"		*Rimsky Korsakow*

(Three violins by Misses Jackson, Covington and Huffman)

Chorus, "Weeping Mary," - *R. Nathaniel Dett*
"Music in The Mines"
(Tenor solo by Mr. Hickman.)
Mr. Dett Conducting

PART II

Chorus, "Heav'n,"	- -	*Arr. by Harry T. Burleigh*
Ladies' Chorus, "Deep River,"	-	*Arr. by Victor Harris*
Group of Songs,	- - - -	*R. Nathaniel Dett*

"Follow Me"
"I'm Glad Trouble Don't Last Always"
"The Land I'm Bound For"
(Dedicated to Mr. Hickman.)
Mr. Hickman

Piano Solos, - - - - *R. Nathaniel Dett*
From "Enchantment Suite"
"Song of The Shrine"
"Dance of Desire"
Mr. Dett

Chorus, "O Holy Lord," - - *R. Nathaniel Dett*
"Chariot Jubilee"
(Tenor Solo by Mr. Hickman.)
Mr. Dett Conducting

Accompanists, Mrs. Elmer Bush, Miss Ernestine Covington
and Theadore Philips.

First concert of Douglass Memorial Chorus, courtesy of Oberlin
College Archives.

PART I

Spirituals of Praise, Adulation and Biblical Narration
Oh, Rise an' Shine, An' Give God the Glory
May the Lord, He will be Glad of Me
(Leads by semi-chorus, and College and Conservatory
Women)
Peter on the Sea
Chorus

Group of Songs:
Eri Tu, from "Un Ballo in Maschera"	-	*Verdi*
Iphigenie - - - - - -		*Gluck*
To Anthea - - - - - -		*Hatton*

Mr. Lloyd Hickman

Spirituals of Joy and Hope
Good News! The Chariot's Comin'
(Lead by Mr. Albert Hodge)
Oh! The Land I'm Bound For
Chorus

Folk-song Scene, on Traditional Airs   *R. Nathaniel Dett*
Music in the Mines
Chorus, with Solo by Mr. Hickman

PART II

Spirituals of Death and Pilgrimage
Were You There When They Crucicied My Lord
Swing Low, Sweet Chariot
(Leads by Mr. Hickman)

Group of Songs—
Follow Me - - - - - -		*Dett*
On Ma Journey - - - - -		*Boatner*
Blow Gabriel - - - - -		*White*

Mr. Lloyd Hickman

Spiritual of Admonition
Motet—Don't be Weary Traveler   *R. Nathaniel Dett*
Chorus, with Solo by Mr. Hickman

Spiritual of Resurrection
Dust, Dust and Ashes
Chorus

Spiritual-Chorale
L'Envoi   -   -   -   -   *R. Nathaniel Dett*
Chorus

Douglass Memorial Chorus concert, Warner Hall, April 29, 1929,
courtesy of Oberlin College Archives.

Morrison, also a composer, violinist, writer, and music educator, took up piano at the age of seventy-nine as therapy for a heart condition. The Douglass Memorial Chorus, a community group open to town and gown of Oberlin, featured outstanding Negro performers, including Dett, on its annual concerts when Dett's vocal solos and choral works were always programmed.

Gently, Lord (SATB with soprano solo, unaccompanied) is described by McBrier as a "borrowed melody used as *cantus firmus*," and is cited (p. 136) as an example of Dett's contrapuntal technique. The original Bahama melody was in 4/4 meter, as is Dett's anthem, but the time values are cut in half and the words begin "Dig my grave long and narrow, make my coffin long and strong." The melody begins in measure 1 with the soprano, supported by alto, then tenor, then bass. At measure 5 the supporting voices join again in this order. At measure 9 the tenor has the melody and similar support is given by bass, alto, and soprano in that order. The various moving lines go mostly step-wise, ascending and descending smoothly, and to achieve such a *legato* effect the choral director might emphasize the importance of staggered breathing. The bass line has some interesting ascending skips from low F to C to A. The score has few accidentals and the harmonies are not unusual. Several phrases are repeated, both word-wise and musically. Though there are few rests after the first sixteen measures, this work should present minimal problems to singers with stamina and concentration.

Choral publications for the year 1926 totalled five: *There's a Star in the East, Son of Mary, Let Us Cheer the Weary Traveler, O Hear the Lambs A-Crying,* all issued by Church, and *Don't You Weep No More, Mary* by Schirmer. *There's a Star in the East* (SSA) is not available and no information has been located concerning it. This piece, however, is possibly an arrangement of *Rise Up Shepherd and Follow*.

Son of Mary (SATB), written especially for and dedicated to the Oberlin Musical Union and its conductor Dr. George W. Andrews, is also unavailable for analysis. Dr. Andrews, mentioned in Chapters I and VI, was Dett's favorite professor at Oberlin. The Musical Union, whose original name was Oberlin Music Association, was founded in 1837 by George Nelson Allen. After 1856 it was renamed the Oberlin Choir, and in 1860 the Musical Union, whose main concerts were at commencements, at which a *potpourri* of good music was offered. During the late nineteenth and early twentieth centuries the Union presented three annual concerts, often featuring professional guest performers. Gradually its repertoire became a prestigious one of masses, oratorios, requiems, and collaborative efforts with major symphonies, according to the Oberlin *Observer*, May, 1982.

Let Us Cheer the Weary Traveler, widely used by the slaves as a signal that one of their number was being helped to escape to freedom, was one of Dett's more popular choral works. His inscription reads: "A Negro Spiritual in the form of a short unaccompanied motet for mixed voices." The melody was taken from the same tune in Dett's *Religious Folk-Songs of the Negro*. Its opening hymn-like statement becomes a theme with variations in measure 9 when the soprano again repeats the theme, joined by the altos and tenors in an ascending eighth-note pattern, then by the basses.

The B strain at measure 17 is in fairly close harmony, until measure 22 when the bass has a step-wise descending eighth-note pattern. Now the A section returns, exactly as it was scored in the opening measures. In the last eight measures, the first two of which are marked *marcato, quasi stretto*, have a barbershop quality, ending in an elongated *allargando*. Rather than be considered an exciting choral piece, it would better show off pure voices in perfect harmony if rendered well, *a cappella*, as intended. (See Musical Example No. 37.)

McBrier (p. 137) shows this same example (meas. 1-8), describing them as "complete spiritual melody harmonized," and measures 9-14 as the same melody "treated contrapuntally." Dett interestingly used a contraction of "heavenly" (heav'nly) in different voices on the same beats, though did not contract "traveler" to "trav'ler."

Let Us Cheer the Weary Traveler has also been set for chorus by H. E. Dann, T. P. Fenner, J. W. Johnson, F. J. Work, and other arrangers. Harry Burleigh's arrangement for solo voice (1919) is included in *The Spirituals of Harry Burleigh*, a collection issued by Belwin-Mills in 1984.

* * *

The plaintive *O Hear the Lambs A-Crying* was dedicated "To the Oratorio Society of New York City, Albert Stoessel, Conductor." This prestigious group was founded in 1873

Let Us Cheer the Weary Traveler

Mus. ex. 37, meas. 1-8.   © 1926, John Church Company.   Used by permission.

by Leopold Damrosch, whose two sons, Walter and Frank, succeeded him as its conductors. After Walter's second stint as conductor Stoessel (1894-1943) took the position in 1922, the same year that he became director of music at the Chautauqua Institute. He appeared widely over the US during the 1920s and 1930s, during which time he was director of the opera and orchestra departments at the Juilliard Graduate School and also headed the Music Department at New York University, where he was awarded an honorary M. A. degree. First trained as a violinist in St. Louis, Stoessel went as a youngster to study in Berlin. His first conducting experience was as a military bandmaster in WWI. He composed an opera (*Garrick*, produced at Juilliard), works for orchestra, chorus, and violin, and authored *The Technic of the Baton* (1920). He was fatally stricken at a performance a few months before Dett's death as he conducted a composition by Walter Damrosch.

O Hear the Lambs A-Crying is structurally interesting. Dett keeps most of the piece in a natural minor, using about an equal number of G sharps and G naturals. Sometimes he uses "feed-a" instead of "feed." Repetition of the minor thirds, a to c and c to a, contributes to the mournful quality pervading this very sustained, unaccompanied piece.

In measure 61 (for "Quartet or Semi Chorus," *ad. lib.*) Dett writes some three-measure phrases for the lines "Lord, I do love thee/ Thou dost know;/ O teach me, Lord, to love thee more." Scored for soprano solo and a six-part chorus of mixed voices, most of the solo's movement is step-wise, with a few small skips. Bass and tenor parts are the heaviest, with *divisi* in measures 19-21, 23-25, 27-28, 47-49, 51-53, 55-57, 81-83, 85-87, and 89-90. McBrier (pp. 134-135) cites *Lambs* as an example of antiphonal writing, wherein Dett pitts the women's choir against the augmentation of the men's parts, and uses the soprano solo as a counterpoint to the choirs.

* * *

Evans classifies *Don't You Weep No More, Mary* (SATB) as easy. Based loosely on biblical text from John 20:11 and 11:17-27, I Corinthians 15:14, Acts 5:30, and Matthew 28:2-3, the piece is set in d minor. It uses only bits of Negro dialect, such as the title, and the lines "Jesus rose third day in-a that morning" and "because he promised for to set me free."

The first stanza resembles a dialogue, announced by soprano and alto, mostly in sixths. After a measure and a half the tenors and basses enter, moving in contrary motion, supporting the melody. Beginning the second verse is a dialogue between alto and tenor while the soprano sustains a hum. After the first two and last two lines a chorus part, harmonized from the melody of the opening refrain, is interjected. Now the first verse is repeated, followed by more humming. Evans' analysis says:

Dialogue between the voice parts serves as an ingenious transtion to the restatement of the phrase, "Rose third day in-a that morning," by the chorus.   Following this section, the altos sing the text: "O Hallelujah on that day the angel rolled the stone away." The soprano section hums a melismatic and embellished line. The basses, humming quarter notes, conclude the section with two measures of a *divisi* on a V-I cadence in B flat major. The tenor line leads back to d minor, singing "He rolled the stone away." The arrangement closes with a sustained, dramatic, and   chromatically altered treatment of chords on the phrase "Rose third day in-a that morning."[44]

Religious Folk-Songs of the Negro (1927)

There was some discussion in Chapter IV about the reception of Dett's *Religious Folk-Songs of the Negro as Sung at Hampton Institute* (full title), published in 1927 by the Hampton Institute Press, which reissued it in 1981. The volume includes 165 songs, most of which are one to two pages in length and have no piano introduction. Some of them are harmonized and others are given only as a melody. Supposedly Dett scored them the way he heard them sung at Hampton, as the title suggests. The first southern Negro students who migrated to other areas of the US for higher education brought with them spirituals, raw material which became the basis of several collections. Traditional singing of them by the Hampton student body each Sunday evening peaked during Dett's tenure.

It is not necessary to restate Dett's lengthy Foreword to this compilation, which may be found in Jon Michael Spencer's *The R. Nathaniel Dett Reader Essays on Black Sacred Music* (1991). To summarize, however, Dett describes the Negro as a religous being whose unshakable faith has tided him through many a storm, travails naturally expressed through song. Unfortunately, Negro music has too long been associated with minstrelsy, and some of its religious-based ditties have conjured an impression of ludicrousness and insincerity. In addition, the primitive elements of early Negro religious music have been foot stamping, hand clapping, and shouting, actions detracting from reverence.

One main problem has been "how to evolve a style of music

that will convey a religious message through a popular medium without at the same time suggesting things of the world," Dett wrote in the Foreword. Continuing, he said:

> What this ability of the black man to improvise his troubles into art-forms has fully meant to him will probably never be told. . . . One of the most outstanding characteristics of all the songs is that, free as the music is from cacophony and discord, just as remarkably free is its poetry from any word of bitterness, anger, or reproach.

Dett further comments on the black/white controversy over origins of the spirituals, the background as related to physical racial characteristics, the Negro's natural feeling for tempo, and of Robert R. Moton's talent as a song leader: "Often, after getting the chorus of a thousand voices going, he would place both hands behind his back, leaving the singers to carry on in their own way. . . . His beat was inconspicuous." In conclusion he points out the difference in interpretation of the spirituals by the Hampton students during his tenure and that of older Negroes who were a part of slavery.[45]

The 1981 edition, titled *Hampton Song Book*, with a Foreword by Nancy B. McGhee, was presented by Hampton choral director Roland Carter at the 1982 NANM convention. It called attention to the "unique hymnic arrangement of the spirituals by topical index analagous to indexes found in major denominational hymn books." The subject indexes are Admonition, Aspiration, Biblical Themes, Christian Life, Christmas, Church Consolation, Death, Death of Christ, Deliverance, Encouragement, Faith and Fellowship, Future Life, Invitation, Jesus Christ, Judgment, Meditation, Occasions, Penitence, Pilgrimage, Praise, Religion, Religious Experience, Ressurection, Second Coming, and Tribulation.[46]

One of the harmonized songs in the volume is *L'Envoi*, "an old Negro melody, transcribed from the singing of Dr. Robert Russa Moton, Principal of Tuskegee Institute, set in the form of a chorale by R. Nathaniel Dett." The second verse is from a hymn by Rev. Horatius Bonar. "Envoi" means "flight" or "soaring." It is one of the more sophisticated harmonizations in the volume, and included in Dett's Appendix.[47] (See Musical Example No. 38.)

L'Envoi

* Second verse added from a hymn by Rev. Horatius Bonar

Mus. ex. 38, entire song.   Courtesy of Hampton University Archives.

Compositions from 1930-1936

Ave Maria, sung by the Hampton Choir on its European tour (see Chapter IV), was published in 1930 by Schirmer. An edited version by Evelyn Davidson White was issued by Hinshaw Music, Inc. in 1978. White's edition will be used in the following analysis. The English text by Frederick H. Martens is set for SATB with baritone solo. Dett's subtitle is "Guide me and lead me," which are the beginning words with the Latin above. It is a tightly knit, short chorale of fifty-two measures, with smoothly moving parts, few rests, interesting progressions, and a few dissonances that resolve subtly. The key is F major, though d minor and g minor are arrived at briefly in a few cadences.

Dett uses characteristic slurs over both quarter and eighth notes to indicate two pitches for one syllable, a device which helps carry the overall rhythm. The bass line is *divisi* only in measure 28, though both a low C and the C above are scored in measure 31. The baritone solo does not begin until measure 44, marked *Con express. ma recitando*. Chant-like words on a repeated A are "Guide me and lead me, O heav'nly Father, Lighten my voyage over life's troubled sea; O let Thy spirit, o'er me abiding, Point me ever to heaven and Thee!" Under this the chorus sings the sustained words "Thy love unending," then all parts have a five-measure "Amen" which closes the piece.

McBrier lists Schirmer's publication of *As Children Walk Ye in God's Love* (SATB) in 1930, though White does not in her study. Dett included it on a Hampton Choir concert at Carnegie Hall on April 16, 1928, though it obviously had not been published at this time. In his program notes for the occasion Dett referred to this work and Burleigh's *Deep River* as settings, or more popularly, arrangements, of Negro melodies. He quoted himself in the notes from his Foreword to *Religious Folk-Songs* (1927), deploring the stigma of minstrelsy attached to the spiritual. The climax in *As Children Walk Ye* is achieved, according to Dett, by the addition of a counterpoint written over the original tune. (A score is not available for further analysis.)

In 1932 the Theodore Presser Company issued *Somebody's Knocking at Your Door* (SSA with soprano or tenor solo), one of Dett's first published works after leaving Hampton. *Sit Down, Servant* (SATB) was also published this year by Schirmer. Fischer published two versions of *Rise Up Shepherd and Follow* (SATB in 1932 and TTBB in 1936), according to the most reliable sources. The TTBB arrangement will be discussed later in this chapter.

Drink to Me Only with Thine Eyes (SATB) and *Go Not Far from Me, O God* (SATB) were issued by Fischer in 1933. Dedicated "To my American Choir of Station WHAM, Rochester, NY," *Drink to Me Only (a cappella)* is not difficult. In ABA form the traditional English air is used by Dett as a theme with embellishments. Interest is immediate. In the first twelve measures of hummed introduction, with breath marks for staggered breathing, Dett departs from the tune by scoring an eighth-note pattern, first in the soprano, next in alto, bass, then tenor.

At measure 13 tenors have the melody and the basses, *divisi*, continue the eighth-note countermelody. In measure 21 the texture thickens as all parts join through measure 47. (See Musical Example No. 39.) Then the melody is taken by the tenor, supported by a *divisi* bass with two sets of words, the rhythm of lower bass serving as an accompanimental figure. Similar treatment continues to the piece's end, the melody always detectable. This is one of Dett's finest arrangements. An undated *Fischer Edition News* (c. 1932 or 1933) announcing the forthcoming *Drink to Me Only with Thine Eyes* and *Go Not Far from Me, O God* boasted that they "maintain the best traditions of this composer's [Dett's] writing." *Drink to Me Only* was called "a setting in Madrigal style . . . most effective when properly rendered."

The original title of *Drink to Me Only* was "To Celia," one of three "Songs to Celia" by the well-known British poet, dramatist, and critic Ben Jonson (1572-1637). Jonson's life was never dull, for he managed to provide his own exciting adventures. A man of unusual brilliance, he was also an argumentative tavern brawler, who was raised humbly, married unhappily, served in the military in Flanders, then settled in London, where his interest in acting and drama writing served him well.

In 1598 Jonson's play *Every Man in His Humour* established him as one of England's finest dramatists, who persisted in following classical rules. His critical writings, *Timber, or Discoveries*, however, are more liberal, and his volumes of poetry, *Under-wood*, *The Epigrams*, and *The Forrest* (1616), the collection which contains "To Celia," are graceful and delicate. Jonson was frequently at odds with Shakespeare, whose drama

Drink to Me Only with Thine Eyes

Mus. ex. 39, meas. 21-26. Copyright © 1933 by J. Fischer & Bro.
Copyright renewed c/o CPP/Belwin, Inc., Miami, FL 33014.
International copyright secured. All rights reserved.

company produced some of his plays. His popularity as a masque writer for the British court waned quickly after Charles I succeeded King James in 1624. An earlier blow came the year before when his personal library burned. In 1628 Jonson was stricken with paralysis and financially depleted, but continued to write and read prodigiously, receiving visitors from his sickbed. He was buried in Westminster Abbey.[48]

Go Not Far From Me, O God (SATB with baritone solo) is dedicated "To the memory of my beloved teacher and friend Dr. George Whitefield Andrews." (Dr. Andrews of the Oberlin faculty was discussed in Chapter VI.) Based on two traditional Negro melodies from his own collection, the work's merit is in contrapuntal effectiveness and contrasts. The *Fischer Edition News* described it well:

> The opening section is plaintively in d minor with a theme of haunting loveliness weaving through the voice parts of the baritone solo. Then comes a change into D major with richly thickened parts and parallel movement, the climax coming at the very end in ten parts. Long years of experience with large choirs trained to do his will have shown Mr. Dett how to make voice leading supremely effective, and this experience shows in every bar. This is *a cappella* music of the finest type, but it needs an adequate choir to do it justice.

Intervals in the soprano's opening statement, repeated in measures 4-6 by the tenor, could be treacherous for inexperienced singers. (See Musical Example No. 40.) Dett uses more intervals of sixths and sevenths for the male voices, and a short passage of consecutive fourths in measure 64 in the D major section. The beginning meter of 3/4 in the d minor section switches to 4/4 after a sustained A major chord. The intervallic movement seems designed for utmost cohesion and continuity. There are only four pauses, marked by *fermatas*: at measure 15 when the baritone solo begins, at measure 37 when the bass voices restate the opening theme, at the key change (measure 58), and three measures before the end, when there is an elongated measure in 6/4. Texture thickens considerably under the baritone solo at measure 58 where the D major section begins. (See Musical Example No. 41.)

Go Not Far From Me, O God

Mus. ex. 40, meas. 1-6. Copyright © 1933 by J. Fischer & Bro.
Copyright renewed c/o CPP/Belwin, Inc., Miami, FL 33014.
International copyright secured. All rights reserved.

Go Not Far From Me, O God

Mus. ex. 41, meas. 58-62. Copyright © 1933 by J. Fischer & Bro.
Copyright renewed c/o CPP/Belwin, Inc., Miami, FL 33014.
International copyright secured. All rights reserved.

* * *

In 1933 Schirmer published *As By the Streams of Babylon* and *Wasn't That a Mighty Day?* The first, *Babylon* (SATB with solo, soprano preferred), was programmed frequently. Originally it was a tune by Thomas Campian (1567-1620), English poet and composer. Some mystery still surrounds Campian's academic qualifications as a medical doctor, which was his real profession as of 1602. He did attend Cambridge and Peterborough, but no degrees have been documented. "As By the Streams of Babylon" was included in Campians's *A Booke of Ayres*, "Set foorth to be song to the Lute Orpherian and Base Violl," the first in a series published in the early 1600s. Besides poetry and song Campian composed masques, and was a scholar of poetic and music theory.

Babylon, only four pages in length, begins with a twelve-measure hum for the choral parts under the solo. At measures 13-22 the chorus sings words as the soloist continues. From measures 23-37 the chorus hums, though the soloist finishes at measure 33. The musical movement is similar to that in Dett's preceding two pieces. The solo line, stated three times, has no accidentals, and is a miniature AB form. The key is g minor, but the B section stays briefly in B flat major. The choral parts have accidentals and are identical for the three AB sections. At the end of each B section and at the end of the piece Dett scores a G major cadence, a feature rarely found in his previous compositions.

Wasn't That a Mighty Day?, also issued by Schirmer in 1933, is essentially an unaccompanied spiritual for mixed voices, adapted for baritone or alto solo, though Fansler describes it as scored for three-part men's ensemble/five voices.[49] He points out the subtle chromatic alterations in the opening chorus, which illustrate Dett's unpredictable harmonic progressions. The solo alto section is accompanied by a series of diminished seventh chords in the other voices. Toward the end the basses sing a rhapsodic quasi recitative, supported by sustained chords in the other voices. The song's message, taken from Matthew 2:1 and Luke 2:18, concerns the birth of Christ. Fansler notices the "blues" effect of this piece.

Evans, who states that *Mighty Day* is scored for SATTB with baritone or alto solo, classifies it as "Difficult." The key is f minor, the meter 4/4. The first section is introduced by three male parts and baritone solo, *ad. lib.* Next the soprano takes the melody, sustained by the lower voices on repeated phrases of "mighty day." Then it is taken by the alto, backed by tenors and basses in thirds. A shifting from quarter to eighth-note patterns offers rhythmic variety.

After a restatement of the first section new material is introduced in the bass line beneath sustained humming in the women's parts. Counter-melodies in soprano and alto close this section as the bass sings "Peace on earth," etc., repeated by full chorus, with harmonic, rhythmic, textual, and dynamic changes. At the end the bass parts are marked *ff, rapido e con fervore,* while the other parts sustain the tonic chord.[50]

* * *

Though Dett's choral arrangement of *Juba* was not as widely performed as the piano piece, he must have enjoyed scoring it so humorously to his own words. Published in 1934 by Summy, it was dedicated to "The Inter-Hi Chorus of Rochester, Alfred Spouse, Director." Music educator Spouse was well-known in the Rochester area, and taught for a number of years at West High School, now Joseph C. Wilson Magnet High School. He collaborated with Frederick Harwood on *Universal Song* (Schirmer), a voice method book still being used in voice classes in Rochester high schools in the 1970s, and with Maybelle Glenn edited *Art Songs for School and Studio* (Ditson). Spouse was founder and conductor of the Inter High Choir from c. 1932 until 1937, retiring from choral work in the mid-1950s.

Donald Hayden, a former member this choir under Spouse, and conductor of the group from 1966-1979, gave the following information:

> The Inter High Choir had about 110 members from its inception until the early 70s when transportation problems, social problems, work problems, and rehearsal space problems got in the way. The group sang for a meeting of the MENC in the Metropolitan Opera House in 1936, . . . for the New York World's fair in 1939, and at concerts with the Rochester Civic Orchestra, and other MENC [Music Educators National Conference] sessions, including one in Chicago in 1952. It was a splendid chorus with a national reputation.[51]

Dett may have arranged *Juba* earlier for a smaller ensemble

Cover. © 1934, Summy-Birchard Music, a Division of Summy-Birchard, Inc. All rights reserved. Used by permission.

Juba

Mus. ex. 42, meas. 33-38. © 1934, Summy-Birchard Music, a Division of Summy-Birchard, Inc. All rights reserved. Used by permission.

Juba

Mus. ex. 42 (cont'd), meas. 51-58.

Juba

Mus. ex. 42 (cont'd), meas. 59-66.

Juba

Mus. ex. 42 (cont'd), meas. 75-82.

Juba

Mus. ex. 42 (cont'd), meas. 111-121.

before Summy's SATB publication, a possibility suggested by Dr. William Loring, editor for Scarecrow Press, Inc., who recalled:

> As a boy in my high school years, about 1926 to 1931, Dett and his travelling quartet or sometimes more singers used to regale us at school assemblies every other year. And Juba was always the foot stomping, hand clapping delight to us young characters, usually as an encore at the end of their performance.[52]

Dett's words, describing the avid dancer King Juba and the gathering frenzy of the exciting Juba dance keep the singers as busy as the solo piece does the pianist. After a four-measure introduction the accompaniment, definitely intended for performance, duplicates the piano score. Dett has skillfully set words and/or syllables to the same rhythms as the accompaniment and added some syncopation. It is a clever piece, understandable as a crowd pleaser, which the following excerpts will show. In today's terms it might be considered a rap song. (See Musical Examples Nos. 42 a, b, c, and d.)

Based on a Christmas spiritual, Dett's anthem *Rise Up Shepherd and Follow* (TTBB with tenor solo) also has an accompaniment. The tune is sometimes called *There's a Star in the East*, since these words are the opening phrase. It was published in 1936 by Fischer. The accompaniment not only carries most of the movement and provides transitions, but alternates with the voice parts and the solo line in a call/response treatment. Marked *Pastorale sed con moto*, it is a far cry in mood from the energetic *Juba*.

The Dett Collection of Negro Spirituals (1936)

Including originals, settings, anthems, and motets, each of the four groups (or volumes) of the Collection, published by Hall & McCreary Company, has a Foreword by Dett. In the First Group Dett emphasizes including Negro spirituals on every type program possible, now that their true merit has been recognized. The spiritual is appealing as a chorale due to its infectious rhythms and easy harmonies. He mentions the addition of harmonies to a single voice, a task to which his professional experience had fitted him. He paid tribute to Mrs. Catherine

Fields-Gay, mentioned in Chapter IX, for providing some of the melodies, and called attention to his setting of "Deep River" as a motet with soprano *obbligato*. The First Group contains twenty-eight songs, fourteen of which had been included in Dett's *Religious Folk-Songs of the Negro*, some with slightly altered settings.

Most of the spirituals in the four volumes, totalling over seventy, are in simple four-part harmony, and several have short solos, always responded to by other voices. (See Musical Example No. 43, "Go Down Moses," First Group.) They are dedicated to Dett's mother, who died in 1937, the year following their publication. Separate titles will be listed in the Catalog of Music.

The Second Group is prefaced with an essay titled "Understanding the Negro Spiritual," in which Dett reiterates the difference between the singing of the spirituals by the slaves and by his contemporaries, i. e., the Hampton students, based on their own life experiences. He applied the same judgment to the white man's less fervent singing of them. Explaining why the spirituals differ in expression from other folk expression, Dett says that "while with other races folk singing was only one of the avenues of soul expression, with the Negro, it was the sole avenue of emotional relief, . . . it was life itself." The Afro-American slaves saw religion as their salvation, their answer. Jesus' resurrection symbolized to them his personal escape, which with faith would make their own freedom possible. Sincerity became the keyword. Of the fourteen songs in this Second Group, nine were included in *Religious Folk-Songs of the Negro*.

In Dett's essay for the Third Group, "The Authenticity of the Spiritual," he discusses the ancient modes mentioned earlier in this chapter. He refutes theories which say that the spiritual derived from revival or other protestant hymns, e. g., those of Moody and Sankey, most of which have not survived. Spirituals are older than our American culture, a fact evident in their rhythmic elements, syncopation, and modal structure. Frugality in melody is another characteristic of their primitivism, obvious in "Standing in the Need of Prayer," which has only three notes, and "Hew 'Round the Tree," with only two. Also, the leader and response format in many of them was transplanted from Africa. Dett reiterated similarities of the spiritual to the Russian folk song as an expression of oppressed peoples.

In essence Dett is saying that practically everything in

Go Down, Moses

2. Thus saith the Lord, bold Moses said
   Let my people go,
   If not I'll smite your first-born dead
   Let my people go.
   CHORUS— Go down, Moses, etc.

8. No more shall they in bondage toil
   Let my people go,
   Let them come out with Egypt's spoil
   Let my people go.
   CHORUS— Go down, Moses, etc.

Mus. ex. 43, copyright © 1938 by Hall & McCreary Co. Copyright renewed c/o CPP/Belwin, Inc., Miami, FL 33014. International copyright secured. All rights reserved.

the art, literature, and music of the spirituals sprang from some source, or is based on what preceded it. Unique to the spiritual has been its harmonies, which Dett believes were naturally there from the beginning, though they were not notated. Ten of the spirituals in Group Three, including two versions of "Roll, Jordan, Roll," were also in *Religious Folk-Songs of the Negro*.

One of the more unusual and most beautiful melodies in the Fourth Group is "Ho Everyone that Thirsts!" a solo for mezzo voice. Dett inscribed it "To Helen," likely his wife or daughter, "Sung by Mrs. Catherine Fields-Gay." With tonal centers of a minor and C major, the song ends on an A major chord. There are no accidentals in the vocal line. Dett's accompaniment, obviously to be used, is largely chordal and does not duplicate the voice line. He uses C major seventh, d minor sixth, a minor seventh, and b minor seventh chords skillfully. The form is ABABA. (See Musical Example No. 44.)

The Fourth Group contains fourteen songs, only four of which were included in *Religious Folk-Songs of the Negro*. Dett's Preface, titled "The Development of the Negro Spiritual," interestingly traces the Negro's recognition in America's musical life before the Civil War, with emphasis on the impact of both Eliza Taylor Greenfield (the "Black Swan"), Thomas Greene Bethune (Blind Tom), and other performers whose prowess was respected. Again, Dett laments the ridicule, prejudice, and mockery attached to serious musical efforts of the Negro. He credits composers Burleigh, Diton, White, the Johnsons, Dawson, Still, Boatner, Work, Ryder, Florence Price, and N. Clarke Smith for their compositions in the Negro idiom, and Dvorak for revealing the "possibilities inherent in plantation tunes."

> This spirit of return to the beginnings of things has been largely my source of inspiration in working with folk song motifs, and while I would in no wise proclaim its dictates as the only way, not to persuade others unwillingly to a similar procedure, I feel I must offer my humble thanks for the favor with which its results have been received by my own people, by the American public, generally, and by those on foreign shores.[53]

Ho Every One That Thirsts!

Mus ex. 44, meas. 1-17. Copyright © 1938 by Hall & McCreary Co.
Copyright renewed c/o CPP/Belwin, Inc., Miami, FL   33014.
International copyright secured. All rights reserved.

The Ordering of Moses (1937)

Dedicated "In High Esteem to the Honorable George Foster Peabody, Distinguished Patron of the Arts and Sciences," *The Ordering of Moses,* Dett's oratorio in fulfillment for his Master's degree at Eastman, was finished in 1932-1933. Not pleased with it at the time, it underwent at least three revisions and was published by Fischer in 1937, the year of its premiere at the Cincinnati Festival. (See Chapter V for the performance in Cincinnati and Chapter VII for subsequent performances.)

Scored for SATB, five soloists, and orchestra (or piano/organ), *Moses* is an approximately fifty-five minute work based on spirituals and the biblical saga of Moses and the children of Israel. There are no spoken parts. It perhaps received more publicity and favorable comment than any Dett works since *Listen to the Lambs* and *Chariot Jubilee.* After its presentation *The Crisis* commented that the story of the Exodus provided a framework "on which is woven a tone pattern depicting the spiritual yearning, sorrows and joys that have attended the rise of his [Moses'] people up from bondage," and called it "the most impressive Negro contribution to music."[54]

Tilford Brooks calls it "the finest result of Dett's successful synthesis of the Black and European musical traditions."[55] Another writer describes *Moses* as reflecting "a fine blend of traditional forms to fit the needs of a new expression on a large scale."[56] Howard Hanson said, on hearing of Dett's death, "I think, without question, that oratorio [*Moses*] is the greatest chorus for Negro voice yet written. In my estimation he [Dett] was one of the greatest composers of Negro music."[57]

In constructing *Moses* Dett burst the bonds of traditional forms and techniques. All voices participating need a wide range, and the conductor must be skilled in directing intricate rhythmic patterns. Alice Anderson, who had sung a role in *Moses* wrote in the Spring, 1954 issue of *Tones and Overtones* (Alabama State College) that the work had even "crept into an examination compiled by the staid American Guild of Organists." *The Southern Workman* reprinted reviews of *Moses'* premiere by leading music critics, among them Olin Downes, who considered it a triumph and wrote of its "growing excitement," "powerful rhythms," "barbaric pulse," and "wordless ululations" on the "Ah" syllable which portrayed the passage through the Red Sea. Other reviewers commented on the packed house, Dett's ovation, and the overall excellence of the production. One of them noticed that from his box seat Dett was keeping time with his head.[58]

Nina Pugh Smith wrote in the *Cincinnati Times-Star*, May 8, 1937, that *Moses* was the "composition of a talented, trained musician," and continued:

> The idiom is vocally that half syncopated, wailing, downtrending line expressed in all the spirituals. The orchestral score is of the impressionistic school, remote, idealized, rather delicate, extremely appealing. As a composition . . . [it] is so human and so interesting that a single hearing of it is not enough for music lovers. It is not of such elaboration but that it can be repeated under conditions not too exacting.

Dett called *Moses* a "Biblical Folk Scene for Soli, Chorus and Orchestra, the Text Based on Scripture and Folk Lore." Sometimes it is referred to as a cantata. In any case, it is an example of extended form of the spiritual. One of Dett's notebooks, filled with fragments of programs, song words, speeches, poetry, and a list of clothing to take on a trip, provided insight into his problems with *Moses*. Not textual, they were more in finding music to portray the cries of a people as elemental as the Jews were during the Exodus, and in counterpointing the fugue on the *Go Down Moses* theme. Special acknowledgements went to "Jewish students of Eastman who made many valuable suggestions," and to Nadia Boulanger, "who helped enlarge my knowledge of the use of antique modes."[59]

In correspondence with the Cincinnati Festival manager Dett wrote that he had no sudden inspiration for *Moses*, but that sometimes words and music did occur to him at the same time.

> The similarity of folk text to the words of Scripture is striking, and the fusion of the two seems natural. . . . In connection with the making of the fugue, a strange and inexplicable thing occurred. I had tried almost everything without satisfaction, when suddenly I realized that the melody I had written for the trio, "God Looking on Israel," was a perfect counterpoint. This discovery filled me with great enthusiasm and the fugato was soon finished.[60]

When Dett admitted to Percy Grainger that it took him "about four years" to write the fugue, Grainger said, "I thought so."[61]

Among the better in-depth studies of *Moses* is McBrier's. She calls it a "union of poetry, vocal, and instrumental music," whose free and continuous style is dictated by the text. With *Go Down Moses* as the main theme Dett uses both fragments and complete quotations for motivic, harmonic, and contrapuntal development. Its several biblical phrases are deftly combined with Dett's original verse. McBrier points out some examples of Dett's technique: major chords moving chromatically (parallelism) in measures 881-882, textual and chordal repetition (especially of fourths) in measures 224-225, use of counterpoint to develop fugal subject, and development of the theme in accompanimental interludes, for example in measures 493-502.

Tilford Brooks was also aware of Dett's use of fourths, diminution and augmentation of various motives, either in the vocal line or in the accompaniment, his ability at descriptive music, e. g. in "March of the Israelites" and "The Egyptians Pursue," and his infrequent use of dissonances.[63]

Georgia Atkins Ryder's "Melodic and Rhythmic Elements of Negro Folksongs as Employed in Cantatas by Selected American Composers Between 1932-1967" includes a section on *Moses*, selected because it was the first oratorio/cantata to incorporate identifiable characteristics of American Negro folk songs, and for its similarity in other cantatas in religious and philosophical elements. Ryder gives Dett credit for predicting that the oratorio form would continue to flourish, thereby making it a perfect vehicle for his expression and creativity in a dignified and ordered manner.

Speaking of Dett's compositional ideas as being "too crude for the formal church," Ryder detects a

> prior concern with dignity and formality rather than the preservation of the folk element. . . . From time to time his statements divulge an unresolved conflict between his deep feeling for the music of his race and his desire to identify with intellectual attitudes which were not hospitable to folk expressions. He deplored the use of "mannerisms or stage tricks" in other artists' concert presentations of the songs; yet his own critics complained that "interpretation more racial in quality would have been welcome."[64]

J. Harrison Wilson's doctoral dissertation was an in-depth study of *Moses*, though he considered Dett a minor American composer because of the restrictions imposed by the contemporary social atmosphere. Wilson's project included a recorded performance of *Moses* on April 12, 1970, at the Second Baptist Church of Los Angeles. Performers were the church's Cathedral Choir, five soloists, and the Angel City Symphony Orchestra, with Wilson as conductor. Logistics pertinent to the performance, discussed by Wilson, are difficulty of orchestral score (requiring foremost a competent cellist), wide vocal range required of singers, and full understanding of dramatic elements and text. *Moses* requires a miminum of sixty amateur or volunteer singers, less if a professional group. For his production Wilson called in two semi-professional soloists, tenor Reginald Fields and bass Wardell Howe. If piano or organ is used Wilson suggests the addition of some percussion. Substitutions for too high or too low notes in vocal parts, as well as revamping of difficult orchestral passages, are permissable.[65]

The principal roles in *Moses* are Miriam (soprano), Moses (tenor), The Voice of God (baritone), The Voice of Israel (alto), and The Word (baritone). The Children of Israel are the chorus. Prefacing the score Dett explains that *his* Moses was "a shepherd on a hillside, undoubtedly a young man," more believable when sung by a tenor than a baritone. He never intended portraying the Moses "familiarized by the other arts; especially by the work of Michaelangelo, whose statue of the patriarch has become symbolic."

The text is based on scripture from Lamentations and Exodus, skillfully entwined with folklore in both rhyme and blank verse. The full orchestration includes first violins (8), second violins (8), violas (6), cellos (6), basses (5); two each of flute, oboe, bassoon, and clarinet, one piccolo; horns (2), trumpets (2), trombones (3), and one tuba; tympani, bass and snare drums, cymbals, tambourine, castanets, triangle, chains; and harp. Wilson points out the chorus' main functions as completing or reflecting on the thought introduced by the solo voice, adding dramatic color, assisting in narration, and reiterating responses.[66]

Space does not permit a detailed analysis of *Moses* such as Wilson's. An examination of the score, however, reveals Dett's dramatic skills and potential as an orchestrator who packed everything possible into the challenging piano/organ accompaniment. The fifty-six measure Prelude opens with a motive described by William Dawson as "a missing link," symbolic of the Negro as a link in the human chain of slavery, one which recurs throughout the work. (See Musical Example No. 45.)

The Ordering of Moses

INDEX

The Word has the opening solo, responded to by the chorus. A conversation between the two follows, then another similar treatment between alto and chorus, both relating the woes of bondage. An instrumental interlude with cello and horn solos leads to a trio (SAB) with chorus, measures 192-313. Now the chorus parts sing in response to each other in a *con fuoco* passage ending at measure 233, after much reiteration of the words "Mercy, Lord." After a grand pause the opening motive is

The Ordering of Moses

Mus. ex. 45, meas. 1-2, 12-13, 23. Copyright © 1937 by J. Fischer & Bro. Copyright renewed c/o CPP/Belwin, Inc., Miami, FL 33014. International copyright secured. All rights reserved.

restated by the orchestra. For the next twelve measures the chorus parts are supported by a flurry of whole-tone scale fragments.

At measure 259 the theme "Go Down Moses," resembling the Hebraic chant, is introduced by the basses in unison. After eight measures the tenors join, then altos, then sopranos, all singing different texts in a fugal treatment. Moses then sings, *recitativo*, "Lord, who am I to go unto Pharaoh, and why should I lead the children of Israel?" He continues to question his own worth, but is reassured by the chorus, then by the Voice of God. The former key of f minor and meter of 4/4 now changes to c minor/E flat major. Dett switches to 6/8 meter for twenty-nine measures, then back to 4/4. At measure 409 triplets and duplets are scored against each other in the accompaniment for six measures. Separated by instrumental interludes the chorus reiterates the words "Let my people go!"

Key signatures of one flat, four flats, then no flats or sharps sustain a longer improvisational instrumental interlude which claims no tonal center. As it ends on a d minor chord at measure 524 the key changes to two flats. The Word now had a short solo, with response by the chorus singing "And when Moses smote the water, the children all passed over, the sea gave way!" Another interlude of chromatic progressions culminates at measure 588 when a variaton of the opening theme is played by a single horn. After a pause and a key change to D flat major in 10/4 meter "March of the Israelites" begins (measure 590). Throughout this movement the only word sung is a repeated "Ah." (See Musical Example No. 46.) Ryder states that these "wordless voices" were "designed to portray the emotional intensity of the Hebrew people during the stated Bibilcal event."[67]

The accompaniment continues to carry triplet patterns through the "March" as the flats are cancelled for seven measures (the "ahs" continuing), then a key signature of A major is established in 4/4 meter. At measure 670 "The Egyptians Pursue" is prefaced by a *commodo* tempo, still in triplet figures in the accompaniment. Finally, at measure 748, the baritone solo announces "And when they reached the other shore." Moses then has a recitative on high F for four measures, then going up to a high B flat with a *fermata.*

Miriam's solo, ushered in by the baritone's words, "And Miriam, gifted with prophecy, answered them, saying:" begins "Come, let us praise him Jehovah." The chorus punctuates this on beats two and three with alternating "Hal-le" and "lu-jah." The solo ends on a sustained high C. Wilson suggests that tambourine would enhance the keyboard accompaniment in this section. Though short, the tessitura of Moses' last solo, "Sing ye to Jehovah," is taxing.

The final chorus "He is King of Kings" begins with the exact melody of the so-named spiritual. It is in F major, interspersed with tenor (Moses) and soprano (Miriam) solos. Some of the

The Ordering of Moses
March of the Israelites
Through the Red Sea

Mus. ex. 46, meas. 590-597.

choral passages are heavily scored and the total effect is even
more massive with Dett's busy accompaniment. At measure 1110
a *declamativo* section between Miriam and Moses is sustained by
prolonged whole notes in the chorus, presumably to be dictated by
the conductor. Closing the work is a twenty-measure postlude,
marked *Presto*, containing all new material in its scale and chord
passages made up of F major ninths.

Dett's orchestration is imaginative and equally as powerful
as the choral parts. Wilson compares it to the lush, late
Romantic instrumental style of other composers. Dett sparingly
uses chords of the fourth, contrapuntal writing (except in the
fugue), tone clusters, and augmented triads. Wilson considers
Moses the perfect textual blend of scripture, folklore, and
spirituals with traditional music techniques. Accompaniment by
harp, horn, cello, and oboe to a few of the solos provides color.
Wilson describes Dett's altered seventh chords as "defying
analysis."[68]

There is little melodic repetition, except for transpositon, for
instance in measures 137-144. (See Musical Example No. 47.) The

The Ordering of Moses

Mus. ex. 47, meas. 137-144.

fugue in "Go Down Moses" involves both singers and players, who
alternate on theme and counter-subject. Some dissonant intervals
of seconds were perhaps used purposefully in "And God spoke to

Moses" to show God's annoyance with Moses (measures 340-343). The "Allegro Marziale" (357-407), just before the reprise of "Go Down Moses," shows Dett's advanced style and technique in use of frequent chord changes, parallel seconds and sevenths, cross relationships within the same measures, chromaticism, and seventh chords with added dissonances. Dett's dramatic effects are enhanced by his careful selection of text to suit voices, and in the orchestral description of Moses and God's struggle in the section "Meditation of Moses" (measures 444-519).

Wilson considers "March of the Israelites," with its Jewish flavor, some of Dett's truly creative writing. The continuing *ostinato* gives the impression of "a large caravan passing very near and gradually moving away into the distance as the harmony loses its thickness and the voices lose their power in the lower register."[69] *Moses* shows a few tinges of opera when Dett uses tremolos for a specific effect, such as the water settling over the Egyptians. He word-paints by moving voices down in half steps, in one instance, to emphasize the depth of the sea. Wilson calls the ending tonality of F major from the work's beginning in f minor a symbol of "changed circumstances of the once captive nation."[70]

Ryder summarizes that such outstanding features as the blending of Negroid musical and Hebraic textual elements, and the parallelism in text and music, in particular "Go Down Moses," work as a unifying theme, a traditional linking of spirituals to the Old Testament of which Dett was surely aware. The style of *Moses* could not be considered Negroid, but rather an assimilated, overall general formality in style and structure, somewhat dictated by the text. Calling it a "matrix" for the oratorio/cantata form Ryder continues: "The whole reflects the composer's knowledge and application of nineteenth-century musical techniques rather than the preservation of folk idioms. Within its genre, it is not diminished by these observations."[71]

Compositions in 1938

Fischer published *The Lamb* and *Now Rest Beneath Night's Shadows*, both for women's voices, in 1938 while Dett was at Bennett College. *The Lamb*, "Idyll for Chorus of Women's Voices Three Part" (SSA) is *a cappella*, set to a poem by William Blake and dedicated "To Mr. Davidson Taylor."[72] Blake's texts have been set by numerous composers, among them Arthur Farwell and Benjamin Britten, though "The Lamb" seems to be his best known poem.

Visionary and mystic artist Blake (1757-1827), brilliant poet and engraver, was considered insane by many of his contemporaries, but was accepted by fellow artists and intellectuals at the Royal Academy. He lived in London on the edge of poverty and died in neglect, having earned most of his living by engraving and illustrating in water color other men's works. He was largely self taught in languages and literature. Struggling constantly to free his soul from reason, law, and organized religion, he was partially able to express himself through poetry and mythological essays. "The Lamb" is in his volume *Songs of Innocence* (1789). Blake was an eccentric, imaginative, and introspective thinker, misunderstood in his time.

Dett's *The Lamb* is unpretentiously beautiful with its close harmonies which spread subtly to more open but not hollow ones. The opening key signature of one sharp which goes through measure 25 establishes the key as e minor, with an occasional G major resolution. At measure 26 E major is confirmed by both key signature and tonal center, with only a few phrases ending in c sharp minor. The alto part is scored very low, including one E sharp and several F sharps and Gs. Even singers with good ears and harmonic knowledge would need to listen carefully for well tuned ensemble. Dett uses Blake's two stanzas as written, separating them by the key change. (See Musical Examples Nos. 48a and 48b.) Unlike his usual settings of spirituals, Dett uses no repetition of words, except in the last twelve measures, on the words "Little lamb, God bless thee!" which might be considered a coda.

* * *

Now Rest Beneath Night's Shadows (SSAA) is a peaceful chorale, marked *Lento molto tranquillo*. Its close harmonies are not unusual. Dett includes an even wider range for Altos II, who sing a low E flat. The beginning thirty-eight measures are duplicated exactly in a second verse. In the final four measures their harmonies are slightly different and a high A flat is sustained by Soprano I on the word "God." Then these words are punctuated: "shall meet" (rest) "no" (rest) "harm."[73]

The Lamb

Mus. ex. 48a, meas. 1-4.

Mus. ex. 48b, meas. 26-29. Copyright © 1938 by J. Fisher & Bro.
Copyright renewed c/o CPP/Belwin, Inc., Miami, FL 33014.
International copyright secured. All rights reserved.

Compositions in the 1940s

In 1940 Hall & McCreary Company, publishers of *The Dett Collection of Negro Spirituals* (1936), published *Hew Down the Tree* (SSAA with contralto solo, *a cappella*). Dett wrote under the title:

> This anthem is based on a two-tone melody. Its comprehensive harmonic setting is modern and has a subtle brilliance which shows the remarkable possibility of religious musical expression. The text includes an excerpt from the Sermon on the Mount and the entire First Psalm which a soloist chants against a choral background of the original two-tone melody.

This two-tone melody was the basis of the previously discussed "Hew Roun' the Tree," a spiritual in the 1936 collection. The opening words demand the cutting and burning of all trees which bear bad fruit. At measure 87 the text compares a wicked man to the undesirable tree, advising his destruction. At measure 95 Psalm I is chanted by the soloist over the chorus' repeated "Hew, hew, hew down the tree." Dett's note says: "The chant should be done rapidly, no special effort to fit it with the other parts," though the marking at this point is *recitando molto allargamente*. Another of Dett's directions allows the lower altos to take optional notes when scored if the part is too low, G being the lowest note.

The words and music are quite repetitive, but *Hew Down the Tree* is an appealing piece, largely carried by its insistent rhythm. The first 38 measures are in c minor ending on G major chords, which one might expect to lead again to this key, but instead Dett states the theme briefly in f minor for a sixteen-measure section, then returns to c minor. At measure 55 he sets up a rhythmic pattern for the words "hew down the tree" to continue in various voices till the piece's end. (See Musical Example No. 49.) A stunning ending is reached by repetition of the words "Hew, hew, hew down the tree," at a dynamic of *ff*.

Ascapezza, Dett's choral piece dedicated to ASCAP, and *So We'll Go No More A-Roving* (both for women's voices) were published in 1940 by Fischer. Unfortunately neither score is available.[74] *Ascapezza* (SSA or SSAA) was sung by the Bennett Choir on some of their regular broadcasts in the early 1940s,

Hew Down the Tree

Mus. ex. 49, meas. 55-62. Copyright © 1940 by Hall & McCreary Co.
Copyright renewed c/o CPP/Belwin, Inc., Miami, FL 33014.
International copyright secured. All rights reserved.

performances confirmed by John G. Paine of ASCAP, according to the *Norfolk (VA) Journal and Guide*, February 22, 1941. It was also sung at the Southern Conference of Music Educators in Charlotte, North Carolina in March of 1941. In attendance, Dett explained that through the years ASCAP had "held a beacon light for those who have the desire and the genius to do creative work in music."[75] Lord (George Gordon) Byron's poem, "So We'll Go No More A-Roving," was written in 1817.[76]

Dett's *a capella* works from 1941, *Ask for the Old Paths* (SATB), *Heavenly Union* (SATB with baritone or tenor solo), and *When I Survey the Wondrous Cross* (SSAA), were published by Mills Music, Inc. *City of God* for mixed chorus with piano/organ accompaniment, was published by Fischer this same year.

Heavenly Union was based on a spiritual, transcribed by Dett from the singing of an unidentified Norfolk, Virginia resident. "Naturally an elaboration of the spiritual pattern, it is most effectively planned from every standpoint."[77] *Ask for the Old Paths* is based on text from the book of Jeremiah 6:16. *When I Survey the Wondrous Cross* was Dett's dedication hymn for the Annie Merner Pfeiffer Chapel at Bennett. (See Chapter V for the dedication program.)

Earlier settings of Isaac Watts' *Wondrous Cross* by Isaac B. Woodbury (1819-1858), Lowell Mason (1792-1872), and one by Edward Miller in 1790 may be found in Methodist, Baptist, and Episcopal hymnals respectively. The work has been used not only as a conversion hymn but in Communion services as well, often listed under *Eucharist*. As a young man, displeased with the music at his Congregational Chapel in Southhampton, England, Isaac Watts (1647-1748) decided to better it. His fervent verse-making became so profuse that his father punished him, an act about which he made further verses, such as: "Oh, father do some mercy take, And I will no more verses make."

Watts later became a minister at London's Mark Lane Independent Church, but continued writing poetry. Some of his well-known hymns are "Joy to the World," "Am I a Soldier of the Cross," "O, God Our Help in Ages Past," and "Alas! And Did My Saviour Bleed." Watts has been most praised for his expressiveness of thought and spiritual reverence. In messages that appealed to the unlettered as well as to the learned, he "spoke the universal language of the heart." Conversion stories related to the four-verse *Wondrous Cross*, first published in *Hymns and Spiritual Songs* (1707), are myriad.[78]

Original words to the five-verse *City of God*, set earlier by T. Haweis (1734-1820), are attributed to Samuel Johnson (1709-1784), English lexicographer, critic, poet, and conversationalist. A version of the song found in some Catholic missalettes of today is based on Bible texts from Ephesians, Isaiah, Matthew, and John I. The refrain says: "Let us build the City of God/ May our tears be turned into dancing/ For the Lord, our light and our love/ Has turned the night into day."

* * *

Negro Spirituals, 1959

Negro Spirituals, fifty-one selections from *The Dett Collection of Negro Spirituals*, issued in 1936 by Hall & McCreary Company, was published in 1959 by Blandford Press in London. Dett's preface is an interesting combination of skillfully placed paragraphs from his prefaces in the four groups of spirituals in the 1936 *Collection*. His former credits to the Fisk and Work Collections, and to the previously mentioned Mrs. Catherine Fields-Gay, Charles Flax, and Mrs. Harriet Washington (Dett's maternal grandmother), as well as to others, remain in the 1959 edition. A few piano introductions are provided, but Dett suggests that the singing should be *a cappella*. Nearly all have multiple verses and most are one to three pages in length, though one anthem titled "On That Sabbath Morn," is twelve pages.

"If I Had Died When I Was a Babe" is dedicated to Josephine (Dett), "Baptism" to Sam (Dett), "Communion" to Hampton organist Ernest Hays, and "Calvary's Mountain" to Carl Senne, who may have been the unidentified "Carl" to whom he dedicated "As His Own Soul" (*Eight Bible Vignettes*). Titles in *Negro Spirituals* are not listed separately in the Catalog of Music, but indicated by a + beside titles from the 1936 *Collection*.

* * *

Unpublished and Undated Choral Compositions

There is no confirmation by the Oberlin College Archives of Dett's submission to the *Songs of Oberlin* collections, but a faded copy of his *The Oberlin Song*, published though undated, is in the Mesiah Papers. Words by Seth L. Strong begin:

Hail, all hail, to the sons of Oberlin
Hail, all hail, to this glorious band, her kin.
Let the gold and crimson standard ever highest rise
The gold for achievement and the crimson for sacrifice.
Welcome back today, ye sturdy sons of toil,
Welcome back to these classic halls from life's turmoil.

Its three verses are in four-part harmony in F major. Ending the song is a thirty-two measure piano Coda in B flat major.

The Oberlin College Archives furnished interesting information concerning the series *Songs of Oberlin,* first published in 1905 under the editorship of Anna Louise Strong and Edna Barrows, graduates of that year. The Foreword to this collection said: "If it is true, as has been stated, that *the* Oberlin Song has not yet appeared, it is our hope that this collection may serve as a stimulus to future efforts in that direction."[79] Dett's *Oberlin Song* must have been his submission for one of the editions of the collection, or written for a reunion, since the words say "Welcome back today."

The Oberlin Alumni Magazine said of the 1905 issue:

It is a neat little volume of seventy-five pages, bound in red silk cloth with gilt edges. In [it] . . . the editors have gathered together the best songs that have appeared in the past years, including the Society Songs, Senior Step Songs and several prize songs that have appeared in recent annuals.[80]

The brilliant Miss Strong (b. 1885), a Phi Beta Kappa at Oberlin, contributed her own "Fair Oberlin" to the 1905 edition. After leaving Oberlin she pursued philosophy and journalism, and was the youngest woman ever to receive a doctorate from Chicago University. She became a longtime friend and supporter of the Communist party chairman, Mao Tse-Tung, and was arrested in 1949 by the Soviets and deported from Russia for spying during the Stalin era. Her father was Sydney Strong, Oberlin class of 1881, possibly an uncle or cousin to Dett's lyricist Seth L. Strong (b. 1884), class of 1909, who later earned a medical degree from Harvard and settled as a physician in Boston.

More editions of *Songs of Oberlin* followed in 1908, 1910, 1911,

1914, 1917, 1921, and 1925, each of which deleted the less popular tunes and added others. If Dett's song were included in any of these, it has not been located by the Oberlin College Archivist, though holdings of these editions are incomplete. Arthur Heacox, one of Dett's professors, wrote a review of the 1914 edition for the May 1914 *Oberlin Alumni Magazine*, mentioning several alumnae whose songs were to be included, but did not name Dett. Heacox was on the selection committee for the 1925 edition, which may possibly have included Dett's song.[81]

There is no evidence that *No Auction Block for Me* (c. 1929-1930), performed on the European choir trip in 1930, was ever published except in short form as "No More Auction Block" in *Religious Folk-Songs of the Negro* (1927). In his programme notes for the Queen's Hall concert in London, May 3, 1930, Dett described this song as "a sigh of relief that in death the trials concommitant with servitude at last are over." The song was orchestrated and performed on a broadcast by the Bennett Choir in February 1940. Other of Dett's unpublished choral pieces from 1943 are *God's Trumpet Wakes the Slumbering World*, a processional hymn written for the high school and chancel choirs of the First Congregational Church of Battle Creek, Michigan, and *Our God is Good in Earth and Sky*, dedicated to that church's pastor, Reverend Carleton Brooks Miller.[82]

Summary

Certain similarities are found in several of Dett's choral works: use of sequences and *fermatas*, call and response, open fourths in the accompanying parts, echo text phrases, parallel inversions, and an overall romanticism. Dett, however, wrote as he felt—in the *a cappella* style popular in the 1920s and '30s, one of European tradition.

Listen to the Lambs and *The Lamb* are still appealing to present-day choirs. There are extreme ranges in *Go Not Far From Me, O God* and in the busy *Juba*, whose articulation of text at the suggested metronome marking might be problematic. Textures seem overly thick in both *Juba* and *Don't Be Weary Traveler*, partly because of their close intervals, often triads for bass and tenor.

Drink to Me Only with Thine Eyes is in the vein of glee club fare, utilizing the then popular rock-along piano style which

Dett instead scored for the voices. Some of his hummed accompaniments are also in this style. *The Lamb* (SSA), with word-oriented rhythm, is scored quite low for alto, and necessary clarity in the *p* and *pp* passages requires a minimum of thirty voices. Such a low range was fairly common, however, due to the long-standing tradition of church choir singing.

* * *

This chapter has covered Dett's choral compositions from 1914 to 1943. Whether they or his piano works have been more successful is debatable, but both genres have proved more viable than his songs for solo voice. With the exception of the longer and more difficult *Chariot Jubilee* and *The Ordering of Moses* most of the choral works are of medium difficulty, and at the time of composition the *a cappella* ones were certainly interesting enough to challenge any choir. In them Dett achieved the pure unaccompanied sound he so much desired. Generous in his dedications, Dett was able to acknowledge his benefactors, friends, and the professional persons/groups who performed these works.

PART THREE:
Catalog of Music and Discography

CATALOG OF MUSIC

Dett's musical works, listed chronologically according to publication date, comprise three categories: *Piano and Other Instrumental Compositions; Songs, Folksongs, and Spirituals for Solo Voice;* and *Folksongs, Spirituals, and Other Choral Works.* The piano works, with the exception of *Nepenthe and the Muse,* were reprinted in 1973 by Summy-Birchard as *The Collected Piano Works of R. Nathaniel Dett,* accessible and containing the suites *Magnolia, In the Bottoms, Enchantment, Cinnamon Grove, Tropic Winter,* and *Eight Bible Vignettes.* Mills Music published *Harp of the Willows II,* likely Dett's last piano piece, in 1942. Most of Dett's unpublished compositions (those from Oberlin and a few later ones) which have been discussed in the text, will appear in the *Index,* but, with a few exceptions, will not be included in the *Catalog of Music.* Some unpublished arrangements of spirituals recorded by Dorothy Maynor will be listed only in the *Discography* and the *Index.*

Sibley Library at the Eastman School of Music has manuscripts of such unpublished works as "Confessional" for violin and piano (1908), and vocal works, "The Crimson and the Gold" (words by Alma M. Penrose), "From the Sea" (words by Dett), "I'm Troubled in Mind" (as sung by a former slave, Mrs. Brown of Nashville), "Lord Have Mercy" (words collected by Dett), "Oh, Stand the Storm" and "Ole-time Religion" (authors of words unknown), and "Oh, Whisp'ring Tree" (words by Dett). Sibley's list of holdings also includes sheet music to Dett's early piano composition "Niagara Falls" (no date or publisher is given). Unfortunately, but understandably, Sibley is not a lending library.

Publishers are abbreviated by the following symbols:

BMC   Boston Music Company, 172 Tremont St., Boston, MA 02111.

BP   Blandford Press, 16 West Central Street, London, W. C. 1

CCB   C. C. Birchard (see Summy-Birchard, Inc., sole agent)

CFS   Clayton F. Summmy (see Summy-Birchard, Inc., sole agent)

GSP   G. Schirmer Publishers, 225 Park Avenue South, New York, NY 10003

HIP   Hampton Institute Press (now Hampton University Press, Hampton University, Hampton, VA 23668)

HMC   Hall & McCreary Company (sole agent CPP/Belwin, Inc., P. O. Box 4340, Miami, FL 33014)

HMI   Hinshaw Music, Inc., P. O. Box 470, Chapel Hill, NC, 27514

JCC   John Church Company (see Theodore Presser Company, sole agent)

JFB   J. Fischer & Bro. (sole agent CPP/Belwin, Inc., P. O. Box 4340, Miami, FL 33014)

MMI   Mills Music, Inc. (sole agent CPP/Belwin, Inc., P. O. Box 4340, Miami, FL 33014)

RAS   Richard A. Saalfield, London, with office in New York as late as 1899.

SBI   Summy-Birchard, Inc., 265 Secaucus Rd., Secaucus, NJ, 07096-2037

SCF   S. C. Fragard, Niagara Falls, NY

TPC   Theodore Presser Company, Presser Place, Bryn Mawr, PA, 19010

VSM   Vander Sloot Music Company, 29 Washington Blvd., Williamsport, PA

Vander Sloot Music Company, Dett's first publisher (spelled Vandersloot, according to a news item in the Williamsport *Sun Gazette*, December 24, 1955), was founded by F. W. Vandersloot shortly before 1900, amusingly enough, in a kitchen at 29 Washington Boulevard. The idea occurred to him after his wife's composition, "Yellow-Kids on Parade," became the rage of local music lovers. As a family business the firm grew to be one of the largest publishers of popular music. Subsequently it moved to other locations in Williamsport, and in 1930 was absorbed by a Philadelphia company. Both Vandersloot and his son Carl were composers.

Donald E. Loker, Local Historian, in Niagara Falls, New York searched diligently for the address of S. C. Fragard, publisher of Dett's *Cave of the Winds March*, but was unable to locate it in City Directories of the early 1900s.

Less than half of Dett's music is no longer available for purchase. Though total catalog information on each entry is not complete, copies of the works may be found at the places whose abbreviated symbols follow:

ACUP   Marian Anderson Collection, Van Pelt Library, University of Pennsylvania, Philadelphia, PA.

AuMU   University of Melbourne, Parkville, Victoria 3052, Australia.

CArcHT   Humbolt State University, Arcata, CA.

CL   Los Angeles Public Library, Los Angeles, CA.

CLobS   California State University, Long Beach, CA.

CLSU   University of Southern California Library, Los Angeles, CA.

CNoS   California State University, Northridge, CA.

CSj	San Jose State University, San Jose, CA.
CSt	Stanford University Libraries, Palo Alto, CA.
Ct Y	Yale University, New Haven, CT.
CU	University of California, Berkeley, CA.
DHU (MS)	Howard University, Moorland-Spingarn Research Center, Washington, D. C.
DLC	United States Library of Congress, Washington, D. C.
ICarbS	Southern Illinois University, Carbondale, IL.
ICN	Newberry Library of Chicago, Chicago, IL.
ILinL	Lincoln Christian College, Lincoln, IL.
InFw	Allen City Public Library, Fort Wayne, IN.
InU	Indiana University, Bloomington, IN.
IU-Mu	University of Illinois, Urbana, IL.
KyLoS	Southern Baptist Theological Seminary, Louisville, KY.
LLafS	University of Southwestern Louisiana, Lafayette, LA.
MB	Boston Public Library, Boston, MA.
MFmT	Framington State College, Framington, MA.
MH	Harvard University Library, Cambridge, MA.
MLC	Siena Heights College, Adrian, MI.

MdBP	Peabody Institute, Baltimore, MD.
MiD	Detroit Public Library, Detroit, MI.
Mi U	University of Michigan, Ann Arbor, MI.
MnDUStS	College of St. Scholastica Library, Duluth, MN.
MoJoM	Missouri Southern State College Library, Joplin, MO.
MoS	St. Louis Public Library, St. Louis, MO.
MsCleD	Delta State University, Cleveland, MS.
N	New York State Library, Albany, NY.
NAuC	Cayuga County Community College, Auburn, NY.
NBuC	State University College at Buffalo, NY
NcD	Duke University, Durham, NC.
NcGA	North Carolina Agricultural and Technical State University, Greensboro, NC.
NCortU	SUNY College at Cortland, NY.
NcU	North Carolina State University Library, Raleigh, NC.
NIC	Cornell University, Ithaca, NY.
NN	New York Public Library, New York, NY.
NN (SC)	New York Public Library, Schomburg Center, New York, NY.

NNia	Niagara Falls Public Library, Niagara Falls, NY.
NRU	University of Rochester, Eastman School of Music, Sibley Collection, Rochester, NY.
OCl	Cleveland Public Library, Cleveland, OH.
ODW	Ohio Wesleyan University, Delaware, OH.
OO	Oberlin College Library, Oberlin, OH.
OrP	Library Association of Portland, Portland, OR.
OrPMB	Mulnomah School of the Bible, Portland, OR.
OrU	University of Oregon, Eugene, OR.
OU	Ohio State University, Columbus, OH.
PAnL	Lebanon Valley College, Annville, PA.
PP	Free Library of Philadelphia, Philadelphia, PA.
PPi	Carnegie Library of Pittsburgh, Pittsburgh, PA.
PPPL	Philadelphia Board of Public Education, Pedagogical Library, Philadelphia, PA.
PSC-Hi	Friends Historical Library of Swarthmore College, Swarthmore, PA.
RPB	Brown University Library, Providence, RI.
TNF	Fisk University, Nashville, TN.
TxFTC	Texas Christian University, Fort Worth, TX.

U   Utah State Library, Salt Lake City, UT.

ViHaI   Hampton University, Hampton, VA.

ViN   Norfolk Public Library, Norfolk, VA.

ViU   University of Virginia Library, Charlottesville,
                 VA.

WHi   State Historical Society of Wisconsin, Madison,
                 WI.

WSU   University of Wisconsin, Madison, WI.

Following the year of publication, each entry is numbered and will include as much information as is presently known. These specific markings or symbols are used to facilitate reader scanning:

* indicates popularity in performance and/or favorable reviews;

** indicates suitability for today's repertoire, without regard to its former popularity;

* ** indicates that both an historical and a current appraisal apply;

P indicates suitability for professional performers only;

S indicates suitability for students or amateurs only;

P,S indicates suitability for both professional and non-professional performers.

Other data following the title include meter; metronome markings (E-eighth note, Q-quarter note, H-half note, DQ-dotted quarter, DH-dotted half); expressive markings; key; number of pages; range (if vocal solo); type voices (if choral

work); accompanied (acc.) or *a cappella* (a cap.); text source or
poet; R (has been recorded); place of publication, publisher, date
of publication; premiere performance; approx. performance time;
dedication; location of holdings; and call numbers from the
Library of of Congress and the Dewey decimal system. The +
symbol by entries under *The Dett Collection of Negro Spirituals*
(1936) denotes inclusion also in *Negro Spirituals* (1959).

Piano and Other Instrumental Compositions

1900

1. S   *After the Cakewalk* (piano); 2/4.
    Williamsport, PA: VSM, 1900; NBuC.

1902

2. S   *Cave of the Winds March* (piano); 6/8; *Con spirito*; G
    major; 5 pp.
    Niagara Falls, NY: SCF, 1902; NNia, NBuC, NN (MYD
    box).

1903

3. S   *Inspiration Waltzes* (piano); 3/4.
    London: RAS, 1903; Mrs. Charlotte Dett; NBuC.

1909

4. S   *My Agnes from Niagara.*
    Niagara Falls, NY: SCF, 1909.

1912

5. *,** P,S *Magnolia* (piano suite); R.
    Chicago: CFS, 1912; Evanston, IL: SBI, 1973; NNia (I-176,
    C-6), MiD (RM785 D48w), OO (768.4M D484C), NN
    (MYD), N, ViHaI, LLafS (M 24.D333), NRU (Box 2),
    AuMU, MB (M 24.D333), OCl.
    "Magnolias"; 4/4; *Moderato molto cantabile*; D

major; 5 pp.; 3:38.

"The Deserted Cabin;" 12/8; *Largo con tristezza, melodia ben sostenuto*; b minor; 2 pp.; 2:17; organ arr. Nevin at NRU (Box 2), MB, OrP, ViHaI.

"My Lady Love;" cut time; *Allegretto grazioso*; A major; 6 pp.; 2:56; NN (SC).

"Mammy;" 4/4; *Lento con tenerezza*; D flat major; 3 pp.; 3:19; organ arr. Nevin at OrP, NN (SC), NRU (Box 2), MB, ViHaI, NN (No. 2 in 8040.I68).

"The Place Where the Rainbow Ends;" 3/8; *Allegro*; G flat major; 12 pp.; 5:19; DHU (MS, ABS-32.505), NN (SC).

1913

6. *,** P,S *In the Bottoms* (piano suite); R; Chicago, 1913, at concert by Fanny B. Zeisler; Mr. & Mrs. Fred Goff (?).

Chicago: CFS, 1913; Evanston, IL: SBI, 1973; LLafS (M 24.D333), OCl, NN (MYD), CLSU, MB, IU, OrP, MiD (RM785, D48w), OO (M 24.D333 I6) NRU (Box 2), NNia, ViHaI, AuMU, MdBP, NN (SC).

"Prelude" ("Night"); 4/4; H=54; *Adagio sostenuto*; D major; 5 pp.; R; 3:48.

"His Song;" 2/2; H=120; *Andante non troppo ma piu patetico*; d minor; 3 pp.; 2:16; Mr. Fred Goff; NNia (I-611, C-6); organ arr. Nevin at NRU (Box 2).

"Honey;" 2/4; Q=100; *Allegretto*; F major; 2 pp.; Paul L. Dunbar; R; 1:00.

"Barcarolle;" 6/8; DQ=56; *Moderto molto grazioso*; C major; 10 pp.; 4:55; OO (M 24.D333 I6 B2).

"Juba" ("Dance"); 2/4; Q=120-144; *Non troppo allegro*; F major; 5 pp.; R; 2:10; re-dedicated to Percy Grainger; DHU (MS, JEM-12.181), NN, NNia (I-23, C-6), ICN, OrP, OO (786.45

MD484J), NN (SC), AuMU.

1922

7. ***,**** P,S *Enchantment* (piano suite); Fisk University, 1923; 12 min.; Percy Grainger.
    New York: JCC, 1922; Evanston, IL: SBI, 1973; LLafS (M24 D.333), MiD (RM785 D48w), NN (MA), ViHaI, NNia, AuMU, NRU (Box 2), NN (SC), OO (786.4M D484C).
    "Incantation"; 2/4; *Un poco agitato, ma moderato*; c sharp minor; 8 pp.; NNia (I-8, C-6).
    "Song of the Shrine"; cut time; *Lento con molto espressione*; E major; 4 pp.; NNia (I-14, C-6).
    "Dance of Desire"; 2/4; *Con moto*; D flat major, E major; 10 pp.; NNia (I-12, C-6).
    "Beyond the Dream"; 3/4; *Andante patetico, quasi notturno*; A major; 8 pp.; NNia (I-13, C-6).

8. S *Nepenthe and the Muse* (piano); 6/8; *Adagio molto tranquillo*; D flat major; 5 pp.; mythology; 2 min.; Dr. Arthur Foote.
    New York: JCC, 1922; AuMU (MGCi/DET-9), NNia (I-578, C-6).

1923

9. ***P,S** *Ramah* (violin and piano); 4/4; *Lento e molto expressivo*; G major; 5 pp.; Bible; 3 min.
    Boston: BMC, 1923; NNia (I-65, C-6).

1924

10. *****   *Cotton Needs Pickin'* (var. for piano); 4/4; F major; unpublished; Oct. 18, 1924, People's Church, St. Paul, MN.
    NNia (I-350, C-6).

1926

11.   *Fair Weather* (piano).
        Bryn Mawr, PA: TPC, 1926.

1928

12.   *   S *Cinnamon Grove* (piano suite); 11 min.
          New York: JCC, 1928; Evanston, IL: SBI, 1973; LLafS (M
          24.D333, NNia (I-76, C-6), PP, MiD (RM785 D48w), OO
          (786.4M D484C), MB (M 24.D333), ViHaI.
             "Moderato molto grazioso"; 4/4 (2/2); *Ma con moto*; F
                 major; 6 pp.; John Donne.
             "Adagio cantabile"; 3/4; D flat major; 10 pp.;
                 Rabindranath Tagore; R.
             "Ritmo moderato e con sentimento, Quasi Gavotte";
                 4/4; b flat minor; 8 pp.; Henry W. Longfellow.
             "Allegretto"; 2/4; F major; 8 pp.; Negro folksong.

1937

13.   *   P *American Sampler* (orchestra); Philip Freneau;
          unpublished; CBS broadcast, Oct. 2, 1937; 20 min.

1938

14.   *   S *Tropic Winter* (piano suite); 18 min.
          Chicago: CFS, 1938; Evanston, IL: SBI, 1973; DHU (MS-
          WCM 4.66, 5.67, 5.70, 5.73), LLafS (M 24. D333), ViHaI,
          NNia, AuMU, DLC (M.24.D3435), MB, MiD (RM785
          D48w), OO (786.4M D484C), NN (MYD).
             "The Daybreak Charioteer"; 4/4; *Pomposo marziale
                 moderato*; no key sig., G flat major tonality; 4
                 pp.
             "A Bayou Garden"; 4/4; *Adagio molto sostenuto*; B
                 flat major; 2 pp.
             "Pompons and Fans"; 3/4; MM Q=96; *Grazioso*; G
                 major; 6 pp.
             "Legend of the Atoll"; 4/4; *Lento, recit. un poco
                 dolente*; D major; 3 pp.
             "To a Closed Casement"; 4/4; MM Q=72; *Andante*

espressivo; C major; 3 pp.

"Noon Siesta"; 4/4; *Lento quasi berceuse;* no key sig., G
major tonality; 1 p.

"Parade of the Jasmine Banners"; 6/8; *Allegretto
grazioso;* E flat major/e flat minor; 8 pp.;
NN(SC).

1941

15. *,** P,S *Eight Bible Vignettes;* R.
New York: MMI, 1941; Evanston, IL: SBI, 1973; LLafS (M
24. D.333), NNia, ViHaI, DhU (MS-ABS-31.489 thru
31.492, 32.494, 32.500, 32.501, 32.504), IU, OCl, MB,
AuMU, MiD (RM785 D48w), OO (786.4M D484C),
NN(SC).

"Father Abraham"; 4/4; *Molto maestoso;* f minor, A
flat major; 6 pp.; Bible; March 17, 1942, Dett
performed it at fiftieth anniversary of
Chamber of Commerce, Niagara Falls, N.Y.;
4:32.

"Desert Interlude"; 4/4; MM Q=88; *Larghetto
patetico;* a minor; 3 pp.; Bible; 3:23.

"As His Own Soul"; 4/4; MM Q=84; *Moderato
semplice quasi volkslied;* G flat major; 4 pp.;
Bible; 3:25; To the memory of Carl.

"Barcarolle of Tears"; 6/4; MM Q=144; *Andante;* c
minor; 4 pp.; 3:46.

"I Am the True Vine"; 3/4; MM Q=138; *Con moto ma
espressivo;* f minor, A flat major; 3 pp.; Bible;
3:33.

"Martha Complained"; 12/8; MM DQ=72-80;
Larghetto; c minor, C major; 5 pp.; Bible; 5:30.

"Other Sheep"; 2/4; MM Q=58; g minor, G major; 12
pp.; Bible; 9:29.

"Madrigal Divine"; 4/4; *Moderato molto tranquillo;* C
major, 3 pp.; 3:52.

Songs, Folksongs, and Spirituals for Solo Voice
with Accompaniment

1903

16.   S *Churning Song*; 6/8; *Andante con moto*; G major; 4
           pp.; D to G; Sillian M. Thompson; unpublished; 2:30;
           Mrs. Flora Pierce-Dennis; NNia (I-581, C-6).

1918

17.   *   S *Go On, Mule!*; 4/4; In slow and well marked time; C
           major; 3 pp.; 2:30; C to E; Fletcher Bryant.
           New York: JFB, 1918; NN(SC), NNia (I-579, C-6).

1919

18.   *   P,S *A Thousand Years Ago or More*; 4/4; MM Q=72;
           Larghetto sostenuto rubato; D flat major; 7pp.; D to A
           flat; Frederick H. Martens; 3 min.
           New York: JCC, 1919; NNia (I-572, C-6).

19.   *,** P,S *Follow Me*; cut time; MM H=96; *Allegro con brio
           ma non troppo*; f min.; 8 pp.; C to F; Negro spiritual;
           R; 3 min.
           New York: JCC, 1919; ACUP (Box 180), NNia (I-173, C-
           6), NN (MP box), NN(SC).

20.   *,** P,S *I'm So Glad Trouble Don't Last Alway*; 4/4; MM
           H=60; Quietly; F major; 4 pp.; F to F; Negro spiritual;
           R; 2:50.
           New York: JCC, 1919; DHU(MS-JEM-12.180, WCM-
           5.69), NNia (I-575, C-6), NN (MP box), NN(SC), NRU
           (Box 1).

21.   *   S *Magic Moon of Molten Gold*; 3/4; *Andante molto
           tranquillo movemento di barcarolla*; C major; 15 pp.,
           D to A flat; Frederick H. Martens; 3:40.
           New York: JCC, 1919; NBuC, ViHaI, NN(SC).

22.   *,** P,S *Somebody's Knocking at Your Door*; cut time; MM
H=72; Very moderately; E flat major; 8 pp.; Negro
spiritual; R; 2:40.
New York: JCC, 1919; NNia (I-35, C-6), ACUP (Box
183b), AuMU, NN (MP box; 784.7-D), MiD (RMS 784.52).

1923

23.   P,S *Poor Me*; Negro spiritual; R.
New York: JCC, 1923; ACLU (Box 183), NN(SC).

24.   *O the Land I'm Bound For*; Negro spiritual; Douglass
Memorial Chorus, Oberlin (1923); Lloyd Hickman.
New York: JCC, 1923.

25.   *   S *The Winding Road*; 4/4; *Moderato*; E flat major; 6
pp.; D to F; Tertius van Dyke; 2 min.
Bryn Mawr, PA: TPC, 1923; NNia (I-574, C-6).

26.   *,** P,S *Open Yo' Eyes*; 2/4; *Andante poco espressivo*; C
major; 6 pp.; C to A; Nathaniel Dett; 2 min.
Bryn Mawr, PA: TPC, 1923; ACLU (Box 194), NNia (I-29,
C-6).

27.   * P,S *Zion Hallelujah*; 4/4; *Lento con molto tranquillo*; D
flat major; 4 pp.; D flat to E flat; Negro folksong;
1:45; Reinald Werrenrath.
New York: JCC, 1923; AuMU, NN(SC).

1924

28.   *P,S *Were Thou the Moon*; 4/2; *Lento, con molt'
espressione*; F major; 3 pp., C to E; Nathaniel Dett;
1:30; Stanley Hoban.
New York: JCC, 1924; NNia (I-66, C-6), ACLU (Box 194),
NN(SC).

29.   *P,S *The Voice of the Sea*; 4/4; *Adagio tristmente*; B flat

major; 4 pp.; A to D; Nathaniel Dett; 1:30; Kathryn Meisle.
New York: JCC, 1924; NNia (I-11, C-6), NN(SC).

30. *,** P,S *A Man Goin' Roun' Takin' Names*; 2/4; *Largo mestamente*; E flat major; 4 pp.; C to F; Negro folksong; 2 min.; Jerome Swinford.
New York: JCC, 1924; NNia (I-171, C-6), NN(SC), MiD (RMS784.52 D48m).

31. *,** P,S *I'm A-Goin' to See My Friends Again*; 2/4; *Lento con molt' espressione*; G major, 4 pp.; D to G; Negro folksong; 1:30; Roland Hayes.
New York: JCC, 1924; NNia (I-570, C-6).

1926

32. *God Understands*; Katrina Trask.
New York: JCC, 1926; OrU.

1929

33. * S *Lead Gently, Lord, and Slow*; 4/4; *Largo con molto espressione*; C major, F major; 4 pp.; low A to D, high D to G; Paul L. Dunbar; 2 min.
New York: JCC, 1929; NNia (I-172, C-6), DHU (MS-ABS-32.499).

34. * S *My Day*, 4/4; *Andante con moto sentimente*; G major; 4 pp.; B to E; Daniel S. Twohig; R; 2 min.
New York: JCC, 1929; NNia (I-9, C-6), NN(SC).

1932

35. * S *Sit Down, Servant*; 2/2; MM H=56; *Lento*; F major; 6 pp.; C to D flat; Negro folksong; 2 min.
New York: GSP, 1932; ACUP (Box 194), NN(SC), ViHal (ms and pub. copies); DHU (MS-JEM-13.186).

1934

36. * S *O Lord, the Hard-won Miles*; 4/4; *Andante*; E flat major, G major; 4 pp. (low A to E flat, high C sharp to G); Paul L. Dunbar; 2 min.
New York; GSP, 1934; ACUP (Box 194), NN(SC), DHU (MS-JEM-13.184), ViHaI (ms and pub. copies).

1935

37. * S *Iorana*; 3/8; *Grazioso*; g minor, G major; 5 pp.; D to G; J. Henry Quine; 3 min.; Robert Gibbings.
Chicago: CFS, 1935; DHU (MS-ABS-32.498), ACUP (Box 194), OO (M1619 C58N4), NNia (I-30, C-6), ViHaI (ms).

1940

38. *,** P,S *Ride On, Jesus*; 2/4; *Marziale marcato*; E flat major; 4 pp.; C to B flat; Negro spiritual; R; Library of Congress, Dec. 10, 1940; 1:38; Dorothy Maynor.
New York: JFB, 1940; DHU (MS-ABS-32.506), NN(SC).

39. *,** P,S *I'm Goin' to Thank God*; high voice; Negro spiritual; R; 3:06; Dorothy Maynor; Library of Congress, Dec. 10, 1940.
New York: JFB, 1940; DHU (MS-ABS-32.496), NN(SC).

1942

40. *,** P,S *Go On, Brother!* 2/2; *Andante serioso*; f minor; 2 pp.; C to A flat; Negro spiritual; 1 min.; Dorothy Maynor.
New York: MMI, 1942; OO (M 1670.D488S65), DHU (MS-ABS-31.493), NN (MO US negro box).

41. S *The Soul of America Defend!*; cut time; *Marziale*; E flat major; 2 pp.; C to F; Nathaniel Dett; 2 min.
New York: MMI, 1942; NN, DHU (MS-ABS-32.507).

42. * S *Hymn to Parnassus*; 4/4; *Andante espressivo*; C major; 4 pp.; C to F; Verse I Anonymous, Verse II Nathaniel Dett; broadcast over North Carolina network, April 2, 1942, Lottie McCoy soloist; 2 min.
New York: MMI, 1942; OO (M 1670.D488 S65), DHU (MS-ABS-31-494), NN(SC).

1943

43. *,** P,S *I'm A-Trav'ling to the Grave*; 2/2; *Ritmo quasi march funebre*; G major; 3 pp.; D to G; Negro spiritual; 1:30; Dorothy Maynor.
New York: MMI, 1943; DHU (MS-ABS-32.495), OO (M 1617.D488 S65), NN(SC).

44. *,** P,S *What Kind of Shoes You Going to Wear?* 2/4; *Un poco allegro*; A flat major; 4 pp.; E flat to F; Negro spiritual; 1:20; Dorothy Maynor.
New York: MMI, 1943; NN(SC), DHU (MS-ABS-32.508), OO (M 1617.D488 W53).

45. *,** P,S *Now We Take This Feeble Body*; 4/4; *Adagio doloroso*; A flat Major; 3 pp.; E flat to B flat; Negro funeral hymn; 1:30; Dorothy Maynor.
New York: MMI, 1943; DHU (MS-ABS-32.502), OO (M 1617.D488 S65).

46. *,** P,S *In That Morning*; 8/8; MM E=72; *Lento espressivo*; g minor; 2 pp.; G to G; Negro spiritual; 1:10; Dorothy Maynor.
New York: MMI, 1943; DHU (MS-ABS-32.497), OO (M 1617.D488 I58).

Folksongs, Spirituals and Other Choral Works

1914

47.   *   S *Hampton, My Home by the Sea*; 4/4; *Con espress.*;
    A flat major; 2 pp., 2 verses; SATB, acc. optional;
    Nathaniel Dett; 2 min.; To all lovers of Hampton.
    Hampton, VA: HIP, 1914; ViHaI, NNia (I-20, C-6 and I-
    562, C-6), NN (SSR).

48.   *,** P,S *Listen to the Lambs*; 4/4; *Moderato*, weirdly; d
    minor; 8 pp.; SATB (8 pts.) w/sop. solo; *a cap.*; Bible;
    R; 5 min.
    New York: GSP, 1914; SSA, New York: GSP, 1923; IU,
    NNia (I-71,C-6), NN(SC), OrP, AuMU.

1916

49.   *   S *O, Holy Lord*; 4/4; *Lento con molt' espressivo*; G
    major; 8 pp.; SATB (8 pts.); *a cap.*; religious folksong;
    R; Hamilton, Ontario, Oct. 5, 1916, Elgar Choir; 4:30.
    New York: GSP, 1916; NNia (I-577, C-6), ViHaI, NcU.

50.   *   S *Music in the Mine*; 3/4; *Andante*; A flat major; 15
    pp.; SATB w/ten. solo; *a cap.*; folksong; prof. prem.
    New York Oratorio Soc., Carnegie Hall, Feb. 21,
    1922:6:30.
    New York: GSP, 1916; NNia (I-91, C-6), NN(SC).

1918

51.   S *America the Beautiful*; 4/4; *Con spirito*; C major; 1
    p. (4 verses); SATB, acc.; Katherine Lee Bates;
    National Victory Sing, Thanksgiving 1918; 2:30.
    New York: JFB, 1918; ViHaI, IU, DHU (MS-JEM-12.176).

52.   *,** S *I"ll Never Turn Back No More*; 3/4; *Moderato di
    molto*; F major; 8 pp.; SATB w/sop. or ten. solo; *a cap.*;
    Bible; R; 3:30; Hampton Choral Union and Hampton

Choir.

New York: JFB, 1918; MB (M 1617.D45I5), ViHaI, NcU, DHU (MS-JEM-12.179), AuMU, OO (378.771 1TZ1908).

53. *,** P,S Weeping Mary; 4/4; Andante espressivo; c minor; 8 pp.; a cap.; Negro folksong; 4 min.; Bruce Carey.
New York: JFB, 1918; DHU (MS-WCM-5.74 and JEM-13.187), NNia (I-175, C-6), NcU.

1919

54. *,** P,S The Chariot Jubilee; 2/2; Adagio; G and D major; 30 pp.; SATB w/ten. solo; organ/piano or orch. acc.; Bible; R; St. Cecilia Soc. of Boston, Apr. 22, 1920; 20 min.; Syracuse Univ. Chorus.
New York: JCC, 1919; NNia (I-573, C-6), NN(SC), MB (M 435.79), OCl, DHU (MS-WCM-4.65).

55. * S Done Paid My Vow to the Lord; 4/4; Molto moderato ed serioso, un poco rubato; g minor; 7 pp.; SSA w/bar. or contr. solo; Negro spiritual; 2 min.
New York: JCC, 1919; ViHaI, OO, NN.

56. * S I'm So Glad Trouble Don't Last Alway; 4/4; MM H=60; Quietly; F major; 4 pp.; SSA, acc.; Negro spiritual; 1:15.
New York: JCC, 1919; ViHaI.

57. *,** P,S Somebody's Knocking at Your Door; SATB; acc.; Negro spiritual; 16 pp.
New York: JCC, 1919, 1939; ViHaI; SSA w/ten. solo; New York: JCC, 1921; NN.

58. O Mary Don't You Weep; SATB; a cap..
Boston: CCB, 1919.

1921

59. *,** P,S There's a Meeting Here Tonight; 4/8; Animato

non troppo allegro; E flat major; 10 pp.; SSA; acc.;
Negro spiritual; 2:30; St. Cecilia Society of Boston.
New York: JCC, 1921; ViHaI.

60. *,** P,S *Don't Be Weary Traveler;* 4/4; *Andante molt'
espressivo;* b minor; 15 pp.; SSATBB (6 pts.); *a cap.;*
Negro folk songs; 4 min.; George Foster Peabody.
New York: JCC, 1921; ViHaI, AuMU, MB.

1924

61. *,** S *Gently, Lord, O Gently Lead Us;* 4/4; *Larghetto,
molto sostenuto;* F major; 15 pp.; SATB w/sop. solo; *a
cap.;* Bahama folksong, adapted by Thomas
Hastings; 3:30; Douglass Memorial Chorus (Oberlin).
New York: JCC, 1924; ViHaI, NNia (I-67, C-6), AuMU.

1926

62. *There's a Star in the East;* SSA; Negro folksong.
New York: JCC, 1926.

63. *Son of Mary;* SATB; Negro folksong; Oberlin Musical
Union and George W. Andrews.
New York: JCC, 1926.

64. * S *Let Us Cheer the Weary Traveler;* 4/4; *Moderato
molto maestoso;* C major; 9 pp.; SATB; *a cap.;* Negro
spiritual; R; 3 min.
New York: JCC, 1926; MB, ViHaI.

65. *,** P,S *O Hear the Lambs A-Crying;* 2/2; MM H=66;
Larghetto; a minor; 10 pp.; SATTBB w/sop. solo; *a
cap.;* Negro folksong; 3:30; Oratorio Society of New
York.
New York: JCC, 1926; NN(SC), DHU (MS-WCM-5.68).

66. *,** P,S *Don't You Weep No More, Mary;* 2/2; d minor; 8
pp.; SATB; *a cap.;* Bible; R; 3 min.

New York: GSP, 1926; NN(SC).

1927

67. * S *Religious Folk-songs of the Negro As Sung at Hampton Institute*; c. 260 pp.; SATB; acc. opt.; Negro folksongs and spirituals.
Hampton, VA: HIP, 1927; ViHaI, CtY (V3 D48-927), IU, ODW, OU, MiU, CU, NN, PP, OO (784.756 MD484R), PSC-Hi, PPPL, DLC, NIC, MB (8057.458), MiD, WHi, ViN, NcGA, MH-AH, TNF, NcD.

A Wheel in a Wheel
Babylon's Fallin'
Band ob Gideon
Bright Sparkles in de Churchyard
But He Ain't Comin' Here t'Die No Mo'
By and By
Children, We All Shall Be Free
Come Down, Sinner
Daniel Saw the Stone
De Church of God
De Old Sheep Done Know de Road
De Ole Ark a-Moverin' Along
De Winter'll Soon Be Ober
Deep River
Dere's a Little Wheel A-Turnin' in My Heart
Did You Hear How Dey Crucified My Lord?
Don't Be Weary, Traveler
Don't Call de Roll
Don't Get Weary
Don't Leave Me, Lord
Don't You View Dat Ship a-Come a-Sailin'!
Down by the River
Dust an' Ashes
Ef You Want to Get to Hebben
Ev'ry Time I Feel the Spirit
Ezekiel Saw de Wheel
Fighting On

Git on Board, Little Children
Go Down, Moses
Go, Mary, an' Toll de Bell
Go Tell It on de Mountain (App. III)
Goin' to Shout All Over God's Heav'n
Going to Heaven
Good Lord, Shall I Ever Be de One?
Good News, de Chariot's Comin'
Grace Before Meat at Hampton
Gwine to Live Humble to de Lord
Gwine Up
Hail! Hail! Hail!
Hard Trials
He Is King of Kings
Hear de Angels Singin'
Hear de Lambs a-Cryin'
He's the Lily of the Valley
I Ain't Goint' Study War No More
I Am Goin' to Join in This Army
I Am Seekin' for a City
I Couldn't Hear Nobody Pray (App. X)
I Don't Want to Stay Here No Longer
I Heard from Heaven Today
I Heard the Preaching of the Elder
I Know the Lord's Laid His Hands on Me
I'll Be There in the Morning
I'm a-Rolling
I'm a-Trav'ling to the Grave
I'm Gwine to Jine de Great 'Sociation
I'm So Glad Trouble Don't Last Alway
I'm Troubled in Mind
If You Love God, Serve Him
In Bright Mansions Above
In Dat Great Gittin'-Up Mornin'
In That Beautiful World on High
In the Kingdom
I've Been a-List'ning All de Night Long
I've Been Toilin' at de Hill
I've Got a Mother in de Heaven

I Want to Be Ready
I Would Like to Read
Jerusalem Mornin'
John Saw Judgment
Keep a-Inchin' Along
Keep Me from Sinkin' Down (App. XII)
King Manuel
Leanin' on de Lord
L'Envoi (App. XIII)
Let de Heaven Light Shine on Me
Let Us Cheer the Weary Traveler
Let Us Praise Him
Like a Rough and a Rolling Sea
Listen to de Lambs
Little David, Play on Your Harp
Live Humble
Look Away
Lord, Have Mercy
Lord, I Want to Be a Christian
Lord, Until I Reach My Home
Most Done Trabelling
Mother, Is Massa Gwine to Sell Us?
My Lord Delibered Daniel
My Lord, What a Morning! (App. VIII)
My Lord's a-Riding All the Time
My Soul Wants Something That's New
My Way's Cloudy
No More Auction Block
Nobody Knows de Trouble I've Seen
Oh, de Downward Road Is Crowded
Oh, de Hebben Is Shinin'
Oh, Freedom!
Oh, Give Way, Jordan
Oh, He Raise-a Poor Lazarus
Oh, Jerusalem!
Oh, Religion Is a Fortune
Oh, Sinner, You'd Better Get Ready
Oh, Stand the Storm
Oh, the Rocks and the Mountains

Oh, Wasn't Dat a Wide Ribber?
Oh, When I Get t' Heaven
Oh, Yes!
Oh, Yes, Yonder Comes My Lord
Ole-Time Religion
Peter on the Sea
Pilgrim's Song
Poor Pilgrim
Prayer Is de Key of Heaven
Put John on de Islan'
'Raslin' Jacob
Reign, Massa Jesus
Ride On Rise an' Shine
Rise Up, Shepherd, an' Foller (App. IV)
Roll de Ole Chariot Along
Roll, Jordan, Roll (App. I)
Run, Mary, Run
Run to Jesus
See Fo' and Twenty Elders
Seek and Ye Shall Find
Slav'ry Chain
Somebody's Knocking at Your Door
Sometimes I Feel Like a Motherless Child
Soon I Will Be Done
Stars in the Elements
Stay in de Field
Steal Away to Jesus (App. VII)
Sun Don't Set in de Mornin'
Sweet Canaan
Sweet Turtle Dove
Swing Low, Chariot
Swing Low, Sweet Chariot
Swing Low, Sweet Chariot (App. V)
Tell Jesus
There Is a Balm in Gilead
There Were Ten Virgins
There's a Meeting Here To-Night
They Look Like Men of War
'Tis Me (App. IX)

'Tis the Old Ship of Zion
View de Land
Walk Togedder, Childron (sic)
Walk You in de Light
Want to Go to Heaven When I Die (App. II)
We Are Almost Home
We Are Building on a Rock
We Are Climbing Jacob's Ladder
We Are Walking in de Light
Were You There When They Crucified My
    Lord? (App. VI)
What Yo' Gwine t' Do When de Lamp Burn
    Down?
When the General Roll Is Called
Where Shall I Be When de Firs' Trumpet
    Soun'?
Who'll Jine de Union?
Why, He's the Lord of Lords
Wonder Where Is Good Ole Daniel
You Goin' to Reap Jus' What You Sow
Zion, Weep a-Low

1930

68.   S *Ave Maria*; 4/4; *Molto moderato e con expressione*;
    F major; 6 pp.; SATB w/bar. solo; *a cap.*; Frederick H.
    Martens; European tour of Hampton Choir, 1930; 2:40.
New York: GSP, 1930; Chapel Hill, NC: HMI, 1978;
ViHaI.

69.   S *As Children Walk Ye in God's Love*; Hampton
    Choir Concert, Carnegie Hall, Apr. 16, 1928.
New York: GSP, 1930.

1932

70.   * S *Somebody's Knocking at Your Door*; SSA w/ten.
    solo; Negro spiritual.
Bryn Mawr, PA: TPC, 1932.

71.   *   S *Rise Up Shepherd and Follow* (see also   1936
          entry); 7 pp.; SATB; acc.; Christmas spiritual; R.
      New York: JFB, 1932.

1933

72.   S *Drink to Me Only with Thine Eyes*; 3/4; *Andante
          expressivo*; G major; 10 pp.; SATB; *a cap.*; Ben Jonson;
          American Choir broadcast, WHAM, Rochester, 1933;
          2:45; American Choir.
      New York: JFB, 1933; NNia (I-68, C-6) DHU (MS-JEM-
      12.177).

73.   *   P,S *Go Not Far From Me, O God*; 3/4; *Larghetto con
          molt' espressione*; d minor, D major; 10 pp. SATB
          w/bar. solo; *a cap.*; traditional Negro melodies; 3
          min.; George Whitefield Andrews.
      New York: JFB, 1933; NNia (I-90, C-6), ViHaI, DHU
      (MS-JEM-12.178).

74.   *   S *As By the Streams of Babylon*; 4/4; Slowly; g
          minor; 4 pp.; SATB w/sop. solo; *a cap.*; R; 1:20.
      New York: GSP, 1933; ViHaI, NN(SC).

75.   *   P,S *Wasn't That a Mighty Day?* 4/4; f minor; 11 pp.;
          SATB w/bar. or alto solo; *a cap.*; Bible; 3:08.
      New York: GSP, 1933; NN(SC).

1934

76.   *   S *Juba*; 2/4; F major; 16 pp.; SATB, acc.; Nathaniel
          Dett; Inter-Hi Chorus, Rochester, NY, 1934; 2:45;
          Inter-Hi Chorus, Rochester, NY.
      Chicago: CFS, 1934; NNia (I-23, C-6).

1936

77.   *   S *Rise Up, Shepherd and Follow*; 2/2; *Pastorale sed con moto*; G major; 6 pp.; TTBB w/ten. solo; acc.; Christmas spiritual; 1:45.
New York: JFB, 1936; ViHaI, DHU (MS-JEM-13.185.)

78.   *   S *The Dett Collection of Negro Spirituals*; SATB, solos; acc. and *a cap.*; Negro spirituals; Charlotte Dett.
Chicago: HMC, 1936; OO (M 1670.D4883, v. 1-4, 1982), MB (8057-462), NN(SC), DLC, IU, OU, ViHaI. The + symbol by the following titles indicates their inclusion also in *Negro Spirituals* (1959).

    Vol. I

        Balm in Gilead
     + Daniel Saw the Stone
        Deep River
     + Don't Call the Roll, John
     + Give Me Your Hand
        Go Down Moses
     + Go Tell It on the Mountain
        I Hope My Mother Will Be There
     + I Know the Lord's Laid His Hands on Me
     + I've Done What You Told Me to Do
        I Want to Be Ready
     + Keep Me from Sinking Down
        Lord I Want to Be a Christian
     + Many Thousand Gone
     + Mary and Martha
     + My Brother, I Do Wonder
     + My Way's Cloudy
        Nobody Knows the Trouble I've Seen
     + Oh, I Got a Light
     + Poor Mourner's Got a Home
     + Rise and Shine
     + Room Enough
     + Shine Along

Somebody's Knocking at Your Door Steal
   Away
+ Sweetest Sound I Ever Heard
Swing Low, Sweet Chariot
+ There's a Meeting Here Tonight

Vol. II

Dust, Dust and Ashes
+ I Am Seeking for a City
+ Let the Heaven Light Shine on Me
+ Murm'ring Word
My Lord, What a Morning!
+ Old Ark's a-Movering Along, The
+ Save Me, Lord, Save Me
+ Stay in the Field
+ 'Tis the Old Ship of Zion
We Are Building on a Rock
+ We Are Climing Jacob's Ladder
+ What You Going t' Do When the Lamp
   Burns Down?
+ Winter'll Soon Be Over, The
+ You're Going to Reap Just What You Sow

Vol. III

+ Appolyon and the Pilgrim
+ Better Be Ready
+ Calvary's Mountain
+ Certainly, Lord
+ Down in Hell
+ Father Abraham
I Ain't Going t' Study War No More
+ I Belong to the Union Band
+ In That Beautiful World on High
I've Got Shoes
+ Lord, Until I Reach My Home
+ My Way's Cloudy
Nobody Knows the Trouble I See, Lord
+ Poor Pilgrim
Roll, Jordan Roll (c. 1860)

> Roll, Jordan Roll (Tidewater version)
> + Run to Jesus
> Steal Away
> + We Are Trav'ling to the Grave

Vol. IV

> + Baptism
> By and By
> + Come to Me
> + Communion
> Ev'ry Time I Feel the Spirit
> + Hew 'Round the Tree
> + Ho, Everyone That Thirsts
> + If I Had Died When I Was a Babe
> + Is There Anybody Here?
> Little David, Play on Your Harp
> + O, Holy Savior
> + On That Sabbath Morn
> + Pray on the Way
> Roll, Jordan, Roll

1937

79. *,** P,S *The Ordering of Moses*; 4/4; *Andante assai*; f minor; 123 pp.; SATB w/soli; acc. piano/organ or orch.; Bible, Negro spirituals, Jewish themes; R; May 7, 1937, Cincinnati Festival; 55 min.; George Foster Peabody.
New York: JFB, 1937; CtY (V3 D48 Orl 2), LLafS (M 2023.D4807), NN (MRH), DHU (MS-ABS-32.503), NN(SC), AUMU, IU, CLSU, OO (M 20031D43307, 1970), MB (ML50.D47 07), CSt, RPB, U.

1938

80. *,** S *Now Rest Beneath Night's Shadows*; 4/4; *Lento molto tranquillo*; A flat major; 8 pp.; SSAA, *a cap.*; Paul Gerhardt; 2:45.
New York: JFB, 1938; ViHaI, DHU (MS-JEM-12.183).

81. *,** S *The Lamb*; 2/4; *Larghetto*; e minor, E major; 6 pp.; SSA; *a cap.*; William Blake; 1:30; Davidson Taylor. New York: JFB, 1938; DHU (MS-JEM-12.182).

1940

82. *Hew Down the Tree*; 4/4; *Moderato assai*; c minor; 15 pp.; SSAA w/contr. solo; *a cap.*; Bible; 3:15. Chicago: HMC, 1940; ViHaI.

83. *Ascapezzo*; women's voices; Nathaniel Dett; Bennett Choir, 1940 broadcast; ASCAP. New York: JFB, 1940.

84. *So We'll Go No More A-Roving*; 8 pp.; SSAA *a cap.*; Lord (George Gordon) Byron. New York: JFB, 1940.

1941

85. *Ask For the Old Paths*; 12 pp.; SATB w/ten. solo; *a cap.*; book of Jeremiah. New York: MMI, 1941; MB (M 2092.4 D48 C45).

86. *Heavenly Union*; 13 pp.; SATB w/bar. solo; *a cap.*; Negro spiritual. New York: MMI, 1941; MB (M 2092.4 D48 C45).

87. *When I Survey the Wondrous Cross*; 12 pp.; SSAA; *a cap.*; Isaac Watts; Pfeiffer Chapel at Bennett College, 1941; Annie Merner Pfeiffer Chapel (Bennett). New York: MMI, 1941; MB (M 2092.4 D48C45), NN(SC).

88. *City of God*; 12 pp.; SATB; acc. piano/organ; Samuel Johnson. New York: JFB, 1941.

1959

89.   *Negro Spirituals;* 79 pp.; SATB, solos, anthems.
London: BP, 1959 (edited reprint of *The Dett Collection of Negro Spirituals,* 1936). CtY (V3 D48 959), CArcHT, CLobS, CNoS, CSjU, CL, ILinL, InFw, KyLoS, MFmT, MLC, MiD, MnDuStS, MoJoM, MoS, MsCleD, NcD, NCortU, NAuC, OCl, OrPMB, PPi, PAnL, PP, RPB, TxFTC, WSU. See entry no. 78, 1936, for separate titles marked by +.

DISCOGRAPHY

Recordings of Dett's works are fairly substantial in number, though most are not readily available today. Unfortunately, complete citations are lacking. For instance, news items reported that the Pathé Talking Picture Company in Paris recorded the Hampton Choir in 1930, but no specific selections were named.

More explicit, however, the *Norfolk Journal and Guide*, November 21, 1970, reported the Hampton Choir's recording of some Dett pieces shortly before they toured Scandinavia that fall. Titled "Music by Dett and [Roland] Carter," the first in a series of Afro-American Recordings, it included *Let Us Cheer the Weary Traveler, O Holy Lord, I'll Never Turn Back No More* (Toni Shaw, soloist), *Don't You Weep No More, Mary, Listen to the Lambs* (Edward Whitting, soloist), and *Go Down Moses* from *The Ordering of Moses* (Eugene Harper, organist).

Recordings of piano works by Clive Lythgoe in 1976 and Denver Oldham in 1988 received reviews. Britisher Lythgoe's *In the Bottoms* was said by *American Record Guide*, November, 1976, to be "played a bit too preciously to achieve maximum charm" (p. 23). Lythgoe's own jacket notes for the Philips label LP reveal that he was originally trained as a singer. His piano debut in London at Wigmore Hall impressed Dame Myra Hess, who commented: "Magnificent technically . . . the grasp and colour of his work are outstanding." Shortly afterwards he debuted with the BBC Symphony Orchestra as soloist in Sir Arthur Bliss' piano concerto. Extensive touring in Europe and North America followed, and his popularity increased with a long running series for British radio and television.

Even more publicity was given Oldham's 1988 CD for New World Records (NW367-2), perhaps because it included not only *In the Bottoms*, but *Magnolia* and *Eight Bible Vignettes* as well. Its jacket notes by Dominique-René DeLerma include concise biographical sketches of Dett and Oldham, plus selected Dett discography and bibliography. Reviews were carried in *EAR* (May 1989), *High Fidelity* (July 1989), *American Music* (Winter 1989), and the *Cleveland Plain Dealer* (December 11, 1988). The latter called pianist Oldham the champion of "a number of neglected American composers [who] plays Dett's pieces fluently and with stylistic understanding." Continuing, the reviewer said:

> This recording of a goodly sampling of Dett's piano music . . . does the composer a real service. It shows that . . . he was thoroughly familiar with the piano as an instrument, writing for it with considerable brilliance and stylistic variety.

* * *

Adagio Cantabile (from *Cinnamon Grove*). Victor 17912 B in set M-764, 1941. Jeanne Behrend, piano.

As By the Streams of Babylon. Nelson Cornell Custom Records. Hampton Institute Choir.

Balm in Gilead. Period SPL-580, c. 1950. Inez Matthews, mezzo, Jonathan Price, piano.

The Chariot Jubilee. Audio House AHS 30F75, 1975. Morgan State University Choir w/Nathan Carter, cond.

Done Paid My Vow. Richmond Sound Stages SWO-626, c. 1970. Virginia Union University Choir, Odell Hobbs, cond.

Eight Bible Vignettes. New World Records 367-1 & 2, CD, 1988. Denver Oldham, piano.

Ev'rytime I Feel the Spirit. Library of Congress, LCM 2141 (CD from 1940 perf., 1990). Dorothy Maynor, soprano, Arpad Sandor, piano.

Follow Me. Victor 6472 B, c. 1919-1920. Reinald Werrenrath, baritone.

Go Tell It on the Mountain. RCA Camden CAL-344, c. 1950. Dorothy Maynor, soprano w/male chorus.

I Couldn't Hear Nobody Pray. Victor 2208 A in Album M879; Reissue RCA Camden CAL344, c. 1950.

I'm A-Trav'lin' to the Grave. London LPS-182, c. 1950. Ellabelle Davis, soprano, Hubert Greenslade, piano.

I'm Goin' to Tell God All My Troubles. Library of Congress, LCM 2141 (CD from 1940 perf., 1990). Dorothy Maynor, soprano, Arpad Sandor, piano.

I'm So Glad That Trouble Don't Last Alway. Smithsonian Collection of Recordings RD 041 (CD c. 1990 made from rec. between 1939 and 1965). "The Art of Roland Hayes." Roland Hayes, tenor, Reginald Boardman, piano.

I'm So Glad That Trouble Don't Last Alway. Columbia 128 D. Carroll Clark, baritone.

I'm So Glad That Trouble Don't Last Alway. Paramount 12040 A. Madam Fairfax-Hurd, mezzo.

I'm So Glad That Trouble Don't Last Alway. Black Swan 7106 B. Hattie King Reavis, soprano, w/orch.

In the Bottoms. New World Records 367-1 & 2, CD, 1988. Denver Oldham, piano.

In the Bottoms. Philips DeLuxe 9500-096, 1976. Clive Lythgoe, piano.

In the Bottoms. Desto 7102/3, 1970. Natalie Hinderas, piano.

Juba. Duo-Art Piano Roll 6339, c. 1920. Percy Grainger, piano. Grainger also recorded *Juba* on Columbia A6145 (Columbia Gramophone, matrix no. 49749-2), 1920; Decca 24159 B (matrix no. 73059) in Album A586, 1945.

Juba. RCA Victor 45-5023 in Album E76. Ardon Cornwell, piano.

Juba. Roycroft 170. Gruen Roycroft, piano.

Juba. University of Washington Press OLY-104, 1976. Victor Steinhardt, piano.

Juba. Musical Heritage Society MHS 3808, 1978. "The Piano in America." David Dubal, piano.

Juba. Vocalion 21001. David Pezetski, piano.

Juba. Recorded in Paris. Maurice Dumesnil, piano.

Juba. Victor 21750, pre-1948. Victor Orchestra, Rosario Bourdon, cond. Music Sound Books 78024, pre-1955, reissued by MGM E-3195 (1955). Hamburg Philharmonia, Hans-Jurgen Walther, cond.

Listen to the Lambs. Columbia 73019D, reissue Columbia ML-2119, 1950. De Paur Infantry Chorus, Leonard DePaur, cond.

Listen to the Lambs. Columbia ML-5048, 1955 and ML-6235/MS-6835, 1966; Philips NBL-5012 and Philips N-02125L, both pre-1956. Mormon Tabernacle Choir w/Philadelphia Orch., Richard P. Condie, cond.

Magnolia. Autograph, QRS (4-roll set). R. Nathaniel Dett, piano.

Magnolia. New World Records 367, 1 & 2, 1988. Denver Oldham, piano.

My Day. Library of Congress, LCM 2141 (CD made from 1940 perf.). Dorothy Maynor, soprano, Arpad Sandor, piano.

The Ordering of Moses. Eastman Festival of American Music, 1960. Eastman Singers, David Fetler, cond.

The Ordering of Moses. Silver Crest TAL-42868-S, 1968. Talladega College Choir, William Dawson, cond. w/Mobile Symphony Orch. and soloists Jeanette Walters, Carol Brice,

John Miles, John Work IV.

The Ordering of Moses. Voice of America, 1951, from perf. in Carnegie Hall by Nat'l Negro Opera Company.

Poor Me. RCA Victor 10-1278A. Marian Anderson, contralto, Franz Rupp, piano.

Prelude (Night). Decca 24195A, Album A586, c. 1945, reissued on Gustafson Piano Library Tape, GPL 102. Percy Grainger, piano.

Ride On, Jesus. BRC Productions, 1986. Veronica Tyler, soprano, Charles Lloyd, piano.

Rise Up, Shepherd An' Foller. Victor 2210A in Album M879. Dorothy Maynor, soprano w/unacc. male choir.

Somebody's Knockin' at Your Door. Paramount 12040B. Madam Fairfax-Hurd, contralto.

Steal Away to Jesus. Victor 2211A in Album M879. Dorothy Maynor, soprano w/unacc. male choir.

Were You There When They Crucified My Lord?. Victor 2208B in Album M879, reissued by RCA Camden CAL344. Dorothy Maynor, soprano w/unacc. male choir.

END PAPERS
Endnotes by Chapters
Appendix
Bibliography
Index

END PAPERS

ENDNOTES BY CHAPTERS

Chapter I

1. Philanthropist Levi Coffin (1798-1877), a native of North Carolina who spent many years in Cincinnati and other parts of Ohio, was the initial leader of the Underground Railroad. Among others his work was carried on by Harriet Tubman (1821-1913), a fugitive slave from Maryland, who in her colorful career was writer, abolitionist, nurse, spy, reformer, and one of the first black women to receive recognition for her efforts. The likelihood that Dett was descended from slaves who came to Ontario via the Underground Railroad as early as the 1830s is also suggested by Gloster B. Current in "National Association of Negro Musicians, Inc., Salutes Nathaniel Dett's 100th Birthday," *The Crisis*, Vol. 90, No. 2 (February 1983), p. 18.

2. Letter from Millie Willson to Anne Simpson, July 4, 1991; William B. Hamilton, *The Macmillan Book of Canada* (Toronto: Macmillan of Canada, 1978), p. 191.

3. *Virginia Pilot and Norfolk Landmark*, September 21, 1919. In this interview Dett also spoke of the poverty years suffered by his family.

4. Hamilton B. Mizer, *A City Is Born: Niagara Falls, A City Matures: A Topical History 1892-1932*, No. 24 (Lockport, NY: The Niagara County Historical Society, 1981), p. 136. *Niagara Falls* (N Y) *Gazette*, July 18, 1918. Phillis Wheatley (born c. 1753) came by ship from Africa to Boston, Massachusetts, in 1761, bought in that city by a prominent merchant, John Wheatley. Her duties were to assist Mr. Wheatley's wife. The Wheatley family, whose name Phillis took, realized that she was intelligent and tutored her well. Her first volume of poetry, *Poems on Various Subjects Religious and Moral*, was published in London in 1773. Publication of other poems and some of her letters followed. She died in 1784. Julian D. Mason, Jr. ed.,

The Poems of Phillis Wheatley (Chapel Hill: The University of North Carolina Press, 1989), pp. 2-3.

5. Vivian Flagg McBrier, *R. Nathaniel Dett His Life and Works 1882-1943* (Washington, D.C.: The Associated Publishers, 1977), pp. 1-3. McBrier's work has been invaluable in preparing this study. Dr. McBrier, (Mrs. Clayton McBrier), a former piano student of Dett's and a member of his Hampton Choir, was born in Lynchburg, Virginia. She received B. S. degrees in Elementary Education and Music from Virginia State College in 1937, the Master of Arts in Music from Columbia University in 1941, and the Ph. D. in Musicology from the Catholic University of America in 1967. As a lecturer and professor she is well known in the public schools of Lynchburg, as well as at Howard and Columbia Universities. To her credit are several published articles. In 1963 she was awarded the Meyer Fellowship for Superior Service in the District of Columbia Schools, and she received an Achievement Award from Alpha Kappa Alpha. Dr. McBrier was choir director and at one time chairman of the Division of Fine Arts at the District of Columbia Teachers College. She has been a professional lecturer at the Howard University School of Religion. She continues to teach piano in Washington, D.C.

6. Undated, unnamed news item in Dett Collection, Local History Department, Niagara Falls, New York, Public Library, hereinafter cited as Dett Collection, NFNYPL.

7. Donald E. Loker, Local History Specialist at the NFNYPL gave this information in letters to Anne Simpson, June 24 and July 11, 1991. Most biographical material on the Dett family erroneously states that Robert Tue Dett operated a tourist home in Niagara Falls, New York.

8. McBrier, *R. Nathaniel Dett*, p. 3.

9. Letter dated October 15, 1991, from Mrs. Mildred Clark to Anne Simpson.

10. R. Nathaniel Dett, "From Bell Stand to Throne Room," *The*

Etude, Vol. LII, No. 2 (February 1934), p. 79.

11.   Deterioration of the August 30, 1898 *Cataract* item, prevented reading details of this art work. Item was found in "Papers and Documents Pertaining to the Life and Work of Dr. Robert Nathaniel Dett," microfilmed by Monroe Fordham, State University College at Buffalo, and Frank B. Mesiah, at that time Director of the Black American Museum and Cultural Center, Niagara Falls, New York, 1974. The collection, donated by Samuel Dett, is in eight folders, unpaginated, often unreadable, and not necessarily in chronological order. These documents will hereinafter be cited as Mesiah Papers and Documents or Mesiah Collection.

12.   Dett, "From Bell Stand to Throne Room," p. 79.

13.   *Ibid.*

14.   *Ibid.*, p. 80. Dett graduated from the Niagara Falls Collegiate Institute on October 31, 1901.

15.   Marjorie F. Williams, *The First Presbyterian Church of Niagara Falls, 150 Years 1824-1974* (Niagara Falls, N Y: First Presbyterian Church, 1974), pp. 16, 22-23.

16.   Dett, "From Bell Stand to Throne Room," p. 79. The Cataract House, as it was first named, was built in 1825. It hosted many of the city's social and cultural events, and dating from 1829 its register included such famous guests as Abraham Lincoln, Grover Cleveland, Franklin D. Roosevelt, King Edward VII, and King George V. In 1945 the Cataract burned. Mizer, *A City Is Born Niagara Falls,* pp. 89-90.

17.   Dett, "From Bell Stand to Throne Room," p. 80. It is not too surprising that Dr. Hoppe's name was not found in an examination of seven biographies of Dvorak.

18.   Quoted in May Stanley, "R. N. Dett of Hampton Institute, Helping to Lay Foundation for Negro Music of Future," from *Musical America*, Vol. XXVIII, No. 4 (July 6, 1918), p. 17.

19. An unnamed news item found in the Dett Collection, NFNYPL stated that Robert Dett purchased and became the proprietor of another Niagara Falls establishment, the Hotel Atlantique, in 1906.

20. Program in Dett Collection, NFNYPL.

21. Paul Gromosiak, *Niagara Falls, Answers to the 100 Most Common Questions about Niagara Falls* (Buffalo, NY: Meyer Enterprises, 1990), pp. 30-31.

22. The diaries are in Folder 2 of the Mesiah Collection.

23. Halstead's letter is in the Dett Collection, NFNYPL. A program in the same collection from the Halstead Conservatory's 1916-1917 graduades indicates that Dett's compositions were still popular there. Several of them were played on the Conservatory's nineteenth commencement, June 26-30, 1917.

24. *Course Catalog* from Oberlin College, 1987-1988, p. 1.

25. Dett later dedicated the poem "Oh Whisp'ring Tree" in *The Album of a Heart* (1911) to Mrs. F. H. Goff of Granville, Ohio, and a piano composition to Mr. Goff.

26. McBrier, *R. Nathaniel Dett*, p. 9. Dett taught piano in his own studio in Oberlin between 1904 and 1908, a statement made in a job application form he filled out after graduation in 1908. This document is in the Dett Collection, NFNYPL.

27. Program in Dett Collection, NFNYPL. The *Niagara Falls Gazette*, October 12, 1904, called it "one of the most enjoyable musical entertainments ever given in this city."

28. Dett, "From Bell Stand to Throne Room," p. 80. More information on Dett's professors at Oberlin will be given in Chapter VI.

29. *Ibid.* A short, unpublished biographical sketch on Dett by

Constance H. Marteena states that Frampton was formerly at Iowa State Teachers' College. On some occasion Frampton had heard Dett play, was impressed, and wanted to help in arranging his entering Oberlin.

30. From *Oberlin College Catalog,* 1906, p. 209, courtesy of Oberlin College Archives.

31. One of Dett's successors as choir director at Mt. Zion Baptist, Dr. Nathaniel Gatlin, was proud of his own insight into Dett and his rapport with choir members and Oberlin's townspeople. Dr. Gatlin delivered a eulogy at Bennett College shortly after Dett's death. It will be included in Chapter V.

32. Dett, "From Bell Stand to Throne Room," p. 80. In this essay no date was specified for the Kneisel Quartet's performance.

33. Adolph Schulz-Evler (1852-1905), Polish pianist and composer, is now almost forgotten, though was very popular around the turn of the century for his brilliant, showy piano pieces which he used mainly in his own performances. His transcription of Strauss' "Blue Danube Waltz," a display piece said to have little musicality, was often used for an encore.

34. McBrier, *R. Nathaniel Dett,* pp. 10-12. McBrier did not specify the winning compositions.

35. Program in Mesiah Papers and Documents, Folder 1.

36. *Ibid.,* Folder 3. The Niagara Falls Public Library has Dett's undated blue book from Oberlin Conservatory for a History of Music exam, and a dim manuscript of Dett's "Fugue," a short piano piece on "a theme of Schreck," dated August 3, 1906. Not difficult to execute for a pianist, except for bringing out the inner voices, the e minor fugue divides its activity between right and left hands as if they were conversing. It ends on an E major chord. The "Fugue" was likely written as an exercise in composition. The name Schreck might have been intended as Franz Schrecker

(1878-1934).

37. Material courtesy of Oberlin College Archives. Mr. Hall was not identified further. On this same questionnaire Dett listed the University of Pennsylvania as one of the other colleges he had attended, but gave no dates or other particulars. It is possible that he audited a course and was not actually registered at the University. A letter dated October 8, 1991, from Gail M. Pietrzyk, University of Pennsylvania Public Services Archivist, to Anne Simpson stated: "I have double-checked all of our resources for information about R. N. Dett. I have still found no indication that Dett was a student at the University."

38. Documents found in Dett Collection, NFNYPL.

39. McBrier, R. Nathaniel Dett, p. 28. *Rosemaiden*, composed in 1870, was one of Britisher Cowen's nine cantatas. Also to his credit are four operas, three oratorios, six symphonies, and numerous chamber works. *Rosemaiden* is a fanciful tale of the Queen of the Flower Fairies who yearns for love and excitement. When she is transformed by Spring into Roseblossom, she falls in love with a forester, marries him, and experiences true love, but is later emotionally unable to deal with his death. The elves bewail the fate of their former Queen, cursing love as fatal to lasting peace and happiness.

40. Anna L. Cooke, *Lane College: Its Heritage and Outreach 1882-1982* (Jackson, TN: Lane College, 1987), p. 24.

41. McBrier, *R. Nathaniel Dett*, p. 14.

42. *The Album of a Heart*, originally bound in vibrant green suede with gold lettering, will be discussed further in the Appendix.

43. McBrier, *R. Nathaniel Dett*, p. 17.

44. *Ibid.*

45. *Ibid.*, p. 23.

46. Dett, "From Bell Stand to Throne Room," p. 80. Mme Hackley's influence on and generosity toward Dett will be discussed more fully in Chapter VI.

47. Anne K. Simpson, *Hard Trials: The Life and Music of Harry T. Burleigh* (Metuchen, N J: Scarecrow Press, Inc., 1990), p. 426 n9. Unfortunately, Mrs. Marshall's birth date is incorrect in Simpson's *Hard Trials*. She was born in 1869.

48. Letter from the Washington Conservatory of Music Records, courtesy of Moorland-Spingarn Research Center, Howard University.

49. *Ibid.*

Chapter II

1. Quoted in McBrier, *R. Nathaniel Dett*, pp. 25-26, from Helen L. Ludlow, *Samuel C. Armstrong, Education for Life* (Hampton, VA: Hampton Normal and Agricultural Institute Press, 1913), p. 12.

2. *The Crisis*, Vol. V, No. 5 (March 1913), p. 219. Mme Hackley, as a professional singer, lecturer, and teacher, had studied with Jean and Edouard de Reszke in Paris. Chapter VI will include a further discussion of Mme Hackley.

3. Dett, "From Bell Stand to Throne Room," p. 80.

4. *Ibid.*

5. Newspaper review in John Lovell, Jr., *Black Song: The Forge and the Flame* (New York: The Macmillan Company, 1972), p. 408.

6. Adolph K. Placzek, ed., *Macmillan Encyclopedia of Architects*, Vol. 2 (The Free Press: New York, 1982), pp. 436-437. To architect Hunt's credit are the Tribune Building in New York City, many other public buildings and libraries in some of the larger U. S. cities, and the

Biltmore Mansion in Asheville, North Carolina. He is said to be the most important figure in the development of architectural professionalism in the United States during the nineteenth century.

7. Eileen Southern lists Fenner's seventeen singers, all but four of whom had been slaves: James R. Bailey, William G. Catus, Sallie Davis, Alice Ferribee, Rachel Elliot, James C. Dungey, Robert Hamilton, John Holt, Hutchins Inge, Lucy Leary, Maria Mallette, Joseph Mebane, Mary Norwood, Carrie Thomas, J. B. Towe (one of the tenors who was both shout leader and improvisator), James M. Waddy, and Whit Williams. Eileen Southern, *Biographical Dictionary of Afro-American and African Musicians* (Westport, CT: Greenwood Press, 1982), p. 163.

8. Lovell, *Black Song*, p. 408.

9. Alice Mabel Bacon, "Works and Methods of the Hampton Folklore Society, *The Black Perspective in Music*, Vol. 4, No. 2 (July 1976, Special Issue), p. 154.

10. John Wesley Work, *Folk Song of the American Negro* (New York: Negro Universities Press, 1969, reprinted from 1915, ed.), p. 95.

11. *Ibid.* When Moton (1867-1940) was a senior at Hampton in 1889 he became assistant commander in charge of the male student cadet corps. "Major" was the name given him in 1891 when he was appointed Commandant, a position held until 1915. That year marked the death of Booker T. Washington of Tuskegee Institute, and also Moton's move from Hampton to become principal at Tuskegee for the following twenty years. In essence, Moton assumed Washington's role as a racial leader, having worked closely with him when they toured the United States. Correspondence as late as 1931 between Moton and Dett, located in the Dett Collection, NFNYPL, indicates that relations stayed quite cordial between the two after Moton went to Tuskegee, and during Dett's dismissal crisis at Hampton.

12.   Miles Mark Fisher, *Negro Slave Songs in the United States* (New York: The Citadel Press, 1969), p. 24.

13.   *The Crisis*, Vol. 7, No. 2 (December 1913), p. 61.

14.   *Musical America*, December 29, 1913, p. 12.

15.   McBrier, *R. Nathaniel Dett*, p. 27.

16.   Placzek, *Macmillan Encyclopedia of Architects*, Vol. I, p. 364.

17.   *The Crisis*, Vol. 7, No. 4 (February 1914), p. 61.

18.   Letter courtesy of Moorland-Spingarn Research Center, Howard University.

19.   *The Crisis*, Vol. 7, No. 6 (April 1914), pp. 268-269. Parts of reviews of the concert in *Musical America, New York Evening Post*, and *New York Evening Journal* were given in *The Crisis*. The *New York Times*, March 12, 1914, called it "an interesting concert and one calculated to stimulate the imagination." Jon Michael Spencer, "The Writings of Robert Nathaniel Dett and William Grant Still on Black Music," (St. Louis, MO: Ph. D. Dissertation, Washington University, 1982). The Editor, "Black Concerts in Carnegie Hall, 1912-1915," *The Black Perspective in Music*, Vol. 6, No. 1 (Spring 1978), p. 86.

20.   Letter courtesy of Moorland-Spingarn Research Center, Howard University.

21.   "Musical," *The Hampton Student*, Vol. 5, No. 4 (May 1, 1914), pp. 4-5.

22.   "Entertainments," *The Southern Workman*, Vol. 43, No. 7 (July 1914), pp. 420-421.

23.   McBrier, *R. Nathaniel Dett*, p. 29.

24.   Dominique-René DeLerma and Vivian Flagg McBrier, *The Collected Piano Works of R. Nathaniel Dett* (Evanston, IL:

Summy-Birchard Company, 1973), p. v. Southern, *Biographical Dictionary*, p. 158, states that Hackney produced two more successful All Colored Composers' Concerts before their discontinuance in 1916, due to World War I involvement.

25. *Musical America*, June 20, 1914, p. 24.

26. These undated news items were found in the Hampton University Archives.

27. *Musical Courier*, Vol. LXIX, No. 23 (December 9, 1914), p. 32.

28. *Herald* item quoted in *The Crisis*, Vol. 9, No. 3 (January 1915), p. 112.

29. Program included in McBrier, *R. Nathaniel Dett*, p. 101.

30. "A Visit to Happy Town," *Musical Courier*, Vol. LXX, No. 4 (January 27, 1915), p. 8. Three photos accompanied the *Courier* article, showing Hampton's Mansion House where Ware was entertained, the "boys" of the chorus, and Dett with Ware, Miss Drew, the vocal teacher, and President Frissell's wife.

31. *Ibid*.

32. *Ibid*.

33. Spencer, "The Writings of Dett and Still," pp. 151-152.

34. "Hampton's Anniversary," *The Southern Workman*, Vol. XLIV, No. 6 (June 1915), pp. 356-363. There is no evidence that these particular arrangements by Dett were published.

35. Application form, courtesy of Oberlin College Archives. The town of Phoebus, now a part of the Hampton Roads area, was named for Harrison Phoebus, a railroad and hotel magnate. Phoebus' huge home on the sea, built around the turn of the century, later burned. Dett's choir

often sang in Phoebus. Though the year was not specified, Dett was also made an honorary member of the Shakespeare Dramatic Club at Hampton, according to his own statement in an update for Oberlin College, c.1924.

36. The Editor, "Black Concerts in Carnegie Hall, 1913-1915," p. 86. *Musical America*, Vol. XXI, No. 24 (April 12, 1915), p. 41.

37. *Musical Courier*, Vol. LXX, No. 22 (May 19, 1915), p. 37.

38. Letter from Dett to Curtis in McBrier, *R. Nathaniel Dett*, pp. 39-40. More will be said of Curtis-Burlin in Chapter VI. The "Negro violin air" was possibly Dett's "Ramah," not published until 1923 by the Boston Music Company.

39. Glenn Dillard Gunn (1874-1963) American pianist and music critic, studied piano at the Leipzig Conservatory with Carl Reinecke, and later concertized in Germany. He returned to the United States in 1900 and taught at Chicago Musical College from 1901-1905. In 1915 he founded the American Symphony Orchestra of Chicago, whose aim was to perform American works with American soloists. Gunn was music critic for the *Chicago Tribune* (1910-1914), the *Chicago Herald Examiner* (1922-1926), and in 1940 for the *Washington Times Herald*. His publications include *A Course of Lessons on the History and Esthetics of Music* (1912) and *Music, Its History and Enjoyment* (1930).

40. *The Crisis*, Vol. 11, No. 2 (December 1915), p. 58.

41. *The Crisis*, Vol. 11, No. 3 (January 1916), p. 119.

42. *Musical Courier*, Vol. XXII, No. 18 (May 4, 1916), p. 38.

43. *The Crisis*, Vol. 12, No. 4 (August 1916), pp. 190-191.

44. *The Crisis*, Vol. 12, No. 6 (October 1916), p. 181.

45. McBrier, *R. Nathaniel Dett*, pp. 40-42.

46. Letter in Dett Collection, NFNYPL.

47. McBrier, R. *Nathaniel Dett*, p. 31. Maud Cuney-Hare, *Negro Musicians and Their Music*, p. 336, indicates that Helen Elise Smith was on the Hampton faculty at the time of her marriage.

48. McBrier, R. *Nathaniel Dett*, p. 33.

49. May Stanley, "R. N. Dett of Hampton Institute, Helping to Lay Foundation for Negro Music of Future," *The Black Perspective in Music*, Vol. 1, No. 1 (Spring 1973), pp. 65-72. Stanley gives no specific date for the Elgar Choir Concert but the *Hamilton* (Ontario) *Herald* reviewed the concert on October 6, 1916. On the concert, featuring Percy Grainger as soloist, Dett's "Listen to the Lambs" was also performed. The reviewer said that this work was "the most strikingly impressive piece of the evening." In years following the Elgar Choir frequently programmed Dett's works.

50. Stanley, "R. N. Dett of Hampton Institute," pp. 65-72.

51. *The Crisis*, Vol. 13, No. 5 (March 1917), p. 242, gave no date for the recent Ithaca concert.

52. *The Crisis*, Vol. 14, No. 3 (July 1917), p. 141. No specific date was given for the *Elijah* performance.

53. *The Crisis*, Vol. 15, No. 1 (November 1917), pp. 10-12.

54. *Musical Courier*, Vol. LXXXVI, No. 24 (June 13, 1918), p. 48.

55. McBrier, R. *Nathaniel Dett*, pp. 42-43.

56. *The Crisis*, Vol. 17, No. 1 (November 1918), p. 32.

57. *The Southern Workman*, (December 1918), p. 606.

58. Verna Arvey, *In One Lifetime* (Fayetteville, AR: University of Arkansas Press, 1984), p. 53.

59. Letter to Anne Simpson from Judith Still, June 21, 1991.

60. Letter to Anne Simpson from Judith Still, June 10,1991.

61. Marguerite Pope, "A Brief Biography of Dr. Robert Nathaniel Dett," unpublished, courtesy of Bennett College. The *Norfolk Journal and Guide,* March 31,1923, quoted Alexander Koshetz, conductor of the Ukrainian National Chorus, on Dett: "This Negro composer's work is colossal in its significance of the cultural possibilities of Negroes. On my return to Ukrainia I shall put Professor Dett's compositions on my program and have my students study and interpret Negro music."

62. When Dett's oratorio, *The Ordering of Moses,* was performed in St. Louis, November 26, 1943, Grant, bass-baritone, sang the "Voice of God" role. Program courtesy of Oberlin College Archives.

63. Southern, *Biographical Dictionary,* p. 286, gives a complete list of the NANM presidents up to 1981.

64. *Ibid.*

65. *The Crisis,* Vol. 17, No. 5 (March 1919), p. 24; Vol. 19, No. 1 (November 1919), p. 341. Eddy was an excellent performer on both piano and organ. The November *Crisis* item was erroneous in stating that the arrangement of "Mammy" was Dett's rather than Gordon Balch Nevin's, one published in 1918 by Clayton F. Summy.

66. Miss Drew's report for 1919 is in the Hampton University Archives.

Chapter III

1. Letters dated September 27, October 8 and 12, 1919, and Dr. Davison's letter are in the Hampton University Archives.

2. Letter from Robin McElheny, Assistant Curator for University and Public Service, Harvard University Archives, to Anne Simpson, July 24, 1991. Dett himself had not mentioned a composition professor at Harvard with

whom he studied.

3. Walter Raymond Spalding, *Music at Harvard, A Historical View of Men and Events* (New York: Coward-McCann, Inc., 1935), p. 125. More will be said of Foote in Chapter VI.

4. Samuel Eliot Morison, *Three Centuries of Harvard 1636-1936* (Cambridge, MA: Harvard University Press, 1937), pp. 168, 229.

5. These specific guidelines for Bowdoin Prizes are given in the bulletin *Harvard University Prizes (1982-83)*, courtesy of Harvard University Archives.

6. News item from the Boston *Post-Gazette*, April 27, 1904; a partial list of Boott winners and their compositions has been available, courtesy of Harvard University Archives.

7. *Cambridge Chronicle*, March 5, 1904. Information on Frank Duveneck supplied by Dr. William C. Loring, Bethesda, Maryland.

8. Spalding, *Music at Harvard*, pp. 197-198.

9. Bulletin, *Harvard University Prizes (1982-83)*, pp. 18-19.

10. Despite the fact that "Chariot Jubilee" was commissioned by the Syracuse University Chorus, though not performed in that city until 1921, the work's premiere in 1920 by the St. Cecilia Society of Boston has not been explained. The all-white St. Cecilia Society of Boston was one of several so named in other cities. The earliest St. Cecilia Society was founded in Charleston, South Carolina, in 1762, under Catholic auspices. The Boston group came about in 1874 by patronage of Harvard University. Without a specific date of the performance it was, however, mentioned in *The Southern Workman*, Vol. XLIX (July 1920), p. 332, according to McBrier, *R. Nathniel Dett*, p. 43.

11. Erb was at the time Director of the School of Music at the University of Illinois. Besides his several publications in

the fields of harmony, theory, and music appreciation, he edited *Songs for the Assembly* (1931) and composed for solo voice, choir, piano, organ, and music for pageants.

12. *The American Musician,* Vol. 21, No. 11 (December 1919), p. 4.

13. *The Crisis,* Vol. 19, No. 4 (February 1920), p. 210.

14. Letter courtesy of Moorland-Spingarn Research Center, Howard University.

15. *The Crisis,* Vol. 21, No. 2 (December 1920), p. 78.

16. Date was omitted from program in *The Hampton Student,* May 15, 1921, p. 18.

17. *The Hampton Student,* May 15, 1921, p. 19.

18. Telegram courtesy of Moorland-Spingarn Research Center, Howard University.

19. Letter courtesy of Moorland-Spingarn Research Center, Howard University.

20. Item courtesy of Detroit Public Library, "Nathaniel Dett Honored at Syracuse," *Negro Musician,* June 1921, n. p.

21. *Buffalo Evening News,* October 3, 1921.

22. Letter from Mrs. Duveneck to Anne Simpson, August 7, 1991. "The baby" was more likely Josephine Elizabeth, the Detts' second born, as Helen would have been three at that time.

23. McBrier, *R. Nathaniel Dett,* p. 48. Dett's "program" for the four movements, titled "Incantation," "Song of the Shrine," "Dance of Desire," and "Beyond the Dream," is idyllic, mysterious, fanciful, and sensuous, ending with the phrase "like smoke from smoldering incense, the still unsatisfied longing for the unattainable." Full text of the program will be included in Part II with Dett's piano

works.

24. *The Crisis*, Vol. 23, No. 6 (April 1922), p. 272.

25. McBrier, *R. Nathaniel Dett*, pp. 49-50.

26. *Ibid.*, p. 50.

27. *Chicago Crusader*, April 25, 1982.

28. Document in Hampton University Archives.

29. Letter courtesy of Moorland-Spingarn Research Center, Howard University.

30. Material on Jesse Edward Moorland courtesy of Moorland-Spingarn Research Center, Howard University.

31. *The Southern Workman*, Vol. LII, No. 4 (April 1923) p. 197.

32. Review quoted in DeLerma and McBrier, *Collected Piano Music*, p. ix.

33. *The Southern Workman*, Vol. LII, No. 6 (June 1923), p. 295.

34. *Ibid.*, p. 299.

35. *Atlanta* (Georgia) *Independent*, December 6, 1923.

36. Letter in Hampton University Archives.

37. Musical Art Society program courtesy of Grainger Museum, Melbourne, Australia. The program stated that Grainger was with the Columbia Artist agency, and that the Columbia Music Shop in Newport News carried a complete stock of his records; Brooklyn program included in Chapter VI, courtesy of Grainger Museum, Melbourne, Australia.

38. *The Southern Workman*, Vol. 53 (March 1924), p. 132.

39. *Ibid.*

40. *The Southern Workman*, Vol. 53 (April 1924), p. 189.

41. *St. Paul Pioneer Press*, February 19, 1924.

42. *The Southern Workman*, Vol. 53 (April 1924), p. 189.

43. *Ibid.*

44. *Ibid.*

45. *Ibid.*, p. 190.

46. *Dayton* (Ohio) *News*, April 10, 1924.

47. Simpson, *Hard Trials*, p. 102.

48. Flyer courtesy of Local History Department, Niagara Falls, New York, Public Library. Further details of this event from an item contained in the Mesiah Collection were not readable.

49. *New York Age*, August 9, 1924.

50. Letter from Dett to Gregg, August 21, 1924, Hampton University Archives.

51. Letter found in Mesiah Papers and Documents.

52. Program for this service is in Dett Collection, NFNYPL.

53. Simpson, *Hard Trials*, pp. 85-86.

54. "At Niagara," from Dett's *The Album of a Heart*, was included in the first edition of Robert Kerlin's *Negro Poets and Their Poems* (1923), and in two subsequent editions. Dett's poem in James Weldon Johnson's *The Book of Negro Poetry* is titled "The Rubinstein Staccato Etude," included in full in the Appendix. Dett's letter to Spingarn courtesy of Moorland-Spingarn Research Center, Arthur B. Spingarn Papers, Howard University.

55. Letter in Dett Collection, NFNYPL.

56. *Buffalo Express*, May 9, 1925.

57. Program in Grainger Museum, University of Melbourne, Australia, and in Dett Collection, NFNYPL. "Gently Lord, Lead Us On" was likely the same choral work as "Gently Lord, Oh Gently Lead Us." More will be said of the May 3 concert in Chapter VI in connection with Percy Grainger.

58. Letter in Hampton University Archives, date incomplete.

59. *The Crisis*, Vol. 30, No. 5 (September 1925), p. 284.

60. Lovell, *Black Song*, p. 544.

61. Unnamed news item in Dett Collection, NFNYPL.

62. *The Crisis*, Vol. 31, No. 2 (December 1925), p. 77.

63. Lee's letter is in the Dett Collection, NFNYPL. The National Memorial Association's purpose, stated on its letterhead, was "To commemorate the heroic deeds of Negro soldiers and sailors who fought in all the wars of our country and the World War." One of its vice-presidents at this time was Mary McLeod Bethune. Its honorary members included a cross section of state officials, ministers, university presidents, and Garnet C. Wilkinson, Assistant Superintendent of Public Schools in Washington, D.C.

64. Lane's favorable opinion of Hampton was made clear in a letter to Dett several months earlier, dated March 23, 1924. He wrote: "Hampton is the white man's best effort in Negro education. . . . It is destined to be America's leading University for Negroes." Both of Lane's letters are in the Dett Collection, NFNYPL.

65. Letter in Dett Collection, NFNYPL.

66. Obituary from Spencer, "The Writings of Robert Nathaniel Dett and William Grant Still," p. 168.

67.   Program in Dett Collection, NFNYPL.

68.   McBrier, *R. Nathaniel Dett*, pp. 92-95.

Chapter IV

1.   Program in Dett Collection, NFNYPL. Though the program did not name the orchestrator, it probably was not Dett, as he rarely felt comfortable in scoring instrumentation.

2.   Unnamed news item in Dett Collection, NFNYPL.

3.   Letter courtesy of Oberlin College Archives.

4.   Citation courtesy of Oberlin College Archives.

5.   Allen B. Doggett, Jr., "Artistic Achievement," *Christian Advocate*, January 20, 1927 (copy with incomplete page citation courtesy of Hampton University Archives). On October 16 Elizabeth Sinkford, Hampton soloist, had shared a recital with Mrs. Dett, sponsored by the Musical Art Society. Both artists performed Dett's compositions as well as those of others, according to McBrier, *R. Nathaniel Dett*, p. 103.

6.   Doggett, "Artistic Achievement," *Christian Advocate*, January 20, 1927.

7.   This item was later carried in the *Newport News Star*, April 29, 1930.

8.   The Engel-Dett correspondence is given in Dominique-René DeLerma, "Dett and Engel, a Question of Cultural Pride," *The Black Perspective in Music*, Vol. 1, No. 1 (Spring 1973), pp. 70-72.

9.   Royalty statement in the Hampton University Archives.

10.   Verna Arvey, *In One Lifetime* (Fayetteville: University of Arkansas Press, 1984), p. 64. De Bose, longtime friend of Still, was later on the faculty at Bethune-Cookman

College (Florida), and chairman of the music departments at both Talladega College (Alabama) and Southern University (Louisiana).

11. *The Crisis*, Vol. 34, No. 3 (May 1927), p. 86.

12. *Louisville* (Kentucky) *Defender*, May 4, 1972. More will be said of this collection of 165 songs in Part II.

13. *The Crisis*, Vol. 34, No. 7 (September 1927), pp. 227-228.

14. George Pullen Jackson, *White and Negro Spirituals* (New York: J. J. Augustin Publishers, 1943), pp. 141-142.

15. *The Crisis*, Vol. 33, No. 4 (February 1927), p. 211. Singers McCormack and Werrenrath had also popularized some of Harry Burleigh's art songs and spirituals.

16. *Christian Science Monitor*, May 21, 1927, n. p.

17. Undated, unnamed news item in Dett Collection, NFNYPL.

18. *New York Age*, September 24, 1927; *Niagara Falls Gazette*, September 13, 1927.

19. Document in Dett Collection, NFNYPL.

20. *The Crisis*, Vol. 34, No. 8 (October 1927), p. 244.

21. Letter from Countee Cullen Papers, Amistad Research Center, Tulane University, New Orleans, Louisiana, used by permission. The Mrs. Deland mentioned in Dett's letter was Mrs. Margaret Wade (Campbell) Deland (1857-1945), novelist, poet, and short story writer. Most of her mature life was spent in Massachusetts. Before her marriage she taught art. She was an avid nature lover and a perfectionist as a writer. Between 1886 and 1941 she produced a novel or volume of short stories every two to three years. Mrs. Deland's visit to the Hampton campus in February of 1922 was reported in *The Southern Workman*, April, 1922. (She had also been at Hampton in the spring of 1920.) Her appearances included the Epitome meeting,

Hampton Chapel services, and some cultural clubs in the city. At each she read from some of her works. At Chapel she emphasized the value of a sound education, such as that offered at Hampton.

22. *The Crisis*, Vol. 34, No. 10 (December 1927), pp. 345-346; Vol. 35, No. 5 (May 1928), p. 159.

23. McBrier, *R. Nathaniel Dett*, p. 55.

24. *The Southern Workman*, Vol. XLVIII (April 1928), pp. 154-158. The Negro Elks Convention in Richmond was in August of 1925.

25. President Gregg's letter and program of the Harmon Award ceremony, courtesy of Dett Collection, NFNYPL; Mrs. Dett's letter courtesy of Hampton University Archives.

26. *The Crisis*, Vol. 35, No. 2 (February 1928), p. 60. Still's receipt of second place must have given Dett mixed feelings, hopefully expelling some of his early bitterness at the younger composer. According to the *New York Herald Tribune*, January 9, 1928, author Benjamin Brawley, a New York school teacher, was given at this time a second place Harmon Award, but refused to accept it, saying that he had always done first class work.

27. Program from Dett Collection, NFNYPL. Rudolph von Charlton, piano soloist for the occasion, will be discussed in Chapter VI.

28. *The Crisis*, Vol. 35, No. 6 (June 1928), p. 199. Programs courtesy of Hampton University Archives. The Lvovsky (spelled Lvosky on the program) piece, published in 1916, was used many times by Dett.

29. Just as Dett used Russian choral music in his concerts, the National Ukrainian Singers and other European choirs touring America in the 1920s programmed spirituals and American folk songs. Dett's "Listen to the Lambs" was one of the more popular ones.

30. *New York Evening Post*, April 17, 1928.

31. *New York Herald-Tribune*, April 17, 1928.

32. *New York Times*, April 17, 1928.

33. *The Southern Workman*, Vol. LVIII, No. 1 (January 1929), p. 46.

34. *The Choir*, Vol. 59 (January 1930), p. 140.

35. *New York Times*, March 5, 1938.

36. *Dictionary Catalog of the George Foster Peabody Collection of Negro Literature and History*, Vol. I (Westport, CT: Greenwood Publishing Company, 1972), Introduction, n. p.

37. *Norfolk Journal and Guide*, January 26, 1929.

38. Date on Henry Wilder Foote's letter to Dett is incomplete. Other letters of praise came from women's clubs and alumni of Hampton and Oberlin.

39. Program in Dett Collection, NFNYPL.

40. *The Crisis*, Vol. 36, No. 7 (July 1929), p. 237.

41. *The Crisis*, Vol. 36, No. 6 (June 1929), p. 201.

42. *Philadelphia Public Ledger*, May 26, 1929.

43. Letter courtesy of Oberlin College Archives. There was no further correspondence available to answer Dett's question. He rightfully may have thought he would be additionally responsible for a speech or a musical performance, either by himself or with the choir.

44. H. Wiley Hitchcock and Stanley Sadie, eds., *The New Grove Dictionary of American Music*, Vol. I (London: Macmillan Press, Limited, 1986), p. 279.

45.   DeLerma and McBrier, *Collected Piano Works*, p. vi.

46.   Margaret Bonds, "A Reminiscence," *The Negro in Music and Art*, ed. Lindsay Patterson (New York: Publishers Co., 1967), pp. 191-192.

47.   Ned Rorem, "In Search of American Opera," *Opera News*, Vol. 56, No. 1 (July 1991), p. 10.

48.   *The Crisis*, Vol. 36, No. 8 (August 1929), pp. 277-278.

49.   *Ibid*.

50.   *The Crisis*, Vol. 36, No. 12 (December 1929), p. 419.

51.   McBrier, *R. Nathaniel Dett*, p. 65.

52.   Letter courtesy of Tuskegee Institute Archives. Among the many announcements of the trip were those found in *Musical Leader* (April 30, 1930), *Richmond* (Virginia) *Newsleader* (April 2, 1930), *New York Times* (January 22, 1930), *Niagara Falls Gazette* (February 8, 1930), *Baltimore American* (March 29, 1930), *Providence* (Rhode Island) *Bulletin* (February 5, 1930), *Baltimore Sun* (March 21, 1930), *Pittsburgh Progress Index* (May 22, 1930), *New York Herald Tribune* (May 21, 1930), and *Christian Science Monitor* (April 24, 1930).

53.   *Musical Courier*, Vol. C, No. 3 (January 18, 1930), pp. 6, 9.

54.   McBrier, *R. Nathaniel Dett*, p. 59.

55.   R. Nathaniel Dett, "From Bell Stand to Throne Room," *The Black Perspective in Music*, Vol. 1, No. 1 (Spring 1973), pp. 78-79.

56.   Correspondence in Hampton University Archives.

57.   Letter from E. Franklin Frazier Papers, courtesy of Moorland-Spingarn Research Center, Howard University.

58.   Telegram courtesy of Tuskegee Institute Archives.

59. "From Bell Stand to Throne Room" was first published in *The Etude*, February, 1934, and later in *The Black Perspective in Music*, Spring, 1973. "A Musical Invasion of Europe," hereinafter cited as "Invasion," was published in *The Crisis*, Vol. 37, No. 12 (December 1930), pp. 405-407, 428.

60. "Invasion," p. 406. *Time*, May 8, 1930, commented that the "forty musicians of a different color . . . carried no fiddles, no trumpets," and that Dett was impressive as a "sophisticated leader of the choir."

61. *Musical Leader*, April 24, 1930.

62. Program is in Hampton University Archives.

63. "Invasion," p. 405.

64. *Ibid.*, p. 406.

65. Dett, "From Bell Stand to Throne Room," p. 79. The Queen of Belgium requested that the choir sing Dett's arrangement of "No More Auction Block for Me," according to Hamilton B. Mizer in *A City Is Born: Niagara Falls, A City Matures: A Topical History 1892-1932*, No. 24 (Lockport, NY: The Niagara County Historical Society, 1981), p. 135. Mizer also mentions, p. 135, that John P. Lang, director of the Music League of Niagara Falls, New York, just happened to be in the audience when the Hampton Choir performed in Paris. He went backstage afterwards to congratulate Dett.

66. David Livingstone (1813-1873) was a Scottish missionary and explorer in Africa. The decorated wreath presented to Dett by the Belgian Band was likely the Palm and Ribbon Award. The European programs are used with permission of the Local History Department, Dett Collection, NFNYPL, and Hampton University Archives.

67. *New York Times*, May 14, 1930.

68.   Letter in Folder 7, Mesiah Papers and Documents.

69.   Lovell, *Black Song*, p. 410.

70.   Item found in Hampton University Archives.

71.   Newpaper clippings in Hampton University Archives.

72.   McBrier, *R. Nathaniel Dett*, pp. 61-62. In the Mesiah Papers and Documents, Folder 6, are numerous programs in French and German from the European performances.

73.   Besides the reviews from McBrier, Maude Cuney-Hare in *Negro Musicians and Their Music* (New York: DaCapo Press, 1974), p. 249, cites this undated comment from *La Feuille d'Avois* in Vienna: "There was absolute mastery of the most difficult passages, incomparable blending, beauty of subtle shading, marvelous discipline, all united into the finest cohesion." The Hampton University Archives has a veritable cache of publicity items from leading US newspapers, journals, and European papers concerning the choir tour. Also drawing attention at the same time was the Hampton Quartet who sang in Manchester and Liverpool Cathedrals, and in schools, colleges, and drawing rooms in England and Scotland between June 1 and July 14, 1930. Hampton's cost for the choir tour was not to exceed $52,000, according to a letter to European manager Albert Morini from the second vice-president of Hampton's Board of Trustees (name not signed on letter). Detailed copies of all bills (food, lodging, transportation, and excursions) as well as a complete itinerary are in the Hampton University Archives.

74.   Letter dated May 14, 1930, in Hampton University Archives.

75.   Mrs. Washington's report is in the Hampton University Archives.

76.   Letter in Hampton University Archives.

77.   *Niagara Falls Gazette*, September 13, 1930.

78. *Niagara Falls Gazette,* October 4, 1930.

79. *Portsmouth* (Virginia) *Star,* November 11, 1930.

80. Letter in Dett Collection, NFNYPL.

81. Item, incomplete citation, courtesy Oberlin College Archives.

Chapter V

1. *The Crisis,* Vol. 38, No. 1 (January 1931), pp. 23-24. Caricaturist Cohen, referred to by Stolberg, was also a crime and mystery writer.

2. *The Crisis,* Vol. 38, No. 2 (February 1931), pp. 63-64.

3. Letter courtesy of Moorland-Spingarn Research Center, Howard University.

4. Program in Hampton University Archives. More will be said of Charles Flax in Chapter VI.

5. Copley's telegram and choir fees found in Hampton University Archives.

6. Letter dated March 10, 1931, in Hampton University Archives.

7. Peabody's letter, dated March 12, 1931, in Hampton University Archives.

8. Review from *New York American,* dated only 1931, in Hampton University Archives.

9. *Oberlin News-Tribune,* February 25, 1931.

10. *Cleveland Plain Dealer,* March 13, 1931.

11. Undated, unnamed news item in Hampton University

Archives.

12. Since he spoke so frankly Cooper was possibly on Hampton's Board of Trustees; letter dated April 13, 1931, in Hampton University Archives.

13. Telegrams in Hampton University Archives.

14. McBrier, *R. Nathaniel Dett*, p. 66.

15. This excerpt and following information from the Dett-Howe correspondence is taken from McBrier, *R. Nathaniel Dett*, pp. 66-69. The letters were filed in the President's Office at Hampton.

16. McBrier, *R. Nathaniel Dett*, p. 67.

17. Letters in Hampton University Archives.

18. One undocumented source said that William Dawson filled in temporarily for Dett, a fact not verified in Dawson's vita, since he had just accepted a position as choral director at Tuskegee in the fall of 1931.

19. Information obtained form Dett's 1935 update for Oberlin College Alumni Records, courtesy of Oberlin College Archives.

20. More will be said of these professors in Chapter VI.

21. McBrier, *R. Nathaniel Dett*, p. 68.

22. News items in Hampton University Archives.

23. *The Crisis*, Vol. 38, No. 12 (December 1931), p. 427.

24. *Rochester Chronicle*, February 12, 1932.

25. McBrier, *R. Nathaniel Dett*, pp. 69-70. McBrier does not state whether Peabody contributed monetary support to Dett at this time.

26. *Niagara Falls Gazette*, March 30, 1933.

27. News item from the *Oberlin Alumni Magazine* (April 1934), n. p., courtesy of Oberlin College Archives.

28. *Niagara Falls Gazette*, April 17, 1934.

29. Composer Boone was John William Boone ("Blind Boone"), a blind pianist who toured the US, Europe, Canada, and Mexico with the Blind Boone Company, a troupe of five or six instrumentalists and singers. Boone (1864-1927) made piano rolls for Q. R. S. Recording Company. Only one of his several piano pieces, "March Tuskegee Cadets," was published, according to the *National Union Catalog of Imprints*.

30. Hildred Roach, *Black Music Past and Present* (Boston: Crescendo Publishing Co., 1973), p. 102; *New York Times*, August 12, 1934.

31. Review cited in McBrier, *R. Nathaniel Dett*, pp. 70-71.

32. *Niagara Falls Gazette*, August 4, 1934. Information from the *New York Times* in 1956, 1960, and 1962 on a Norman S. Wright refers to him as an agriculturalist concerned with nutritional problems, with no mention of his interest in pageants.

33. McBrier, *R. Nathaniel Dett*, pp. 72-73. Choral societies and clubs named for Dett, such as the one in Washington and the R. Nathaniel Dett Club in Chicago did not enjoy the same longevity. The Dett Club in Chicago functioned as late as 1987, according to its publication *Whispers of Love*, an account of the club from 1922-1987.

34. Advertisement courtesy of Oberlin College Archives; news item from *Oberlin Alumni Magazine* (March 1935), n. p.

35. Letters courtesy of Oberlin College Archives.

36. *Afro-American* (Chicago), April 2, 1935.

37. Unnamed newspaper item, dated May 4, 1935, in Hampton University Archives.

38. Many references list Samuel Huston College as Samuel (or Sam) Houston, which is a college in Huntsville, Texas, named for General Sam Houston. The year of Dett's visiting professorship at Samuel Huston has erroneously been given by some biographers as 1937. Dett himself gave the years 1935-1936 in the 1935 Oberlin alumni files. The *Norfolk Journal and Guide*, March 23, 1935, stated that Dett would teach at Langston University in Langston, Oklahoma in the summer of 1935. If this position materialized, it has not been mentioned on Dett's vita.

39. Letter in Dett Collection, NFNYPL.

40. Letter from Dett to Arvey courtesy of Judith Still, daughter of William Grant Still. Ms. Still was unable to identify the "Nathan" mentioned in the letter.

41. Arvey, *In One Lifetime*, pp. 103-104.

42. *Ibid.*, p. 126.

43. McBrier, *R. Nathaniel Dett*, p. 77. An item in the *Niagara Falls Gazette*, July 17, 1937, stated in "Federation Convention News" that a tree had been planted on July 4 in Mrs. Dett's memory in Rochester's Highland Park by the Book Lover's Club of that city.

44. McBrier, *R. Nathaniel Dett*, p. 78. Letter dated April 27, 1937. More information on Grainger's mother and the Dett-Grainger correspondence will be given in Chapter VI.

45. DeLerma and McBrier, *Collected Piano Works of R. Nathaniel Dett*, p. vii. Concerning this matter, Dett wrote in a letter to Grainger, dated April 27, 1937: "It is interesting to hear about your work which you propose to do with the National High School Music Camp. Of course I should love to do something for the band along the more expressive lines. However, I have had no experience with band writing, and consequently am not sure I could make a

success of it." Letter courtesy of the Grainger Museum, Melbourne, Australia.

46. *Musical America*, Vol. LVII, No. 10, (May 25, 1937), p. 8.

47. McBrier, *R. Nathaniel Dett*, p. 81, does not cite Bicknell's newspaper, nor the date of his review. McBrier, p. 50, wrote that Mrs. David Jones, wife of Bennett College's president, noticed Dett's humility during the overwhelming ovation. He later said to her: "My mother would have said 'twas good but you can do better."

48. *The Crisis*, Vol. 44, No. 4 (June 1937), p. 175.

49. McBrier, *R. Nathaniel Dett*, p. 80.

50. *New York Age*, April 2, 1938.

51. McBrier, *R. Nathaniel Dett*, p. 81; *New York Times*, October 24, 1937. McBrier, p. 81, gives no dates for either the performances or the *Stockton Evening Record* review, which was carried in the *Norfolk* (Virginia) *Journal and Guide*, September 11, 1938.

52. *New York Times*, October 2, 1938.

53. *The Crisis*, Vol. 47, No. 1 (January 1940), p. 4.

54. McBrier, *R. Nathaniel Dett*, p. 85.

55. Program courtesy of Jean Snyder, University of Pittsburgh.

56. *The Crisis*, Vol. 46, No. 6 (June 1939), p. 184.

57. *Norfolk Journal and Guide*, February 10, 1940.

58. *Ibid.*

59. News item sent from Greensboro to unnamed paper, December 30, 1939, Hampton University Archives.

60. *Ibid.*

61. *Ibid.*

62. *Norfolk Journal and Guide,* February 10, 1940.

63. Item from *Atlanta World,* March 10, 1940, courtesy of Detroit Public Library. Dett's compositions were not named.

64. Letter courtesy of Judith Still.

65. April 29 and May 5 news items courtesy of Rochester Public Library.

66. Marguerite Pope, "A Brief Biography of Dr. Robert Nathaniel Dett," unpublished, courtesy of Bennett College Library; DeLerma and McBrier, *Collected Piano Works of Robert Nathaniel Dett,* p. vii.

67. *Norfolk Journal and Guide,* February 22, 1941.

68. McBrier, *R. Nathaniel Dett,* p. 85.

69. *Washington Tribune,* April 26, 1941. Various news items gave the choir's personnel to have been anywhere from thirty-two to fifty voices.

70. Unnamed news item dated April 19, 1941, courtesy Detroit Public Library.

71. McBrier, *R. Nathaniel Dett,* p. 86.

72. Organ dedication program courtesy Greensboro Public Library. *The Crisis,* December 1941, p. 371, carried an item concerning the organ's dedication.

73. Chapel dedication program courtesy Greensboro Public Library.

74. *The Crisis,* Vol. 49, No. 2 (February 1942), p. 43.

75. *The Crisis,* Vol. 49, No. 5 (May 1942), p. 148. "Father

Abraham" would later be one of Dett's *Eight Bible Vignettes; Niagara Falls Gazette,* March 17, 1942.

76. Program courtesy of Jean Snyder, University of Pittsburgh.

77. McBrier, *R. Nathaniel Dett,* p. 150. "A Gypsy's Christmas Gift" will be included in Fritz Malval's edition of Dett's poetry (Hampton University).

78. *Battle Creek Enquirer and News,* October 4, 1943.

79. DeLerma and McBrier, *Collected Piano Works,* p. vii.

80. *Battle Creek Enquirer and News,* October 4, 1943.

81. McBrier, *R. Nathaniel Dett,* pp. 33-34.

82. Information from Hampton University Archives.

83. Gatlin's eulogy courtesy of Bennett College Library.

84. Many obituaries list Dett's civic, religious, and pro-fessional affiliations, most of which are not confirmed by a date or city of his joining. Other than the NAACP, NANM, ASCAP, and the Samuel Coleridge-Taylor Choral Society (honorary) which have been documented in this biography, Dett is said to have been a member of Knights of Pythias, Elks, Masons, Rosicrucians, National Education Association, National Association of Teachers of Colored Schools, National Association of American Composers and Conductors, and a life member of Pi Kappa Lambda, honorary music fraternity. Answers to queries concerning some of those affiliations revealed no record of Dett as a member, i. e., the Knights of Pythias, the Elks, the two teaching associations, and the National Association of American Composers and Conductors. Ellen Meltzer, spokesperson for ASCAP wrote to Anne Simpson, September 16, 1991: "We have checked our records and cannot locate information about an organization in the name of the National Association of American Composers and Conductors." Confirmation of Dett's Pi Kappa Lambda membership from the national secretary, Lilias C. Circle,

however, states: "Robert Nathaniel Dett was indeed made a member of Pi Kappa Lambda Music Honor Society. He was, in fact, a member of the charter class at Oberlin when the chapter was installed in 1927." By his own statement in "Invasion" (Chapter III), Dett was also made an honorary member of the English Samuel Coleridge-Taylor Choral Society with the presentation of a pin, when the Hampton Choir sang in London in 1930. Mention was made of Dett's activities as a Rosicrucian in a 1943 issue of the *Rosicrucian Magazine* (full citation incomplete), which stated that he had given a lecture in San Jose, California (as listed on the 1942 brochure), and illustrated it with piano music. McBrier, p. 87, states that at the time of Dett's death he had been a Rosicrucian for many years, especially active in the Rochester Chapter of the Ancient Mystical Order Rosae Crucis. She quotes a letter, February of 1957, from Arthur C. Piepenbrink, Extension Director of the Society: "The Rosicrucian philosophy which was so much a part of Dr. Dett's life is unique in the field of classical study today. Free from dogmas and religious and political alliances, the Rosicrucian Order AMORC instills in its members a sensitivity to their own divine heritage. It helps the individual to help himself—to discover a philosophy of life suitable to his needs and understanding based on a thorough knowledge of the universe in which he lives. It is one of the truly great international organizations working for the betterment of humanity without respect for race or creed." But an inquiry to Lucia Grosch, president of this Society, concerning Dett's affiliation brought this answer (letter dated July 30, 1991): "Our records do not show a Dr. Dett as ever having been a member of our Society. The name 'Rosicrucian' is not patented or copyrighted, therefore any esoteric group can use it." A letter dated August 12, 1991, from Pamela Scheffel, Local History Division of the Rochester Public Library, said: "I am unable to find any current listing for a branch of the Rosicrucian Society in Rochester, nor could I discover who might have kept the records. The last reference to the society being active in the city was 1981."

Chapter VI

1. Unless otherwise stated all information on the Oberlin professors is by courtesy of the Oberlin College Archives, taken from the *Oberlin Alumni Magazine*, or from documents in the Oberlin College files.

2. *The International Cyclopedia of Music and Musicians*, 10th ed., ed. Bruce Bohle (New York: Dodd, Mead, and Company, 1975), p. 1227.

3. Biographical material courtesy of Oberlin College Archives.

4. *The International Cyclopedia of Music and Musicians*, 10th ed., p. 572.

5. *Ibid.*, p. 72.

6. Eileen Southern, *Biographical Dictionary of Afro-American and African Musicians* (Westport, CT: Greenwood Press, 1982), p. 157.

7. *Musical Courier*, Vol. LXIX, No. 23 (December 9, 1914), p. 32. The Hackley Collection at the Detroit Public Library, oddly enough, has few documents concerning Dett's association with Mme Hackley.

8. Anne Billington Hisey, "Happy Birthday, Karl Gehrkens," *Oberlin Alumni Magazine* (April 1962), pp. 16-18; Grove, *Dictionary of American Musicians*, Vol. II, p. 195; *Baker's Biographical Dictionary of Music and Musicians*, p. 808; J. E. van Peursem, "In Memoriam: Karl W. Gehrkens," *Music Educators Journal*, Vol. 61, No. 9 (May 1975), pp. 30-31.

9. John W. Beattie, "The Unknown Peter Dykema," *Music Educators Journal*, Vol. XXXVII (June-July 1951) pp. 11-12; Grove, *Dictionary of American Musicians*, Vol. I, pp. 668-669.

10. In Chapter II it was mentioned that Dett wanted Andersen to edit his arrangement of "Listen to the Lambs" for a Chicago performance, though it may not have materialized. Information on Andersen is from an undated *American Conservatory of Music Catalog,* courtesy of Leo E. Heim, President Emeritus of that conservatory in Chicago.

11. *International Cyclopedia of Music and Musicians,* pp. 1286-1287.

12. John Bird, in his biography *Percy Grainger* (London: Paul Elek, 1976), gives a revealing, frank, and fascinating account of Percy Grainger's relationship with his own mother. He minces no words about Percy's own madness, rather preferring to expose it.

13. Harold Schonberg, *The Great Pianists from Mozart to the Present* (New York: Simon & Schuster, Inc., 1987), pp. 346-347.

14. *New York Times,* September 9, 1930.

15. *The Southern Workman,* Vol. 49 (November 1919), p. 90. Grainger subsequently performed "Juba" in Chicago and Boston.

16. Program in Dett Collection, NFNYPL.

17. Card found in Dett Collection, NFNYPL.

18. Bird, *Percy Grainger,* p. 191. A first "Room Music" concert the preceding April featured only compositions by Grainger. His transcriptions of folk tunes were usually programmed on his solo piano recitals.

19. *New York Times,* May 4, 1925.

20. Program in Dett Collection, NFNYPL.

21. *New York Times,* August 11, 1928.

22. *New York Times,* December 19, 1916.

23.   Bird, *Percy Grainger*, p. 249.

24.   Nathaniel Dett, "Ethnologist Aids Composer to Draw
      Inspiration from Heart of People," *Musical America*, Vol.
      XXX, No. 3 (May 31, 1919), p. 36.

25.   *Ibid*.

26.   "Natalie Curtis-Burlin at Hampton Institute," *Resound*
      (Quarterly of the Archives of Traditional Music), Vol. 1,
      No. 2 (April 1982), pp. 1-2.

27.   *The Crisis*, Vol. III, No. 4 (February 1912), p. 143. In
      Burlin's article "The Negro's Contribution to the Music of
      America: The Larger Opportunity of the Colored Man of
      Today," *The Craftsman*, Vol. 23 (March 1913), pp. 660-669,
      she reiterated the natural musical ability of the Negro.
      Fully aware of the contemporary craze with ragtime, she
      credited for its origins not only the Negro but the native
      music of other peoples as well. As exemplary contributors
      to American music she cited James Weldon Johnson for
      astutely assuming Negro abilities in his *T h e
      Autobiography of an Ex-Colored Man*, and the efforts of
      Hampton Institute, Fisk Institute, Mrs. Gibbs Marshall, the
      Music School Settlement in New York, the Clef Club
      Orchestra, Samuel Coleridge-Taylor, Anton Dvorak,
      Harry Burleigh, Will Marion Cook, and J. Rosamond
      Johnson.

28.   Natalie Curtis-Burlin, "Black Singers and Players,"
      Musical Quarterly, Vol. V, No. 4 (1919), pp. 499-501. A
      fuller description of Burlin's four-volume *Negro Folk Songs*
      is given in "New Vocal and Instrumental Music," *Musical
      America*, Vol. XXX, No. 1 (May 3, 1919), p. 44.

29.   Arthur Foote was given some discussion at the beginning of
      Chapter III. He graduated from Harvard in 1874.

30.   Walter Raymond Spalding, *Music at Harvard* (New York:
      Coward-McCann, Inc., 1935), pp. 164, 275.

31.   Grove, *Dictionary of American Musicians*, Vol. II, p. 150.

32.   *Sonneck Society Bulletin*, Vol. XVII, No. 2 (Summer 1991),
      p. 77. These edited works were "At Dusk" (1920) for flute,
      cello, and harp, and "Sarabande and Rigaudon" (1920), a
      trio for oboe (or flute), viola (or violin), and piano.

33.   Grove, *Dictionary of American Musicians*, Vol. II, p. 150.

34.   Letter in Hampton University Archives.

35.   Information found in Hampton University Archives. Mr.
      Spalding may have been author Walter Raymond
      Spalding, n 30.

36.   Minneapolis *Twin City Star*, June 23, 1917. Davison visited
      the Hampton campus again in 1919.

37.   Letter in Hampton University Archives.

38.   Patricia Turner, *Dictionary of Afro-American Performers*
      (New York: Garland Publishing Co., 1990), pp. 262-263;
      Southern, *Biographical Dictionary*, p. 269.

39.   *New York Times*, August 10, 1939.

40.   *Ibid.* For many years Straus remained an ardent fan of
      Maynor, though continuing to review her less than perfect
      performances candidly. The *New York Times*, August 13,
      1939, carried Straus' interview with Maynor.

41.   *New York Times*, November 20, 1939.

42.   *New York Times*, February 29, 1940.

43.   *New York Times*, October 24, 1940.

44.   *New York Times*, December 15, 1947. On November 19,
      1959, in Town Hall, Maynor sang a tribute to Noel Straus,
      who had died the previous November.

45.   *New York Times*, January 15, 1953.

46. *New York Times,* April 5, 1966; Gary Diedrichs, "A Respect for Talent," *Opera News,* Vol. 39, No. 4 (October 1974), pp. 39-42.

47. Southern, *Biographical Dictionary,* p. 269.

48. This is the opinion of Professor George Brown, University of Southwestern Louisiana, retired music historian and organist, who was studying at Eastman during the time Dett was there.

49. *Baker's Biographical Dictionary of Music and Musicians,* p. 1945; Charles Riker, *The Eastman School of Music, Its First Quarter-Century 1921-1946* (Rochester, NY: University of Rochester, 1948), p. 69.

50. Spalding, *Music at Harvard,* p. 200.

51. *New York Times,* May 22, 1931.

52. *Musical Quarterly,* Vol. XXXIII, No. 2, pp. 219-221.

53. Gilbert Chase, *America's Music,* 2nd ed. (New York: McGraw-Hill Book Company, 1966), pp. 640, 552.

54. Grove, *Dictionary of American Musicians,* Vol. II, p. 320.

55. *Ibid.,* pp. 320-321.

56. *American Composers' Concerts and Festivals of American Music 1925-1971* (Rochester, NY: University of Rochester, 1972), p. 5. This booklet was compiled in part to celebrate Hanson's seventy-fifth birthday in 1971. The Howard Hanson Award was one outgrowth of the American Composers' Concerts.

57. *Ibid.,* p. 16.

58. Turner, *Dictionary of Afro-American Performers,* p. 46.

59. Information on Boatner was taken from Alice Tischler,

Fifteen Black American Composers (Detroit, MI: Information Coordinators, Inc., 1981), pp. 15-34; Turner, *Dictionary of Afro-American Performers*, pp. 45-49; Southern, *Biographical Dictionary*, p. 39; William Arms Fisher, *Seventy Negro Spirituals* (Boston, MA: Oliver Ditson Co., 1926), p. xxi. As mentioned in Chapter III, Boatner and Burleigh were the only composers whose spirituals were included in Fisher's *Seventy Negro Spirituals*.

60. Southern, *Biographical Dictionary*, p. 385. An inquiry to Florida A and M University concerning Von Charlton's faculty position there brought no response. He helpfully supplied sheet music for De Lerma and McBrier when they edited *Collected Piano Works of R. Nathaniel Dett* in 1973.

61. Phenix's letter in Hampton University Archives.

62. Southern, *Biographical Dictionary*, p. 299. Pankey was born in Pittsburgh, Pennsylvania in 1905 and died in an automobile accident in Berlin, 1971, according to an obituary in the *New York Times*, May 11, 1971. He had been expatriated from Paris in 1953 for supporting spies Ethel and Julius Rosenberg.

63. Flax's obituary courtesy Hampton University Archives. In March of 1930 Flax shared an all-Dett recital at Hampton with Mrs. William E. Stark, a reader. Flax sang *Lead Gently, Lord, and Slow, Flower in the Crannied Wall, The Winding Road, God Understands, Magic Moon of Molten Gold, The Voice of the Sea, Were Thou the Moon, My Day,* and a group of spirituals arranged by Dett. Mrs. Stark read poems from Dett's *The Album of a Heart*. The program, too damaged to reprint, is in Hampton University Archives.

64. *Ibid.*

65. *Ibid.*

66. *Ibid.*

67. Funeral program courtesy Hampton University Archives. Marjorie S. Johnson, "Noah Francis Ryder: Composer and Educator," *The Black Perspective in Music*, Vol. 6, No. 1 (Spring 1978), pp. 19-27.

68. Johnson, "Noah Francis Ryder," p. 21.

69. *Ibid.*

Chapter VII

1. McBrier, *R. Nathaniel Dett*, p. 4.

2. *Ibid.*, p. 88.

3. "Personal," *Journal of Negro History*, Vol. XXVIII, No. 4 (October 1943), p. 509.

4. Program courtesy of Oberlin College Archives.

5. Letter, dated November 30, 1943, courtesy of Oberlin College Archives. An excerpt from an undated letter in the Oberlin College Archives from Hutchins obviously pertaining to the St. Louis performance read: "In this half-Southern town, this event seemed to be a miracle. Do you happen to have a sketch of Dett's life? I didn't know till last night that he had died."

6. *Musical Courier*, Vol. CXXVIII, No. 9 (December 20, 1943), p. 13.

7. Greensboro, North Carolina *Daily News*, March 4, 1944.

8. Southern, *Biographical Dictionary*, p. 98.

9. Baltimore, *Afro-American*, February 16, 1952.

10. *Roanoke World-News*, March 9, 1954.

11. Item from unnamed Roanoke paper in *Musical America*, April, 1955.

12. Thomas J. Corcoran, in a letter of December 10, 1991, supplied an address for Dr. Feinstein and sent further information that the Mary C. Terrell school is located at 55th and State Streets. At least a dozen other schools were completed or under construction at the time, some named for Anton Dvorak, composer Florence Price, and actor Ira Aldridge.

13. Tillman (b. 1899) enjoyed a productive career as a commercial artist and portrait painter. His work has been shown in several US cities, including St. Louis and Washington, D.C. One of his better known portraits, exhibited in Cleveland, is of Jane Hunter, founder of the Phillis Wheatley Association.

14. Hampton, Virginia, *Daily Press*, August 5, 1969.

15. Southern, *Biographical Dictionary*, pp. 286, 509.

16. *Ibid.*, pp. 98-99.

17. Dominique-René De Lerma, *Reflections on Afro-American Music* (Kent, Ohio: Kent University Press, 1973), pp. 203-204.

18. *Ibid.*, p. 204.

19. *Ibid.*, p. 255.

20. Letter courtesy of Oberlin College Archives.

21. Letter courtesy of Oberlin College Archives.

22. *Cleveland* (Ohio) *Plain Dealer*, April 29, 1973. Cuyahoga Community College was established in 1963.

23. Gordon's and Bigglestone's letters courtesy of Oberlin College Archives. Gordon's work was still in manuscript form as of 1977. There has been no listing of it in Bowker's *Books in Print*.

24. Letter from Mrs. Clark to Anne Simpson, October 15, 1991.

25. Arlene E. Gray, *Listen to the Lambs* (Ridgeway, Ontario, Canada: Smith-Davison Litho., Ltd., 1984), p. ii.

26. Arlene E. Gray, Prologue to *Nate, My Son* (Niagara Falls, NY: In and Out Printing: 1987), p. 4; interview with Gray, September 11, 1991. Gray's statement that Dett was on the Eastman School of Music faculty was not confirmed by Sibley Library Archivist Mary E. Rame, who answered the query on January 15, 1992: "According to the Eastman School of Music Catalogues, I find no reference to Dett as a member of the faculty nor as a graduate instructor in the departments of composition and musicology. Perhaps he did some teaching as an assistant to a faculty member."

27. Gray, *Nate, My Son*, p. 4.

28. *Buffalo* (New York) *News*, July 22, 1985; *Niagara Falls Gazette*, March 13, 1979.

29. *Buffalo News*, July 22, 1985.

30. Letter in Dett Collection, Local History Department, NFNYPL.

31. Maynor's address is reprinted in the *National Music Council Bulletin*, Vol. 36 (1977), pp. 7-8.

32. *The Black Perspective in Music*, Vol. 6, No. 1 (Spring 1978), pp. 91-92. A query in the *New York Times*, August 6, 1978, indicated that another biography of Dett might be in progress, though there is no evidence that it materialized. Sent in by Colin H. Davis, Jr. of Arverne, New York, it sought letters, essays, speeches, information on performances and recordings of Dett's works, his membership in the Rosicrucians, any memorabilia from the Hampton Choir's European trip, "such as posters, programs and photographs including rare French Pathé sound newsreel film of the Choir."

33. *Niagara Falls Gazette*, February 18, 1980. In the news

account a fragment of Dett's verse paying tribute to the Falls was included: "My heart is strangely heavy;/ I'm so possessed./ Forgive me, leave me alone/ I shall go stand in the shadowed gorge." Program courtesy of NFNYPL.

34. Eaton's letter, dated March 31, 1982, courtesy of Oberlin College Archives.

35. *Niagara Falls* (Ontario) *Review*, October 9, 1982; George A. Seibel, *The Niagara Portage Road: A History of the West Bank of the Niagara River* (City of Niagara Falls, Canada, 1990), p. 278. Program courtesy of NFNYPL. Dett's photo on the program cover was the same one used for the February 17, 1980, program in Niagara Falls, New York. Insufficient paper quality prevented reprinting.

36. Material courtesy of Hampton University Archives. Actual dates of the October celebration were not on the program found in the archives.

37. *The Crisis*, Vol. 90, No. 2 (February 1983), p. 70.

38. Mrs. Cumbo, founder of Triad Presentations, was the wife of cellist Marion Cumbo of the American String Quartet of Harlem.

39. *New York Times*, October 20, 1982.

40. Seibel, *The Niagara Portage Road*, p. 258. Seibel's book contains a photo of the small, quaint B. M. E. Church, now the R. Nathaniel Dett Memorial Chapel, which in 1986 became an historical site. Program of ceremony courtesy NFNYPL.

41. *Informer and Texas Freedman* (Houston, Texas), October 3, 1987.

42. Hampton University News Release, Hampton University Archives.

43. Mrs. Love, a retired teacher and pianist living in Detroit, Michigan, is still active in cultural events in the Detroit

area. She continues to write and accept public speaking engagements when her work as Curator of Your Heritage House permits. As one of its treasures her establishment, a black cultural museum for children, features the hand-made toys of William Grant Still, donated by his daughter Judith Still.

44. Interview with George Brown, a retired Music History professor from the School of Music, University of Southwestern Louisiana in Lafayette, September 2, 1991.

Chapter VIII

1. From DeLerma's notes included with Denver Oldhams's CD of "R. Nathaniel Dett Piano Works," New World Records, NW 367-2.

2. DeLerma and McBrier, *Collected Piano Works of R. Nathaniel Dett*, p. ix.

3. *Ibid.*, p. x.

4. *Ibid.*, p. ix.

5. *Ibid.*

6. *Ibid.*

7. "Freda," another unpublished piano composition from 1908, was listed on an Oberlin program, courtesy of Oberlin College Archives.

8. Raoul Abdul, *Blacks in Classical Music: A Personal History* (New York: Dodd, Mead, & Company, 1977), p. 165.

9. The parts of Dett's piano suites were usually printed separately before being issued as a whole and cost from $.25 to $.85, according to a 1940 price list from the National Recreation Association (New York) found in the Hampton University Archives. These prices were also applicable to other of Dett's works for solo piano, violin, and organ. An

entire suite under one cover cost from $1.25 to $1.50 at this time. In 1912 Summy also issued *Magnolia* through Weekes & Co. in London, and by 1913 Summy's New York office was able to issue *In the Bottoms*.

10. Southern's review, *The Black Perspective in Music*, Vol. 2, No. 2 (Fall 1974), p. 218.

11. From Robert Kerlin, *Negro Poets and Their Poems*, quoted in the brochure on Dett (Hampton Institute, 1925), courtesy of Oberlin College Archives.

12. Frederick H. Martens, "The Chariot Jubilee and Other Compositions of R. Nathaniel Dett," *The Southern Workman*, Vol. 48, (1919), p. 663. At this time Martens was a contributing editor to *Musical America*. Dett later set Martens' poem "Magic Moon of Molten Gold" as a vocal solo.

13. Playing time for the *Magnolia* suite is approximately fifteen minutes.

14. Maud Cuney-Hare, *Negro Musicians and Their Music* (New York: Da Capo Press, 1974), p. 338.

15. McBrier, *R. Nathaniel Dett*, pp. 20-21.

16. Pianist/teacher Ernest Hutcheson in *The Literature of the Piano* (New York: Alfred A. Knopf, 1948), p. 361, lists *In the Bottoms* as Dett's best known work but erroneously gives its publisher as G. Schirmer. "Bottoms" is a word pertaining to flatland areas where cotton is grown, particularly in Southern Arkansas, East Texas, North Louisiana, and parts of South Carolina, Georgia, Alabama, and Mississippi. Dett, raised as a Northerner, was never involved in cotton farming, but was aware, nevertheless, through his ancestral slave background of the tribulations of his race as plantation workers.

17. Bloomfield-Zeisler's so-called premiere of *In the Bottoms* in Music Hall, Chicago, was in 1913, according to critic Glenn Dillard Gunn, cited in McBrier, *R. Nathaniel Dett*, pp. 21-22.

18. Letter from Dr. Krummel, University of Illinois, to Anne Simpson, August 2, 1991.

19. Harold C. Schonberg, *The Great Pianists* (New York: Simon & Schuster, Inc., 1987), pp. 353-354.

20. Dett said that "Honey" was inspired by Dunbar's "A Negro Love Song."

21. *Musical America*, November 29, 1913, p. 12.

22. Debra Ann Miles, "R. Nathaniel Dett's In the Bottoms Suite: An Analysis with Historical Background," Master of Music Theory, 1983, North Texas State University, Denton, Texas.

23. McBrier, *R. Nathaniel Dett*, p. 22.

24. Jay Martin and Gossie H. Hudson, eds., *The Paul Laurence Dunbar Reader* (New York: Dodd, Mead & Company, 1975), p. 292.

25. McBrier, *R. Nathaniel Dett*, p. 16.

26. Dominique-René DeLerma, *Black Music in Our Culture* (Kent, OH: Kent State University Press, 1970), p. 86.

27. Lynne Emery, *Black Dance in America* (Palo Alto, CA: National Press Books, 1972), p. 189.

28. *Ibid.*, p. 188.

29. McBrier, *R. Nathaniel Dett*, p. 95. "March Negre" is also listed among Dett's works in the *ASCAP Biographical Dictionary*, 4th ed. (New York and London: Jacques Cattell Press, R. R. Bowker Company, 1980), p. 123. To date no publisher for the piece has been located.

30. Organ score by Nevin courtesy of Hampton University Archives.

31. McBrier, R. *Nathaniel Dett,* p. 95; DeLerma and McBrier, *Collected Piano Music,* p. x.

32. De Lerma and McBrier, *Collected Piano Music,* p. x.

33. *Ibid.,* p. 61.

34. *Ibid.,* p. x.

35. "A New Romantic Piano Suite on Original Program by R. Nathaniel Dett," was the title of the review, source and date not fully cited, courtesy Oberlin College Archives.

36. *Ibid.*

37. Claire R. Reis, *Composers in America* (New York: The Macmillan Company, 1947), p. 98. It is not surprising that Dett may have conceived some scale and arpeggio passages for the harp as well as for the piano. Reis' estimated playing time for the harp version is eighteen minutes, suggesting that Dett may have added some harp passages to the original piano score.

38. *Bulfinch's Mythology* (New York: Avenel Books, 1979), p. 930. The piano score of *Nepenthe and the Muse* is among the Grainger Museum holdings.

39. In Arlene Gray's *Listen to the Lambs,* p. 38, the contract date is given as January 20, 1921.

40. Letter printed in 1925 brochure on Dett issued by Hampton Institute, courtesy Oberlin College Archives.

41. Reis, *Composers in America,* p. 98.

42. Letter to Anne Simpson from Thomas Broido, January 31, 1992. McBrier lists *Fair Weather* in *Collected Piano Works.*

43. Information on Sousa given by Sousa scholar Paul Bierley in letter to Anne Simpson, January 5, 1992. Strasser's

arrangement is not published, according to Bierley, who did not state the publisher of Sousa's arrangement.

44. Southern, review of *Collected Piano Works*, in *The Black Perspective in Music*, p. 217, fully cited in Endnote 10.

45. McBrier, R. *Nathaniel Dett*, p. 92, did not specify the arranger as Dett. A two-piano four-hand arrangement (no date given) was listed in *Negro Spirituals and Music Composed by Negroes* (a bulletin) (New York: National Recreation Association, 1940), p. 8.

46. Letter courtesy of Grainger Museum, Melbourne, Australia.

47. These titles were listed on a brochure for Dett, compiled c. 1942, Dett Collection, NFNYPL.

48. Paul Robert Lieder, Robert Morss Lovett, and Robert Kilburn Root, eds., *British Prose and Poetry* (Boston, MA: Houghton Mifflin Company, 1928), p. 326.

49. *Gitanjali* was published in 1912, one of over two dozen of Tagore's literary volumes, most of which remain untranslated. American composer John Alden Carpenter used some poems from *Gitanjali* for his vocal cycle of the same name (1913). Two others, "On the Seashore of Endless Worlds" and "The Sleep That Flits on Baby's Eyes," were taken from Tagore's *Crescent Moon*. *Collected Poems and Plays of Rabindranath Tagore* (New York: The Macmillan Company, 1943), p. 3.

50. *Encyclopedia Americana*, Vol. 26 (Danbury, CT: Grolier Incorporated, 1989), p. 226.

51. Edith Hamilton, *Mythology Timeless Tales of Gods and Heroes* (New York: New American Library, 1969), pp. 68-69.

52. *Bullfinch's Mythology*, p. 940.

53. *The Complete Poetical Works of Longfellow* (Boston, MA: Houghton Mifflin Company, 1922), p. 186.

54.   Though his father tried to dissuade his son's writing or teaching as a profession, Longfellow was one of first American poets to make a living as such. *Encyclopedia Americana*, Vol. 17, pp. 728-730.

55.   Letter from Dr. Vitzthum to Anne Simpson, September 4, 1991. McBrier, *R. Nathaniel Dett*, p. 84, took her "allusions" from material provided by Bennett College.

56.   *Dictionary of Canadian Biography*, Vol. I, ed. George W. Brown (Toronto: University of Toronto Press, 1966), pp. 412-413.

57.   *Ibid.*, p. 413.

58.   *Norfolk Journal and Guide*, October 1, 1938.

59.   *Ibid.*

60.   *Ibid.* Unfortunately, CBS did not guarantee publication of "American Sampler," nor of Dett's orchestration of the spiritual "No Auction Block for Me" (1940), discussed in Part I, Chapter V.

61.   DeLerma and McBrier, *Collected Piano Works*, p. x.

62.   *Ibid.*

63.   Gunn's review as quoted in the *Rochester Democrat and Chronicle*, June 20, 1943.

64.   *Musical America*, Vol. LXII, No. 1 (January 10, 1942), p. 32.

65.   DeLerma and McBrier, *Collected Piano Works*, p. 150. The reference to Moody and Sankey, American evangelists, concerns their gospel type music. Dwight Lyman Moody (1837-1899) planned and established a chain of educational institutions and worked extensively with Ira Sankey (1840-1908), organist and singer, in revivals in the US and Britain, where Sankey's collections of gospel hymns were extremely popular. Sankey's autobiography, *My Life and*

the Story of the Gospel Hymns (1906), describes their work.

66. DeLerma and McBrier, *Collected Piano Works*, p. 150.

67. *Ibid.*, p. 170.

68. *Ibid.*, p. 180.

Chapter IX

1. Dett's opinions from essays and program notes cited in McBrier, *R. Nathaniel Dett*, pp. 43-44, 47-48.

2. Dett, "From Bell Stand to Throne Room," p. 80.

3. *Ibid.*

4. *Ibid.*

5. Gray, in *Listen to the Lambs*, gives poet Thompson's first name as Lillian, not Sillian. No substantive information on these persons has been located, though poet Lillian B. Thompson collaborated with Burleigh on an art song in 1907. Sillian Thompson's poem, "Churning Song," was published in *The Argosy* in September of 1901, according to a hand-written note at the end of Dett's ms. Flora Pierce-Dennis may have been a friend or teacher at the Halstead Conservatory.

6. *The Southern Workman*, Vol. 47 (December 1918), p. 414.

7. *Baker's Biographical Dictionary of Music and Musicians*, p. 1463; *International Cyclopedia of Music and Musicians*, p. 1336.

8. *The Southern Workman*, Vol. 48 (December 1919), p. 665.

9. Curiously, mention was made in the *New York Times*, February 21, 1961, of a Revella E. Hughes, heiress to the bulk of an estate of the grandaughter of a chewing gum company founder. Hughes had met Evelyn V. Adams, the granddaughter, in Paris and subsequently shared housing

with her in Garden City, New York. Hughes was shot accidentally by a friend who was examining a WWI pistol, the account said. Hughes was sixty-four at the time, so she could possibly have been the singer, Ravella Hughes, despite the discrepancy in spelling. No other references to Hughes as a singer have been found, though she may have been a student at Hampton in the early 1920s.

10. *The Southern Workman*, Vol. 48 (December 1919), p. 665.

11. R. Nathaniel Dett, *The Dett Collection of Negro Spirituals*, First Group (Chicago: Hall & McCreary Company, 1936), Foreword.

12. *New York Times*, March 1, 1958.

13. *New York Age*, February 9, 1924.

14. Edward B. Moogk, *Roll Back the Years* (Ottawa, Canada: National Library of Canada, 1975), pp. 58, 275.

15. *Encyclopedia of Music in Canada*, Helmut Kallman, Gilles Petrin, and Kenneth Winters, eds. (Toronto, Canada: University of Toronto Press, 1981), p. 432. Sue McBerry, a former Hoban student residing in Portland, Oregon in 1992, placed Hoban's death in the early 1980s. Dr. Ed Baird took over his NATS workshop activities in 1978.

16. Henry Pleasants, *The Great Singers* (New York: Simon & Schuster, Inc., 1981), p. 346.

17. K. J. Kutsch and Leo Reimens, *A Concise Biographical Dictionary of Singers* (New York: Chilton Book Company, 1969), p. 282.

18. *New York Times*, August 1, 1929. Other soloists for *Requiem* included Jeanette Vreeland, Arthur Hackett, and Reinald Werrenrath.

19. A reviewer for *Musical Courier*, Vol. 10 (March 9, 1935), pp. 15, 30, wrote that as Acuzena Meisle was not nervous, rather "in full possession of her dramatic and vocal faculties. . . . The enthusiasm of her hearers waxed

throughout the evening until after the fourth act she was called before the curtain seven times. . . . The management is probably wondering why they did not add this outstanding native artist to the Metropolitan roster before this."

20. Information on Brown courtesy of Hampton University Archives.

21. *New York Times*, September 29, 1918.

22. *Musical America*, Vol. XXXVII, No. 8 (December 16, 1922), p. 23.

23. These comments from the *Buffalo* (NY) *Courier*, May 1, 1923, were in *Musical America*, Vol. XXXVIII, No. 4 (May 19, 1923), p. 18.

24. *New York Times*, October 12, 1929. Reviews from the *Times* indicated that Swinford sang a variety of lieder and art songs from all periods.

25. *New York Times*, May 11, 1944; *Sarah Lawrence College Alumnae Magazine*, February, 1962, p. 23.

26. Dett's credit to Bryant on the score is "From the Singing of Reverend J. Fletcher Bryant, Pueblo, Colorado." Bryant continued his ministry in Pueblo after WWI.

27. Southern, *Biographical Dictionary*, p. 173. MacKinley Helm's *Angel Mo' and Her Son Roland Hayes* (1944) provides more complete information on Hayes.

28. Gray, *Listen to the Lambs*, pp. 37, 150.

29. Unfortunately, no information has been located on Twohig.

30. Ms of "Sit Down, Servant" is in the Dett Collection, NFNYPL. McBrier's list of works includes the solo *Melody*, published by Church in 1932, a score of which is no longer available.

31.   Edgar Rogie Clark, *Negro Art Songs* (New York: Edward B. Marks Music Corporation, 1946), Introduction.

32.   *New York Times*, October 26, 1930.

33.   *New York Times*, November 22, 1921.

34.   *Dictionary of National Biography*, E. T. Williams and Helen M. Palmer, eds. (Oxford: Oxford University Press, 1971), p. 409. Other information on Gibbings is from the *Oxford Companion to Art*, Harold Osborne, ed. (Oxford: At the Clarendon Press, 1970), p. 475. Gibbings' *Lovely is the Lea*, about Ireland, was a co-selection of the Book-of-the-Month Club for December, 1945. He was largely resspsonsible for founding the Society of Wood Engravers.

35.   *Detroit Free Press*, January 19, 1941.

36.   This wording is on the first page of Dett's score.

37.   Newman I. White, *American Negro Folk-songs* (Hatboro, PA: Folklore Associates, Inc., 1965), p. 107.

Chapter X

1.   "R. N. Dett of Hampton Institute, Helping to Lay Foundation for Negro Music of Future," *The Black Perspective in Music*, Vol. 1, No. 1 (Spring 1973), p. 65.

2.   Article titled "Dr. Dett's Artistry Removes Color Line in World of Music."

3.   Stanley, "R. N. Dett of Hampton Institute," p. 65. McBrier, in *R. Nathaniel Dett*, p. 54, stated that Dett considered the most basic surviving form of the spiritual one in which a solo leader carries the theme followed by a refrain from the chorus with little variation in tone. Resembling call and response type singing, this form originated in Africa.

4.   *The Southern Workman*, Vol. 56 (July 1927), p. 305.

5.   Carl Gordon Harris, Jr., "A Study of Characteristic

Stylistic Trends Found in the Choral Works of a Selected
Group of Afro-American Composers and Arrangers," PhD
Dissertation, University of Missouri-Kansas City, 1972, pp.
34-37. Harris was at this time director of the Virginia
State College Choir in Petersburg, Virginia. This group
performed Dett's *Listen to the Lambs* at his alma mater in
Kansas City on April 29, 1971. He refers to Dett, Burleigh,
John W. Work, Jr., Frederick J. Work, Clarence Cameron
White, Rosamond Johnson, and James Weldon Johnson as
"Black Trail Blazers" in their dedication "to presenting
and preserving traditional Negro music in the authentic
style of its creators" (p. 9). Eileen Southern wrote that
these same pioneer composers broke down some barriers
when they gradually began to receive publicity and
acknowledgement for their publications. Southern,
"America's Black Composers of Classical Music," *Music
Educators Journal*, Vol. 64, No. 3, pp. 46-48. Comparable to
the "Russian Five," Warner Lawson (cited in White, n 14)
included Dett, Burleigh, White, and William Dawson in
his "Afro-American Five," in their successful bridging of
the gap between raw folk music and concert music. Lawson,
pianist, choral conductor, and educator, was schooled at
Fisk, Yale, and Harvard universities, and in Berlin with
Artur Schnabel. He received two honorary doctoral
degrees (1954 and 1966). His last position was Dean of the
School of Music/Fine Arts at Howard University.

6. McBrier, *R. Nathaniel Dett*, p. 46.

7. *Ibid.*, p. 47.

8. Dett set each of these in *The Dett Collection of Negro
    Spirituals* (1936). Some are solos with accompaniments,
    but most are in four-part harmony with no separate
    accompaniment.

9. Harris, "A Study of Characteristic Stylistic Trends," p. 40.

10. Arthur Lee Evans, "The Development of the Negro
    Spiritual As Choral Art Music by Afro-American
    Composers with an Annotated Guide to the Performance of
    Selected Spirituals," PhD Dissertation, University of

Miami School of Music, 1972, p. 60.

11. *Ibid.*, pp. 82-83.

12. *Ibid.*, p. 82.

13. Fansler, "The Anthem in America 1900-1950," PhD Dissertation, North Texas State University, Denton, Texas, 1982, p. 197.

14. McBrier, *R. Nathaniel Dett*, p. 36, cited this quote from Dett's notebook, one also cited by Evelyn Davidson White, *Choral Music by Afro-American Composers* (Metuchen, NJ: Scarecrow Press, Inc., 1981), p. 3. White, in her extensive study, categorizes *Lambs* as medium to difficult level.

15. Harris, "A Study of Characteristic Stylistic Trends," pp. 44-45.

16. Evans, "The Development of the Negro Spiritual as Choral Art Music," p. 83.

17. Fansler, "The Anthem in America 1900-1950," p. 198.

18. Harris, "A Study of Characteristic Stylistic Trends," pp. 45-46.

19. McBrier, *R. Nathaniel Dett*, p. 38.

20. Benjamin Brawley, *The Negro in Literature and Art* (New York: Duffield & Company, 1930), pp. 168-169.

21. Edith Borroff, *Music in Europe and the United States A History*, 2nd ed. (New York: Ardsley House Publishers, Inc., 1990), p. 603.

22. Cook's undated letter was quoted in James G. Spady, ed., *William L. Dawson: A Umum Tribute and a Marvelous Journey* (Philadelphia, PA: Creative Artists' Workshop, 1981), n. p. Unfortunately, Spady gives no date for Cook's letter, likely written in October of 1927, however, since Mencken's article "The Dark American" was carried in a

late September, 1927 issue of the *New York World*. By October 1 several eastern papers were aware of it and printed critical letters by others.

23. Royalty statement found in Dett Collection, NFNYPL.

24. "Musical Successes of R. Nathaniel Dett," *The Southern Workman*, Vol. 51, No. 4 (April 1922), p. 200.

25. Evans, "The Development of the Negro Spiritual as Choral Art Music," p. 159.

26. See n 14.

27. Frederick H. Martens, "The Chariot Jubilee and Other Compositions of R. Nathaniel Dett," *The Southern Workman*, Vol. 48 (month missing, 1919), p. 663. *Voulez ouir les cris de Paris* was one of several later descriptive pieces of Clément Jannequin (c. 1475-1560).

28. See Chapter VI for biographical information on Grainger and his appreciation for this dedication.

29. Evans, "The Development of the Negro Spiritual as Choral Art Music," p. 155.

30. Martens, "The Chariot Jubilee and Other Compositions of R. Nathaniel Dett," p. 663.

31. *Baker's Biographical Dictionary of Music and Musicians*, p. 411.

32. *The Crisis*, Vol. 17, No. 2 (December, 1918), p. 68. Dominique-René DeLerma, however, in his notes to Denver Oldham's CD "R. Nathaniel Dett Piano Works," New World Records 367-2, suggests without naming them that Dett completed "several wartime patriotic works for Canada and the United States."

33. Martens, "The Chariot Jubilee and Other Compositions of R. Nathaniel Dett," p. 663.

34. *Reader's Digest Family Songbook* (Pleasantville, NY: The Reader's Digest Association, Inc., 1969), p. 245.

35. Lina Mainiero, ed., *American Women Writers*, Vol. I (New York: Frederick Ungar Publishing Co., 1979), pp. 123-124.

36. Martens, "The Chariot Jubilee and Other Compositions of R. Nathaniel Dett," p. 664.

37. *Ibid.*, pp. 663-664.

38. DeLerma, notes from Oldham's CD, n 32.

39. Quoted in Maud Cuney-Hare, *Negro Musicians and Their Music*, p. 337.

40. Benjamin Brawley, *The Negro Genius* (New York: Dodd, Mead and Company, 1942), p. 303.

41. Martens, "The Chariot Jubilee and Other Compositions of R. Nathaniel Dett," p. 664.

42. *Baker's Biographical Dictionary of Music and Musicians*, p. 1409.

43. Information on the Cecilia Society was given in Chapter III, n 10, in connection with its performance of Dett's works.

44. Evans, "The Development of the Negro Spiritual as Choral Art Music," pp. 154-155.

45. Dett's Foreword to *Religious Folk-Songs of the Negro As Sung at Hampton Institute* (Hampton, VA: Hampton Institute Press, 1927).

46. Gloster B. Current, "National Association of Negro Musicians, Inc., Salutes R. Nathaniel Dett's 100th Birthday," *The Crisis*, Vol. 90, No. 2 (February, 1983), pp. 19-20.

47. Separate titles in *Religious Folk-Songs of the Negro* will be included in the Catalog of Music, Part III of *Follow Me*.

48. *Encyclopedia Americana,* Vol. 16 (Danbury, CT: Grolier Incorporated, 1989), pp. 162-163.

49. Fansler, "The Anthem in America 1900-1950," p. 200.

50. Evans, "The Development of the Negro Spiritual as Choral Art Music," pp. 160-162.

51. Letter to Anne Simpson from Donald Hayden, May 27, 1992. In 1966 Hayden became Rochester's Supervisor of Vocal Music, and in 1976 its Director of Music. As a high schooler (1935-1938) he and William Warfield sang with the Inter-High Choir. Though not familiar with *Juba,* Hayden recalled singing other of Dett's choral music, and mentioned that there had been "a bond of friendship" between Dett and Spouse. Ronald H. Bogardus, another member of Spouse's chorus and classmate of Dett's daughter Helen, recalls Dett's directing *Listen to the Lambs* and *Juba.* He wrote: "Dr. Dett and Alfred Spouse were close friends and worked together in a professional manner. . . . Mr. Spouse died in 1981 in Montreal, Canada." Letter from Bogardus to Anne Simpson, June 1, 1992.

52. Letter to Anne Simpson from Dr. William Loring, March 22, 1992.

53. R. Nathaniel Dett, *The Dett Collection of Negro Spirituals,* Fourth Group (Chicago: Hall & McCreary Company, 1936), p. 4.

54. *The Crisis,* Vol. 44, No. 4 (June 1937), p. 175.

55. Tilford Brooks, *America's Black Musical Heritage* (Englewood Cliffs, NJ: Prentice-Hall, Inc., 1984), p. 213.

56. Margaret Just Butcher, *The Negro in American Culture* (New York: Alfred A. Knopf, 1969), p. 89.

57. *Rochester Democrat and Chronicle,* October 4, 1943.

58. "Estimates of Dett's *The Ordering of Moses," The Southern*

Workman, Vol. 66 (September 1937), pp. 304-310.

59. Notebook in Hampton University Archives.

60. *Cincinnati Enquirer*, May 7, 1937.

61. McBrier, R. *Nathaniel Dett*, p. 83.

62. *Ibid.*, pp. 134-147.

63. Brooks, *America's Black Musical Heritage*, pp. 210-213.

64. Georgia Atkins Ryder, "Melodic and Rhythmic Elements of Negro Folk Songs as Employed in Cantatas by Selected American Composers Between 1932-1967," PhD Dissertation, School of Education, New York University, 1970, pp. 192-197. Mrs. Ryder was the wife of Noah Ryder, mentioned in Chapter VII of *Follow Me*.

65. J. Harrison Wilson, "A Study and Performance of *The Ordering of Moses* by Robert Nathaniel Dett," PhD Dissertation, University of Southern California, 1970, pp. 66 ff.

66. *Ibid.*, pp. 26-27.

67. Ryder, "Melodic and Rhythmic Elements of Negro Folk Songs," p. 102.

68. Wilson, "A Study and Performance of *The Ordering of Moses*," pp. 32-39.

69. *Ibid.*, p. 56.

70. *Ibid.*, p. 66. Wilson's excellent and thorough analysis of *Moses* is a valuable study for Dett scholars.

71. Ryder, "Melodic and Rhythmic Elements of Negro Folk Songs," p. 105.

72. Davidson Taylor (1907-1979) was mentioned in Chapter V in connection with Dett's "American Sampler." As the son of

a minister he grew up in Mississippi, received a Master's in Theology from Southern Baptist Seminary in 1930, but soon forsook ministerial plans for radio announcing. Based in St. Louis from 1930-1933 at Station WHAS, Taylor wrote radio criticism for the *Louisville Courier-Journal*. From 1933-1938 he rose from announcer to director of Columbia Broadcasting System in New York, a position facilitating promotion of American compositions over radio.

After service in WW II Davidson returned to CBS, but left in 1950 to set up The Voice of America for the State Department. In 1951 he joined the National Broadcasting Company, holding various high positions there until 1958, leaving then to be a consultant in planning the Lincoln Center Library-Museum of the Performing Arts. Davidson co-founded Columbia University's School of the Arts in 1966, organized its curriculum, and by 1969 had been made Dean, a position held until his death. Obituary, *New York Times*, July 28, 1979. The multi-gifted Taylor was described in the *Times* as "an advocate of the arts who dabbled in poetry and painting, . . . [and] who turned to broadcasting in an era when the phenomenon of radio was captivating the nation."

73.   Taken from words by Paul Gerhardt (1607-1676) *Now Rest Beneath Night's Shadows*, written in 1656, was one of his 134 poems or translations set to music by hymnists. German-born Gerhardt studied theology at the University of Wittenberg (Lutheran), became a private tutor, and assumed his first ministry in 1651. By 1657 he was Deacon at the Church of St. Nicolai in Berlin where Johann Crüger (1598-1662), his future chief collaborator, was cantor. Gerhardt's first fifteen chorales were included in the second edition (1647) of Crüger's *Praxis pietatis melica* (Practice of Piety in Song), and eighty-one more appeared in the fifth edition (1653). This work was considered the most influential Lutheran song book of the mid-1660s. Neither it nor its successors, however, was conceived for congregational singing but for home use.

In 1666, due to disagreement with Friedrich Wilhem, the Great Elector, over a Calvinist declaration, Gerhardt was dismissed from hIs Berlin post. In 1669 he became Deacon at Ludden, where he remained until his death.

Several of his hymns have remained in Protestant hymnals for the past 300 years. As late as 1982 four of them were in *The Hymnal*, used in many Episcopal churches. Most commonly retained in Methodist, Baptist, and Presbyterian hymnals have been his "Jesus, Thy Boundless Love to Me" (1653), "All My Heart This Night Rejoices" (1656), and a translation of "O, Sacred Head Sore Wounded." Gerhardt, largely responsible for survival of the chorale form, has been called the "principal hymnist of the century, second only to Luther, and in fertility his superior." Donald Jay Grout, *A History of Western Music*, 3rd ed. (New York: W. W. Norton & Company, 1980), p. 363. *Grove's Dictionary of Music and Musicians*, Vol. II, 5th ed., ed. Eric Blom (New York: St. Martin's Press, Inc., 1954), p. 273.

74.   ASCAP was not able to locate a copy of *Ascapezzo*. Other information on Dett's 1940 compositions, is in Chapter V of *Follow Me*.

75.   *Richmond Afro-American*, March 29, 1941.

76.   As a successful poet, respected among hIs British peers, Byron (1788-1824) had an incredibly adventuresome career. He was a member of the House of Lords, an avid traveler, a friend of the Percy Shelleys, Leigh Hunt, Thomas Moore and other eminent literary figures, who enjoyed the romantic, Bohemian life, defying everything which confined the spirit. On a trip to Portugal and Turkey he swam the Hellespont, at once becoming enamored of Greece. In an effort to aid Greek independence by raising a regiment, he contracted a fatal fever and died in 1824. Byron, on whom volumes have been written, is best known for his longer poems *Childe Harold's Pilgrimage, Mazeppa, The Prisoner of Chillon, The Vision of Judgment*, and a poetic drama, *Don Juan*.

77.   *Musical America*, January 10, 1942, n. p. on item sent from Oberlin College Archives.

78.   W. Thorburn Clark, *Hymns That Endure* (Nashville, TN: Broadman Press, 1944), pp. 68-75.

79.   Material from Oberlin College Archives.

80.   *The Oberlin Alumni Magazine*, Vol. 1, No. 4 (January 1905), p. 107. It is doubtful that Dett's song had been written this early.

81.   *The Oberlin Alumni Magazine* (May 1925), p. 19.

82.   *Battle Creek Enquirer and News*, October 4, 1943.

APPENDIX

Poetry

A collection of Dett's poetry, containing *The Album of a Heart* (1911), *The Song of Seven* (a heretofore unpublished manuscript begun in 1928), and a dozen or so miscellaneous short poems, is in preparation for issue by Hampton University Press. Dr. Fritz Malval, Hampton Archivist and editor of the collection, has granted permission for using some of the poetic content in *Follow Me*.

In his Foreword to *The Album of a Heart* Dett refers to the human heart as "a gallery in which many pictures indeed are hung," a place where small memories are stored and remain precious miniatures. Romantic in style, most of the volume's thirty poems are in four-line stanzas of abab or abbcc rhyme scheme, and a few are of thirteen lines, unrhymed. In them Dett expresses his love of nature with reference to the moon, the sun, lanscapes, the sea, and birds. His main themes are those of striving, love, relation to God, inward unrest, self doubt, aspiration, and loneliness.

The shortest poem, aptly titled "Bagatelle," says: "Life's a spindle;/ Both ends dwindle." Two of the poems have French titles, "Au Matin" ("To Morning") and "Au Soir" ("To Evening"). "A Romance Sonata," the longest one, is in seven parts, each named in musical terms, e. g. *Andante Teneramente, Largo con Tristezza*, etc. New love is compared to sunrise and lost love to moonset, his inner pain and resentment to the raging elements.

Only one of the poems, "Pappy," is in dialect. Dett effects both humor and sadness in "The Gossip or The Old Maid's Story," a longer narrative in rhymed couplets which could well be spoken in today's rap style. It is the tale of a spinster and her beloved gentleman friend who spat over a pan of cornbread. When she unwittingly tosses it at him, he leaves. Unreconciled, she begins to grieve over her foolish behavior. She never sees him alive again, for he dies from burns in a train wreck. She identifies the body only by a ring he wore and some cornbread clinging to his hand. The humorous "Conjured" describes the malaise of one in love. The last eight lines say: "And when I talk, my voice/

Seems all out of pitch;/ When I think about her, my pulses, they twitch./ I'm in love or I'm crazy,/ I can't tell quite which;/ But I know I've been conjured/ By that little witch."

Dett set to music "Oh Whisp'ring Tree," "To the Sea," "Twilight," and "Yield But Thy Love to Me." Several of the poems are dedicated: "The Traumerei" to Olga (no last name); "I Stood by the Caves of Memory" to Prof. P. D. Sherman, Oberlin College; "The Mountain" to O. B. Payne, a student at Lane College; "The Rubinstein Staccato Etude" to Prof. G. C. Hastings at Oberlin; "To the Sea" to Prof. George W. Andrews at Oberlin; "Berceuse" to Kathryn Barnes, a child of Oberlin friends; "Oh Whisp'ring Tree" to Mrs. F. H. Goff; and "Remembrance" to his mother. One titled "Elegy" was written on the death of a sixteen-year-old student, Suella Person, and another, "Bishop Isaac Lane," in tribute to this longtime Methodist Bishop and founder of Lane College. "Ode" and "Lane College Song" were for Lane students and the Lane student body, respectively.

Each first line of the four-stanza "Remembrance" says "Mother Dear, I'm not forgetting," followed by thankful remembrances of Mrs. Dett as an exemplary mother. The last stanza reads:

> Mother Dear, I'm not forgetting__
> But the climb is long and drear,
> Oft the mount-crag's fierce down-frowning
> Change most ardent hope to fear;
> Yet the Crown for which I'm striving__
> Call my own? I could not dare!__
> Mother Mine, to you I'll bring it;
> None but you that Crown shall wear!

"At Niagara," reprinted in Robert Kerlin's *Negro Poets and Their Poems* (3rd ed. 1935), shows Dett's introspective side. Possessed by a strange mood, he chooses meditative solitude near Niagara's tumbling waters, under the stars and the moon, in preference to being with a dear friend.

"The Rubinstein Staccato Etude," in humorous vein, was reprinted in James Weldon Johnson's anthology *The Book of American Negro Poetry* (1931). Anton Rubinstein (1830-1894) composed two sets of Etudes for piano, Op. 23 and Op. 81, though Grove does not specify separate titles. "Staccato" might have been Dett's own name for one of the Etudes, resembling such appropriate dubbings as the "Black Key," "Cello," and "Winter Wind" Etudes of Chopin. Dett's poem says:

Staccato! Staccato!
Leggier (sic) agitato!
 In and out does the melody twist
Unique proposition
In this composition.
 (Alas! for the player who hasn't the wrist!)
Now in the dominant
Theme ringing prominent,
 Bass still repeating its one monotone,
Double notes crying,
Up keyboard go flying,
 The change to the minor comes in like a groan.
Without a cessation
A chaste modulation
 Hastens adown to subdominant key,
Where melody mellow-like
Singing so 'cello-like
 Rises and falls in a wild ecstasy.
Scarce is this finished
When chords all diminished
 Break loose in a patter that comes down like rain;
A pedal-point wonder
Rivaling thunder,
 Now is all mad agitation again.
Like laughter jolly
Begins the finale;
 Again does the 'cello its tones seems to lend
Diminuendo al molto crescendo.
 Ah! Rubinstein only could make such an end!

* * *

The eighteen-page manuscript of *The Song of Seven* has been preserved in a notebook in the Hampton University Archives. Malval places the date of completion in the late 1930s after Dett left Bennett. Dett's Preface, written in 1928 at Hampton, states in part:

> . . . in the art of music, rhythmic change, without disturbance of unity, has long been old.
>
> One wonders, therefore, why the thought that a variety of forms may add to the emphasis of one central idea has not earlier carried over into literature, as it has into drawing and architecture; for its exploitation centuries ago, in the works of Bach, was even then no novelty.
>
> This is the device employed in the "Song of Seven," almost every movement or canto of which is different from the other, while the relation which binds them together remains more or less obvious. Certainly, elasticity is given the expression of any general idea and individuality gained for the various parts by having each constituent element assume a form and meter peculiar to itself. The frequency with which poetry has been attuned to sadness prohibits an imaginative study of one who by suicide succumbs to a ravaging despair from being presented as a new idea in art; and since the intention in creating the "Song of Seven" was not to declare a new principle or raise a disturbing question, but rather to furnish entertainment for an idle, passing hour, if the old story appearing here but pleasantly persuade the reader by its originality of vesture, the author will be content.

In three sections, *The Song of Seven* is an intimate examination of Nature's powers over the human spirit. Sitting beside the sea Dett ponders not only the omnipotence of its vastness, but also the mysteries of wind and sun, and his own identity in relation to them. A few lines from the first stanza are:

O wide and boundless Bitter Sea,__
How dark, how deep thy mystery!
Thy tree of dreams of things which may not be,__
Star-melodied with fancies,__
Scar-foliaged with fears,__
What ills it omens him who sees or hears!

Miscellaneous poems to be included in Malval's edition are "In the Bottoms," "To a Mountain," "Victory Song," "Winter Grass," "A Prayer," "To Roland Hayes," "A Gypsy's Christmas Gift," and half a dozen untitled poems. "To a Mountain" was printed in *The Southern Workman* (December, 1929, p. 545) with an illustration of trees, mountains, and rocks by Allan R. Freelon. The mountain symbolizes goals yet unattained. "A Gypsy's Christmas Gift" and its inspiration were mentioned in Chapter V of *Follow Me*. (The complete poem is in McBrier, *R. Nathaniel Dett*, pp. 151-152.)

A manuscript of the twenty-eight line "To Roland Hayes," in rhymed couplets, is in the Mesiah Papers. Undated but obviously written after Dett had heard Hayes in concert, it praises Hayes' musicianship which recalls both sweet and sad personal memories for Dett. The last lines are: "The song ends, but remembered years/ Have filled my eyes with mists of tears."

Essays

Jon Michael Spencer's *The R. Nathaniel Dett Reader, Essays on Black Sacred Music* (Duke University Press, 1991) contains most of Dett's available literary output. Not included are: Dett's poetry, his book review of James Weldon Johnson's *Fifty Years and Other Poems*, and two essays, "Ethnomusicologist Aids Composer to Draw Inspiration from Heart of People" (*Musical America*, May 31, 1919), and "From Within" (*The Hampton Student*, September 15, 1923).

Dett's literary works are listed as follows:

The Album of a Heart. Jackson, TN: Mocowat-Mercer, 1911.

"As the Negro School Sings." *The Southern Workman*, Vol. 56 (July 1927), pp. 304-305.

The Dett Collection of Negro Spirituals. Chicago: Hall & McCreary Company, 1936.

"Ethnologist Aids Composer to Draw Inspiration from Heart of People." *Musical America*, Vol. XXX, No. 3 (May 31, 1919), p. 36.

"From Bell Stand to Throne Room." *The Etude*, Vol. 52 (February 1934), pp. 79-80.

"From Within" (An Idyll of Hampton). *The Hampton Student*, September 15, 1923, p. 6.

"John W. Work." *The Southern Workman*, Vol. 54 (October 1925), p. 438.

Miscellaneous poems, to be issued with *The Album of a Heart* and *The Song of Seven* by Hampton University.

"A Musical Invasion of Europe." *The Crisis*, Vol. 37 (December, 1930), pp. 405-407, 428.

"Negro Music" (Bowdoin Prize thesis, Harvard University, 1920) in four parts: "The Emancipation of Negro Music," "The Development of Negro Secular Music," "The Development of Negro Religious Music," and "Negro Music of the Present."

"Negro Music." Thompson, Oscar, ed. *The International Cyclopedia of Music and Musicians*, 1st ed. 1939, 3rd ed. 1944, 6th ed. 1952. New York: Dodd, Mead, and Company.

Negro Spirituals. London: Blandford Press, 1959.

Program notes. Concert by the Hampton Institute Choir. Carnegie Hall, New York, April 16, 1928.

Program notes. Concert by the Hampton Institute Choir. Symphony Hall, Boston, March 10, 1929.

Program notes. First appearance in London of the Hampton Institute Choir. Queen's Hall, London, May 3, 1930.

Religious Folk-Songs of the Negro As Sung at Hampton Institute. Hampton, VA: Hampton Institute Press, 1927.

Review of James Weldon Johnson and Rosamond Johnson's *The Book of American Negro Spirituals. The Southern Workman,* Vol. 54 (December 1925), pp. 563-565.

Review of James Weldon Johnson's *Fifty Years and Other Poems. The Southern Workman,* Vol. 47 (1918), pp. 406-407.

Review of Howard W. Odum and Guy B. Johnson's *Negro Workaday Songs. The Southern Workman,* Vol. 56, No. 1 (1927), pp. 45-46.

The Song of Seven. Hampton University Archives.

Having already discussed Dett's views put forth in most of these essays and program notes, a brief summary of the four Bowdoin Prize essays seems in order. For reasons not explained, nevertheless amusing, Dett signed his pseudonym, Toussaint L'Ouverture, on the typewritten manuscript, now in the New York Public Library. In the first one, "The Emancipation of Negro Music," Dett, still deploring the stigma of minstrelsy, traces the history of the better Negro choirs, and questions Stephen Foster's role as a composer for Christy's Minstrels. He chastizes the slavish following of American composers in the European tradition, rather than exploring their own native resources, a practice somewhat righted by Coleridge-Taylor and MacDowell, however, after Dvorak pointed the way.

Still lamenting the fact that minstrelsy and ragtime were in vogue, in "The Development of Negro Secular Music" Dett is leery of the role of Jewish ragtime composers, some of whom also owned publishing houses which promoted Negro music.

Suggesting that these Jews either had sympathy for Negroes as a
minority group like themselves, or desired to make money from
Negro talent, he wishes that they might have capitalized on
their own music. He praised the efforts of the Music School
Settlement in New York City, and those of James Reese Europe's
classy orchestra, which perked up the ears of music publishers
eager for new and marketable works. Dett's categories of secular
song included Love Songs, Cradle Songs, Incendiary Songs (those
reflecting anger, passion, urges, and hard work), Wordless Songs
(those hummed), etc. Pauses, cries, and other punctuation were
discussed in regard to meter.

   In the third essay, "The Development of Negro Religious
Music," Dett points out the intensely personal nature of most
Negro folk songs, a trait making them unsuitable in a formal
church service or overly dramatic setting. Regarding concerts of
Negro music as fund raisers, he warns of losing the innermost
spirit of the songs through commercialization. The search for a
song form to bridge this gap is necessary, resulting in a product
usuable for all functions, one showing the artistic treatment of
inherent characteristics in Negro music. Favorable signs of this
"cause of preserving and dignifying a native asset" were already
showing, thanks to the efforts of Burleigh, Hackley, recording
companies, and college choirs which had increased their
repertoire in the Negro idiom.

   Finally, in "Negro Music of the Present," Dett commends
Dvorak, the Negro American composers who had studied and
performed abroad, himself for *Listen to the Lambs* and his first
two piano suites, and the progress of the Washington
Conservatory, "entirely officered by colored people," including a
colored woman (Mrs. Marshall) as its principal. Accounting for
the past reticence of black composers, he lists: (1) general
indifference to native origins, and a clinging by composers, critics,
and publishers to European ideas in music and art; (2) lack of
Negro literary masterpieces suitable for opera librettos and
other large idiomatic musical works; (3) lack of proper musical
and academic training among Negro composers; (4) ignorance of
Indian and Negro source materials; and (5) the non-lucrativeness
of music as a profession, necessitating supplementary jobs for
musicians. He advocates a national American philanthropy

whose main purpose would be the education of native-born Indians and Negroes. An edited version of this essay appeared in *Musical Courier*, July 11, 1918.

Dett's entry, "Negro Music," for *The International Cyclopedia of Music and Musicians* (lst, 3rd, and 6th editions in 1939, 1944, and 1952) elaborated on the material in the Bowdoin Prize essays. An excellent piece of writing, "Negro Music" includes specific titles of compositions and more details pertaining to their composers.

Though Dett was a staunch admirer of James Weldon Johnson, his review of *The Book of American Negro Spirituals* (1925) was not entirely favorable. Besides some criticism of Johnson's "new guises" for old spirituals, he noted a lack of "perfect co-operation among all the collaborators," saying that the song texts did not follow the Preface's stipulations. The book, Dett felt, did not settle what place the Negro spiritual should have in the scheme of music as a whole, but it nonetheless was a valuable step toward the race's artistic progress.

Dett had been a bit more complimentary about Johnson's *Fifty Years and Other Poems* (1918), saying that it presented various writing styles, ones allowing the Negro to express himself. He considered Johnson's own poems the most serious, ones "in which he pleads the cause of justice and recognition for his race." He called the book "most eloquent."

Dett considered *Negro Workaday Songs*, compiled by University of North Carolina professors Howard W. Odum and Guy B. Johnson, a unique collection of *outré* songs of the Negro laborer. The collection was intentionally structured from an incisive sociological viewpoint, not toward presenting a higher class of Negro music. Dett realized that the volume added "a new ray to the increasing galaxy of scientific and literary searchlights which are constantly being brought to bear upon Negro psychology."

"Ethnologist Aids Composer to Draw Inspiration from Heart of People" makes clear Dett's awareness that the ethnologist and ethnology share equally in aiding the composer. Ethnologists have sought and found the truth in "the heart of the common people." Unfortunately, the art of ethnological research has not been as esteemed as that of artistic creation. Records made by these "ambassadors of the unlearned" serve as bridges between nations. Dett praised Natalie Curtis-Burlin, "one of the foremost figures in contemporary music history," citing her *Indian's Book*, which established her as an "ethnologist of extraordinary powers," and "surpassed anything of a previous nature."

Hampton, the Album in Dett's Heart

Somewhere between poetry and prose, "From Within" (An Idyll of Hampton) was published in *The Hampton Student*, September 15, 1923. As the writer, Dett relates his thoughts while viewing the Hampton campus from inside the auditorium, most likely Ogden Hall. His truly poetic prose says:

> The quiet notes of birds from among the deep foliage is as the distant echo of music, when, inspired by sacred solitude, the musing organist seemingly draws from billowing clouds of incense the low-breathed tones of flutes.
> It is so peaceful now, thus to dream on this rare August afternoon, while the delicious fragrance of the scarcely moving winds ever add new delights.

This gentle reverie, interrupted by noisy student activities, quietens again with evening singing. "Then the lights will flicker at the windows, and evening prayers be said; and night, like a great dark mother, will gather the world in her arms." The whole piece reflects Dett's fondness for Hampton, his home by the sea.

BIBLIOGRAPHY

Books

Abdul, Raoul. *Blacks in Classical Music: A Personal History*. New York: Dodd, Mead and Company, 1977.

American Composers' Concerts and Festivals of American Music 1925-1971. Rochester, NY: University of Rochester, 1972.

Arvey, Verna. *In One Lifetime*. Fayetteville, AR: University of Arkansas Press, 1984.

ASCAP Biographical Dictionary, 4th ed. New York and London: Jacques Cattell Press, R. R. Bowker Company, 1980.

Ballanta, Nicholas George Julius. *Saint Helena Island Spirituals*. New York: G. Schirmer, 1925.

Bird, John. *Percy Grainger*. London: Paul Elek, 1976.

Bohle, Bruce, ed. *The International Cyclopedia of Music and Musicians*, 10th ed. New York: Dodd, Mead & Company, 1975.

Borroff, Edith. *Music in Europe and the United States*, 2nd ed. New York: Ardsley House Publishers, Inc., 1990.

Brawley, Benjamin. *The Negro Genius*. New York: Dodd, Mead & Company, 1942.

_____. *The Negro in Literature and Art*. New York: Duffield & Company, 1930.

Brooks, Tilford. *America's Black Musical Heritage*. Englewood Cliffs, NJ: Prentice-Hall, Inc., 1984.

Brower, Grover. *International Library of Music for Home and Studio Use*. Entry, "Afro-American Composers." New York: The University Society, Inc., 1966.

Brown, George W., ed. *Dictionary of Candian Biography*, Vol. I. Toronto: University of Toronto Press, 1966.

Bullfinch's Mythology. New York: Avenel Books, 1978.

Burek, Deborah M., ed. *Encyclopedia of Associations*, 25th ed. Detroit: Gale Research, Inc., 1991.

Butcher, Margaret Just. *The Negro in American Culture*. New York: Alfred A Knopf, 1969.

Butterworth, Neil. *A Dictionary of American Composers*. New York: Garland Publishing Co., 1984.

Chase, Gilbert. *America's Music*, rev. 2nd ed. New York: McGraw-Hill Book Company, 1955.

Claghorn, Charles Eugene. *Biographical Dictionary of American Music*. West Nyack, NY: Parker Publishing Company, Inc., 1973.

Clark, Edgar Rogie. *Negro Art Songs*. New York: Edward B. Marks Music Corporation, 1946.

Clark, W. Thorburn. *Hymns That Endure*. Nashville, TN: Broadman Press, 1944.

Cohen-Stratyner, Barbara N. *Biographical Dictionary of Dance*. New York: Schirmer Books, 1982.

Cohn, Arthur. *Recorded Classical Music*. New York: Schirmer Books, 1981.

Collected Poems and Plays of Rabindranath Tagore. New York: Macmillan Company, 1943.

The Complete Poetical Works of Longfellow. Boston, MA: Houghton Mifflin Company, 1922.

Cooke, Anna L. *Lane College: Its Heritage and Outreach 1882-1982.* Jackson, TN: Lane College, 1987.

Course Catalog 1987-88 from Oberlin College.

Cuney-Hare, Maude. *Negro Musicians and Their Music.* New York: Da Capo Press, 1974.

Darrell, R. D. *The Gramophone Shop Encyclopedia of Recorded Music,* 2nd ed. New York: Simon and Schuster, 1942; 3rd ed. New York: Crown Publishers, 1948.

DeLerma, Dominique-René. *Bibliography of Black Music Reference Materials,* Vol. I. Westport, CT: Greenwood Press, 1981.

_____. *The Black American Musical Heritage.* Columbus, OH: Midwest Chapter of the Music Library Association, 1969.

_____. *Black Music in Our Culture.* Kent, OH: Kent State University Press, 1970.

_____. *Concert Music and Spirituals: A Selective Discography,* Occasional Papers, 1. Nashville, TN: Fisk University Institute for Research in Black American Music, 1981.

_____. *Reflections on Afro-American Music.* Kent, OH: Kent State University Press, 1973.

_____. *A Selective List of Master's Theses in Musicology.* Bloomington, IN: Denia Press, 1970.

_____ , and McBrier, Vivian Flagg, eds. *The Collected Piano Works of R. Nathaniel Dett.* Evanston, IL: Summy-Birchard Company, 1973.

DeMille, Agnes. *America Dances.* New York: Macmillan Publishing Co., Inc., 1980.

Dett, R. Nathaniel. *The Album of a Heart*. Jackson, TN: Mocowat-Mercer, 1911.

Dictionary Catalog of the George Foster Peabody Collection of Negro Literature and History, Vol. I. Westport, CT: Greenwood Publishing Company, 1972.

Dictionary Catalog of the Negro Collection of the Fisk University Library. Boston, MA: G. K. Hall, 1974.

Eagon, Angelo. *Catalog of Published Concert Music by American Composers*, 2nd ed. Metuchen, NJ: Scarecrow Press, Inc., 1969.

Emery, Lynne F. *Black Dance in the United States*. Palo Alto, CA: National Press Books, 1972.

Encyclopedia Americana. International Edition. Danbury, CT: Grolier Incorporated, 1989.

Fisher, Miles Mark. *Negro Slave Songs in the United States*. New York: The Citadel Press, 1969.

Fisher, William Arms, ed. *Seventy Negro Spirituals*. Boston, MA: Oliver Ditson, 1926.

Floyd, Samuel and Reisser, Marsha J. *Black Music in the United States: An Annotated Bibliography*. Millwood, NY: Kraus International Publications, 1984.

Gray, Arlene E. *Listen to the Lambs: A Source Book of the R. Nathaniel Dett Materials in the Niagara Falls Public Library, Niagara Falls, N. Y.* Ridgeway, Ontario: Smith Davison Litho, Ltd., 1984.

_____. *Nate, My Son*. Niagara Falls, NY: In and Out Printing, 1987.

Greenfield, Edward, Layton, Robert, and March, Ivan, eds. *Penguin Stereo Record Guide*, 2nd ed. Middlesex, England: Penguin

Books, 1978.

Gromosiak, Paul. *Niagara Falls, Answers to the 100 Most Common Questions about Niagara Falls.* Buffalo, NY: Mayer Enterprises, 1990.

Grout, Donald Jay. *A History of Western Music,* 3rd ed. New York: W. W. Norton & Company, 1980.

Haas, Robert Bartlett, ed. *William Grant Still The Fusion of Cultures in American Music.* Los Angeles: Black Sparrow Press, 1975.

Hamilton, Edith. *Mythology Timeless Tales of Gods and Heroes.* New York: New American Library, 1969.

Hamilton, William B. *The Macmillian Book of Canadian Place Names.* Toronto: Macmillan of Canada, 1978.

Handy, W. C. *Negro Authors and Composers of the U. S.* Ann Arbor, MI: University Microfilms International, 1978.

Hurston, Zora Neale. *The Negro in Music and Art,* ed. Lindsay Patterson. Entry titled "Spirituals and Neo-Spirituals." New York: New York Publishers Company, Inc., 1967, pp. 15-17.

Hitchcock, H. Wiley, and Sadie, Stanley, eds. *The New Grove Dictionary of American Music,* Vols. I-IV. London: Macmillan Press, Limited, 1986.

Hughes, Langston. *Famous Negro Music Makers.* New York: Dodd, Mead & Company, 1955.

Hutcheson, Ernest. *The Literature of the Piano.* New York: Alfred A. Knopf, 1948.

Index to Negro Spirituals, CMBR Monographs No. 3. Rev. ed. from 1937. Chicago: Columbia College Chicago, 1991.

Jackson, Blyden. *A History of Afro-American Literature, The Long Beginning 1746-1875,* Vol. I. Baton Rouge, LA: Louisiana State University Press, 1989.

Jackson, George Pullen. *White and Negro Spirituals.* New York: J. J. Augustin Publishers, 1943.

Jackson, Irene. *Afro-American Religious Music.* Westport, CT: Greenwood Press, 1979.

Johnson, James Weldon. *Along This Way.* New York: Viking Press, 1933.

_____. *The Book of American Negro Poetry.* New York: Harcourt, Brace & Company, 1931.

_____. *The Book of American Negro Spirituals.* New York: The Viking Press, 1925.

Kallman, Helmut, Potvin, Gilles, and Winters, Kenneth, eds. *Encyclopedia of Music in Canada.* Toronto: University of Toronto Press, 1981.

Kerlin, Robert. *Negro Poets and Their Poetry,* 3rd ed. Washington, D.C.: Associated Publishers, Inc., 1935.

Krave, Richard. *A History of the Dance.* Englewood Cliffs, NJ: Prentice-Hall, Inc., 1969.

Kutsch, K. J., and Reimens, Leo. *A Concise Biographical Dictionary of Singers* (New York: Chilton Book Company, 1969).

Lieder, Paul Robert, Lovett, Robert Morss, and Root, Robert Kilburn, eds. *British Poetry and Prose.* Boston, MA: Houghton Mifflin Company, 1928.

Locke, Alain. *The New Negro.* New York: Atheneum, 1970.

Logan, Rayford W. and Winston, Michael R., eds. *Dictionary of*

American Negro Biography. New York: W. W. Norton & Company, 1982.

Lovell, John, Jr. *Black Song: The Forge and the Flame*. New York: The Macmillan Company, 1972.

Low, W. Augustus, and Clift, Virgil A., eds. *Encyclopedia of Black America*. New York: McGraw-Hill Book Company, 1981.

Mainiero, Lina, ed. *American Women Writers*, Vol. I. New York: Frederick Ungar Publishing Co., 1979.

Mapp, Edward. *Directory of Blacks in the Performing Arts*. Metuchen, NJ: Scarecrow Press, Inc., 1978.

Martin, Jay, and Hudson, Gossie H., eds. *The Paul Laurence Dunbar Reader*. New York: Dodd, Mead & Company, 1975.

Mason, Julian D., Jr., ed. *The Poems of Phillis Wheatley*. Chapel Hill: University of North Carolina Press, 1989.

Matney, William C., ed. *Who's Who Among Black Americans*, 5th ed. Lake Forest, IL: Educational Communications, Inc., 1988.

May, Hal, and Trosky, Susan M., eds. *Contemporary Authors*, Vol. 124. Detroit, MI: Gale Research, Inc., 1988.

McBrier, Vivian Flagg. *R. Nathaniel Dett His Life and Works 1882-1943*. Washington, D. C.: Associated Publishers, Inc., 1977.

Mizer, Hamilton B. *A City is Born: Niagara Falls, A City Matures: A Topical History 1892-1932*, No. 24. Lockport, NY: The Niagara County Historical Society, 1981.

Moogk, Edward B. *Roll Back the Years*. Ottawa: National Library of Canada, 1975.

Morison, Samuel Eliot. *Three Centuries of Harvard 1636- 1936*.

Cambridge, MA: Harvard University Press, 1937.

National Union Catalog Pre-1956 Imprints. London: Mansell Publishing, The American Library Association, 1971, 1980.

Niagara Falls, Canada: A History. Niagara Falls, Ontario: The Kiwanis Club of Stamford, Ontario, Inc. 1967.

Odum, Howard W. *American Sociology.* New York: Longmans, Green and Co., 1951.

Oja, Carol J., ed. *American Music Recordings: A Discography of 20th Century U. S. Composers.* Brooklyn, NY: Institute for Studies in American Music, 1982.

Osborne, Harold, ed. *Oxford Companion to Art.* Oxford: At the Clarendon Press, 1970.

Patterson, Lindsay, ed. *The Negro in Music and Art.* New York: Publishers Company, Inc., 1967.

Patterson, Willis C., ed. *Anthology of Art Songs by Black American Composers.* New York: Edward B. Marks Music Company, 1977.

Placzek, Adolph K., ed. *Macmillian Encyclopedia of Architects,* Vols. 1, 2. New York: The Free Press, 1982.

Pleasants, Henry. *The Great Singers.* New York: Simon & Schuster, Inc., 1981.

Ploski, Harry A., and Williams, James, eds. *The Negro Almanac: A Reference Work on the African American,* 5th ed. Detroit, MI: Gale Research, 1989.

Pratt, Waldo Selden, and Boyd, Charles N., eds. *Grove's Dictionary of Music and Musicians,* American Supplement, Vol. 6. New York: The Macmillan Company, 1944.

Reis, Claire R. *Composers in America.* New York: The Macmillan Company, 1947.

Riker, Charles. *The Eastman School of Music. Its First Quarter Century 1921-1946.* Rochester, NY: University of Rochester, 1948.

Roach, Hildred. *Black Music Past and Present.* Boston, MA: Crescendo Publishing Co., 1973.

Seibel, George A. *The Niagara Portage Road: A History of the Portage on the West Bank of the Niagara River.* Niagara Falls, Ontario: The City of Niagara Falls, Canada, 1990.

Sharecross, John T., ed. *The Complete Poetry of John Donne.* New York: New York University Press, 1968.

Simpson, Anne K. *Hard Trials: The Life and Music of Harry T. Burleigh.* Metuchen, NJ: Scarecrow Press, Inc., 1990.

Slattery, Thomas C. *Percy Grainger The Inveterate Innovator.* Evanston, IL: The Instrumentalist Co., 1974.

Slonimsky, Nicolas, ed. *Baker's Biographical Dictionary of Music and Musicians,* 7th ed. New York: Schirmer Books, 1984.

Southern, Eileen. *Biographical Dictionary of Afro-American and African Musicians.* Westport, CN: Greenwood Press, 1982.

_____. *The Music of Black Americans: A History.* New York: W. W. Norton & Company, 1971.

_____. *Readings in Black American Music.* New York: W. W. Norton & Company, Inc., 1971.

Spady, James G., ed. *William L. Dawson: A Umum Tribute and a Marvelous Journey.* Philadelphia: Creative Artist's Workshop, 1981.

Spalding, Walter Raymond. *Music at Harvard, A Historical View of Men and Events*. New York: Coward-McCann, Inc. 1935.

Stearns, Marshall and Jean. *Jazz Dance, the Story of American Vernacular Dance*. New York: Schirmer Books, 1964.

Terry, Walter. *The Dance in America*. New York: Harper & Row Publishers, 1971.

Tischler, Alice. *Fifteen Black American Composers A Bibliography of Their Works*. Detroit, MI: Information Coordinators, Inc., 1981.

Turner, Patricia. *Afro-American Singers: An Index and Preliminary Discography of Long-Playing Recordings of Opera, Choral Music and Song*. Minneapolis: Challenge Productions, Inc., 1977.

_____. *Dictionary of Afro-American Performers*. New York: Garland Publishing, Inc., 1990.

Vitzthum, Richard C. *Land and Sea The Lyric Poetry of Philip Freneau*. Minneapolis: University of Minnesota Press, 1978.

Wake, Arthur N. *Companion to Hymnbook for Christian Worship*. St. Louis, MO: The Bethany Press, 1970.

Westlake, Neda M., and Albrecht, Otto E., eds. *Marian Anderson, A Catalog of the Collection at the University of Pennsylvania Library*. Philadelphia: University of Pennsylvania Press, 1981.

Whispers of Love, A History of the Nathaniel Dett Club of Music and Allied Arts, 1922-1987. Chicago: The Club, 1987.

White, Evelyn Davidson. *Choral Music by Afro-American Composers*. Metuchen, NJ: Scarecrow Press, Inc., 1981.

White, Newman I. *American Negro Folk Songs*. Hatboro, PA:

Folklore Associates, Inc., 1965.

Williams, E. T., and Palmer, Helen M., eds. *Dictionary of National Biography.* Oxford: Oxford University Press, 1971.

Williams, Marjorie F. *The First Presbyterian Church of Niagara Falls, New York, 150 Years 1824-1974.* Niagara Falls, NY: First Presbyterian Church, 1974.

Winks, Robin W. *The Blacks in Canada.* Montreal: McGill-Queen's University Press, 1971.

Wittke, Carl. *A History of Canada,* 3rd ed. New York: F. S. Crofts & Co., 1942.

Work, John Wesley. *Folk Song of the American Negro.* New York: Negro Universities Press, 1969. Reprint from 1915.

Journals and Periodicals

American Record Guide, XL/1 (November 1976), pp. 22-23.

AMICA News Bulletin, (March/April 1991), p. 25.

Anderson, Alice. "R. Nathaniel Dett." *Tones and Overtones* (Spring 1954). Montgomery, AL: Alabama State College Press, pp. 33-36.

Bacon, Alice Mabel. "Work and Methods of the Hampton Folklore Society." *The Black Perspective in Music,* 4/2 (July 1976, Special Issue), pp. 151-155.

Beattie, John W. "The Unknown Peter Dykema." *Music Educators Journal,* XXVII (June-July 1951), pp. 11-12.

Brooks, Tilford. "The Black Musician in American Society." *Music Journal,* XXXIII/6 (July, 1975), pp. 42-43.

Christian Advocate, (January 20, 1917), n. p.

Cockerell, Dale. "Of Gospel Hymns, Minstrel Shows, and Jubilee Singers: Toward Some Black South African Musics." *American Music,* 5/4 (Winter 1987), pp. 424-427.

The Crisis, 1/1-50/12 (November 1910 through December, 1943).

Current, Gloster B. "National Association of Negro Musicians, Inc., Salutes R. Nathaniel Dett's 100th Birthday." *The Crisis,* 90/2 (February 1983), pp. 18-20.

Curtis-Burlin, Natalie. "Black Singers and Players." *Musical Quarterly,* V/4 (1919), pp. 498-506.

_____. "The Negro's Contribution to the Music of America: The Larger Opportunity of the Colored Man of Today." *The Craftsman,* 23 (March 1913), pp. 660-669.

Dean, Alison. "Record Reviews." *American Music,* 7/4 (Winter 1989), pp. 484-485.

DeLerma, Dominique René. "Dett and Engel, A Question of Cultural Pride." *The Black Perspective in Music,* 1/1 (Spring 1973), pp. 70-72.

Dett, R. Nathaniel. "John W. Work." *The Southern Workman,* 54 (October, 1925), p. 438.

_____. "Book Reviews." *The Southern Workman,* 56/1 (1927), pp. 45-46.

_____. "As the Negro School Sings." *The Southern Workman,* 56 (July 1927), pp. 304-305.

_____. "Ethnologist Aids Composer to Draw Inspiration from Heart of People." *Musical America,* XXX/3 (May, 31, 1919), p. 36.

_____. "From Bell Stand to Throne Room." *The Black Perspective in Music*, 1/1 (Spring 1973), pp. 73-81; reprinted from *The Etude*, LII/2 (February 1934), pp. 79-80.

_____. "A Musical Invasion of Europe." *The Crisis*, 37/12 (December 1930), pp. 405-407, 428.

_____. "Folk Song of the American Negro." *The Southern Workman*, 45 (1916), pp. 125-126.

_____. "The Emancipation of Negro Music." *The Southern Workman*, 47 (1918), pp. 176-186.

_____. "Negro Music of the Present." *The Southern Workman*, 47 (1918), pp. 243-247.

_____. "St. Helena Island Spiritual." *The Southern Workman*, 54 (1925), p. 527.

Diedrichs, Gary. "A Respect for Talent." *Opera News*, 39/4 (October 1974), pp. 39-42.

Doggett, Allen B., Jr. "Artistic Achievement." *Christian Advocate* (January 20, 1927), n. p.

EAR, 14 (May 1989), p. 52.

The Editor. "Black Concerts in Carnegie Hall, 1912-1915." *The Black Perspective in Music*, 6/1 (Spring 1978), pp. 71-88.

The Etude (Obituary), LXI/11 (November 1943), pp. 697, 763.

Fischer Edition News, c. 1932-1933.

Gordon, Douglass. "And the Truth Shall Make You Free." *The Southern Workman*, 57 (1928), pp. 154-158.

Graham, Shirley. "Spirituals to Symphonies." *The Etude*, 54/11 (November 1936), pp. 691 ff.

The Hampton Student, V/4 (May 1, 1914), pp. 4-5; XI/4 (May 15, 1921), n. p.

"Hampton's Anniversary." *The Southern Workman,* XLIV/6 (June 1915), pp. 356-363.

Harris, Carl G., Jr. "Three Schools of Black Choral Composers and Arrangers, 1900-1970." *The Choral Journal,* XVI/8 (April 1974), pp. 11-12.

Herrema, Robert D. "Choral Music by Black Composers." *The Choral Journal,* X/5 (January 1970), pp. 15-17.

High Fidelity, XLIX (July 1989), p. 65.

Hisey, Anne Billington. "Happy Birthday, Karl Gehrkens." *Oberlin Alumni Magazine* (April 1962), pp. 16-18.

Johnson, Marjorie S. "Noah Francis Ryder, Composer and Educator." *The Black Perspective in Music,* 6/1 (Spring 1978), pp. 18-31.

Journal of Negro History (obituary), XXVIII/4 (October 1943), pp. 507-509.

Martens, Frederick H. "The Chariot Jubilee and Other Compositions of R. N. Dett." *The Southern Workman,* 48 (1919), pp. 662-665.

Maynor, Dorothy. "Honoring the Memory of R. Nathaniel Dett." *National Music Council Bulletin,* 36 (1977), pp. 7-8.

McGinty, Doris. "Book Reviews." *The Black Perspective in Music,* 6/1 (Spring 1978), pp. 91-92.

Musical America, pertinent material from 1914-1943.

Musical Courier, pertinent material from 1914-1943.

"Musical Successes of R. Nathaniel Dett." *The Southern Workman,* LI/4 (April 1922), p. 200.

R. Smith. "Natalie Curtis-Burlin at the Hampton Institute." *Resound, A Quarterly of the Archives of Traditional Music,* 1/2 (April 1982), pp. 1-2.

"New Music Vocal and Instrumental." *Musical America,* XXX/1 (May 3, 1919), p. 44.

"New Operas and Premieres and American Operas." *Central Opera,* XX/1 (1977-1978), n.p.

"A Notable Negro Concert." *The Southern Workman,* 43/7 (July 1914), pp. 381-382.

Oberlin Alumni Magazine, pertinent material from 1916-1962.

Oberlin Review, May 6, 1921, n. p.

"Personal." *Journal of Negro History,* XXVIII/4 (October 1943), pp. 507-509.

"A Rare Treat for Music Lovers." *The Open Door* (Wickliffe, OH), XI/62 (April 1934), pp. 1-2.

Review, "Estimates of Dett's The Ordering of Moses." *The Southern Workman,* 66 (1937), pp. 304-310.

Rosicrucian Magazine, 1943 (incomplete citation on clipping sent from Oberlin College Archives).

"The School Year in Music." *The Hampton Student,* XI/4 (May 15, 1921), pp. 18-19.

Schwann, 42/1 (Winter 1990), p. 120.

Sonneck Society Bulletin, XVII/2 (Summer 1991), p. 77.

Southern, Eileen. "America's Black Composers of Classical Music." *Music Educators Journal*, 62/3 (November 1975), pp. 46-59.

The Southern Workman, 43/7 (July 1914), p. 420.

Spearman, Rawn Wardell. "The Joy of Langston Hughes and Howard Swanson." *The Black Perspective in Music*, 9/2 (Fall, 1981), pp. 125-126.

Spencer, Jon Michael. "R. Nathaniel Dett's Views on the Preservation of Black Music." *The Black Perspective in Music*, 10/2 (Fall 1982), pp. 133-145.

Stanley, May. "R. N. Dett of Hampton Institute: Helping to Lay Foundation for Negro Music of the Future." *The Black Perspective in Music*, 1/1 (Spring 1973), pp. 65-69.

Time, XXX/20 (May 17, 1937), pp. 44-45; XXXII/16 (October 17, 1938), pp. 45-46.

Van Peursem, J. E. "In Memoriam: Karl W. Gehrkens." *Music Educators Journal*, 61/9 (May 1975), pp. 30-31.

Untitled item. *The Hampton Student*, V/4 (May 1, 1914), pp. 4-5.

Yancy, Henrietta Miller. "The Contribution of the American Negro to the Music Culture of the Country." *The School Musician Director and Teacher*, 42/7 (March 1970), pp. 60-61.

Yuhasz, Sister Marie Joy, O. P. "Black Composers and Their Piano Music." *American Music Teacher*, 19/4 (February-March 1970), pp. 24-25.

Unpublished Dissertations

Evans, Arthur Lee. *The Development of the Negro Spiritual as Choral Art Music by Afro-American Composers With an Annotated Guide to the Performance of Selected Spirituals.*

Miami, FL: 1972 (Ph. D. Dissertation, University of Miami School of Music).

Fansler, Terry Lee. *The Anthem in America, 1900-1950.* Denton, TX: 1982 (Ph. D. Dissertation, North Texas State University).

Harris, Carl Gordon, Jr. *A Study of Characteristic Stylistic Trends Found in the Choral Works of a Selected Group of the Afro-American Composers and Arrangers.* Kansas City, MO: 1972 (D. M. A. Dissertation, University of Missouri).

Jackson, Raymond T. *The Piano Music of Twentieth Century Black Americans As Illustrated Mainly in the Works of Three Composers.* New York: 1973 (Dissertation, The Juilliard School).

Miles, Debra Ann. *An Analysis of Robert Nathaniel Dett's In the Bottoms.* Denton, TX: 1983 (Master of Music Thesis, North Texas State University).

Raichelson, Richard M. *Black Religious Folksong: A Study in Generic and Social Change.* Philadelphia: 1975 (Ph. D. Dissertation, University of Pennsylvania).

Ricks, George Robinson. *Some Aspects of the Religious Music of the United States Negro.* Evanston, IL: 1980 (Ph. D. Dissertation, Northwestern University).

Ryder, Georgia Atkins. *Melodic and Rhythmic Elements of American Negro Folk Songs as Employed in Cantatas by Selected American Composers Between 1932 and 1967.* New York: 1970 (Ph. D. Dissertation, University School of Education).

Spencer, Jon Michael. *The Writings of Robert Nathaniel Dett and William Grant Still on Black Music.* St. Louis, MO: 1982 (Ph. D. Dissertation, Washington University).

Wilson, J. Harrison. *A Study and Performance of The Ordering of Moses by R. Nathaniel Dett.* Los Angeles, CA: 1970 (D. M. A.

Dissertation, University of Southern California).

Unpublished Essays

Gordon, E. Harrison. "Black Classical Musicians of the Twentieth Century." Edison, NJ: 1977.

Marteena, Constance H. "R. Nathaniel Dett." Ms in Bennett College Library.

Pope, Marguerite. "A Brief Biography of Dr. Robert Nathaniel Dett." Ms in Bennett College Library.

Newspapers

Afro-American (Baltimore, Richmond and Chicago)

Amsterdam News (New York)

Atlanta Daily World

Atlanta Independent

Battle Creek Enquirer

Buffalo Evening News

Buffalo Express

Cambridge Chronicle

Chicago Defender

Chicago Evening Post

Cincinnati Enquirer

Cincinnati Times-Star

Cleveland Plain Dealer

Daily Cataract Journal (Niagara Falls, NY)

Dayton News

Free Press (Detroit)

Greensboro (North Carolina) *Daily News*

Greensboro (North Carolina) *Record*

Informer and Texas Freeman (Houston)

London Guardian Weekly

Louisville (Kentucky) *Defender*

Michigan Chronicle (Detroit)

New York Age

New York Evening Post

New York Herald-Tribune

New York Times

Niagara Falls (New York) *Gazette*

Norfolk Journal and Guide

Oberlin News-Tribune

Philadelphia Public Ledger

Portsmouth (Virginia) *Star*

Roanoke World-News

Rochester Democrat and Chronicle

St. Paul Pioneer Press

Suspension Bridge Journal

Twin City Star (Minneapolis)

Virginia Pilot and Norfolk Landmark

Washington (D. C.) *Evening Star*

Washington (D. C.) *Tribune*

INDEX

The following Index intends to aid the reader in locating pertinent information on Dett's professional activities, his family, his music, and the associates with whom he worked during his career. Some less pertinent names, titles, and places mentioned in the text will not be listed; neither will record labels, record review journals (see Discography and Bibliography), or places holding copies of Dett's music (see Catalog of Music). Compositions in quotes are (1) Dett's unpublished works or (2) parts of a large work whose title immediately follows. Other entries in quotes are mainly Dett's poems or essays, or works by other composers. All book titles and Dett's published compositions are in italics.

References to the Dett Collection in the Niagara Falls, New York, Public Library (NFNYPL), the Hampton University Archives, the Oberlin College Archives, the Moorland-Spingard Research Center, and the Mesiah Papers will be indexed as found in Chapters I through X and the Appendix. Their citations in the Chapter Endnotes will not be indexed.

ABOUT THE AUTHOR

ANNE KEY SIMPSON holds degrees in Piano Performance (B.S.) and Musicology (M.A.) from Texas Women's University. Since retiring in 1986 from the University of Southwestern Louisiana as Staff Accompanist for the School of Music, she has been a free-lance writer and accompanist, an adjudicator, and a lecturer/recitalist. Simpson is a member of Sigma Alpha Iota and Pi Kappa Lambda music fraternities, the College Music Society, and the Sonneck Society. Since 1981 over thirty of her articles on accompanying and art song composers have been published in music journals. She has authored two biographies, *Hard Trials: The Life and Music of Harry T. Burleigh* (Scarecrow Press, 1990), and *A Gathering of Gaines* (Center for Louisiana Studies, 1991).